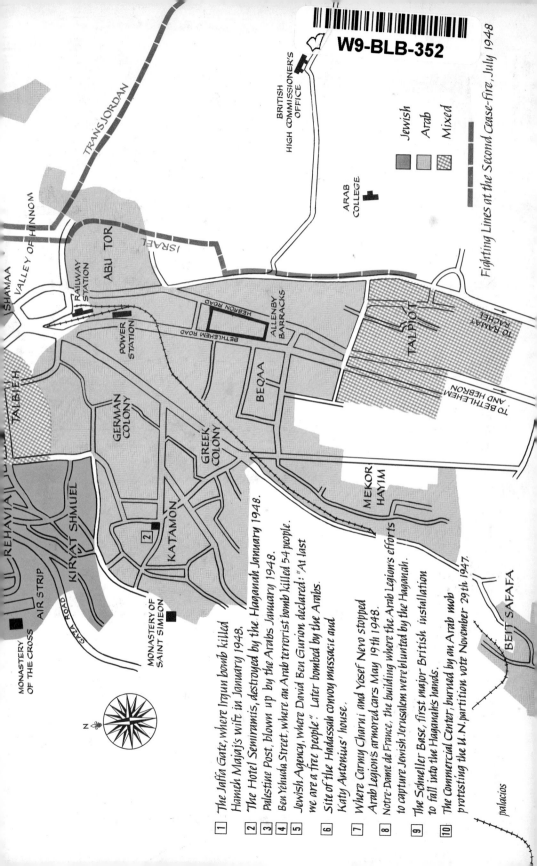

W9-BLB-352

Fighting Lines at the Second Cease-Fire, July 1948

Jewish
Arab
Mixed

BRITISH HIGH COMMISSIONER'S OFFICE

ARAB COLLEGE

TRANSJORDAN

ISRAEL

ABU TOR

SHAMAA

VALLEY OF HINNOM

TALBIEH

RAILWAY STATION

POWER STATION

HEBRON ROAD

BETHLEHEM ROAD

ALLENBY BARRACKS

BEQAA

TALPIOT

TO RAMAT RAHEL

TO BETHLEHEM AND HEBRON

MEKOR HAYIM

GERMAN COLONY

GREEK COLONY

REHAVIA

KIRYAT SHMUEL

AIR STRIP

GAZA ROAD

KATAMON

2

MONASTERY OF THE CROSS

MONASTERY OF SAINT SIMEON

BEIT SAFAFA

palacios

N

1 The Jaffa Gate, where Irgun bomb killed
   Hameh Majaj's wife in January 1948.
2 The Hotel Semiramis, destroyed by the Haganah in January 1948.
3 Palestine Post, blown up by the Arabs January 1948.
4 Ben Yehuda Street, where an Arab terrorist bomb killed 54 people.
5 Jewish Agency, where David Ben Gurion declared: "At last
   we are a free people." Later bombed by the Arabs.
6 Site of the Hadassah convoy massacre and
   Katy Antonius' house.
7 Where Carmy Charvi and Yosef Nevo stopped
   Arab Legion's armored cars May 19th 1948.
8 Notre-Dame de France, the building where the Arab Legion's efforts
   to capture Jewish Jerusalem were blunted by the Haganah.
9 The Schneller Base, first major British installation
   to fall into the Haganah's hands.
10 The Commercial Center, burned by an Arab mob
   protesting the U.N. partition vote November 29th 1947.

BY LARRY COLLINS AND DOMINIQUE LAPIERRE

O JERUSALEM!
OR I'LL DRESS YOU IN MOURNING
IS PARIS BURNING?

O JERUSALEM!

LARRY COLLINS
AND
DOMINIQUE LAPIERRE

 SIMON AND SCHUSTER · NEW YORK

FIRST PRINTING
SBN 671-21163-3
Library of Congress Catalog Card Number: 77-185063
Manufactured in the United States of America
Printed by Murray Printing Company, Forge Village, Mass.
Bound by H. Wolff Book Mfg. Co., Inc., New York, N.Y.
Maps by Rafael Palacios

Portions of this book have appeared in *Reader's Digest*.

CONTENTS

5

CONTENTS

PART FOUR

JERUSALEM: A CITY DIVIDED

6

How shall we sing the Lord's song in a strange land?
If I forget thee, O Jerusalem, *let my right hand*
forget her cunning.
If I do not remember thee, let my tongue cleave to the
roof of my mouth;
if I prefer not Jerusalem above my highest joys.

> The song of the exiled children of Israel,
> sung by the waters of Babylon
> Psalm 137

O Jerusalem, *Jerusalem, thou that killest the prophets and stonest them*
which are sent unto thee, how often would I have gathered thy children
together as a hen gathereth her chickens under her wings, and ye would not!

> Jesus contemplating Jerusalem
> from the Mount of Olives
> Matthew 23:37

O Jerusalem, *the choice of Allah of all his lands! In it are the chosen of his*
servants. From it the earth was stretched forth and from it shall it be rolled
up like a scroll.
The dew which descends upon Jerusalem is a remedy from every sickness
because it is from the gardens of Paradise.

> The Hadith, the sayings
> of the Prophet Mohammed

PROLOGUE

THEY KNEW THE SOUND. For months before this afternoon in May 1948, the forlorn wail had symbolized the frontiers of their existence. It was the skirl of British bagpipes, and now its call reverberated for the last time down these ancient stone passageways, piping away the few British soldiers left inside the old walled city of Jerusalem. They marched in columns, silent and unsmiling, the rhythmic tramp of their boots blending with the dying notes of the bagpipes. At the head and the rear of each column one soldier, a Sten gun crooked in his elbow, broke the pattern of their unwavering stares, his restless eyes scanning the hostile stone façades around them.

Along the Street of the Jews, from the sculptured stone windows of their synagogues and the mildewed hallways of their sacred houses of learning, the bearded old men watched them go. Their ancestors had watched other soldiers march out of Jerusalem: Babylonians, Assyrians, Romans, Persians, Arabs, Crusaders and Turks, the martial predecessors of these departing British soldiers whose brief thirty-year reign over Jerusalem was now ending. Rabbis, Talmudic scholars, interpreters of the Law, pale and stooped from years of unremitting study, those old men and their forebears had huddled for centuries under the walls of Jerusalem, a forgotten fragment of Jewry, living on the charity of their scattered brethren, caretakers of the Jewish heritage of the City of David. They had kept the Sabbath and conformed every action of their poor lives to the precise prescriptions of the Law. They had memorized their Torah verses and painstakingly copied down the Talmudic texts they passed from generation to generation. And daily they had bowed before the stones of the Temple Mount, beseeching the God of Abraham to bring His people back one day to the Land of Zion from which they had been cast.

That day had never been so close For other eyes, too, followed those British soldiers, peering from sandbagged windows and concealed gunports chiseled into the quarter's venerable stones. Impatient with the ways of the Divine, armed men stood poised to hasten the fulfillment of His prophecies with the homemade hand grenades and Sten guns they clutched by their sides. As the last British soldiers disappeared, they would dash to seize the

9

positions the Englishmen had held for months, a little string of vantage points sealing off the Old City's Jewish Quarter from the hostile Arab quarters surrounding it.

Suddenly, as the last British column moved down the street, it stopped and veered left up a twisting cobblestone alley leading toward the vast domain of the Armenian Patriarchate. It stopped in front of the arched stones crowning the entry to No. 3 Or Chayim Street.

Inside, surrounded by his collection of ancient books and silver Jewish artifacts, Rabbi Mordechai Weingarten, the senior citizen of the Jewish Quarter, had passed the afternoon in the reassuring company of his sacred texts. Lost in his thoughts, he hesitated a moment at the knock on his door.

He got up, put on his black vest and jacket, adjusted his gold-rimmed spectacles and his black hat, and stepped into the courtyard. There before Weingarten stood a middle-aged British major wearing the yellow-and-red insignia of the Suffolk Regiment. From his right hand dangled a bar of rusted iron almost a foot long. With a solemn gesture he offered it to the elderly rabbi. It was a key, the key to Zion Gate, one of the seven gates of the Old City of Jerusalem.

"From the year 70 A.D. until today," he said, "a key to the gates of Jerusalem has never been in Jewish hands. This is the first time in eighteen centuries that your people have been so privileged."

Weingarten extended a trembling hand to accept the key. Jewish legend held that on the night the Roman Emperor Titus destroyed the Temple, its despairing priests had thrown the keys of Jerusalem to heaven crying "God, henceforth be Thou the guardian of the keys." Now the improbable agent of their return to Jewish hands stood to attention and saluted.

"Our relations have not always been easy," he said, "but let us part as friends. Good luck and goodbye."

"Blessed art Thou, O Lord," murmured Weingarten, "Who had granted us life and sustenance and permitted us to reach this day." Then, addressing the Englishman, he said, "I accept this key in the name of my people."

The Englishman turned. With a quick order he marched his men out of the rabbi's little courtyard. Already the shadows of evening stretched across the Old City. Soon a new sound rose to replace the echoes of the bagpipes. Hearing it, Weingarten, still clutching the key to Zion Gate in his hands, stiffened. The sound was a reminder of how tenuous was his people's title to the gates it opened, and how short-lived might be their new domain over these stones from which they had been cast in exile so many centuries before. Once again, Jerusalem was about to become a battlefield. While the

10

rabbi listened in the gathering darkness, the noise grew and multiplied until it seemed to rise from every corner of the Old City.

Sinister and terrifying, it was the sound of gunfire.

The Arab woman instinctively tensed at each bullet passing overhead and quickened the pace carrying her up the deserted street. Ahead of her, at the crest of the rise in Julian's Way, was her destination, the six-story stone building in which Assiya Halaby had spent so many of her working days. Its ugly bulk dominated New Jerusalem's skyline as its occupants had dominated the city's life. Named for the Jewish king who had chosen to build his capital in these Judean hills, it was the seat of the British mandatory authority in Palestine.

This morning the lobby of the King David Hotel was almost deserted. Yellow dust covers shrouded its heavy armchairs and sofas. Its usually immaculate floor was littered with scrap paper. Half a dozen filing cabinets, their locks sealed with red wax, waited at the door for the truck that would confine the once hopeful edicts they contained to the dusty oblivion of some British archive. In one corner of the room, a final handful of British civil servants chatted together with the faintly embarrassed air of the last hangers-on at an official cocktail party.

Assiya Halaby had risked her life walking to the King David to say goodbye to them. As she stepped into the hotel, she realized she was the only one of their colleagues, Arab or Jewish, who had come to make that gesture to the men who had ruled the land of her birth for a third of a century.

The afternoon before in her third-floor office in the King David, she had performed her last official act for them as a servant of His Majesty's government. She had signed a special supplementary expenditure warrant authorizing the Agricultural Department to spend 650 Palestine pounds for the services of two additional guards for the forest of Jenin. The certain knowledge that the trees of that forest would never know the protective glance of those guards had not stayed for a second the swift stroke of her bureaucrat's pen. Perhaps it was fitting that it had not, for in many ways Assiya Halaby was a product of the British administration in Palestine.

The daughter of a middle-class Christian Arab family, she owed much to that administration. Above all, she owed it her emancipation as a woman, a fact symbolized by a brief ritual in Jerusalem's motor-vehicle registry one spring morning in 1939. When it was finished, Assiya had become the first Arab woman in Palestine to own and operate her own car.

Like many Palestinian Arabs, Assiya Halaby had not really believed the

11

British were going to leave. It seemed incomprehensible that the men who had taught her to love the orderly administration of human affairs would "run away and leave behind a vacuum." Yet now, after a parting handshake with Assiya, they climbed, one by one, aboard their waiting bus. In their haste to leave, they did not think to offer a safe passage home to the only individual in Jerusalem who had come to bid them farewell. Their convoy rolled off down Julian's Way toward Damascus Gate and their own safe passage home. Behind them, alone, Assiya Halaby waved a last goodbye. The King David was empty now. All that remained of Britain in the building that had been the citadel of her civil power in Palestine were a few scraps of paper scuttling like dry autumn leaves along an empty corridor.

When Assiya Halaby got home, she found a message from her brother urging her to join him in the safety of the Moslem Quarter of the Old City. She packed up a few belongings: a portable typewriter, her baby pillow and teddy bear, a green two-piece suit. As she left her house, she snatched a book from her library shelf to read in the days ahead.

For Assiya Halaby, as for many others in Jerusalem, a new life was beginning in that dawn. Soon a wall would lacerate Jerusalem's heart, and its stones would make Assiya Halaby an exile in the city of her birth. Instead of a few days, she would have years to ponder the message of the book she had taken with her that morning. Its title was *The Arab Awakening*.

Stiff and solemn in the freshly pressed uniform of a general of His Majesty's Royal Artillery, the Scot stepped out of the formal entrance of his residence and paused an instant to savor the spectacle spread before him. Some long-forgotten bureaucrat with an eye for a view and a gap in his knowledge of the Bible had chosen to build the official residence of the British high commissioners in Palestine on the Hill of Evil Counsel. The irony of that gesture had not been lost on those whose lives had depended on the decisions of the men who had lived in it. Now Sir Alan Cunningham, the last of their line, let his eyes enjoy a parting glance at that magnificent panorama at his feet, the Old Walled City of Jerusalem, ancient and unchanging, spread upon its barren hilltop.

Sir Alan had little time for contemplation, however. His last ritual as British high commissioner awaited him. As surely as the churches of the city sprawled below, the authority he represented had its faithfully prescribed liturgy, and even failures could not end without the appropriate closing ceremony. This morning, the ceremony over which Sir Alan was presiding would mark the end of British rule in Palestine.

Great Britain had eagerly sought that rule in the aftermath of World War I during which she had been lured to Palestine by two strategic objectives, securing the northern approaches of the Suez Canal and casting a bridgehead toward the desolate wastes of Iraq with their promise of a new and fabulous treasure, petroleum. Her rule had been formalized after the war by a League of Nations mandate, substituting her authority for that of the conquered leaders of Ottoman Turkey.

That rule had begun with high intent. Britain had promised to succor the wandering Jew here, to tutor the native, to replace Turkish misrule with an example of enlightened Christian colonialism. But it had not worked out that way. The problems she had encountered in Palestine had proved insurmountable, and, as no one knew better than her last High Commissioner, the legacy Britain was leaving behind on this May morning was chaos and the promise of war. With his last glance at Jerusalem, an agonizing thought struck Cunningham: there, below his garden wall, 160,000 people awaited only his departure to start killing one another.

He turned away. A score of people—army officers, government officials and a handful of newsmen—waited for him. Scanning their faces, Cunningham sadly realized that not a single representative of either Jerusalem's Arab or Jewish community had come to bid him farewell. He took his place in front of the residence. On its balcony, five soldiers of the Highland Light Infantry stood to attention. It was seven o'clock. A bugle sounded in the clear morning air. Sir Alan drew to attention. Slowly and majestically, the bagpipes began to play the Union Jack out of the blue sky of Jerusalem.

Watching it come down, Sir Alan felt "an overwhelming sadness" sweep over him. "So much effort expended," he thought, "so many lives lost to such little purpose finally. Thirty years and we achieved nearly nothing."

The black limousine that would carry him to the airport drove up. It was a four-ton armored Daimler built for George VI's tours of Blitz-ridden London. Clement Attlee had sent it to Jerusalem for Cunningham's safety. The stubborn Scot had always refused to ride in it. On the formal orders of his security officer, it would take him on his last, sad journey across Jerusalem.

Before getting in, he spun around. He could not leave without a parting stroll along the paths of the Residence garden he had loved so well during his three years in Palestine. How often, here among his roses, had he pondered the fate of a condemned Jewish prisoner or struggled to forget the sight of British bodies mangled by a terrorist's bomb. He knew every clump of lavender, every rose climbing the garden walls, every meticulously thinned Aleppo pine.

13

"And now," he wondered, "who is going to look after it all now?"

It was May 14, 1948. A page was turning in the history of the Holy Land. With the departure of a British general, an ancient state would be reborn upon it and the struggle for its soil between Arab and Jew would take on a new, an overt form. For two decades its ramifications would trouble the Middle East and preoccupy the world.

PART ONE

JERUSALEM: "A TIME TO MOURN AND A TIME TO DANCE"

November 29, 1947 — December 20, 1947

1

DECISION AT FLUSHING MEADOW

IN THE AFTERNOON of Saturday, November 29, 1947, in a cavernous gray building that had once housed an ice-skating rink, in Flushing Meadow, New York, the delegates of fifty-six of the fifty-seven members of the General Assembly of the United Nations were called upon to decide the future of a sliver of land set on the eastern rim of the Mediterranean. Half the size of Denmark, harboring fewer people than the city of St. Louis, it had been the center of the universe for the cartographers of antiquity, the destination of all the roads of man when the world was young: Palestine.

No debate in the brief history of the United Nations had stirred passions comparable to those aroused by the controversy over that land to which each of its members might in some way trace a part of its spiritual heritage. Before the General Assembly was a proposal to cut the ancient territory into two separate states, one Arab, one Jewish. That proposal represented the collective wisdom of a United Nations special committee instructed to find some way of resolving thirty years of struggle between Jew and Arab for the control of Palestine.

A mapmaker's nightmare, it was, at best, a possible compromise; at worst, an abomination. It gave fifty-seven percent of Palestine to the Jewish people despite the fact that two thirds of its population and more than half its land was Arab. The Arabs owned more land in the Jewish state than the Jews did, and before immigration that state would contain a majority of barely a thousand Jews. Each state was split into three parts linked up by a series of international crossroads upon whose functioning the whole scheme depended. Both states were militarily indefensible. *

Most important, the United Nations plan refused to both states sovereignty over the city of Jerusalem, the pole to which, since antiquity, the political, economic and religious life of Palestine had gravitated. Holding the

* Twenty years later, after the Six-Day War, ruling a territory three times the size of that allocated her in the partition plan, the state of Israel would actually have frontiers half as long as those accorded her in 1947.

17

attachment to Jerusalem too widely spread and deeply felt, its potential for prompting strife too great to entrust it to one nation's care, the United Nations Special Committee on Palestine had recommended that the city and its suburbs be placed under an international trusteeship.

The proposal had been a staggering blow to Jewish hopes. Re-creating a Jewish state in Palestine without Jerusalem as its capital was anathema to the Jewish people, the resurrection of a body without its soul.

Two thousand years of dispersion were summed up in the phrase "If I forget thee, O Jerusalem." The most important wall of the synagogues of the Diaspora faced east to Jerusalem. A patch of wall in every orthodox household went unattended in Jerusalem's name. The Jewish bridegroom crushed a glass under his foot at his wedding to show his grief at the destruction of the Temple, and prayed that his marriage would provoke joy and dancing in the streets of Jerusalem. The traditional words of Jewish consolation, "May the Almighty comfort you and all the mourners of Zion and Jerusalem," evoked the City. Even the word "Zionism," defining the movement to reassemble the Jews in their ancient homeland, was inspired by a hilltop in Jerusalem, Mount Zion.

Through the generations, men with neither the interest nor the intent— nor even the remotest possibility—of ever gazing on Judea's hills had nonetheless solemnly pledged to each other at the end of their Passover feast, "Next Year in Jerusalem."

Beyond those spiritual concerns lay strategic ones. Two out of every three inhabitants of Jerusalem were Jewish. They represented almost one sixth of the entire Jewish settlement in Palestine. With Jerusalem and a wide access corridor to the sea, the Jewish state would have a firm foothold in the Judean heartland of Palestine. Without it, the state risked becoming a coastal enclave clinging to the Mediterranean.

Urged by the Vatican, the Catholic nations of Latin America had made it clear to the Jews that the price of their votes for the plan to partition Palestine would be the internationalization of Jerusalem. Without them, the Jews had no hopes of mustering the ballots needed to pass partition. With a heavy heart, they had yielded, and Jerusalem's loss was the measure of the price they were willing to pay for a Jewish state.

Despite the loss of Jerusalem, the partition plan proposed by the United Nations Special Committee on Palestine still promised the Jewish people— and, above all, the 600,000 Jews of Palestine—the fulfillment of a two-thousand-year-old dream and an urgent present need. With a constancy, a tenacity, unequaled in the annals of mankind, the Jews had clung to the memory of the Biblical kingdom from which they had been driven in A.D. 70

as the centuries of their dispersion had stretched toward an eternity. In their prayers, in their rites, at each salient moment in the passage of a lifetime, they had reminded themselves of their attachment to that Promised Land and the transient nature of their separation from its shores.

Their ancestors, the first wandering Hebrew tribes fleeing Mesopotamia, had barely set foot on that land before history condemned them to ten centuries of warfare, migration and slavery. Finally, fleeing Egypt under Moses, they began their forty-year trek back to the hills of Judea to found their first sovereign state.

Its apogee, under David and Solomon, lasted barely a century. Living at the crossroads of the caravan routes of Europe, Asia and Africa, installed on a land that was already a beckoning temptation to every nearby civilization, the Hebrews endured a millennium of unremitting assaults. Assyria, Babylon, Egypt, Greece, Rome, each in turn sent its cohorts to conquer their land. Twice, in 586 B.C. and in A.D. 70, their conquerors inflicted upon them the supreme ordeal of exile and destroyed the Temple they had built in Jerusalem's Mount Moriah to Yahweh, their one and universal deity. From those dispersions and the suffering accompanying them was born their tenacious attachment to their ancient land.

Reinforcing its appeal, giving it a continual contemporary urgency, was the curse of persecution which had followed the Jews into every haven in which they had taken shelter during their dispersal. The roots of Jewish suffering grew out of the rise of another religion dedicated, paradoxically, to the love of man for man. Burning in the ardor of their new faith to convert the pagan masses, the early fathers of the Christian Church strove to emphasize the differences between their religion and its theological predecessor by forcing upon the Jews a kind of spiritual apartheid. The Emperor Theodosius II gave those aspirations legal force in his code, condemning Judaism and, for the first time, legally branding the Jews a people apart.

Dagobert, King of the Franks, drove them from Gaul; Spain's Visigoths seized their children as converts; the Byzantine Emperor Heraclius forbade Jewish worship. With the Crusades, spiritual apartheid became systematic slaughter. Shrieking their cry *"Deus vult! God wills it!,"* the Crusaders fell on every hapless Jewish community on their route to Jerusalem.

Most countries barred Jews from owning land. The religiously organized medieval craft and commerce guilds were closed to them. The Church forbade Jews to employ Christians and Christians to live among Jews. Most loathsome of all was the decision of the Fourth Lateran Council in 1215 to stamp the Jews as a race apart by forcing them to wear a distinguishing badge. In England it was a replica of the tablets on which Moses received the Ten Commandments. In France and Germany it was a yellow *O,* forerunner of the yellow stars with which the Third Reich would one day mark the victims of its gas chambers.

Edward I of England and later Philip the Fair of France expelled the Jews from their nations, seizing their property before evicting them. Even the Black Death was blamed on the Jews, accused of poisoning Christian wells with a powder made of spiders, frogs' legs, Christian entrails and consecrated hosts. Over two hundred Jewish communities were exterminated in the slaughters stirred by that wild fantasy.

During those dark centuries, the only example of normal Jewish existence in the West was in the Spain of the Caliphate, where, under Arab rule, the Jewish people flourished as they never would again in the Diaspora. The Christian Reconquista ended that. In 1492 Ferdinand and Isabella expelled the Jews from Spain.

In Germany, Jews were forbidden to ride in carriages and were made to pay a special toll as they entered a city. The republic of Venice enriched the vocabulary of the world with the word *ghetto* from the quarter, Ghetto Nuovo—New Foundry—to which the republic restricted its Jews. In Poland, the Cossack Revolt, with a ferocity and devotion to torture unparalleled in Jewish experience, wiped out over 100,000 Jews in less than a decade. When the czars pushed their frontier westward across Poland, an era of darkness set in for almost half the world's Jewish population. Fenced into history's greatest ghetto, the Pale of Settlement, Jews were conscripted at the age of twelve for twenty-five years of military service and forced to pay special taxes on kosher meat and Sabbath candles. Jewish women were not allowed to live in the big city university centers without the yellow ticket of a prostitute. In 1880, after the assassination of Alexander II, the mobs, aided by the Czar's soldiers, burned and butchered their way through one Jewish community after another, leaving a new word in their wake: *pogrom.*

Bloody milestones on the road to Hitler's gas chambers, those slaughters succeeding one another through the centuries were the constant of Jewish history, the ghastly heritage of an oppressed race to whom the crematoriums of the Third Reich might seem only the final, most appalling manifestation of their destiny.

Yet, by a strange paradox, the event which produced the decisive Jewish reaction to that bloodstained history was not a pogrom, not a slaughter, not a Cossack troop's brutality. It was a military ceremony, a ritual whose killing was spiritual, the public humiliation of Captain Alfred Dreyfus in Paris in January 1895.

In the midst of the crowd massed on the esplanade of the Champ de Mars to watch the ceremony was a Viennese newspaperman named Theodor Herzl. Like Dreyfus, Herzl was a Jew. Like Dreyfus, he had led his life in comfortable, seemingly unassailable assimilation into European society, little concerned with his race or religion. Suddenly, on that windy esplanade, Herzl heard the mob around him begin to cry, "Kill the traitor! Kill the Jew!" A shock wave rolled through his being. He had understood. It was not just for the blood of Alfred Dreyfus that the crowd was clamoring; it was for his blood, for Jewish blood. Herzl walked away from that spectacle a shattered man; but from his anguish came a vision that modified the destiny of his people and the history of the twentieth century.

It was Zionism. With the energy of his despair, Herzl produced its blueprint, a one-hundred-page pamphlet titled *Der Judenstaat*—"The Jewish State."

"The Jews who will it," it began, "shall have a state of their own."

Two years later, Herzl formally launched his movement with the First World Zionist Congress in the gambling casino of Basle, Switzerland. The delegates to Herzl's congress elected an international Jewish executive to guide the movement, created a Jewish National Fund and a Land Bank to begin buying land in the area in which he hoped to create his state, Palestine. Then they picked two indispensable symbols of the state whose foremost claim to existence was in the fervor of their speeches, a flag and a national anthem.

The flag was white and blue for the colors of the tallith, the shawl worn by Jews at prayer. The title of the Hebrew song chosen as a national anthem was even more appropriate. It represented the one asset Herzl and his followers disposed of in abundance. It was "Hatikvah"—"The Hope."

• • •

At no time had Jewish life wholly disappeared in the Palestine to which Herzl's followers proposed a return. Even in the darkest hours of the dispersion, small colonies of Jews had survived in Safed, Tiberias and Galilee. As elsewhere, their cruelest sufferings had come under Christian rule. The early Christians had had them banned from Jerusalem, and the Crusaders burned the Holy City's Jews alive in their synagogues.

Palestine's Moslem rulers had been more tolerant. The Caliph Omar had left them relatively unmolested. Saladin had brought them back to Jerusalem along with his Moslem faithful; under the Ottoman Turks, they had been able to take the first steps toward a return to the Promised Land. Sir Moses Montefiore, an English philanthropist, built the first Jewish suburb

21

outside Jerusalem's old walls in 1860, offering his kinsmen a pound sterling to spend a night beyond the ramparts. By the winter day in 1895 when Theodor Herzl witnessed the degradation of Alfred Dreyfus, thirty thousand of Jerusalem's fifty thousand inhabitants were already Jewish.

A series of pogroms in Russia just after the turn of the century sent a new wave of immigrants to Palestine. They represented the fruit of the first decade of Herzl's movement. Practical idealists, those immigrants were Zionism's first pioneers, and from their ranks would come half a century of leadership for the movement. They were men like Reuven Shari, a lawyer from the Crimea; his wife was a concert pianist. "I took my law degree and went out and dug ditches," he would recall, "and my wife took the hands that had been trained to play the concerts of Brahms and Mozart and used them to milk cows, because that was the way we could develop this land."

Among them was a nineteen-year-old lawyer's son named David Green from Plonsk, a small Polish factory town thirty-eight miles northwest of Warsaw. He had absorbed his Zionism eavesdropping at the door of his father's study, the favorite meeting place of Plonsk's Lovers of Zion. Unlike the men who debated in his father's study, however, David Green wanted to live Zionism, not talk it.

He lived it hard. Like so many others of his generation in Palestine, he learned at first hand the pains of hunger, malaria and exhausting physical labor struggling to reclaim the soil of the land he had sworn to develop.

A year after he had arrived in Palestine, he made a two-and-a-half-day hike from Jaffa through the gorge of Bab el Wad to discover for himself the symbol of the cause to which he committed his life, the walls of Jerusalem. What he discovered was a Tower of Babel. At the spiritual center of Judaism the shocked young man found Jews "speaking to each other in forty different languages, half of them unable to communicate with the other half."

Without the bond of a common language, the diverse communities of Jewry, he was persuaded, could never hope to found a modern nation. Shortly afterward, he returned to Jerusalem as an editor of a Zionist trade-union paper committed to a revival of the Hebrew language. As he finished his first editorial he stared at his own signature at the bottom of the page. There was little that was Hebrew about "Green." He thought for a moment, then he scratched out his last name and replaced it with a new one in Hebrew, the name he would carry for the rest of his life. It meant "son of a lion cub." It was Ben-Gurion.

22

Partly out of a sincere sympathy for Zionism, partly in an effort to rally Jewish support for the Allies in World War I, Great Britain offered David Ben-Gurion and his fellow Zionists the first concrete opportunity to realize their dream. In a 117-word note to Lord Walter Rothschild, head of the British branch of the great Jewish banking family, Arthur Balfour, Lloyd George's Foreign Secretary, promised, "His Majesty's Government view with favour the establishment in Palestine of a national home for the Jewish people." The promise, soon known as the Balfour Declaration, contained one condition: that the development of a Jewish national home did not prejudice "the civil and religious rights of existing non-Jewish communities in Palestine." The promise was of grave importance: Great Britain was, at the moment it was issued, in the process of seizing Palestine from Germany's wartime allies, the Turks. Balfour's solemn pledge was incorporated into the terms of the League of Nations mandate assigned to Britain in Palestine after World War I ended.

Slowly at first, the national home in Palestine promised to the Jews grew. Immigration, disappointing to the Zionists in the first decade after the Balfour Declaration, leapt up with the rise of persecution in Poland and Nazi Germany, reaching a peak of sixty thousand in 1935–36. Jewish investment went along with it. In the first fifteen years of Britain's mandate, it totaled eighty million pounds sterling, almost double the British budget for the period.

Beyond the ties of history, the promise of Britain and the beginnings of a Palestine national home, however, a ghastly tragedy had driven the Jews to demand of the United Nations a state of their own in the autumn of 1947. The end of the war had brought the Jewish people face to face with a reality so overwhelming in its horror that not even a history which seemed a catalogue of the cruelties man was capable of imposing on man had prepared them for it. It was the systematic slaughter of six million of their kind in the gas chambers of Nazi Germany. One central preoccupation obsessed the Jews at the United Nations: to gather the survivors of the catastrophe into Palestine as swiftly as possible, and to construct there a society so strong and self-reliant that a similar disaster would never again menace the Jewish people. The United Nations' recognition of their right to such a state seemed to the Jews no more than just reparation for the sufferings the world had inflicted on them.

.   .   .

For the Arabs, and above all for the 1.2 million Arabs of Palestine, the partitioning of the land in which they had been a majority for seven centuries seemed a monstrous injustice thrust upon them by white Western imperialism in expiation of a crime they had not committed. With few exceptions, the Jewish people had dwelt in relative security among the Arabs over the centuries. The golden age of the Diaspora had come in the Spain of the caliphs, and the Ottoman Turks had welcomed the Jews when the doors of much of Europe were closed to them. The ghastly chain of crimes perpetrated on the Jewish people culminating in the crematoriums of Germany had been inflicted on them by the Christian nations of Europe, not those of the Islamic East, and it was on those nations, not theirs, the Arabs maintained, that the burden of those sins should fall. Beyond that, seven hundred years of continuous occupation seemed to the Arabs a far more valid claim to the land than the Jews' historic ties, however deep.

In Arab eyes, the Balfour Declaration had been an act of pure imperialism, a mortgaging by Britain of the future of a land to which she had no rightful claim, without any effort to consult the wishes or the desires of the Arabs who had constituted ninety-two percent of Palestine's population when the declaration was issued. For the Arabs, the Palestine conflict was the outgrowth of an era supposedly laid to rest in World War II, an era whose excesses now had to be righted: that period in which the colonial powers of Europe had felt free to dispose of the destinies of the nonwhite peoples of the Afro-Asian world.

Like so many of those peoples, the Arabs had their claim to lay before the nations which had so long dominated their affairs. Less than a year after David Ben-Gurion had signed his first editorial in Jerusalem on the eve of World War I, seven young Arabs, two of them Palestinians, had met in Damascus to found a secret society. They gave it the seductive name Al Fatat—"Young Girl." * Its aim was the liberation of the Arab world from Turkey's Ottoman Empire. More important, it represented the first manifestation of a renascent Arab nationalism that disputed Jewish claims to Palestine for half a century.

The Arabs too had their Balfour Declaration. Anxious to foment an Arab uprising against Germany's Turkish allies, Great Britain pledged her support to Arab claims to a vast independent state in return for an Arab revolt against Ottoman Turkey. The pledge was contained in an exchange of eight letters between Britain's Resident in Egypt, Sir Henry MacMahon, and the dominant spiritual leader of the Arab world, the Sherif of Mecca.

Remarkable for the diplomatic imprecision of their language, MacMahon's letters failed to mention the word "Palestine," but their tone left

* Not to be confused with Al Fatah, the contemporary Palestine liberation movement.

the Arabs persuaded that it was included in the area promised them for their state. In 1916, spurred by T. E. Lawrence, they launched their famous revolt.

As they did, Britain, in secret negotiations with France, was in the process of substantially diluting the promises her Resident in Egypt had made to the Arabs. If the Ottoman Empire was to be dismembered after World War I, the French insisted on their share of the spoils. A secret treaty known as the Sykes-Picot Agreement, for the two men who signed it, Sir Mark Sykes for Britain and Jacques Georges-Picot for France, finally awarded to the French, without the Arabs' knowledge or consent, a "sphere of influence" in much of the area in which Britain had promised to support an independent Arab state.

Feeling themselves betrayed by the British and the French, their claim to Palestine thwarted by the Balfour Declaration, the Arabs lived a rude awakening in the aftermath of World War I. As was perhaps inevitable, the focal point of their fury became the Zionist return to a land the Arabs felt had been promised to them.

For their part, the Jews coming to Palestine to build the national home promised them by the British tended to imagine the country in terms not unlike their Biblical image of the land. That it was already settled by an alien people prepared to dispute their claims to it often came as shock. Officially, the Arab presence and claim to the land were not recognized by the Zionist leadership for years. Herzl never mentioned the Arabs in any of his speeches to the World Zionist congresses, and he dismissed the Arab problem as unimportant in his writings.

It was not until 1925, eight years after the Balfour Declaration, that Chaim Weizmann warned: "Palestine is not Rhodesia and 600,000 Arabs live there who . . . have exactly the same rights to their homes as we have to our National Home."

Influenced by the first prophets of Marxism, with whom they had shared the scourge of Czarist persecution, Zionism's early pioneers longed to build a state that would marry Jewish tradition and social democracy. They had transformed Zionism into something far more substantial than a religious movement and had imbued its followers with a sense of social discipline and communal responsibility vital to its later success.

One of their fundamental concepts was the idea of a kind of redemption of the Jewish race through a return to manual labor, a flushing out of the mentality of the ghetto in the sweat of tasks long unperformed by Jews. Ditch-diggers were as important to their idea of a Jewish state as were philosophers. Determined to build a Jewish working class with a wide variety of skills, they called for Jewish labor for Jewish enterprises. The Histadrut, the Jewish trade-union organization, compelled Jewish firms to limit their hiring to Jewish workers. As the Zionists acquired land, much of it from absentee Arab landlords in Beirut, they evicted the Arab tenant farmers living on it, to make way for Jewish settlers. Those peasants displaced by one Zionist policy drifted to the cities, where they found that another Zionist policy, Histadrut's, prevented them from working in the predominantly Jewish-owned commerce and industry.

Anxious to promote a Hebrew language and cultural revival, the Jews maintained their own highly effective school system. Through the Jewish Agency for Palestine, they managed their own political affairs independent of the Arabs. There was a tendency of the Jewish community in Palestine to act as a separate entity and, with its higher standard of living and education, to regard the Arabs as inferior.

For the Arabs, those cultural institutions of which the Jews were so proud seemed an alien intrusion in their land. Zionist labor policies inevitably led to the creation of a new class of dislocated urban poor. The Jewish tendency to live within the framework of their own social systems, their tendency to patronize the Arabs, stirred Arab bitterness and suspicion, and helped widen the gap between the two communities.

Half a century behind their Zionist neighbors in the development of their own nationalist aspirations, industrially and socially underdeveloped, having just emerged from centuries of repressive colonial rule, the Arabs responded to the situation simply and unsophisticatedly. They consistently refused every compromise offered them, insisting that since the Jewish claim to Palestine was invalid in the first place, any discussion of the subject would merely give it a validity it did not have. Repeatedly, their attitude, made unbending by the fanaticism of their leaders, lost them opportunities to set a limit on Jewish growth in Palestine and to define with precision their own rights there. Instead, Arab resentment periodically erupted in outbursts of violence, in 1920, in 1929, in an outright revolt against British rule in 1935–36.

Now, bitterly opposed to the partitioning of Palestine into two separate states, the Arabs had advanced a proposal whose lack of reality reflected the stance they had adopted for three decades. It was the creation of a single, Arab state in which, they declared, the Jews would be allowed to live as a minority. To head it, they proposed a fanatic Arab political leader who had participated in Nazi Germany's slaughter of six million Jews.

For Britain, the nation that had ruled Palestine for thirty years, the debate offered an end, however inglorious, to what had become a nightmare.

Palestine, on that November afternoon two years after the end of the Second World War, was the only place on the globe where British soldiers were still dying in combat.

Britain had been caught in Palestine between the contradictory promises she had made to Jew and Arab to ease her coming in the first place. Since the war, her persistent refusal, out of concern for Arab reaction, to allow the survivors of the Nazi holocaust to immigrate to Palestine in substantial numbers had brought her into open conflict with the Jews. So grave had the conflict become that 100,000 British soldiers, one for every six Jews, were now required to maintain a precarious order in Palestine. Unable to resolve the problem herself, she had finally cast it into the lap of the United Nations.

None of the nations supporting partition as a solution to the Palestine dilemma had been as forceful in its advocacy of the plan at Flushing Meadow as the United States. Feeling the intense pressures of the most numerous and most influential Jewish community in the world, America's lawmakers had let burst a flood tide of petitions, declarations and statements in favor of partition and the unrestricted immigration of displaced Jews into Palestine. It was an ironic comment, however, on the hypocritical aspects of America's Palestine policy that while the General Assembly's debate was evoking the misery of hundreds of thousands of displaced persons, the United States Congress was refusing to allow its own refugee relief bill out of committee, and that during the first eight months of 1946 the same American legislators who were so freely urging a quarter of a million Jewish immigrants on Palestine's 1.2 million Arabs had allowed exactly 4,767 refugees, barely the number aboard the illegal Palestine immigrant ship the *Exodus,* onto America's promised shores.

By direct order of the White House, the United States had exerted every form of pressure available to it on those nations in the United Nations opposed to partition or hesitant in their support of it. President Truman had personally warned the United States delegate to the United Nations, Herschel Johnson, to "damn well deliver the partition vote or there will be hell to pay." His adviser Bernard Baruch had shocked France's United Nations delegate Alexandre Parodi with a blunt threat to cut United States aid if France opposed partition.

Despite those efforts, the supporters of partition were faced with the prospect of defeat on the day originally set for the General Assembly vote, Wednesday, November 26, 1947. A two-thirds majority was required to pass the resolution. To offset the votes of the Arab-Moslem nations alone, the leaders of the Jewish Agency, representing the Zionist movement, needed

27

twenty-two votes, more than a third of the General Assembly. For each additional vote against partition, they needed two in favor. Calculating the probable votes of the Assembly's fifty-seven member nations that Wednesday morning, Moshe Sharett,* the Agency's "Foreign Minister," warned his followers, "It's too dangerous. We must stall."

After waiting two thousand years for a state, the Jewish people had now to find a way to wait a little longer, to find the additional time needed to secure the votes which would assure partition's passage. The tactic that Sharett chose was a filibuster which finally forced an adjournment of the Wednesday session before the vote could be called. The respite they won gave the Jewish Agency leadership not only an extra night but a Thanksgiving recess as well in which to muster their missing votes.

During that crucial interlude, four nations opposed to partition, Greece, Haiti, Liberia and the Philippines, were subjected to a deluge of diplomatic pressures and menaces. The United States, again acting on the instigation of the White House, threw the full impact of its tremendous prestige behind the Jewish cause. Two justices of the United States Supreme Court personally cabled Philippine President Carlos Rojas warning that "the Philippines will isolate millions and millions of American friends and supporters if they continue in their efforts to vote against partition." Twenty-six senators cabled Rojas and urged him to change his nation's vote. The Philippine ambassador was summoned to a blunt but intensive briefing at the White House. Finally Rojas ordered his delegation "in the higher national interest" to switch its vote from against to for partition.

Threatened with a Jewish boycott of his firm's products, Harvey Firestone of the Firestone Rubber Company intervened personally with William Tubman, President of Liberia. If Liberia didn't change her vote, Tubman was told, the company would have to reconsider plans to expand its rubber acreage there. Senior statesman Adolf A. Berle's help was enlisted in bringing pressure to bear on the government of Haiti. The Greeks were torn between pressures from an ally on whose aid Greece was increasingly dependent in prosecuting a civil war and fears of reprisals on the large Greek colonies scattered through the Arab countries.

Still, as the first delegates began to file into their improvised assembly hall for the final vote Saturday afternoon, November 29, the issue remained

---

* Moshe Sharett's surname was then Shertok. But in his case, and in the case of other well-known people who Hebraicized their names after May 14, 1948, it was decided, in the interest of simplification, to use the names by which they are now generally familiar to the public.—L. C. and D. L.

in doubt. Long before the first black limousines drew up in front of the massive old skating rink, the singing, chanting crowds had built up in the streets outside, waving Zionist banners and billboards.

Slowly, the three hundred seats reserved for the delegates began to fill up. The stately figure of Emir Faisal ibn Abd al-Aziz of Saudi Arabia, moving with solemn grace in his black-and-gold abayah, led the Arab delegations to their places. So crowded was the assembly hall that several members of the Jewish Agency delegation had been forced to squeeze into the press gallery to watch the proceedings. Missing from their ranks was the patrician scientist who was their leader, Dr. Chaim Weizmann. The elder statesman of Zionism for a quarter of a century, Weizmann had been the principal artisan of the negotiations which had led Britain to the Balfour Declaration. His whole life had been a voyage to this moment. Yet when three young colleagues had called for him at his hotel suite, he had been too overwhelmed with emotion to leave. Clasping the door for support, Dr. Chaim Weizmann had begun to weep.

The preliminaries were brief. The positions of the principals were all well known now, endlessly declared and restated in the months of debate that had led to this Saturday afternoon.

Britain's Sir Alexander Cadogan, aloof and imperturbable, maintained an air of studied indifference. Ten days before, he had carefully spelled out Britain's policy. She would leave Palestine on the day and hour of her choosing. The General Assembly could look for no help from His Majesty's Government in implementing any plan that had not been accepted by both Arab and Jew, a likelihood so inconceivable—as no one knew better than the British—that Cadogan's statement made it clear that England was washing her hands of Palestine. Since then, the sole contribution made to the debate by His Majesty's delegation had been the addition of a comma to a committee report.

Shortly after five o'clock, the Assembly President, Oswaldo Aranha of Brazil, gaveled down the last speaker and solemnly informed the men before him that the vote on the recommendation to partition Palestine would now be taken. From his seat in the spectator's gallery, Moshe Sharett stared with concern at the banks of silent men about to take the most important decision in the history of his people. For the hundredth time, he studied his calculations, not daring to imagine the cost of failure, knowing, as he had warned the Assembly, that his people would "never submit to any attempt to subjugate them to an Arab majority."

Not far away, in the same spectator's gallery, Jamal Husseini, the representative of Palestine's Arabs, also waited impassively for the vote to begin. A few minutes before, in the delegates' lobby, he had reiterated the threat he had made so often in the past weeks: If the General Assembly voted partition, the Arabs of Palestine, supported by the Arab states, would go to war against its decision as soon as the British left.

An aide set a basket before Aranha. In it were fifty-six slips of paper, each bearing the name of one of the nations represented in the hall. Aranha extended his hand and slowly drew from the basket the name of the nation whose vote would begin the poll. He unfolded the slip of paper and stared an instant at the men ranged before him.

"Guatemala," he announced.

At his words, a terrible silence settled over the Assembly. Even the press gallery fell quiet. For an instant, the three hundred delegates, the spectators, the newsmen, seemed united in awe of the moment before them, in their awareness of the grave and solemn decision about to be taken.

The delegate of Guatemala rose. As he did, suddenly, from the spectators' gallery, a piercing cry sundered the silence of the Assembly hall, a Hebrew cry as old as time and the suffering of men: "*Ana Ad Hoshiya*. O Lord, save us."

2

"AT LAST WE ARE A FREE PEOPLE."

SIX THOUSAND MILES from the converted skating rink in which a handful of men were about to decide the fate of the land of which it was the heart, the sacred city of Jerusalem waited impassively for the newest sign of its destiny.

Whether in the sacrifice of animals on the altar of her ancient Jewish Temple, the sacrifice of Christ upon a cross, or the constantly renewed sacrifice of men upon her walls, Jerusalem had lived as no other city in the world, under the curse of bloodshed. Yet her name, according to legend, came from the ancient Hebrew "Yerushalayim," meaning "City of Peace," and her first settlements had stretched down from the Mount of Olives under a grove of palm trees whose branches would become a universal symbol of peace. An unending stream of prophets had proclaimed here the peace of God to man, and David, the Jewish king who had made the city his capital, had celebrated it with the words "Pray for the peace of Jerusalem."

Sacred to three great religions, Judaism, Christianity and Islam, Jerusalem's stones bore the stigmata of her sanctity and her walls the memory of the crimes committed within them in the name of religion. David and Pharaoh, Sennacherib and Nebuchadnezzar, Ptolemy and Herod, Titus and the Crusaders of Godefroy de Bouillon, Tamerlane and the Saracens of Saladin, all had fought and burned and killed here.

Now, in the midnight blue of this November night, Jerusalem offered a deceptively peaceful appearance. A ring of distant lights surrounded the city like satellites: to the north, those of Ramallah; far to the east by the Dead Sea floor, Jericho; to the south, Bethlehem. Closer by, a second chain of lights leaped from hilltop to hilltop like lighthouses in the night standing guard over the approaches to Jerusalem. Most important among them were the lights of Kastel, blinking from the peak from which the village dominated the sole road linking Jerusalem to the sea, the artery along which virtually every vital supply for the 100,000 Jews of Jerusalem flowed. Those few miles of twisting asphalt were the hinge upon which

31

Jewish Jerusalem's existence hung that November evening. And, almost without exception, the lights along its route belonged to Arab communities.

Jerusalem began where the highway became Jaffa Road. The city's principal commercial artery, the road ran through a mixture of banks, stores, coffeehouses and cinemas blending in their unique manner the Orient and the Jewish quarters of Central Europe. To the north, huddled around the domes of their numerous synagogues, the zealous guardians of a Hasidic sect of orthodox Jewry lived in Mea Shearim. To the south were the city's modern Jewish quarters, and beyond them another set of equally modern and largely Arab quarters.

At the end of Jaffa Road lay the walls of old Jerusalem, proud and imposing, imprisoning the Old City in a splendid belt of stone. Wrapped inside a vast puzzle of vaulted alleyways and hidden passages were fifty thousand people sealed by race and rite into separate ghettoes. Jewish, Armenian, Christian and Moslem, those traditional quarters were the nervous tissue around the three sacred sites that were Jerusalem's glory and its curse.

Two hundred yards east of the Jewish Quarter, enclosed in an alley barely ten feet wide, was a façade of huge, uneven stone blocks. Those stones, granitic remnants of Solomon's Temple, were the spiritual center of Judaism, the Wailing Wall, the symbolic beacon toward which twenty centuries of Jewry had turned to mourn their exile. Caressed to an ochre sheen by the reverent touch of thousands of hands, lips and foreheads, they had resisted every calamity, natural and man-made, that had battered Jerusalem through the centuries. A handful of black-coated orthodox Jews, bobbing up and down to the rhythmic singsong of their ancient prayers, stood perpetual guard at that shrine to a glorious and dolorous history. Stuck into the cracks and crevices of the great stone blocks were dozens of scraps of paper, memoranda from the faithful to the Lord, petitioning for his blessing on a newborn son, an ailing wife, a flagging enterprise and, above all on this November night, the deliverance of his people.

A few hundred yards away, two stone cupolas and a Romanesque belfry crowned the dark and incense-filled caverns of another beacon calling to generations of humanity, the site for which the masses of Europe had hurled themselves into the adventure of the Crusades. Those stones spanned the most sacred shrine in Christendom, the Church of the Holy Sepulcher, built over the hilltop on which Jesus Christ is presumed to have been crucified. There, in a profusion of stairways, pillars, altars and sanctuaries, priests of all the sects of Christianity met, Greek, Russian, Coptic, Latin,

Armenian, Chaldean, Syriac, kneeling in mutual aversion, chanting their similar litanies to the resurrected Savior each claimed as his own.

The symbol of Jerusalem's importance to another faith lay to the east. The Qubbet es Sakhra, the Dome of the Rock, stood serene and stately at the center of its spacious esplanade. Below its gracious ceiling, covered with its inscriptions to Allah, the One, the Merciful, was a clump of gray stone, the Mount Moriah of antiquity. A faint impression upon that rock bound it to Islam, the handprint of the Angel Gabriel for the faithful, holding the rock to the earth on the night the Prophet Mohammed on his white steed El Burak ascended from it into heaven.

Ringing over the Old City's rooftops with equally sonorous fervor, the carillons of her church towers, the piercing call of her minarets, the cry of the shofar from her synagogues called Jerusalem to a perpetual prayer. For thousands in the city, they were a reminder that Jerusalem was only a way stop on a mystic journey, a journey whose destination was a deep ravine running below the city's eastern walls. There, below the spare slopes of the Mount of Olives, ran the Biblical Valley of Jehoshaphat to which the trumpets of the Last Judgment would call the souls of all mankind at the end of the world. Anticipation of that event had made Jerusalem a city where men came to die as well as to live, and generations of Christians, Jews and Moslems slept scattered under a sea of whitened stone around the valley, achieving in death in Jerusalem what they had so often failed to achieve in life: a peaceful reconciliation of their claims to its ramparts.

To Jerusalem's traditional divisions, another had been added recently. Demarcated by British barbed wire, it had grown out of the conflict between Jerusalem's Jewish population and its British authorities, and divided the community into a series of British-controlled security zones. They included the huge central compound which enclosed its vital installations. It had been scornfully dubbed Bevingrad by the city's Jews, after Britain's Foreign Secretary Ernest Bevin. For all its divisions, however, as the evening of November 29, 1947, stretched into night, Jerusalem enjoyed a blessing it had known rarely in the past third of a century: unity. In homes, in cafés, in clubs, linked together by an electric cable and a common sense of anguish and anxiety, the people of Jerusalem, Arab and Jew alike, sat by the radio, following word by word the distant debate on which the future of their city depended.

As they had almost every evening of their married life, Ambara and Sami Khalidy had gathered that night before the fireplace of their library,

33

Ambara at the fragile writing desk at which she had made the first Arabic translation of Homer, Sami in his leather wing chair by the fire. In circling ranks on the walls around them, their leather bindings burnished to a mahogany glow, were the silent witnesses to the right by which they occupied that room, the texts of the oldest Islamic library in the world. Since the day in A.D. 638 when Khalid ibn al-Whalid had ridden into the Holy City at the head of a column of the Caliph Omar's conquering warriors, there had been Khalidys in Jerusalem. Latest representative of a stream of scholars, teachers and sheikhs the family had produced to provide the intellectual leaven of Jerusalem's Moslem community, Sami Khalidy was the president of Jerusalem's Arab college. Shopkeepers' sons, the scions of Jerusalem's old Arab families, the progeny of Bedouin sheikhs —Sami Khalidy had gathered them all into his college, the hopeful raw material from which he might fashion a new generation of leaders for the Arabs of Palestine. Now, his bright-blue eyes clouded with concern, Sami Khalidy clung to every word coming from his radio and wondered if destiny was about to deprive his young pupils of the country he had prepared them to lead.

In their little apartment near Herod's Gate, thirty-six-year-old Hameh Majaj and his young wife softened the impact of the news flowing from their radio by contemplating the blueprints of the little house they planned to build in the spring just outside Jerusalem. All fall they had dreamed of that house, which bore the promise of a final ration of happiness for Hameh Majaj.

An orphan as a child, a shy and lonely man as an adult, Majaj's happiness dated from the moment three years earlier when a pretty girl had appeared at his post-office desk looking for a job. The job he had given her was that of his wife. She had since given him two children. He had just completed payments on the parcel of land on which their new house would take form. Even the number of its lot, thirteen, seemed a harbinger of good luck.

Around her feet, Katy Antonious' servants spread their cloths over the uneven stones that would serve as a table for the myriad little dishes of an Arabic *mezze*. Even on this fateful night, the widow of the foremost Arab historian of his generation remained faithful to the role that had been hers for two decades: that of the first hostess of Arab Jerusalem. Rare was the distinguished visitor who had not passed under the Arabic inscription "Enter and be welcome" on the stone arch above the door to her home.

Over her parquet floors had passed a sampling of international society, bishops and Arab princes, scholars and generals, poets and politicians.

Determined to mark this night with a gesture worthy of her tenacious devotion to Jerusalem's ancient stones, Katy had gathered her dinner guests around her and marched them off to an al-fresco supper on the squared roof of the Stork Tower. That tower was anchored in the northeastern corner of Jerusalem's old walls, hard by the spot where, eight centuries before, an earlier generation of Arabs had resisted another invasion of Jerusalem, that of the Crusaders of Godefroy de Bouillon.

On the opposite side of Jerusalem, in a simple stone house in one of the city's new Jewish quarters, another woman puffed nervously on a cigarette and fretted with the pencil and paper before her. She too was a renowned Jerusalem hostess, although of a different sort. Her salon was her kitchen, and the measure of her hospitality the endless cups of coffee she poured for her guests from the pot on her stove. Two generations of Zionists had met in that kitchen to laugh and argue, curse and cry, plan and despair. Chain-smoking her cigarettes, pushing forward her coffee and cakes, she had been the eternal Jewish mother in the adolescence of a new kind of Jew.

In a sense, she had been born to live this night. Her father was a carpenter whose talented hands had earned him the privilege of living in Kiev, outside the Pale of Settlement in which Czarist Russia had confined its Jews. Slender that privilege, for it gave a Jew only the chance to starve a little more slowly than his less fortunate kin. Five of the six children who had preceded her birth in 1898 had died in early childhood. Her father brought her to another Promised Land, and there, in the streets of an American city, at the age of seventeen, collecting funds for the victims of a World War I pogrom, she had found her Zionist faith.

She had devoted her life to that cause. To her, this evening might represent the culmination of everything she had lived for, a justification of her very existence. Normally, she was the most gregarious of women. Yet so precious were the emotions of these hours that Golda Meir had chosen to spend them alone with a cup of coffee, her endless cigarettes, and the note pad on which she would register each vote that brought her closer to a lifetime's dream.

Not far from Golda Meir's home, thirty of the most wanted men in Palestine followed the news on an old upright Philips radio placed in the center of a table spilling over with platters of omelette, great brass coffeepots and a dozen uncorked bottles of vodka. Barely a quarter of a mile away, wrapped in its protective layers of barbed wire, was the headquarters of the British Security Police, whose officers had spent two years chasing them up and down Palestine.

At the head of the table, his bald head ungraced by so much as a curl of hair, his massive chest heaving with each word he uttered, was the man who had summoned them to this room. He had been a wrestler in the circus, the foreman of a rock quarry, an art dealer, a journalist and a doctor of philosophy. It was not, however, his mastery of any of those diverse crafts that had excited the admiration of his fellows and the dedicated pursuit of the British police. Yitzhak Sadeh was the spiritual father of the Haganah and the founder of its elite striking force, the Palmach.

He had molded the Palmach on his own Marxist-Socialist principles. It was an army without insignia, indifferent to uniform and drill, relaxed in its discipline; an army in which rank had only one privilege, that of getting killed first.

Now someone asked Sadeh what he thought the result of the vote just beginning would be.

He was solemn and unsmiling. "I do not care," he said. "If the vote is positive, the Arabs will make war on us. Their war," he said, his eyes sweeping the faces of his young officers, "will cost us five thousand lives."

In the hush that followed he added, "And if the vote is negative, then it is we who shall make war on the Arabs."

Silence filled the room. The radio began to announce the passing votes. Sadeh reached out and very deliberately poured himself a tumbler of vodka from the bottle before him.

He raised it to his young subordinates.

"My friends," he said with a sad half-smile, "you might as well toast all of the votes with a glass of vodka."

In the wire room of the Palestine Broadcasting System, the news of each nation's vote was ripped from a teletype machine as it came in. A Jewish runner raced one copy across a small courtyard to the studios of the Hebrew service. An Arab runner raced a second across the same courtyard to the Arabic studios eight yards away.

There Hazem Nusseibi scribbled an Arabic translation for his waiting broadcaster. Watching the votes come in, Nusseibi thought, It can go either way. Suddenly, an urgent bulletin fell on his desk. Nusseibi translated it for his broadcaster. Only as the man read out his words did the full impact of what he had just written strike Nusseibi.

"The General Assembly of the United Nations," the broadcaster read, "by a vote of thirty-three in favor, thirteen against and ten abstentions, has voted to partition Palestine."

"A milestone has passed," thought Nusseibi; "a curtain has fallen upon our heads." From across the courtyard, he heard the first jubilant shouts of his Jewish colleagues.

Outside the night was still. From his balcony, Israel Rosenblatt stared with an almost mystic awe at the panorama spread before him in the cool dark air: Suleiman's Citadel, the Tower of David, Old Jerusalem's walls, the domes of her churches and synagogues, her slender minarets, all glowing with an alabaster sheen in the moonlight. Then, from some hidden courtyard, a sound sundered the silence. It was the primeval bleating of a shofar, the ram's-horn trumpet with which Joshua's hosts had laid down the walls of Jericho. Hearing it, Rosenblatt remembered the words of a solemn Yom Kippur prayer. "My God," he whispered, "the shofar has sounded our freedom at last." From courtyards and synagogues all across the city, other shofars took up the call until that harsh and primitive sound seemed to claw apart the night, a cry thirty-five centuries old adding its ancient message to that just relayed by radio. At that moment, like many another man in Jerusalem that night, Israel Rosenblatt turned his regard eastward toward that wall of stone that was the repository of so many of Judaism's sacred memories. Softly, almost imperceptibly, he began to mumble a prayer of thanksgiving.

In the sitting room of her stone house, Golda Meir's note pad rested on her knees, the last figures she had written on it staring up at her. The woman who had worked so hard for this moment could no longer read those figures. As the fateful announcement had come over her radio, Golda Meir's eyes had overflowed with tears.

The Arab educator Sami Khalidy had gotten up from his wing chair and crossed his library at the news. With a sharp snap, he turned off his radio. He looked at his wife. "A tragedy is now beginning," he said.

On the other side of Jerusalem in the Arab quarter that bore his family's name, young Nassereddin Nashashshibi heard his father declare at the same instant, "This means war." In the years to come, he would always remember the grim prophecy of Syria's United Nations delegate Fares el Khoury coming from the radio in his living room. "The Holy Places," said the Syrian, "are going to pass through long years of war, and peace will not prevail there for generations."

37

As Paris had lived its liberation night, as London and New York had reveled at the end of the war, Jewish Jerusalem now erupted in its own special explosion of joy, the most exuberant perhaps in its history, a wildly happy outburst to herald the end of a two-thousand-year wait.

In his little bar, Fink's, David Rothschild had listened to the news with two pretty girls. When the results came in, the three of them rushed out into the still-deserted streets. Giggling like children, they skipped down King George V Avenue, banging on doors, shouting up at the silent walls and windows, "We have a state, we have a state!" Two young Haganah officers, Mordechai Gazit and Zelman Mart, leaped into Mart's old Chevrolet and went careening through Jerusalem, their horn blaring, until Gazit thought "we had woken up the entire city."

Everywhere, as the impact of the news registered, lights snapped on, windows were flung open, neighbors called to each other in the dark. In pajamas and slippers, with a bathrobe or an overcoat tossed over the shoulders, Jerusalemites invaded the streets. At a corner of Ben Yehuda, Uri Avner joined a group of students rushing down the street. As they ran along, people flowed out of the doorways to join them. At the corner of Jaffa Road a British patrol car stopped their procession.

"Do you realize it's after midnight?" an officer asked them.

"Do you realize we have a state?" they shouted back.

Another group of youngsters commandeered a truck with a loudspeaker and drove through the city calling people out to celebrate. A British armored car stopped them too, then swung in behind them, adding the voice of its loudspeaker to theirs.

On Ben Yehuda Street, Reuven Tamir, a member of the Jewish settlement police, and a group of friends pried open a kiosk that sold cakes and soda during the daytime. As they started distributing cakes to their friends, the angry owner ran up. Then, understanding that on this night everything was free, he joined them, passing out his stock. At that instant a crowd rushed by, carrying a Jewish member of the British police on their shoulders and crying, "He'll be our first police minister!" Tamir blinked. It was his father.

Bars and restaurants opened as their owners rushed to join the celebration. The director of the Carmel Mizrachi wines rolled an enormous vat of red wine into the middle of Ben Yehuda Street and began passing out free drinks to the crowd. In the ultra-religious quarter of Mea Shearim, yeshiva students with their curly side locks and bearded rabbis stood in the streets toasting *lechayim*—life—with bottles of cognac. Drivers ran to their buses and began bringing people free into the city. By two o'clock, thousands of deliriously happy Jews had poured into the heart of Jerusalem. Exultant young people stamped and swirled through the hora at every street corner. Arm in arm, others marched through the streets singing the Zionist anthem, "Hatikvah." In Russian, Czech, German, Hungarian, Yiddish, Hebrew, in almost every tongue of the human race, the old hymns of Zionism's pioneering days echoed through the night. Strangers embraced and kissed. Uri Cohen, a biology student at Hebrew University, happily kissed his way from his home to the city center.

Even the British joined in. On King George V Avenue, Yaacov Salamon saw a British armored car rolling up the street. He froze. He had been on guard duty for the Haganah, and on his hip was a canteen in which he had hidden a hand grenade and a pistol, enough to earn him a life sentence in a British jail if he were caught with them. As he wondered what to do, a group of young people swarmed over the armored car and began to embrace the British police. The stunned Englishmen smiled and embraced them back. "The first time," thought Salamon, "the British have stood by while the Jews went mad with happiness."

So contagious was the mood that some English soldiers even reached into their pockets for a handful of shillings to put into the collection boxes of the Jewish National Fund, then happily pinned its pale-blue emblem to their uniform. Rabbi Ezra Spicehandler offered a swig of cognac to a British soldier. "Oop the Jews!" he cried and gulped down a third of the bottle.

Long before sunrise, the whole of Jewish Jerusalem seemed to be awake and celebrating. Synagogues opened at three and were thronged with grateful assemblies offering a prayer of thanksgiving. Everyone reacted differently to the emotion of those moments. As the first faint light of dawn softened the sky, Zev Benjamin thought of the words of the Bible for the creation of the world: "And the evening and the morning were the first day." Watching the young people dance, Russian-born Reuven Ben-Yehoshua remembered "the early pioneers who never imagined this night," thinking, "If they hadn't come, perhaps this night would never have taken place." Even the most agnostic of Jews might have felt the hand of God upon them that night.

Yet, in that happy carousel, there were the voices of dissent. Bowing in the dark sanctuary of their synagogue, the leaders of the rabidly fanatic Neturei Karta sect of orthodox Jewry were in virtual mourning. To those deeply religious men who believed the Divine alone could order the homecoming of the Jews, the state their fellows were celebrating was an abomination, a miracle wrought by the hands of man when only those of God would do. The dissent of a young student, Netanel Lorch, an officer in the Haganah, was of a different order. Lorch had few illusions of what the Arabs' reaction to tonight's news would be. Watching his fellows whirl through their horas, Lorch thought, "Dancing is for the innocents."

Along Ben Yehuda Street, a tall distinguished man wandered alone, an island of concern in the midst of the jubilant crowds. While they celebrated the promise of a new Jewish state, every fiber of Eleazar Sukenik's being was concentrated on an old one, the one that had died almost two millenniums before on the mountaintop of Masada. That afternoon, in the shop of an Arab souvenir dealer near the Church of the Nativity in Bethlehem, Eleazar Sukenik's fingers had caressed a few scraps of ancient leather. Trembling with emotion, he had realized he held in his hand the most precious remnants ever found of that dead civilization. Tomorrow he was to meet the Arab souvenir dealer to negotiate their purchase. Now he despaired that tonight's pledge of a new Jewish state in Palestine would destroy his only link with those priceless ties to its long-dead predecessor. They were the first scraps of the most important archeological discovery of the twentieth century, the Dead Sea Scrolls.

Everywhere, the Jews of Palestine shared the joy of Jerusalem. Tel Aviv, the first Jewish city of the world, was like some Latin capital on carnival night. In kibbutzim around the country, young people danced and prayed. In the settlements of the Negev and on the Syrian border in the north, watchmen in their lonely sentry posts blessed the night above them.

In Jerusalem, the celebration built toward a crescendo in front of a fortresslike structure whose stone wings had enclosed for years Jewish hopes for a state in Palestine. Bathed in the glow of searchlights, the Jewish Agency building and its courtyard were the scene of an exultant happening. When the white flag of Zionism with its pale-blue star of David proudly crept up the building's flagstaff, an explosion of noise burst from the crowd.

Brusquely the tumult quieted and, like a breaking wave, a strange silence rolled over the sea of faces as the bulky silhouette of a woman appeared on the balcony above them.

"For two thousand years," cried Golda Meir, "we have waited for our deliverance. Now that it is here it is so great and wonderful that it surpasses human words." Then, her voice hesitant with emotion, her heart overflowing, the carpenter's daughter from Kiev become the Pasionara of Zionism grasped for the two words her people had used for generations to mark the passage of life's gay and solemn moments. "Jews," she cried, "*mazel tov!* Good luck!"

. . .

In the Arab quarters of Jerusalem, the echoes of those triumphant Jewish cries rang like a tocsin through the deserted streets. Peering into the night, listening to the distant sound of merriment rising from the Jewish quarters, many an Arab pondered the change in his own destiny that those cheers foretold.

Oppressed by gloom and bitterness, Gibrail Katoul, an officer in the Education Department of the mandate, announced to his wife, "Everything is lost. The streets of Jerusalem will run with blood." Then, with Arab fatalism, Katoul opined, "It is the fault of the British. They let us down. The whole world has conspired to defeat us."

The reaction of Sami Hadawi, another mandate civil servant, was similar to that of many Arabs. Drawing tight the shutters of his new home in Katamon, Hadawi struggled to recover from the news. Then, from somewhere in his subconscious, a firm and reassuring voice told him it was all a lie, it would never come to pass. "The British," he thought in a rush of comfort, "will never leave Palestine."

From his bedroom window, Zihad Khatib, a twenty-one-year-old accountant, watched the flickering orange glow of torchlight dancing on the walls of nearby Mea Shearim and listened to the din of his neighbor's revelry. "It is like V-Day," he told himself. Then, bitterly, he thought, "But it is they who are the victorious ones, not us."

Leaving his studio, Hazem Nusseibi, the Arab who had translated the momentous news, heard a voice beside him whisper in the darkness, "When the day comes, there will be Arabs ready to perform their duty."

Turning, Nusseibi looked at the owner of that voice, a Bedouin officer of the unit guarding the Palestine Radio. He belonged to an elite corps whose cannon would soon exact a heavy price from the Jews of Jerusalem for the state they celebrated this night: the Arab Legion.

Of all the Arabs who witnessed Jewish celebrations that night, none witnessed them in stranger circumstances than a young captain in the Syrian Army wandering in civilian clothes through the exulting crowds of Tel Aviv. As the first rays of dawn lightened the city, Captain Abdul-Aziz Kerine stood at the window of his little hotel peering down in fascination at the happy throng still dancing the hora in the street below. Fascinated he well might be, for a special mission had brought Captain Abdul-Aziz Kerine to Tel Aviv. In a few hours, at Lydda Airport, he would set off for Prague. There he planned to buy ten thousand rifles and one thousand machine guns, the first consignment of the arms with which the Arabs hoped to shatter the dreams of the dancers below the young captain's hotel window.

"So what if we won?" hissed the middle-aged woman in her bathrobe. "Let the old man sleep." Yet, to awaken him, Gershon Avner, a young bureaucrat of the Jewish Agency, had driven twenty-five miles from Jerusalem to the Jewish potash works on the Dead Sea. In his briefcase he carried the draft of an official declaration by the Jewish Agency welcoming the United Nations' historic vote. More than any other individual of his generation, the sleeping man before Avner was responsible for that triumph. With the implacable determination of a hunter stalking a quarry, he had pursued the goal of a Jewish state in Palestine. Coaxing, cajoling, threatening, inspiring, he had led his people toward it with the zeal of a Messianic prophet and the realistic cunning of a Biblical warrior. Avner looked down at the small round stomach and the strands of white hair standing out from his head that identified him to millions around the world. Gently, he shook his shoulder.

"Mazel tov," he whispered to David Ben-Gurion. "We won."

Ben-Gurion got up, slipped on a bathrobe, and plodded to a small writing table. Adjusting his glasses, he began to study the declaration Avner handed him. Then his pen started to fly over its 150-word English text. Soon the paper was covered with its scratchings, giving, Avner noted, the emotional content of the original a more sober tone.

"More paper," Ben-Gurion called, the first words he had uttered to Avner.

With Ben-Gurion's wife, Paula, Avner began a frantic search while the old man waited with fast-rising impatience. Finally, in despair, Avner grabbed the only sheaf of paper he could find, a strip of brown toilet tissue taken from the bathroom next door. Ben-Gurion started to write on it the text of his historic declaration.

As he finished, a group of excited young people from the potash works burst into the room. Circling the stubby little figure of their leader, they began to dance a wild, happy hora. His fists thrust into the pockets of his worn bathrobe, Ben-Gurion watched them with a heavy heart. He well knew the price the Jewish people would have to pay for the state the United Nations had promised them this night. When the young people beckoned him to join their hora, he shook his head.

"I could not dance," he would later recall. "I could not sing that night. I looked at them so happy dancing and I could only think that they were all going to war."

As the Jewish leader knew, the United Nations vote was not in itself a guarantee that a Jewish state would actually come into existence. Between the vote this November night and the actual end, some months away, of Britain's rule in Palestine lay a difficult time of trial. Both sides, Ben-Gurion was persuaded, would try to use it to strengthen their forces and improve their positions for the conflict he felt must follow Britain's eventual withdrawal. In Jerusalem, the first preparations for a showdown still far in the future were already beginning. About the same time Gershon Avner's Austin had driven up to the potash works, another car had slipped through the darkened streets of a Jewish suburb on the city's western outskirts. It stopped in front of the outpatient clinic of the Histadrut Medical Aid Society. A squat, heavyset man strode to the door of the clinic and rapped softly. From the shadows inside, the white-coated figure of a medical orderly emerged. The two men walked through the deserted clinic to a small office at the rear. There the gray-haired man set to work.

His name was Israel Amir, and he was the Jerusalem commander of the Haganah. The medical orderly who had opened the door was one of his soldiers. For over a year the clinic had provided the Jerusalem commander a cover to hide his headquarters from British surveillance. Amir scanned the sheaf of intelligence reports telephoned during the night to his headquarters. They indicated no unusual activity in the Arab city, but Amir was not reassured. The Arabs, he felt, could not let this occasion pass without some reaction. Like most Haganah headquarters, his command had an informal but carefully prepared system to bring his forces into readiness. Quickly he made the three seemingly innocent telephone calls that put his forces on alert.

The outburst which Israel Amir feared was already brewing. Clasping slips of paper marked with a crescent and a cross adjoined at an identical angle, each signed with the Arabic initials "E.G.", Arab messengers were already moving through Old Jerusalem's darkened alleys. The initials belonged to Emile Ghory, a member of Jerusalem's sizable Christian Arab community and a graduate of the University of Cincinnati. Ghory was the leader of the Arab city's unofficial ruling body, the Arab Higher Committee.

The destination of the men who bore his slips of paper were as diverse as Old Jerusalem. One was near the Wailing Wall, another at a mosque next to St. Stephen's Gate, a third behind the Holy Sepulcher. Soon Ghory's messengers aroused from their sleep sheikhs, obscure shopkeepers, peddlers, even women, the widows of conservative religious families whose piety placed them above all suspicion.

They passed Ghory's slip of paper to each sleepy figure and in turn were guided to the hiding place of the objects for which they had come. They unfastened false panels, pulled up floorboards, dug into cellars, chipped away the mortar of caches hidden in walls, opened crates of cheap religious souvenirs, picked apart kilns and baking ovens. By sunrise their work was completed. While the Jews of Jerusalem had danced the night away beyond the Old City walls, they had removed from their hideaways the secret arsenal of Jerusalem's Arab Higher Committee, the eight hundred rifles they had carefully sealed away after the last Arab uprising in Palestine almost a decade earlier, a bloody three-year revolt against the British in 1936–39.

For some Arabs and Jews, however, the aftermath of the U.N. vote led to a kind of sad reaching out to each other, a grasping toward the hope that the conflict to which they seemed condemned might still be avoided. Making their rounds at Government Hospital the morning after the vote, two old friends, Drs. Rajhib Khalidy and Edward Cooke, studied the long rows of beds soon to be filled with the victims of their fratricidal war. "Must we really fight each other?" sighed Cooke. "It will be too horrible."

On King George V Avenue, an Arab dentist named Samy Aboussouan got a jarring response of his own to that same thought. A cultivated man, an accomplished violinist, Aboussouan was one of those Arabs who had always lived in harmony with the Jewish community, and he persisted in his belief in the ultimate reconciliation of Jew and Arab. Suddenly, amidst the jubilant dancers, Aboussouan saw an old friend, violin professor Isaac Rottenburg, a man he had long admired for his "calm, his serenity, his pacifism." Wrapped around the peaceful violin professor's biceps was the armband of the Jewish Home Guard.

Zihab Khatib, the twenty-one-year-old accountant who had watched the celebration in Mea Shearim, lived a disappointment of a different nature that morning. The Jews in his office were in the midst of an impromptu

44

party when he arrived for work. Among them was a lovely blond Rumanian named Elissa who dominated the young accountant's hopeful dreams. They whispered together for a moment. Then Elissa brought him a cake and, taking him by the hand, led him over to join the dancing. Khatib tried, but his heart would not let him. A few minutes later, sadly aware that the events of the night had erected a barrier between them that could never be bridged, Khatib drifted out of the office. The young Arab would see the blond Jewish girl he had hoped to love only once again in his life, in April, behind a rifle pointing from the sandbags of a Haganah guard post in the Montefiore quarter.

In the rest of the Arab world, a rising tide of fury at the U.N. vote was already erupting in violence. Angered by a decision they felt deprived them unjustly of a part of the Arab patrimony, the youth of Damascus had rampaged through the Syrian capital since dawn, chanting, "We want arms." The Prime Minister, fifty-five-year-old Jamil Mardam, offered them the chance to display their patriotism with acts, not words. He promised that a recruiting office would open to enlist volunteers to fight in Palestine. They preferred other activities, however. By noon they had sacked the United States and French legations and, protesting Russia's vote for partition, burned the headquarters of the Syrian Communist Party. In Beirut, capital of Lebanon, similar crowds smashed their way into the offices of the Arabian-American Oil Company. In Amman, capital of the kingdom of Transjordan, only a last-minute effort by police saved two American professors from a lynching at the hands of an angry mob. From his desert palace in Riyadh, King Ibn-Saud of Saudi Arabia proclaimed that his last wish was "to die at the head of my troops fighting in Palestine."

Curiously, the capital of the most important country in the Arab world, Egypt, took the news most calmly. By customary arrangement, a courier from the Prime Minister's office brought King Farouk's chamberlain a bribe and a dispatch with the news. The bribe was the guarantee needed to get the chamberlain to set important documents before the King at the only moment he was disposed to read them—around noon, when he awoke from his usual night of revelry.

Egypt's Prime Minister, Mahmoud Nokrashy Pasha, pondered the news with concern. A former history professor, a man as modest as his sovereign was profligate, Nokrashy was a rarity among Egyptian politicians. He was honest. A lifelong foe of the British, he felt with deep conviction that the only proper concerns of his nation were securing the English evacuation of the Suez Canal Zone and union with the Sudan under the Egyptian crown. Under no circumstances did Nokrashy Pasha want Egypt's army to get involved in a war in Palestine.

Circumstances, however, would deprive the Egyptian Prime Minister of his wish. Spurred by genuine emotion, exhorted by cynical politicians unwilling to restrain the passions unleashed by their reckless rhetoric, led by men living a charade based on careless illusions, the Arabs were soon to be embarked on the high road to disaster. Already, in the streets beyond the Egyptian Prime Minister's palace, two forces were at work sowing the wind whose tempest would bring Egypt to revolution and Mahmoud Nokrashy to a rendezvous with an assassin's bullet.

In the narrow byways of Cairo's ancient bazaar, the Khan el Khalil, the rectors of Al Azhar, the world's oldest Islamic university, drafted the decrees which would sanction the ancient call that had driven the warriors of the caliphs from Baghdad to Poitiers and Saladin to the Horn of Hattin. Debased by overuse, eviscerated of much of its spiritual appeal, still no cry could stir Arab opinion as readily as that ancient call to jihad, the holy war.

In those same Cairo souks the fanatic messengers of a newer Islam, the Moslem Brothers, stirred, too. They saw in the United Nations' decision the seeds of the popular upheaval they awaited to carry them to power.

Soon the walls of Damascus, Beirut and Baghdad would be splashed with the slogans of those Knights Templar of a renascent Islam, calling their followers to a new crusade with the Koran, the dagger and the machine gun.

. . .

David Ben-Gurion returned to Jerusalem at dawn. Seeing the celebrations, he said to himself, "They are silly. They think that a war is for dancing." He went straight to his office to work. By forenoon, an enormous crowd had built up once again in the courtyard of the Jewish Agency, clamoring for the appearance of their leaders.

Determined to infuse them with some of the urgency he himself felt at this hour, Ben-Gurion finally stepped out onto the Agency balcony, surrounded by fifty of his senior aides. As he began to speak, someone whispered to Golda Meir a piece of news to justify Ben-Gurion's caution. Three Jews had just been killed in an ambush outside Tel Aviv.

Yet, as the applause, the happy shouts, the almost physical pleasure of the crowd below swept up to him, Ben-Gurion's stern façade began to dissolve. Suddenly he too felt the overwhelming emotion of that hour, the grandeur of being alive at that rendezvous between the Hebrew race and the two-thousand-year-old promise they had sworn to the Judean hills.

When he finished, he turned to the blue-and-white Zionist flag beside him. Gently, almost reverently, he caressed its folds.

"At last," he murmured in a half-whisper, "at last we are a free people."

3

"PAPA HAS RETURNED."

NEITHER THE ARABS nor the Jews were completely unprepared for the struggle which the U.N. vote made inevitable. Grimly mindful of the prospect of violence, both sides had been quietly girding themselves for months.

In the early spring of 1945, David Ben-Gurion had received a visitor in the cluttered study of his modest house at 15 Keren Kayemet Street. Surrounded by thousands of books of philosophy and history through which his restless mind had prowled, Ben-Gurion greeted his caller and waved him to a chair. Beyond an open window the two men could hear the wash of the Mediterranean sliding down the beaches of Tel Aviv half a mile away. That book-lined study was Ben-Gurion's private citadel, the sanctuary into which he retired every night to read and work. Rare was the event or man that could deprive the Jewish leader of even thirty minutes of that nightly ritual.

Ben-Gurion's visitor was an American and he was a senior official of the United States government. A few weeks before, he had participated in a meeting designed to lay the outlines of the postwar world, the Yalta Conference. As Ben-Gurion listened with growing intensity, his visitor related the details of a private conversation to which he had been a party at that conference. Its participants were Franklin Roosevelt, Winston Churchill and Joseph Stalin. The subject was Palestine.

Suddenly, he said, the Russian dictator had turned to Churchill. There was only one solution to the Arab–Jewish problem in Palestine, Stalin told the Englishman, the solution the Soviet Union was going to support. "It is a Jewish state," he said.

Hearing his visitor recite the Russian dictator's words, Ben-Gurion started. Years later he would recall that at that instant, for the first time, he had the absolute certainty that the Jewish people would have a state in Palestine. Between the combined pressures of the Soviet Union, ruled by the dictator whose thoughts on Palestine had just been revealed to Ben-Gurion, and a United States responsive to public opinion, Britain would eventually be compelled to yield to Jewish desires.

Sitting back, Ben-Gurion calculated the impact of what he had heard. For years the brunt of Zionist diplomacy had been concentrated on obtaining world acknowledgment of the Jewish people's right to a state. From this moment forward, it would have to have another, even more important objective, preparing to defend such a state at the point of a gun. For if the major powers could give his people legal sanction for a state, Ben-Gurion knew only they themselves could bring it into being. That, he was certain, would have to be done in a military showdown with the Arab states. Their survival and their dreams of a state would depend on their being prepared for that showdown.

On the morning of April 6, 1945, shortly after David Ben-Gurion had received his American visitor, a crucial turning point came, too, in the existence of the man whom fate had destined to oppose him, Mohammed Said Haj Amin el Husseini, the Mufti of Jerusalem, spiritual leader of Jerusalem's Moslem community. It took place at a lunch in the capital of Nazi Germany. Once, in his own villa on Goethestrasse in Berlin's Selendorf West, Haj Amin had played host to the leaders of Hitler's Germany. That morning, in a friend's apartment, the only representative of the Third Reich at the table was the S.S. bodyguard-chauffeur who had driven the Mufti to Berlin from Badgastein, Austria, in a wood-burning Mercedes. And the plate set before the man whose table had a few months before been laden with the delicacies of occupied Europe was a staple of the Egyptian fellaheen, a mash of red kidney beans soaked in vinegar, called *foul,* which the Germans considered fit only for livestock. Gathered around Haj Amin in the lugubrious gloom of mourners at a funeral banquet were a dozen of the Arabs who had followed him in October 1941, when, disguised as the female servant of an Italian diplomat, he had escaped a British dragnet and walked from Teheran to the Turkish frontier and thence made his way to Berlin.

Convinced that a German victory would secure the aims to which he had devoted his political life—driving the Jews from Palestine and the British from the Middle East—Haj Amin had thrown in his lot with the Nazis. Placing at their disposal the prestige of his person and the influence of his religious office, the Mufti had done everything he could to secure a German victory. He had recruited Arab agents to drop behind the British lines as saboteurs. He had helped raise two divisions of Yugoslavian Moslems for the S.S. He had facilitated the German entry into Tunisia and Libya. His agents had provided the Wehrmacht with a forty-eight-hour warning—ignored—of the Allied landings in North Africa. Fully aware of the finality of the Final Solution, he had done his best to see that none of its intended victims were diverted to Palestine on their way to Reichsführer Heinrich Himmler's gas chambers. In 1943 he intervened personally with Reich Foreign Minister Ribbentrop to prevent the emigration of four thousand Jewish children from Bulgaria to Palestine.

Haj Amin Husseini had lost his wager. A reminder of his defeat and that of the ally to whose cause he had joined his could be heard just beyond the windows of the villa in which he lunched, the insistent drone of Allied planes methodically bombing Berlin. Like David Ben-Gurion, Haj Amin had now to prepare for the next round in the struggle between their two peoples. With a gesture, he sent his S.S. bodyguard to his car. The German returned toting a burlap sack stuffed with Red Cross prisoner-of-war parcels. Silently the Mufti distributed them to the men around the table. Then he reached into the folds of his black robe and drew out a leather pouch. From it he pulled a thick clump of bank notes: Swiss francs, U.S. dollars and British gold certificates. Carefully he counted them out into a dozen packets, one of which he set before each man.

His pale-blue eyes as impassive, as imperturbable as they had been three years before at those exalting moments when the armies of Germany had seemed within reach of victory, Haj Amin told his followers, "It is finished for us here now. Each of you must try to find his way back home as best he can. There our struggle must begin again in different circumstances."

Then he rose and, with the quick mincing walk for which he was famous, slipped from the room as furtively as a nursing nun gliding from the bedchamber of a dying man.

Haj Amin Husseini was a man of many and diverse qualities, but a deep religiosity had never been one of them, not even on the March day in 1922 when he was summoned to the office of Britain's first High Commissioner in Palestine, Sir Herbert Samuel, to receive at his Jewish hands his appointment as mufti, a kind of bishopric of the third most important city of Islam. Two years of study at Cairo's Al Azhar had revealed little of the theologian in young Haj Amin. Bored, he had turned to a dissimilar but more suitable calling as a cadet officer in the Turkish Army. With his bright-red hair, his sharp blue eyes, a sword dangling from his belt, he cut a dashing figure; so dashing that he quickly attracted the attention of Jerusalem's Arab nationalists and through them that of the British, for whom he was soon working as an intelligence agent. Aware of Britain's promises to the Arabs, convinced that they were destined to be the liberators of his people, he became a passionate Anglophile.

The passionate convert became a passionate apostate when Haj Amin saw evidence of British perfidy on the publication of the Balfour Declaration and the Sykes-Picot Agreement. Thereafter, in the hierarchy of Haj Amin's hatred, the British would always enjoy pride of place before that accorded to his Jewish enemies. Quitting his job as an adviser to the British in the Sudan, he returned to Jerusalem. In the streets and souks of his native city, stirring with the first vague resentment against Jewish immigration, Haj Amin Husseini at last found his true vocation. He took those ill-defined emotions and patiently coaxed the expository anger of the coffeehouse into the fury of the mob.

On Easter Sunday 1920, his manipulations of the city's discontent reached their logical culmination: bursting from the crowded souks and alleys of the Old City, an Arab street mob turned on the Jews at Jaffa Gate.* Twelve people were killed in the ensuing riot. Six were Jews. Six were Arabs. Theirs was the first blood spilled in the Semitic struggle for Jerusalem between Jew and Arab. Henceforth, the strong points and the open countryside of Arab Palestine might belong to the British, but the villages and the souks would be fiefs of Haj Amin Husseini.

His role in the riot earned him a ten-year jail term in absentia. With the guile that would become his personal hallmark, Haj Amin escaped arrest and fled to Transjordan.

His exile was brief. Soon the most important Moslem religious office in Palestine, that of mufti of Jerusalem, fell vacant. It was Britain's responsibility to fill the post from one of three nominees proposed by a college of Moslem notables. E. T. Richmond, a rabid anti-Zionist and the mandate's political secretary, resolved to give Haj Amin the post. He persuaded the High Commissioner, Sir Herbert Samuel, striving as a Jew to be impartial, to support him on the grounds that the job might convert its holder to responsibility.†

Thus the British installed their most implacable foe for life in the central Moslem office in Palestine, their High Commissioner accompanying the

---

* The news was announced to the city's British administrators gathered for Easter services in Jerusalem's Anglican cathedral by a captain named Naylor who galloped up to the church door, dismounted and tiptoed into the pew behind the chief secretary of the government. "Sir," he whispered, "you may be talking about peace on earth and goodwill to men in here, but down at the Jaffa Gate the Jews and the Arabs are beating bloody hell out of each other."

† The regard in which his fellows held Haj Amin's qualifications for the post was revealed when, despite British pressures, he failed to win a place among the top three nominees. The British fixed that, however. As Sir Alec Kirkbride, then a young Arabist, later recalled, "We simply told the two top names on the list they were off and that was that."

appointment with only one admonition: he told Haj Amin to go home and grow a beard to give his twenty-eight-year-old face a dignity worthy of his new post.

For a while, it appeared that the British decision had been a wise one. Haj Amin was silent. He had better things to do than harass his foes. He labored patiently to build his power base. He secured his election to the post of president of the Supreme Moslem Council, capturing with it un-fettered control over all Moslem religious funds in Palestine. He took over the courts, the mosques, the schools, the cemeteries, so that soon no Moslem in Palestine could be born or die without being beholden to Haj Amin. No shiekh, no teacher, no official however petty, received an ap-pointment in Haj Amin's domain without first establishing his total personal loyalty to the Mufti. Scornful and suspicious of the country's educated classes, he built his following in the souks and villages, upon the solid rock of ignorance, binding his followers to him with the promise of alms and arms.

On Yom Kippur, September 24, 1928, Haj Amin found the pretext for which he had been building his organization and biding his time. It was the Wailing Wall. That day, the Jews erected a portable screen by the wall to separate men and women at prayer. A minor gesture, but no one knew better than Haj Amin that the mind of Jerusalem had been conditioned for centuries to attach major political importance to minor religious gestures, and that every status quo was a citadel to be zealously protected; after all, the city's Christians had struggled for generations for a privilege so small as scrubbing one step of the Holy Sepulcher. Accusing the Jews of violating Islamic property, insinuating that their aim was to take over the Dome of the Rock, the Mufti orchestrated a growing wave of religious fanaticism.

It spilled over on a Friday, the Moslem Sabbath, a year later. The Mufti's noonday sermon at the Dome of the Rock that day was unexcep-tional. He was too wise to let the British catch him exhorting the crowd that his deputies had shepherded to the mosque. Besides, the crowd knew what it had come for. So did Haj Amin. After the service, from the balcony of his little garden above the Wailing Wall, his silent black-robed figure stared down as the crowd did its work on the Jewish worshipers below.

This time, the rioting he had provoked spread all across Palestine. When it was finished, over one hundred Jews were dead and Haj Amin Husseini was the undisputed leader of Arab Palestine.

In 1935, some of his followers started small-scale guerrilla activities to protest the rising tide of Jewish immigration from Nazi Germany. The people, Haj Amin decided, were ready to die. He would offer them that chance in a jihad, its aims no less ambitious than driving the British from Palestine and settling the Jewish problem at leisure on his own terms.

His bold undertaking began with a six-month general strike. When that failed to budge the British, the strike became an armed uprising. Aimed at first at the British and the Jews, the Mufti's rebellion soon turned from its original targets to his fellow Arabs. Those offered a chance to die were now the Mufti's enemies from the Husseinis' rival clans, and finally anyone whose social situation or skills aroused Haj Amin's suspicions. Landowners, schoolteachers, government officials, clerks, at times anyone accused of reading and writing English too well, all were gunned down. Men began to hire the Mufti's gunmen to exterminate personal enemies. In the towns, the murders usually took place at the open-air market, early in the morning, when the men, following Arab custom, did the shopping. A figure would glide up behind the victim, pull a pistol from the robes of his abayah, shoot and glide away. In the country, they took place at night, a gang bursting into a man's house and killing him in his bed.

Over two thousand people died in that vicious intramural bloodletting. While the Jews of Palestine were developing the young leaders and the social institutions that would be their greatest resource, Haj Amin Husseini methodically deprived the Arabs of theirs. Throttling progress and any drift to rational thought with his angry fanaticism, cowing with the guns of his ignorant villagers the educated elite, he reduced a generation of Arab leadership to fear and silence.

Soft-voiced and courteous, serene and elegant, Haj Amin stood at the center of it all, never raising his voice, proffering his visitors their ritual coffee cup with his exquisite gestures, condemning a man to death with a barely perceptible wave of his immaculately manicured fingers. He protected his own life with extraordinary precautions. He never went out without his bulletproof vest and six black bodyguards. When he traveled, it was in an armored Mercedes. He was always early or late for his appointments; never on time.

When the British finally decided to arrest him, the Mufti escaped from the Old City disguised as a beggar and fled to Jaffa, whence a fishing boat smuggled him to Lebanon.

From Beirut, under France's benign regard, the Mufti carried on his rebellion until World War II broke out. That September evening in 1939, contemplatively sucking on an olive, he asked a friend, "Do you think the Germans will be any better than the British?"

The Mufti's mind was already made up. He had been in contact with the Germans since 1936. The French politely chased the Mufti from Beirut to Baghdad, where he aided in a plot to overthrow a pro-British government with Axis help. When the plot failed, he fled to Teheran ahead of the onrushing British, and from there, when the British and the Russians invaded Iran in September 1941, to his rendezvous with Adolf Hitler in Berlin.

Six weeks after his final luncheon in Berlin in April 1945, Haj Amin Husseini and two of his followers were in Paris' Cherche Midi prison. They had fled Klagenfurt, Austria, in a Luftwaffe training plane, hoping for asylum in Switzerland. Rebuffed, Haj Amin had elected to turn himself over to the French. From Paris his path seemed destined to lead to a place of honor in the Nuremberg war-crimes trial and a sentence which would remove him from Palestine politics, thus opening the way to power to a more moderate Arab leadership.

There was ample evidence for such a trial. Much of it had been patiently amassed by Haj Amin's favorite chambermaid in Badgastein, a Jewish woman who was an operative of the Jewish Agency planted to shadow his activities. So successful had she been, so ignorant the Mufti of her role, that on his departure he had rewarded her with the mark of his affection: a substantial tip.

But Haj Amin never reached Nuremberg. The French, furious at their British-inspired eviction from Syria and Lebanon, were not displeased to hold in their custody such a potential source of embarrassment to the English. General Charles de Gaulle, the Mufti was told, "is interested in your case." Instead of prison, the Mufti and his followers were allowed to stay in a private villa outside Paris under discreet police surveillance.

The British, unwilling to risk Moslem ire in their colonies, did little, despite a series of pious public pronouncements, to get him on the road to Nuremberg. Finally, in the spring of 1946, Léon Blum on a United States visit was told by Zionist leaders that handing the Mufti over to the war-crimes trials would be an expected quid pro quo for United States economic aid. Sympathetic to the Zionist cause, Blum agreed. His Premier, Georges Bidault, did not. The Mufti was discreetly informed that it would be best if he slipped quietly away. On May 29, 1946, his beard shaven, in a business suit, bearing a forged Syrian passport and an American travel priority, he boarded a TWA plane for Cairo.*

Four days later, a three-word telegram arrived in his Jerusalem head-

---

* Twelve years later, the Paris paper *Paris Presse* claimed that the quid pro quo for his escape was the Mufti's pledge to regard benevolently France's role in her North African colonies of Morocco, Tunisia and Algeria.

quarters. It read: "Papa has returned." From that moment forward, the leadership of the Arabs of Palestine returned to his fanatic, uncompromising person. The bright, Western-educated young men Britain had groomed to take over from him began to look over their shoulders at who might be following them, and suddenly found pleasant things they had long forgotten to say about the Mufti.

For the next year and a half, Haj Amin Husseini, like David Ben-Gurion, devoted himself to preparing his people for the conflict both leaders knew would come. In a hotel room in the Lebanese mountain resort of Aley, he had followed, word by word, the final stages of the United Nations Palestine debate. At dawn, in a telephone call to Jerusalem, he issued the orders for the first action in the fight he had vowed during his last lunch in Berlin to resume. As he had twenty-seven years earlier at the outset of his career, he chose to begin that newest phase in his lifetime's struggle in the bastion he knew best, the souks of Jerusalem.

The crowds began to assemble in the souks at dawn December 1. "The street" was going to provide Haj Amin's reply to the United Nations vote. The city's Arab merchants shuttered their shops and whitewashed their storefronts with a crescent or a cross to shield them from the fury of the mob ready to answer the Mufti's call for a three-day general strike. For Jerusalem's Jewish population, the binge of Partition Night was over. The Arab crowd, its volatile emotions fired by the rumors deliberately spread on such occasions—this morning's claimed that two Arab women had been raped by the Jews at Jaffa Gate—quickly escaped control. Picking up supporters as they rolled along, a stream of workers, drifters, peasants in black-and-white checkered kaffiyehs, excited adolescents, curious shopkeepers in business suits, howling women, flowed toward the Jewish areas like a rush of water bursting from a dike. Sixteen-year-old Nadi Dai'es, a coffee boy at the bus company near Barclays Bank, felt "a surge of national feeling" fill his soul as the mob swept by. Suddenly elated, he dropped his coffee tray and rushed off to join it.

Yelling their slogans in a rhythmic Arabic singsong orchestrated by hand-clapping cheerleaders, the mob drove forward waving a forest of clubs and iron bars. One unlucky Jewish journalist caught on its route, Asher Lazar, was dragged from his car and badly wounded.

Watching them push up Princess Mary Avenue, Zvi Sinai, a Haganah observer, thought that at any moment the British would step forward and bar their progress. Like so many others, he had seen those same police drinking with and congratulating Jerusalem's Jews twenty-four hours earlier.

Now, to his stupefaction, they stared at the advancing demonstrators as indifferently as if they were a few drunken undergraduates celebrating the Oxford–Cambridge boat race at Piccadilly Circus.

Sensing the police's indifference, the mob swung into a sprawling marketplace full of Jewish shops, called the Commercial Center. Clubbing its terrified Jewish shopkeepers, smashing windows and ripping doors from their hinges, the rioters plunged into its stores, tearing goods from the shelves by the armful. Kids scampered into confectionery shops, stuffing their mouths and pockets with sticky wads of candy and halva. Adults tossed the cheap merchandise aside to reach for the best goods they could find—bolts of cloth, hats, bedspreads, shoes, cases of canned food. Some British policemen even gave a helping hand by shooting the locks off doors or, on at least one occasion, smashing open an iron grill with one of their armored cars.

With the shops half looted, the burning began. Before long, tight black spirals of smoke drifted up from every section of the quarter, sending a mist of ashes over the New City. A few of the area's Arab residents tried to check the damage. Samy Aboussouan, the violin-playing dentist, put out a fire in the store below his own apartment, then went off and discreetly painted a cross on a few shops left undamaged by the mob. They belonged to his Jewish friends.

Such efforts were whistling against a windstorm. Soon most of the quarter was ablaze, and a cordon of British police kept the Haganah from entering it.

Determined to revenge the Arab violence, a commando group of the illegal Irgun Zvai Leumi broke into the projection room of the Rex Cinema. They littered the floor with spools of film and set them on fire. In a few minutes the enormous theater was ablaze, its flaming shell sending the biggest, blackest column of smoke in the city up into Jerusalem's skyline.

A few blocks away, an Arab calmly stood on his balcony recording the spectacular blaze with his camera. Antoine Albina's pictures would find their way into Albina's family photo album. He was the owner of the theater going up in flames before his camera, its marquee still proclaiming the film Albina had been offering to his fellow Jerusalemites that week: *It's a Pleasure.*

4

TWO PASSENGERS TO PRAGUE

SWISSAIR FLIGHT 442 lifted off the tarmac and headed out over the dark green waves of orange groves toward the sea. From his window, Captain Abdul-Aziz Kerine stared down at the regular rectangles of Tel Aviv's city blocks where a few hours before he had stared in fascination at the exulting crowds celebrating the promise of a Jewish state. The captain unsnapped his seat belt and lit a cigarette. He was safely underway at last. In seven hours he would be in Paris, where he would catch another plane to his final destination, Prague.

The young captain owed his presence in the Swissair DC-4 to the fact that Syria's recently won independence gave her a prerogative she shared with only one other Arab state, Lebanon: the right to buy arms openly on the international arms market. Since independence, a horde of manufacturers' agents, middlemen, quasi-smugglers, all the fauna of the strange world of international arms traffic had laid siege to the office of Syria's M.I.T.–trained Defense Minister Ahmed Sherabati. A Belgian offered fifty thousand submachine guns at fifty-two dollars each, Spain twenty thousand used German Mausers for thirty-seven dollars apiece, Switzerland 81-millimeter mortars. An Italian of dubious reputation tried to peddle Sherman tanks. There were rifles without firing pins, machine guns without barrels, tanks without guns, airplanes without engines. Europe was, in fact, in those postwar days a gigantic secondhand arms store open to anyone with national credentials and cash in his pocket.

Syria's Defense Minister had finally decided to ignore the opportunists crowding his office and place his first order with one of Europe's most experienced arms manufacturers, the Zbrojovka Brno works of Czechoslovakia. The Syrian captain was on his way to Prague to confirm the order and arrange for its shipment to Damascus. By the standards of World War II, the ten thousand rifles it called for might seem a pittance. By the standards of the Jews of Palestine against whom those arms were to be used, however, it was enormous. The order, a copy of which was tucked into Captain Kerine's briefcase, represented, in fact, more than twice the number of arms in the entire Haganah central reserve.

A few seats behind the Syrian officer, another passenger, his shirt sleeves stretching well past the cuffs of a suit coat manifestly small for even his stubby figure, pored over the Hebrew daily *Davar.* Together with a toothbrush, a leather-bound Bible and a copy of *Faust,* that newspaper constituted the entire baggage of the absorbed reader. The Palestinian passport in his coat identified him as George Alexander Uiberall, a commercial director of the Jewish public-works firm Solel Boneh. In fact only two aspects of that passport were authentic: the passenger's age, thirty-one, and the photograph of his round, frowning face dominated by a pair of quietly determined eyes staring out from under two furry eyebrows.

His name was Ehud Avriel. He was not a commercial director of Solel Boneh or any other business enterprise. It was business, however, that was taking him to Europe, exactly the same business that had ordered Captain Abdul-Aziz Kerine's voyage. Ehud Avriel was flying to Europe in search of ten thousand rifles. His were for the Haganah.

A few hours earlier, a battered gray Ford had driven up to Avriel's kibbutz at Nahariya in northern Palestine. "Wash up and change," the driver told him. "I'm taking you to Jerusalem. The boss wants to see you."

Avriel had displayed no surprise. For ten years the quiet Austrian intellectual had devoted himself to the Zionist cause, achieving some of its most spectacular triumphs. From Vienna, then Istanbul, Athens and finally Paris, Avriel had supervised one of the most extraordinary adventures of the Jewish movement, the illegal immigration of thousands of European Jews into Palestine. In the middle of the war, he had succeeded in smuggling his men into Hitler's death camps. Over one hundred thousand Jews from every country in Europe were personally indebted to Avriel and his organization for having gotten them out of the Nazi inferno and onto the shores of the Promised Land. Now, barely two months after his own return to Palestine, he was once again being called away from his family and his kibbutz.

Three hours later, Avriel had entered a book-lined office on the second floor of the Jewish Agency Building in Jerusalem. Behind the desk, as quietly composed as the freshly pressed folds of his white open-necked shirt, David Ben-Gurion waited for him. With a gravity of tone Avriel had rarely remarked in the Jewish leader, Ben-Gurion told him that the very existence of the Jewish settlement in Palestine might depend on the success of the mission he was now assigning him.

"Listen, my young friend," he said. "War is going to break out here very soon. The Arabs are getting ready. They have five armies preparing to invade us sooner or later. After the United Nations' vote, we are going to have an Arab revolt on our hands right here in Palestine. What happened in 1936 was just child's play."

He was, he told Avriel, sending him to Europe to put his experience in the illegal immigration service to work buying arms. "We've got to change our tactics. We haven't got time any more to stuff four rifles into a tractor and wait for them to get to Haifa. We have to work fast and decisively.

"You have one million dollars at your disposal at the Union de Banques Suisses in Geneva," Ben-Gurion said. Then, taking from his pocket a meticulously folded piece of paper bearing six typewritten lines, he added, "Here is the list of what we need."

Avriel looked at the list: ten thousand rifles, one million rounds of ammunition, one thousand Sten guns, fifteen hundred machine guns. When Avriel glanced up, Ben-Gurion took a second piece of paper from his desk. It was a letter.

"There is a Jewish businessman in Paris named Klinger who says he can get it for us," said Ben-Gurion. "Go see him in Paris right away."

Then, getting up, the Jewish leader walked around his desk and clamped his heavy hand on Avriel's shoulder. "Ehud," he said, "you've got to get us those ten thousand rifles."

At about the same time Ehud Avriel's flight neared its final destination, two of the men who would be responsible for the use of the arms he had been sent to get met in a faded-pink stucco house on the Tel Aviv seafront. Known as the "Red House," that nondescript building at 44 Hayarkon Street was the secret headquarters of the Haganah. One of the two men was a brilliant archeologist, the son of the man who forty-eight hours earlier had seen the first scraps of the Dead Sea scrolls. In the summer of 1947, David Ben-Gurion had summoned Yigal Yadin from his studies of ancient Arabic inscriptions to the study of contemporary Arabic intentions as the chief planning officer of the Haganah.

Mishael Shacham was a Haganah workhorse. He had carried a gun in the Jewish cause since the age of eleven, when he had taken for the first time his turn as a guard in the settlement in which he had been born. Shacham had set up the Haganah's first primitive ammunition factory. Marrying his skills as a carpenter, electrician and plumber with the theoretical genius of the scientists at the Weizmann Institute, he had helped develop in 1938 a revolutionary explosive that could be detonated even when it was water-soaked.

The two men had been summoned to the office of Yaakov Dori, the chief of staff of the Haganah. Already the Haganah possessed a primitive communications system, and the Red House was linked to every Jewish settlement in Palestine by wireless. Its regional commanders reported daily on activities in their areas to Tel Aviv, where their reports were recorded in a central logbook.

The entry in the logbook for that winter day that had most concerned the commander of the Haganah did not, surprisingly, bear on the Arab riots in Jerusalem. It dealt with a minor incident, but an incident which was, it seemed to Yaakov Dori, a fatally ordained precursor of the struggle about to open. A Jewish bus driving from Natanya to Jerusalem had been ambushed by Arab riflemen near Lydda Airport. Three women and two men had died in the attack. Indicating the logbook entry that recorded the ambush, Dori told Shacham he was giving him the responsibility of guaranteeing the roads for Jewish transport.

"The war will be won or lost on the roads of Palestine," he said. "Our survival will depend on our transportation. You must keep the roads open."

Shacham and Yadin withdrew to Yadin's office. Spread around its walls were the sixteen sheets of a 1:100,000 survey of Palestine drawn up in 1945 by the 512th Survey Company of the British Army. Scattered to every corner of that enormous map was a field of red-tipped pins whose locations indicated the magnitude of the problem just assigned Mishael Shacham. From the Lebanese frontier in the north to the tip of the Negev in the south, from the Mediterranean to the Dead Sea, each of those red pins represented a Jewish settlement for whose lines of communication Shacham was now responsible.

Underneath each pin was a white tag bearing a few lines in Hebrew. They summarized the objectives assigned the settlement by the plan which Yadin had been summoned from his studies six months earlier to prepare. It was the Haganah's primary strategic document. Known as Plan D, Dalet, its basic premise was that warfare would break out in Palestine if the British withdrew and an attempt was made to establish a Jewish state. It also assumed that warfare would spread to Jerusalem along with the rest of the country, whatever the arrangements that might be made to hold the city out of the conflict.

The plan foresaw a temporary vacuum preceding and coinciding with Britain's withdrawal. During that vital first stage, the plan assigned to each settlement the task of static defense, of assuring its own survival until forces for a mobile war had been brought into play. The ability of those scattered settlements to survive would depend on whether the Haganah could get them the men and materials required for their defense before the British left Palestine.

Stretching from pin to pin, covering the map like irregular threads of some gigantic cobweb, were the miles of roads on which the Haganah chief of staff believed the war would be won or lost. To get to their destinations, most of those roads passed through large stretches of territory entirely under Arab control. There, over dozens of miles, the slightest curve, the merest hill or gully, a cluster of houses by the side of the road, could provide the cover for a disastrous ambush.

None of the isolated highways, however, represented a danger as grave as that posed by the route heading southeast across the heart of sheet number ten of the map spread out before Yadin and Shacham. The thickness of the wiggling red line it traced across the map indicated its importance. Forty-five miles long, rising from sea level to 2,500 feet, it was the artery leading to the men, women and children who represented the largest, most important Jewish settlement in Palestine, the 100,000 Jewish residents of Jerusalem.

In turn a caravan route of antiquity, a Biblical highway, the Via Maris of the legions of Rome, a passage to the heights of Judea for pilgrims, Crusaders, Saracens, Turks, every milestone along its path was engraved with the tortured history of the land it crossed. From the outskirts of Tel Aviv and Jaffa the road glided through the rich green orange groves to the first village on its route, an assemblage of ancient masonry bleached gray-white by the Mediterranean sun called Beit Dagon, after the fish god of the Philistines. Half a dozen miles farther on, it passed the dozens of acres of Palestine's largest British military camp, Sarafand. From there the road passed into Arab territory, its passage marked by the slender spire of a minaret beckoning from a town on the eastern horizon.

Founded by Suleiman the Magnificent, captured by Richard the Lionhearted, destroyed by Saladin, rebuilt by Egypt's Mamelukes, stormed by Napoleon, the community of Ramle, first major Arab town along the route, had been for generations the repair of caravan raiders and bandits. Just beyond, past a bald, sun-bleached hill, was the site of the Biblical city of Gezer, dowry of the daughter of Egypt's Pharaoh for her marriage to Solomon. From there the road skirted the Biblical Valley of Sorec, where Delilah was born and Samson's jackals with their flaming tails fired the crops of the Philistines. Sweeping along an easterly arc past an expanse of vineyards and wheatfields, the road entered the Valley of Ayalon, over which the sun had stood still for Joshua. At its exit stood two contradictory symbols of Palestine in 1947: the barbed-wire-encircled blockhouse of a

British police station dominating from its hillside eight miles of road, and, across a little draw, the red-tiled roof of the Trappist Monastery of the Seven Agonies of Latrun.

Below the monastery's terraced vineyards was a pumping station for Jerusalem's water supply and the ruins of an old hostelry. On both sides of the route, a stand of pines soared abruptly above the flat plains, the aged sentinels that marked the road's entryway into the narrow gorge which would carry it up two thousand feet to the heights of Judea. It was a green and pleasant place, called, in Arabic, Bab el Wad, the Gate of the Valley—in a few months, the name would symbolize for a generation of Palestine Jewry the price they had had to pay for a state called Israel.

From there, for twenty miles, the road twisted its way up a series of tight curves, its path buried at the foot of the valley, each of its sides a sheer, impenetrable descent of rock and forest. There every rock could hide a rifleman, every curve an ambush, every clump of trees a company of attackers. Even the communities dominating from their rocky perches the valley floor were in Arab hands: Kastel, hugging its heights by the ruins of a Crusader castle built in its turn upon the Roman fort that guarded the western approach to Jerusalem in Christ's time; Abu Gosh, where David had kept the Ark of the Covenant for two decades waiting to enter Jerusalem; Kolonia, rest area for Titus' legionnaires during the siege of Jerusalem.

It was not until the road had reached the heights of the Judean plateau and the kibbutz of Kiryat Anavim that a Jewish traveler could feel safe again. Four miles farther on, the road crested up to its culminating point. There, at the end of a long left-hand curve, the suburbs of Jerusalem promised safety at last.

Successors to the camel caravans of Biblical times, the chariots of the Romans, the zealous columns of the Crusades, wheezing lines of Jewish trucks and buses now struggled up that gulch to Jerusalem, carrying in their vans the ingredients vital for the city's life. Protecting that fragile communication line was an immense, almost insurmountable problem.

While Shacham and Yadin pondered its future, Jerusalem tied up the wounds of a day's rioting. A severe curfew had finally cleared the Commercial Center of Arab looters. The once prosperous quarter was a black jumble of damp and rancid ruins. Standing at the window of his apartment above the Jewish shop he had saved earlier in the day, Samy Aboussouan stared into the night contemplating the results of his countrymen's wrath. His electric power, his telephone, his gas were cut. Now, in the darkness, he listened to a series of sharp reports coming from the still-smoldering cinders of a nearby grocery store. That disconcerting noise would haunt the blackened quarter all night long. It was the intermittent explosion of hundreds of cans of sardines. Angrily, Aboussouan decided he had had enough. He would leave the Commercial Center for a safer refuge as soon as he could.

The bedroom of the Hotel California on Paris' Rue de Berri, across the street from the offices of the Paris *Herald Tribune,* was gray with the haze of cigar smoke. On the edge of the bed, the man whom David Ben-Gurion had sent to Paris to buy ten thousand rifles caressed his bald head in despair. The merchant who had been going to open the gates to Europe's arsenals to Ehud Avriel had turned out to know as much about buying rifles as Avriel knew about buying roses. In a desperate search for a replacement, Avriel had spent the day interviewing it seemed every spurious arms merchant in Europe.

His last interviewee, a Rumanian Jew operating a small import-export business in Paris, now sat before him. Somewhat shamefacedly, Robert Adam Abramovici explained to Avriel that he had smuggled himself into Palestine aboard a small sailing boat in 1943 but had not stayed. The Promised Land had been too confining, too spartan for his tastes. "I like the good life," he confessed. "I like horses, women. So when the war was over, I came to France. If I hadn't been so demanding, I would still be a Palestinian and it would be I, not you, Ben-Gurion would have sent to buy arms." He had been the Rumanian representative of one of Europe's biggest arms manufacturers before the war, he revealed, and the managers of that firm remained his close friends. "They will sell us what we need," he told an astonished Avriel.

He drew out of his briefcase two catalogues. Avriel, his eyes bulging with wonder, skimmed their pages crammed with the photographs of an arsenal so vast, he thought, even David Ben-Gurion's fertile imagination could not have conceived of it.

There was, Abramovici warned, one major restriction on the purchase of those arms. The manufacturers could not deal with an individual, but only with the authorized representative of a sovereign nation. Since a Jewish state would not officially exist for months to come, Avriel would have to get them official credentials from some other nation.

Avriel pondered for a moment, then ordered an aide to the office around the corner at 53 Rue de Ponthieu from which he had directed the clandestine immigration operations for the Jewish Agency. In the bottom drawer of his old desk was a file which might contain a solution to their problem. That file bore the name of a nation whose only ties to Jewry lay in the Biblical era, in the days of Solomon and Sheba. One year earlier, for the sum of one thousand dollars offered to the White Russian prince who was Haile Selassie's special envoy in Europe, Avriel had purchased one hundred signed and sealed blank letterheads of the Paris legation of Ethiopia. He had used them to draw up false visas for Jewish immigrants crossing France to the secret ports of embarkation.

The aide returned with the file. There were exactly eight letterheads left. As Abramovici looked at them, a warm and knowing smile spread over his face. They were exactly the documents they needed.

Abramovici drew two envelopes out of his pocket. He kept one and handed the other to Avriel. The Rumanian epicure had thought of everything. They contained plane tickets to the capital in which the headquarters of his former employers' arms industry was located.

As Avriel congratulated himself on his good luck in his Paris hotel room, fifteen hundred miles away a beaming Arab captain was congratulating himself, too, on the success of his own European mission. While Avriel and Abramovici had been talking, Abdul-Aziz Kerine had been buying arms from his Czech manufacturers in their modern office building at 20 Avenue Belchrido in Prague. In less than twenty-four hours after his arrival, he could note with satisfaction, he had secured his country's order for ten thousand Model E-18 Mausers and one hundred MG-34 submachine guns and had started to make arrangements to ship them to Damascus.

The young captain's satisfaction would have been less complete had he been aware of the identity of the next client who would enter the modern office building in which he had spent the afternoon. At the moment Captain Kerine sat down to dinner in his hotel, the other client was packing his toothbrush, his Bible and his volume of *Faust* for a trip to Prague, where, the next morning, Ehud Avriel was scheduled to have his own conference at 20 Avenue Belchrido with the directors of the Zbrojovka Brno arms works.

• • •

Ehud Avriel's appearance at 20 Avenue Belchrido marked the beginning of the newest phase in a struggle which had been, for the Jews of Palestine, as relentless as the pursuit of water to irrigate their fields: the search for the arms with which to defend them. Until 1936, the armories of their kibbutzim and fortified villages had been filled with a random assortment of rifles bought from the Arabs whose marauders they were meant to repulse. The arrival in the port of Haifa that year of a seemingly routine shipment of tractors, road rollers and steam boilers marked the end of the helter-skelter procurement of arms and the beginning of a more systematic effort to furnish the Haganah equipment. Every hollow space in that array of machinery was stuffed with arms and ammunition.

It had been placed there by a former police inspector turned orange exporter, an elegant man whose talent for intrigue was rivaled only by his taste for beautiful women. To cover his activities in his Warsaw headquarters, Yehuda Arazi had taken control of an agricultural machine shop by saving its debt-ridden owner from the public auctioneer's hammer. Every Saturday after the last worker had left, Arazi and the grateful owner stripped down a week's production of tractors and road rollers, jammed them full of arms, then welded them back together again. Over the course of three years, Arazi's little machine shop managed to smuggle to Palestine 3,000 rifles, 226 machine guns, 10,000 hand grenades, three million cartridges, hundreds of mortar shells and, his proudest achievement, three small planes.*

The end of World War II, however, led to the most extraordinary adventure in the Haganah's arms procurement program. It began, in a sense, in a Tel Aviv sidewalk café one evening in early summer 1945. Scanning his newspaper that night, the eyes of Haim Slavine fell upon a brief news item datelined Washington, D.C. Seven hundred thousand practically new machine tools of the U.S. armament industry would be converted to scrap metal in the next few months, it said. Slavine got up, went home and drafted a letter to David Ben-Gurion. Before the Yishuv, he said, was an opportunity that history would not offer twice. Get those machines, he urged, and smuggle them into Palestine to provide the foundations of a modern armament industry.

A cantankerous, irascible genius, Slavine had a mastery of chemistry, physics and engineering which, with the already impressive contribution he had made to the Haganah's arms program, assured his letter a careful reading. By day the director of Palestine's most important power station, Slavine became by night the Haganah's mad chemist. Using the kitchen of his two-

---

* Only one of Arazi's shipments failed to reach its destination on time. Warned that the British Intelligence Service was preparing to intercept a delivery of machine tools designed to manufacture bullets, Arazi diverted his shipment at the last moment to a notably inhospitable destination, Beirut. By some miracle, the Lebanese customs never investigated the delivery, which sat in a bonded warehouse for two years. Finally smuggled into Haifa, the equipment was assembled after the war in a tiny underground munitions factory built under the fields of a kibbutz. By late 1945, it was turning out the first munitions manufactured locally by the Jewish settlement in Palestine.

room flat as a miniature arms lab, he produced TNT detonators and experimented with the manufacture of hand grenades. His letter reached Ben-Gurion while the Jewish leader was still digesting the information imparted him a few weeks earlier by his American visitor en route home from Yalta. To Ben-Gurion, it offered a concrete way to prepare his people for the showdown he foresaw with the Arabs.

He ordered Slavine to leave for New York immediately. There he put him in contact with the aristocrat scion of one of the United States' most prominent Jewish families. Since his first visit to Palestine as a young naval lieutenant just after World War I, two preoccupations had dominated the life of Rudolf G. Sonneborn—Zionism and his family's chemical concern. At Ben-Gurion's behest, he had assembled a score of American Zionist leaders into a body already dubbed the Sonneborn Institute. Chosen by Sonneborn because they could keep a secret, its members were men of means who represented a broad breakdown of the United States both geographically and industrially.

With their help, Slavine set to work. He began by locking himself into a hotel room with stacks of back issues of *Technical Machinery,* a publication he had discovered by chance on a New York newsstand. Meticulously he memorized from the photographs in those old magazines the technical details of the machines needed for an armament industry. Then, passing himself off as deaf and dumb so that his limited and heavily accented English would not stir suspicions, Slavine set out on a pilgrimage to the machine-tool centers of the United States. From city to city he made his way, buying up drill presses, lathes, grinders, borers in his new role as a scrap-metal dealer. Some machines whose only function was producing munitions had already been broken down as required by American law and their parts widely scattered. To find the parts he was not able to purchase, Slavine organized a team of scavengers who scoured the nation's junkyards. As each machine was bought, it was shipped back to Slavine's headquarters, an abandoned dairy plant at 2000 Park Avenue.

By the time his prodigious purchasing mission was finished, Slavine had acquired the machinery to mount a daily production of fifty thousand rifle or machine-gun bullets, the machine tools needed to perform the 1,500 operations necessary for assembly-line production of a machine gun, and equipment to manufacture 81-millimeter mortar shells. Bought by weight at its value as scrap metal, that mass of machinery had cost Slavine $2 million. In terms of what such machinery had cost new only months before, its value was over $70 million.

Shipping it back to Palestine was an enormous problem. Its bulk was so tremendous that Yehuda Arazi's tactic of stuffing a few bits and pieces into a steam boiler was hopelessly outmoded. After devoting all his skill and patience to assembling his machines in his dairy, Slavine set about stripping them down to the last nut and bolt. When he had finished, 75,000 pieces of machinery had been scattered about the dairy floor. Slavine personally classified each piece according to a code he invented. Then, chosen at random, the bits and pieces were mixed up and crated for shipment to Palestine under an official import permit for thirty-five tons of textile machinery taken out in the name of an imaginary Arab manufacturer. So completely had the pieces been scrambled that only an engineering genius could have detected the real nature of the machines at a customs inspection. Crate by crate, they were slipped past British customs, their passage occasionally expedited by a well-placed bribe.*

By the night when the United Nations had voted to partition Palestine, those crates were safely hidden in kibbutzim throughout Palestine, waiting to be unpacked and assembled. The long delay between the vote and the date the British would actually leave Palestine posed a dilemma for the Jewish leadership. Should they assemble Slavine's equipment immediately so as to have it in full production by the time of the British departure, at the risk of having the British discover and confiscate it? Or should they keep it safely hidden until the British had gone, knowing that it would not be in production when they would need it most, in the first weeks of their state's life?

Finally the risks of losing it seemed too great. For the engineer who had envisaged an arms industry in a Tel Aviv café, that decision postponed the proudest moment of a lifetime. When the last of his machines was finally assembled and operating, Haim Slavine would be able to boast that he had not lost a single bolt, a single screw, a single washer in shipping 75,000 pieces of machinery from his New York dairy plant to the kibbutzim of Israel.

---

* Those customs officials were among the few beneficiaries of that troubled time. In New York in the fall of 1969, Rudolf Sonneborn estimated to one of the authors of this book that as much as $250,000 of his institute's funds had wound up in the Swiss accounts of British officials as the price for their inattention when vital shipments were sent into Palestine.

5

TWO PEOPLES, TWO ARMIES

NO JEW IN PALESTINE awaited the arms Ehud Avriel had been sent to Europe to purchase more anxiously than Israel Amir, commander of the Jerusalem Haganah. In Jerusalem, as everywhere else, the Haganah's shortage of arms was a crippling problem. Jerusalem's pitiful little arsenal was squirreled away in two dozen *slicks*,* secret caches, scattered around the city, their whereabouts known to only one man on Amir's staff—his arms expert, a Yemenite cheesemaker. They were toted around the city by Amir's girl soldiers, the parts tucked into bras or girdles or strapped between their legs. There were more men than weapons and sometimes, it seemed, as many types of arms as there were potential users.

Eight days after the partition vote, thanks, as Amir would later recall, to "a little planning and a lot of confusion," the Jerusualem Haganah had mobilized five hundred men on a full-time basis. Instant soldiers, those men had been plucked from civilian life with a phone call, a message on a scrap of paper or a whispered order on a street corner.

Amir assembled them in the Jewish high school of Rehavia. He held some there as a reserve for his Home Guard, composed of older, less trained men. The rest he stationed in exposed neighborhoods or in mixed quarters where trouble was likely to break out. In dark-olive corduroy trousers and old work shirts, they took up posts on rooftops, in gardens, behind doorways and windows, surveying every incident, studying the comings and goings of the population, following the movements of strangers. With a girl beside them they patrolled the sidewalks like loitering lovers, the girl hiding a pistol under her blouse.

Netanel Lorch, who had thought "dancing is for the innocents" on Partition Night, was sent to the ultra-religious quarter of Mea Shearim with twenty boys and six girls. He classified his girls according to the size of the weapon they could smuggle. The range went from a pistol carrier up to a girl so big she could, Lorch thought, have smuggled him a field gun—if

---

* The Haganah nickname for a hiding place, taken from the Hebrew verb *lesalek,* meaning to dispose of.

only he had had a field gun to smuggle. The presence of the boys and girls together in one small apartment outraged the moral dignity of the conservative religious community. Lorch finally had to set up two guard systems, one to protect him from a nearby British police station, the other to protect him from Mea Shearim's angry rabbis.

Eliyahu Arbel, another of Amir's officers, also ran into the conservatism of those religious communities. After an exhausting argument with a rabbi who wanted a written guarantee that his students would not fight on the Sabbath, Arbel threw up his hands. "Look," he said, "if you really want that pledge, it's the Arabs who'll have to give it to you, not I."

The task of forming a new battalion fell to Shalom Dror, a soft-spoken German Jew with the girth of a stevedore. To equip his nonexistent battalion, he sent girl soldiers to take up a door-to-door collection for blankets, cots, clothes and utensils. To feed his first recruits, he printed up a series of meal tickets for use in the neighborhood restaurants. For most of his manpower he turned to the white stone buildings of Hebrew University, set in a grove of pines on the heights of Mount Scopus dominating the northwestern approaches of the city. That university was a lodestone for some of the most capable youth in Palestine. It had also become a magnet attracting Jewish youth from all over the world. The Haganah now turned to some of those young men to bear witness to the solidarity of the world Jewish community in the coming struggle for Jerusalem.

Bobby Reisman should not have been at Hebrew University at all. He really wanted to be at the Sorbonne in Paris. A businessman's son from Buffalo, New York, Reisman had served with the 101st Airborne in World War II until a wound ended his military career. After the war he had decided to go to Paris to study on the G.I. Bill, but en route, a friend had persuaded Bobby to go instead to Jerusalem because he was sure they would speak English at the university there. To their dismay, the two discovered on their arrival that at Hebrew University they spoke Hebrew, not English. His friend left, but Bobby stayed, studying philosophy and, before long, a dark-haired sabra named Leah. By December 1947, they were married, living in a room of a student boardinghouse in Bet Hakerem.

Stretched out on his bed one night, Reisman heard a rustling of paper. It was a note being slid under his door. He picked it up. The note was in Hebrew, a language he still could not read. He passed it to his wife. She read it silently. Then she lowered it and looked at him for a long and thoughtful instant. It was an invitation, she said, an invitation to join the Haganah.

Reisman sank wordlessly back onto his bed. He had not come to this land to fight. He had had all the war he ever wanted in Europe. Yet he could feel the dark eyes of his wife watching him, waiting for his answer. A few feet away, under a pile of clothes in their bureau, was a small pistol, the badge of her own membership in the organization. He looked into her waiting eyes, and as he did he knew he could not be a spectator in his wife's war. "All right," he sighed, "I'll do it."

Carmi Charny's situation was just the opposite. Carmi desperately wanted the Haganah; the problem was, the Haganah didn't want Carmi. Carmi had been born next to the Bronx Zoo on New Year's Eve 1925, the son of a rabbi. Like his father, he had been destined for the rabbinate. In the Bronx of the depression, that meant a bleak and cheerless life of study. Carmi paid the price. He grew up shy, introspective, frail. With his thick glasses, his pale sensitive face, his stooped shoulders, he was every neighborhood bully's idea of the helpless Jew, the target on which to show off one's fists by the corner drugstore. Carmi took his solace in the dreams of the Land of Zion that rose from his texts and the poems he wrote in Hebrew, a language he had mastered before he was an adolescent. After the war, as naturally as if he were getting on the downtown subway, he boarded the S.S. *Marine Carp,* leaving behind forever the crowded tenements of the Bronx, and set out for the land to which he had felt himself destined since childhood.

Since his arrival in Jerusalem he had tried to enlist in the Haganah. The pale, scholarly Carmi, however, was not the kind of recruit the Haganah was looking for. Finally, thanks to a girl friend who belonged, Carmi found himself in the darkened basement of Rehavia High School, sitting opposite three men whose faces he could not see. When they had finished questioning him, he was taken into a cell-like chamber. On a table before him were two candles, a Bible and a pistol. A projector cut through the blackness, drenching him in light. Carmi could feel in the darkness beyond the projector the presence of other men watching. He placed one hand on the Bible, the other on the cold pistol butt, the metallic embodiment of his schoolboy's visions. Shivering with emotion, the frail rabbi's son from the Bronx swore, by the "supreme conscience of Zionism," his allegiance to the underground army of the Haganah.

By that brief and memorable ceremony a generation of Palestinians had entered the organization that was the common denominator of their existence. Known by its code name "The Aunt," the Haganah was tightly woven into every structure of the community to which it belonged. Aware of the numerical superiority of the Arabs, the Haganah from its beginning had accepted women on an equal footing with men. It had spawned its own youth organization, the Gadna, which under the cover of Girl Scout and Boy Scout troops prepared youngsters for Haganah service. As a result, by the time the United Nations decided to partition Palestine the majority of Palestine's Jewish youth had been exposed to some form of Haganah training.

For some like Netanel Lorch, Haganah service was a tradition passed from father to son. His first exposure to the organization came carrying bullets in the lining of his schoolboy's jacket to his Haganah soldier father during the Arab uprising in 1936. For others, the swearing in ceremony at sixteen was a kind of temporal bar mitzvah, a symbolic step toward Palestinian manhood. For still others, victims of Nazi persecution, the Haganah underground in Europe represented a first contact with Palestine.

The Haganah's primary rule was secrecy. There were no photographs, and written records were held to a minimum. Its training centers were in the basements of Jewish institutions, usually schools or trade-union clubs. Protected by a triple tier of guards, members met once a week to practice judo, learn to break down weapons, climb ropes, burst into houses, jump from moving cars, always ready at any hint of a British raid to convert themselves into studious schoolboys or card-playing workers. Then they served an apprenticeship carrying messages or tracking the movements of key Arab and British figures. Finally they began field training two or three days a month, usually in some remote wadi reached by a punishing march under the sun, where the wastes of the desert might muffle the crack of a rifle shot. Oranges and potatoes stuffed with detonators served as dummy hand grenades. So desperately short was ammunition that the most solemn moment in a recruit's rifle course often came when he was given a single round to fire as a kind of graduation present. In the summer, disguised as extra field hands, Haganah units were sent out to kibbutzim for two weeks or a month's advanced training. Guerrilla tactics and the night fighting the Arabs loathed became their specialties. The Haganah command even managed to install, despite British surveillance, a two-month officers' course, processing one hundred and fifty men at a time at an experimental agricultural station in the Valley of Jezreel. The texts that inspired that course were culled from a collection of little red books patiently pilfered from the barracks of the mandatory power, the training manuals of the British Army.

By the Second World War, the Haganah had an embryonic general staff, its members scattered around Tel Aviv, in the Housing Bureau of the Histadrut trade union, an architect's office, a bank, the office of an importer of agricultural machinery, the Water Supply Bureau. Its few archives were locked in an underground hideaway built into the foundations of a Tel Aviv apartment building. World War II gave its men combat training. Largely at its bidding, forty-three thousand Palestinian Jews served in the war.

Paradoxically, Jerusalem, the center of Zionist aspirations in Palestine, had never been fertile ground for the Haganah. British surveillance had been stricter there than elsewhere. Urban youth simply did not respond to the Haganah with the fervor of kibbutz youth. Jerusalem's orthodox communities were often indifferent or even hostile to its aims.

Yet in Jerusalem, as elsewhere in Palestine, it was one of the principal motors of Jewish society. More than its training courses, more than its organization, more than any of its clandestine accomplishments, the real strength of the Haganah lay in the spirit it had engendered among the Jews of Palestine. Egalitarian yet individualistic, organized yet guided by an agile sense of improvisation, the Haganah was an accurate reflection of the community it sought to defend. The best young men produced by the Jewish return to Palestine unhesitatingly provided its leadership. By their example, they had given the Haganah a tradition of sacrifice and service to which Carmi Charny had bound himself laying his hands on a Bible and a pistol in the darkened basement of Rehavia High School.

* * *

No comparable tradition animated Jerusalem's Arab community. Young males of the Arab bourgeoisie who had had any systematic exposure to arms or military training were rare. Such activities had been traditionally disdained by the Arab bourgeoisie, who left to other classes the tasks of soldiery. When Hazem Nusseibi the young radio editor and his neighbors discovered there was not even a pistol in their dozen villas near the road to Mount Scopus, their reaction was typical. Each rushed to the souks to buy a firearm from the illegal gun merchants flourishing there, driving even higher their already inflated prices. Then Nusseibi led a neighborhood delegation to the offices of the Arab Higher Committee, seeking protection. After a long session of haggling interspersed with cups of coffee, the committee agreed to furnish them ten peasant riflemen from a village in Samaria for the fee of ten Palestine pounds per man per month.

In Upper Beqaa, a middle-class community south of the railroad station, three brothers, George, Raymond and Gaby Deeb, sons of Jerusalem's Buick dealer, set out to form a home guard. From Upper Beqaa's five thousand inhabitants they were able to raise barely seventy-five volunteers. Most of the families found an excuse to keep their sons and husbands out of its ranks. Some of the neighborhood's wealthier merchants sent their sons to school in Beirut or Amman to keep them out of the force.

Resigned, the Deebs filled out the ranks of their home guard from the only source of manpower available in Jerusalem, the armed bands of the Mufti. For the going rate of ten pounds a man a month, they hired twenty-eight men from a village in the north. They housed them in the neighborhood's garages and attics and fed them out of its kitchens. To lead their mercenaries the Deebs hired a former police sergeant with a rasping voice, a quick temper and a fondness for Scotch whiskey, named Abou Khalil Genno.

The colorful Genno and his band soon became a nightmare for the Deebs and their neighbors. The accidental explosion of a hand grenade caused the first casualties in the neighborhood, and the mercenaries seemed to spend as much time searching abandoned houses for liquor as they did on guard. A leaping cat, an unusual noise, a probing shot from a Jewish post was usually enough to unleash a wild burst of their fire, terrifying with indiscriminate equality the Arabs of Upper Beqaa and their Jewish neighbors.

Those wild bursts of gunfire expressed, to a certain degree, the mentality of the Arab villagers. For them, the possession of a firearm was as sure a proof of its owner's masculinity as his first male heir. Part weapon, part plaything, it was used to mark weddings, funerals and village feasts with a copious barrage of noise and lead. From that upbringing came a natural familiarity with arms but a tendency to fire off ammunition recklessly that was markedly different from the habits inculcated in their Jewish foes, to whom each cartridge was a minor treasure.

Often only a generation or two removed from the Bedouin existence, those villagers were frequently men of real courage endowed with an instinctive capacity for the ambush and the guerrilla raid. Properly led, they could be a ferocious adversary, and it was from their ranks that the Mufti had always drawn his most faithful followers. His Jerusalem representatives had tried to group their clans into a coherent force capable of becoming the Arab answer to the Haganah. Haj Amin himself had recently officially baptized the organization the Jihad Moquades, the Holy War Strugglers. Its members, like the young Jews of the Haganah, were taken secretly to the woods and wadis to learn to operate the astonishing variety of weapons the war had left scattered throughout Palestine. Like the Haganah, it had a youth group, called the Futweh, to funnel to it young recruits.

73

What the Mufti's men took to be an operational force, however, was in fact just an improvised paramilitary organization thrown over Palestine's village and tribal structures. Chained to the villages which sustained it, its members ignorant of anything except elemental military techniques, its command structure based on clan and family rather than ability, it was an ill-disciplined force of limited effectiveness.

Above all, the prime requisite for membership was allegiance to the Mufti, and it was the clans, tribes and villages whose loyalty was already well established that were called on to furnish its manpower. Unlike the Haganah with its deep roots in the Jewish community, the Mufti's warriors were a kind of private army whose function was as much to remind Palestine's Arab community who their leader was as it was to fight the Jews.

Mediocre at its best, abysmal at its worst, its leadership was barely literate, more suited to uttering threats at their Jewish neighbors than to leading their men in the field. Their chief was a forty-two-year-old inspector in the Palestine police force, the scion of an old Jerusalem family, named Kamal Irekat. He had a professionally fierce scowl, a Pancho Villa moustache, burning black eyes and a predilection to be photographed in front of his men in riding breeches and a flowing Arab headdress. Irekat had achieved the dubious distinction of being the first Arab leader to vow to "throw the Jews into the sea."

These glaring shortcomings in their social and military structures did not unduly alarm the Arabs of Jerusalem. They knew that in Palestine they belonged to a community twice as large as that of the Jews. They had, in the Middle East, far more access to arms than the Jews. With their strategically situated villages ringing Jerusalem, they had the advantage of superior terrain.

More than anything else, however, they believed that the key to their salvation lay elsewhere. For weeks, the radio and press of the Arab capitals around them had been assuring the Arabs of Palestine that their plight was the plight of all the Arabs. Never would their Arab neighbors allow Palestine to fall to the Jews. As once the warriors of Omar and Saladin, they would come to the rescue of their brothers in Palestine and with their artillery, their aviation and their armor rescue them by the force of Arab arms.

6

"WE WILL STRANGLE JERUSALEM."

AS THEY HAD every night all during the week of December 1947, crowds gathered along Cairo's main street, the Kash el Nil, to stare up at the lights blazing from the palace of Kamal Adin Husseini, office of the Egyptian Ministry of Foreign Affairs. Their charcoal braziers glowing in the mid-December dusk, the street vendors wandered among them selling grilled watermelon seeds and ears of freshly roasted corn. In the palace, under a bank of Aubusson tapestries, eight angry men, the objects of the crowd's curiosity, argued around a rectangular table in the main salon.

Seven of those men represented the seven nations of the Arab League —Egypt, Iraq, Saudi Arabia, Syria, Yemen, Lebanon, Transjordan; the eighth was the secretary general of their organization. Prime ministers or foreign ministers of their nations, they were the leaders upon whose pledges the Arabs of Palestine were counting for their deliverance. They represented a potentially impressive force. Together, the men gathered in the salons of the Egyptian Foreign Ministry ruled some forty-five million people spread over three million square miles, an entity thirty times more populous and two hundred times larger than Palestine. Under their desert wastes lay the world's most important proven reserves of petroleum. They had at their command five regular armies, three of them, in Iraq, Egypt and Transjordan, of some importance.

Bound together by common ties of language, history and religion, they offered a deceptive appearance of strength and solidarity. Two nations, Syria and Lebanon, were French-style republics. Three, Saudi Arabia, Yemen and Jordan, were quasi-feudal kingdoms evolved from desert tribal patterns. Two, Egypt and Iraq, had constitutional monarchies of British inspiration.

They were riven by rivalries: the historic rivalry between Cairo and Baghdad, dating to the caliphs; modern, economically inspired rivalries between oil-rich Saudi Arabia and her poorer neighbors; tribal, national and personal rivalries such as those that led Syria to covet Lebanon, and

Iraq, Syria and their leaders to indulge in a continual conspiracy for pre-eminence in their fractured society.

For four years those leaders had vied with each other in the extremism of their declarations on Palestine, turning the issue into the yardstick by which an Arab politician's patriotism might be measured, encouraging with their extravagant threats the unbending stance of Palestine's Arabs. "The United Nations," Lebanon's Riad Solh had boasted, "will have to station a foreign soldier in front of every Jew in Palestine to make their state work."

Now the time had come to start translating their bellicose threats into action. For a long and clamorous week they had argued in this room, their debates revealing what they all well knew: that a considerable gap lay between their public threats and their private sentiments. The nobility of sentiment with which some of them proclaimed their bonds to their Palestine brothers was limited by the covetous regard they themselves cast upon that ancient land. For them, action in Palestine would be undertaken with an eye to its effect on their own rivalries and conflicting interests. Disdainful of their foes, they did not feel the need for sacrifice and strain to prepare themselves for a showdown with the Zionists.

Night after night, in the position of honor reserved for the delegate of the host country, Egypt's Prime Minister Mahmoud Nokrashy Pasha had reiterated his stand: he was prepared to send to Palestine arms and money, but not the force the men around him clamored for, the Egyptian Army. Proud of their pharaonic heritage, Nokrashy's countrymen tended to regard their Arab neighbors with a somewhat patronizing air, and few Egyptians were deeply concerned by the Palestine problem. Palestine was assigned a secondary role in the Egyptian press.

Behind Nokrashy's attitude was Egypt's conflict with Britain over the Suez Canal. Without Britain's accord he felt he could not commit his army to a struggle in which his lines of communication would have to pass through the British-controlled canal zone.

Next to Nokrashy was the representative of the wealthiest nation in the Arab world, Prince Faisal of Saudi Arabia. His father was a legendary warrior, an old-style desert caliph who could slit a rival's throat with his own hands or welcome him with the elaborate courtesy of his Bedouin upbringing. He had established his kingdom by driving from Arabia the family that ruled two of the nations sharing the table with Faisal, the Hashemites of Iraq and Jordan.

An able and soft-spoken diplomat, Faisal was the antithesis of the public's image of an Arab prince. Scion of the blood in a land in which a man's rank might be measured by the size of his harem, Faisal had had one wife all his life and lived as frugally as any New England banker serving up his codfish cakes with a homily on thrift. The persistent pain of the stomach ulcer he nursed with the milk of an ass had creased his face and darkened his melancholy eyes until, peering out from under the hood of his black-and-gold abayah, he seemed the incarnation of some mournful El Greco Christ.

His father's wish to die at the head of his troops in Palestine was a noble sentiment, but not a particularly helpful one. Ibn-Saud didn't have any troops worth speaking of. What he did have was oil, and the threat that stopping its flow represented in the West, particularly in the United States. Each time his son had been urged to cut the flow of that oil—and the revenues it produced—as Saudi Arabia's contribution to the conflict, his reply had been, "The problem is Palestine, not petroleum."

Opposite Faisal was the representative of the man who ruled Iraq as surely as Faisal's father ruled Saudi Arabia, Nuri as-Said Pasha. He had ridden with Lawrence and had chosen since 1917 to cast his destiny with the British he so admired. Short, stubby, with a little white Chaplinesque moustache, Nuri Pasha was given to tweed suits, the striped ties of his numerous London clubs, and, with the onset of age, a growing deafness to noise and advice he did not like. He was above all a prodigious manipulator of men. No officer in Nuri Pasha's army, no politician in his government, no merchant or landlord in his nation acquired a new mistress, a late-blooming taste for camel boys or a disproportionate slice of baksheesh without that fact coming to Nuri Pasha's attention for use at some propitious moment in the future. Those tactics had earned Nuri Pasha few friends; but they had provided him with a host of devoted followers.

No Arab leader was more ready to do the Jews verbal violence than Nuri Pasha. But, while he was reviling them publicly, he had been whispering to his friends in the British Foreign Office that he would accommodate their state if the price of his agreement were British support for his annexing Syria to Iraq and realizing his dream of a fertile Arab crescent from the Mediterranean to the Persian Gulf.

Nuri Pasha's representative at the conference had put forward a plan designed to stall for time. Wait until the British left Palestine, he counseled; then the Arab armies, with Iraq's at their head, would sweep to Tel Aviv. His suggestion had raised more suspicion than support. Nuri Pasha's rivals saw in all his moves the hand of the British, and they suspected that his proposal was designed as much to use his army to extend British influence into Palestine as it was to shatter plans for a Jewish state.

77

His maroon fez cocked at its usual jaunty angle, a broad smile accenting his prominent cheekbones, Riad Solh, representative of the smallest country at the table, Lebanon, was the foremost advocate of an immediate guerrilla campaign in Palestine. He spoke with considerable authority. He was the architect of Lebanon's proudest claim, that of being the first Arab country to win its independence from the West. Six times Solh had been condemned to death by the French and Turkish occupants of his country. On the day he became an independent Lebanon's first prime minister, he could look back on half a lifetime spent in jail or exile. He had himself already made his personal contribution to the conflict, a gesture of a dimension appropriate to the land he represented in Cairo. Over his wife's furious objections, he had helped convert his next-door neighbor's print shop into a miniature arms plant to make bullets for the Palestinians.

Beside Solh sat his close friend and political ally, a gentleman farmer whose passionate devotion to Arab independence had earned him too half a lifetime in jail or exile. Syria's Jamil Mardam had, in fact, been one of the first members of the Al Fatat secret society founded to win Arab independence from Ottoman Turkey before World War I. He too was a passionate advocate of opening an immediate guerrilla campaign in Palestine. Under Syrian guidance he hoped it would provide a means to counterbalance the influence and ambitions of his rivals in Iraq.

At the center of the table, nervously clicking his amber worry beads between his fingers, Abdurrahman Azzam Pasha, the secretary general of the Arab League, had striven all week to ride herd on the divergent opinions and personalities gathered around him. A lean, courtly man with a soft voice and a receding chin, he was, despite his title, a revolutionary. While Lawrence had led the Arabs against the Turks, Azzam, aided by the Turks, had led his own uprising against Egypt's British overlords. He was surely the first Arab to appeal for Soviet aid for the Arab cause, asking Lenin for assistance in his rebellion the day news of the October Revolution reached Constantinople.

Now on the table before him was a four-page memorandum. Stamped "SECRET," it was largely the product of Azzam's patient efforts to effect a compromise between the viewpoints represented in the salon of the Egyptian Foreign Office. Slowly Azzam began to read it to the men around him.

The first paragraph represented the very essence of the problem that had brought them to Cairo. "The Arab League," it proclaimed, "is resolved to prevent the creation of a Jewish state in Palestine and to conserve Palestine as a united, independent state."

The secretary general looked up. He well knew that at least three men at the table around him had grave reservations about committing themselves to that course of action, and an even graver reluctance to pay the price to carry it out. A week of debate had revealed neither the conviction nor the coordination the Arabs would need to realize such a resolution. As they had debated, however, they had released a daily stream of belligerent communiqués. As had happened so often in the past, as would happen so often in the future, Arab leaders were unable to avoid the consequences of their own careless rhetoric. In a chorus, the men at the table gave their approval to the resolution.

Azzam continued. The countries around the table were to furnish to the League, on a predetermined basis, ten thousand rifles, three thousand volunteers and one million pounds sterling to provide an immediate beginning for guerrilla operations in Palestine, as Mardam and Solh had insisted. Then, with a glance at Nuri as-Said's representative, Azzam read a last clause. The League, it said, would assign to a fifty-two-year-old Iraqi general, a veteran of the Turkish Dardanelles campaign, the responsibility of preparing a plan for the coordinated intervention of the Arab armies in Palestine.

Hanging over the debate of the Arab League leaders had been the image of the soft-spoken, red-bearded leader who stood at the very center of the Palestine drama, Haj Amin Husseini. He had followed their meeting with zealous attention from the cluster of stone villas in suburban Cairo in which he had installed his headquarters. One by one, each of the men assembled in Cairo had made his discreet pilgrimage to that headquarters to confer with Haj Amin. He had received them all under an enormous photograph of Jerusalem, his gold pocket watch hanging on a chain around his neck, urging on them the course of action he himself sought.

Haj Amin did not want their Arab armies in Palestine. With armies, he knew, went authority, and he had no intention of sharing his authority in Palestine with anyone, above all his rivals who commanded the armies of Iraq and Jordan. His aim was to build up his own guerrilla forces so that they could defeat the Jews without outside help.

The League's decisions suited him well. His goal now was to get control of the arms, the money and the volunteers they had called for, and to have guerrilla operations in Palestine placed under his supreme command. To justify such a claim, he was sending to Palestine as his hand-picked field commander the most able fighter his rebellion against the British in 1936 had produced. In a few days he would leave Cairo, ordered to carry out a follower's boast that the Mufti had adopted as his own: to "drive the Jews into the sea."

. . .

Two candles, one at either end of the plain wooden desk, lit the room. Behind the desk, the white wisps of his hair glowing in the candlelight, David Ben-Gurion stared at the knot of men seated before him. No curious crowds had watched their coming as one by one they had made their way to their secret rendezvous in a Jewish high school in the suburbs of Jerusalem.

They were the city's Haganah commanders. Ben-Gurion had summoned them to this meeting because he was convinced that it was here in Jerusalem that the Jews of Palestine faced their gravest trial in the months ahead. Isolated, depending for its existence on one exposed highway, Jerusalem was the Achilles' heel of the Yishuv, the Jewish settlement, the one place where all Ben-Gurion's hopes could be shattered by a single, decisive blow.

Looking at the faces peering at him through the candlelight, he solemnly warned that if the Arabs could lock Jerusalem into their stranglehold, "they can end us, and our state will be finished before it is born."

After that grim preamble, he turned his thoughts to the wider aspects of the struggle. It was the measure of the Jewish leader's genius that on that December evening, while the leaders of the Arab League were completing their debate in Cairo, he had already perceived what the Arab leaders themselves had not yet fully comprehended, the climax to which their entangling skein of rhetoric would inevitably force them.

"It is time," he told the men before him, "to start planning for a war against five Arab armies."

His words fell on them like a gust of winter wind. Some were incredulous.

"Do you think the Arabs of Jenin are going to attack us in tanks?" someone asked, half laughing. To Eliyahu Arbel, the former Czech officer in charge of Haganah planning in Jerusalem, it seemed fantastic: "Ben-Gurion was talking about planning a war against five Arab armies and we were still being arrested by the British for carrying a pistol down the street."

Ben-Gurion persisted. He never made the mistake of underestimating his foes. Nothing could menace his people more than a concerted attack on them by five Arab armies. But if Ben-Gurion did not underestimate his foes, he did not overestimate them, either. He knew their tendency to believe their extravagant boasts, to accept rhetoric as reality, to prepare themselves for a trial with speeches rather than sacrifice. Their threat of war presented to his people a terrible menace; but it also presented them a great opportunity.

The United Nations partition of Palestine had not been a really satisfactory solution from his point of view, but it had been one with which he could live. The internationalization of Jerusalem had left its ache in Ben-Gurion's heart, as it had in the heart of almost every Jew. The long and tortured frontiers assigned to the Jewish state were a military catastrophe. Some Jewish leaders favored fighting to expand the area assigned to the Jewish state, regardless of what the Arabs did. Ben-Gurion and a majority of the Jewish Agency Executive were opposed to their ideas.

If the Arab states insisted on going to war, however, the situation would change. Then the frontiers of their state would not be the boundaries assigned them by the United Nations, but those they could seize and hold by force of arms in the Arabs' war.

Ben-Gurion had often seen Arab intransigence inadvertently become the handmaiden of Zionist aspirations, "helping us by attacking us, helping us make important achievements we otherwise might have missed." The first Arab attacks on their settlements had forced Palestine's reluctant Jewish landlords to begin employing Jewish labor. Arab attacks on Jews in Jaffa had led to the establishment of Tel Aviv. The Arabs' refusal to allow the survivors of Hitler's death camps into Palestine had led to world backing for a Jewish state. But the greatest error the Arabs could make on their behalf, Ben-Gurion thought, would be refusing the United Nations' decision. That "would change everything for us," he thought. That would give his people "the right to get what we could." From that moment on, what their state would be would depend on arms, and not the United Nations decision.

Across the Jordan River from Jerusalem, beyond the dark ridge lines of the mountains of Moab, an enigmatic Arab sovereign sat, as he did every night, in the sitting room of his palace overlooking the eastern edge of Amman and pondered the problem on a chessboard. King Abdullah ibn-Hussein el Hashimi was an accomplished chess player. His favorite piece was the unpredictable knight, and the tactics he preferred in that game paralleled those he had used to arrive at his current station in life: subtlety, indirection and surprise.

81

The kingdom over which he ruled this December evening was three-quarters desert. It contained barely half a million people, and its national budget, before British subsidies, was a million and a half pounds sterling. From that sparse domain, however, had sprung the pieces Abdullah could move on the chessboard of the Middle East: the men of its only truly professional army, the army David Ben-Gurion feared above all the others, the Arab Legion.

Yet, paradoxically, no Arab leader understood Ben-Gurion better than the monarch who commanded that army. Abdullah was the only Arab chieftain who had had any real contact with the Jews of Palestine over the past decade. The electric current which illuminated for this descendant of the Prophet the verses of his Koran at dawn each day was furnished by a Jewish power plant in the northwestern tip of his kingdom. On the eve of the U.N.'s partition vote he had had a cordial and secret meeting with Golda Meir in the home of the power plant's director. The two had agreed that their common enemy was the Mufti and to maintain contact with each other. He frequently called on his Jewish neighbors for advice and technical help. Abdullah had, in fact, tended to regard the Jewish return as a return of one Semitic people persecuted in the West to aid another Semitic people whose development of their ancient homeland had been held back by a Western institution, colonialism.

The realistic little monarch harbored no illusions of the Arabs' chances of thwarting partition. Unlike the Mufti, who tended to think of the Jews of Palestine in terms of the pale rabbinical students of Mea Shearim fleeing before his bullies' clubs, or the Syrians and Iraqis who judged them by their own peaceful Jewish communities, Abdullah well knew the vigor and capacity that lay behind their settlement.

The short, cherubic monarch had only the deepest scorn for his fellow leaders of the Arab League wrangling in Cairo. The League he characterized as "a sack into which seven heads have been thrust." He despised Egyptians in general and King Farouk in particular. "You do not make a gentleman of a Balkan farmer's son simply by making him a king," he liked to remark. The Syrians, whose land he coveted, he considered a cantankerous and quarrelsome people. A natural hatred had flourished between Abdullah and the Mufti of Jerusalem since their first meeting in 1921. "My father," Abdullah continually reminded his followers, "always told me to beware of preachers."

The life of the pale, fragile monarch had been an unending series of frustrations. It was he who had first whispered the words "Arab rebellion" to the British in 1914. But T. E. Lawrence had preferred to confide the rebellion's leadership to his more malleable younger brother, and its glory had passed Abdullah by. The Saudis had driven him and his family from their ancient throne by the Red Sea. The dusty kingdom he ruled had been lopped off Palestine by Winston Churchill and tendered to him as a consolation prize when the French drove his brother Feisal from Damascus. To add to the indignity, Churchill would often boast: "I created Transjordan with a stroke of a pen on a Sunday afternoon in Cairo."

Its inhabitants had welcomed their new emir to his domains with a barrage of eggs and tomatoes, and for years his residence had been a Bedouin tent on the hilltop overlooking Amman where his palace now stood. It was not until 1934, when the British suddenly rediscovered Abdullah tucked away in his little emirate and decided to build him up as a counterweight to the troublesome Mufti, that his fortunes began to rise.

Those had been trying years for Abdullah, for, above all else, he burned with ambitions: the ambition to avenge his humiliated family, to hold sway over a domain worthy of his proud ancestry. He was, in the words of one of his contemporaries, "a falcon trapped in a canary's cage, longing to break out, to realize his dreams and passions of being a great Arab leader; but there he was, pinned up in the cage of Transjordan by the British."

Now, perhaps, partition offered him the chance that had been denied him for a quarter of a century, the chance to get out of that cage, to become the leader he longed to be, to obtain a kingdom to the measure of his ambition and his heritage. Abdullah longed for the sacred city beyond the mountains of Moab, Jerusalem. With Jerusalem he would gain international stature for himself, and for his Hashemite kin a return to the central role in Islam from which the Saudis had cast them. Without it he was condemned to remain what he was, the inconsequential sovereign of a lot of sand.

As carefully as if he were shifting the pieces on his chessboard, Abdullah thought through the moves that might lead him to his goal. One December morning, while, in Cairo, the Arab League colleagues he so despised talked their way through another of their meetings, he pushed forward his first pawn. Shortly before noon, his hand-picked Prime Minister called at a modest residence not far from the King's palace. It was the home of Britain's jovial and distinguished resident minister in Transjordan, Sir Alec Kirkbride.

What, politely inquired the Prime Minister, would be His Majesty's gov-

83

ernment's reaction if King Abdullah annexed to his kingdom the part of Palestine allocated to the Arabs by the U.N.'s partition order?

Slumped in an armchair by the fire, the pensive figure listened to the majestic strains of a Bach organ fugue filling his sitting room. Sixty miles from Amman, in his luxurious residence looking down upon the city at the heart of Abdullah's ambitions, Britain's High Commissioner in Palestine enjoyed a nightly ritual. Regularly, before dinner, Sir Alan Cunningham locked himself into his sitting room to savor the music of Bach, Vivaldi or Beethoven and contemplate, in their consoling strains, the problems weighing on him.

Sir Alan was a glum and bitter man during those evening sessions in December 1947, and he had much to contemplate. His administration in Palestine had been a terrible frustration for the Scots general. From the day he had left London to take up his assignment until the past week, he had not been given a policy to follow. Indeed, dismayed by the lack of clear-cut direction he had received in his conversations at the Foreign and Colonial Offices, Cunningham had bluntly asked Prime Minister Clement Attlee on the eve of his departure what policy directives he was to follow in Palestine.

"Oh," answered Attlee with a shrug, "just go out and govern the country." Then, sensing Cunningham's shock, he got up and, walking him to the door, threw his arm around the Scot's shoulders. "You know, General," he said, "I'm sorry to give you a politician's answer to your question. But it's the only answer I can give."

Ernest Bevin, Britain's Foreign Minister, had been "completely surrounded by Arabists and got all his reports from the same old group of pro-Arab hands," Cunningham felt. His undersecretary, Harold Beeley, he considered "a very dangerous man."

Now at last he had received a policy, the policy which he was to carry out in the closing stages of the British mandate in Palestine, and, above all, toward the United Nations partition decision. He was "to keep the situation as calm as possible consistent with a minimal involvement physically." He was "to have nothing to do with Partition in any way, shape or form."

Those instructions reflected the fact, as Beeley would later recall, that Britain had accepted the partition of Palestine "with an absolute minimum of enthusiasm." From now on, Britain would align her interests in the Middle East as closely as possible with the Arabs. The new Jewish state she would "just forget about for a while, as assuredly it was not going to be very friendly to Britain in the years to come."

In fact, the only aspect of partition which the Foreign Office supported was the internationalization of Jerusalem. The reason was simple. With the United States labeled as pro-Jewish and Russia as anti-God, any big-power role in the internationalized city was bound to fall to Britain.

To give teeth to that policy, the British delegation in the U.N. had been instructed to make itself the forthright advocate of the Arab viewpoint. And, on the eve of the Arab League's Cairo meeting, Britain had announced she would forcibly maintain her restrictions on Jewish immigration into Palestine until she left.*

To Sir Alan those instructions were a cruel disappointment. Unlike Bevin and Beeley, Cunningham favored partition as the only way out of the dilemma into which their tergiversations had led Palestine. An introspective man with the stern Calvinistic sense of duty of his Scots forebears, he felt strongly Britain's obligation to close out her rule in Palestine in the most orderly manner possible and leave behind her some hope of peace. Yet the policy for which he had waited so long now enjoined him to studiously ignore the only plan he thought offered the Holy Land any hope of peace.

Peace, he knew, would be precious in the Holy Land in the months to come. In the first two weeks since the partition vote, ninety-three Arabs, eighty-four Jews and seven Englishmen had been killed in the ancient territory over which he presided. Their deaths, Sir Alan feared, were only a harbinger of a ghastly harvest to come. Locked into the desk drawer of his office adjacent to his sitting room was a three-page British Army order stamped "MOST SECRET" and dated December 6. As much as the policy instructions he had just received from London, the phrases set down in that order preoccupied the dour Scot. The order laid out the principles which would govern the withdrawal of the only effective instrument Cunningham had with which to maintain order in the coming months, the British Army. It contained one deliberate omission. It made no mention of the British Army being responsible henceforth for law and order in Palestine.

Harassed, humiliated, shot at and insulted for the past two years, that army was fed up with maintaining law and order in Palestine. With an end to the mandate now set, its commander, one of Cunningham's fellow Scots, Sir Gordon MacMillan, was determined not to risk the lives of any more of his soldiers in Palestine except in the pursuit of British interests.

Only one phrase in that document had brought to the High Commis-

---

* From 1946 to February 1948, according to a report submitted to the War Office by Sir Gordon MacMillan, the last commander in chief of British forces in Palestine, the British intercepted forty-seven shiploads of illegal immigrants, interning 65,307 illegal immigrants in their detention camps on the island of Cyprus.

sioner's face an amused half-smile to relieve the concern with which he had read it. It was the work of some zealous quartermaster in the army that Cunningham knew so well, and in the midst of the agonies of policy and command it was his good clerk's contribution to Britain's coming Palestinian posterity.

Careful and precise, it was the estimate of the materials which would be required to pack up the remnants of thirty years of British rule in Palestine: four thousand tons of timber and twenty-eight tons of nails.

• • •

The message was whispered at dawn in the shadows of the mosques as the faithful slipped off their shoes before the morning prayer: "Abou Moussa is coming back." At those words, the men set out. From Jaffa, Haifa, Nablus, Jenin and Tulkarm, from twenty key towns to which the message had been sent by that special Islamic grapevine, traveling alone or in small groups so as not to arouse British curiosity, they set off. Their diverse routes led to the village of Beit Surif, southwest of Jerusalem, to which Abou Moussa had promised his return.

Just before noon, a dusty black Chrysler came bouncing and scraping up the dirt road leading to the village. At the sight of the middle-aged man in a blue-and-white checkered kaffiyeh sitting beside the driver, the mob in front of the house sprang forward, warbling the shrill undulating battle cries of the Arab warrior. The man stepped from the car into a shoving sea of hands and faces stretched out to embrace or even touch him. He was of medium height, stocky, with a round, mournful face and the first hint of a paunch in the strained buttons of his brown business suit. Visibly moved, constantly touching his forehead and heart in an Arab gesture of welcome, he struggled through the crowd toward the simple stone house where his followers waited.

No Arab in Palestine, not even his cousin Haj Amin Husseini, commanded the admiration and affection stirred by the man hailed as "Abou Moussa"—the father of Moussa. He was the man the Mufti had sent to Palestine to take command of his Holy War Strugglers. Like his cousin, Abdul Khader Husseini was a member of Jerusalem's Husseini clan. He was, on that December morning, barely forty years old. He was a born leader of men. He possessed great physical courage. Unlike most of the Mufti's lieutenants, he was educated; yet he retained an instinctive understanding of the qualities and shortcomings of his peasant people. He had, despite a limited military background, an intuitive ability to mobilize and use their qualities and resources to their best advantage. Above all, the

86

quiet, almost stolid man in the brown business suit walking away from his dusty Chrysler possessed a priceless asset for an Arab leader. Abdul Khader Husseini had charisma. He had the charisma to galvanize a battalion of Dutchmen. Upon his excitable countrymen its effect was electric. Soon, at the mention of his name, hundreds, thousands of peasants, clutching their rifles by their sides, would come swarming from the souks and their rocky villages to do his bidding.

In the stone building, spread over a mound of steaming rice, the whole roast lamb of a *mensif,* a Bedouin banquet, waited to welcome him. Abdul Khader squatted cross-legged on the floor at the head of a circle of men. The host stretched out his right hand, plucked an eye from the skull of the sheep and offered it to Abdul Khader. Then, in a babble of excited conversation, the banquet began.

For most of the men sitting on the floor around Abdul Khader, it was their first sight of their leader in almost a decade. Twice during the Arab revolt in 1936–39, Abdul Khader had been wounded at the head of his *guerrilleros.* After his second wound, in 1938, he was smuggled to Syria bleeding and half dead on camelback. From there he had gone to Iraq, where his participation in another anti-British rising had earned him four years in jail. Even his presence in Beit Surif was illegal; he was still technically barred from Palestine by the British.

The British had dominated most of Abdul Khader's life. His father had been deposed by them as mayor of Jerusalem in 1920 for his opposition to their mandate. In 1933, after graduating in chemistry from the American University in Cairo, he had participated, at his aging father's side, in his first anti-British demonstration. Since then, in Palestine, Iraq and Egypt, he had spent most of his life fighting or plotting against them. In 1938, the Mufti had even sent him abroad with a hand-picked group of his other followers to polish in the finishing schools of the Third Reich the knowledge of explosives he had first acquired in the chemistry labs of Cairo's American University.

Now he had returned to Palestine for the first time in nine years to take command of the fight against a new foe. Wiping his lips with the edges of his kaffiyeh, he signaled to the men around him that the banquet was over and the time for serious conversation had arrived. Unlike most of the Mufti's lieutenants, Abdul Khader was not given to explosive bursts of hyperbole, nor was he inclined to work himself into a frenzy vowing to incarnadine the Mediterranean with Jewish blood. He was a serious, soft-spoken man, and he knew exactly what he wanted to say.

"Diplomacy and politics," he told his listeners, "have failed to achieve our goals." The Arabs of Palestine, he said, had only one choice: "We shall keep our honor and our country with our swords."

Quietly, methodically, he began to outline his strategy for the fight the Mufti had sent him to lead. Like Yigal Yadin, the planning officer of the Haganah, Abdul Khader Husseini knew that the fight for Palestine would be won or lost on its roads. No fight could be better suited to the means at Abdul Khader's disposal. The military tactic his villagers knew best was the ambush. The lure of loot in trapped trucks and convoys would be a powerful spur to their ardor. Spreading a map of Palestine on the carpet before him, he pointed a finger at a chain of exposed and isolated Jewish settlements circled in red. Harassing Jewish communication with those colonies, ambushing their supplies, finally closing the roads to their convoys, would be their first objective.

Then Abdul Khader's finger moved to the center of the map, to the dark stain at the heart of Palestine, the city of Jerusalem. As well as David Ben-Gurion, Abdul Khader Husseini realized that the one hundred thousand Jews living there constituted the most vulnerable Jewish target in Palestine. As soon as the men and the arms were ready, they would, he announced, lay siege to Jerusalem.

Driving his hands together as though to throttle with his gesture that dark spot on the map of Palestine, he vowed, "We will strangle Jerusalem."

JERUSALEM: THE HOLY CITY AT A TRAGIC HOUR

On May 28, 1948, after ten weeks of violent fighting following the proclamation of the state of Israel, the Jewish Quarter of the Old City of Jerusalem is in flames. The pillar of smoke marks the end of almost 2,000 years of Jewish residence in the ancient alleys beside the western wall of King Solomon's Temple, the famous Wailing Wall.

Mount Zion

Church of the Dormition

El Aqsa Mosque

Jewish Quarter

Armenian Quarter

Wailing Wall

Moslem Quarter

King David Hotel

The Dome of the Rock

THE MOST BITTERLY DISPUTED CITY IN HISTORY

St. Stephen's Gate

Via Dolorosa

Valley of Jehoshaphat

Notre-Dame de France

Courtyard of the Temple

Couvent des Soeurs Réparatrices

Arab Headquarters

Church of the Holy Sepulcher

3   THE WAILING WALL

4   THE DOME OF THE ROCK

THREE SANCTUARIES: THE GLORY AND CURSE OF JERUSALEM

Jerusalem harbors the most important shrines of the world's three great mono-
theistic religions, Judaism, Christianity and Islam: for Christians, the Church of
the Holy Sepulcher, at the end of the Via Dolorosa, the Way of the Cross, erected
on the site where Saint Helena allegedly discovered the remains of Christ's Cross;
for Jews, the Wailing Wall; for Moslems, the Dome of the Rock, the Mount
Moriah of antiquity from which the Prophet Mohammed allegedly ascended to
heaven on his white steed El Burak.

THE CHURCH OF THE HOLY SEPULCHER

6

7

9

10

12

13

15

16

ENEMIES IN THE STRUGGLE FOR AN ANCIENT LAND

[6] Yigal Yadin, 32, an archaeologist. As Chief of Operations of the Jewish Army, the Haganah, he was responsible for preparing the plans with which his ill-equipped countrymen would meet an invasion of five Arab armies.

[7] Vivian Herzog, 29, a veteran of the British Army. His intelligence work was vital in securing the center of Jerusalem for the Haganah.

[8] Teddy Kollek, 37, a fisherman from Lake Tiberias. The man who is now mayor of Jerusalem directed clandestine arms purchases in the United States for the Haganah.

[9] Hadassah Limpel, a 19-year-old Polish girl. She walked across the Soviet Union to reach the Promised Land, where she died in a half-track trying to open a road to Jerusalem's 100,000 besieged Jews.

[10] Shlomo Shamir, 33, commander of a brigade of survivors from Europe's death camps which twice, at a terrible cost, tried to drive the Arab Legion from the heights commanding the only road to Jerusalem.

[11] Eliahu Sacharov, 33, one of the founders of the clandestine arms industry with which the Jews of Palestine sought to prepare for the war with the Arabs.

[12] Ismail Safwat Pasha, 52, the Iraqi general appointed by the Arab League to coordinate the Arabs' military efforts to destroy the state of Israel in May 1948.

[13] Nimra Tannous, 24, "The Tigress," an Arab telephone operator. To the despair of the Haganah intelligence, she sought to warn the Arabs' talkative leadership that their enemies might be listening to their telephone conversations—which they were!

[14] Emile Ghory, 40. A graduate of the University of Cincinnati, he was one of the Arab leaders in Jerusalem in 1948.

[15] Samy Aboussouan, 29, a dentist and an accomplished violinist, whose family was wiped out in the dynamiting of a Jerusalem hotel mistaken by the Haganah for an Arab headquarters.

[16] Ibrahim Abou Dayieh, 29. An illiterate shepherd from the hills of Hebron, he fought with notable courage in Jerusalem, leading his men while strapped to a chair when wounded.

[17] Assiya Halaby, 35. The only Arab to say farewell to the last British civil servants leaving Jerusalem, she saw in their departure the first stirrings of her people's nationalism.

8

11

14

17

19

May 14, 1948: General Sir Alan Cunningham, Britain's last High Commissioner, embarks from Haifa harbor at the expiration of Britain's Palestine mandate.

December 6, 1917: General Sir Edmund Allenby enters Jerusalem on foot after capturing the city from the Ottoman Turks.

20

THE BRITISH PRESENCE IN THE HOLY LAND

One hundred thousand British troops were unable to maintain order in Palestine. Soldiers of the Royal Military Police [20] search Arabs for arms in the streets of Jerusalem. Men of the Suffolk Regiment [21] seal Zion Gate to prevent the Jews from bringing arms and supplies to the besieged Jewish Quarter of the Old City.

21

THE POLITICIAN AND THE WARRIOR:
LEADERS OF ARAB PALESTINE

Haj Amin Husseini, the Mufti of Jerusalem [22], led the Palestinian Arabs' crusade against the Jews' return to their Promised Land.

22

He appointed his kinsman Abdul Khader Husseini to command the Arab military forces in Palestine. Abdul Khader was a legendary figure, venerated by his followers, respected by his adversaries. After his marriage in 1934 [23], he was expelled from the country by the English. He returned secretly in 1948 [24], convinced, like the Haganah, that Jerusalem would be the key to the struggle. He was killed on April 6, 1948; his funeral [25] was a day of mourning for every Palestinian Arab.

23   24

A 42-year-old former sergeant of the Palestine police, Kamal Irekat commanded the Arab irregulars between Jerusalem and Bethlehem. Much given to pageantry and menacing prose, Irekat enjoys the dubious claim of being the first Arab leader to vow to "throw the Jews into the sea."

AN AMBITIOUS MONARCH AND HIS
UNLIKELY LAWRENCE

Son of the man Colonel T. E. Lawrence helped persuade to sponsor the
Arab revolt of 1916, King Abdullah of Transjordan [27] was the one
Arab leader prepared to deal with a Jewish state in Palestine in 1948.
In two secret meetings with Golda Meir and in a series of covert negotiations with the British, he sought agreement to his plan to annex to his
kingdom the Arab portion of a partitioned Palestine. His greatest bargaining counters were the Bedouin soldiers of his Arab Legion, commanded by John Bagot Glubb (Glubb Pasha), shown with Abdullah.
One of Lawrence's most distinguished heirs, the soft-spoken Glubb
sought to hold his soldiers out of the 1948 Arab–Israeli conflict. On
May 18, however, the danger of a Haganah takeover in Jerusalem forced
him to send his troops to the city and enter a war he had hoped to avoid.
A few days later King Abdullah, surrounded by his fellow Arab leaders
[28], arrived in triumph in the city to pray at the Mosque of Omar and
herald the annexation of its Arab quarters to his kingdom.

29

NEW BLOOD ON AN ANCIENT ALTAR

Jerusalem, in the unhappy spring of 1948, revived one of its most terrible traditions, human bloodshed. Whether Arabs [29] torn apart by a Jewish terrorist's bomb or Jewish settlers [30] massacred and mutilated after the ambush of their convoy on the Bethlehem road by Arab guerrillas, the city's residents paid a frightful toll for the passions stirred by their city.

30

PART TWO

JERUSALEM: A HOUSE AGAINST ITSELF

December 1947 — March 1948

7

"ARE WE NOT NEIGHBORS . . . ?"

BY THE MIDDLE of December 1947, the exaltation of the night the United Nations had partitioned Palestine had become little more than a memory. Along Ben Yehuda Street the bright-blue banners dangled from the lampposts like the faded ribbons of an old funeral wreath. The hopeful pronunciamentos that had been plastered to Jewish Jerusalem's walls were already covered with a new set of tracts—black-and-white mobilization notices ordering every Jewish male in the city from seventeen to twenty-five to register for military service.

A few hundred yards away, in the Arab quarter, an elderly hatmaker struggled to keep abreast of the orders for tarbooshes pouring into his shop. Not since 1936 had Phillip Arouk sold those maroon conical felt hats as he had been selling them since partition. To his fellows they were a badge that stamped them as Arabs for the Mufti's gunmen drifting into the city in increasing number.

Life in Jerusalem in mid-December remained, during the daytime, relatively tranquil. In confusing streams the throngs crowded the heart of the Jewish city, peering into shop windows sheltering a range of merchandise as diverse as the city's population. There were piles of Persian rugs, hand-embroidered silks, spun-silver brooches from the Yemenites, art galleries, music shops with the records of Paris, London, Hollywood and prewar Eastern Europe. The delicatessens were stocked with bottles of wine from the Rishon vineyards, the first Jewish agricultural enterprise in Palestine, the dairy products of the Tnuvah cooperative, sparkling boxes of Elite chocolates. The florists' windows blazed with tall gladioli drooping on their slender stalks and scarlet and gold roses from the hothouses of Sharon.

Rich and pungent, the aroma of roasting coffee drifted over the crowds from the cafés lining Ben Yehuda and George V. There were the Imperial and the Royal, where the British went; the Atara, whose owners had refrained from getting a liquor license to keep the British out and whose top floor was tacitly reserved for members of the Palmach; the Brazil, where students hung out.

Around them, rabbinical scholars from Mea Shearim, orthodox Jews in white shirts with a hand-knit *kippah*—a skullcap—pinned to their heads, girl kibbutzniks in khaki shorts and sweaters, Yemenite laborers, German refugees proud and poor in their shiny double-breasted suits, flooded off the sidewalks, ignoring the imprecations of the police and the impatient honks of British Army patrol cars.

Missing from those crowds now, however, were the Arabs who had given them still another colorful dimension: the bank of shoeshine boys lined up by Zion Cinema banging their brushes on their boxes to attract customers, the coffee vendors jingling the bells of the bulbous brass urns strapped across their shoulders, the Sudanese roasting peanuts by the curbside on a glowing brazier. Gone, too, were the villagers carting in for sale on their spindly legged donkeys mounds of oranges, tomatoes, carrots, radishes.

Partly from fear for their own security, partly in response to the Mufti's orders, they had all begun to avoid Jerusalem's Jewish areas. Each community already had its own bus service, the faded-blue vehicles of the Egged Line for the Jews and the dull-silver buses of the National Company for the Arabs. Jewish taxis refused fares for Arab areas, and Arab cabs wouldn't enter Jewish neighborhoods. Going from one to another, a foreign correspondent noted, was "like crossing between two foreign countries."

Arab and Jewish civil servants, many of whom had worked side by side for years, now greeted each other on arriving at the office in the morning with a reciprocal search for arms. For Jews, access to the law courts and the city's principal bank, Barclays, both entered through Arab areas, became increasingly dangerous. For Arabs, a visit to government offices in the Jewish areas was a hazardous experience. Even children began to pelt each other with stones on the way to and from school.

The key installations, the General Post Office, the telephone exchanges, Government Hospital, police headquarters, the broadcasting studio, the prison, were all behind the barbed wire of "Bevingrad." Only one back entrance to the G.P.O. remained open, reached by passing through a crooked line of barbed wire. Heinz Kraus, an out-of-work Jewish technician, was on guard duty there every day with an Arab and a British soldier. The Arab, he noted, even searched for arms under the tarbooshes of his fellows.

On December 15, the Arabs gave the population a chilling reminder of the stranglehold in which they might eventually hold Jerusalem by blowing up the pipes delivering the city's water. While the British repaired them, the Jewish Agency ordered a secret survey of the cisterns in the Jewish areas of the city.

Even the one refuge in which Arab and Jew had always found harmony, the graveyard, was troubled in the first weeks following the partition vote. Jewish funeral processions winding their way up to the Mount of Olives, some behind the coffins of the first victims of the sporadic shooting ringing out in the city, often came under Arab sniper fire.

More than any other facet of its daily existence, however, a ritual accomplished each evening at the Egged bus station on the outskirts of town had become the symbol of Jewish life in Jerusalem. The struggle for the roads, foreseen by the chiefs of the Haganah and by Abdul Khader Husseini, had begun. The Arab ambushes were still sporadic and unorganized, but they had already forced the Haganah to rely on daily convoys to link Jerusalem with the coast. The steel-plated buses used in the convoys weighed eight tons each. They could go no faster than ten miles an hour climbing up to Jerusalem from Bab el Wad, and rare was the convoy that escaped without being at least sniped at.

Long before sunset each night, the crowds began to gather in the bus station waiting for the incoming convoy to arrive. As its vehicles ground to a halt, the crowds swarmed over them, every eye fixed on their locked doors waiting for the results of a sinister lottery. The first figures to appear in those doorways were often covered with blood, candidates for the ambulance that waited for each convoy. The last were sometimes dead, laid out on the bus station's asphalt apron to be identified by the pathetic scream of the friend or relative who had come to the station to welcome them back to Jerusalem.

And yet normally those December weeks were a time of joy in Jerusalem as the Jews celebrated Hanukkah, the feast of lights, marking the triumph of the Maccabean revolt, and the city's Christians prepared for Christmas. Usually at this season Jewish Jerusalem blazed by night with lights from eight-tipped menorahs snapped on one by one as each day of the Hanukkah feast passed. Relay racers rushed blazing torches to the city from the tombs of the Maccabees, and there was public dancing of the hora and communal parties with piles of steaming *latkes,* potato pancakes.

This year, Jerusalem was dark for the feast of lights. There was no dancing in its deserted streets, and all public ceremonies were canceled. Feeling the chill hostility of the night around them, many a Jew in the security of his home might well have prayed for a contemporary renewal of the ancient blessing he commemorated with a prayer each night of the

109

feast as he lit the candles of his menorah: "We kindle these lights to mark the marvelous victories and wonderful liberation which Thou didst achieve for our ancestors."

. . .

It was the shortest bus ride in Palestine. It lasted barely five minutes. But the half-mile route covered by Jerusalem's No. 2 bus was the most dangerous trip a Jew could take in those first days after the U.N. partition vote. That bus ride ran from the center of Jerusalem through Jaffa Gate, along the rim of the Old City's Armenian Quarter, down to the southern end of an oversized alleyway at the heart of the most ancient Jewish settlement in Palestine, the Jewish Quarter of the Old City. It was the only physical link open between New Jerusalem and the Jewish Quarter, and its half-mile route was ringed by hostile Arab throngs.

The quarter lay in the southeastern corner of the Old City, on a slope of ground running down from Mount Zion toward the Temple Mount. Its southern flank was the Old City wall. To the west was a settlement of Arab families from North Africa, to the north the Moslem Quarter. Barely the size of fifteen football fields, it sheltered only a symbolic parcel of Jewry, two thousand people, a tenth of the Old City's total population.

For centuries there had been Jewish scholars living in it. They had built as their monuments to their dispersed nation and the faith that sustained it the twenty-seven synagogues that dominated the quarter. Sometimes built underground because "from the depths you will call to God," sometimes on the high ground because "there is no building a synagogue except at the height of a city," those synagogues were studded through the quarter, the solid anchors on which it depended.

There was Eliyahu Hanavi, where, according to legend, Elijah the Prophet had appeared to complete a minyan, the ten-man quorum required for a public prayer. In one musty corner of the synagogue a crumbling chair still awaited the Prophet's return. Next door, under the large dome and latticed windows of Ben-Zakai Synagogue, were the shofar on which, tradition held, Elijah would sound his people's freedom and the flask of oil with which he would rekindle the lamp of the rebuilt Temple. There was the Stambuli Synagogue, built by Turkish Jews, in which impaired or damaged sacred texts were guarded. Once a year, thirty men marched out from the synagogue in a candlelit procession to bury those texts and to guarantee a year's rain for Palestine's crops. And, of course, there was the Hurva, the most beautiful of all, under whose magnificent dome were kept the battle flags of the Jewish Legion that had fought in World War I.

110

Arab–Jewish relations in the Old City had always been good. Most of the property in the quarter was Arab-owned, and one of its familiar sights was the Arab rent collector making his way from house to house, pausing in each for the rent and a ritual cup of coffee. Here the Islamic respect for men of religion had been naturally extended to the quarter's scholars in their yeshivas. As for the quarter's poor artisans and shopkeepers, the most natural of bonds, poverty, tied them to their Arab neighbors.

On Friday evening, Arab youngsters would go to the homes of their devout Jewish friends and kindle for them the oil lamps a Jew could not light on the Sabbath. Many an Arab and Jewish youngster would always remember the exchange of gifts traditionally performed between the communities at feast times, the Jews bringing to their Arab neighbors heaps of cut, dried almonds at Sukkoth, the harvest festival, Arabs offering trays of bread and honey to help their Jewish neighbors mark the end of Passover.

Between the religious leadership of the Old City and the Zionist leadership of the New, however, relations were often strained, and, as a result, the Haganah was weak inside the Old City. On the night that partition was voted, there were exactly eighteen Haganah men in an area where the Arab potential could be numbered in the thousands.

A Belgian-born arms expert sent to study the quarter's needs after the vote returned with a dismaying report. The entire armory of the quarter consisted of sixteen rifles of which fourteen worked, twenty-five pistols and three Finnish submachine guns. At any moment, Amir knew, the Arabs might decide to blockade the route of the No. 2 bus and sever his only tie to the Old City. While it remained open, he vowed to use it to funnel into the Jewish quarter all the men and arms his strained garrison could spare.

He was not too soon. Already the same simple, emotional natures that linked the Old City's Arabs and Jews were becoming conductors of the sentiments that would shortly drive them apart. The handful of Arabs in the Jewish quarter moved out. One Arab baker left with his dough still in the oven, handing his key over to the Haganah as he went. Fist fights and shooting erupted.

Nadi Dai'es, the sixteen-year-old coffee boy who had rushed off to join the mob streaming past his office the day the Commercial Center was burned, was one of the Arabs living in the Jewish Quarter. His family's relations with their Jewish neighbors had always been friendly, but in those days after partition, he remembered, "our feelings were electrified and slowly we began to understand and believe that every Jew was an enemy intent on taking our lives and our land."

111

Nadi went to the souks and bought himself a pistol. One night in December, firing erupted in his neighborhood. The sixteen-year-old boy rushed to the window and emptied his pistol into the night. As he did, he heard, coming up to him in the darkness, a pathetic cry from across the alleyway, from the woman whose Sabbath lamps he had lit for a decade.

"Do not shoot, do not shoot," she cried. "Are we not neighbors since many years?"

In Jerusalem, as elsewhere in Palestine, the Haganah's basic strategy reflected a philosophy propounded by David Ben-Gurion. What the Jews had, they must hold. No Jew was to leave his home, his farm, his kibbutz, his office without permission. Every outpost, every settlement, every village, no matter how isolated, was to be clung to as though it were Tel Aviv itself. Despite this, Jerusalem's Jewish population began to drift away from mixed neighborhoods in which they were a minority.

The best way to stop that trend, Amir decided, was to drive the Arabs out of those neighborhoods first. At the same time he resolved to chase them from a few small Arab enclaves embedded in Jewish areas.

His first tactics were psychological. His men would sneak into the areas at night and plaster the walls and doors of Arab houses with threatening posters. Handbills telling their owners to "leave for your own safety" were stuck to the windshields of Arab cars. Anonymous threatening calls were made to Arab leaders in each neighborhood. Ruth Givton, a secretary at the Jewish Agency, was assigned the job of threatening Katy Antonious, the Arab hostess who had thrown a dinner party on the Old City's walls on Partition Night. The ploy didn't work. The garrulous Arab woman's line was always busy.

Those psychological tactics produced only a limited success. Amir then raised the pressure. Haganah raiding parties would go in at night, cutting telephone and electric wires, throwing hand grenades onto the ground, firing into the air, striving to create a general air of insecurity. At Sheikh Badr, an Arab settlement below the hilltop where the Israeli Knesset would one day rest, the tactic was repeated several nights running. Finally one morning, Amir's men noted, the Arabs in Sheikh Badr packed up and fled.

At about the same time, the Arab guerrillas of Abdul Khader Husseini undertook their first organized action in the city. As in Amir's case, its aim was primarily psychological—"to give the Jews a warning," as one of Husseini's leaders told his men. The objective was a Jewish house in Sanhedria in which a group of Haganah men had been stationed. To make the attack, 120 Holy Strugglers were brought to Jerusalem by truck from Hebron. In a drenching rainstorm they made their way through a wadi to a point two hundred yards from the house. Abdul Khader stood up and gave the signal for the attack with a single shot, the first symbolic shot of the campaign beginning that night. The Arabs fired for fifteen minutes, until a British armored car appeared. Then they withdrew, after suffering their first casualty. One of their number had been bitten by a snake.

"They're attacking!" the driver yelled.

At his words, Eli Greenberg, a Czechoslovakian survivor of the Dachau death camp, turned and peered through the slit in the steel plates covering the bus's windows. Outside, on the open square before the pillars of Jaffa Gate, Eli saw what looked like a mob of "scores" of screaming Arabs barring their bus's route through the gate.

At almost the same instant, he heard the driver shout, "The bastards have left us!" The British armored car that was to have convoyed their No. 2 bus through Jaffa Gate had just gone scuttling off down the Bethlehem Road.

Fortunately for their fellow passengers, Greenberg and ten others on board were members of the Haganah. He leaped up and opened a ventilating plate. With a quick gesture he lobbed a grenade at the feet of the advancing mob. Taking advantage of the panic it caused, the driver shot through the gate, skidded past Suleiman's Citadel and careened along the rim of the Armenian Quarter down to the Street of the Jews.

That night Greenberg and the men who had entered the Old City with him were taken along the black and menacing alleys to the outposts ringing the quarter. Greenberg was assigned a sandbagged corner of the roof of the Warsaw Synagogue. An officer passed him an enormous Colt and a clip of bullets. "The password is 'Judith,' " he whispered. Then he pointed to a trench of darkness below the position, the alleyway separating the synagogue walls from the row of buildings opposite Greenberg. "They are there," the officer whispered.

Greenberg drew himself in as close to the sandbags as he could, as if to make his shadowy figure melt into theirs. Thirty months after an American soldier had found him half dead on a slab of wood in Dachau, the Czech jeweler's son realized he faced death again, this time defending a country about which he knew almost nothing, which had become his almost by accident. As he peered out at the shadowy line of roof opposite him, a curious memory came to Greenberg. It was a Biblical quotation he had learned as

113

a child in Prague. "On your ramparts, Jerusalem, I have appointed watchmen."

Greenberg was just one of the many such watchmen ordered into the Jewish Quarter by Israel Amir. Almost fifty had been sent in, in two buses and three taxis, thanks to half a dozen bribed British guards. Every trip of the No. 2 bus brought in a few more disguised as students, workers or yeshiva scholars. Any cover was valid. Moshe Russnak rode in by ambulance, disguised as a doctor and escorted by a pair of British armored cars. By mid-December, the Haganah had managed to run one hundred and twenty men into the quarter.

A special air reigned among them. Most were members of Jerusalem's Palmach reserve, composed largely of students at Hebrew University. Their relations with the quarter's elderly rabbis in these early days were congenial. The rabbis extended to the Haganah men the privilege of using their *mikveh,* the religious baths. Food was limited but not scarce. There was one café, the Europa, where everybody gathered to sample one of its two dishes, Arabic coffee and a sticky yellow pudding.

The synagogues, because of their size and strategic locations, became the bulwarks of the Haganah's positions. Inspecting the posts installed in Nissan Bek, Shalom Dror saw some two-hundred-year-old Talmudic scrolls and texts pressed into service as sandbags. An old door had been suspended from the dome to serve as a plank from which a sharpshooter could peer through the synagogue's latticed windows into the street. Shivering in the cold, wrapped in a blanket, the guard lay on the door with a pistol in one hand and the text he was studying in the other. Below him, his fellow yeshiva students pondered their lessons.

A stream of new arrivals poured into the Arab city too: men of the Mufti's forces called in from the countryside, volunteers from Iraq, Syria, Transjordan burning with an ardor for Jerusalem no less fervent than that inspiring the men of the Haganah. With their arrival, the nightly exchanges of fire between the outposts of the two sides increased in intensity. Those exchanges drew a third wave of outsiders into the Old City's walls, the green-kilted men of one of Britain's most distinguished regiments, the Highland Light Infantry.

Their presence, however, did little to stem the nightly tide of firing or its inevitable consequences. One bitter blue December day a score of men marched up the slopes of the Mount of Olives, bearing on their shoulders a shrouded body laid upon a plank. The name of the man to whom it had belonged was Salamon. He came from a kibbutz in the north, and he was the first Haganah casualty in the latest struggle of the Jewish people for Jerusalem. He had been killed defending a post by the Old City's Nissan Bek Synagogue, the Haganah position closest to the western wall of King Solomon's Temple.

• • •

To Gaby Deeb, the son of Jerusalem's Arab Buick dealer, the man looked like one of those sketches of the local peasantry that artists sent back to their papers from the Middle East in the nineteenth century. His beautifully waxed black moustache curled up a wrinkled brown face. He wore a black Syrian tunic buttoned to his throat, baggy black cotton bloomers and a white Arabic headdress. Two bandoliers glistening with bullets were slung across his sixty-year-old chest. His belt bulged with a pair of Parabellums and an ornate gold dagger. Strapped to his back was a fat black cylinder that resembled nothing so much as a stovepipe.

He had walked alone all the way to Jerusalem from Aleppo in northern Syria, because, he told Deeb in formal Arabic, he wanted to participate in the crusade for El Kuds, the Holy City. He could not let his first night pass without striking a blow in the struggle.

Deeb obligingly took the old Syrian to the outskirts of the Jewish quarter of Mekor Hayim along with his nightly party of snipers. There he indicated a water tower frequently used by Haganah riflemen.

"I shall destroy it," proclaimed the old man. Before Deeb's dumb-founded eyes, he unslung the stovepipe from his back. It was an ancient World War I French mortar, lit by a fuse at its base, held in place by wires fixed to the stakes which the Syrian proceeded to noisily hammer into the ground.

"Be prepared!" called the old man in a booming voice Deeb thought must have warned every Jew in Mekor Hayim to be prepared. He and his men ducked.

An ear-shattering explosion shook the ground on which they lay. The old man and his mortar disappeared in an enormous cloud of black smoke. Deeb studied the dark night, waiting to see a shell streaking toward the water tower. Nothing appeared. Seconds ticked by, and the star-filled Jerusalem sky remained despairingly empty, the water tower defiantly intact. Finally the cloud of black smoke began to settle and Deeb started toward it.

There was nothing left. The old Syrian and his mortar were mixed in a thousand scraps of flesh and metal scattered over the earth of the city he had walked six hundred miles to defend.

The blue-and-white box of Lux soap powder was there where it should be, before the left-hand pane of the lower window. Seeing it, Uri Cohen, the biology student who had kissed his way to town on Partition Night, turned and entered the shanty. The seven others were already there. The first one in had indicated that the meeting place was secure by placing the soapbox in the window before a predesignated pane. The last one to leave would remove it.

To those seven men Uri was known only by his code name, Shamir. They were all members of a cell of the Irgun Zvai Leumi, an underground, illegal Jewish organization, hated by the British, feared by the Arabs, disowned by a good majority of their own community. Heirs to the philosophy of a Zionist zealot named Vladimir Jabotinsky, they clung to the dream of a Jewish state running from Acre to Amman, from Mount Hermon to the Suez Canal. For them, Churchill's decision to create the emirate of Transjordan with a stroke of his pen on a Sunday afternoon in Cairo had been a mutilation of the Balfour Declaration. They wanted it all, all the land that had once belonged to the Biblical kingdom of Israel, and they wanted it, if possible, without the encumbering presence of its Arab inhabitants.

While the Jewish Agency, representative of the majority of the Jewish community, had pursued its goals with negotiations and self-restraint, the Irgun and its smaller offshoot, the Stern Gang, had gone to the gun. They had not scrupled at murder and terrorism to obtain their aims. Their escutcheon was a rifle thrust aloft by a clenched fist ringed by the motto "Only Thus." In the accomplishment of that pledge, they had already splattered on it the blood of over three hundred victims, most of them innocent—like the ninety Arabs, Jews and Britons they had killed in their most famous exploit, the destruction of a wing of the King David Hotel on July 22, 1946. They had shocked the world and outraged their fellow Jews by hanging two British sergeants, then booby-trapping their bodies, in reprisal for the execution of one of their number. Their excesses were largely responsible for the anti-Jewish sentiment which permeated the British forces in Palestine. Those excesses had produced other fruits, however. They had helped disgust the British public with Britain's role in Palestine, and thus played an important role in leading Clement Attlee to his decision to leave.

For the Irgun, the United Nations' partition of Palestine was only an invalid dismemberment of the larger homeland they sought. Above all, they condemned the internationalization of Jerusalem, which they proclaimed "was and will forever be our capital." Just before the vote, Menahem Begin, the bespectacled, meek-looking head of the Irgun, had told his commanders in a secret meeting that Jerusalem "was to take precedence over everything else in the months ahead." They were to destroy any hope of internationalizing the city by their actions there. As they had spattered Palestine with British blood in pursuit of a Jewish state, so would they now spatter Jerusalem with Arab blood in pursuit of its Jewish capital.

Their first actions had been directed against the Arabs of Lifta and Romema, on the western edge of Jerusalem, whose inhabitants they accused of passing information on the movements of Jewish convoys to Tel Aviv. Then they turned their attention to the Arab crowds in the center of the city. On December 13, one of their commandos hurled two bombs into a mass of Arab shoppers at Damascus Gate, killing six people and wounding forty more.

It was the willingness to participate in such actions that bound the disparate members of the Irgun together. The eight men of Uri Cohen's cell gathered in their shanty in Jerusalem's poor Yemenite Quarter were a typical cross section of the organization's membership. One was an elderly man who sold roses from a baby carriage on Ben Yehuda Street. As he did he meticulously gathered much of the intelligence the organization needed for its activities. One was a Yemenite laborer who could barely read and write. Another, the most fanatic member of the group, was an Orthodox Polish Jew from Mea Shearim.

Uri Cohen was in the Irgun because he wanted to be where the action was. He always had. He had spent most of his life satisfying his craving for action on the sports field. At eighteen he had joined the Royal Air Force, looking for action, just as he had joined the Irgun for the same reason four years later. His appetite had gone unfulfilled. "The Haganah is doing nothing," he regularly complained, "and now we are doing nothing, too."

For Uri Cohen, however, this meeting would not be like all the others. He had, his cell leader announced, been selected to begin the next day in an Irgun commanders' course. It would prepare him for the action for which he had clamored so long.

It was a ritual as unvarying as his daily reading of a passage of the Bible. Every Friday at noon, a staff officer hand-carried to the office of the Chaplain General of the British armed forces in Palestine one of the twenty numbered and registered copies of a "Most Secret" document called "Order of Battle and Location Statement." Its half-dozen pages gave the exact location and the movements anticipated for the coming week of every British unit in the Middle East.

117

After a careful perusal of its contents, the chaplain locked the document in his safe and headed to the officers' mess of the King David Hotel. Before his return an hour later, a photocopy of the document was on its way to Haganah intelligence.

That exploit, carried out by a secretary, was one of the first achievements of an intelligence service whose accomplishments would one day dazzle the world. Given their numerical inferiority, it was not on the primitive bomb-and-run tactics of the Irgun that the Jews of Palestine would have to depend in their struggle with the Arabs. Long before the Irgun had placed its first bomb in the midst of an Arab crowd, the Haganah had sought to mobilize the diverse resources of Palestine's Jewish community for the sophisticated tasks of intelligence warfare.

The head of Jerusalem's Uri net was a twenty-six-year-old German-born physicist named Shalhevet Freir. Freir had learned at first hand the ways of the British military as a sergeant in the Eighth Army fighting his way across Africa. Later, disguised as an English major or colonel, he had run illegal immigrants past Britain's forces in Italy. Now, from an office in an obscure Institute for the Study of Social Affairs on Jerusalem's Bezalel Street, he directed twenty agents filtered into every level of Britain's civil and military establishment. He had even, thanks to an Armenian secretary, succeeded in penetrating the office of the High Commissioner.

The key to the Haganah's successes lay in the brilliance and the variety of the individuals who served it. With his bushy moustache, his penetrating blue eyes, his worn tweed sports jackets, his quietly superior Oxbridge accent, twenty-nine-year-old Vivian Herzog could pass anywhere for a young British officer in civilian clothes. Born in Dublin, Herzog, the son of the Chief Rabbi of Palestine, was officially responsible for liaison between the Haganah and the British Army. His real assignment was establishing a network of strategically located pro-Jewish officers inside the British establishment. If Herzog was to enjoy an extraordinary success in his task, it was not surprising. He brought to it the highest of qualifications. He had been an officer in that most British of British units, the Guards, and he had prepared for his Haganah assignment by serving for a year and a half as a captain in British military intelligence.

Herman Joseph Mayer, the German-born eldest son of Jerusalem's most distinguished bookseller, had spent the war with a pair of earphones clamped to his head, moving from El Alamein to Monte Cassino monitoring the conversations of Luftwaffe pilots for the R.A.F. Now, in the basement of his father's home at 33 Ramban Street, Mayer was busy monitoring other conversations. This time, however, the voices filtering through the static of his earphones were English. Mayer presided over an auxiliary of Jewish intelligence called Arnevet, "the Rabbit." The Rabbit, manned by English-speaking Haganah girls, functioned twenty-four hours a day, its specially adapted radio fixed to a wavelength of 58.2 meters, the channel of the British police.

With the passage of time, the accomplishments of those varied intelligence units would grow to impressive dimensions. Already the flow of information into Freir's headquarters was highly significant. It included the weekly intelligence estimate of the British Army for the Middle East, most of the letters exchanged between Sir Alan Cunningham and his superiors in London, the orders and circulars sent to the subordinate commands of G.H.Q. Palestine, and the British Army's periodic evaluation of the state of Jewish and Arab preparations.

More vital for the future was the penetration established by Jewish intelligence inside the Arab ranks. Within a fortnight of each meeting of the Arab League, a copy of its minutes was in the hands of the Jewish Agency in Jerusalem. Even the Cairo headquarters of Haj Amin Husseini had been penetrated with a paid informer.

In the basement of the Jewish Agency, in two closely guarded rooms, a curly-haired young man named Yitshak Navon was organizing what would become the most precious source of information of all. Those two rooms were linked by a special cable to the central switchboard of the Jerusalem Post Office. There the Post, Telephone and Telegraph's largely Jewish technicians were quietly setting taps on key Arab and British telephones in Jerusalem and on the trunk lines linking Palestine to Europe and the rest of the Middle East. Soon Navon would have a score of operators on duty around the clock in his basement hideaway, carefully transcribing the conversations of every key Arab and British official in the city.

Adjunct of that secret war was a propaganda war that both sides were beginning to wage through clandestine radio stations. The Arabs' radio, called Voice of the Revolution, broadcast every evening at seven o'clock from a small transmitter hidden under a pile of carpets in the delivery van of an Armenian rug dealer.

The Haganah's transmitter was hidden in a private home. To fool the British detection services, it was located in a neighborhood without electric current. Current was supplied by a wire stretched from house to house from a nearby hospital. The Haganah's order for its concealment was: "Hang out more undershirts." The housewives along its route had all been asked to keep it covered with laundry.

119

8

THE SANTA CLAUS OF THE HAGANAH

THE SNOW CLUNG to the old tile roofs and built up in irregular layers along the city walls. Overhead, the star which 1,947 years earlier had guided the shepherds of Judea and the Three Magi to Bethlehem's stable flickered like a distant beacon in the winter sky. Wrapped in its mantle of snow, Jerusalem prepared to celebrate one of the most uncertain Christmastides in its history.

Seldom had peace seemed more remote and men of goodwill rarer than in that Jerusalem of 1947. Regularly, as December waned toward Christmas, the sound of gunfire shattered the city's peace. The skirmishes that gunfire betokened had grown in intensity and frequency with each passing day. By the end of the year, violence in Palestine would have claimed the lives of 175 Arabs, 150 Jews and fifteen British soldiers.

Arabs and Jews rivaled each other in their ferocity in compiling those figures. As a reprisal for Arab sniper fire into Jewish areas, one Haganah officer set up a Bren gun in an office window and sent a clip of bullets into a crowd of Arab shoppers at Jaffa Gate. Gershon Avner, the young man who had brought David Ben-Gurion news of the partition vote, saw two British soldiers shot before his eyes on a crowded street in the heart of Jewish Jerusalem. Israel Schreiber was kidnapped by a band of Arab teenage hoodlums in the Old City souks. A few hours later his body, stuffed into a burlap bag, was dumped outside Damascus Gate. Nuria Alima, a half-crippled Jewish newspaper dealer, was murdered by an Arab gunman who had just bought one of his papers. Robert Stern, a popular columnist of the *Palestine Post,* was shot on the threshold of the Press Office. In the last article he had submitted to his paper, the British-born Stern had inadvertently composed his own epitaph. "If I die," he had written, "rather than a monument to my memory, I would prefer people make an offering to help care for the animals in the Jerusalem zoo." The next day, as the first contributions began to flow into the zoo, the unfortunate newsman's funeral convoy was machine-gunned by Arab sharpshooters.

Beyond the city gates, along the same road the carpenter of Nazareth and Mary, his wife, had plodded with their ass toward Bethlehem, Arab riflemen ambushed a Jewish convoy, killing ten Jews, then mutilating their bodies.

Even Christmas Eve had its ration of gunfire. Driving through the Jewish neighborhood of Mekor Hayim, Samy Aboussouan, who had just played the violin in the Palestine Broadcasting System's annual Christmas Eve concert, came under fire. By the time he reached his destination, a modest hotel in Katamon, his car was pockmarked with bullets. Aboussouan had moved his family into the Hotel Semiramis a few days after the burning of the Commercial Center. The three-story, bougainvillea-covered hotel, owned by his uncle, was so discreet that it had seemed to Aboussouan the surest refuge in Jerusalem.

Inside, with a fire blazing in the fireplace, the atmosphere was a cheerful contrast to the sinister and deserted streets through which Aboussouan had just passed. Determined to forget the situation with a traditional Christmas feast, Aboussouan's uncle, mother, aunts and cousins had set up an enormous Christmas tree in the hotel's sitting room, its branches covered with candles and glittering ornaments. At midnight, Aboussouan's family would march off to the nearby Chapel of St. Theresa for midnight mass, caroling in the darkness as they went the ancient hymns that celebrated the birth of a Savior nineteen centuries earlier in a stable a few miles from where their hotel now lay. Then they would return for an enormous Réveillon, a Christmas feast, at the hotel's banquet table glowing with silver and porcelain. As she always did at Christmas time, Samy's mother had prepared for their feast one of his favorite dishes, *karshat,* tripe stuffed with rice, garlic and chick-peas.

Just before eleven o'clock, an astonishing apparition appeared at the foot of the stairs leading to the hotel's upper floors. A plumed bicorn on his head, a cape over his shoulders, a sword buckled around the black-velvet and gold braid of his diplomat's dress uniform, it was the figure of Manuel Allende Salazar, vice-consul of Spain, off to represent his nation at the solemn midnight mass celebrated each year before Jerusalem's diplomatic corps and mandatory authorities in the basilica of the Church of the Nativity in Bethlehem.

Seeing the surprised and laughing faces of his fellow guests, the young Spanish diplomat gaily whirled back his cape, pulled his sword from its scabbard and profiled himself before the figure of an imaginary bull.

"As Manolete on the eve of his death," he proclaimed. Then, with a rush, he swept out the door into the night. In a few days' time, the laughter he had left behind was to have a tragic echo, and his parting joke the semblance of a ghastly premonition.

A British armored car shepherded the column of automobiles up the winding road, its headlights licking the white fields of snow covering the hills. Stiff and erect in his own diplomat's uniform, the representative of the latest nation to fail to bring peace to this particular parcel of earth sat lost in his melancholy reminiscences. It was a wet December night such as this thirty years before that James H. Pollock, the Jerusalem district commissioner, had seen the hilltop village of Bethlehem for the first time. He had been a young lieutenant in the vanguard of Allenby's army then, standing on the threshold of his life and his career. From that December night until this, both had been associated with the British mandate in Palestine. Now, Pollock sadly reflected, it had fallen to him to be the last Englishman to represent his nation's authority at the ceremony which seemed to symbolize so much of this difficult land he had entered as a conqueror and would leave as a disheartened civil servant.

When Monsignor Vincent Gelat entered the basilica of the Church of the Nativity at the head of the traditional parade of prelates, the strains of the Gloria burst from the assemblage of uniformed diplomats and faithful. As always, the first notes of that militant hymn were the signal that set the church towers of Bethlehem ringing out once again their ancient tidings of the birth of a Messiah.

Only a handful of pilgrims stood outside the basilica, ready to answer the call of the bells with their carols from Sheperds Fields or .the square before the church. Hearing the bells in his home a few streets away, Dr. Mikhail Malouf, the Arab head of Palestine's psychiatric hospitals, stood up.

Normally, Christmas Eve was a joyful feast in the Malouf home. Dozens of their friends dropped in to celebrate around the dishes of the Arabic *mezze* that Berthe Malouf spread over every table in her house. As they feasted, they would listen to the distant caroling rising from Sheperds Fields. And at the sound of Bethlehem's bells they too would walk singing up to Basilica Square.

This year there was no *mezze* and no feasting in the Malouf home. It had not seemed appropriate. The only sound drifting up to their home that night had been that of a few British soldiers on pass singing loudly off in the distance.

Now, with the chimes of the Church of the Nativity ringing through

122

his living room, Dr. Malouf solemnly wished his wife a traditional Arabic greeting, "May all your feasts find you in good health." Then he kissed her. Arm in arm they stood at their living-room window peering into the darkness through the lightly falling snow. From the center of Bethlehem they heard again the shouts and singing of the British soldiers, a little drunker now, ringing through the night. "But in the houses," Berthe Malouf thought, listening to them, "there is only sadness."

. . .

While Jerusalem paced through those age-old Christmas rituals, 2,500 miles away, near the Belgian port of Antwerp, a stumpy young man in a black mackintosh stepped out of a hired Buick, his arms wrapped around the bottles that were to be his offering of the Yuletide season. With a gesture of his head, Xiel Federmann indicated to the solitary guard at the gate of a sprawling line of warehouses that the cognac filling his arms was for him. Grateful at his unexpected visitor's generosity, the guard threw open his gates and waved Federmann inside.

Booming "Merry Christmas," Federmann unloaded the cognac and rubbed his hands in happy anticipation of the task before him. He was, on this Christmas morning, about to become the Santa Claus of the Haganah. Before Federmann stretched the acres and acres of the most fantastic bargain-basement store in the world in December 1947.

There were hundreds of halftracks, ambulances, water tanks, jeeps, trailer trucks, bulldozers, staff cars, ammunition carriers. There were tents in a dozen different sizes to hold one to one hundred men; an ocean of helmets, miles of cables, hose and wire, thousands of radios, field telephones, walkie-talkies, hand-cranked generators. There were carloads of cartridge belts, underpants, socks, combat boots, sweaters, fatigues, flashlights, first-aid kits, prophylactics—equipment enough, it seemed to the wondering Federmann, to fit out half the Jews of the world in the service of the Haganah. As Ehud Avriel had been sent to Europe to buy arms and ammunition, Federmann's task was to find and buy the rest of the material needed to equip immediately an army of sixteen thousand men.

The choice was a marvelous mix of man and mission. Despite his youth, Federmann had installed himself in Haifa running a café for British servicemen on his arrival in Palestine in 1940. Before long, the sale of coffee constituted only a minor part of his commercial activities. Using the contents of the *Standard Requirement Book for Equipment and Ordnance* as his bible, the extraordinary Federmann became a prime furnisher for the British Army and the Royal Navy.

Rare was the item, no matter how esoteric, that Federmann could not furnish his clients. His most notable achievement was furnishing the Royal Navy with one hundred thousand sailors' caps on short notice. Nowhere in the entire Middle East was there a press capable of blocking the hats into their unique, flat shape. Federmann prowled the suburbs of Tel Aviv until he found an aging Polish hatmaker accomplished in making the *straimel,* the round flat hat the orthodox Jews of Poland wore to mark the Sabbath. The elderly craftsman rounded up for Federmann his fellow hat-makers who had escaped the ghettoes of Poland, and soon the fingers that had shaped the *straimel* were busy pressing into form the flat cap of the Royal Navy.

A few months after the last cap was delivered, Federmann was able to detect during an official ceremony aboard H.M.S. *Warspite* the presence of those products of his inventive genius. It poured rain that day, and as he watched the admiral review the guard of honor Federmann's nose began to twitch. Rising from the ranks of the men before him was an unmistakable stench. Federmann recognized it immediately. It was the stench of glue dissolving in the rain, his glue, a paste made of crushed cattle bones redolent of the institution in which he had bought it, the Tel Aviv slaughter-house.

Now the wondering Federmann began to survey the immensity of the display spread before him, preparing his shopping list for the soldiers of his still-unborn country. In one of the first warehouses he entered, he stumbled on a strange device. It was a U.S. Army pack rack designed to help a man carry a heavy load. Federmann hesitated for a moment. They might be useful, he thought, and they cost only twenty cents apiece. With a shrug, he marked three hundred down on his list and walked on. One day, Federmann's twenty-cent pack racks would save the Jews of Jerusalem from starvation.

9

JOURNEY TO ABSURDITY

THE WOMAN STALKED up to the British major searching the bus.

"What is this?" she demanded.

"We're searching for arms," he replied.

"You can't do that," she announced.

"I can't?" asked the major.

The woman was not to be put off. She demanded the major's card. Like a proper Englishman, he drew it from his pocket and handed it to her. Behind his back, a few of his men began to snicker. Despite her heated protests, the search continued.

Finally the major said, "O.K., the bus can go."

"Wait a minute," said Golda Meir. "What about the girl in the car over there?" The car had carried the Haganah escort of the Jerusalem–Tel Aviv bus on which Golda was a passenger. The British had captured one of its occupants, a girl, and a Sten gun.

Golda Meir's intervention had been more than just a personal protest. The situation on the Jerusalem–Tel Aviv road was one of her major political concerns. Given Jerusalem's importance, its international stature, the planners of the Haganah had assumed the British would keep its vital road link to the sea open as long as they remained in Palestine. The Haganah's definition of an open road and that of the British Army had turned out to be two different things, however. For Britain's army commander, Sir Gordon MacMillan, an open highway was one on which his convoys could pass unmolested.

Sensing the nuance, the Arabs allowed British patrols and convoys to pass unscathed, saving their fire for Jewish vehicles. On behalf of the Jewish Agency, Golda had demanded British police escorts for their convoys, arguing that Britain remained responsible for security on the roads. The British had finally agreed, but at a price: they insisted on the right to control the convoys' contents to prevent the Haganah from bringing

125

arms and men into Jerusalem. Since that was one of their principal tasks, the Agency had started instead to place Haganah guards on them. In return, the British had begun to search the convoys for arms, a move infuriating to the Agency, where it was thought English energies might be put to better use preventing Arab ambushes.

Finally Golda Meir had wrung from Sir Henry Gurney, the government's Chief Secretary, a reluctant agreement to end the searches. Now, having found that the agreement was not being carried out, she got a second unpleasant surprise. The British major announced that he was taking his girl prisoner to a police station deep in Arab territory. Golda shuddered.

"In that case," she declared, "I'm going with you."

Irritated, the major told her, "You can't do that. I'll have to arrest you."

"That, young man, is precisely what I want you to do," Golda snapped, and climbed onto the seat beside the arrested girl.

The two women, thanks to her insistence, were finally taken to a Jewish police station. The British desk sergeant on duty noted down the details of their case. Then he asked Golda her name. "Oh, my God!" he sighed softly on hearing it, and clapped his hands to his head.

A few minutes later, a chief inspector arrived to offer her a drink and a safe passage to Tel Aviv in his armored car. At the outskirts of Tel Aviv she motioned the inspector to stop. "It is you who are in danger now," she said, and climbed down from the car. As the inspector started to back away, Golda remembered that it was December 31, 1947, and that for her English escort a New Year was about to begin. Turning, she cupped her hands before her mouth and cried "Happy New Year!" to the unknown British policeman.

Then she strode briskly off toward Tel Aviv.

• • •

The new year opening before the inhabitants of Jerusalem would be the most turbulent of modern times. No calling, not even that whose traditional role was easing the suffering of men, would be spared its ramifications.

At high noon one day, three Arab gunmen stepped from behind a clump of bushes at the Arabic Beit Safafa Hospital and murdered Dr. Hugo Lehrs, a physician who despite the pleas of his Jewish colleagues had refused to abandon his Arab patients. Hearing the news minutes later on the Palestine radio, Dr. Mikhail Malouf, the Bethlehem psychiatrist, exclaimed, *"Ya Allah!"* And he lamented to his wife, "This should never have happened."

At high noon the next day, the Biblical ration of vengeance, an eye for an eye, a tooth for a tooth, was exacted on the Arab medical community. On his way to visit the inmates of a little insane asylum outside Bethlehem, Mikhail Malouf was murdered, wrapping in a new sadness the home in which a few nights before he and his wife had celebrated their melancholy Christmas together.

To not a few Jerusalemites, those opening days of the new year meant a sudden uprooting. The regrouping of the city's population sought by the tactics of the Haganah and the snipers of Haj Amin Husseini had begun. It was on the villa-covered slopes of the middle-class Arab neighborhood of Katamon that the situation deteriorated most rapidly.

Inhabited largely by Christian Arabs and a minority of well-to-do Jews, Katamon was cursed by the strategic value of its high ground and its geography. Separating the Jewish quarter of Mekor Hayim from the neighborhood of Talbiyeh, it was, for the Haganah, a kind of Arab abscess in the southern flank of the city, breaking the continuity of their settlement, providing a constant threat to Jewish Jerusalem's integrity. For the Arabs, conversely, Katamon was a valuable stronghold in enemy territory, the bridgehead from which they might one day launch the thrust that would cut Jewish Jerusalem in two. Arab gunmen regularly machine-gunned passing Jewish cars and sniped into Mekor Hayim from its rooftops.

Seeking to provoke an Arab exodus from the quarter, the Haganah had blown up eight abandoned Arab houses on its fringe New Year's Eve. That gesture, and the rifle fire sweeping through its streets, had its effect. Without further provocation, a number of Katamon's Arab bourgeoisie left the area for the safety of Beirut, Amman and Damascus. Gibrail Katoul, the civil servant who on Partition Night had seen in the United Nations vote a kind of worldwide conspiracy, was among them. Forty-eight hours before his departure, his next-door neighbor's eldest son appeared in his doorway. During the 1936 Arab rebellion, Katoul had made the armed guards he hired to protect his home swear to extend their protection to the home of his Jewish neighbor.

"Now," sighed Katoul to the neighbor's son, "it is too late. We can do nothing to help you and you can do nothing to protect us. You are in danger here in this Arab quarter. You too must leave."

Two days later, a horse cart drew up in front of the Jewish home to pick up the family's belongings. The same morning, a truck came for the carefully packed wooden cases of the Katouls. From their windows the neighbors watched the two families go, two sad little caravans, the Jews moving off in one direction, the Arabs in another.

For the second time in a month, Mishael Shacham found himself in front of the chief of staff of the Haganah in the underground army's Tel Aviv headquarters. This time the matter that had brought him there was a report from a special Haganah envoy to Jerusalem. Its implications were so grave that Yaacov Dori had decided to relieve Shacham of his transportation task for the time being and send him to Jerusalem.

The situation in the city, the report said, was deteriorating daily. Despite the Haganah's efforts, Jews were leaving the outlying areas and mixed quarters for the densely populated Jewish areas in increasing numbers. Something, Dori was convinced, had to be done immediately to stop that flow. David Ben-Gurion's order that every parcel of land had to be defended was not just a ringing phrase to rally a beleaguered people. For the Jews of Palestine, there were no Ammans, no Beiruts, no Damascuses. There was only the sea. If a psychology of abandonment were allowed to take hold of the population, the whole Jewish settlement in Palestine might simply start to unravel. Jerusalem was the first place where that problem had arisen, and it was there it had to be stopped. Dori told Shacham to go to Jerusalem immediately. With whatever tactics he wished, he was to stop the deterioration in the situation and, if possible, reverse the flow.

Within hours after getting his orders, Shacham was at Israel Amir's headquarters. Jews were now leaving new areas from which they had not previously retreated, Amir told Shacham, and were hiring British policemen to get them and their belongings out past the Mufti's gunmen.

Amir's intelligence staff believed that the only swift and effective way of altering the situation was to strike a major blow inside Arab Katamon. The shock of such a mission, they held, might force the Arabs out of the quarter and change the psychological climate in the city.

"All right," said Shacham. "Where is the main Arab headquarters in Katamon?"

The Arab leadership was no less concerned than the Haganah with the fate of Katamon. The day following the Haganah's destruction of eight abandoned houses in the area, the local defense committee began to organize a home guard. More important, Abdul Khader Husseini summoned up from Hebron one of the Mufti's most faithful followers, an illiterate shepherd named Ibrahim Abou Dayieh. Abou Dayieh had distinguished himself during the 1936 revolt. Since then he had been responsible for the south of Palestine, running a little peasant army of his own in the hills around Hebron.

On Saturday, January 3, the day of Mishael Shacham's arrival in Jerusalem, Abou Dayieh, Abdul Khader and Emile Ghory prowled the streets of Katamon in a jeep, planning the disposition of the one hundred men Abou Dayieh planned to smuggle into the neighborhood on Jerusalem's No. 4 bus. At sunset, the three men stopped for tea and a conference with Katamon's leaders at a pleasant, bougainvillea-covered three-story building. Its discreetly quiet sitting room made it one of their favorite meeting places. A plaque over its stone doorway indicated its name. It was the Hotel Semiramis.

Israel Amir's intelligence staff had the answer to Mishael Shacham's question ready for the daily staff conference at 10 A.M. on Sunday, January 4. One of their Arab informers had furnished the information. There were two Arab headquarters in Katamon, he reported. One was a little boarding-house called Claridge's. The other was the Hotel Semiramis. The informer had himself seen the sand-colored jeep of Abdul Khader Husseini parked in front of the hotel for over an hour the evening before. Shacham located the two buildings on a map of Jerusalem. Its proximity to the Jewish lines made one of the two the easier target. Looking up from his map, Shacham announced his choice—the Hotel Semiramis.

Outside, leaden ridges of cloud rolling up from the plain pushed across the Sunday morning sky, bringing the promise of a furious storm. At almost exactly the same moment Israel Amir's officers had sat down to their daily staff conference, the eighteen members of the Aboussouan family who were gathered at the Hotel Semiramis had set out for ten-o'clock mass at their little neighborhood Chapel of St. Theresa. There Samy Abousouan's pious mother urged everyone in the family to confession and Communion as "the only real protection against the perils menacing us all."

After mass, still another member of the family arrived at the hotel, Wida Kardous, the teenage daughter of the governor of Samaria, sent to Jerusalem for the end of her Christmas vacation. Shortly before lunch Manuel Allende Salazar, the Spanish diplomat living in the hotel, came up to Samy Aboussouan with a book he had borrowed a few days before. The two men chuckled over how apt a description of their own situation its title was. It was called *Journey to Absurdity*.

Heralded by a cracking roll of thunder, the storm that had been building up all day finally burst loose at sunset. While jagged streaks of lightning lashed the sky, a deluge hammered the city, swiftly turning the streets of Katamon into muddy torrents. The first waves of wind and rain tore out the power lines, plunging the quarter into blackness. Terrified, two of Samy Aboussouan's elderly aunts began to recite the rosary in the darkness while the hotel's domestics scuttled around looking for candles.

Dinner was a lugubrious affair. Outside, the rain beat on the windows and the reverberating thunderclaps set the flames of the candles on the dining table swaying. Suddenly, halfway through the meal, there was a loud banging on the front door. Two armed Arab guards, their water-filled boots squishing on the floor, marched into the room looking for the proprietor's twenty-three-year-old son, Hubert, to take his turn on guard duty. His mother shrieked, then began to cry.

"Not tonight," she pleaded. "Take him tomorrow night, the night after tomorrow, every night of the week, but not tonight."

Furious, the guards stalked back out into the storm.

Barely one thousand yards away, in the top floor of the Rehavia residence of a Jewish surgeon, four men gathered around a Jerusalem street map. With a finger, Mishael Shacham traced out the route that would take them to their target. The four-man demolition team would be covered by a squad of Haganah riflemen. In the rain-swept street outside were the black Humber and the prewar Plymouth they would use to get to the Semiramis. Once there, Shacham explained, they would have exactly ten minutes to break open the cellar door, get their two suitcases containing 175 pounds of TNT into the basement and up against the hotel's key supports, light them and get out. H hour was one o'clock.

The rain continued to beat down on the city. It was, in the terms of an old Arab adage, "raining from the earth and the sky." In the Hotel Semiramis, Samy Aboussouan and three cousins sat down by candlelight to play a few desultory hands of bridge. The Spanish consul came in early and went directly upstairs. In one corner of the room, the two elderly aunts continued to pray. Shortly after eleven, everyone went to bed. The last words Wida Kardous, the teenager who had arrived that morning, heard as she climbed the stairs was a reassuring whisper in the dark from one of her cousins: "Don't be afraid." By midnight the last candle in the hotel was snuffed out.

There was no letup in the storm. Normally, thirty young men of the hastily assembled local militia guarded Katamon in ten key checkpoints. In a storm like this, they reasoned, there was no chance of a Jewish attack. Most of them were sent home to bed. At midnight, his tour finished, twenty-year-old law student Peter Saleh went home to bed, too. No one relieved him. There were, huddled in the rain and darkness, exactly eight guards left on duty in three of Katamon's ten checkpoints.

The Humber and the Plymouth were fifteen minutes early. Not a single Arab had been on duty at the only roadblock along their way. From the courtyard of the Orthodox convent opposite the hotel, a watchman saw one of the cars stop in front of the Semiramis kitchen. He noticed two figures leap out carrying satchels and run toward the building.

The door to the hotel cellar was locked. Cursing in the darkness, Avram Gil pulled a grenade from his belt and fixed it to the door. With a sharp roar it blew the door from its hinge. Gil and two other members of the commando plunged into the smoking basement carrying their satchels of TNT.

A rain of falling glass caused by the grenade's explosion woke up Wida Kardous. In the darkness she heard her Aunt Maria calling out to her. Then another voice called out, "Lie on the floor!"

The same sound of falling glass woke Samy Aboussouan. For an instant he thought there was a fight out in the street. Then he heard footsteps crunching over the broken glass in the courtyard below his window and a voice in Hebrew calling, "*Od lo, od lo*. Not yet, not yet." At that sound, Samy leaped from his bed. In the darkened hallway beyond his bedroom he found his parents, an uncle, and an aunt rushing up and down in their bathrobes, babbling to each other in fear and worry. He told them to go down to the sitting room, the safest place in the hotel, then ran to the telephone.

As quickly as he could, Samy dialed 999, the number of the motorized police. "They've attacked the Hotel Semiramis with hand grenades!" he cried to the sleepy English voice that answered.

In the cellar of the hotel, the explosive charges had already been carefully set against the building's principal supports. Avram Gil and his aide could not light the fuse, soaked by its brief exposure to the pouring rain. It was their voices Samy Aboussouan had heard calling back their cover squad, which had started its withdrawal.

131

Nervous, sweating, they did not know what to do. "Yoel," Gil whispered to their commander, who was standing guard at the door, "we can't light the fuse."

The commander came down "very relaxed, very composed." He sat down cross-legged in front of the explosive. "This is what you have to do in such operations," he explained. "Take it easy, don't get nervous, then all will be well." Patiently he cut the soggy fuse with his pocketknife and began to make up a new one.

Upstairs, Wida Kardous' Aunt Maria let go of the young girl's hand and told her, "I'm coming right back. I'm going to get a bathrobe." Frightened, Wida watched her disappear in the blackness. Samy Aboussouan hung up the telephone and started toward the sitting room. On the floor above him, his brother Cyril gave his hand to their mother to guide her down the stairs to the salon. Their father, putting on a dressing gown, followed.

It had taken about four minutes to make the new fuse, but now it was ready. The commander went to the entry, picked up a still-glowing splinter from the wreckage of the door and walked back to the explosive. Softly he blew on the scrap of wood until it glowed yellow-orange. He pressed it against his new fuse. It sputtered. He waited a moment. Then he said, "The fuse is lit. Run!"

Wida Kardous did not hear a thing. She would only remember for the rest of her life opening her eyes on an incredible spectacle. Above her "there was only the sky."

"Where is the roof? Where are the people?" she murmured.

Samy Aboussouan was blinded by an immense blue light, followed by a violent shock and a sharp whistling. He had the impression the walls were tumbling in on him "in a monstrous race." Picked up by the blast, hurled to the ground, he found himself lying on a heap of plaster looking up at the lightning flashes streaking across the sky. He lifted his head for an instant toward the doorway through which his parents should have entered the sitting room. All he could see was a pile of broken stones and one step of the staircase dangling from a broken beam. For a long moment the ghastly scene before him was "wrapped in a frightful silence." Then, rising from some corner of the ruins, he heard the anguished voice of his brother begging for help.

The shattering roar of the explosion awakened most of Katamon. From his nearby bedroom window, law student Peter Saleh, the guard who had just gone to bed, saw the hotel lift up with a roar, then collapse on itself. A cloud of smoke and dust rose from the ruins while the shock waves rolled back and forth over the Judean hills. As it died away, Saleh heard again the steady splash of the rain and, from underneath the pile of rubble almost below his window, a first pathetic moan.

Awakened by the noise of the first hand grenade, Kay Albina, the wife of the man who had filmed the destruction of his own movie house a month earlier, had seen the whole drama from her bedroom window. She had heard the Haganah cars flee and had watched in awe as the terrible explosion seemed to lift the roof of the hotel slowly up into the air, then drop it back to earth. A first-aid student, Kay Albina swept up her Red Cross kit and a handful of sheets and rushed through the rainswept streets to help the wounded.

None of her first-aid manuals, however, had prepared her for the horror of the first sight she saw in the ruins of the hotel. It was the figure of a woman stumbling hysterically through the rubble, cradling in her arms the severed head of her infant daughter.

Twenty-six people died in the explosion of the Semiramis Hotel. Samy Aboussouan and Wida Kardous survived, but the Aboussouan family was virtually obliterated. Samy's mother and father, his two aunts and his three uncles died. Hubert Lorenzo, the twenty-three-year-old son of the proprietor, died along with the parents who would not let him take his turn on guard duty.

Three days after the explosion, the frantic scratching of a dog who had not left the ruins since the blast led the searchers to the body of the last innocent victim still buried in the rubble. Hidden under a heap of masonry and broken beams, it was the corpse of his master, the young Spanish diplomat who on Christmas Eve had laughingly compared himself to Manolete on the eve of his death. Victim of a drama which was not his, Manuel Allende Salazar had completed the last steps of his own Journey to Absurdity.

Journeys of a different sort had ended in those early days of January. There would be no more No. 2 buses to run men and supplies from New Jerusalem into the Jewish Quarter of the Old City. On New Year's Eve the Arabs cut the bus route with a massive roadblock at Jaffa Gate, and the quarter's residents began to endure in modern form one of the oldest traditions of the ancient city they so esteemed, the siege.

Not an ounce of food, fuel or ammunition had reached the quarter since the Arabs had erected their roadblock. The unburied dead accumulated in a week of blockade lay just beyond the Haganah's headquarters. Kerosene, used by the quarter's residents for cooking, was almost gone. So, too, was milk for the children.

Alarmed, the Jewish Agency had protested daily to the British, for whom it would have been an easy matter to force the Arabs to remove the roadblock. The British reply had been a request to the Agency to temporarily evacuate the quarter. The Agency refused. The British then proposed a compromise. They would escort a supply convoy to the quarter through Zion Gate once a week, providing they could search it for arms and ammunition. They would escort anyone who wanted to leave out of the quarter, but no one would be allowed in.

The proposal was against almost all the principles the Jewish Agency was trying to maintain in its dealings with the British. The situation in the quarter was desperate, however. The residents were already beginning to blame the Haganah for their difficulties and clamoring to leave with or without a British escort. Reluctantly, the Agency agreed to the British suggestion.

For the handful of Haganah officers assigned to defend the most sacred acres the Jewish people possessed in Palestine, those days constituted a rude descent into reality. They were trapped in one of the most exposed positions in Palestine with a garrison of only one hundred and fifty Haganah men, fifty men of the Irgun and Stern Gang, and a force for which they would be increasingly grateful in the months to come, threescore girl soldiers of the Haganah.

Those winter nights gave Isser Natanson, the quarter's Irgun commander, many a moment to ponder his last exchange with the man who had ordered him into the quarter.

"What will we do there?" he had asked.

With a sour smile his superior had replied, "You'll be a sacrifice. What other reason is there for being there?"

. . .

January seventh was always a special day in the life of Hameh Majaj. It was his wedding anniversary. Normally, he and his wife celebrated the event with a festive dinner at the home of his uncle. Festive dinners, however, did not seem appropriate in the troubled January of 1948. They had decided instead to celebrate with a quiet dinner in their own dining room. When it was finished, they would begin their nightly contemplation of the

134

blueprints of the dwelling in which a year hence they would celebrate their anniversary for the first time in a home of their own.

Hameh Majaj had a surprise for his wife, however. It was a three-tiered gold harem ring he had bought in the souks. On his modest salary, its price represented a considerable sacrifice, and it was a measure of his devotion to her. He had planned to give it to her at dinner, but, seeing her smiling at the breakfast table that morning, he could not resist. He leaped up, rushed to his bedroom and got the ring. Shyly, he slipped it onto his surprised wife's finger, then watched with pride and pleasure as she held it up to the morning sunlight.

January seventh, 1948, would be a special day in the life of Uri Cohen too. His persistent demand for action had at last been accepted by his superiors in the Irgun. Before him, on a bed in the one-room shack of a Yemenite porter at the Jerusalem bus station, were three stolen British police uniforms. They would provide disguises for Cohen and his companions in the mission to which he had been assigned.

The commander of their mission was an Oriental Jew only a couple of years older than Cohen. He had, Uri knew, "done this thing several times before." Looking at him in his suit and tie, the young biology student suddenly thought he was "just like a businessman getting ready to go to work."

The commander led them next door, to the back room of an automobile repair shop. There, sitting on the floor, were the instruments of the action for which Uri Cohen had been clamoring: two fifty-gallon oil drums packed tight with old nails, bits of scrap iron, hinges, rusty metal filings. At their center was a core of TNT whose explosion would turn the barrels into a vicious weapon, hurling those rusty shards of iron at a velocity sufficient to shred to ribbons any human being unlucky enough to stand in their way. The firing device was a plain cotton fuse wrapped in a dozen wooden matches. Scraping a matchbox over them would light the fuse.

Quietly, the commander assigned each man his job. Uri Cohen's stomach sickened when he was given his. He was going to be the bomber. When the time came, his job would be to light the fuses with a matchbox and push the oil barrels onto their target.

At precisely four o'clock, Cohen arrived in his uniform in front of a high school in the Rehavia quarter. The police van that would carry them on their mission was waiting. It had been stolen from a Ford garage where it was being repaired. Cohen got into the police van. The commander sat in front next to the driver. On either side of Cohen, armed with machine

135

guns they would fire from the slit along the side of the van, were two other men.

Their route had been carefully planned so that they would enter the Arab part of the city through an Arab Legion checkpoint. Cohen peered through the slit as they rode by, the Arab Legionnaires staring impassively at them, assuming they were British. Suddenly they were inside Arab Jerusalem, heading up the Bethlehem Road under the slopes of Mount Zion toward the walls of the Old City.

As they started up the hill, Uri began to tremble. "What am I doing here?" he asked himself. Suddenly the whole thing seemed crazy, farfetched. "Here I am, a biology student; I study life and in a few minutes I'm going to kill people," he thought. The wheels in his mind turned over faster and faster and a slick of nervous sweat dampened his forehead. "What am I doing this for, what am I doing this for?" he asked himself again and again.

It was too late for those questions now. In the stolen police van there was no talk. Ahead, through the windshield, Uri saw an Arab roadblock and, a hundred yards beyond, the target for the first of the two bombs beside him. He saw an Arab raise his hand to flag them to a stop. Very calmly, the commander turned to the driver. "Drive right on through," he said.

Hameh Majaj looked at his watch. He and his wife had cut short the ritual courtesy visit they paid each year, on their wedding anniversary, to his wife's elderly aunt inside the Old City. With the situation, and the work still to be done for their dinner, Hameh's wife was in a hurry to get home. In three minutes, he knew, a No. 3 bus was due at Jaffa Gate. They could just catch it, if they hurried. Taking his wife by the hand, he tugged her along the narrow passageways. Half running, they turned out of the Old City and rushed toward the knot of people waiting at the Jaffa Gate bus stop.

The commander told the driver to stop, then turned and looked back at Cohen. "Light your bomb," he said.

Cohen reached into his pocket, then stiffened. He was a nonsmoker, and in his excitement he had forgotten to put into his pocket a matchbox to light the bomb. The commander coolly stood up, walked to the back of the van and handed Cohen a pack of matches from his own pocket. Cohen scraped the box over the matches ringing the fuse. Then he threw open the rear doors of the police van and looked out for the first time on his target.

A sea of surprised faces stared up at him. At his feet the fuse sputtered. For a second, Cohen peered out at those figures of what seemed to him like "hundreds of people, a real crowd, all shocked and startled." They were the evening crowd of Arab bus riders waiting for the No. 3 bus at the Jaffa Gate stop.

"They have seen the devil," Cohen thought. "They see the bomb right in front of them with the fuse burning." He reached down and with his athlete's arms began to twist the bomb gently down onto the pavement in their midst. It thudded to the ground, sparks spitting from its fuse. The crowd seemed paralyzed with terror, staring first at the bomb, then at Cohen as if he were "a figure in a nightmare," as if, Cohen thought, they were all "in a movie that has suddenly stopped."

He reached out to close the door, his arms passing within hand reach of those stunned Arab bus riders about to be killed by the bomb he had just set down among them. The door closed, and Cohen could still see their uncomprehending faces as he snapped it shut.

The explosion went off at the instant Hameh Majaj and his wife won their race for the No. 3 bus. Still holding hands, they were hurled backward by the shock. Struggling up into a sitting position, Majaj gagged at the horrible spectacle all around him. The enormous square was littered with bodies, bits and pieces of them strewn across the pavement like chunks of meat. Next to the bus stop was a store whose owner had been cranking down his metal shutter when the bomb went off. The explosion had driven his body into the screen, impaling it on its raw metal edges in a grotesque crucifixion. He turned to his wife on the pavement beside him. She was covered with blood, her eyes half open.

"Something is falling inside me," she mumbled. Then her eyes closed.

Hameh spoke to her, but there was no answer. He knelt over her and took her limp hand in his, begging her for a reply. There was none. Even her convulsive shudders had stopped. Screaming, Hameh Majaj leaped to his feet pleading for help, for an ambulance to get her to a hospital.

Three hours later, a duty surgeon at the hospital came out of the operating room into which they had wheeled Majaj's wife. "He looked at me," Majaj would later recall. "I couldn't talk, but I knew what his eyes were telling me."

Hameh Majaj went into the emergency room for a last look at his wife's body. With tear-blurred eyes he stared down at the remains of the woman who had brought him so much happiness. His hands shaking with his sobs, he bent over and withdrew from her finger the keepsake by which he would remember her for the rest of his life, the three-tiered gold harem ring he had so proudly offered her for their wedding anniversary that morning.*

* A few moments after the explosion at Jaffa Gate, Uri Cohen's stolen police armored car struck a traffic island as he was preparing to unload the second bomb. Cohen and his companions abandoned the car and, under British fire, attempted to flee across Mamillah Cemetery to the safety of a Jewish neighborhood. Three were killed. One escaped, only to die a few months later in another Irgun action. Uri Cohen was wounded and was taken to a hospital, from which he was later rescued by the Irgun. From that wound he would keep his own souvenir of the tragic explosion which had taken the lives of seventeen people on January 7, 1948—one leg two inches shorter than the other.

10

"BAB EL WAD ON THE ROAD TO THE CITY"

Every time we go to sleep, we are not sure we are going to wake up. It is not the bullets we mind so much, but the dynamiting when you're asleep. People wake up in the middle of the night under the debris of their houses. Your father has to go to work in an ambulance. Every time we hear the door knock we are scared stiff that they have come to blow up our house. We stay home every evening from six o'clock on and lock all the doors and windows.

THUS DID AN ARAB MOTHER writing to her son at the American University of Beirut describe what life had become for her in Jerusalem two months after the United Nations partition vote. Her words might well have summarized existence in the city for many another housewife, Arab or Jewish, in January 1948. "Jerusalem," wrote a correspondent of *The New York Times,* "is becoming virtually isolated behind a curtain of fear. No one comes to Jerusalem or leaves his neighborhood except for an emergency."

In Jewish Jerusalem, food was now beginning to disappear. Milk, eggs, meat and vegetables were in short supply. Most restaurants were open only at noon. Fink's restaurant remained the hangout of Jerusalem's newsmen and night owls, but its cuisine was limited to a kind of hamburger liberally mixed with flour. Max Hesse kept his restaurant, the most elegant in Jerusalem, functioning because of his good relations with the Arab merchants who had supplied him for years. They delivered Max's daily order to a kind of neutral ground, the burned-out ruins of the Rex Cinema, where his chef picked it up.

It was a bitter cold winter, and in most Jewish homes fuel was desperately short. Even more serious for the city's housewives was the shortage of kerosene for cooking. The most elegant among them began to carry a pail or tin can when they went out, in case a donkey-towed kerosene tanker should cross their route.

Little mail was delivered; cable communications were chaotic, and international telephone calls were held up for hours and sometimes days;

139

Jewish lawyers refused to attend court, because their safety was not assured, and the court system ground to a standstill; the District Health Office ceased registering deaths, births and contagious diseases at the beginning of the year. The cemetery on the Mount of Olives was now inaccessible to Jerusalem's Jewish population. Covered with sheets, laid out on litters, their dead were borne off instead to the burial grounds of Sanhedria where their ancestors had laid the judges of an earlier Israel to rest.

For members of both communities, physical security was an almost daily concern. Few, however, led lives as exposed as Ruth and Chaim Haller, one of the few Jewish couples left in Katamon. Their only access to their home was by a trench dug through their garden up to their back door. At night Ruth stood guard at a ground-floor window, clutching in her hand a cowbell with which to rouse the Haganah guard upstairs in case of danger. Yet, like so many others, they learned to adapt their life to the circumstances. One evening as they prepared to leave for a concert, the Haganah warned the Hallers they would dynamite a nearby Arab home that night. The pair debated a moment. Then, opening their windows so that the blast would not shatter them, they set out for the concert anyway.

More than anything else, however, the somber mood of Jewish Jerusalem that winter was reflected in a square white handbill. Like a blight upon a leaf, those white scraps of paper began to fleck the walls, the telephone poles, the shop windows of the Jewish city. They were pasted there by the Haganah, the Irgun or the Stern Gang. Whatever the source, the stark black letters they bore inevitably began with the same phrase: "We stand to attention before the memory of our comrade . . ."

Jerusalem's Arab population, living in a city surrounded by Arab countryside, suffered none of the food and fuel shortages plaguing the Jewish neighborhoods. Their preoccupation with security was no less urgent, however, than that of the Jews. In the book-lined library in which they had followed the partition debate, Ambara and Sami Khalidy continued to read and study nightly. Now, however, Ambara's chair was placed before the window, blocking the view of her husband. The assassination by profession touched off by the murders of Drs. Lehrs and Malouf had spread to the academic community, and Ambara feared that some Jewish gunman might slip into their garden bent on killing her husband to avenge a murdered Jewish professor.

Even her children had been affected by the deterioration in Jerusalem life. Watching the arrival of the guards whom her father had requested for his Arab College, Sulafa, the eldest daughter, thought, "Now the good days are gone."

Unlike the Jewish quarters, where relations between the populace and their Haganah defenders were naturally close, a kind of uneasy truce existed in the Arab areas between the middle-class population and their essentially mercenary peasant protectors. Each neighborhood had its warlord loyal to Haj Amin but not necessarily to his fellow warlords. They squabbled constantly, extorted protection money from the citizens they were hired to defend. To their ranks had been added the stream of gangs flowing into Jerusalem from Syria, Transjordan and Iraq. Ostensibly there to defend the Holy City, they were often as anxious to pillage it as they were to fight for it. A thieves' market developed in the souks to handle the goods they looted from abandoned Arab and Jewish homes. Untrained, undisciplined, they would respond to a few random Jewish sniper shots with a wild barrage of rifle fire, then spend hours searching the souks for ammunition to replace the rounds they had wasted.

"Jerusalem," the city's Lebanese consul noted with despair in a dispatch to his Foreign Office, "is subject to a disorder unequaled anywhere in the world. Arms of every kind are passed from hand to hand under the eyes of the authorities. Public life is practically paralyzed. Stores and markets close at noon. The Arab bands have one chief here, another there, all acting independently without any contact between them."

One place in the city stood apart from the rancor and chaos of Jerusalem, however—a little island all its own in which a handful of Jews and Arabs lived together in peace and harmony. It was the government insane asylum. After observing its inmates' indifference to the strife sundering their peoples, Jacques de Reynier, the delegate of the International Red Cross, made a melancholy entry in his diary: *"Vive les fous!"* (Long live the nuts!)

•　•　•

"We must make the Jews live hell." That threat, uttered by the secretary of Jerusalem's Arab Higher Committee, summed up the ambitions of the Mufti's partisans in the city in the winter of 1948. Yet, with the British still present in Jerusalem in impressive strength, the Arabs no more than the Haganah could contemplate actually seizing and holding enemy ground. And so the two sides nightly sent their forces on destructive commando raids into each other's territory, striving to accomplish psychologically what they could not yet accomplish militarily.

141

The favorite Haganah tactic was to send a small, select commando team deep behind Arab lines, to the rear of a village or quarter suspected of harboring the Mufti's gunmen. While a second group of men drew the Arabs forward by opening fire on the front of the area, the commandos slashed into the rear. The idea, in the words of Abbras Tamir, a young Haganah officer, was "to go in fast with surprise, blow up some houses, kill some people and get out."

Despite their inferiority in men and arms, the well-trained and disciplined Haganah had the better of those forays, and a psychosis of fear began to overtake the Arabs in the city. Those who could afford another sanctuary, the upper and middle classes, began to drift away, leaving behind a leadership gap that would have serious consequences later.

In Sheikh Jarrah, an Arab neighborhood north of the Old City, Katy Antonious marked her going by asking all her friends to a last luncheon. Two successive assaults on the house next to hers had given reality to the threat the Haganah had been unable to deliver verbally because her phone was always busy. Now the walls of her villa were scarred with bullet holes, and her guests shivered in the February air rushing through its shattered windows. They sat on shaky bridge tables scattered among the packing cases that contained the silverware and crystal with which she had given so many brilliant receptions. Looking at those guests, Katy thought, "How sad it is. This house has known so much laughter and gaiety and now it is the last party, with an air of Brussels on the eve of Waterloo."

She left the next morning, persuaded, as so many others would be, that her departure was temporary. She was wrong. Katy would enter that house only once again in her life, during a brief lull in the fighting months hence. Its roof would be riddled with shell holes, its doors and windows gone, the parquet floor on which her guests had danced charred with cooking fires and covered with bloodstains and human excrement. She would sit on a crate and weep. She would never be able to go back.

In Romema, the largely Arabic community on the edge of the Tel Aviv road that had been the object of repeated Irgun bombings, the Arabs' departure was organized under the protection of the Haganah. For forty-eight hours before they left, little groups of Jews and Arabs stood haggling on the sidewalks, negotiating the sale of the fixtures in the shuttered shops behind them, terminating leases, arguing over the price of the furniture the Arabs could not carry away with them. Then, one morning, the Arabs left en masse and the community's new Jewish residents moved in behind them. Down came the Arabic signboards. A new set, in Hebrew this time, went up in their place. Soon there was a new Jewish grocer, a new Jewish gas station, a Jewish coffeehouse. The wicker stools on which the old Arab men had squatted in front of their café went off to a secondhand furniture dealer, their nargilehs to an antique shop. Within three weeks the last traces of the community's generations of Arab inhabitants had disappeared. Romema looked as though it had been Jewish since the day it was built.

It was not, however, in the fight for a few shattered houses or an isolated neighborhood that the key to the struggle for Jerusalem lay in those winter weeks of 1948. It was elsewhere, before a pair of black eyes gazing out from under the folds of a kaffiyeh wrapped around the face of a shepherd stumbling with his flock along a ridge of the Judean hills. For almost a week, the man had wandered the ridge line, pondering the terrain before him, intently studying each craggy slope, each clump of fir trees, each rocky promontory.

Haroun Ben-Jazzi was not, however, a shepherd. The animals at his feet were a borrowed flock picked up from a villager to cover his activities. Ben-Jazzi was a sheikh of the Howeitat Bedouin tribe, a first cousin of Abou Taya, the Arab chieftain who had ridden with Lawrence, and the sight upon which his windburned Bedouin eyes gazed with such intensity was a strip of black asphalt, the road to Jerusalem. That was the key to the city's existence, and the struggle for it was now to enter a new phase, the phase foreseen by Abdul Khader Husseini a few weeks earlier when, with a gesturing of his hands, he had vowed, "We will strangle Jerusalem." The disorderly, unorganized assaults on the road which had already exacted their toll on Jewish traffic were now to be replaced by more systematic, planned attacks. Abdul Khader had personally ordered Ben-Jazzi to survey every foot of ground along the road from Bab el Wad to the Arab village of Kastel. With his borrowed flock nibbling the grass at his feet, Ben-Jazzi had drifted from crest to crest, silently staring down at the Jewish convoys snaking up to Jerusalem, calculating each natural ambush site along their route, each spot where "one man could do the work of one hundred."

Abdul Khader's original plan to throttle that Jewish traffic had called for a semipermanent roadblock he could defend with a relatively small number of his Holy Strugglers. He abandoned the idea for two reasons. First, the British, he realized, would be compelled to break the roadblock. Second, Abdul Khader wanted to draw the villagers in the communities along the road into his campaign. And so he decided to launch individual

143

attacks on each passing convoy and to allow the villagers who had aided the attack to join in looting the convoys afterward. Knowing well the mentality of his people, he knew that each success and its spoils would provide a spur to draw into his ambushes an ever larger number of village fighters. Their growing numbers would give him a steadily expanding strength to match the certain growth in the size of the convoys' escorts.

Using the information Ben-Jazzi provided, Abdul Khader opened his campaign. He led the first major attack himself. His kaffiyeh streaming behind him, he raced ahead of his men toward the passing convoy, gesticulating with his rifle to the rhythm of his Arabic war cries. Improvised at first, his attacks began to take on a well-planned pattern. One group of Abdul Khader's men stationed near the foot of Bab el Wad would rush out as soon as the convoy passed and would throw up a roadblock to cut its escape route. Up ahead, the bulk of his men would hastily erect another barricade to force it to a halt. As Abdul Khader had predicted, the news that a convoy was trapped, the sound of gunfire, drew hundreds of screaming villagers to the site. While his guerrillas manned the roadblocks, the villagers, scenting the loot ahead, swooped down like a swarm of locusts on the convoy.

Abdul Khader soon developed a relatively effective intelligence system. He hid a wireless set near the village of Hulda, the key assembly point for the Jewish convoys. A weatherbeaten shepherd, a dirty-faced little boy, a black-robed woman were formed into a rotating guard to observe Jewish movements. They scampered back to the radio set with information on each departing convoy, its size, its length, its contents. That information was radioed to Abdul Khader's headquarters, where it was relayed to Ben-Jazzi through a smaller transmitter hidden in one of the dozens of grottoes tucked into the cliffs above the Jerusalem road.

His offensive caused the British little concern. For the British Army, the Jerusalem–Tel Aviv road had assumed a secondary importance to their main evacuation routes, in the north to Haifa, in the south to the Suez Canal. A squadron of the Life Guards' armored cars based in Jerusalem ran a two-car patrol twice daily down the road. The patrol was called a "swan." "You'd boom down in the morning and boom back," recalled the squadron's commander. "Then you'd do the same thing again just before nightfall." The safe passage of those patrols was sufficient, in the eyes of the British command, to constitute an open road. Abdul Khader's men were careful to interfere with them as little as possible.

For the Jews, each convoy to Jerusalem was an ordeal, a brutal, desperate struggle to claw one more load of goods past Abdul Khader's

increasingly effective ambushes. The survival of the one hundred thousand
Jews in the City of David depended on the Haganah's ability to force
thirty trucks a day up the gorge of Bab el Wad to Jerusalem. Thirty
trucks; yet as each week passed, the daily average fell under the pressure
of Abdul Khader's attacks.

As the weeks of that terrible winter dragged on, Jewish Jerusalem's
well-being lay in the hands of a band of boys and girls of the Palmach.
Called "Furmanim" because all their orders were addressed to an imaginary
Mr. Furman in Room 16 of Jerusalem's Jewish Agency building, they
were the permanent guards of the convoys. They rode in the Haganah's
flimsy homemade armored cars, six cars to each convoy, and the insignia
they proudly sewed onto their uniform was one of those armored "sandwiches" in a pair of wings. They were kids like Yehuda Lash. It was one
of the paradoxes of that strange winter that his mother could cook breakfast for him before he left his Jerusalem home at 4 A.M. each day to risk
his life in Abdul Khader's ambushes. He would always remember his
mother walking him to the door in the predawn blackness, "her eyes full
of concern." He was a convoy commander. He had just turned twenty.

The return trip was always the more difficult. Crammed with sacks
of flour, sugar, rice, concealed munitions, the heavily loaded trucks crawled
up the road in low gear. The sixteen-mile trip from Bab el Wad to Jerusalem averaged three hours. To smash the roadblocks along the route, the
Haganah used trucks equipped with bulldozer blades. The Arabs began
to mine the roadblocks and the shoulders of the road so that the besieged
trucks couldn't extricate themselves. From their high perches they poured
fire into the thin, unprotected roofs of the Jewish armored cars.

Reuven Tamir, another of the young Palmachniks making that run,
recalled how in his car "we would always sing as we came to Bab el Wad.
Then the singing would stop and the silence was overwhelming. It was
a terrible feeling. The only noise left was the sound of our motor."

Tamir was caught in a disastrous ambush while escorting one convoy
up the Bab el Wad gully. Through the slits of his armored car, he could
see the Arabs leaping from rock to rock, gesturing at them, daring them
in Hebrew to come out of their cars. Behind them, two trucks were already
ablaze, their Arab assailants leaping through the flames around them in
a kind of frenzied, exultant war dance. One truck had been loaded with
eggs. Egg yolks poured down its flanks in gashes of yellow sludge, steaming
and spitting in the heat. Within half an hour, the ammunition in Tamir's
car was gone, and the Arabs were hurling grenades at them from only a
few feet away. Suddenly Tamir realized he "didn't even have one bullet

left to commit suicide." That day, however, the British intervened just in time to save Tamir and his convoy.

Such intervention was rare. As the weeks passed, the road up from Bab el Wad was littered with burned-out vehicles. Scorched by Molotov cocktails, torn apart by mines, looted of every movable part, those stark metallic skeletons were a constant reminder of the price the Haganah was paying to supply Jerusalem. To the kids of the Furmanim riding past their swelling ranks twice a day, each blackened wreck was a memorial to some friend whose youth had ended there in the gulch of Bab el Wad.

"On both sides of the road our dead are piled up," wrote one of the Furmanim, a poet.

> The iron skeleton is as quiet as my friend.
> Bab el Wad!
> Remember our names forever.
> Bab el Wad on the road to the city.

•   •   •

Abdul Khader Husseini was on the verge of realizing his goal. Jerusalem was slowly being strangled. For the city's Jews, the prospect of having to endure the rigors of a siege was becoming a real threat. Three years after the end of World War II the city that was supposed to be a symbol of peace for mankind had in its turn to face the prospect of food shortages, rationing, blackouts, all the appurtenances of civilian suffering that the cities of Europe were at last beginning to forget. The task of preparing Jerusalem and its citizens to withstand that suffering was assigned by the Jewish Agency to its legal counselor, a taciturn lawyer named Dov Joseph.

It was a fitting choice. Joseph had borne Jerusalem a special devotion since his youth in Montreal. For four hours every afternoon during the long Canadian winters of his boyhood, while the rest of his neighborhood played in the snow, Joseph had attended Hebrew school, his youthful eyes staring up at the focal point of his classroom, a drawing of Solomon's Temple as it might have been in the days of the Jewish kingdom. He had seen the city first in 1919, in the pith helmet and bush jacket of a sergeant in the Jewish Legion. When, for the first time, he saw before him the stone remnants of the building that had called to him during the dark winter afternoons of his boyhood, Joseph felt an "overpowering" emotion and his body began to tremble. Two years later he was back in Jerusalem for good with, as his bride, the first Jewish woman to immigrate to Palestine from North America. He was an intense, often irritable man, tenacious in the pursuit of his goals. Above all, Dov Joseph was not a man to indulge his own weaknesses; in the painful days that lay ahead, he would show little inclination to indulge the weaknesses of his fellow Jerusalemites.

His first act was to order an inventory of all the food stocks in the city's warehouses and stores. From then on, every truckload of food coming into Jerusalem was stored under his supervision in the safest warehouses he could find.

With a pair of nutrition experts, Joseph calculated the basic foodstuffs Jerusalem would need to survive on a minimum ration for a day, a week and a month. Then he and his aides set about the grim task of secretly printing up the cards which, in an emergency, would entitle the city's population to the pitifully small rations they had allotted them.

Even graver than the risk of famine in a besieged Jerusalem, however, would be the risk of dying of thirst. Ninety percent of the city's water came from the springs of Ras el Ein, sixty miles to the west. The eighteen-inch pipe and the four pumping stations required to get the water up three thousand feet to Jerusalem lay in territory as Arab as the slopes of Bab el Wad. Even the little additional water available to the city from one of its most ancient sources, King Solomon's Pools, lay in Arab-controlled territory. Once the British left, the Arabs could cripple Jewish Jerusalem and force its surrender without a shot by depriving the city of the most vital element of daily existence, water. A bundle of dynamite sticks would be all they would need to do it.

Fortunately for Joseph, one of the first regulations of the British mandate in Jerusalem had called for the construction of a cistern in every new dwelling built in the city. In December he had made a secret survey of those cisterns. Now Joseph confiscated them all. He ordered Zvi Leibowitz, a German-born water expert, to begin quietly diverting a part of the incoming water into them, sealing and locking each cistern as it was filled. Those cisterns, Joseph was convinced, would be his city's only means of hanging on if the Arabs cut the water.

The city's sole electric-power plant was also vital to the Jews of Jerusalem, who absorbed ninety percent of its output. It lay in a kind of no man's land just south of the city. Thirty tons of fuel a day were required to keep its diesel generators operating. While waiting for the moment the Haganah could take the plant, Joseph ordered its supervisor, Alexander Singer, to start building up an emergency fuel supply.

Finally, since the city's principal hospital facilities on Mount Scopus might be cut off from the rest of Jerusalem by the Arabs, Joseph prepared

147

a series of emergency operating theaters and clinics inside the Jewish city. To help supply them, a blood bank was opened.

None of Joseph's tasks, however, was to cause the dour Canadian lawyer as much anguish as one lonely decision he took early in February. With the tempo of Arab assaults on the road rising daily, Joseph came under considerable pressure to evacuate Jerusalem's women and children to the coast while they could still escape. There were sound reasons for doing it. Their evacuation would make the food and water problem immensely easier. The decision not to let them go was Joseph's alone. He took it because he reasoned the fighting spirit of Jerusalem's men would be raised if they knew that their homes and families lay helpless just behind them. Those men would have no illusions about their families' fate if the city were overrun. The pain of that decision, the awareness of the terrible moral burden that would be his if Jerusalem fell, would weigh on Joseph for months to come. But, as he would remark years later in recalling that decision, "We did not favor the easy way."

Six thousand miles and a world away, another group of men wrestled, too, with the problems of Jerusalem. They labored in the standardized dreariness of the committee rooms of the United Nations, and the problem before them was represented by an object as banal as a calendar. While Dov Joseph was deciding whether to evacuate Jewish women and children from his city, the members of the United Nations Working Committee on Jerusalem agonized over the fact that if the official holidays of all the religious communities and national bodies represented in Jerusalem were to be honored as such, the holidays of the little international city they were planning would exceed the number of days on the calendar.

That preoccupation was indicative of the trivialities into which the United Nations' planning for an international Jerusalem had slid. For six weeks, while the situation in the city deteriorated daily, the members of the United Nations Working Committee on Jerusalem had argued their way paragraph by paragraph through the legal charter with which they would order the birth of the world's first international city. They extended its limits to include Bethlehem and three Arab communities so that its population would be made up of an equal number of Arabs and Jews. It was to be divided into three boroughs, one for the Arabs, one for the Jews, and one, made up of the old walled city at the heart of it all, for the world. It would be demilitarized and run by a United Nations–appointed governor aided by an elected legislative council. Justice would be administered by a court system complex enough to bewilder Jerusalem's most abstract theologians. The committee had even thoughtfully provided it with a flag, the United Nations flag with the seal of Jerusalem imposed upon it, and a Latin term to define its legal status for the world to which it would belong—*corpus separatum.*

The Arabs remained adamantly opposed to the city's internationalization as just another manifestation of a partition plan they rejected as illegal. "The people of Jerusalem, who are not sacred, should not be punished because their city is," one of their leaders told the United Nations.

The Jewish position, however, had shifted. The Jewish Agency, originally opposed to internationalization, was now actively fighting for its accomplishment. With the Arab ring around the city tightening, internationalization had begun to appear to some as perhaps the best way of assuring the physical safety and well-being of the city's Jewish population. The Agency now sought to place before those nations and forces which had clamored for Jerusalem's internationalization the consequences of their action. If the Christian West wanted Jerusalem, it would have to pay a price for it, and that price would be men to keep its peace, specifically men for an international police force.

From chancellery to chancellery, the Agency's representatives pleaded for men to man such a force. They got nowhere. Finally, despairing, the Agency's leadership, in a secret meeting at the United States Consulate, asked for the rapid dispatch of five hundred U.S. Marines as the best way of bringing a police force into being. Their suggestion provoked nothing but consternation in Washington. The Truman Administration, whatever its sympathies for the Jewish cause, did not want to bear the onus of sending American troops abroad in an election year.

The greatest source of concern to the Jewish leadership, however, was the Palestine policy of the great power still in physical occupation of the land. The partiality displayed by the British police during the burning of the Commercial Center had not proven to be a passing phenomenon. Instead, to the angry Jewish population it seemed that the British administration was growing increasingly anti-Semitic on the personal level and pro-Arab on the political plane.*

---

* There were, of course, exceptions. The Jewish Agency had an unknown ally in its campaign for a Jerusalem police force, British High Commissioner Sir Alan Cunningham. Despairing of maintaining order in the rest of Palestine, Cunningham hoped at least to salvage Jerusalem. That winter he wrote to all the archbishops he could think of, urging them to bring pressures to bear for the creation of a 3,000-man police force. His campaign was no more successful than the Agency's. The Archbishop of Canterbury's response was to write a letter to *The Times,* an action which, the High Commissioner grimly noted, "shook absolutely no one to the core." Francis Cardinal Spellman, Archbishop of New York, didn't even answer his letter. Cunningham's

There was justification for the Jews' suspicions. In the two months since partition, fifty Haganah men and women had been arrested in Jerusalem alone for bearing arms and had been sent to jail for it. At the same time, as Lebanon's consul had noted, the British authorities made little effort to prevent armed Arabs from circulating in the city. Richard Catling, the head of the Criminal Investigation Department, summed up British policy by observing, "We didn't mind the Arabs moving around with grenades all over their chests and cartridge belts hanging from their shoulders, just so long as they didn't bother us."

When the Palestine government's Central Security Committee complained to Jerusalem's district commissioner about "the increasing freedom with which armed Syrians and others congregate in public areas in Jerusalem," the only action the district commissioner was told to take was warning Arab leaders "to keep their soldiers as unobtrusive as possible."

Britain enforced a strict ban on importing arms into Palestine on the grounds that its onus fell equally on Arab and Jew. Yet, on January 9, she signed a major arms contract with Iraq, accompanying the sale with a secret codicil authorizing the use of those arms "to discharge Iraq's responsibilities vis à vis the Arab League." There was no doubt in anyone's mind that those responsibilities were in Palestine.

While the Royal Navy maintained its rigorous patrols of Palestine's coastal waters to intercept illegal immigrant ships which might bring military-age renforcements into the country for the Haganah, the British Army was closing its eyes to the infiltration of hundreds of armed Arab guerrillas into the country. Britain's spokesmen at the United Nations and in Jerusalem piously denied any knowledge of that infiltration. The Jewish Agency knew very well the British were lying. The British Army's intelligence summaries stolen by the Haganah's agents each week revealed that not only did the British know the infiltration was taking place, but they knew the date, the time, the location and the approximate size of each infiltration.

Behind that attitude lay the fact that Britain's Foreign Secretary, Ernest Bevin, and his coterie of Arab experts were not yet resigned to partition's inevitability. If it proved unworkable, then the Palestine problem might yet be thrust back into their laps for resolution along lines more to Bevin's

---

attachment to Jerusalem, however, led him to one decision that proved of capital importance to Jewish hopes in the city. By the end of January, he came under heavy army pressure to evacuate the city entirely and administer the mandate until its close from the port of Haifa. He refused and threatened to resign if London forced him to do so. Given the state of Jewish preparations at the time, his acceptance would probably have led to an Arab takeover of Jerusalem.

liking. Nothing seemed more certain to demonstrate partition's fundamental unworkability than serious Arab military opposition to it. Increasingly, the reports flowing into the Foreign Office predicted just that eventuality.

The author of many of these reports was Brigadier C. K. Clayton, Britain's senior intelligence officer in the Middle East. A Blimpish hang-over from Lawrence days, Clayton was, as one of his colleagues remarked, "so absent-minded he could forget to wear his pants to the office," a mental trait not, after all, highly prized in intelligence agents. Still, Clayton had been around a long time, and his signature had appeared on the bottom of so many dispatches that it had begun to take on an aura of infallibility. After all, hardly a meeting of importance took place in the Arab world without his portly silhouette drifting around its fringes in ponderous pseudo-anonymity. From his gleanings at these meetings came the grist for his dispatches, and in the winter of 1948 they were telling Bevin what he and his entourage wanted to hear: the Arabs were going to war with the Jews and they were going to win.*

With that perspective looming on the Middle Eastern horizon, the Foreign Office was more than ever determined to do nothing to help parti-tion along. Beyond that, the Foreign Office wished to adopt an attitude toward the Arabs' evolving military schemes which would not jeopardize the cornerstone of Britain's future Middle Eastern policy, Anglo–Arab friendship.

To the frustrated Jews, however, it seemed that Britain's real aim in Palestine was to give substance to a prediction uttered one winter morning in the United States Consulate General by the government's Chief Secre-tary, Sir Henry Gurney. Looking calmly at his American host, Gurney declared it was a useless waste of time to talk about the United Nations role in Palestine.

"By the time the United Nations arrives," Gurney predicted, "Palestine will be up in smoke."

---

* Like many British military men in the Middle East, Clayton tended to over-estimate the Arabs and underestimate the Jews. It was a natural error. The British had, after all, trained the principal Arab armies and, as tutors, could hardly be expected to disavow the value of their teaching.

11

GOLDA MEIR'S TWENTY-FIVE "STEPHANS"

THE TRUCK SLIPPED through the black winter's night up to the edge of the lawn. Five men armed with planks and coils of rope leaped out and advanced cautiously through the darkness. One of them switched on a flashlight. Its beam fell on two massive metal silhouettes. Behind them an inscription over a doorway revealed the name of the institution to which those shadowy figures belonged, Jerusalem's Menorah Club, the meeting place of the men who had served with the Jewish Legion during the First World War. They were relics of that war. For thirty years enshrined there on the clubhouse lawn, they had been the proud incarnation of Britain's victory over the Ottoman Empire and of the legion's part in it. Now Eliahu Sochaczever, a Polish engineer of the Haganah, had come to claim these souvenirs for a new struggle. Stripped down, sawed into pieces, the two captured Turkish cannons of the Menorah Club were going to serve as barrels for the first artillery pieces of Jerusalem's Haganah.

The fact that the Haganah had to steal them from their honored moorings in the middle of the night—indeed, the fact that anyone could label the instruments for which they were destined "artillery"—was indicative of the Haganah's poverty in heavy weapons. So urgent was the need for them that Jerusalem's Chief Rabbi had granted the workers in Sochaczever's secret workshops a dispensation to labor on the Sabbath while they converted these Turkish cannons into homemade mortars. Called the Davidka after their inventor, David Leibovitch, an agronomist from Siberia, those mortars constituted the sole piece of heavy artillery in the Haganah's arsenal during the winter of 1948. They fired a shell made from water pipes and packed with explosives, nails and bits of scrap metal. Their range and accuracy, in the words of one Haganah man, "were about the same as David's slingshot." In addition to the fact that they existed, the Davidkas had one signal advantage. They made an incredible amount of noise, enough to terrify anybody within hearing range.

In garages, locked into attics, in apartments hastily converted into makeshift laboratories, other Jerusalemites labored that winter to turn out

152

improvised arms for the defense of their city. In that enterprise, the Jewish community could call on the services of some of the world's best-known scientists. Joel Racah and Aaron Kachalski, for example, abandoned their pursuit of the secrets of nuclear physics and molecular chemistry to give themselves over to more elementary tasks. In an apartment in Rehavia the two masters of matter's most complex secrets worked day and night developing a better gunpowder for the Davidka. Nearby, two students in the chemistry and physics department at Hebrew University, Jonathan Adler and Avner Treinin, turned out homemade hand grenades and a variety of booby-trap devices for use in the Arab quarters of the city. To develop a detonator for his grenades, Adler used as a textbook the manual of another clandestine body, the Irish Republican Army. In a room lined with rubber sheeting in the orthodox quarter of Mea Shearim, a deaf and dumb student named Emmanuel turned out lethal fulminite of mercury for Adler's detonators.

Far more substantial were the efforts deployed by the Haganah along the coastal plain, where security was more promising. They were supervised by a Jerusalemite, Joseph Avidar, the son of a Ukrainian miller who had immigrated to Palestine at the age of nineteen. Using some of the machinery purchased in the United States by Haim Slavine, and benefiting from the technical counselors furnished him by the Sonneborn Institute, Avidar ran, among other things, a munitions plant covering almost one thousand square feet of floor space. It was hidden underneath the kibbutz of Maagan Michael, north of Tel Aviv, built for the express purpose of providing a cover for its activities. The entrance to the factory was concealed in a laundry in which the kibbutzniks supplemented their income by laundering uniforms for the British Army. Its extraordinary consumption of electric current was concealed by passing its cables through the kilns of the community's bakery. The bakery's smokestack was the underground factory's air vent.

Avidar's greatest problem had been finding cartridge cases for the nine-millimeter bullets he wanted to manufacture. He solved it by a unique stratagem—importing millions of lipstick tubes from an English cosmetics concern. By July 1948, his little clandestine factory would have produced three million cartridges.

Outside Hadera, another workshop under Avidar's command made shells for a small mortar. The crating room of a Haifa orange grove served as a cover for the assembling of fifty thousand hand grenades. One of the most important enterprises directed by the busy Avidar assembled the "sandwich" armored cars upon which the Haganah depended to keep the road to his adopted Jerusalem open. The "armor" that protected those cars was made of two four-millimeter-thick steel sheets "sandwiched" around fifty millimeters of wood. Avidar was constantly besieged by inventors offering him a better lightweight plastic sheeting. He proposed to each of them a quick test to measure the efficiency of their inventions. He told them to hold a sheet of their plastics in front of their chest while he fired a revolver at them from twenty-five yards. He never found a better armor plate than his heavy sandwich.

In Tel Aviv, Haifa and, above all, Jerusalem, the Haganah added to its arsenal by buying arms from its enemies. Hidden under truckloads of carrots or cauliflower, a few rifles and cases of ammunition thus reached the Haganah's hands, sold to them by the Arabs through Armenian intermediaries. The British in Jerusalem also turned out to be a worthwhile source of arms. At the end of January, a pair of British noncoms delivered to the Haganah a truckload of explosives and ammunition for nothing more concrete than a glass of cognac and a grateful handshake. Another noncom sold the Haganah his armored car, its turret packed with shells, gasoline and small arms, for one thousand Palestine pounds.

A few carefully planned raids on the British Army's arms depots supplemented those acquisitions. Inspired by the purchase of their first armored car, the Jerusalem Haganah sent a group of men disguised as British soldiers into the Bevingrad security zone. They drove out with a brand-new Daimler armored car. Like the Flying Dutchman, the car began to mysteriously appear and reappear, until Jerusalem's Arabs were persuaded the Haganah possessed a whole fleet of armored cars.

The British also served as an excellent source of arms for the Arabs of Jerusalem. For a thousand pounds one British sergeant offered to close his eyes to their activities while he stood guard over his regiment's armory. A pair of policemen negotiated the sale of their armored car for the same sum during a stopover in a tobacco store in Upper Beqaa. On the lonely roads beyond the city, "holdups" of British trucks were regularly arranged in return for a few pounds. Prostitutes were sometimes used to take an arms-depot sentry's mind off his work while Haj Amin's men helped themselves to a few cases of the ammunition he was supposed to be guarding. Arab manual laborers in those depots patiently pilfered small arms and spare parts.

The Jerusalem Arab community simply did not have intellectual resources to match those furnished the Haganah by the Jewish community's galaxy of distinguished scientists. They were not, however, without their armaments experts. A British intelligence report signaled early in the winter of 1948 the arrival in Jerusalem of twenty-five Yugoslavian Moslems, veterans of the Wehrmacht. Their task, the report said, was to aid the city's defenders in making mines and explosives.

Above all, the Arabs had the advantage of long, desolate frontiers across which it was relatively easy to smuggle arms. One such shipment was forwarded by Ibn-Saud, King of Saudi Arabia. When Abdul Khader Husseini opened the shipment he was speechless with fury. Saud had sent him a consignment of the primitive pre–World War I rifles with which he had conquered the Arabian desert. Angrily, Abdul Khader broke them one by one over his knee.

The Arabs' principal local source of arms in early 1948 were the battle-fields of Egypt's Western Desert. Even there, the intramural feuding that handicapped so many of their other endeavors came into play. Egyptians, Moslem Brothers, Palestinians, acquisitive army merchants, squabbled among themselves for the desert's harvest, outbidding each other with the Bedouins who scavenged the arms from the sands, hijacking each other's purchases. By Bedouin camel train, under truckloads of fruits and vege-tables, in the trunks of automobiles, along the desert tracks used by genera-tions of hashish smugglers, those arms found their way back to Palestine. One way or another, a great number of them wound up on sale in Jeru-salem's souks. During that winter of 1948 the demand for them was so great that prices lost all relation to value. By midwinter, a single rusty Mauser was sold for one hundred pounds, four times the price of a brand-new Mauser in the Czechoslovakian paradise of Ehud Avriel and Abdul-Aziz Kerine.

• • •

Set firmly astride the historic Baghdad–Cairo axis, Damascus, capital of Syria, was the epicenter from which by tradition the multiple explosions of a turbulent past had radiated through the Arab world. A verdant miracle rising from the desert floor, Damascus could inspire such awe that, legend held, the Prophet had turned away from its gates proclaiming, "One can-not enter Paradise twice." From the conquests of the Omayyad caliphs to the conversion of Saul of Tarsus on a street called Straight and to the collapse of the Ottoman Empire in 1918, three thousand years of history were written upon its walls. Nothing was more natural than that in the early winter of 1948 Damascus should become the focal point of the Arab League's campaign to aid the Arabs of Palestine, the staging area upon which converged a strange migration of merchants, mercenaries and impassioned volunteers. Capital of a politically and militarily independent nation, Damascus offered the perfect sanctuary in which to assemble, furnish and train those volunteers, the base from which they could slip into Palestine, the headquarters in which the Arabs could prepare for a major assault on Palestine once the British left.

The half-lit, teeming labyrinth that was Damascus' souk concealed the Middle East's most flourishing arms market. Prewar French rifles, British Sten guns, Mausers of the Wehrmacht, even American bazookas were on sale there. Scraps of the uniforms of six different armies were heaped in indiscriminate piles next to the bolts of silk brocade for which the souk was known.

Above all, Damascus was the theater in which the rival factions of the Arab world contended for its leadership. In the city's suburbs, not far from the modest mausoleum of the greatest Islamic general in history, Saladin, another general had set up headquarters in an old French Army barracks. Appointed by the Arab League at its December meeting in Cairo, Ismail Safwat Pasha, a fifty-two-year-old Iraqi, was supposed to be the supreme commander of all the Arab forces destined to intervene in Palestine: the Jihad Moqhades of Haj Amin Husseini, the volunteer Liberation Army being raised and armed by the Arab League and, eventually, should they enter the war, the regular armies of the Arab states. In fact, as Safwat Pasha soon discovered, in that anthill of conflicting political interests and ambitious men his effective command was limited to the handful of officers who made up his headquarters staff.

Like so many of his political counterparts, Safwat Pasha combined a mastery of hyperbole and the extravagant phrase with a determined refusal to face reality. Already he had promised his troops "a triumphant parade to Tel Aviv." Confronted by a group of Palestinians who complained they lacked arms with which to attack passing Jewish convoys, he roared, "Then destroy them by throwing stones at their armored cars!" Warned by his able young operations officer, a Jordanian veteran of the British Army named Wasfi Tell, that his triumphant march on Tel Aviv might turn to disaster "because of the deplorable state of our forces," Safwat took only one precaution. He made sure Tell's report did not reach any Arab leaders, confidentially advising his young aide, "If some of the Arab governments read this they will refuse to take the risk of sending their armies to Palestine."

Everything was in short supply in Safwat's headquarters except for the cases of papers and files which spilled through the offices. Chairs, tables, telephones were lacking. There was no radio to link the headquarters to the field. A swarm of Syrian and Iraqi officers buzzed around the building, seemingly more familiar with the science of political intrigue than with that of warfare. The distribution of funds, of commands, of rank, of operational zones, of arms and materials, all were objects of bargaining as intensive as any displayed in the city's souks.

When the palavering at the headquarters was finished, the officers adjourned to the salons of the other pole of Damascus' political life, the Orient Palace Hotel. Half a century of plots had been hatched on the worn velvet easy chairs and sofas of the hotel's sitting room. In that winter of 1948, the Orient Palace remained faithful to its conspiracy-cluttered past. An air of intrigue permeated the place. It was ringed by an ominously evident collection of bodyguards watching over the enigmatic figures who drifted in and out. Groups whispered intently in corners, then froze into blatant silence at the appearance of some figure in the doorway. Through hastily opened and closed doors came glimpses of other men in rooms adjoining the salon huddled over tables covered with coffee cups and maps. Perched on their stools in the bar, the intelligence agents of the Western powers observed the proceedings with feigned disinterest which deceived no one.

The arrival, early in February, of a client of particular mark signaled the importance of the role Damascus and the Orient Palace had assumed in Palestine's affairs. Together with his senior aides, Haj Amin Husseini moved into an entire floor of the hotel. Wrapped in that air of intrigue which seemed to flow so naturally from him, Haj Amin began to glide along its corridors, his movements carefully screened by half a dozen bodyguards. Occasionally, an indiscreet twist of his abayah revealed that he wore another garment under its folds. It was a bulletproof vest, the personal gift of the man who had until recently been his protector, Adolf Hitler.

Haj Amin had reason to wear a bulletproof vest, for he had many a bitter enemy in Damascus. His undisguised ambition to turn Palestine into his personal fiefdom, the wave of assassinations which had accompanied his rise to power, his intransigence, the ferocity with which he could turn on his foes, had left him with few true friends among his Arab brothers. He was, commented Sir Alec Kirkbride, Britain's knowledgeable minister in Amman, "like the Red Queen in *Alice in Wonderland*. He had so stirred up extremist sentiment in Palestine that he had to keep running faster, getting more and more extreme, just to stay where he was."

Since the Arab League meeting in Cairo in December, Haj Amin had insisted that the arms and money being collected by the League be placed

157

at the disposal of his organization. He had come to Damascus to achieve two things. First, he wanted to convert his Arab Higher Committee into a provisional Palestine government to rival the Jewish Agency. Second, he wanted to thwart the plan, set in Cairo, to raise a volunteer Liberation Army. Operating from Syria with recruits raised in the Arab world, the army was supposed to begin a guerrilla campaign in Palestine before the British withdrew. If he could not block its creation, Haj Amin at least wanted its commander to be one of his faithful lieutenants.

He had little success. Safwat Pasha accused him of misappropriating funds, of stealing arms, of nepotism, of substituting political loyalty for military skill in making appointments. The Mufti's organization, he shouted in one angry meeting, was swallowing up the arms and the money to support two thousand men in Haifa alone, yet there were barely two hundred fighters in the city.

His fellow political leaders realized that with world opinion overwhelmingly in favor of the Zionists as a result of the Nazi holocaust, the Palestinians would elicit little sympathy for their cause as long as they were led by one of Hitler's collaborators. The British and Haj Amin's political foes in the councils of the Arab League did not want an abundance of weapons in Haj Amin's untrustworthy armories. Besides, the British hoped that by the shifting of the Palestine problem from Haj Amin's uncompromising hands into the more responsible chancelleries of the Arab governments, some solution to the question might eventually be found. The British had led the Arab League's secretary general, Azzam Pasha, and Syria's Prime Minister Jamil Mardam to understand that they would oppose the Liberation Army if it were Mufti controlled, but were prepared to take a more lenient view of its activities if it was not.

Faced with that array of opposition, Haj Amin's plans ran into trouble. King Abdullah's insistence that he wanted no part of a Mufti-led government in Palestine helped stifle that scheme. The Liberation Army had already gained so much momentum it could not be stopped. Bound to grow in importance, it would clearly have first claim on the Arab League's finances and arms. After a series of angry arguments presided over by Syrian President Shukri al Kuwatli, the army was given the responsibility for operations in all northern Palestine. Abdul Khader Husseini retained control of the Jerusalem area and another faithful Mufti subordinate the countryside around Jaffa. But his fellow Arabs' choice for the commander of the Liberation Army was Haj Amin's cruelest disappointment in Damascus.

With his scarred face, his thick neck and his closely cropped red hair,

Fawzi el Kaukji bore a closer resemblance to a Prussian major than to an Arab chief. He was closemouthed and uncommunicative. Among the many decorations which on occasion graced his uniform, the one he esteemed most was a black metal cross—the only mark of a true warrior, in his opinion. He had won the Iron Cross second class thirty years earlier as a lieutenant in the Ottoman Army in another Palestine campaign, fighting alongside the Prussians of General Otto von Kreiss against the British. Since then he had been an unqualified admirer of things German, a sentiment he had affirmed by marrying a German girl he met in Berlin during the Second World War.

Convalescing in the German capital from a wound he had received in Iraq, Kaukji had become a familiar figure in the nightclubs of the wartime Reich. One night on his cabaret rounds, his eyes fell on a striking young blonde. To win her attention, the elegant Oriental ordered to her table two of the rarest commodities in the Nazi capital, a bottle of Veuve Clicquot champagne and a package of Camel cigarettes. From that night on, the pretty German girl and the fifty-five-year-old Arab adventurer thirty years her senior were an inseparable couple.

Born in northern Lebanon, Kaukji had served his military apprenticeship in the Turkish Army. When the Ottoman Empire began to crumble, he went to work spying on the Turks for the British. Then, successively, he spied on the French for the British, on the British for the French, on the French and the British for the Germans. The high point of his military career had come during the Arab revolt against the British in Palestine in 1936. His frequently demonstrated prowess won him fame among the Arab population and the esteem of Haj Amin Husseini. His popular following, however, was not altogether to the Mufti's liking, and, equipped with arms and money, he was shunted off to Iraq to foment a rebellion there. Instead of promoting an uprising, the Mufti's aides later claimed, "he swallowed up the arms, the money and the rebellion."

The Mufti prized servility and loyalty above all else in his aides, and Kaukji had failed on both counts. As a result, when the two men met again in wartime Berlin, relations between them were cool and soon deteriorated to a deep mutual dislike. In the chaos of defeat, Kaukji had managed to slip into France and later escape into Egypt. There he had announced he was "at the disposition of the Arab people should they call on me to take up arms again."

And so they had, as commander of the Liberation Army, as much for his value as a counterbalance to his enemy Haj Amin Husseini as for his capacity as a military chief. After all, if his career had inspired a popular legend, it had not inspired an inordinate amount of confidence in his fellow Arab leaders. The measure of their trust was the one stipulation that went with his appointment. At the request of the Syrian government, Kaukji was not to take command of his troops on Syrian soil, but only inside Palestine. The Syrian government feared that, bought at the last moment by some rival political faction, Kaukji might be persuaded to make a wrong turn and march on the ministries of Damascus instead of the kibbutzim of Palestine.

On the radio, by enormous newspaper ads, with fiery speeches in their mosques and coffeehouses, the young men of the Arab world were called to volunteer for Kaukji's army and for the defense of El Kuds, the Holy City of Jerusalem, whose spires were woven into the rugs upon which so many of them recited their daily prayers. Those calls promised to volunteers the not inconsiderable sum of sixty Syrian pounds a month for private soldiers and Syrian Army pay scales for noncoms and officers. From the crowded slums of Cairo, from the cavernous souks of Aleppo, from the banks of the Tigris and the Euphrates, the Red Sea and the Persian Gulf, the volunteers responded, setting out on the road to Jerusalem, adventure and loot.

From the south, up the routes used by pilgrims to Mecca, from the west out of Mosul and Baghdad across the wastes of the Iraqi desert, from the east past the snow-tipped crest of Mount Hermon, a noisy migration descended on Damascus. They came in convoys of open trucks and dilapidated old buses, covered with flags and flowers and old bedsheets painted with patriotic slogans. They rode through the city, a jubilant cavalcade of noise, of shouting men, chanting rhythmic slogans, singing, above all firing their weapons into the air. There were the huge silver buses of the Nairn Company, their flanks eroded by sandstorms from their trips across the desert from Damascus to Baghdad. There were taxis from all over the Arab world, some so overloaded that their mufflers seemed to scrape the asphalt. There were motorcycles and bicycles, camels, horses and even an occasional mule. Often a bold banner hanging from the flanks of a truck or bus identified its occupants as the "Lions of Aleppo" or "Falcons of Basra."

Packed into that stream of vehicles parading through the streets of Damascus was an incredible array of human beings. There were young students from Beirut, Cairo and Baghdad burning with youthful fervor. There were idealists and patriots, middle-class intellectuals in business suits or jodhpurs and a kaffiyeh out to avenge what they considered an injustice to their people. There were young Syrian politicians, like Akram Hourani and Michel Aflak, founders of the Baathist Party, persuaded that Palestine would prove the ideal crucible in which to mold their ideas. There were Egyptian Moslem Brothers as anxious to overthrow their country's rulers as they were to march on Tel Aviv; Iraqis thrown out of the army after Nuri as-Said had crushed the Rashid Ali uprising; notorious Syrian Francophiles who had served all the French and Vichy secret services; veterans of the Mufti's 1936 rebellion; Circassians, Kurds, Druzes, Alaowites, spurred more by the lure of pillage than by a passion for the Mosque of Omar; Communists out to infiltrate the fledgling army. There were thieves, adventurers, brigands, homosexuals, nuts, all the quacks of the Arab world with a hate in their hearts for the British, the French, their local governments and even the Jews; the pariahs of the Arab world for whom the *jihad* was a call to plunder instead of to arms.

Their destination was a bleak, rolling plateau of red sandstone foothills and windblown topsoil thirty miles southwest of Damascus. Set in that desolate scene, behind a village of flat-roofed mud houses, were a few dreary remnants of Syria's French occupation, the barracks of the Katana military camp. Soon some six thousand volunteers had been assembled in its primitive stone buildings. To their ranks were added a small group of British deserters, escaped German prisoners of war, Yugoslav Moslems sentenced to death by Tito for having served in the Wehrmacht, men for whom this crusade offered above all a refuge from the police forces searching for them.

No central authority governed the camp or instilled a common discipline in its disparate recruits. Trained officers were desperately short. Command was more or less abandoned to the self-styled leaders arriving at its gates at the head of their private bands. The new arrivals were thrown into a semblance of a uniform from the leftover stocks of the Syrian Army and scraps of American, British and French apparel dredged from the souks. Arms and ammunition were lacking and when they were available often failed to work. One section of recruits was set to work doing nothing but cleaning rusty rifles with the lemons of the Palestine they had come to conquer. Training was haphazard. The shortage of ammunition limited rifle instruction. Recruits who were able to fire half a dozen rounds at a target and toss a hand grenade or two were considered well trained.

In the shortest supply of all was money to pay for Katana's burgeoning operations. The states of the Arab League which had been so quick in Cairo in December to vote for a one-million-pound-sterling war chest (to which they had subsequently added an additional one million pounds) had actually paid in little more than a tenth of their pledges. Azzam Pasha, secretary general of the League, sometimes felt his days were divided between writing promissory notes to sustain Katana and writing letters urging the Arab governments to honor their commitments.

The clamor and confusion of the Syrian scene in that winter of 1948 would inspire diverse reactions, but none more succinct than that of the little Englishman who, from the hilltop of another Arab capital, commanded the Middle East's most professional military force. To John Bagot Glubb, Glubb Pasha, commander of the Arab Legion, Damascus that winter had become "a madhouse."

• • •

The same problem preoccupying the harassed Secretary General of the Arab League in Damascus would disturb the leaders of the Jewish Agency in Tel Aviv that winter. One January evening they were summoned to hear a report by Eliezer Kaplan, their treasurer. Kaplan had just returned from a fund-raising trip to the United States with his pockets virtually empty. The American Jewish community, so long the financial bulwark of the Zionist movement, was growing weary of the incessant appeals for aid of their Palestine brothers, he reported. The time had come, Kaplan said, to face a bitter reality. In no case could they count on more than five million dollars from America in the critical months ahead.

That figure hit the group gathered around Kaplan like a thunderbolt. One by one, their glances turned toward the stubby man who had followed Kaplan's report with ill-disguised impatience. David Ben-Gurion was better placed than any of them to understand how serious were the consequences of what Kaplan had just said. The rifles and machine guns for which he had sent Ehud Avriel to Prague could hold back the Palestinian Arabs; but against the tanks, artillery and aircraft of the regular Arab armies he was sure the Yishuv would one day face, they would be useless, however courageous its soldiers might be. Ben-Gurion had drawn up a plan to equip a modern army. To carry it out, he needed at a minimum five, six times the sum mentioned by Kaplan. Springing from his seat, he growled to the men around him, "Kaplan and I must leave for the United States immediately to make the Americans realize how serious the situation is."

At that moment a quiet female voice interrupted him. It belonged to the woman who had found her Zionist faith taking up a collection in Denver, Colorado.

"What you are doing here I cannot do," Golda Meir told Ben-Gurion.

"However, what you propose to do in the United States I can do. You stay here and let me go to the States to raise the money."

Ben-Gurion reddened. He liked neither interruptions nor contradictions. The matter was so important, he insisted, he and Kaplan should go. The other members of the Agency Executive, however, supported Golda. Two days later, with no more baggage than the thin spring dress she wore and the handbag she clutched in her hand, she arrived in New York on a bitter winter's night. So precipitate had her departure been that she had not had the time to take the convoy up to Jerusalem to fetch a change of clothes. The woman who had come to New York in search of millions of dollars had in her purse that evening exactly one ten-dollar bill. When a puzzled customs agent asked her how she intended to support herself in the United States, she replied simply, "I have family here."

Two days later, trembling on a podium in Chicago, Golda Meir found herself facing a distinguished gathering of the members of that family. They were the leaders of the Council of Jewish Federations, drawn from the forty-eight states of the Union. Their meeting and her arrival in the United States had been a fortuitous coincidence. Before her in one Chicago hotel room were most of the financial leaders of the American Jewish community, the very men whose aid she had been sent to seek.

For the carpenter's daughter from the Ukraine the task before her was an intimidating challenge. She had not been back to the United States since 1938. On her earlier trips, her associates had been dedicated Zionists and Socialists like herself. Now she faced the whole enormous spectrum of American Jewish thought, much of it indifferent or even hostile to her Zionist ideals.

Her friends in New York had urged her to avoid this confrontation. The council's leadership was not Zionist. Its members were already under great pressures for funds for their own American institutions, for hospitals, synagogues, cultural centers. They were weary, as Kaplan had discovered, of appeals from abroad for money.

Yet Golda Meir had insisted. She had telephoned Henry Montor, director of the United Jewish Appeal, in Chicago and, despite the fact that the speakers' program of the meeting had been drawn up long in advance, announced that she was on her way. Then, pausing only to buy a coat with which to face the American winter, she had set out for Chicago.

Now Golda Meir heard the toastmaster announce her name. At the sight of her simple, austere figure moving to the speakers' stand, someone in the crowd murmured, "She looks like the women of the Bible." Then, without a text, the messenger from Jerusalem began to speak.

"You must believe me," she said, "when I tell you that I have not come to the United States solely to prevent seven hundred thousand Jews from being wiped off the face of the earth. During these last years, the Jewish people have lost six million of their kind, and it would be presumptuous indeed of us to remind the Jews of the world that seven hundred thousand Jews are in danger. That is not the question. If, however, these seven hundred thousand Jews survive, then the Jews of the world will survive with them, and their freedom will be forever assured." But if they did not, she said, "then there is little doubt that for centuries there will be no Jewish people, there will be no Jewish nation, and all our hopes will be smashed."

In a few months, she told her audience, "a Jewish state will exist in Palestine. We shall fight for its birth. That is natural. We shall pay for it with our blood. That is normal. The best among us will fall, that is certain. But what is equally certain is that our morale will not waver no matter how numerous our invaders may be."

Yet, she warned, those invaders would come with cannon and armor. Against those weapons "sooner or later our courage will have no meaning, for we will have ceased to exist," she said.

She had come, she announced, to ask the Jews of America for twenty-five to thirty million dollars to buy the heavy arms they would need to face the invaders' cannon. "My friends," she said in making her plea, "we live in a very brief present. When I tell you we need this money immediately, it does not mean next month, or in two months. It means right now. . . .

"It is not to you," she concluded, "to decide whether we shall continue our struggle or not. We shall fight. The Jewish community of Palestine will never hang out the white flag before the Mufti of Jerusalem . . . but you can decide one thing—whether the victory will be ours or the Mufti's."

A hush had fallen on her audience, and for an instant Golda thought she had failed. Then the entire assembly of men and women rose in a deafening wave of applause. While its echoes still rang through the dining room, the first volunteers scrambled to the platform with their pledges. Before coffee was served Golda had been promised over a million dollars. They were made available immediately in cash, a fact without precedent. Men began to telephone their bankers and secure personal loans against their own names for the sums they estimated they would be able to raise later in their communities. By the time that incredible afternoon was over, Golda was able to telegraph Ben-Gurion her conviction that she would be able to raise the twenty-five "Stephans"—twenty-five million dollars, in the code they had chosen (using the name of American Zionist leader Rabbi Stephen S. Wise).

Astounded by her Chicago triumph, the American Zionist leadership urged her to set off on a cross-country tour. Accompanied by Henry Morgenthau, Jr., Franklin D. Roosevelt's former Secretary of the Treasury, she set a grueling pace, speaking sometimes three and four times a day. From city to city she moved on her pilgrimage, renewing before each of her audiences her dramatic plea, eliciting from each the same spontaneous, overwhelmingly generous reaction she had produced in Chicago. And from each stop a telegram went back to Tel Aviv tallying the "Stephans" raised during the day. From time to time along the way other telegrams went out from her hotel room. To Ehud Avriel in Prague, Xiel Federmann in Antwerp, and others seeking to buy equipment for a Jewish army, they brought the most reassuring news those men could hope to receive—the details of the bank transfers which would allow them to go on with their purchases.

Only once in her extraordinary pilgrimage did she falter. It was in Palm Beach, Florida. Looking at the elegance of the dinner crowd before her, their jewels, their furs, the moon playing on the sea beyond the banquet hall's windows, she suddenly thought of her soldiers of the Haganah trembling in the cold of the Judean hills that night. Drinking black coffee on the dais, thinking of the contrast between that scene and the one before her, tears came to her eyes. "These people don't want to hear about fighting and death in Palestine," she thought. But they did, and so movingly that before the evening was over the gathering at Palm Beach had pledged her a million and a half dollars, enough to buy a winter coat for every soldier in the Haganah.

The woman who had arrived in the United States one bitter January night with ten dollars in her pocketbook would leave with fifty million, ten times the sum Eliezer Kaplan had mentioned, twice the figure set by David Ben-Gurion, three times the entire oil revenues of Saudi Arabia for 1947. Waiting for her airplane at Lydda Airport was David Ben-Gurion, the man who had wanted to go in her place. No one appreciated better than he the magnitude of her accomplishment in the United States or its importance to the Zionist cause.

"The day when history is written," he solemnly told her, "it will be recorded that it was thanks to a Jewish woman that the Jewish state was born."

12

"SALVATION COMES FROM THE SKY."

WITH GRATIFYING REGULARITY, the bellhop delivered the little slips of paper to the client in Room 121 of Prague's Hotel Alcron. Issued by the city's Zivnostenska Bank, they confirmed the transfer, from the Chase Manhattan Bank in New York via a Swiss bank, of a steady stream of dollars to the bank account of Ehud Avriel. That was his share of the harvest of Golda Meir's American trip, a prodigious flow of funds which in a month and a half had allowed Avriel to purchase 25,000 rifles, 5,000 Bren guns, 300 machine guns and 50 million cartridges. The mind of the man who had come to Europe with a toothbrush and a copy of *Faust* to buy arms, however, no longer thought "in terms of ten thousand rifles, but of dozens of tanks, airplanes and guns." Avriel had learned of the change in the Haganah's fortunes in a flying visit to Tel Aviv to acquaint Ben-Gurion with the possibilities he had discovered in Czechoslovakia.

"You don't have to worry about money any more," Ben-Gurion told him. "Just tell me what we can do." A new phase in the purchase activities was opening. Now they were going after heavy weapons wherever they could find them.

Golda Meir's dollars were sent to Geneva's Pictet and Company, a bank in which the Haganah, capitalizing on the fluctuating exchange rates of Europe's currencies, converted them into Swiss francs, then to Italian lira, gold, and back to dollars, a complex circle whose profits would allow Ehud Avriel to buy a few extra rifles with each purchase he made.

To direct the expanded arms-buying operations, Ben-Gurion set up a full-scale purchasing mission with its own experts, organization and communications system. Geneva with its reputation for discreet financing was headquarters. Ben-Gurion sent to Geneva to run it one of his most trusted friends, a Russian with a mania for secrecy so deeply rooted that before opening his safe he looked in the mirror to make sure who he was. Shaul Avigour was a Haganah legend. A survivor of the first Zionist combat on the soil of Palestine, the battle of Tel Hai, founder of the first illegal immigration network, his most recent exploit had been successfully smuggling fifteen thousand Rumanias and Bulgarians into Palestine.

Shaul Avigour in his Geneva headquarters soon began to run up one of the biggest telephone bills in Switzerland, calling New York, Prague, Buenos Aires, Mexico. The telephone was his only means of communication, as the Haganah had felt it imprudent to install in Switzerland one of the secret radio transmitters with which it linked most European cities to Tel Aviv. The network's code name was "Gideon," for one of the judges of Biblical Israel. It had been established for the illegal immigration program, and now it provided secure communications for Avigour's arms buyers. It was located on the roof of an orphanage in Monte Mario, one of the seven hills of Rome. Five times a day its thirty-six-foot antenna relayed to "Shoshana"—the Haganah's Tel Aviv headquarters—the reports of Avigour's agents filtering across Europe in search of arms for the soldiers of Jerusalem.

If those reports confirmed the success of Avigour's and Avriel's purchasing activities, they spoke increasingly that winter of another problem facing the Haganah's arms agents. It was one thing to buy arms in Europe; it was another to find a ship willing to risk running them past a British naval blockade into Palestine.

Most maritime insurance was written or rediscounted in London, and agents prepared to insure Palestine-bound ships were hard to find. Besides, losing a precious cargo of arms to Britain's naval blockade was a disaster the Jewish Agency could not afford. And so Ben-Gurion's arms purchasers concluded they would have to stockpile arms in Europe until the British mandate expired, then try to rush them eastward before the state they were meant to defend could be overrun.

Ben-Gurion grew more impatient with the problem as every day went by. He bombarded Avriel and Avigour with insistent, angry cables urging them to find a way to smuggle at least some of their arms past the British into Palestine.

It was not easy. Xiel Federmann, the Santa Claus of the Haganah, finally chartered a Danish freighter, by pretending its destination would be Istanbul, not Tel Aviv. Federmann turned it into a cornucopia of military stores with all the supplies he had plucked from the war-surplus warehouses of Antwerp: halftracks in wooden crates labeled "TRACTORS" in Turkish with an Istanbul address; jeeps, trucks, water tankers, helmets, socks, tents, camouflage nets, pack racks, all neatly crated and marked with a fictitious Turkish destination. Then he ordered forty tons of soft coal brought to the dock. Federmann's men patiently dumped the contents of

167

the coal sacks one by one into the ship's holds until a dusty black mattress covered Federmann's Istanbul-bound shipment. When he had finished, he announced to the ship's master that the coal was destined for Tel Aviv, implying that if he didn't want to go there before heading for Istanbul, he could unload the coal himself piece by piece.

On the eve of the ship's sailing, the indefatigable Federmann learned of the existence of a lot of field telephones in perfect condition that he had somehow overlooked in his foragings around Antwerp. Their asking price was $40,000 cash. Federmann didn't have that sum. The only banker he knew in the city refused to give it to him. Federmann, however, was a resourceful young man. He went to a Jewish survivor he knew in what had been Antwerp's world-famous diamond-cutting center. At Federmann's friend's request, the quarter's Jewish diamond merchants began drifting into his shop bringing all their available cash with them wrapped in old newspapers or tucked in little suede diamond sacks or battered jewelry boxes. In half an hour, Federmann had his $40,000.

Ehud Avriel spent three months looking for a ship willing to take a proportion of his purchases to Palestine. He finally located a tramp steamer called the *Nora* in the Yugoslavian port of Brno. To get his cargo of Czech rifles past Britain's customs inspectors, Avriel covered them with a commodity chosen to dull their professional curiosity: six hundred tons of Italian onions.

Avriel's wretched tramp steamer, however, provided him with more than transport. One day in the offices of the Yugoslavian shipping agent who had located the *Nora* for him, a clerk whispered to Avriel, "Congratulations. I see you found another ship. We wrote orders to put your second shipment of rifles on the *Lino*."

Avriel's bushy eyebrows raised just a bit. He had ordered no second shipment of arms through Brno. But he had a very good idea who had. Abdul-Aziz Kerine, the Syrian officer who had preceded him in the offices of Prague's Zbrojovka Brno arms works, must, he reasoned, have found a ship to carry his arms to Syria. No British blockade would hinder the movements of his ship. Someone else would have to undertake that job. Instead of simply trying to run a blockade, Avriel would now have the problem of setting up one of his own.

"*Yakum purkan min shemaya*—salvation comes from the sky," promised an old Aramaic prayer in the language that was the lingua franca of Palestine in Christ's time. In contemporary Palestine, no one was a firmer believer in a modern interpretation of that ancient adage than David Ben-

Gurion. He had been in London during the Blitz and knew what air power meant in modern warfare. Even in the reduced scale of the combat that his people faced in Palestine it could prove decisive. Air transport might well be the only reliable means of supplying the isolated Jewish colonies scattered through Palestine, and even, if worse came to worse, Jerusalem itself. The Jewish leader had been obsessed with the idea of laying the foundations for an air force, but he had been unable to solve one problem: How do you build an underground air force in an occupied country?

The answer was given to him, surprisingly, by his next-door neighbor in Tel Aviv, a twenty-nine-year-old R.A.F. veteran whom Ben-Gurion had once bounced on his knee. Aaron Remez had flown for the R.A.F. for four years, providing air cover at the Normandy landings, escorting Bomber Command flights over Germany, attacking the V-bomb sites. None of those experiences, however, had produced a shock to rival the one he had received on his return to Palestine. It came on his first sight of his father. He was behind the barbed wire of a British concentration camp, guarded by men wearing the uniform of the country for which Remez had risked his life for four years. Embittered, Remez returned to Tel Aviv and drafted a fifteen-page memorandum for his next-door neighbor. It was a proposal for the establishment of a Jewish air force.

That document, four private pleasure planes, an air taxi and twenty pilots were the foundations of what would become, two decades later, the most proficient air force in the world. Remez' memorandum had, in a sense, answered the question that had plagued Ben-Gurion, by ignoring it. You didn't build an underground air force in an occupied country, he wrote. You build it up outside while preparing inside the country the structures to receive it.

Set up a foreign-based organization to buy planes, he urged. They would have to rely at the outset on recruiting non-Palestinian volunteers, Jewish and non-Jewish, to fly them. Conceal them on secret airfields, using fictitious companies to provide them a cover. Negotiate landing and fueling rights for those dummy companies.

In Palestine, Remez proposed setting up a Haganah Air Service. Its cover would be an organization whose headquarters were in a simple office building at 9 Montefiore Street—the Palestine Flying Club. The club had a primitive hangar at Lydda Airport sheltering its four monoplanes and a De Havilland Dragon Rapide used as an air taxi between Tel Aviv and Haifa. The club's president became the Haganah Air Service's first commander, and Remez his operations officer. Remez began rounding up all the Palestinians he could find with flying experience. Around the country, settlers set to work building ten primitive dirt landing strips to receive the Air Service's planes—when they had them. With a longer perspective, Remez began to lay plans to occupy the R.A.F.'s Palestine bases when the mandate expired.

The most notable achievement of his fledgling service in those early weeks, however, took place not in Palestine but in the office of the War Assets Administration in Washington. There, one morning shortly after the partition vote, the Air Service's first foreign recruit, a thirty-one-year-old flying enthusiast from Bridgeport, Connecticut, named Adolph (Al) Schwimmer handed the W.A.A. a check for $45,000 and received in return three gray slips of paper. They were the titles to the Haganah's first real planes, three practically brand-new Constellations each of which had cost half a million dollars to build.

To that trio of planes Al Schwimmer soon added fifteen C-46s for short-haul transports. His burgeoning little collection of planes, painted with the insignia of two companies that the former U.S. Air Transport Command major had established, Service Airways and Panamanian Air Lines, were hangared in Burbank, California, and Millville, New Jersey.

There was no question, however, of using those planes in Palestine. Yet as Abdul Khader Husseini's attacks on Jewish transport increased in numbers and effectiveness, the need for some kind of air service, however limited, grew. One day Remez learned that the British wanted to sell twenty R.A.F. Auster observation planes for scrap metal. They were not C-46s, but they had wings and a motor and some of them at least could be made to fly. He arranged for their purchase by a friendly scrap-metal dealer, who handed them over to the Palestine Flying Club. By cannibalizing their parts, Remez' mechanics were able to put a dozen of them into flying condition. As each plane was finished, it was painted in exactly the same manner as one of the Flying Club's pleasure planes, a Taylorcraft to which the Austers bore a fortunate resemblance. Then Remez and his men stenciled onto its wings the serial letters of their Taylorcraft, *VP-PAI*, and put it into service. Soon a fleet of thirteen *VQ-PAI*s, twelve Austers and the original Taylorcraft were flying around Palestine. The British Civil Air inspectors never discovered the explanation behind the astonishingly active life of *VQ-PAI*.

Thus, salvation of a limited sort at least began to arrive from the sky for Palestine's isolated kibbutzim. Those planes scouted the countryside around them for Arab ambushes, flew water to the Negev and dropped emergency supplies to ammunition-short settlements. They even began night flights into primitive strips illuminated by the headlights of parked trucks.*

In Jerusalem, the Haganah carved a rough two-thousand-foot dirt runway out of a wadi floor next to the Monastery of the Cross, below the hill on which an Israeli parliament would stand one day. Getting in and out of that little strip was the most difficult challenge the pilots of the Air Service faced.

For the Jews of Jerusalem, the *put-put* of their little planes slipping regularly in and out of the improvised strip became a comforting part of daily existence. Soon they had given them an affectionate nickname, inspired by their triangular landing gear. They called them "Primus" because they looked as fragile and unstable as the little three-legged kerosene stoves on which so many Jewish housewives cooked that winter.

---

* The effectiveness of the Flying Club's delivery service was limited by the accuracy of its aim and its drop techniques. Carmi Charny, the rabbi's son born next to the Bronx Zoo, who had had such difficulty talking his way into the Haganah, witnessed one unfortunate drop at the kibbutz of Har Tuv outside Jerusalem. It consisted of a sack of World War II German arms. The sack fell into the kibbutz's one, outdoor bathtub, shattering the tub and bending the rifles hopelessly out of shape.

13

"WE SHALL BECOME AS HARD AS STONE."

"TONIGHT, Lipshitz, you don't go."

Shimshon Lipshitz was not a man to ignore lightly such an injunction from the woman who had ordered every detail of his orthodox household for eighteen years. Above all, his wife's warning concerned his own safety. Like hundreds of other Jerusalemites in the winter of 1948, Lipshitz could not make the half-mile walk from his home to his place of work without exposing himself to sniper fire.

Yet his wife's words threatened something that was a source of great pride to Shimshon Lipshitz. Since December 1, 1932, he had never missed a day's work. He did not intend to miss one now. Resting a chunky hand on his wife's shoulder, he announced, "Lipshitz has never missed a day. I am going."

The destination to which Lipshitz' determination drove him was an ordinary three-story red stone building on Hasollel Street a few steps from Zion Square and the heart of New Jerusalem. It was the headquarters of the *Palestine Post,* the foremost English-language newspaper north of Cairo. Caught between the Jewish extremists whose terrorism it deplored and a mandatory administration whose policies it criticized, the *Post* was Zionism's most articulate public voice in the Middle East. Since its first edition had reached the streets of Jerusalem in 1932, Lipshitz had been the *Post*'s chief printer.

With his soft gray eyes that could sweep over banks of inverted type as surely as a rabbi scanning the verses of his Torah, and with his deft, heavy hands, Lipshitz had assembled the blocks of lead that had recorded an epoch period in his people's history. From Nazi Germany's Crystal Night to the triumph of Partition Night two months ago, those hands and eyes had followed the ghastly tragedy of the death camps and the struggle for a Jewish salvation. In a few months' time, they would hold the type announcing the fulfillment of his and Zionism's dream, the announcement of the birth of a Jewish state.

On this January night, the columns of lead awaiting his hands con-

172

tained only a liturgy of Palestine's petty violence. The Haganah, in "preventive retaliation," had dynamited an Arab home in Sheikh Jarrah. The British had seized a Haganah post in Yemin Moshe. An Arab ambush had damaged an undisclosed number of trucks at Bab el Wad.

As he did every evening, the *Post*'s assistant editor, Ted Lurie, paused at Lipshitz' bank to check the layout of the night's story. Then Lurie cast an eye at the front page. In the outer right-hand column of that page was a little box held open until the last moment for late news breaks. Tonight it was empty. On such a quiet evening Lurie had every reason to hope it would remain so. Satisfied with his paper's latest compilation of the minutiae of Palestine life, Lurie picked up his coat and set out for a ritual evening cup of coffee at the Café Atara.

Two miles away, in the Arab village of Shofat on a ridge north of Jerusalem, an anxious man paced the side of the road. In the darkness, Abou Khalil Genno could see the black figures of the village women, squatting on their haunches along the road. They stared at him as he puffed nervously on the first cigarettes he had ever smoked. Those cigarettes and the British police uniform he was wearing were keys to the act Genno was soon to perform. He was, in a sense, going to fill the little blank space in the front page of the *Palestine Post* for February 2, 1948. He was going to offer Jewish Jerusalem Abdul Khader Husseini's reply to the destruction of the Semiramis Hotel and the Irgun bombs at Damascus and Jaffa Gates.

Terror bombing had been contemplated by the Mufti's men as early as October 1947, when his subordinates submitted to the Arab League a map of Jerusalem and a list of 160 objectives they boasted they were prepared to destroy. Nothing had come of that initiative, however, and it was not until the wave of successful Jewish bombings threatened to shatter Arab morale that Abdul Khader ordered his men to "organize terror bombings inside Jewish civilian areas wherever possible." In Jerusalem, he mixed a team of spies into the city's street cleaners to look for a suitable target for his first effort.

To prepare his explosives, Abdul Khader called on an intense thirty-one-year-old Jerusalemite with blue-green eyes and straight blond hair deeded to him by some forgotten Crusader forebear. The most remarkable aspect of the un-Arabic appearance of Fawzi el Kutub, however, was his fingers. They were lean and strong, and they were never still. They were forever picking apart some object, dancing over some irregular form as though their nervous movements represented the only means of expression available to the dour, taciturn personality that commanded them. Since Kutub's

173

adolescence their principal activity had been playing with explosives, and Kutub's life seemed to have been given over to one maniacal obsession: blowing up his Jewish neighbors.

Using hand grenades he had made from old Turkish artillery shells, Kutub began his career at fifteen attacking the primitive buses shuttling back and forth between the New City and the Old. Later he decided to celebrate with a dinner the purchase of his first British Mills grenade. Before the first course was served, however, Kutub grabbed the grenade and dashed off to hurl it into a nearby Jewish café; only then could he savor his meal. During the 1936 rebellion he would boast he had personally hurled fifty-six grenades at his Jewish neighbors.

With his restless fingers and inventive mind, he became the master of the hand grenade, constantly devising ways to render it more murderous and more effective. Using a rope and a coil he discovered a technique to lower a grenade from a rooftop and explode it outside some unsuspecting Jew's window. One of his favorite tricks was to stuff a homemade grenade into a child's rubber balloon. Its fuse was set so that the balloon would catch fire first. The puff of flame would bring people running to see what was burning—just in time to have a grenade explode in their faces.

The British finally became aware of Kutub's activities, and he fled to Damascus and then Baghdad. Later, during the war, he went to Nazi Germany on the Mufti's invitation. There the Mufti provided him a unique opportunity to develop his savage talents, by enrolling him in an S.S. commando course in Holland. After a year's training in the most refined techniques of terrorism, he was ordered to lead a four-man team of German saboteurs into Palestine. He refused. The German reaction to his ingratitude was swift. Blindfolded and handcuffed, he was taken by the Gestapo to an unlikely location for a young Arab terrorist. Kutub was dumped into a Jewish concentration camp outside Breslau.

There he starved and suffered for three months along with the wretched human skeletons around him. Only the Mufti's personal intervention with Heinrich Himmler prevented him from accompanying them on their final journey to the gas chambers. Released from the concentration camp, he went to Berlin to prepare Arabic propaganda for the Nazis. When the Russians surrounded the city, Kutub stole the uniform from the body of a dead German soldier, put a fake bandage on his arm and headed south. He got as far as Salzburg, Austria, where he was taken prisoner by the Americans. Four months later, his real identity established, he was released.

Kutub made his way from port to port, looking for a boat to take him to Palestine. The one he found in Marseilles was already crowded with passengers. Undismayed, Kutub called upon his concentration-camp experience and managed to pass himself off as a survivor of the gas chambers. Thus, with fifteen hundred Jewish refugees as traveling companions, he finally set sail for the Promised Land.

Since Abdul Khader Husseini's return, Kutub had been at his old friend's side as the Arabs' explosives expert, the intensity of his anti-Jewish sentiments in no way diminished by memories of his concentration-camp days. His first assignment had been to pack with half a ton of TNT the stolen British police pickup truck that Abdul Khader counted on using to open his Jerusalem offensive. To get the truck into the Jewish city, Abdul Khader had the services of two British deserters, Eddie Brown, a former police captain who claimed that his brother had been killed by the Irgun, and Peter Madison, a blond former army corporal.

Because Abdul Khader did not fully trust the Englishmen, Abou Khalil Genno had been chosen to follow the truck in a second car and light with a cigarette the fuse peeping from the driver's panel. Now, still puffing uncertainly on his practice cigarette, Genno awaited the arrival of the booby-trapped truck. In the darkness he heard one of the villagers whisper, "That's the one who's going to do something big in Jerusalem tonight."

"My God," thought Genno, "if they know, everybody in the city must know."

Silently he reviewed the plan. The two British deserters would go in first, passing a British and a Haganah checkpoint on their way. They would park the truck in front of the target and wander off as if they were going to get a drink in a nearby café. Five minutes later Genno would follow. He would park a hundred yards from the target, light a cigarette, casually stroll back and light the fuse.

The booby-trapped police van finally arrived. With the two Englishmen at the wheel it set off to deliver its load of TNT to Jerusalem. Genno started the Vauxhall. As he did, a group of black-robed women rushed wailing out of the shadows. Like priestesses chanting the incantations of some ancient rite, they mumbled a verse of the Koran. Then, in a final blessing, they splashed a bowl of goat's milk under the wheels of the departing car.

Ted Lurie was crossing Jaffa Road when he noticed a British police truck swing into Hassolel Street, clipping the concrete traffic island with its rear wheels as it went. "That guy," thought the assistant editor of the *Palestine Post,* "is in a helluva hurry to get somewhere."

He crossed Zion Square and marched up Ben Yehuda Street to the Café Atara. At the instant Lurie began to push open the door of the café, a deafening roar shook the center of the city. Lurie stumbled; then, with his newspaperman's instincts, he jumped up and sprinted to the phone to find out what had happened. To his fury, the *Palestine Post*'s number was busy. He hung up and called again. It was still busy. Seething with impatience, he was starting to dial it a third time when an excited voice behind him furnished Lurie the explanation for his busy signal. "My God," the voice shouted, "the bastards have blown up the *Post!*"

By the time Lurie reached his newspaper, sheets of flame were already gushing out of the pressroom and a stream of his wounded friends were staggering up the smoke-clogged stairs. The street around the building was a sea of broken glass. Its red stone façade had been scorched sand yellow by the blast, and, like ink blots, great black splotches stained its surface. From the buildings around the *Post,* householders stared unbelievingly through their shattered windows at the scene below them.

A pair of American newsmen, Fitzhugh Turner of the New York *Herald Tribune* and John Donovan of NBC, helped pull the wounded from the pressroom. Lurie rushed to the clinic where they were taken, to oversee their treatment.

At midnight, Lurie's wife tugged his sleeve. "Ted," she said, "what are you going to do to get the paper out?"

He looked at her, his blue eyes incredulous. "Are you crazy?" he asked.

"Your job is to get the paper out," she replied coolly.

Lurie realized she was right. He set up a temporary newsroom in a nearby apartment. Within an hour he had located another printing press. Two of his reporters picked their way through the debris looking for carbons of the night's stories while their girl friends retyped the scraps they were able to salvage.

By six o'clock in the morning, faithful to its daily rendezvous with the people of Jerusalem, the paper was on the street. It was a bedraggled, sad little sheet reduced to one page, but it proudly bore the logotype of the *Palestine Post*. Abdul Khader Husseini had demonstrated he was capable of penetrating the heart of the city, but he had not succeeded in his major goal. He had not silenced the *Palestine Post.*

In the Hadassah clinic, the gray eyes that had swept over so many banks of type were swathed in bandages. Shimshon Lipshitz was one of the score of victims of Abdul Khader Husseini's bomb. The man whose wife had tried to keep him from going to work would be half blind for the rest of his life. Yet, like the paper he worked for, Shimshon Lipshitz would have his triumph over the disaster of this night. His one remaining eye bolstered by a magnifying glass, he would be back at his printer's bank in time to set in place the blocks of type announcing the birth of a Jewish state.

. . .

Whether he was in Jerusalem, Damascus, Beirut, Berlin or, as now, Cairo, the daily routine of Haj Amin Husseini never varied. Precisely at sunrise, he rose from three brief hours of sleep, turned east and, kneeling upon the threadbare prayer rug given him four decades earlier by his father, began the first of his daily prayers. That prayer rug was the only material possession to which the ascetic Haj Amin attached any importance. Money and physical goods were for him tools with which to bend others to his will, never vehicles for his own pleasure.

His prayer accomplished, Haj Amin performed the series of calisthenics which, along with an abstemious diet, had kept his fifty-five-year-old figure as trim as it had been in his days as a cadet officer in the Turkish Army. Then he exercised a curious passion for a man who had condemned scores of people to death with a nod of his head. He walked to the chicken coop he constructed in all of his residences and happily scattered a ration of grain before his favorite animals.

His chickens fed, Haj Amin withdrew to a private sitting room, where for three hours he read and wrote reports. Then, just before ten o'clock, he made his way to the core of his headquarters, an enormous sitting room, its walls lined with dozens of spindly wooden chairs. There, in an atmosphere impregnated with the haze of cigarette smoke, the pungent aroma of Arabic coffee and the hiss of whispered conversations, the Mufti's supplicants waited, shifting from seat to seat in a mysterious game of musical chairs whose rules only they seemed to understand, whose moves were signaled by a quick nod, a hand pressed deferentially to the heart, or a cautiously overblown Arabic greeting. Among the men who had waited there that winter to offer their services to Haj Amin was a young captain in the Egyptian Army. "Patience," the Mufti had counseled the ardent young captain, "your time will come." He was right. The captain's name was Gamal Abdel Nasser.

This morning, a special excitement animated the salon. Abdul Khader was coming. He had returned to Cairo to make his first report to the Mufti

177

on the progress of his campaign in Palestine. When his stocky figure appeared at the door, he was almost swept off his feet by his excited admirers and was accorded the supreme honor of being passed through the salon directly into the office of his kinsman Haj Amin.

The report he had to deliver was bound to please the man who had sent him to Palestine "to drive the Jews into the sea." His efforts to close the road to Jerusalem were increasingly successful. With the *Palestine Post* explosion he had demonstrated his capacity to penetrate the heart of the Jewish areas of the capital. Encouraged by that success, he announced that he was preparing to strike a new blow in the heart of Jewish Jerusalem, a blow so devastating that this time he hoped it would drive the city's Jews to sue for peace and deliver Jerusalem to the Arabs.

The Mufti was elated. Bestowing a paternal blessing on his kinsman, he ordered him to spend a few days in Cairo checking on arms supplies and visiting with his family, installed in a villa not far from his own.

A bachelor's degree from the American University in Cairo had not kept Abdul Khader from the social traditions of his people. He had met his wife for the first time in her father's house on the morning of his wedding when he timidly lifted the veil from her fifteen-year-old face. Since then she had given him four children and, despite a strict observance of custom that kept her veiled in front of all but her husband's most intimate friends, she was his most fervent supporter. The laundry, the linen closet, the cupboards of her home, were crammed with rifles, detonators, pistols and explosives confided to her keeping by her husband's friends.

For five days she followed with an understanding complicity his efforts to scavenge a few extra rifles and machine guns for his partisans. On the morning of his departure, she pressed into his hand a miniature Koran. Wherever he went he always carried a Koran which she had offered him. His first he had lost just after his serious wound in 1936, and the second he had misplaced just before returning to Cairo. She begged him to keep this newly purchased Koran in his shirt pocket, over his heart, where she was sure it would keep him safe in the days ahead.

She followed his departure from the terrace of their house, her four children lined up beside her. Seeing him wearing the gray suit they had bought together in calmer days at Cairo's Sednaoui's department store, she suddenly thought it might be an omen of better times to come.

Abdul Khader waved. Then, with a last smile, he climbed into his car, off to Jerusalem, off to strike the blow he had promised the Mufti, the blow he hoped would drive the Jews of Jerusalem to surrender.

• • •

At about the same time, in a beautiful February dawn 360 miles north-east of Cairo, another man and wife prepared to bid each other farewell. They stood side by side in Tel Aviv's central bus station, their hands barely touching, seemingly bound by a troubled silence in a world of their own. The man wore a khaki shirt and shorts. He was of medium height, with horn-rimmed glasses and a prominent nose. At the first sound of the armored bus's engine, he bent down and kissed his wife. *"Shalom,"* he said and climbed aboard.

David Shaltiel too looked back for a last glimpse of his wife, but he did not smile. He had good reason not to. Twenty-four hours earlier David Ben-Gurion had entrusted to him the most important command in Palestine. He had chosen him to replace Israel Amir as the Haganah's commander in chief in Jerusalem.

The Jewish leader had personally briefed Shaltiel on his assignment. Reiterating his order that no Jewish soil was to be abandoned, he ordered Shaltiel to defend the Jewish areas in the city, house by house and street by street. The population must be obliged to stay put. If some families had to be evacuated, they would have to be replaced by others. Where possible, he would put Jews into abandoned Arab houses to stake out a claim to the areas the Arabs had left.

Militarily, he was to strive to build a continuous line of Jewish settlement in the city by occupying Arab neighborhoods jutting in between Jewish quarters. If he could do it without getting into a clash with the British, he was to take over Sheikh Jarrah and secure communications with the Jewish institutions of Hebrew University and Hadassah Hospital on Mount Scopus. Above all, he was to maintain open communications with the Jewish Quarter of the Old City, Mount Scopus, the Dead Sea Potash Works and the satellite settlements around the city. Ben-Gurion had then reminded him that the Jewish Agency accepted internationalization of the city. He was to acknowledge the authority of the United Nations Commission if it arrived, and cooperate with it.

It was a staggeringly difficult assignment, and no one knew it better than the worried man who climbed aboard the Jerusalem bus on February 6, 1948. David Shaltiel was a man whose career had been an accumulation of contradictions, but perhaps the greatest among them was that he should have been chosen to defend the city that meant so much to so many Zionists. No one could have been more unrepresentative of that movement than he. He had received his military training not only in the Haganah's clandestine ranks but also in one of the world's harshest proving grounds, the enlisted ranks of the French Foreign Legion. The setting in which he had learned at first hand the rigors of combat bore a haunting resemblance to the Judean hills to which he was now destined. It was the Rif Mountains, and his foes then as now were Arabs, the savage warriors of Abdel Krim.

Shaltiel was the offspring of an old Sephardic family that had settled in Hamburg, Germany. His father ran a modest leather-goods business. Their adherence to the tenets of orthodoxy was so rigorous that on the Sabbath, all work being forbidden, the young Shaltiel could not even carry a handkerchief in his pocket; instead, it was sewn into the sleeve of his coat by his mother, making it a part of his clothing and reducing the effort required to use it. He revolted early against his religious upbringing. At the age of fifteen, on Yom Kippur, the holiest day of the Jewish calendar, he deliberately ate his way through his first piece of nonkosher food, selecting for his act of defiance the impurest dish of all, a slice of pork. Then he sat back and waited to see if God would punish him. God's failure to do so developed in Shaltiel a lifelong scorn for institutional religion.

His rebellion soon extended to his parents' bourgeois existence, and he emigrated to Palestine. For a while he worked in the tobacco fields, his home one-half of a rented cot slept in during the day by the worker who paid the other half of the rent. He later became a hotel bellhop and, briefly, the first butler employed in Tel Aviv. Without any deeply rooted Zionist ideals to sustain him, he soon grew bored with the spartan, unsophisticated Palestinian existence. Fed up because "everything's already done," he drifted to Milan, where he spent a year working for a textile firm. Industry held no more attraction for him than Palestine's tobacco fields, however, and on his first vacation Shaltiel decided to try to find a shortcut to prosperity on Monte Carlo's gambling tables. The shortcut he found was to poverty. Despairing, ready for a new adventure, he celebrated his twenty-third birthday by enlisting in the Foreign Legion.

Five years later he emerged as a master sergeant with the Médaille de la Mérite on his chest. Exercising a privilege open to him as a Legion veteran, he settled in Paris, working as a salesman for Shell Oil. There he developed a deep and lasting appreciation for things French and above all for those things coming from the kitchens and vineyards of France.

The rise of anti-Semitism in Nazi Germany drew him back to the Zionist movement. He helped build camps to prepare young people to emigrate to Palestine. In those camps he developed his first real sense of belonging to Zionism, and it eventually returned him to Palestine. He found a job guarding the cats and rabbits awaiting vivisection in the laboratories of Hebrew University. The veteran of the Rif War, however, turned out to be a singularly inept guardian for those animals. Touched by their plight, he opened their cages one day and let them flee.

He became a construction worker. One day he was spotted by a friend standing in line looking for a new job and was sent to the Haganah. Soon he was back in Europe purchasing arms. In November 1936 he was arrested on a train at Aachen by the Gestapo as he was trying to smuggle 100,000 marks out of Germany.

For weeks he was shifted from one prison to another, until he had known torture in twenty-four different Gestapo headquarters. He kept his sanity by studying Hebrew from a little grammar he hid under his straw mattress. It was at Dachau, however, that the best in David Shaltiel's character came out. The man who had such a deep love for life's pleasures found in that ordeal spiritual resources he had not thought he had. He became a prison leader, bringing hope and a sense of shared, collective existence to his compound. It was a measure of the horror of that existence that the best job in the compound was burying the dead, because the gravediggers divided the corpses' clothes among themselves. Shaltiel reorganized things so that the fittest dug the graves and the neediest got the clothes.

Finally, released shortly before the Second World War, he returned to Palestine. He quickly rose through the ranks of the Haganah, launching its counterintelligence, where he became an avid foe of the Irgun. In 1942, when Rommel's army menaced Cairo, he was named the Haganah's commander in the port of Haifa.

Through all those adventures, Shaltiel remained a fastidious, elegant man with a fine appreciation of life's pleasures. He was an adamant epicurean in a land where gefilte fish and dried beans was considered a gastronomic dish, an aspiring aristocrat in a society whose idols were trade-union secretaries and farm managers. Two bibles, one of his closest friends remarked, were always at his bedside: the real one and the *Guide Michelin.*

In the Haganah he remained, despite his rank, essentially an outsider. The long marches under the Sahara sun, the spartan barracks of Sidi-bel-Abbès, had left Shaltiel an apostle of orthodoxy in military matters. His kind of officer was the coolly poised young St.-Cyriens of the Legion who had marched him off to fight the Rif in polished boots and freshly pressed uniforms, not the indifferently dressed sabras of the Palmach, who were as ready to argue about an order as to execute it.

His concept of soldiering, the enemies he had made in the Irgun as a counterintelligence officer, his lack of old Zionist ties—all those things would work against David Shaltiel in Jerusalem. None of them, however, would prove as much of a handicap as one salient shortcoming, a shortcoming overlooked by David Ben-Gurion when he had picked him for the Jerusalem command. In his long military career, David Shaltiel had never exercised direct command over more than a platoon of men in battle.

The first battle David Shaltiel fought in Jerusalem was not with Abdul Khader's partisans but with the bureaucrats of the Jewish Agency. His predecessor had operated from two rooms in the Agency basement, running his command like a big informal tribe. Shaltiel wanted at least five times that.

"It is impossible in these difficult times," an Agency official wrote him, "to destroy our administration . . . and nothing must be done in relation to rooms without the decision of the proper committee." Shaltiel walked in and "requisitioned" the rooms he wanted.

He set up a formal chain of command. Everyone on his staff was assigned a specific title and function. All orders were to be written down, he decreed. He instituted uniforms with ranks clearly marked for his headquarters and insisted on a gesture that was an anathema to the easygoing soldiers of the Haganah, the salute.

Less than a week after his arrival, Shaltiel faced his first crisis. A sergeant major of the Highland Light Infantry arrested four Haganah men in a post involved in frequent exchanges of fire with the Arabs. An hour later, the four were handed over to an Arab mob. One of the four was fortunate: the mob killed him with a bullet. His three companions were stripped, emasculated, then hacked to death.

A furious Shaltiel issued a proclamation saying: "Four Jews were murdered in cold blood by the British." And he ordered: "From now on, every Haganah man in Jerusalem must oppose with his arms any attempt of arrest or search by the British forces."

The next day he summoned his officers to a formal command conference. Jerusalem, he reminded them, was built of a stone so hard the Arabs called it *mizzi Yehudi,* the head of a Jew. "We shall become as hard as that stone," he vowed.

The result of Shaltiel's first reforms, his apparent toughness, was to give a new sense of purpose to his subordinates. "For the first time," thought one young officer, "we have a commander who knows where we are going."

Despite that outward boldness, however, Shaltiel was deeply concerned by the situation he had found. The measure of his concern was the first request sent by the new commander of Jerusalem to Tel Aviv. It was for three thousand sweaters. So ill-equipped were his men that some of them were catching pneumonia standing guard during the bitter Jerusalem winter nights. Everything seemed to be in short supply: arms, ammunition, men, food—everything, Shaltiel mused, except the growing ranks of his enemies around him.

"Jerusalem," he sardonically confided to a friend, "is going to become our bloody little Stalingrad."

· · ·

At least one corner of Jerusalem was already undergoing an ordeal so harsh that it would indeed enter the city's legends as its little Stalingrad. Since the Arabs had cut the route of the No. 2 bus line, their sole link with the rest of the city, the inhabitants of the Jewish Quarter of the Old City seemed condemned to fall sooner or later in the ruins of their besieged ghetto.

To galvanize its residents, the Haganah sent the quarter a new commander, a thirty-three-year-old officer of Russian origin. Avraham Halperin was a particularly fortunate choice for the assignment. He was a pious young man, the scion of a family of Russian rabbis. Smuggled into the Old City with the aid of a bribed British soldier, Halperin was shocked by his first glimpse of his command. A group of his new soldiers, clutching long poles in their fists, were threatening to drive an unruly pack of civilians back into the quarter.

Since the Arabs had barricaded the area, five hundred of its 2,200 residents had taken advantage of the British offer of a safe one-way passage out of the Old City. If that flow continued, Halperin thought, soon the only things left in the quarter for the Haganah to defend would be the stones of its synagogues.

Halperin was determined to avoid using force to hold his frightened civilian population in the quarter. They were, for the most part, either very young or very old members of the different communities of orthodox Jewry. Keep their lives as normal as possible, he reasoned, and they'd forget their desire to flee. He summoned the chief rabbi of the Ashkenazi community and offered him Haganah funds to pay his followers for sitting and studying in a yeshiva, a religious study group. When the chief rabbi of the Sephardic community heard the news, he immediately demanded equal treatment from Halperin. Then a third rabbi came to see him. The members of his community were too old to study, he said. What could the Haganah commander do for them?

Halperin reflected for an instant. Set them to reciting the psalms, he told the rabbi, and he would pay them a shilling a day.

The older children were integrated into the defense of the quarter. They stood watch on the rooftops while the Haganah trained. Those roofs were their natural playgrounds, and when the British imposed a curfew it was the youngsters who circumvented it, scurrying from rooftop to rooftop with messages. They learned judo, how to climb walls and how to jump from house to house. Above all, they were sent out to buy and filch bullets from the British for the Haganah's dwindling stores.

Each morning a band of them would assemble at Haganah headquarters for a few shillings, then scamper off to the British strongpoints. "They would come back," one Haganah girl soldier remembered, "a wild grin on their faces, crying, 'I bought bullets, I bought bullets. Give me more money!' And," she could add, "we lived on those bullets."

Halperin put most of the rest of his population to work building fortifications and linking up the tightly packed houses of the quarter by knocking holes in the walls between them. A passionate student of archaeology, he had found in his ancient texts hints of underground passageways that could give his men a safe and secret means of moving from one strongpoint to another. He set dozens of people to work uncovering them, building an invaluable network of secret tunnels. One of the best of those tunnels passed through the women's section of the *mikveh,* the religious baths. The quarter's rabbis were horrified at the thought that Halperin's men might come plunging through that passage while their women were bathing. To pacify them, Halperin installed a locked grill in the passage, keeping the key himself. He would not open it, he promised, except in case of *Pikuach Nefesh*—life or death.

Halperin's communications were woefully primitive. The two telephones in the quarter were tapped by the British. Anyone in Jerusalem, if he knew the correct wavelength, could eavesdrop on his lone transmitter. For a while, Halperin's only means of getting his secret messages out of the quarter was by stuffing them into the ear of a dog who liked to go into the New City. The tactic worked well until one day the suspicious Arabs caught and killed the dog.

Above all, the existence of Halperin's command depended on the twice-weekly convoys the British escorted into the besieged quarter past the Arab barricades. The Haganah used every trick imaginable to sneak arms and ammunition aboard those convoys under the prying eyes of the British inspectors. A few men were even smuggled in on a false-bottomed truck, until their hiding place was discovered. Soap bars were packed with gelignite. One day the Haganah's mess hall received several sacks of a strange grain that looked like rice. When, at lunchtime, a cook sprinkled a few grains on a hot skillet, they began to explode. "I knew then the stuff wasn't for making soup," he later recalled.

Water was short. Each man received one pail of hot water a week in the *mikveh*. Beyond that, he had to make do with a few drops splashed on his face and beard every morning.

Those painful days had their memorable moments. One of them occurred just before Purim. The quarter's population was enriched by the unexpected arrival of a barber and a prostitute. "Ah, there was such happiness!" remembered one Haganah boy. "We all stood in one line waiting for a shave and a haircut, then we stood in another line waiting our turn for her."

Inevitably, Halperin's efforts to bring the quarter's civilian population under his control led him into conflict with the elderly rabbi who had presided over the quarter since 1935, Rabbi Mordechai Weingarten. Weingarten was a short, stout man with a full beard, plain-rimmed glasses and a slow, ponderous manner. For over two hundred years his family had lived in the Old City, and five generations of Weingarten women had been married in the sprawling home on the edge of the Jewish Quarter which was now his. Since his election as chairman of the quarter's Jewish Council he had run the area like a patriarch, his style far closer to that of the Arab sheikhs who shared the Old City with him than it was to the socialistically inclined young Zionists beyond the Old City's walls. Through his hands were funneled the five thousand pounds' worth of charitable assistance provided to the quarter each month by the Jewish Agency. With that money he ran his schools, a hospital and a kitchen for the quarter's destitute, presiding over them all with the firm, paternalistic hand of a man who could remember the birthday and wedding anniversary of almost every citizen in the quarter.

Weingarten's role had led him into close and sympathetic relationships with the British and the Arabs, relationships which the Haganah had found increasingly disturbing in the changing circumstances since partition. One day, shortly after Halperin's arrival, Weingarten's five thousand pounds failed to arrive. Perplexed and angry, he called on Halperin to demand why. Halperin informed the aging rabbi that he, Halperin, would henceforth administer those funds. Weingarten was shocked. He was, he knew, being deliberately cut off from the source of his authority.

Some time later, Halperin in turn called on Weingarten. As the two men chatted over a cup of coffee, there was a knock on the door. Wein-

185

garten got up to answer. Halperin glanced out the window and saw a British officer.

A few minutes later, as he stepped out of the rabbi's courtyard into the street, Halperin was surrounded by British soldiers. The officer who had knocked on Weingarten's door moved forward.

"You're under arrest," he said.

14

A FLASH OF WHITE LIGHT

NO ARAB MILITARY VICTORY in Palestine during the winter of 1948 would rival that represented by a single sentence in an official document issued in the distant corridors of the United Nations. "Only armed force," it read, "will be able to enforce the Partition plan." That phrase constituted the principal conclusion of the first report submitted to the Security Council by the United Nations' Operating Committee on Palestine. More than his ambushes at Bab el Wad, more than his penetration of Jewish Jerusalem, it was Abdul Khader Husseini's most significant achievement since his return to Palestine.

The Jewish Agency had tended to publicly dismiss the Arabs' threats to oppose partition by force during the debates of autumn of 1947. The conviction had arisen among many states that once the world body had made its official pronouncement, the Arabs could somehow be brought to accept it by diplomatic pressures and the lure of economic aid. Now Abdul Khader's campaign had made it clear that the Arabs really meant to fight, and a wave of consternation had begun to sweep through the ranks of partition's backers.

There was a serious question whether the United Nations had the right under its charter to employ force to implement partition. In any event, no one wanted to provide men for such a force. Britain was out of the question; France was exhausted; Truman had ruled out the use of United States troops and was horrified at the thought of Soviet troops in the Middle East; the smaller nations had no desire to pull the Big Powers' chestnuts from a fire of their own making.

Yet the idea that the fledgling international body, at the United States' behest, had thrown up an unworkable resolution to its first grave problem was a dismaying thought. In the United States the Administration was split into hostile camps over partition, with the White House supporting it and the State and Defense Departments opposing it. So bitter were their arguments that Truman's White House aides accused their State Department rivals of basing their decisions on anti-Semitism rather than diplomacy, and the others reciprocated by charging that the White House viewed the issues in terms of United States domestic politics instead of United States national security.

The rallying point of the State Department's opposition to partition was the chief of the department's Near and Middle Eastern Affairs Division, Loy Henderson. A courtly old-school veteran of service in the Soviet Union, Henderson viewed the issue in terms of the deepening Cold War. The Arabs' resentment, he reasoned, would prove so profound they would open the Middle East to Soviet penetration and ultimately, perhaps, to Soviet control of its immense oil reserves.

Like his colleagues in Britain's Foreign Office, Henderson was not resigned to the finality of the U.N.'s partition plan. He had, in fact, resolved to make one more effort to stop it. The unhappy prospects conjured up by the United Nations report gave him the occasion for which he had been searching. He ordered the State Department planning staff to reappraise the chances of partition's success in the light of what had happened since the plan was voted.

Not surprisingly, the memorandum produced by the planning staff concluded that partition as set up was unworkable. The United States, it pointed out, was not obliged to support partition if force was required to make it work. Therefore, it recommended that the Administration take steps as soon as possible to suspend the partition plan.

The memo won the support of Secretary of Defense James V. Forrestal III. Like Henderson a foe of partition, he was above all concerned with partition's effect on the United States' access to Middle East oil. Without it, he feared, the Marshall Plan would fail, the United States would not be able to sustain a major war, and in a decade, he predicted, "the nation could be forced to convert to four-cylinder cars."

Forrestal arranged a meeting with Henderson and Assistant Secretary of State Dean Rusk. There was already sufficient evidence, he argued, to publicly declare partition unworkable. Henderson agreed, but he was wise enough to know that any such declaration would get nowhere unless it was accompanied by an alternative proposal. He provided it.

It called for a ten-year United Nations–run Palestine trusteeship in the hope that somehow, after a decade of communal existence under United Nations rule, Palestine's two warring communities might agree between themselves on a formula for their future. Paradoxically, implementing that plan would require the forces the United States was unwilling to provide to make partition work. The Joint Chiefs of Staff estimated that one hundred thousand troops would be needed to impose it, and a substantial

United States contribution would demand a partial call-up of reserves.

Henderson and his colleagues put the plan into a formal memorandum to be submitted to the White House for Presidential approval.

It was a zealously guarded secret. Such a sudden and complete reversal of policy on the part of the nation primarily responsible for getting partition through the United Nations would stun and shock the world; and its premature disclosure, Henderson realized, would bring intense Zionist pressure on the White House. Despite all precautions, however, the Jewish Agency realized the United States was beginning to have second thoughts about the resolution that had promised their long-sought Jewish state.

The United States had already imposed an embargo on all arms shipments to the Middle East. With Britain still freely selling arms to the Arab states, the move was bitterly resented by the Zionists. If the United States should now reverse itself on partition and, above all, push a new plan through the United Nations, it could be a deadly blow to Jewish hopes. The Zionists might find themselves forced to abandon their plans for a state, or carry them through in defiance of the United States and the United Nations.

To their dismay, the Zionist leadership discovered that at that crucial juncture the doors to the office of the man who had been their greatest bulwark in the United States and in whose hands a decision to abandon partition would ultimately lie were closed to them. Exasperated by the continual pressures to which they had subjected him, prompted by a cordial personal dislike for their principal American spokesman, Rabbi Abba Hillel Silver, Harry S Truman stubbornly refused to meet with the movement's leadership.

Despairing, the Agency sent an SOS to London to the elderly, half-blind scientist who had led the Zionist movement for so many years. If anyone could get into Truman's office, the Agency leadership reasoned, it was Chaim Weizmann. He had met Truman only once, in November 1947, but between the two had passed an extraordinary current of sympathy and understanding.

Weizmann sailed immediately for New York and, for over two weeks, confined to his bed in the Waldorf-Astoria with a fever, strove to arrange a meeting with Truman. He failed. The doors of Truman's office remained closed even to him.

Brokenhearted, Weizmann was preparing to leave the United States when, late one evening, the president of B'nai B'rith visited his hotel suite. A year before, he recalled, he had met in the office of a Kansas City lawyer a man who might be able to help them. He was not a Zionist, he warned, and in calling him they might be clutching at straws. Still, anything seemed worth trying. While Weizmann watched, he walked to the telephone.

Hundreds of miles away, a telephone rang in a darkened bedroom. The rumpled figure on his bed groping for the call was the most ordinary of men. His concerns that night had been those he shared with millions of other Americans just like him: his family, his income tax, wringing a living from the modest men's-wear shop he ran at Main and Thirty-ninth Streets in Kansas City, Missouri. He was Jewish, but, apart from an interest in "my suffering people across the sea," he had never been an ardent apostle of Zionism.

Yet all the ambitious hopes of that movement were going to hang on the answer he gave to his telephone ringing in the night. For Eddie Jacobson once had been the business partner of Harry Truman, and on that winter night in 1948 he was one of the few men in the world to whom the office door of the President of the United States was never closed.

• • •

For David Rivlin, as for hundreds of other Jerusalemites, the Saturday night of February 21, 1948, on Ben Yehuda Street would always seem like a miracle. Saturday night on Ben Yehuda was one of Jewish Jerusalem's most faithfully cherished customs. It marked the end of the city's rigorously observed Sabbath, when, its shops shuttered, its streets deserted, Jerusalem scrupulously honored God's day of rest. At Sabbath sundown, the city burst back to life. Lights winked on, cinema marquees lit up, restaurants opened their doors, and by the hundreds Jerusalemites swarmed to the city's center to wander up and down Ben Yehuda Street, drifting from café to café in a happy, talkative, bustling crowd.

That Saturday night the crowds were back on Ben Yehuda, celebrating, it might seem, the few days of quiet the city had just enjoyed. Even the weather had cooperated. It was a lovely, star-speckled winter's night, softly warm after weeks of penetrating cold.

David Rivlin decided to spend the night in his favorite café, the Atara. There he met one of his closest friends, Avram Dorion. A special bond united the two men. Rivlin, a seventh-generation Palestinian, had married Dorion's sister—the only other member of his family to survive Hitler's gas chambers—so that the girl could get a Palestine immigration certificate.

Learning that Dorion was taking the early-morning convoy down to Tel Aviv, Rivlin suggested he spend the night in a spare bed in Rivlin's

190

room a few steps up Ben Yehuda Street. That would save him the dangerous walk back to his hotel in the Arab neighborhood of Talbieh. Dorion accepted. He drifted out of the café early to get a good night's sleep. Rivlin stayed until closing time. Walking up the street to his flat, he stared up again at the clear, dark sky and exulted in the quiet of the night. What a blessing, he thought, to pass a Saturday night on Ben Yehuda Street, its pleasures unmarred by the sound of gunfire or explosions.

His eyes half closed, Avram Dorion stumbled over the unfamiliar route to his friend's bathroom. He turned on the tap and splashed a handful of cold water onto his face. Sleepily, he stared up into the mirror before him and for a moment studied the outlines of that face. It was a strong, commanding face with a prominent nose and sorrowful, brooding eyes hinting at the tragedies that had marred his life. That face was also the key to the career to which he had so long aspired. Dorion wanted desperately to be an actor.

In his suitcase in the next room was the negative of his first film, his first concrete step toward his life's goal. Its celluloid coils could permit him to dream that February morning that the face framed in the simple bathroom mirror before him might one day stare down upon the crowds from the marquees of New York, Paris and London. Perhaps it might even be his destiny to represent on the screens of the world the face of a new, a Jewish nation. No actor, after all, had a better claim to portraying the spirit of that nation than he did. He had fought in the Jewish Brigade. His family had died in Hitler's ovens. Stirred by his thoughts, Avram Dorion sleepily reached for his razor and began to shave the dark stubble from his face.

A few doors down the street, forty-two-year-old Mina Horchberg clamped her hands on her hips and stared at the youth before her. "Eat," she commanded her young nephew. He too was off to Tel Aviv in the morning convoy, and Mina Horchberg was not going to send him back to his mother on a cold February morning without a warm breakfast in his stomach.

A mile away, over at the Haganah's Romema roadblock at the western entrance to the city, Shlomo Chorpi had been on duty barely half an hour when the three-truck British Army convoy headed by an armored car labored up the incline from Bab el Wad. Affixed to the bumper of each truck were the metallic yellow squares that were the identifying code for British military traffic moving in Jerusalem that Sunday. A tall fair-haired young man in the greatcoat and blue cap of the Palestine police leaned down from the turret of the armored car and jerked a thumb toward the trucks behind him.

"They're O.K.," he shouted to Chorpi. "They're with me."

One of Chorpi's guards poked his head into the cab of the first truck and exchanged a word with its British driver. Then he pulled back and nodded to Chorpi. With a friendly gesture, the roadblock commander waved them on down the Jaffa Road toward the center of Jerusalem.

The tall blond young man in the turret of his armored car was not English. He was an Arab named Azmi Djaouni, and the act he was about to accomplish was so ghastly he would spend the rest of his life atoning for it in a Cairo insane asylum. The three trucks trailing along behind his armored car were the instruments of the decisive blow Abdul Khader Husseini had promised the Mufti a fortnight earlier, the blow he hoped would force the Jews of Jerusalem to clamor for peace.

There were, however, real Englishmen in the convoy. Eddie Brown and Peter Madison, the two deserters who had helped destroy the *Palestine Post,* rode in the trucks behind Djaouni's armored car. This time it was money, not vengeance, which accounted for their presence in Abdul Khader's convoy. They and two comrades were essential to the mission. In fact, Brown and Madison had refused to leave until they had received half of the one thousand pounds sterling they had been promised by the Mufti for their part in the action.

Each of their trucks had been carefully packed with over a ton of TNT by Fawzi el Kutub, Abdul Khader's explosives expert. He had seeded each charge with a vicious addition of his own devising, a mixture of two hundred pounds of potassium and aluminum powder packed in a dozen oil cans. Their presence, he had calculated, would raise substantially the temperature of the explosion and send a spray of miniature Molotov cocktails through the damaged area. His fuses were fixed onto the dashboard of each truck. Kutub had passed them through a metal tube so that, once ignited, they could not be cut or ripped from their charges. They peeped now from the panel before each driver. A quick gesture of the drivers' well-paid fingers just before they jumped from their trucks, and the fuses would begin an irreversible sixty-second burn.

A sharp report somewhere out in the street woke David Rivlin. He staggered sleepily onto his little balcony overlooking Ben Yehuda. It was, he would always remember, "a lovely, bright morning." He looked up toward King George V. The only person he saw in the deserted, silent street was a milkman carrying his bottles from door to door. He looked to the right. Zion Square stood empty, the rooftops that ringed it catching the first rays of a beautiful, sunny day. Then he looked down into Ben Yehuda directly below his balcony. Three military trucks were stopped there. One was in front of the Hotel Amdursky a few doors away. The second was just behind it, in front of the Vilenchick Building. The third was right under his window.

Rivlin went back into his bedroom and sat down on the edge of his bed. As he did, a thought overwhelming in its simplicity struck him.

"My God!" he gasped. "We are going to be blown up!"

At almost that instant, Fawzi el Kutub's TNT exploded in a blinding flash of white light. The stone façade of the six-story Vilenchick Building bulged slowly outward, then tumbled into the street. The interior of the Hotel Amdursky collapsed in one slow, majestic movement. Across the street, two apartment buildings crumbled to the ground as if they had been clouted by some gigantic sledgehammer. Hundreds of people were hurled from their beds. For almost a mile around, windowpanes were shattered. Then, as the echo of the explosion ricocheted across the shocked city, the first sheets of flame began to scamper over the wreckage.

Mina Horchberg had been on her balcony watching her departing nephew when the trucks blew up. The image of the young man for whom she had just prepared a warm breakfast disappearing down the street was the last she saw. She was instantly decapitated by the force of the blast.

At No. 16 Ben Yehuda, on the fifth floor over Goldman's restaurant, Uri Saphir, a young Haganah soldier, woke up on his bedroom floor in a cloud of dust, smoke and plaster. Saphir's first thought was for his dog. He called out to the animal. There was no answer. Before him was a gaping hole where the bedroom window had been. He dragged himself to it and peered down through the dust and smoke to the street below. There, running nervously around the wreckage, he saw his dog. Part of the window frame still dangled from the ledge beside him. Flapping from it "like a flag over Ben Yehuda Street" were the trousers he had been wearing the night before.

A blood-soaked figure staggered into the room. It was his father. Uri wrapped him in a blanket and started carrying him downstairs. Everything along the way seemed totally destroyed except for one sight which struck Saphir's eyes: a dozen eggs resting serenely intact on someone's kitchen table.

David Rivlin remained where he was, seated on the edge of his bed without a scratch, thinking to himself as he gasped for breath in the settling dust, "I'm alive, I'm alive." The balcony on which he had been standing thirty seconds before had completely disappeared. Then, from the apartment next door, he heard someone groaning. He staggered toward the sound. It came from a Stern Gang prison escapee buried under a heap of plaster. Rivlin helped drag his naked body out of the rubble, then went to look for a blanket to cover him.

Groping his way through the smoke and dust toward his apartment, he came on the figure of a half-naked man swaying uncertainly in a doorway. His face had been shredded into an unrecognizable mass by the explosion. From the hole where the man's mouth might have been, Rivlin heard a gurgling noise that he thought was his name. He looked down and saw that the man was wearing a pair of his own pajama bottoms. Rivlin began to cry, because he had realized at that instant that what he saw before him was all that was left of the handsome face of his friend who had longed to be an actor, Avram Dorion.

As the magnitude of what had happened on Ben Yehuda Street became apparent, the stunned population's fury turned on the British. The Irgun issued orders to shoot any Englishman on sight. Gunfights broke out all over the city. At noon, after losing almost a dozen men, the British finally did something they had never done before—they ordered their troops to stay out of Jewish Jerusalem.

The explosion was by far the heaviest blow the Arabs had succeeded in directing against the Jews of Jerusalem. Yet, for all its horror, its results were the opposite of those Abdul Khader Husseini had set out to achieve. Instead of driving them to sue for peace, the tragedy united Jerusalem's Jews in a new determination to resist. Their outburst against the British would aid that determination by leading the mandatory authorities to more or less abandon their efforts to patrol the Jewish areas of the city, as they had weeks earlier its Arab neighborhoods.

All day, the search for the living and the dead went on in the ruins of Ben Yehuda. In the Hotel Atlantic, on the wall above what had been its staircase, a Zionist flag had somehow survived the explosion. It hung there all day in the winter sunshine. Someone had placed a cardboard sign underneath it. On it, in large letters, were the words "Silence—so we may hear the wounded still under the rubble."

Late that night, two drunken Englishmen huddled morosely over a bottle of whiskey in the Auberge des Pyramides, one of King Farouk's favorite nightclubs, on the outskirts of Cairo. Eddie Brown and Peter Madison had come to Cairo to collect the balance of the wages due them for their day's work. Now, their usefulness ended, the Mufti of Jerusalem had nothing for them but a cold smile and an empty hand. Instead of the five hundred pounds sterling they had come for, they were contemptuously thrown out of his villa.

Slobbering in their Scotch, they prepared to disappear for the rest of their lives, condemned to live in fear of the vengeful hand of the Irgun wherever they would go. For Eddie Brown and Peter Madison had given the Irgun much to avenge. Fifty-four people had been killed by the explosives they had helped deliver to Ben Yehuda Street that quiet Sunday morning. Reckoned in terms of their wages, that came to just under ten pounds sterling a human life, not quite the price of the whiskey they would drink that night in Cairo.

15

AN UNLIKELY LAWRENCE

JOHN BAGOT GLUBB, Glubb Pasha, commander of the Arab Legion, stared with unconcealed distaste at the gray city slipping past the windows of his Humber. Those were not his domains, those chill and dreary streets. His kingdom lay elsewhere, in the solitude of the desert. It was only there, on the silent wastes, under an unending sky, that John Glubb was truly at home.

He was an unlikely Lawrence, this little man with a high-pitched voice who was sunk into the leather upholstery of his diplomat's Humber. Yet of all the long line of British Arabists that had followed the master east, he was indisputably the greatest. No Westerner alive had mastered the intricacies of the Bedouin dialect as completely as Glubb. He could hear a Bedouin's history in the inflections of his accent and read his character in the folds of his kaffiyeh. He knew their lore, their customs, their tribal structure, the complex web of unwritten law governing their lives.

Glubb had discovered his life's passion in the aftermath of World War I. His face still bearing the scars of the bullet that had clipped off the tip of his chin, he went out to Iraq as a tribal-affairs officer. Summoned to Transjordan to sort out the warring Bedouin tribes on the country's southeastern frontier, he had fallen in love with the tribesmen whose disputes he was supposed to arbitrate. Their life had become his. Mounted on fast-moving Hajeen camels, Glubb led the elite members of his Long Range Desert Patrol himself, matching his endurance to theirs. He slept wrapped in a goatskin on the desert floor, a rock for a pillow. His rations were their meager patties of desert bread made of meal dampened with water, baked over an open fire with camel's milk and rancid sheep's butter. Through the lonely nights he squatted cross-legged by their campfires, listening and questioning, patiently accumulating his enormous knowledge of their disappearing race.

So complete was Glubb's emulation of their habits that whenever he sat down to a meal or a conference with his Bedouins he began to pluck imaginary lice from his chest and squash them, Bedouin style, between his thumbnails. Over the years he had grown into a kind of Bedouin himself, preferring solitude to company, silence to small talk. Glubb shunned Amman's social life, preferring to save himself for the moments he could escape the city and flee back to his Bedouins and their silent sands.

In March 1939 he had been given command of the Arab Legion when its founder, Colonel F. G. Peake (Peake Pasha), retired. Against everyone's advice, Glubb had decided to build his illiterate Bedouin tribesmen into an elite mechanized force as the core of the Legion. Under his supervision, the Legion grew from two thousand men in 1939 to sixteen thousand in 1945. They fought alongside the British against the Vichy French in Syria and against their brother Arabs in Iraq, winning the admiration of friend and foe alike in both conflicts.

Their commander was a complex, complicated man. His face was anything but fierce: a small, unmilitary moustache, plump cheeks, pale-blue eyes and graying hair parted neatly in the middle of his head. He had soft, almost feminine hands and a shy, reserved manner. Yet he had a ferocious temper. Once, in a fit of fury, he had beaten a sheikh so badly with a camel stick that he had to send him twenty camels the next day to make amends. More than one of his officers had fled his office with an inkwell or paperweight flying past their ears. He was a hard-driving ascetic man who insisted on meddling in every aspect of the Legion's affairs.

Few of the men who had served with him would ever claim to have fully understood him. "You never knew what was going on with Glubb," one of them later commented. "His mind had begun to work like an Arab's. He was all subtleties. He had the kind of lucid mind that could understand the illogic of the Arabs and anticipate it. He knew they would act from their emotions, and he knew what those emotions were. He dealt as an Arab with the King's palace, as a Bedouin with the tribes, as a British officer with London. No one except Glubb knew everything that was going on."

Glubb's presence in the black Humber was the measure of that. Beside him was King Abdullah's Prime Minister, Tewfic Abou Hoda. Their destination was Whitehall and a secret meeting with Britain's Foreign Secretary, Ernest Bevin. Abou Hoda had chosen to entrust the task of serving as his interpreter to Glubb rather than to a fellow Arab.

The two men were immediately ushered into the enormous office in which on so many occasions over the decades the map of the world had been altered with a few words or a judicious pen stroke. As soon as he was seated, Abou Hoda began his plea for another alteration in that map, a minor one by the standards of that somber room, but one of major concern to the sovereign who had sent him to London.

King Abdullah, he told Bevin, was being urged by numerous Palestinians to move into the west bank after the British mandate in Palestine expired and to lay claim to those areas assigned to an Arab state under the partition plan. He carefully stressed the interest shared by England and Transjordan in preventing the return of Haj Amin Husseini to Jerusalem. Obviously, he pointed out to Bevin, Abdullah would never undertake so major an action without the concurrence and support of his principal ally.

The British Foreign Secretary thought for just an instant. Like John Glubb, who had translated Abou Hoda's words, he was persuaded of the value to Britain of a stable Hashemite monarchy in Transjordan united by blood to Britain's other Middle East ally, Iraq.

"It seems the obvious thing to do," he told the Prime Minister. Then, almost as an afterthought, he appended one word of caution to the approval he had just given to Abdullah's program. "Don't go and invade the areas allotted to the Jews," he said.

John Glubb now had an additional approval to secure in London if Abdullah's hopes were to be realized. The Arab Legion, on which King Abdullah was going to have to rely in the months to come, had been allowed to run down from its wartime peak of sixteen thousand men to four thousand. Glubb wanted to build it up to seven thousand, and to expand its mechanized regiment to a division by purchasing fifty to seventy-five armored cars. Even more important, the Legion had always relied on the British Army in Palestine to provide its maintenance support, workshops and logistics. All that would have to be replaced when the British withdrew.

He turned to his countrymen. Three months later, on the eve of Britain's departure from Palestine, the results of John Glubb's visit to London would become apparent. Thanks to a threefold increase in the Arab Legion's subsidy, John Glubb and his Bedouin warriors would hold in their hands the fate of Jerusalem.

It was not the discomfort that annoyed Pablo de Azcarate quite so much as the indignity of it all. His rank and the eminence of the organization he represented entitled him, it seemed to the Spanish diplomat, to a more elaborate welcome to the city than the one he was getting. Azcarate had frequently thought about his official entry into Jerusalem, ordering it in his imagination with the loving concern for detail and protocol absorbed in his years as an international civil servant. Often had he dreamed of his first magic glimpse of its marvels, the Mount of Olives, Gethsemane's gardens, the ancient ramparts. Reality was turning out to be considerably less romantic than all that, however. The only spectacle to greet the first representative of the United Nations to reach Palestine on his official entry into Jerusalem was a pair of hobnailed boots and the imperious buttocks of a British policeman.

Over Britain's vigorous objections, Azcarate had been sent to Jerusalem along with a Norwegian colonel, an Indian economist, a Greek lawyer and two secretaries to establish a United Nations presence in the city and prepare the way for partition. The only representative of the Palestine government at the airport to welcome his party, an indifferent second lieutenant, had ordered the Spaniard onto the cold metal floorplates of an army truck at the feet of a police sergeant. Whenever he tried to raise his head for a glimpse at the passing scenery, the sergeant reminded him with a gesture of his Sten gun to keep it fixed between his knees for his own "protection."

Whatever illusions Azcarate had left about the treatment he was going to get in Jerusalem were dispelled when his truck drew up to the official "residence" the British had prepared for his group. It consisted of a few rooms in the ground floor and cellar of a small two-story house across the street from the King David Hotel. When Azcarate marched into the building to take possession of it in the name of the worthy international body which had sent him to Palestine, he found a plumber installing their toilet, the electric current off and a pair of workmen happily knocking a hole in a wall. The shabby scraps of furniture heaped here and there looked to him as though they had been pillaged from a monk's cell or a prison. There was not even a bottle of ink or a scrap of paper to write on. The Arabs, the only servants allowed inside the British security zone, refused to have anything to do with them, he was informed; one of their number would be taken under guard to the Y.M.C.A. at mealtimes to fetch a hot meal.

Azcarate's astonishing reception was a calculated humiliation fashioned by the British to impress upon the Spaniard the distaste with which they viewed his and the United Nations' presence in Palestine. His Majesty's civil servants, as they had already made clear, did not propose to share their authority in Palestine with the United Nations or anyone else until their mandate expired.

Shocked by their attitude, Azcarate debated making an official protest. Finally, deciding that the best policy would be to "show unconcern and goodwill," he ordered his group to unpack.

The next morning, the principal secretary of the United Nations Palestine Implementation Commission officially inaugurated his mission by addressing himself to the first task at hand, washing his breakfast dishes and making his own bed. Then, thinking it fitting that the United Nations' presence, however unwanted, be properly signaled to the city, Azcarate unpacked the lovely new blue-and-white United Nations flag given him just before he left New York.

Proudly conscious of the drama of the moment, the short, bespectacled Azcarate marched up to a second-floor window to unfurl the banner of the of the parliament of man over the sacred city.

Even Azcarate, who by now had understood the limits of his mission's popularity, was taken aback by the reaction his gesture provoked. A flurry of sniper fire began zipping past the flag. The unfortunate diplomat had overlooked a vital point. The blue and white of the United Nations flag closely resembled the colors chosen by Theodor Herzl decades before for his Zionist banner. Every Arab sniper in Jerusalem was convinced he had just decorated his house with the Jewish flag.

* * *

As he did every morning at precisely seven-thirty, General Sir Gordon MacMillan, commander in chief of the British forces in Palestine, ate a Jaffa grapefruit as he read the overnight messages delivered to his mess by the King David signals room. The dispatches awaiting the general's eyes on Saturday morning, March 6, 1948, were going to spoil the taste of his grapefruit. They announced the arrival in Palestine of the delegate of another concert of nations, riding, too, in a military vehicle. At midnight, at the head of a column of twenty-five trucks and five hundred men, Fawzi el Kaukji had rolled over the Allenby Bridge into Palestine, absolutely unmolested by the troops MacMillan had stationed there. The general was furious. However tolerant the Foreign Office view of Kaukji might be, he could not be allowed, MacMillan well knew, "to go openly rampaging over territory in which Britain considered herself a sovereign power."

As he feared, he had barely finished breakfast before he began to receive "all kinds of screaming messages from London saying Kaukji and his people had to be run off and no nonsense about it."

That was precisely what Sir Gordon MacMillan did not want to be obliged to do. Concerned above all with the lives of his men, he saw "no point in getting a lot of British soldiers killed in that kind of operation." Since Kaukji was already inside Palestine, the best tactic, he reasoned, would be to persuade him to lie low and avoid stirring an international incident until the British had left. MacMillan convinced High Commissioner Sir Alan Cunningham to send a district officer along with one of his generals to try to reason with Kaukji.

Kaukji was in a cordial and expansive mood when the British delegation caught up with him late in the afternoon. The essence of MacMillan's message was quite simple. We are responsible for law and order, Kaukji was told, and if you start stirring things up we will have no choice but to run you off. After all, you shouldn't even be here in the first place; but we'll make an exception this time if you promise to behave.

Kaukji smilingly agreed and offered his visitors a cup of coffee to seal their agreement. He had, of course, no intention of keeping it, but his formal pledge to behave himself was enough for MacMillan. As he had hoped it would, it "placated His Majesty's Government for a while and got us off the hook."

In any event, Kaukji was not in a great hurry to open operations. He had, thanks to the regular infiltrations of the past two months, four thousand armed men under his command. Grouped into four regiments, they were concentrated in the Galilee and around Nablus. So openly acknowledged was their presence in Nablus that six hundred of them had paraded before ten thousand residents of the city, then received an official welcome from the mayor.

By Palestine standards, his men were relatively well armed. Communications and logistics, however, were primitive. Runners ran word-of-mouth commands or handwritten messages from post to post. The shortage of food and other essential items did not unduly concern Kaukji. He intended to let his army live off the plunder of conquered Jewish settlements. Nor did the fact that his medical supplies consisted of aspirin, bandages and laxatives worry him. He anticipated neither a long campaign nor serious casualties.

"I have come to Palestine to stay and fight until Palestine is a free and united Arab country or until I am killed and buried here," he announced. His aim, he declared, borrowing the slogan that was becoming the leitmotiv of the Arab leadership, was "to drive all the Jews into the sea."

"Everything is ready," he proclaimed. "The battle starts when I give the word."

. . .

The commanding general of the British Army in Palestine was not the only person seeking to establish a dialogue with Fawzi el Kaukji on March 6, 1948. Yehoshua Palmon had been trying to arrange a secret meeting with the Arab leader for weeks. One of the most skilled linguists in Palestine, Palmon had lived for months in the desert with Bedouin tribes. For a year, disguised as an Arab peddler, he had wandered around Syria with a mule and a case of dry goods. From those experiences had come a wealth of Arab contacts. Through them he was aware of the bitter rivalry dividing Kaukji and the Mufti. If only he could use his contacts to arrange a meeting with Kaukji, he thought, he might achieve something of great consequences for his employers. Palmon was one of the Jewish Agency's most effective intelligence agents.

Kaukji's arrival in the north of Palestine had immediate repercussions in Jerusalem. Until his army's value had been measured in the field, the leaders of the Haganah could not risk withdrawing men from the Galilee to reinforce the city. Yet Jerusalem's new commander, David Shaltiel, had come to the conclusion that he had to have more men or reduce the area he had been assigned to defend. His first month in the city had revealed numerous shortcomings in his command.

Jerusalem's local peculiarities had left the Haganah markedly less effective than it was elsewhere in Palestine. Years of rigid British surveillance had hampered training. The complex mosaic of ethnic communities in the city made unity difficult. The orthodox sects which composed a large part of Jerusalem's population had never been a fertile source of Haganah recruits. The Jerusalem contingents of the Stern Gang and the Irgun, the largest and most influential in the country, resisted the city's internationalization and thus made impossible the kind of cooperation that was growing between these organizations and the Haganah elsewhere.

All of those factors led Shaltiel to write Ben-Gurion early in March asking for reinforcements. The three thousand men under his command, he said, were not enough to defend the city. Many of his commanders, he declared, were not up to their tasks, and he asked permission to change them. Unlike Dov Joseph, Shaltiel felt that the fact that Jerusalem was being defended by her own sons was a disadvantage. "Every time a Jerusalemite is killed," he wrote, "it affects the morale of everyone."

He had just enough arms for his fixed posts. "Every time I have to equip a convoy," he reported, "I have to take arms from my positions. If the convoy is ambushed, I lose the arms."

A few days later, summing up the city's situation in a report to Eliezer Kaplan, treasurer of the Jewish Agency, Shaltiel said Jerusalem was unprepared for war in its water reserves, its fortifications and the organization of its manpower. Whether or not Jerusalem would even be able to hold out until the British withdrew would depend, he warned, on their ability to solve several problems. For Shaltiel, the most important was to bring the Irgun and the Stern Gang under Haganah discipline. His efforts met with little success, however.

"No compromise," Yoshua Zetler, local commander of the Stern Gang, snapped at him at a secret meeting arranged between the two men. "You [the Jewish Agency] were willing to internationalize Jerusalem. You will get no help from us in that."

Shaltiel begged him to station some of his men in the villages protecting the city's flanks. Zetler refused.

"I'm not interested in villages," he said. "Jerusalem is the only thing that interests me."

The Haganah commander's relations with Jerusalem's numerous orthodox communities were equally unsatisfactory. Their good rabbis were convinced that the thousands of young men in their Talmudic schools would serve Jerusalem's cause better reciting psalms and praying for victory than bearing arms or digging trenches. Shaltiel ordered a young diplomat named Jacob Tsur to try to change their attitude.

Wearing a new black hat purchased for the occasion, Tsur marched into the home of the Chief Rabbi of Palestine to address Jerusalem's most eminent religious leaders. Summoning up all his erudition, Tsur began to recite, chapter and verse, the words of the great Jewish philosopher Maimonides, who wrote of total wars in which the people's existence was imperiled and "every man, even the bridegroom under his canopy, should be mobilized." After several hours of intense casuistical debate, the rabbis finally agreed to allow their students to spend four days a week digging fortifications. For the remaining three days, they decreed, they would devote themselves to prayer "so God may grant us victory." *

All of Shaltiel's problems paled, however, before the complications

---

* In defiance of their professors, several hundred of the young students would volunteer for combat with the Haganah. The medical examination to which the organization submitted its recruits revealed a sad fact. An astonishing number of those Talmudic scholars were stricken with tuberculosis.

arising from his prime responsibility, defending a command that embraced settlements around the city, the besieged Jewish Quarter of the Old City and the Dead Sea Potash works twenty-six miles away where David Ben-Gurion had heard the news of the partition vote. Almost a third of his men were tied up either in those outposts or in keeping communications with them open.

The frustrated Shaltiel decided to urge on Tel Aviv a move which contradicted Ben-Gurion's order that no Jewish territory was to be abandoned for whatever reason. He urged that the Jewish Quarter and settlements west and south of the city be abandoned and the men and weapons thus saved concentrated in Jerusalem. The Arabs, he predicted, would enjoy "a steady increase in numerical strength . . . so that by May 1 their ratio to us will be as high as five to one. Our deteriorating military situation, which includes bad training, lack of experience, poor leadership, considerable losses and a continuing increase in the enemy's strength does not allow room for any sentiment." The evacuations had to be carried out, he said, and "political considerations must not be taken into account, because they are contradictory to our military imperatives."

• • •

"The only reason he's come to us is we're better customers," thought Nahum Stavy, watching the British major before him nervously wipe his glasses. The major was stationed in a vital compound of buildings on the northeastern fringe of Jewish Jerusalem, the Schneller School, an orphanage confiscated by the British from a German charity. Stavy, one of Shaltiel's officers, had just explained to him the Haganah's need for those buildings and, above all, its overwhelming desire that they not fall into Arab hands.

Without looking up, the major told Stavy he might be disposed to help them, but, he indicated, there would be "some expenses involved." Stavy had expected that. He was prepared, he informed the Englishman, to cover in cash any reasonable sum. The major mentioned two thousand dollars. Stavy nodded his agreement.

His transaction was the opening skirmish in the only offensive operation in which David Shaltiel was prepared, for the time being, to engage his forces. It was an offensive in which guile would be more important than guns, whiskey more effective than munitions, and it would occur during what Shaltiel foresaw would be the most crucial twenty-four fours of his command, the day the British left the city.

On that day, the British Army would evacuate the vital complex of buildings and strongpoints from which they had dominated Jerusalem for so many years. Those buildings, selected for their strategic value and their role in the functioning of the city, were the key to the control of central Jerusalem. The side that seized them when the British withdrew would be well on its way to the conquest of the city. There was Bevingrad, at the very heart of Jerusalem, a fortresslike barbed-wire-ringed compound which contained the General Post Office with its telephone exchanges, police headquarters, the courts, the city administration, the prison, the broadcasting station, the Russian Orthodox Compound, two hospitals, banks. There was the Italian Hospital, whose spires looked over an entire corner of the city; the massive French Hospice of Notre-Dame, its great stone wings dominating the walls of the Old City; Allenby and El Alamein Barracks, the King David Hotel. Generally situated along the dividing line between the Jewish and Arab sections of the city, the entrances to most of those buildings from the Jewish side were a tangle of barbed wire, barricaded doors and roadblocks. The approaches from the Arab side, however, were relatively thin and Haj Amin Husseini's followers would be able to pour through them in seconds when the British left.

It was essential, therefore, that the Haganah make sure the British took the easy course and marched out through the Arab side, so that they could move in behind them as they departed. They would need to know minute by minute the evacuation schedule of each building so that Shaltiel's men could move with utmost precision. Vivian Herzog, the former Guards officer working with Haganah intelligence, was assigned the task of persuading the British to withdraw through the Arab rather than the Jewish side. He was also told to determine what British officers were ideologically sympathetic to the Jewish cause or could be persuaded by a judicious bribe to furnish them evacuation schedules.

Because it was isolated from the rest of their positions in the city, the British had decided to evacuate the Schneller Compound two months before they left the rest of Jerusalem. As he had promised Stavy he would, the Schneller major telephoned early one March morning. "We are leaving," he said. "Be outside the gate at ten o'clock with the money."

Stavy was there precisely at ten. The two men toured the compound together, Stavy studying the place as though taking an inventory. Then the major reached into his pocket and handed him a ring of keys. Stavy passed him an envelope containing two thousand dollars. When he had received the money a few minutes earlier from Shaltiel's procedure-conscious adjutant, Stavy had been told to ask for a receipt. The major smiled. It was a perfectly lovely administrative procedure, he admitted, but hardly an appropriate one under the circumstances. "Good luck," he said and walked away.

Before the major's car had disappeared, the Haganah had occupied the compound. Fifteen minutes later the furious Arabs, realizing what had happened, attacked the buildings. It was too late. Within days they would be the Haganah's main base in Jerusalem.

16

THE HABERDASHER FROM KANSAS CITY

AURA HERZOG CONTEMPLATED with satisfaction the gray flannel suit she had purchased as part of her trousseau at Cairo's Sicurel department store. Today was one of her rare opportunities to wear it. She and her husband were taking to lunch the Norwegian colonel who had arrived in Jerusalem along with the United Nations' Pablo de Azcarate. If the British had welcomed the United Nations to the city with studied contempt and the Arabs had welcomed it with gunfire, the Jewish Agency was eager for the international body's support. Vivian Herzog had been assigned to serve as the Norwegian's liaison officer.

His wife had decided, on her own initiative, to leave early for her noontime rendezvous with her husband at his Jewish Agency office and spend an hour conferring with the Agency's legal adviser about her work for the Haganah. At the instant Aura Herzog stepped from her bedroom, her eyes fell on a pair of gold earrings. She swept them into her pocket. How fortunate, she thought; in those difficult circumstances they were just the touch needed to help show the Norwegian visitor the kind of elegance of which the women of Jerusalem were still capable.

Another piece of gold jewelry was the center of Fawzi el Kutub's attention. It was a lady's wristwatch, once destined for the arm of an Arab girl in Jaffa, bought by the Arab demolition expert in wartime Berlin. Kutub's discovery that the girl's affections had not withstood the war intact had kept the watch from its original destination. Now Kutub was about to put it to a use not intended for it by its Swiss manufacurer.

Having removed its crystal and its hour hand, he had attached a wire to the remaining minute hand. With painstaking care he worked a hot needle into its face just above the number six, then attached a second wire to the needle. When the minute hand reached the needle, it would detonate, by closing an electric circuit, Kutub's latest bomb, a quarter of a ton of TNT packed in the trunk of the gray-green Ford beside him.

As he had in his Ben Yehuda Street bomb, Kutub had sought to augment his explosive's power with his amateur chemistry by boosting the mass of his detonators with a powder left from the interaction of a mixture of mercury, nitric acid and alcohol. He had even concealed two extra detonators in the car. One was a pressure detonator set to explode if anyone tried to lift his case of TNT. The other would go off in case the driver panicked and ripped the wires on the face of his lady's wristwatch.

His work finished, Kutub turned to Daoud, the driver. "It's ready," he said. "Get in!"

Before he did, the man walked up to the car's right front fender and screwed into place the insignia which would guarantee the gray-green Ford swift passage through any roadblock, Arab, British or Jewish, in the city. It was the American flag.

Daoud's destination was the most heavily guarded Jewish building in Jerusalem, the headquarters of the Haganah and the Zionist movement, the same stone building toward which Aura Herzog had set out a few moments before, the Jewish Agency.

To Abdul Khader Husseini, as to a whole generation of Jerusalem Arabs, its imposing façade towering near the end of King George V Avenue was the symbol of their ills, the granite incarnation of an alien authority come to lay claim to their lands. Its dark cellar contained the archives of three generations of the Zionist movement. From its offices had gone out a long line of fervent emissaries to recruit funds, immigrants, supporters and finally the caution of the United Nations at Lake Success. It was from its balcony that David Ben-Gurion had proclaimed on Partition Day, "At last we are a free people."

Its courtyard was surrounded by a steel fence ten feet high. Visitors were screened and searched before being allowed inside. A platoon of the Haganah stood a discreet but constant guard on the building. Yet now a timid Christian Arab from Bethlehem was about to drive a quarter of a ton of TNT into the heart of the Agency's compound under the approving eyes of those Haganah guards.

Daoud himself had suggested the plan to Abdul Khader. One of the United States Consulate's two regular drivers, he called at the Agency every day to pick up two Jewish secretaries employed at the consulate. He was so familiar a figure that the building's Haganah guards had suggested he sell them arms, and, with Abdul Khader's connivance, Daoud had begun a small traffic in pistols and hand grenades.

Then, a few days ago, the opening for which Daoud had been waiting arrived. The guards asked him to buy them Bren guns. He agreed, providing he could bring his car into the Agency compound to deliver them so that no one could witness their transaction.

Daoud rolled unmolested into the Agency courtyard and parked his car directly in front of the Haganah headquarters. Beside him was a clanking burlap bag containing the most expensive Bren gun the Haganah would ever purchase. While the guard went inside to get his money, Daoud announced he was going to the café across the street to buy a pack of cigarettes.

As he disappeared, an alert guard noticed the car parked outside Haganah headquarters. He got in, snapped off the hand brake and rolled it across the courtyard to a new location almost directly under the office window of Vivian Herzog.

That action cost the guard his life, but probably saved the lives of David Shaltiel and most of his subordinates. Thirteen people, all of them in the civilian wing of the Agency, were killed by the explosion.

The life of the man who should have been the first among them was spared by an extraordinary coincidence. At the moment the guard had started to roll the booby-trapped car toward his office window, Vivian Herzog had gotten up to go to the bathroom. Untouched by the explosion, he began to work his way from room to room helping the injured. As he stepped into the ruined office of the Agency's legal adviser, Herzog started to tremble. He recognized the gray flannel skirt on the blood-covered body lying on the floor. "My God!" he whispered as he sank to his knees. "What are you doing here?"

There was no answer from his wife's inert figure. Tenderly he bent over and brushed away some of the blood spilling down her handsome face. As gently as he could, he slipped his arms under her body and carried her downstairs to an ambulance.

Two and a half hours later, precisely at one o'clock as he had promised, Vivian Herzog called at United Nations headquarters to take Colonel Roscher Lund to lunch. He excused his injured wife's absence and apologized for his bedraggled appearance. Then the two men left for the home of Reuven Shiloah, a senior official of the Agency. He too had been injured by Daoud's bomb, and his lacerated head was swathed in bandages that left only four small holes for his eyes, his nose and his mouth. The three men had a glass of sherry, then they sat down to lunch: Shiloah, sipping soup with a straw through one of the holes in the mummylike mask enveloping his face; Herzog, his shirt dark with the dried bloodstains of his injured wife; the Norwegian, his mood shifting from astonishment to awe.

"We must convince these people we are capable of managing our nation when the English leave," Herzog thought. And so not once during the entire lunch did they mention the disaster that had very nearly taken both their lives that morning. Instead, for an hour and a half they talked of their dreams for the new state they would build in Palestine in the next twenty years. As he listened to those two brave men ignoring a cruel present to plan a different future, tears came to the wondering Norwegian's eyes.

"My God," he whispered. "No one will stop a people like yours."

Two days later, on Saturday, March 13, thousands of miles away, in Washington, D.C., the Zionist cause was about to receive another setback, this one diplomatic.

The Kansas City haberdasher who had been summoned from his bed by a midnight telephone call in February was utterly downcast. In all the years of their friendship, Eddie Jacobson had never heard Harry S Truman talking as he was now—angrily and bitterly. Perhaps for the first time, the man who had once been Jacobson's business partner was refusing him a personal favor. Truman was not prepared, he told Jacobson, to see Chaim Weizmann or any other Zionist leader.

The need for such a meeting had become urgent. A few days earlier, Truman had given his reluctant approval to an outline of the State Department's proposal to jettison partition in favor of a United Nations trusteeship over Palestine. That approved memorandum was already being acted upon by the State Department.*

The President had given a hint of his shifting attitude in his answer to the telegram Jacobson had sent him after his midnight phone call on February 20. "The situation has been a headache to me for two and a half years," Truman wrote. "The Jews are so emotional and the Arabs are so difficult to talk to that it is almost impossible to get anything done. . . . I hope it will work out all right, but I have about come to the conclusion that the situation is not solvable as presently set up. . . ."

Despite the discouraging tone of the President's reply, Jacobson had come to Washington to intervene with him personally. Now, as all Tru-

---

*Nor were the department's activities limited to trusteeship. The day before Truman's meeting with Jacobson, three officers of the State Department had held a secret meeting with Camille Chamoun in the Lebanese United Nations delegate's New York hotel room. The aim of their meeting, according to a cable sent by Chamoun to his superiors in Beirut, was "to begin a confidential exploration of other solutions to Palestine than partition." The three Americans had indicated, Chamoun said, that if he could get Arab acceptance of a single federal state composed of Jewish and Arab cantons, American support for the plan would be forthcoming.

man's resentment at the pressures to which some American Zionist leaders had subjected him rose to the surface, Jacobson found himself thinking, "My dear friend, the President of the United States, is at this moment as close to being an anti-Semite as a man can possibly be." Jacobson was particularly saddened by the thought that it was the actions of a handful of Jewish leaders who had "slandered and libeled" Truman that were responsible for his attitude. The President's reaction, the firm, angry manner in which he was turning him down, left Jacobson "completely crushed." Stunned, he pondered the President's desk for a moment, despairing at the turn which their conversation had taken. As he did, his gaze fell upon a statue of Andrew Jackson astride a horse.

"Harry," he said, "all your life you have had a hero. You are probably the best-read man in America on the life of Andrew Jackson . . . When you built the new Jackson County Courthouse in Kansas City, you put this statue," Jacobson said, indicating the statue on the President's desk, "life size, on the lawn, right in front of the courthouse, where it still stands. Well, Harry, I have a hero, too, a man I've never met but who is, I think, the greatest Jew who ever lived—Chaim Weizmann. He's a very sick man, almost broken in health, but he traveled thousands and thousands of miles just to see you and plead the cause of my people. Now you refuse to see him because you were insulted by some of our American Jewish leaders, even though you know Weizmann had absolutely nothing to do with those insults and would be the last man to be a party to them. It does not sound like you, Harry," Jacobson sadly remarked.

As he finished, Jacobson noticed that the President had begun drumming the desk with his fingertips. Truman swiveled around in his chair and stared out the window at the barren stalks of the White House rose garden. "He's changing his mind," Jacobson thought.

All of a sudden, Truman whirled around again. "All right, you bald-headed son of a bitch," he said smiling. "I'll see him. Tell Matt * to arrange a meeting as soon as possible after I get back from New York."

Five days later, in strictest secrecy, Chaim Weizmann slipped through the east gate of the White House for his meeting with Harry Truman. The two men talked for forty-five minutes. Once again, the extraordinary current of mutual respect and sympathy which had animated their first meeting dominated their conversation.

Weizmann did most of the talking. He pressed Truman for three things:

---

* Matt Connelly, the President's appointments secretary. Truman was going to New York March 17 to address a Saint Patrick's Day dinner at the Hotel Astor.

lifting the arms embargo, support for partition and Jewish immigration into Palestine.

The President told Weizmann the State Department was considering the first point. As for immigration, his position in its favor had always been clear. It was on the second point, however, that this meeting would bear its fruit. The moving plea on behalf of his people by the half-blind Zionist leader nearing the end of his life and his forces weighed more heavily in the mind of Harry Truman than the reasoned memorandum of his State Department counselors. Truman changed his mind again and returned to his original convictions. He would keep faith with this elderly man and the thousands of his kinsmen still behind the barbed wire of Europe's displaced-persons camps. The United States, he promised Weizmann, would continue its support of the partition of Palestine.

On the afternoon of Friday, March 19, not quite twenty-four hours after Weizmann left the White House, Warren Austin, the United States delegate to the United Nations, slipped into his Security Council seat and asked permission to address the body. The speech he was about to deliver had been drafted by Loy Henderson, the State Department author of the trusteeship plan. Secretary of State George C. Marshall had forwarded it to Austin on Tuesday, March 16, with instructions to deliver it "as soon as possible." Its substance differed little from the memorandum the President had seen and approved shortly before his meeting with Weizmann. Austin, like everyone else in the State Department, had remained totally ignorant of that meeting.

Now, as, sentence by sentence, he officially unfolded the United States plan to adjourn the partition of Palestine *sine die,* a shocked and bewildered silence fell over the Council. In the visitors' gallery, many American Zionists were close to tears. The Arab delegations, at first uncomprehending, were soon exultant.

The United States government, Austin said, was formally asking the Security Council to suspend all action on partition and call a special session of the General Assembly to consider placing Palestine under a United Nations trusteeship when the British mandate ended May 15. It had become apparent, Austin declared, that partition could not be implemented peacefully "as long as existing Arab resistance persists." Unless emergency action were taken, he warned, violence and bloodshed would descend upon the Holy Land, violence which could infect the entire Middle East and even menace the peace of the world.

To embittered Zionists, the United States' action was a betrayal, a "capitulation" in the face of Arab opposition to partition. The following day, Saturday, services of mourning were held in synagogues across the country. For the jubilant Arab delegations, partition was "dead" and victory theirs.

In Jerusalem, exultant Arab irregulars sent a triumphant barrage of bullets into the air. From Beirut, Haj Amin Husseini proclaimed he had never doubted that "sooner or later the United States would return to the path of virtue and justice." An angry David Ben-Gurion called the speech a "surrender" and promised his people that when the time came they would proclaim a Jewish state with or without United States support.

Nowhere, however, was the reaction to Austin's speech more vigorous or more angry than it was in the White House. Truman was furious. In approving the State Department's trusteeship memorandum, the President had assumed he was reserving to himself the decision on the manner and timing with which it would be made public. Therefore he had felt no urgency to communicate to the State Department the second thoughts on trusteeship that his conversation with Weizmann had inspired and his conviction that the United States would have to stick to its commitments on partition. He was persuaded that the release of the speech was a deliberate attempt by the antipartition faction in the State Department to force his hand by placing him publicly before a *fait accompli.*

Indeed, to a certain degree he was. Clearly, he could not disavow Austin's speech. One complete reversal of American policy in the United Nations had already shaken confidence in his Administration's leadership. Another would destroy it completely. He would have to ride along with trusteeship for the time being.

Privately, however, Truman was determined to make his views known and his anger felt. At eleven o'clock on the morning after Austin's speech, he ordered Judge Samuel Rosenman, a frequent visitor, to "go find Chaim Weizmann wherever he is. Tell him I meant every word of what I said," the President declared. "I promised him we would stick to our guns on partition and I meant it."

White House adviser Clark Clifford was instructed to conduct an investigation into how and why the speech was made. Marshall and Undersecretary Robert Lovett both felt the cutting edge of the President's wrath. But, above all, Warren Austin's speech was going to provide its author with an occasion to undertake some enriching foreign travel. By special appointment of the President, Loy Henderson was shortly named to a new post— U.S. minister to Katmandu.

213

17

THE CONVOY WILL NOT ARRIVE

EVEN JERUSALEM'S OLDEST RESIDENTS could not remember a month as cold as March 1948. For nights on end, the thermometer slipped below zero. The soldiers of David Shaltiel and Haj Amin Husseini shivered through those bitter nights, drenched by storms of sleet and hail, often unable to see beyond the tips of the rifles they clutched in their trembling hands.

The cold, unfortunately, did nothing to stifle the intensity of their struggle. They had turned parts of Jerusalem, like the Mamillah Road stretching down to Jaffa Gate from the edge of the New City, into shooting galleries. One morning, an elderly German Jewish woman, unable to put up with the firing any longer, piled the contents of her little antique shop on a cart and started down the street. She had covered barely fifty yards before an Arab sniper concealed on the Old City walls killed her. A few days later Ibrahim Dajani saw a sixty-five-year-old friend shot in almost the same spot by a Jewish sniper hidden at the opposite end of the street.

David Shaltiel intensified the campaign to register all men in the city from eighteen to forty-five. Haganah delegates in armbands began to patrol cafés, restaurants and movie houses checking registration cards. One family which sent its eighteen-year-old son to England to escape services was fined four thousand dollars and ordered to bring the boy back. The training of the Gadna, the Haganah's volunteer youth movement, was expanded. The organization set up a permanent training base in Sheikh Badhur, an Arab village abandoned after a series of Haganah attacks in late December. Called Givat Ram, Commander's Hill, the base was by mid-March providing instruction for two hundred young men and women a day.

For the Arabs of Jerusalem, as indeed elsewhere in Palestine, the slow but steady drift of the middle classes out of the country was a source of growing concern. On March 8, Haj Amin Husseini noted in a letter to the governments of Syria, Egypt and Lebanon the tendency "of a great number

214

of Palestine's sons to leave their cities and settle in neighboring Arab countries." The Arab Higher Committee, he declared, had decided that no one would be allowed to leave Palestine without its approval. "The numerous Palestinians who have left their country since the start of fighting," he wrote, were to be compelled "in the national interest" to return. He requested the three governments to refuse to extend their residence permits and to refuse to issue new ones without his committee's consent.

Unfortunately, the first exceptions to that rule were inevitably made for Haj Amin's political allies. Jerusalem's Lebanese consul noted in a March report to Beirut a growing bitterness among the population toward the Arab Higher Committee, whose political leaders were accused of fleeing the country. Equally bitter, he said, were the population's sentiments toward the Arab states accused of "not giving them any effective help, of not keeping their promises, and of having made vain threats over the past few years. The Arab states," he warned with rare clairvoyance, "had better start either to aid the Arabs of Palestine in an effective manner or to begin trying to calm them down."

Few aspects of the city's life escaped change. Its Jewish schoolchildren managed to celebrate Purim commemorating their ancestors' deliverance from a massacre during the Babylonian exile, with their traditional costumes and disguises, but this year they were forbidden to use two instruments of juvenile joy—fireworks and cap pistols.

For many, the geography of daily living changed. Harry Levin and his neighbors in one of the city's most exposed Jewish quarters had to sleep in corridors to avoid stray bullets. Ambara and Sami Khalidy too were forced to find a new, less exposed bedroom. Their daughter sorrowfully noted the disappearance of the family rose garden, dug up to fill the sandbags that now marked the boundary between her father's Arab College and the Ben Zvi Agricultural School with which it shared its Judean hilltop. On its grounds she could see the students who used to toss her back a missing balloon or ball with a shy *"Shalom"* digging slit trenches, young people like her father's students trained for leadership but condemned to war.

In downtown Jerusalem an institution of another sort closed its doors. Informed that the Haganah had to take over his premises, Max Hesse sadly packed away the Bavarian porcelain, Mosar Czech glassware and Wilna silver that had given his restaurant an appearance as elegant as its cuisine, and shuttered one of the few places in the city where Arabs, Britons and Jews still gathered freely.

In the growing chaos, some men displayed a rare prescience. Dov Zwettels, a post-office employee, began collecting telephones. Patiently he made his way from one disorganized government office to another, snipping phones from the wall and depositing them in a black satchel. Soon his supply of telephones, hidden away against the future needs of a Jewish state, exceeded the reserve of the post office itself.

His activities may have contributed to the slow collapse of Jerusalem's communications. One angry resident noted that a cable took two days to reach Jerusalem from London and six days to reach his home from the post office five hundred yards away. Some messages reached their destination through curious channels. Shalom Dror, one of the city's Haganah officers, was trapped in an Arab ambush when his armored car's wireless cackled out the most welcome message he had ever received: his parents, whom the German-born Dror had not seen since the eve of World War II, had arrived in Haifa. Dror had fought for years to wrest them from Hitler's death camps and get them to Palestine. How ironic, he thought, that they should have arrived in the Promised Land on this March morning. Now he would never be able to welcome them to the soil of the country they had taught him to love. Dror was certain he would not survive the desperate fighting around his armored car.

That fighting was part of the combat dominating all phases of life in Jerusalem, the struggle for the roads. Steadily, inexorably, Abdul Khader Husseini was winning the struggle. The price the Haganah was paying to get its convoys through was exorbitant. The amount of food reaching the city had dwindled to a trickle. Its reserves were disappearing. Unmentioned, but increasingly present, was a specter which now loomed over the Jewish city—hunger.

Sabine Neuville, the wife of France's consul general in Jerusalem, cast a satisfied glance at the sparkling elegance of her table. Jerusalem may have been a hungry city, but on this March evening twenty-eight of its inhabitants at least were going to savor a memorable meal. From its gold-embroidered damascene tablecloth with its garland of roses to its Limoges porcelain and Baccarat crystal, the dining table was a tasteful blend of the refinement of the Orient and the grace of France. Yet none of the Neuvilles' guests would be Arab or Jewish. They were all Europeans, representatives of two nations, France and England, which had spent a century and a half vying with each other for ascendancy in this area. Neuville's formal dinner tonight was an acknowledgment that the influence they had sought to exercise here had passed to other hands, to those of two Semitic peoples whose fight for this land, however cruel, was far more justified than theirs had been.

No site could have provided a more moving setting for a *soirée d'adieu* than the dining room of the French Consulate. From its vast bay windows, Madame Neuville's guests would look across the Jewish neighborhood of Montefiore to the sacred Old City in its crown of ramparts that had called out to ten centuries of their forebears.

Madame Neuville would serve her guests *filets de dorade,* roast beef Sauce Périgueux, surrounded by fresh vegetables "the way the British prefer it," and *foie gras.* To accompany that feast, René Neuville had brought out the best bottles of his cellar, carefully selected with his connoisseur's palate from the wines of Alsace and Bordeaux.

Madame Neuville scrutinized a last time the place she had assigned each of her guests: Sir Alan Cunningham, Chief Justice Sir William Fitzgerald, Cunningham's two aides, "seductive, charming young men with their impeccable French," she thought, her mind drifting back to an earlier era, "and how cleverly Perfidious Albion always chose them."

Within a couple of hours, the men in white tie with decorations and the women in evening dresses would file into her dining room in the flickering glow of four sterling-silver candelabra set along her table. The sight of those candelabra brought a final, faintly sardonic smile to Sabine Neuville's face. They belonged to her husband's collection of personal memorabilia of a Frenchman toward whose memory he bore a special veneration. Her British guests would, she hoped, recognize the initial stamped on the base of the candelabra presiding over her little *soirée d'adieu.* Proud and disdaining, it was the great gold "N" of their original owner, Napoleon Bonaparte.

Five hundred yards from the bay windows of Sabine Neuville's dining room, just behind the crenellated ridge of David's Tower, a pair of men carried on a heated discussion. Its subject was the half-empty bottle of Haig and Haig whiskey one of the two clutched in his hands. Just behind them was a stolen British Army truck, another of Fawzi el Kutub's boobytrapped vehicles.

This time, to drive its ton of TNT to its target, Kutub had selected from among several volunteers a former French Army corporal from Tunis, Kadour Mansour, known to everyone as El Tunsi, the Tunisian. El Tunsi's price had been the bottle of whiskey Fawzi el Kutub clutched in his hands. Distressed by the speed with which the thirsty El Tunsi had gulped down half the bottle, Kutub had begun to fear that if he drank any more he'd be as likely to deliver his load of TNT into the middle of some Arab village as to the target Abdul Khader Husseini had selected for him.

El Tunsi begged for his bottle back. Finally Kutub relented. "Promise if you come back you'll never touch another drop," he said.

El Tunsi agreed. Then, as he drained the last of the bottle before Kutub's unbelieving eyes, he made a last request. "If I come back and give up drinking," he said, "tell me you'll find me a wife."

Anything, Kutub assured him, pushing him up into the cab.

Covered by half a dozen machine guns on Mount Zion, El Tunsi's truck, weaving slightly, rolled across the Valley of Hinnom toward its target. Abdul Khader Husseini had selected it because from its old stone houses the Haganah was able to snipe at his Bethlehem-bound traffic. It was the storied Jewish neighborhood of Montefiore, right under Madame Neuville's dining-room windows.

The farewell dinner of the representatives of France and Great Britain was consigned by Kutub's explosion to a setting appropriate to the chaos into which Jerusalem was slipping. The bomb shattered thirty houses and injured fifteen residents of Montefiore. Only the Haganah's foresight in evacuating some of the quarter's most exposed homes had prevented a disaster.

When the shock waves subsided, Madame Neuville rushed to the dining room. The floor was awash in blown-out bay window, shattered porcelain and shredded crystal. Only Napoleon's candelabra, she noted with satisfaction, seemed unscathed. Heaving a sigh, she walked to a nearby telephone and pressed a button on its base.

"Chéri," she announced to her husband, "please call our guests and tell the ladies to bring their furs. There are no windows left in the dining room."

Haroun Ben-Jazzi stared into the darkness toward the sound rising up the valley he had prowled a month before with his flock of borrowed sheep. It was the low, insistent rumble of motors. For hours Ben-Jazzi and his followers had lain shivering in the last watches of the night, waiting for it. A message from their transmitter hidden in Hulda, the Jewish assembly point, had warned that the Jews would try today to drive a major convoy through Bab el Wad to Jerusalem.

Ben-Jazzi was ready for them. Three hundred men were hidden in the slopes above the barricade of stones and logs thrown up in the middle of the road. The closest of them were fifteen feet from the roadside, waiting to spring on the leading cars with grenades if the land mines hidden in the roadblock failed to stop them. On each side of the road a Vickers machine gun was trained on the barricade.

Lieutenant Moshe Rashkes, riding in the armored car leading the convoy up the gorge of Bab el Wad, contemplated the dark forms of the trucks trailing along behind him. There were forty of them strung out for almost a mile down the road to Hulda. Crammed into those trucks were hundreds of sacks of flour, thousands of cans of meat, sardines, margarine; there was even one truck whose panels were spilling over with a fruit the people of Jerusalem had not seen in weeks—oranges. For those 100,000 Jerusalemites the forty truckloads of food in Rashkes' convoy represented far more than a series of meager meals. Their safe arrival would be proof that the lifeline on which they depended, the road to the sea, was still theirs, that it could still deliver to them the ingredients of their survival.

Ben-Jazzi's first sight of the convoy was Rashkes' armored car lumbering slowly forward through the fading dawn. It was just half a mile beyond the pumping station marking the entrance to Bab el Wad when he saw it. Inside the car, Rashkes heard the shots ring out, then a dull thump as the blockbuster moving up to thrust aside Ben-Jazzi's barricade hit one of his hidden mines. At that moment, over his car's wireless, Rashkes heard the convoy commander announcing to Hulda, "We are surrounded but continuing to move."

The cars were soon so close that Ben-Jazzi could see the Stens peeping through their steel slats firing onto the hillside. With a whistle, he signaled his men hidden in the roadside ditch to rush the cars with grenades and force the windows shut.

It became suffocatingly hot inside the cars. The clang of bullets striking Rashkes' vehicle rose to a steady din. Through a narrow gun slit Rashkes strained for a glimpse of his attackers, but all he could see were the huge rocks and the dense pine forests rising above the road. Ahead of him Rashkes saw the blockbuster, tossed into the gulley by the force of the mine. A second truck moving up behind it had hit another mine. Spun at right angles to the axis of the road, it barred the way up to Jerusalem. From all along the column he heard the dull thump of exploding tires. As the morning sky lightened he could see white plumes of steam spurting out of half a dozen trucks whose radiators had already been hit. The convoy commander, in a Hillman, scurried along the line of trucks like a sheepdog yapping at his flock, shouting at his drivers to stop closing up on each other. They ignored him, and the tail end of the convoy pressed insistently forward until the gaps between trucks was cut to a few yards, offering the Arabs a neat, compact target.

Rashkes' "sandwich" was ordered forward to evacuate the crew of the blockbuster. The five men managed to slip from their overturned vehicle and sprint to the safety of his car. Then they moved toward the second truck, which was lying on its side, the door to its armor-plated cab shut. From the bottom of the door Rashkes saw a thin dark stream of blood dropping onto the pavement. Its van was on fire and the flames were working their way toward the cab and the gas tank just behind it.

Rashkes shouted to the truck's two drivers to open the door. There was no answer. The fire moved closer. "They're dead," someone said. Then, as his armored car started to draw away, Rashkes saw the doorknob of the cab move.

Two of the men in his car slipped out the emergency door and crawled to the truck. While the Arabs sent a stream of fire at them, they struggled to open the door. "Someone's tapping inside!" one of them shouted. Rashkes saw the horror and frustration contorting their faces as they tugged at the jammed door. Below the cab, the little maroon trickle continued to drop onto the pavement. The fire grew stronger, reaching out for the edge of the gas tank. Finally Rashkes ordered his two men to flee the flames.

Horror-stricken, everyone in his car stared at the overturned truck. The thin stream of blood continued to seep onto the pavement. Once again, almost imperceptibly, the doorknob moved. Then the fire reached the gas tank and the cabin was engulfed in orange flames.

By now the convoy was hopelessly stuck. Half a dozen trucks had tumbled into the gully trying to turn around. Ben-Jazzi's roadblock and the two vehicles cast up against it eliminated any hope of moving forward.

Swarms of villagers, alerted by the noise of gunfire, had joined Ben-Jazzi's men. From the pine grove above, shrill and terrifying, the undulating war cry of their women drove them on. Rashkes could hear screams in broken Hebrew ringing down the hillside: "Yitzhak, Yitzhak, today death will find you!"

One hour, two hours, six hours passed. The heat was unbearable. Inside the cars, men stripped to their undershorts. In Rashkes' vehicle the ammunition was almost gone.

Finally the order came over the wireless to withdraw. The trucks that could move began to roll back down the incline in reverse, most of them, tires shot out, riding on their rims. The armored cars covered their withdrawal, pushing into the gully the trucks that couldn't move, to clear the road. As his car inched back down the road to Hulda, Rashkes saw the Arabs swarm down the hillside. Shrieking their jubilant cries of victory, they flung themselves on the abandoned trucks, ripping them to pieces. Frantic hands grabbed at sacks of flour, cases of sardines, cans of meat. Bobbing and tumbling like pearls spilling from a broken necklace, dozens of oranges rolled down the hillside. Soon, like the industrious files of their ancestors carrying stones to erect some prehistoric citadel, long columns of villagers began twisting up the hillside, bent by the weight of the booty they carried away. Tonight in Beit Mahsir, Saris, Kastel, in all the poor villages clinging to the Judean heights above the road, there would be a rare and unexpected banquet on the food which Jerusalem's hungry Jews so desperately awaited.

The Haganah left along the road nineteen vehicles, almost half the number that had set out from Hulda. They included sixteen trucks and two armored cars. The nineteenth vehicle, towed away by his men, would become Haroun Ben-Jazzi's personal souvenir of his victory. It was the Hillman of the convoy's commander.

As he always did, Dov Joseph in Jerusalem had received a coded message at dawn informing him that a forty-truck convoy was on the way. Shortly before nightfall, his secretary brought him the news that it would not arrive. For the first time since November 29, a convoy had completely failed to break through to Jerusalem. Joseph sank into a chair "profoundly depressed." Slowly a realization came upon him. "We are now under siege," he thought.

PART THREE

JERUSALEM: A CITY BESIEGED

March 20, 1948 — May 13, 1948

18

A HOUSE IN THE MIDDLE OF HELL

FROM THEIR BARREN HILLTOP, the settlers' barracks looked down upon a road almost as old as the wanderings of man. Nine miles south of Dov Joseph's office windows, they stood midway along the ancient highway linking Jerusalem, the city of David, to Hebron, the city of the Patriarchs. The four hundred and fifty men and women of Kfar Etzion were supposed to constitute the southernmost anchor of Jerusalem's defenses. So exposed was their position, however, that they had lived in a state of quasi-siege for months and David Shaltiel had already recommended to Tel Aviv the abandoning of their settlement.

Abraham had grazed his flocks on Kfar Etzion's ridges. David had marched past this place on his way to the conquest of Jerusalem and the unification of the tribes of Judah and Israel. Jehoshaphat's warriors had gathered in the little vale above which the settlement was perched, to give thanks for their victory over the Moabites and deed it its name, the Valley of Brakha.

Ancient spawning ground of the chiefs of the Hebrew nation, the hills had become over the centuries the stronghold of a deeply felt and often violent Arab nationalism. In Hebron to the south, sixty-six Jews, most of them helpless yeshiva scholars, had been slaughtered during the Mufti-inspired riots of 1929. The survivors had straggled back, but a fresh outburst in 1936 had finally driven the last Jews from the city that sheltered the tomb of the father of the Hebrew people, and had ended its centuries-old tradition as a center of Jewish learning.

The four interrelated colonies which now constituted the settlement of Kfar Etzion represented a fragile effort to reestablish a Jewish foothold in the land of the Patriarchs and at the same time provide a strategically situated southern buttress to Jerusalem. It had been a difficult enterprise. To the Arabs of Hebron, Kfar Etzion was an alien intrusion on ground that had been wholly Arab for centuries. The colony's struggle to survive was a vital illustration of that unique institution sired by the Zionist return to Palestine, the kibbutz.

The land had been first bought in 1928 from an Arab sheikh by a group of orthodox Jews from Jerusalem. Their tentative efforts to settle it were abandoned after the Hebron massacres in 1929. A wealthy citrus grower from Rehovot purchased the land, added a few further tracts acquired from nearby Arab villagers and settled forty workers on it to lay the foundations of a fruit plantation. Once again an Arab uprising, this one in 1936, ended the Jewish settlement.

To prevent the land from falling back into Arab hands, the Jewish National Fund took it over from the disillusioned citrus grower. In 1942, by a complex legal maneuver, the Fund circumvented the restrictions on Jewish land purchases set out by the British government's 1939 White Paper and acquired the land of a nearby German monastery whose monks had been interned as enemy aliens by the British. On an April night one year later, three women and ten men slipped through the darkness to lay claim to the monastery and officially establish the settlement of Kfar Etzion.

Those first settlers were orthodox Jews, members of a movement founded in Poland and dedicated to combining a rigorous observance of the precepts of the Torah with a collective existence. Its members had earned the title deeds of Kfar Etzion's inhospitable ridges with seven years of back-breaking labor clearing land in Samaria. "Our fellow Jews are experiencing a horrible fate in Europe," they wrote on that night when, almost as conspirators, they came to claim their land. "With our efforts we will build a haven for those who survive."

This prophecy proved accurate. Two years later, sixty emaciated men and women arrived at Kfar Etzion to begin a new life alongside its original settlers. As a spiritual bond had united its first pioneers, so a physical one linked the new arrivals, the dark-blue concentration-camp numbers tattooed into their flesh. Akiva Levi, a nineteen-year-old Czech, had finished his education at thirteen and spent his adolescence staring at the gas-chamber doors of a Silesian death camp. Blond, strikingly pretty Zipora Rosenfeld was one of Auschwitz's few survivors. Netanel Steinberg's memory was still haunted by images of the destruction of Warsaw's ghetto. To Yitzhak Ben-Sira, one of Etzion's original founders, their arrival ended a bitter personal pilgrimage. At the war's end, Ben-Sira had left Palestine for Europe to seek the survivors of his family of twelve brothers and sisters. He found five. Four of them had come back with him to reimplant the Ben-Sira family in the hills of Hebron.

A grueling existence awaited the newcomers. In the winter, a cutting wind tore at Kfar Etzion's slopes, sometimes wrapping them in a dank shroud of mist. By summer, a harsh sun seared the moisture from the land and stifled the settlers in their primitive shelters. There was no water. For two years the kibbutzniks survived on the wintertime hoardings of the monastery's cistern, sacrificing to their withered plants the water their own bodies craved. Each acre had to be cleared by hand with the help of four mules, and the spare topsoil terraced with a complex series of stone walls to prevent the winter rains from carrying it away. Soon it became apparent that fruit trees and vineyards were the only crops their rocky soil could sustain.

Planting their first orchards, the settlers paused to dedicate themselves and their saplings to a pledge drafted by one of their number. "We have taken this oath upon settling in Kfar Etzion," they solemnly intoned. "We shall not rest or know peace until we cast off the shame of barrenness from these highlands, until we shall cover them with fruit and forest trees . . ."

Even the orthodox faith that united the settlers added its special problems to those that nature had given them. A complex system had to be devised so that their cows would be milked on the Sabbath without human labor. Almond roots grafted onto apple trees took hold more readily on their unpromising land, but, as the Bible enjoined men against grafting alien roots, a special rabbinical dispensation was required before the settlers could employ the technique. Since the Torah specifically prohibited harvesting fruit trees during the first four years of their life, the settlers were forced to find a nonagricultural source of income. In spring and summer they moved back into their tents and rented their stone huts to Jerusalemites anxious for a spell in the country.

Despite all those obstacles, the settlers steadily developed their kibbutz. As their number grew, they established three satellite colonies called Massuot (Torch), Ein Tsurim (Rocky Spring) and Revadim. The four interdependent settlements became known as the Etzion bloc.

The partition vote on November 29, 1947, greeted with so much joy by their fellow Jews elsewhere in Palestine, was welcomed with mixed feelings by the settlers of Kfar Etzion. The kibbutz they had labored so hard to build would not be a part of the new Jewish state. It had been assigned to its Arab neighbor.

The decision had marked the beginning of a cruel winter. Well aware of the menace that the settlement posed to their lines of communication, persuaded—correctly—that Kfar Etzion had been settled for military as well as agricultural reasons, the Arabs lost no time in attacking it. Within a fortnight after the vote, a convoy en route to the colony was ambushed outside Bethlehem. Ten of its twenty-six passengers were killed and all its vehicles lost. Since that date, Kfar Etzion had been in a virtual state of siege. In January women with young children were escorted back to Jerusalem by the British. Shortly after they left, the Arabs launched a concerted attack on the colony. They were thrown back in a day of bitter fighting, but that night in the *Neve Ovadia,* the "house of God's worker," which served as the kibbutz's synagogue and communal center, someone recorded in the settlement's diary: "A series of miracles saved us today, but how long can we hold out? We are a tiny island in a stormy sea of Arabs."

Four days later, the stone floor of the *Neve Ovadia* served as an improvised morgue to receive the mutilated bodies of thirty-five Haganah men wiped out trying to reach the colony from Jerusalem. It was the worst defeat the Haganah had yet suffered at the Arabs' hands.

As winter stretched toward spring, the settlers and the Palmach men who had been assigned to the colony laid aside their farm tools to cover their barren lands with slit trenches, crude stone pillboxes and barbed wire. They prepared a primitive landing strip, and the isolated settlement became one of the first beneficiaries of the ancient Aramaean prayer become the Haganah Air Service's byword, "Salvation comes from the sky."

Still the settlers' spartan existence had its compensations. Their fields burst into an incredibly beautiful carpet of flowers with the arrival of spring. Each evening, Yitzhak Ben-Sira and his rediscovered brothers and sisters wandered the fields together, stuffing their knapsacks with scarlet anemones, lavender cyclamen and golden buttercups. Purim arrived and, without their children to perform for them, the settlers staged the Purim play themselves. That evening, when the play was over, they stood together in the *Neve Ovadia* and drank together *"Lechayim"*—the toast to life. Never again would that toast have the same meaning for their settlement that it had that night. The springtime upon them was the spring of Kfar Etzion's first harvest.

That same night, ten miles away, the officers of Jerusalem's Haganah anguished over a decision which would determine whether the settlers would have a chance to reap the first fruit of their orchards or not. Dov Joseph's premonition that Jerusalem was under siege had proved premature by exactly twenty-four hours. The flaming wreckage of the trucks lost by Moshe Rashkes' convoy had not marked the real beginning of the siege of Jerusalem. The following day, while the settlers at Kfar Etzion prepared for Purim, the Haganah had managed to run sixty vehicles up the road, drawing only sniper fire from the Arabs, who were still exulting over their triumph of the day before.

Their arrival concentrated in the city almost all of the trucks, armored cars and buses used by the Jerusalem Haganah to keep the road open. It also put the city's commanders before a crucial decision. Should they seize the occasion to gamble those vehicles in a massive effort to resupply Kfar Etzion?

Shaltiel and his Czech planning officer Eliyahu Arbel both opposed the idea. Getting the colony the two hundred tons of supplies it would need to survive for three months would require sixty-five trucks and twenty-five armored cars. "A loss of thirty to fifty percent in such a convoy can be calculated," Shaltiel prophesied. As he had earlier, he urged that the colony be evacuated under British cover and its forces concentrated in Jerusalem.

In Tel Aviv, however, the young archaeologist in charge of the Haganah's operations overruled Shaltiel. To Yigal Yadin, Kfar Etzion was "the bastion holding Jerusalem from an attack to the south." He personally ordered Shaltiel to send the convoy in and put into it everything the Jerusalem command could spare. To lead it, he sent back to the city Mishael Shacham, the man who had destroyed the Hotel Semiramis.

Its success would depend above all on one thing: speed. "The operation's plan has to be as precise as the workings of a Swiss watch," Arbel warned. "If everything doesn't work right on time, the Arabs will have cut the way back." Originally, Shacham proposed to spend an hour inside the colony. Shaltiel's intelligence officer, a wiry, intense man named Yitzhak "Levitza" Levi, exploded at that. Give the Arabs an hour, he warned, and they would mobilize hundreds of men to send stones pouring down into the road. Stubborn, unyielding, he literally tore the minutes away from Shacham until finally it was agreed that the convoy would spend exactly fifteen minutes in the settlement. In groups of five, settlers would line the road up to Kfar Etzion so that the truckers could start throwing things out of the trucks before they had even stopped rolling. Four vehicles of the armored-car escort would stay behind to patrol the road outside the colony and hold the Arabs back while the convoy unloaded.

The Schneller School, "purchased" a fortnight earlier by Nahum Stavy, was turned into the convoy's assembly point. Tons of food, medicine, munitions, cement, iron bars, barbed wire, barrels of fuel were hastily stockpiled in the school's courtyard. Over a hundred men of the Sixth Palmach Battalion were assigned to protect the convoy. To give them firepower superior to anything the Haganah had previously put on the roads, Shaltiel stripped his command of its best arms: eighteen machine guns, two mortars, forty-seven modern rifles, forty-five submachine guns. A barricade buster, a crane, four armored buses, forty trucks and nineteen armored cars, virtually every vehicle at the Jerusalem command's disposal, was assigned to rush the two hundred tons of supplies and a 136-man relief force to Kfar Etzion. Four wireless sets were scattered through the convoy. Its commander, Mishael Shacham, was given one of the Haganah's precious Austers so that he could control its movements from the air.

Its departure was set for 6 A.M. Easter Saturday, March 27, in the hope that a rare Sabbath action might catch the Arabs unprepared. All night long a frantic activity animated the Schneller Compound. The task of organizing a convoy far more important than anything they had yet put on the road proved too much for the Jerusalem Haganah, however. At six o'clock a dozen trucks remained to be loaded. The convoy was not ready to leave until a few minutes before eight.

Looking at that long line of trucks, the noise of their motors beginning to wake up half of Jerusalem, a sense of the enormity of their gamble overtook Arbel. Grabbing his map, he sought out the man who would command the convoy's escort. Once again he pointed out to him the worst danger spots along his route, the sites he would have to patrol with particular care while the convoy was unloading. His finger slid along the map to a point just beyond Solomon's Pools where the road narrowed to a bend lined by a high wall. "Here," he said. "Here is where the Arabs are going to try to get you."

Sent off with a burst of applause and anxious waves, the enormous convoy slid outside Jerusalem toward the silent hills. It rolled past the Greek Monastery of Mar Elias, and Rachel's Tomb down to Bethlehem, where, to its commander's relief, a handful of Arab guards, apparently stunned by its size, fled their barricades as it moved into view. As each mile passed, the convoy's wireless set recorded its progress for the worried Haganah command in Jerusalem. Past Solomon's Pools; then past the dangerous bend indicated by Arbel. Finally, within ninety minutes, the lead trucks started rolling up the dirt road to Kfar Etzion without a shot having been fired at them.

A joyous shout of triumph from the settlers greeted the sight. Exactly as they had planned, the truckers began tossing their first packages to the ground before their vehicles had lurched to a stop. In Jerusalem, the Haganah's commanders were jubilant. They were going to win their gamble.

The convoy's trip out had been unimpeded, but it had not been un-observed. From a window of the Mar Elias Monastery, Kamal Irekat, a forty-two-year-old former police inspector, had watched the trucks crawl by with satisfaction. Abdul Khader's lieutenant south of Jerusalem had been waiting for this convoy. All the way down to Hebron he had men and explosives like the mines stocked behind him in the monastery, waiting for its arrival. Irekat had no intention of trying to stop it on its way into Kfar Etzion. He would wait and fall on it on its way back, when it would be far from Jerusalem and help. Before the first trucks had reached the gates of Kfar Etzion, Irekat's messengers were already miles away, rushing from village to village calling the men to arms. Irekat himself had leaped on a motorcycle and headed toward the site he had already picked for his ambush. As he did, he glanced at his watch. It was nine-thirty. For once, an Arab leader's estimate was more conservative than that of Shaltiel's intelligence officer. Bouncing down toward Kfar Etzion, Irekat guessed he would need two hours to turn his ambush into a fatal trap.

In Jerusalem, Shaltiel, Arbel and Levitza, the intelligence officer, fol-lowed each step of the unloading operation on the wireless set linking them to Kfar Etzion. Fifteen minutes came and there was no indication that the convoy was ready to leave. "Mishael, Mishael," Levitza pleaded into the microphone, "for God's sake, hurry!"

At Kfar Etzion, the unloading had gone exactly as planned. Two unexpected problems, however, were delaying the convoy's departure. The first was an order from Tel Aviv that Shacham had received when he had landed his Auster at Kfar Etzion. A Haganah plane had crashed-landed on the same strip a few days before. Shacham was told to load it into one of his trucks and get it back to Jerusalem.

The second problem was being caused by the sudden and stubborn refusal of the only member of the settlement authorized to leave with the convoy to board his waiting transport. Despite the frantic efforts of half a dozen settlers, Zimri, Kfar Etzion's seed bull, refused to enter the truck destined to take him to a sniper-free pasture in the plains of Sharon.

While sixty vehicles and two hundred men waited on a reluctant bull and a broken airplane, Irekat's call to arms spread with feverish excitement to every corner of the Hebron hills. In mosque after mosque, muezzins mounted to their minarets to send the word warbling across the village rooftops. On horseback, in creaking jalopies and new American cars, on donkeys and by foot, the men of Nahlin, Beit Fajar, Hallul, Artas, Beit Sahur and Beit Jalla came swarming toward the road. Fathers fought with sons for the honor of taking the family rifle to the fight. Men rushed from their stone huts with a firearm and a handful of bullets stuffed into their trousers. There was no thought of food or water or first-aid equipment. No one told them where to go or how to get there or what to do. Command went to the oldest or to the man who ran fastest or shouted loudest. But they came, first dozens, then scores, then hundreds and finally thousands. In Bethlehem and Hebron, honking trucks summoned men from shops, coffeehouses and souks. Fiercely firing their weapons to the sky, they too joined the rush to the road.

The very nature of his tumultuous army imposed its limitations on Irekat's well-laid plans. When he got to his ambush site he discovered that a couple of hundred men were already sending a stream of boulders bouncing onto the road half a mile away. He shrugged, then ordered his followers to pick up their mines and join the others. Like a cancer growing on the site nature had chosen for it, his ambush would now take place on the curve to which his village warriors had instinctively gravitated.

Sweeping over the area in a Haganah spotter plane, Daniel Beckstein gasped. For miles back into the hills he could see the lines of men converging on the road. He radioed a frantic warning to Jerusalem to get the convoy moving before it was too late.

By now an almost unbearable tension united the men around the wireless set in Shaltiel's headquarters. "We are all going to explode," Arbel thought. Over and over again they repeated into the microphone, "When are you going to leave? Why are you taking so much time?"

At Kfar Etzion the settlers continued to struggle with Zimri the bull and the Haganah's airplane. The British by now were aware of what had happened and of the fast-building Arab efforts to block the convoy's route back. Furious that the Haganah had sent the convoy out without British knowledge or permission, the district commissioner's office sent a police officer to the Jewish Agency with a stern warning to keep the convoy in the colony or accept the consequences. Shaltiel hesitated a moment, then decided to continue the operation. He could not contemplate leaving the vehicles on which his command depended isolated at Kfar Etzion.

An hour, an hour and a half dragged by. As each minute clicked past, the silent knot of men gathered around Shaltiel's wireless grew more pessimistic. "The worst is going to happen," thought Arbel, standing beside the Jerusalem commander. The four armored cars left behind to patrol the road reported that the Arabs were now so numerous they could no longer hold them back.

Finally Kfar Etzion announced that the convoy was ready to leave.

232

At its head was a scout car followed by the barricade buster and its crane. A hundred yards back came the first of the empty trucks, then the four armored buses full of Palmach men, then the rest of the trucks. Like sheepdogs, the armored cars were scattered protectively through the convoy. One of them brought up the rear, just behind the truck bearing away Kfar Etzion's seed bull. It was eleven-thirty. Instead of fifteen minutes, the convoy had spent two hours at Kfar Etzion, just the time Kamal Irekat had calculated he needed to cut off its way back to Jerusalem.

The convoy's wireless operator kept Shaltiel's headquarters abreast of its progress minute by minute. The barricade buster cut a path through a first Arab barricade, then a second and a third. The tension eased in the convoy. Three more barricades were successfully pushed aside. Ahead was the seventh, the biggest one the convoy had encountered. Under a steady Arab fire, the barricade buster moved up to attack its boulders. Suddenly, without warning, a rock slide spilled off onto the buster. The heavy vehicle trembled an instant, then tumbled over on its side into a ditch. From a slit in the rear of its cab an injured crewman saw the entire convoy, like a dying snake with its head cut off, writhing to a stop two hundred yards behind. A sheet of Arab fire poured onto the stalled vehicles, the roar of gunfire now punctuated with the report of exploding tires. The trap had snapped shut.

"Where are you?" Jerusalem radioed the convoy.

"Nebi Daniel," came the reply. At those words, Eliyahu Arbel sank morosely into his chair. Nebi Daniel was the name of an old Arab house. It sat on a hillside just beyond Solomon's Pools, at exactly the spot Arbel had indicated on his map to the convoy commander four hours before.

The echoes of a different fusillade rang out that same Saturday afternoon in another set of hills just south of Jerusalem, only a few miles from the ambushed Kfar Etzion convoy. This fusillade, however, was a joyous outburst of noise designed to welcome into the little Arab village of Al Maliha eight hundred residents of a neighboring community. Dressed in the traditional red velvet robes of the Keis tribe, Alia Darwish, the fifteen-year-old daughter of one of Al Maliha's patriarchs, heard the noise with a tremor of excitement. It marked the end of her childhood. Those neighbors had come for her. In a noisy, happy procession they would lead her back to their village, where a man she had never seen, a handsome, dark-eyed stonecutter named Mohammed Moussa Zaharan, awaited her. This March Saturday was Alia Darwish's wedding day.

Alia Darwish was seated astride a horse harnessed in gold. Her

233

father placed in her hands a long sword whose blade she pressed to her lips and forehead over the white veil hiding her face. She would not remove it until the moment of her marriage, when her husband would symbolically take possession of her by cutting the veil from her face with the sword.

Singing traditional nuptial hymns to the shrill atonal pipings of their flutes and the vibrant thump of the *kakabeh,* a kind of guitar, the procession, Alia at its head, wound its way out of Al Maliha. Behind the bride, the women of her village, their long robes embroidered in velvet and satin, coins jangling in their headdresses, danced the *zafeh,* the wedding dance.

The little community toward which they bore Alia Darwish clung to a rocky ledge on the other side of a deep wadi from Al Maliha. Its slopes, covered by almond trees, were scarred by gaping white holes, the rock quarries which had for decades constituted the village's principal source of wealth and repute. Generations of villagers like Alia's fiancé had worked the stone from those quarries, and their skilled stonecutters' hands were a legend through all the Middle East. From Jerusalem to Baghdad there was scarcely a city which did not boast at least one house whose finely chiseled white stones had come from that quarry.

For years, the village inhabitants had cultivated friendly relations with their Jewish neighbors of Givat Shaul, Motza and Montefiore. They went to each other's feasts, danced and sang together over cups of coffee and glasses of arak. Even in that troubled springtime of 1948, the village which was now to become Alia Darwish's new home had managed to remain a strangely calm oasis at the gates of Jerusalem. With quiet but firm resolve, her new neighbors had kept the Mufti's men from their peaceful village, named after one of the notables who had founded it. It was called Deir Yassin.

There was no longer any hope of breaking the barricade barring the road back to Jerusalem for the convoy which had resupplied the settlement of Kfar Etzion. The Arabs had slipped down to within three hundred yards of the trapped vehicles, and inside their cabins the drivers could now hear them calling to each other.

Rather than risk total disaster, the convoy commander ordered every vehicle that could move to fall back on the settlement. It was already too late for most of the vehicles. Only five armored cars, carrying thirty-five men, and five trucks managed to break away. One of them was the vehicle carrying Zimri the seed bull whose stubborness had helped delay the convoy's departure.

For the one hundred and eighty men and women left behind in Irekat's trap, the only hope of saving themselves lay in the thick walls of the abandoned Arab house for which their ambush site was named. The trucks that could still move closed up on Nebi Daniel, ringing it two deep in a circle like a wagon train drawn up to hold off an Indian raid.

The gate was blown open. Men rushed inside to barricade windows and set four machine-gun positions on the roof. The armored cars that could still move inched from truck to truck along the line of stricken vehicles, rescuing their crews and bringing them into the besieged compound.

No one could reach the men trapped in the barricade buster. All afternoon its crewmen, several of them wounded, held off the steadily advancing Arabs. After six hours their ammunition was gone and the men lay listless and exhausted on the floor. Toward sunset a pair of Molotov cocktails thumped against the car. Calmly, Zerubavel Horowitz, the commander, told his men they were free to make a break for safety any way they could. He would stay behind with his wounded. One by one, the others leaped out. As Yaacov Ai, the last man to leave, pushed through the door he caught a final glimpse of Horowitz standing among the wounded like "the captain of a sinking ship who refuses to desert his helpless passengers." Seconds later the burning vehicle exploded.

As the afternoon wore one, the messages from the men and women trapped in the Nebi Daniel house grew increasingly desperate. Shaltiel asked Tel Aviv to mobilize the Haganah Air Service to "bomb" the Arabs' positions. The Haganah offered the best it could: an Auster and a Tigermoth, from whose windows Uzi Narciss and Amos Chorev dropped lengths of pipe stuffed with dynamite and fitted with a screw device that, hopefully, would explode them on impact.

The news of the disaster swept rapidly through Jewish Jerusalem, casting a pall of gloom through the community. Few of its members did not have a friend or relative among the besieged. In Bet Hakerem, Benjamin Golani, a Russian-born mason, played with the dials of his radio set to intercept the voice of his son, the Haganah's radio operator in the besieged Old City. The voice he found that afternoon was not his son's, but it was almost as familiar. It belonged to his son-in-law Moshe, to whom, the evening before, Golani had confided his revolver, a magnificent Parabellum. Through his words from one of the ensnared armored cars, Golani learned he was caught in the Arab ambush less than ten miles away from his living room.

The Jerusalem Haganah had put practically all its mobile forces into the trapped convoy. There was no reserve in the city capable of breaking through to the besieged men and women. Only one way of saving the one hundred and eighty people and the precious vehicles caught at Nebi Daniel was available. Shaltiel had to turn to the British for help.

Their reaction to his first pleas was not enthusiastic. As District Commissioner James Pollock had already found out, the Palestine police "were not inclined to be very helpful." A group of them had practically mutinied when Pollock had ordered them out to study the situation. The Haganah, they had replied, had run their convoy against British orders and had left Kfar Etzion against British advice. Now they would just have to pay for the consequences of their "bloody-mindedness."

Dublin-born Isaac Herzog, the Chief Rabbi of Palestine, violated the sanctity of the Sabbath by picking up his telephone to personally intervene with Sir Alan Cunningham, the High Commissioner. His son Vivian, the former Guards officer, raced from office to office beseeching the men whose uniform he had worn so long to save his fellows from a massacre.

Both the British commander, Sir Gordon MacMillan, and his Jerusalem deputy, Brigadier C. P. Jones, were in Athens that weekend for a regional conference. The officer left in charge, Colonel George W. Harper of the Suffolk Regiment, had on earlier occasions proven helpful to the Haganah. Today he was caught in a dilemma. If he lost British soldiers extricating a convoy that had gone out against regulations, there would be hell to pay when MacMillan returned. On the other hand, if the men and women at Nebi Daniel were all murdered and the British had done nothing to save them, there would be hell to pay, too.

Harper pushed a unit up the Hebron road until it ran into Arab mines. With darkness falling, he felt he could not risk going on. He ordered the unit back. The besieged Jews would have to get through the night as best they could.

In the building at Nebi Daniel, the situation worsened steadily. The wounded littered the floor. Morphine, virtually the only medical supply the men had salvaged from the trucks, was almost gone. Yehuda Lash watched one dying man cling to a girl, caressing her body, "trying to hold on to her warmth as though it was life itself." When he died Lash heard the girl murmur, "It was all that I could do for him."

Outside, the Arab ranks continued to grow. Under the cover of darkness they crept steadily closer to the ring of trucks protecting the house. Irekat saw one man from Bethlehem hurl his body and a Molotov cocktail into an armored car. Set ablaze by his own bomb, he rolled off into a ditch and died. Just after midnight, Irekat's men, led by Sheikh Hamoud of Hebron, tried to rush the house with a huge mine. The Jews spotted them seventy yards from success and drove them off with hand grenades. That stopped the Arabs' assaults. All night, however, the people trapped in the house could listen to them talking just beyond their ring of armored cars, waiting for dawn and the assault with which they would overwhelm Nebi Daniel.

As bright and clear as the spring sunshine, a joyous wave of sound spilled over the rooftops of Jerusalem, driving for a moment the echo of gunfire from the Judean hills. As they had for centuries, the church bells of Jerusalem were announcing once again the miracle of Jesus Christ's resurrection from the tomb of Joseph of Arimathea.

The gaps between the symbolic promise of Christ's sacrifice and the harsh human realities of Jerusalem that morning did not modify in any way the solemn liturgy of the day. Preceded by a deacon bearing a massive silver cross, the Latin Patriarch led the traditional parade of prelates and notables through the shadowy corridors of the Church of the Holy Sepulcher to the marble-faced chamber of Christ's Tomb. Tall and dignified, conscious of the fact that a Britisher was accomplishing this rite for the last time, District Commissioner James Pollock marched at the head of the diplomatic corps. In the district commissioner's pocket was a telegram, still another plea to the United Nations for an international police force for the city. The heads of Jerusalem's Christian communities, Armenian, Coptic, Greek and Latin, had presented it to Pollock. It was the first time in history, he thought sardonically, that the august heads of those communities had ever been able to agree on anything.

The procession shuffled to a stop before the darkened tomb. The Patriarch bowed low, then solemnly proclaimed, "Christ is risen."

"Christ is risen," came the reply from the line of men behind him. "Allelujah, peace to all mankind." Another Easter Sunday morning had come to Jerusalem.

There was no peace at the gates of Jerusalem. The messages reaching the city from the house at Nebi Daniel were tense and faint now, as though the depleted batteries of the besieged men's radio had become the barometer of their own condition. Exhausted, dizzy with hunger, plagued by heat and smoke, the defenders rushed from gunport to gunport, sometimes tripping over the dead and dying lying on the floor.

Outside, the ferocity of the Arabs' attacks intensified. They too had been without food for twenty-four hours. Some, who had gone without water since the battle started, dipped their kaffiyehs into dried-up wells to get them damp, then sucked the moisture from them to ease their thirst. But they had the promise of victory to drive them on. Toward ten o'clock, hundreds of them, covered by a smoke screen, began advancing on the house. At the same time, the defenders received a grim piece of news. A second British relief column en route to the site had stopped.

Colonel Harper had stopped this time to begin negotiations with the Arabs for their surrender. It was going to be a costly one. Communicating by radio with the Mufti in Cairo, Irekat demanded that everyone in the building be handed over as a prisoner of war. The British refused. Finally Irekat and the British agreed on terms that the Jewish Agency felt compelled to accept. Shaltiel's estimates of the risks of running a convoy out to Kfar Etzion would be proven low. To save the men and women trapped in Nebi Daniel, the Jerusalem commander was going to have to give up every one of his command's precious vehicles and all the arms he had culled from his strongpoints.

Colonel Harper ordered the column forward again, fourteen half-tracks and five trucks preceded by an armored car. Behind it came a line of Red Cross ambulances for the dead and wounded.

At Nebi Daniel, the firing was still going on. As the column rounded a curve, Jacques de Reynier of the Red Cross suddenly saw the house "small and alone in the middle of hell." On the road leading up to it, he noted "a sprawl of shattered, blackened vehicles and burned bodies, their heads and sexual organs carefully mutilated."

The end came quickly. Colonel Harper explained the surrender terms and gave the Haganah commander three minutes to organize his people. Already the Arabs had begun to seep down the hillside to savor the spectacle. Inside the house, someone smashed the radio with an ax and tossed the bolts of the machine guns into a well. Then, blinking at the sunlight, covered with grease and smoke, the first man staggered out the door.

The rest followed quickly, throwing their arms in a heap at Harper's feet. On the hillside, the Arabs watched the growing pile with noisy impatience. When the last of the thirteen dead and forty wounded had been carried from the house, Harper turned to Irekat.

"It's all yours," he said.

Less than an hour later, the survivors' convoy reached Jerusalem. Seeing the stunned, shocked faces staring up at them from the sidewalks, the men in the first truck began to sing. The others behind them joined in, until the echoes of their song rang through the streets. They were coming back from the worst defeat the Haganah had suffered at the hands of the Arabs, but to the worried citizens of Jerusalem they had decided to sing "Hatikvah," the Hope.

The echoes of other songs rang over the desolate hills around Kfar Etzion. From their rocky ridge the settlers stared in silence at the spectacle passing before them. Jubilant and triumphant, Kamal Irekat's warriors rolled down to Hebron in the remains of the powerful convoy that had come to succor them, brandishing the scores of captured arms they would soon turn on the colony.

Late that evening, a shaken young man arrived at the home of Benjamin Golani. It was Moshe, the son-in-law to whom Golani had given his prized Parabellum thirty-six hours earlier. The gun was gone, Moshe sadly revealed, but no Arab would use it on the settlers of Kfar Etzion. Solemnly he reached into his pocket and passed his father-in-law a piece of metal. It was the hammer of his Parabellum.

• • •

Two of the most disconsolate young men in Palestine sat glumly before David Ben-Gurion. Yigal Yadin, who had ordered the Jerusalem command to put everything available into the Nebi Daniel convoy, and Mishael Shacham, who had commanded it, had come to examine the consequences of the disaster with the Jewish leader. To Yadin, the convoy's loss would always be "the darkest moment of our struggle."

Indeed, wherever they might look in those last days of March 1948, the leaders of the as yet unborn Jewish state could find cause to despair. The Arabs were winning the battle for the roads. Communications with the Yishuv's isolated settlements were cut or being maintained at great sacrifice. The whole north of Palestine was threatened by the still-unmeasured menace of Fawzi el Kaukji's Liberation Army. Internationally, the tide of public opinion which had helped sustain the Zionist cause in November had receded as Arab resistance had made a peaceful application of the partition plan appear unlikely. The Zionists' principal diplomatic

239

ally, the United States, had turned on them with a damaging arms embargo and the trusteeship proposals.

There were, of course, bright spots in the picture. No Jewish-held ground had been lost to the Arabs. The local arms factories, the need for which Ben-Gurion and Haim Slavine had foreseen three years before, were coming into production. In Europe, Ehud Avriel and his colleagues had been remarkably successful in purchasing arms. Not a single shipment of those arms, however, had yet reached Palestine.

Still, the fact remained that the Haganah was almost everywhere on the defensive and that the defeats inflicted on it had come, not from the enemies Ben-Gurion feared most, the regular Arab armies, but from the guerrillas of Abdul Khader Husseini. The able Arab chieftain was on the verge of making good his vow to strangle Jerusalem. Since the convoy whose trucks had been lost at Nebi Daniel had slipped into the city, not a single Jewish vehicle had gotten through Bab el Wad. One small convoy had been wiped out. Two others, much larger, had been beaten back by the Arabs. With the road cut, one sixth of the entire Jewish settlement in Palestine was now isolated and menaced by starvation. Clearly the current was running against the Jews, and if it were not reversed, the Yishuv was going to face disaster.

To David Ben-Gurion, Jerusalem was the foundation on which all else would stand or fall. The loss of the Nebi Daniel convoy, Abdul Khader's success in closing the road at Bab el Wad, gave the city's plight an immediacy which could not be ignored. "The High Commissioner," Ben-Gurion told his visitors, "gave us a solemn promise to keep the road open and he has failed to keep his word. Now it is up to us to open it."

Yadin proposed a scheme to Ben-Gurion that, by the standards to which the Haganah was accustomed, was bold and imaginative. It called for the use of four hundred men, far more than the Haganah had ever employed in a single operation.

Ben-Gurion blew up. "What do you mean, four hundred men?" he barked at Yadin. "That's not going to open anything up. The Arabs," he told his young planning officer, "understand the importance of Jerusalem even if you don't. They know if they can get Jerusalem and one hundred thousand Jews in their clutches it will be all over for us, and this state of ours will be finished before it's even begun. We can't save Jerusalem with these little efforts of four hundred men."

Call all the regional commanders of the Haganah to Tel Aviv immediately, he ordered Yadin. Together they would draw up a proper plan to relieve Jerusalem.

240

When Yadin and Shacham had left, Ben-Gurion went to his desk and drafted a message to the devoted Viennese he had ordered to Europe to buy arms four months before. If ever the Yishuv needed those arms, it was now, and there was no trace of the affection he bore Ehud Avriel in the angry words soon spurting to Europe over the transmitter "Shoshanna."

"Your arms will not save Jerusalem in Prague," Ben-Gurion declared. "Get them to Palestine any way you can."

19

"HANG ON TO JERUSALEM WITH YOUR TEETH."

JERUSALEM'S PLIGHT could be measured in a chart wrapped in an orange folder and locked into the upper right-hand desk drawer of Dov Joseph, the Canadian lawyer who had been ordered to prepare the city for a siege. It recorded the quantity of twenty-one basic commodities ranging from flour to laundry soap, tea and dried meat available in Jerusalem's warehouses. On Monday March 29, 1948, the day David Ben-Gurion called for a meeting of the commanders of the Haganah to open the road to Jerusalem, Joseph's chart showed that the city had on hand a five-day supply of margarine, four days of macaroni, ten days of dried meat.

There were no fresh meat, fruit or vegetables available in its markets. If eggs could be found, they were sold for twenty cents apiece. The city was living off its slender reserves of canned and packaged food: sardines, macaroni and dried beans. David Shaltiel's Haganah soldiers received a daily ration of four slices of bread covered with a syrupy spread called Cocozine, a bowl of soup, a can of sardines and a couple of potatoes. They were the best-fed people in Jerusalem.

Dov Joseph had avoided instituting rationing as long as possible so as not to create a climate of insecurity in the city. Now it began with a vengeance. Adults were allowed, for example, two hundred grams, about four slices, of bread a day. For children, Joseph proclaimed a special supplementary ration. It consisted of one egg and fifty grams of margarine a week.

Nor was food the only staple in short supply in the city. No kerosene had reached Jerusalem since February. Housewives had begun using DDT and Flit as cooking fuel. People learned how to improvise. Anyone with a patch of land or a window box tried to grow a few vegetables. For those who did not even own a flowerpot, a handful of erudite biologists at Hebrew University suggested hydroponics, a technique for growing vegetables in water without soil. Soaked cotton was recommended for nurturing seedlings.

In the cafés among the ruins of Ben Yehuda Street where off-duty

242

Haganah soldiers gathered, the standard drink was a "champagne" which would have curdled the palate of a French vintner. It was a mixture of a little white wine, lemon squash and a splash of soda water. Every Haganah soldier received three cigarettes a day; members of the elite Palmach got five. Usually a cigarette was passed from hand to hand among half a dozen soldiers so no precious wisp of smoke was wasted.

Occasionally help came from the enemy. One night Chaim Haller heard a soft whistle coming from beyond the barbed wire ringing his home in Katamon. Creeping to the sound in the dark, he found Salome, the elderly Arab woman who had been his maid for years. She passed him a few tomatoes through the wire, whispering, "I know you have nothing."

In view of the city's plight, the United Nations Security Council called for a truce in Jerusalem. The Mufti's Arab Higher Committee, however, sensing that victory was within its grasp, vehemently rejected the plea. The position of the city's one hundred thousand Jews would become untenable, its spokesman boasted, "when we cut off the water supply and put three hundred barricades between Jerusalem and the sea." For its part, the Jewish Agency gratefully announced it would accept a truce from any source whatsoever provided it left the approaches to the city open. The Agency had, in fact, tried once again on March 26 to get the Christian West to accept the obligations implicit in internationalizing Jerusalem, by calling for a force of ten thousand Danish and Norwegian troops. That request got no more response than had the similar pleas which preceded it.

Clearly, the Jews of Jerusalem could count only on their own determination to survive and on whatever help the rest of the Yishuv could bring them. Studying the figures in his little orange folder, Dov Joseph knew that rationing the supplies he had encouraged householders to build up at home could stretch a bit here, save a bit there. Those measures would only be palliatives, however. Unless the Haganah could reopen the road to the city, the one hundred thousand Jews of Jerusalem were going to be starved into submission long before the British left Palestine. There was no more concrete evidence of that than the last entry on the first line of Dov Joseph's chart. It showed that on Monday March 29, 1948, his warehouses contained exactly thirty-four tons and 226 kilograms of flour, enough to provide each Jewish resident of Jerusalem with just six slices of bread.

．　．　．

For a pastry cook from Toronto, Canada, Julius Lewis was demonstrating an extraordinary interest in the technical jargon of the three Americans beside him in the bar of Paris' Hotel California. They wore

243

identical dark-blue uniforms still bearing the brass buttons of the organization from which they had bought them second hand, Pan American World Airways. Together with an aging DC-4 hangared at Le Bourget Airport, they constituted the corporate executives, flying personnel, shareholders and capital resources of Ocean Trade Airways, a chartered airline incorporated in Panama. With their old DC-4, the three men made a modest if adventuresome living on the fringes of legality by flying items like nylons, cigarettes, perfume and whiskey around Europe.

They accepted Lewis' offer of a drink with the same alacrity with which they accepted his subsequent invitation to dinner at the Jour et Nuit, a restaurant a few doors away at the corner of the Champs-Elysées. There, over coffee, Lewis revealed that he was in fact an Englishman, a six-year veteran of the R.A.F., and that his real name was Freddy Fredkens. His occupation had little to do with baking pastries. He was an agent of the Haganah and he had received his current assignment from Ehud Avriel a few minutes before coming downstairs to the California bar. The presence of the three owners of the Ocean Trade Airways in the bar had been a fortunate coincidence for all concerned. Fredkens had a charter to propose. It would be the most highly paid assignment Ocean Trade Airways had ever undertaken. Fredkens suggested they fly, for ten thousand dollars, a cargo of Czech arms from Prague to Palestine.

One by one, the commanders of the Haganah crowded into the little second-floor study of the house on Keren Kayemet Street where three years earlier David Ben-Gurion had received his American diplomat heading home from Yalta. As each man arrived, Paula Ben-Gurion passed him a cup of tea. When the last of them had settled into place, Ben-Gurion began.

"We are here," he said, "to find a way to open the road to Jerusalem. We have three vital centers, Tel Aviv, Haifa and Jerusalem. We can still survive if we lose one of them—provided the one we lose is not Jerusalem. The Arabs have calculated correctly that the subjection of Jewish Jerusalem, its capture or its destruction would deal a severe and possibly fatal blow to the Yishuv and break its will and its ability to withstand Arab aggression. We are going to have to take risks. We have got to get the Jerusalem road open no matter how great the risks involved are."

To do it, the Haganah would have to do something it had never done before, he said. It would have to cast off the techniques of an underground army and operate for the first time in the open, in strength, in pursuit of a precise geographic objective. Ben-Gurion wanted fifteen hundred men assembled for the operation by taking the best troops and best equipment from each of the Haganah's regional commands.

When he had finished, there was a moment of silence. The forcefulness of Ben-Gurion's exposition, his concern for the safety of Jerusalem, had struck each man in the room. The need for the operation he proposed was evident; but so were the risks it involved. He was asking them to commit a terrible share of their men and arms to a single action. Every other front in Palestine would be critically exposed while it went on. If it involved the loss of a substantial number of arms it would be a disaster. Listening to him, Joseph Avidar, the Ukrainian miller's son running the Haganah arms stores, knew that the Jewish Army that night could count on barely ten thousand modern weapons in all of Palestine. The Golani Brigade in the exposed north had, according to Avidar's figures, 162 rifles and 188 Sten guns. Above all, after the loss of the Kfar Etzion convoy, the Haganah could not risk another defeat. Whatever its outcome, the operation that Ben-Gurion proposed would be a turning point in the struggle for Palestine.

At midnight, Ben-Gurion at their head, the Haganah commanders got into two cars and drove to their Red House headquarters to begin requisitioning the arms and men the operation would require. All night long, messengers on bicycles pedaled back and forth between Red House and their transmitter hidden behind a toilet in the basement of a nearby radio repair shop. As each message left, Joseph Avidar noted down the number of arms and rounds of ammunition it called for with the anxiety of a man watching his life's savings being swept from his bank account by some unforeseen emergency.

Shortly before dawn, one of the weary men in Red House proposed a name for the hazardous operation they had agreed to undertake. They would call it Operation Nachshon, after the first Hebrew who, according to legend, dared accept the challenge of the unknown by marching into the parting waters of the Red Sea during the flight from Egypt.

For a man who had come to Palestine to drive all the Jews into the sea, Fawzi el Kaukji was displaying a disarming civility toward his Jewish guest. Yehoshua Palmon, the astute Haganah intelligence agent, had finally realized his ambition. For almost two hours he had been squatting cross-legged on the floor of Kaukji's headquarters in the village of Nuri Shams, chatting amiably with him about theology, the history of the Middle East, and the conflict between their peoples. Now Palmon delicately turned the subject to the Mufti.

To his surprise, Kaukji, despite the presence of a dozen of his subordinates, launched into a bitter tirade against "the manner in which the Husseinis murder people." Haj Amin, he said, had "political ambitions in Jordan and Syria which are not in the interests of the Arab nation and which every patriotic Arab should oppose."

Palmon cautiously inserted Abdul Khader's name into the conversation. Abdul Khader, Kaukji said, was scheming against him, too. Then he let slip two sentences which in themselves justified all the risks Palmon had taken in striving for this meeting. "I don't care if your people fight him," Kaukji told Palmon. "In fact, I hope you do fight him and give him a good lesson. If you do, he is not going to be able to count on me for any help."

With that, the Arab general launched into a further, astonishingly frank declaration. "I must avenge myself for the defeat of my forces at Tirat Zvi," he said. "I must fight you and beat you in the Valley of Jezreel in a few days." Palmon was sure Kaukji would be true to his word. He had realized that Kaukji, like the Mufti, had political ambitions, and victories were the fuel he needed to sustain them.

Back in his own base, Palmon reflected on the extraordinary conversation. In addition to what Kaukji had told him, he had come away with one distinct impression. His stay in Germany had influenced Kaukji far more than Palmon had realized. The man who prized the Iron Cross above all other decorations wanted desperately to run the kind of battle the Germans ran, to be a German general. The only problem was that Kaukji's soldiers were Arabs, not Germans, and they were trained for guerrilla actions, not blitzkriegs. For the moment one thing remained to be done. That night every Jewish settlement in the valley of Jezreel was placed on the alert.

Operation Nachshon, the drive to open the road to Jerusalem, rested on a simple strategy. Since it was clear that the road could not be reopened by ramming bigger convoys into Bab el Wad, Nachshon would try to temporarily establish a Jewish-held corridor on both sides of the road, six miles wide in the plains, one to two miles broad in the hills beyond. That belt of land would encompass the dozen Arab villages upon whose support Abdul Khader Husseini depended in his campaign to close the road.

From Deir Mahsir in the west to Kastel and Kolonia in the east, that chain of villages represented a Palestine far older than the British mandate and Zionism's early pioneers. Their stone huts, bleached the color of stale milk chocolate by decades of sun, clung like barnacles to the desolate hills of Judea. Scattered around them, sad little beads of broken-stone fences terraced the land in a vain effort to fix the few patches of topsoil that still remained on to the hillside. Those villages grew figs and olives, and, a few months before, the hands that were now striving to close the road to Jerusalem had cultivated the vegetables that had nourished the city. On the hillsides the villagers pastured sheep destined for the animal souk of Herod's Gate in Jerusalem during the Moslem feast of Bairam marking the end of Ramadan.

Few of the villages had electricity; none of them had water or telephones. The primary means of communication between them remained horseback and foot. Their social structure was primitive, but it had proven impervious to the mandate's efforts to change it. Two buildings dominated each town, a mosque and the home of the mukhtar, the headman, a post usually passed from father to son. The mukhtar ran the village, and in his house the men gathered daily to sip coffee and argue and, if they were fortunate, to listen to news of great consequence on a battery-powered radio.

Abdul Khader's bands could not operate without those villages as their base. They provided him food and a pool of supplementary manpower that could be swiftly called into battle. While the Haganah was moving convoys up to Jerusalem through its Operation Nachshon corridor, the Palmach's Har-el Brigade under Yitzhak Rabin, a young officer of whom the world would hear a great deal two decades later, would have the mission of razing those villages. By "not leaving stone on stone and driving all the people away, there was not going to be a village for anybody to come back to," Rabin realized, and "without those villages the Arab bands were not going to be able to operate effectively any more." Then, when the operation was finished, the Haganah could safely go back to the convoy system.

Shimon Avidan, the commander of the Palmach's Givati Brigade, one of Orde Wingate's first pupils, a heavyset man who had spent the war training Palestinian saboteurs to drop behind the German lines, was assigned to command Nachshon. Despite the requisitions from the regional commands, Avidan's arms situation remained crucial. Many of the men assigned to his operation were young recruits just out of training. Iska Shadmi, one of his company commanders, recalled that the troops assigned to him were "like kids on a youth movement outing. They came with their suitcases and boxes, they were romantic boys and girls. They carried no ammunition, but they had their possessions in small cases, the girls all with their books of Rachel, the poetess of the Kinneret."

Shadmi lined them up and informed them that henceforth each person would carry just one knapsack. "Decide what you want, flowers or your clothes," he announced. Some of the girls started crying. "In a few days, with these kids, ten rifles and four machine guns," Shadmi thought, "I am going to have to go to war for a road to Jerusalem."

The Arabs of Beit Darras had shown little interest in the run-down airfield handed over to them by its departing owners, the R.A.F. Its single landing strip was pocked with holes and scarred with clumps of grass. There was no control tower, no electricity, no fuel pump, no radio. Its only equipment consisted of two small wooden hangars. Yet as soon as darkness fell one night at the beginning of April, a column of trucks, lights out, drew up to the airstrip. Half of the men they carried silently set to work filling in the holes on the runway, while the others took up defensive positions around the field.

As soon as the strip was serviceable, a chain of electric lights hooked to a portable generator was strung around the field. Then the men unloaded dozens of jerricans of aviation gasoline and stacked them in a hangar. Finally someone rigged up a control tower. It consisted of a portable radio transmitter set in the back of a truck. At ten o'clock, after just two hours of intensive efforts, the renovated airport of Beit Darras was ready to receive its first traffic.

The radio operator began sending out his call signal. It was *"Hassida,"* Hebrew for stork. If the Arabs had not been interested in the airfield, the Haganah was. Aaron Remez, the R.A.F. veteran who had promised his next-door neighbor David Ben-Gurion that "salvation comes from the sky," had borrowed the Arab airfield for a daring one-night operation. His hastily repaired airstrip was designed to share in the salvation of Jewish Jerusalem.

Beside Remez, his radio operator repeated their insistent call, *"Hassida."* There was no reply. As the minutes dragged into hours and his calls to "Stork" remained unheard, a gradual sense of despair gripped Remez. Along the runway, the men who had worked so hard preparing the strip sat silently in the darkness listening for the sound of an airplane engine. They heard only the wind.

The DC-4 for which they were waiting was miles away, droning steadily southward under an intermittently cloudy sky. The crew and owners of Ocean Trade Airways had come a long way from the bar of Paris' Hotel California. Their first stop after leaving Le Bourget Airport had been Prague. Ehud Avriel had been waiting for them to supervise the loading of the first of his arms destined to go into action against the enemy. Manifested as agricultural machinery bound for Addis Ababa, they were packed in the fuselage behind the crew, one hundred and forty Czech M-34 machine guns taken out of their crates to save weight, and thousands of rounds of ammunition.

A fourth crewman had also joined the three Ocean Trade Airways owners—Amy Cooper, a Palestinian R.A.F. veteran with hours of flying time in the Middle East. The well-trained Cooper had been appalled by the condition of the DC-4. Its radio was so weak that it couldn't even receive the weather bulletins. Their celestial navigation had been hindered by a substantial cloud cover over most of their route, and Cooper feared it had been a highly approximate effort. Now, six hours out of Prague, they stumbled through the sky searching for a glimpse of the Palestine coast.

Suddenly the pilot poked Cooper in the ribs. "Hey!" he shouted. "We're there! There's Tel Aviv!"

The R.A.F. veteran stared down at the lights coming up under the starboard wing. Cooper was not a chauvinist, but the lights blinking below seemed to him rather feeble for the Jewish city. He grabbed a map and studied it intently.

"My God!" he yelled after a moment. "That's Port Said! We're heading straight into Egypt!"

The pilot abruptly swung the plane northward. Thirty minutes later they were over Tel Aviv. Cooper picked up the despairing calls for "Stork" and ordered the field to flash its lights three times when they heard the sound of the plane's engines. A few minutes later, gobbling up every inch of the little runway, the Ocean Trade Airways DC-4 settled down at Beit Darras.

From his window, Cooper could see the men alongside the runway jumping up and down at the miraculous sight of the plane gliding to a landing on their strip. Seconds later they swarmed over the aircraft. The astonished Italian, Irishman and Jew from New York who had flown arms to Beit Darras as they might fly cigarettes to Naples were acclaimed like heroes, a greeting markedly in contrast to that which they were accustomed to receiving.

Shimon Avidan, the commander of Operation Nachshon, expressed his own deep relief in a different manner. He climbed into the DC-4's fuselage and began to kiss his one hundred and forty new machine guns one by one.

Samir Jabour was the son of a cobbler in Jaffa, a lean young man with a luxuriant black pompadour, tawny skin and melancholy brown eyes. Jabour had not wasted his youth at his father's cobbler's bench. He lived at night, in the half-lit little bars along the sea where Jaffa blended into Tel Aviv and sex did not distinguish between Arab and Jew. On one of his rounds, he met a dowdy, unhappy brunette named Rachel P. Despite her appearance, Jabour rarely left her side after their first encounter. It was her occupation that interested the young Arab. Rachel was a secretary at the Jewish Agency in Tel Aviv. Jabour was a clandestine agent of the Arab Higher Committee.

Twenty-four hours after Ehud Avriel's plane had made its brief visit to Beit Darras, Jabour was able to inform Abdul Khader Husseini's headquarters that the Jews had held a major meeting in Tel Aviv to prepare a "big onslaught" on the road to Jerusalem. They would try to drive the Arabs from the heights above Bab el Wad. They were going to use an "enormous" number of men to do it and there were reports that they had received new arms to help them. For an intelligence service as primitive as the Arab Higher Committee's, it was an astonishingly accurate report.

Abdul Khader had been expecting a major Jewish effort on the road. His foes, he knew, could not allow him to isolate the city. What alarmed him more was Jabour's report of "new arms." With the exception of the arms seized at Nebi Daniel, his armament was the same heteroclite collection of weapons with which he had started his campaign, supplemented by occasional gleanings from the Western Desert. Given his great numerical superiority, that had been enough to keep the poorly armed Jerusalem Haganah on the defensive. A major assault from the coast with new arms was a different matter.

Abdul Khader immediately set out for Damascus to demand the delivery of the modern weapons he had been promised for weeks. Husseini and his aide Emile Ghory found the atmosphere in the Syrian capital "depressing." The United States' trusteeship proposal had prompted the Arab leaders, it seemed to Ghory, to "overreact as always, to behave as though the war was won and they could now throw up their hands and wait for the General Assembly to save them." The rivalries dividing the Arabs were as intense as ever, and Abdul Khader noted a growing hostility to his kinsman Haj Amin.

He opened his first meeting in Damascus by describing the military situation. Then he revealed his information on the forthcoming Jewish attack. The Haganah's aim, he predicted, would be to capture the hilltop village of Kastel, because, he said, "whoever holds Kastel controls the road to Jerusalem." Once the Haganah had succeeded in reopening the road to the city, they would be free to strike at Jaffa and Haifa, he declared.

"We are prepared to fight to the last man," Abdul Khader vowed, "but we have no effective arms. You have been promising us modern arms for months, but all you have sent us is a lot of camel shit from the Western Desert." Give him artillery and modern rifles, he pleaded, and his guerrillas would turn back the Jewish attacks.

His pleas left Ismail Safwat Pasha, the Iraqi named to head the Arab League's military effort, unmoved. The regular Arab officers around Safwat did not esteem Abdul Khader's capacities as highly as did his Jewish foes. Nor did his allegiance to the Mufti encourage their confidence. His men, Safwat told Abdul Khader, were not experienced enough with artillery to be trusted with it. The Jews, he said, would probably overrun their positions and capture the guns. As for arms, the shipload of Czech rifles heading for Beirut was already earmarked for Kaukji's Liberation Army. Abdul Khader would have to get along with what he had. In any event, Safwat assured him, 'if the Haganah captures Haifa or Jaffa, we'll hand them back to you in two weeks."

Normally Abdul Khader was an undemonstrative man, but at Safwat's words he quite literally turned red with fury. Seizing a folder of papers from the desk between them, he smashed it over the Iraqi's head. "You are a traitor!" he shouted.

"You will hang on to Jerusalem with your teeth," David Ben-Gurion growled to Dov Joseph. His tone was more controlled than Abdul Khader Husseini's in Damascus had been, but the passion behind it was no less intense. The Canadian lawyer had flown from Jerusalem to Tel Aviv on Ben-Gurion's order, in the fragile Piper Cub that linked the city to the coast. The success of Operation Nachshon would be measured, Ben-Gurion knew, by the amount of food thrust into Jerusalem while the road was open. He wanted one man in charge, one man who would be totally responsible, who would see to it that at all costs Jerusalem would not be forced in the future to give in from lack of food.

He had designated Joseph as that man. He would have absolute authority, Ben-Gurion told him. He instructed the Jewish Agency's treasurer, Eliezer Kaplan, to make available whatever sums Joseph needed.

"When can you start?" Ben-Gurion asked.

"When do you want?" replied Joseph.

"Right now!" said Ben-Gurion.

It was after midnight. Joseph got up, filled with a terrible sense of apprehension. Ben-Gurion's charge had been powerful and bruising, and Joseph realized the problem was now his alone. "Good God!" he thought. "How horrible if I don't succeed."

Joseph took over an office in a nearby building and called in a number of Haganah men. They worked all night. The Canadian calculated that if he could get three thousand tons of food to Jerusalem, he could feel safe. He gave his Haganah colleagues a rough outline of what Jerusalem needed. They, in turn, gave Joseph a list of all the food wholesalers in Tel Aviv. At dawn, carrying an order from Joseph, Haganah men placed a seal on every food warehouse in the city. Not a can of beans was to leave them until Joseph had first made his selections for Jerusalem.

Two Haganah veterans of the British Army, Harry Jaffe and Bronislav Bar-Shemer, were assigned the job of organizing the convoys that would carry Joseph's supplies to Jerusalem. The Canadian told them they would need a minimum of three hundred trucks. After two days of scouring Tel Aviv's trucking firms, Bar-Shemer had managed to assemble barely sixty vehicles. To get the rest, he chose a simple expedient. He decided to hijack them.

"I took the Haganah boys from their training camps and sent them to the busy intersections," he later recalled. "They started stopping every truck that came along. I don't know who was more scared, the drivers or the soldiers pointing their guns at them, telling them to drive to a big empty field at Kiryat Meir."

Every time a score of trucks had collected in his playing field, Bar-Shemer formed their loudly protesting drivers into a convoy and, under the command of his teenage soldiers and their Sten guns, packed them off to the assembly point for the Nachshon convoys, an abandoned British Army camp called Kfar Bilu. The drivers were the most disgruntled group of human beings Bar-Shemer had ever seen. "They hated our guts," he remembered. "None of them had any idea of what was happening." Some of them, Bar-Shemer knew, "had wives who were giving birth and here we'd kidnapped them at high noon or in the middle of night." Fortunately for Bar-Shemer, most of those drivers owned their trucks, and the vehicles represented their livelihood. They were not inclined to abandon them to Bar-Shemer, not even for a wife in childbirth.

Feeding his group of captive drivers soon became a serious problem. A firm believer in direct action, Bar-Shemer walked into one of the Tel Aviv's most popular restaurants, Chaskal's. "The Jewish nation needs you," he told its owner, Yecheskel Weinstein. In about three minutes' time Bar-Shemer explained what he required and placed a truck and a squad of soldiers at Weinstein's disposition. It was eleven o'clock in the morning. At five o'clock in the afternoon Weinstein was ladling out a hot meal to four hundred men at Kfar Bilu.

20

SIX WORDS ON A BUMPER

THE LEGIONS of Rome had been the first to fortify the rocky outcropping at the summit of the steep slope up which the men stealthily picked their way. To the north, across the gorges of Bab el Wad, was the peak of Nebi Samuel, where, according to legend, the Prophet had sat in judgment on the fallen nation of Israel, the Maccabees had fasted before their assault on Jerusalem, and Richard the Lionhearted had wept at his first view of the Holy City. To the east, the naked eye could glimpse Jerusalem's outskirts. Just below the 2,500-foot-high peak, as exposed and vulnerable as an open nerve, lay the road to Jerusalem.

For twenty centuries, as a Roman camp, a Crusader castle, a Turkish bunker, that lonely, windswept promontory has been a strategic height, the natural guardian of Jerusalem's western approaches. Now, on this dark and rainy April night, the 180 men of the Palmach's Har-el Brigade climbing through its groves of fig trees were fresh proof of its eternal vocation. A few feet above their heads slept Kastel, the village that Abdul Khader had prophesied in Damascus would be the Haganah's first objective.

Operation Nachshon's plan called for two preliminary operations: a diversionary attack near Ramle, to lure back into the town the Arab guerrillas deployed north of the Jerusalem road just before Bab el Wad, and the capture of Kastel.

Uzi Narciss, one of the two men who had "bombed" the attackers at Kfar Etzion, posted a machine gun at either end of the village. Just after midnight he attacked. The fifty-odd armed men in the village were no match for Narciss' force. Rounding up the villagers, they abandoned Kastel and fled into the night. For the first time since partition, an Arab village was in Jewish hands.

Shortly after noon the following day, Saturday, April 3, seventy men of the Jerusalem Haganah arrived to relieve Narciss' Palmach force. Their commander was a stern curly-haired Latvian named Mordechai Gazit who aspired to be one of the Jewish nation's first diplomats. Narciss ordered Gazit to set up a defensive perimeter around the area, then to destroy the village so that the Arabs could no longer use it as a base for their forays on the road.

When word of Kastel's fall reached Damascus, Abdul Khader Husseini immediately ordered his Jerusalem headquarters to retake the village. Once again the messengers of Kamal Irekat rushed from hamlet to hamlet, this time calling for men to help free Kastel.

By sundown, Irekat was ready to begin his attack. The procedure was simple. He shouted, *"Nashamdi!* Let those who are ready go!"* and started to run for the first Jewish positions, in the Tzuba rock quarry in front of Kastel. Four hundred men followed him, crying, *"Allah akhbar!* God is great!"* Many insisted on wearing their white kaffiyehs even though they were easily visible in the darkness, because tradition held it a shame for a Bedouin to remove his headdress in battle. They swept the Jews from their trenches and forced them back into the quarry buildings. All night the Arabs tried unsuccessfully to drive them out of that refuge.

The arrival at dawn of reinforcements under Ibrahim Abou Dayieh, the Hebron shepherd commanding the Arabs in Katamon, recharged their spirits. A new assault drove the Haganah from the quarry buildings. Then, with another whooping rush, Irekat's men swept the Jews back to the outskirts of Kastel itself. By now, however, the Arabs were exhausted. Most of them had been without food for twenty-four hours.

Irekat sent messengers to the villages near Kastel for help. Within an hour, singing and chanting the undulating Arab war cry behind their veils, the black-robed village women came streaming up to the battle site balancing on their heads baskets of eggs, leban cheese, olives, tomatoes and flat round loaves of Arabic bread.

The attack resumed. Gazit's men had not had time to start destroying the village, and now they turned each house into a strongpoint to hold off Irekat's attackers. Halfway through this assault, the Arabs suddenly ran out of ammunition. Just as no one had thought of food in the headlong rush to Kastel, so, too, no one had been concerned with the ammunition supply. Another swarm of messengers fanned out across the countryside.

John Glubb, commander of the Arab Legion, saw one of them in Ramallah running through the streets shouting, "Has anyone ammunition for sale? I pay cash." Before the Englishman's astonished eyes, he bought two hundred rounds of ammunition, some Turkish, some German, some English, then leaped into his car and set off to repeat the process in the next town.

By sunset, enough new ammunition had been hauled up to the outskirts of Kastel on muleback to allow the assault to begin again. Shortly after midnight, with his men within hand-grenade range of Gazit's seventy beleaguered Haganah troops, Irekat was wounded. His only medic, a hospital employee from Bethlehem, treated the leader with the sole first-aid kit available to his five hundred villagers. Then, over Irekat's loud protests, the medic strapped him onto a mule for the trip back to Jerusalem.

Irekat knew well the psychology of his village warriors. Products of the hierarchical structure of their villages, they tended to magnify the importance of the leader, to erect around his person a kind of cult. Guided by an able man, those villagers were capable of acts of great bravery. Without a galvanic presence to rally them, however, their organization risked rapid disintegration.

As Irekat had feared it would, that was exactly what happened on that night of Sunday, April 4. Gazit and his men, bracing for the Arabs' final assault, suddenly saw their foes start to wander off the battlefield. They were going home to their villages. By dawn Monday, barely a hundred of them remained. Kastel was still firmly in Jewish hands.

• • •

Three men whispered together like conspirators in the predawn darkness on Jerusalem's King George V Avenue just opposite the shuttered windows of Yarden's coffeehouse. They represented the Stern Gang, the Irgun and the Haganah. The Haganah man noted with satisfaction that there was no one in the deserted street to observe their conversation. Yeshurun Schiff had every reason to cloak their meeting in secrecy. He was the adjutant of a man who bore a special loathing for the two dissident groups, David Shaltiel. Yet Schiff had invited them to this darkened street corner to ask them to come to Shaltiel's aid.

The Jerusalem commander's forces were stretched so thin he had no reserves to relieve Gazit's harassed men at Kastel and those in an equally difficult situation at the Jewish settlement of Motza below the captured Arab village. Schiff wanted the Stern Gang and the Irgun to employ their forces in an attack on the rock quarries at Tzuba and thus relieve Arab pressure on Kastel and Motza.

As Schiff expected, his request did not arouse the sympathy of the two organizations. Neither was inclined to come to the aid of a man whom they considered almost as much of an enemy as the Arabs. Jealous of their independence, wary of Shaltiel's motives, they had maintained their refusal to cooperate with his command. They told Schiff they would give him an answer the following night. If they agreed, however, there would be a price to pay. They would expect the Haganah to reward them with a substantial supply of arms and grenades.

The following night, the two organizations conveyed their agreement to Schiff and claimed the materiel promised them. Neither group, however, had any intention of attacking the rock quarries at Tzuba. Yoshua Zetler, leader of the Stern Gang, and Mordechai Ra'anan, chief of the Irgun, wanted Shaltiel's additional arms to secure a victory of their own, a dramatic victory that would demonstrate their dynamism to Jewish Jerusalem and force its leadership to recognize their claims in the city. They had settled upon a target for their action. Its reputation, its size and proximity, promised a victory as easy as it would be dramatic. It was a community of stonecutters on Jerusalem's western outskirts, the village of Deir Yassin to which Alia Darwish had been borne for her wedding a few days before.

Redolent with the stench of rotting onions, the dumpy little tramp steamer sailed up to a berth in Tel Aviv harbor. A sniff of her cargo hold assured the port's British customs inspectors of the accuracy of the S.S. *Nora*'s manifest. As soon as they cleared her for unloading, a horde of stevedores swarmed over the ship. Frantically they clawed aside the onions to get at her real cargo, thousands of Czech rifles and machine guns. Chartered after so many difficulties, Ehud Avriel's first freighter had arrived with providential timing. Operation Nachshon was due to begin in just twenty-four hours. The *Nora*'s arms could mean the difference between victory and defeat in the hours ahead.

As fast as the stevedores could pull them out of the *Nora*'s hold, the weapons—still enclosed in a thick coat of grease—were packed onto trucks and rushed to the Haganah units assigned to Nachshon. Iska Shadmi, who had ordered the recruits of his company to choose between clothes or flowers, got his consignment at ten o'clock at night. He had nothing with which to clean off the grease, and his unit was scheduled to go into action before dawn. Like many others of his generation of Palmachniks, Shadmi had been nourished on a book on the conquest of Kazakhstan, *The Men of Pompillo*. Seek the dramatic, the unexpected solution, was its message.

Shadmi pondered a moment. Then he called his company together. He ordered the men to strip off their undershorts. That solved the problem of cloths to wipe off the grease. The girls he told to unravel strands of barbed wire so that they would have a tool to ram the cloths down the rifle barrels.

For the first time since he had joined the Palmach, Shadmi had enough ammunition, but he had nothing in which to carry it. He ordered his recruits to fill their socks with cartridges, then tie them to their belts.

Haim Laskov, a British Army veteran commanding another infantry company, received a consignment of MG-34 machine guns. None of his men knew how to fire them. Laskov found a former British Army machine-gunner to demonstrate them for the company. To Laskov's horror, he discovered that the guns would fire only one round at a time. Laskov rushed a car to Tel Aviv to locate an ordnance expert. While his men awaited the order to move out, the expert scratched away on the guns' defective firing pins with an old file, putting as many of them as he could into working order.

Assembled into three battalions of five hundred men each, the Jewish forces opened their attack at nine o'clock in the evening of April 5. The first companies quickly seized an abandoned British Army base and two Arab villages in the area adjacent to the convoy's planned departure point. The men behind them moved up into the hills above Bab el Wad to seize the heights dominating the road. They encountered ferocious resistance from the Arabs. The villages of Saris and Beit Mahsir repulsed their attacks, but the Jewish soldiers were finally able to seize positions between the villages and the road.

Farther east, the key village of Kastel was already in Haganah hands, but just beyond it Arab forces crossed the road and attacked the Jewish settlement of Motza. Their action threatened to cut at that one vital point the highway now open along the rest of its length.

Despite the setbacks, the operation's opening phase was a success. By midnight, the gorge of Bab el Wad and its flanks were controlled by the Haganah. The order was radioed back to start the first convoy through.

The former British Army camp of Kfar Bilu swarmed with Bronislav Bar-Shemer's kidnapped truck drivers, mechanics, Haganah men, all milling around the stocks of goods commandeered on Dov Joseph's orders from Tel Aviv's warehouses. To load them onto the waiting trucks, the Haganah had rounded up a team of Salonikan stevedores from the port of Tel Aviv. Squat, heavily muscled men whose leaders had ordered them a special diet of sardines, rice, apples and cheese, they set to work by the flickering glare of torches.

"It was like an automatic chain belt," the wondering Tel Aviv restaurateur Yecheskel Weinstein recalled. "Every five minutes they loaded a truck. Two young boys stood beside them playing a guitar while they worked. Greek music filled the night and those stevedores kept heaving crates and sacks of food to one another without a break in their rhythm."

257

Standing by the side of the road in the darkness, Bar-Shemer watched the trucks set off. There was an incredible variety of vehicles in that line passing before his eyes. There were vans from the Tnuvah dairy, Bedfords, Fords, factory trucks, delivery vans, heavy Mack dump trucks, open kibbutz farm trucks, White semitrailers, Rio hay wagons. They came in every size, shape and color imaginable, many of them splashed with posters advertising soap, baby food, a kosher butcher in Haifa, a brick kiln in Ramat Gan or a shoe factory in Tel Aviv. The light ones came first. The heavier, slower vehicles brought up the rear, each rigged out with a steel cable to take in tow the trucks that faltered along the way.

None of them had its lights on. Bar-Shemer had seen to that. His men had meticulously removed the bulbs from every headlight in the convoy so that no panicky flick of a light switch would illuminate the column for Arab snipers. Their escorts swung on board as they rolled past the kibbutz of Hulda. Iska Shadmi landed in a load of potatoes and quickly dug himself a foxhole.

Looking up at the sullen, fearful faces of those drivers his men had kidnapped a few days before, Bar-Shemer thought, "If looks could kill, I'd be dead." From his vantage point he followed their progress, a long column stretching out in the moonlight like an immense caterpillar. "The delicious odor of orange blossoms," he noted, "filled the night." Ahead, the road ran straight and flat for six miles up to a gentle hilltop rising on the left. There the steeple and the ochre façade of the Trappist Monastery of Latrun towered above a stand of olive trees. Then an easy arc to the right past the monastery's vineyards brought the column to the foothills marking the entry to Bab el Wad. Waiting for the last truck to leave Hulda so that he could fall in at the end of the convoy, Bar-Shemer noted far off in the distance the echo of sporadic rifle fire. "They're moving into Bab el Wad," he thought.

Riding at the head of the column, Harry Jaffe, the convoy commander, heard three of those rounds clang into the panel of his new blue 1947 Ford. He prayed they were only the work of an isolated sniper. The trucks strung out behind him had none of the protective armor of the vehicles that had been used previously on the Jerusalem road. Huddled in his pile of potatoes, Iska Shadmi angrily scanned the dark forests above him for some sign of a foe. All the way up to Jerusalem, he would see only one human being in those pines, an old Arab with a white beard.

As Jaffe had hoped, apart from a few snipers there were no Arab forces in the hills. Shaking the night with the steady drone of their engines, the trucks ground slowly up the pass toward Jerusalem. Some

258

lurched along with two or three tires flattened by sniper fire. From others, overheated by the long, slow trip, Jaffe saw jets of steam squirting into the air. All along the column, like huntsmen spurring on a pack of hounds, his men shouted, "*Kadima, Kadima!* Forward! Forward!" to the harried truckers.

In Jerusalem, the news that a convoy was coming rippled through the city. Hundreds of people ran down Jaffa Road to watch it come in: women in bathrobes and slippers and pincurlers, schoolchildren, religious Jews coming from morning service in the synagogues, their prayer shawls still draped over their shoulders. They hung out of windows, clambered onto rooftops and balconies, to watch in awe and gratitude. They sang and cheered and clapped as the convoy hove into sight. They were a desperate, hungry people existing that week on a ration of two ounces of margarine, a quarter of a pound of potatoes and a quarter of a pound of dried meat. For two weeks not a single vehicle had reached the city, and now they were rumbling forward in a steady stream as far back as the eye could see—dozens of trucks bumper to bumper, their swaying vans crammed with supplies.

Mature men watching them from the curb wept openly. Children scrambled up onto the trucks with flowers. Women sprang onto dashboards to kiss the drivers. In front of the Sephardic Home for the Aged an elderly woman embraced Yehuda Lash, and the young veteran of so many Jerusalem convoys sighed, "If only it could have been her daughter." Riding on his pile of potatoes, Iska Shadmi remembered all his lessons in the Palmach and the youth movement about "how, if we were strong, we would become a nation." Suddenly, seeing those grateful Jerusalemites, that theory became reality for Shadmi. Even the sullen truck drivers Bar-Shemer had forced to make this journey were transformed. Rolling down the corridor of ecstatic human beings, they understood they had saved a city.

Above all else, one memory would remain engraved upon the minds of those Jerusalemites watching the convoy stream down the streets of their city that happy April morning. It was the first glimpse many of them had of the convoy—the front bumper of the blue Ford of Harry Jaffe.

On it, Jaffe had painted six words: "If I forget thee, O Jerusalem . . ."

21

"ONE OF THE ARABS WE KILLED LAST NIGHT"

BARELY A MILE and a half from the happy throngs welcoming Operation Nachshon's first convoy to Jerusalem, in the bedroom of a house in the Arab quarter of Bab el Zahiri near Herod's Gate, an embittered Arab leader wrote to his wife in Cairo. Abdul Khader Husseini had returned to Jerusalem just in time to learn that his foes had broken at last the stranglehold he had so patiently fastened on the city. In the back of his car were fifty rifles given him by the Syrian Army and three Bren guns purchased with his own money in the souks of Damascus. They were the only modern weapons he had been able to obtain on his trip to Syria.

Abdul Khader's last days in Damascus had been as disillusioning as the earlier ones had been. Despite the angry conclusion of their first encounter, he had met again with Safwat Pasha. It was during one of their conferences that the news of Irekat's failure at Kastel arrived.

"If your men cannot retake Kastel," Safwat Pasha had remarked, "then we will ask Kaukji to do it."

Abdul Khader had made still another plea for weapons. The answer was the fifty rifles he had brought back to Jerusalem, offered not by Safwat but by Syrian President Shukri al Kuwatli. "The blood of Palestine and its people shall be on your head," Abdul Khader had angrily told the unyielding Iraqi general as he stamped out of their meeting. Late that night, he had left Damascus.

Now, in his brother's Jerusalem home, he finished his letter to his wife. His words were shaped in the ornate rhetoric of his language, but they were an accurate reflection of those traits and emotions which had made Abdul Khader Husseini such an effective leader of his people.

MY DARLING WAJIHA,

We have written great and glorious pages of history, and this was not easy but only with great sacrifice and efforts day and night. When we act,

every man forgets himself and his relatives and his sons, his food and
his sleeping. . . .

The enemy is strong, but we will reach the final victory, if God wills.
[*inch' Allah*]

Then he slipped into the envelope a poem he had written to his son the
night before in Damascus.

This land of brave men
Is our ancestors' land.
On this land
The Jews have no claim.
How can I sleep
When the enemy is upon it?
Something burns in my heart.
My country is calling.

When he had finished, Abdul Khader summoned one of his lieutenants,
a wiry schoolteacher named Bajhat Abou Gharbieh. Never had Abou
Gharbieh seen his chief so bitter. "We have been betrayed," he said.
His last sight in Syria, Abdul Khader recounted, was a warehouse full of
arms at Al Mazah Airport, for his rival Kaukji. "They have left us three
choices," he remarked angrily. "We can go to Iraq and live in disguise.
We can commit suicide. Or we can die fighting here."

He told Abou Gharbieh to send him two of the Haganah armored
cars captured at Nebi Daniel and to order Ibrahim Abou Dayieh with one
hundred of his men to meet him at the Tzuba rock quarry. Whatever
happened, Abdul Khader had his mind set on one thing. He was going
to take Kastel back even if he had to lead the attack himself.

At Kastel, Mordechai Gazit and his seventy Haganah defenders were exhausted. They had been under constant fire for four days. Abdul Khader's
attack against them began at ten o'clock on the evening of April 7. The
Arab leader had almost three hundred men. He positioned most of them,
under Abou Dayieh, directly in front of the village. The others, split into
two groups, he posted on the flanks. To replace the cannon Safwat had
denied him, Abdul Khader had four mortars operated by a quartet of
British deserters.

Gazit and his men suddenly found themselves caught in a devastating
barrage of fire from those mortars. Before it had lifted, Abou Dayieh and

261

his followers were moving forward against their advance posts. After an hour of heavy firing, the Arabs had driven Gazit's men from the first row of houses in the village and were barely one hundred yards from his key position in the house of the village's mukhtar. Sensing his foes weakening, the Hebron shepherd sent a messenger to Abdul Khader. Then he sent forward a mining party to dynamite the mukhtar's house.

A few minutes later, Gazit heard his troops in the house call for help. Taking a party of men, Gazit scrambled toward the position. No one was there. Just in front of it, he stumbled on a big tin can, the kind used by the Arabs to carry olive oil. It was filled with a reddish powder, and attached to it he found an unignited fuse. Obviously his men's cries had frightened off Abou Dayieh's mining party. Reassured, Gazit returned to his command post.

As he slipped inside, he heard his sergeant major, Meyer Karmiol, scramble to his feet on its little balcony. "Who's there?" he called in English.

"It's us, boys!" came the answer in Arabic. Through the window, Gazit watched Karmiol arm his Sten gun and fire a burst along the slope before the house. Twenty-five yards down the incline, Gazit saw the outline of a body falling to the ground.

Despite the failure of his mining party, Abou Dayieh pressed his attack against Gazit's positions all night long. Just before dawn, a messenger arrived from his eastern flank. Instead of reinforcements, however, he brought bad news: a party of Haganah men was moving up the hill behind Kastel.

Abou Dayieh had had no response from his message to Abdul Khader. Dejectedly he decided to withdraw. For the fourth time, the Arabs had failed to reconquer Kastel.

Meanwhile a dozen Palmach, led by Uzi Narciss, the original conqueror of Kastel, finally reached Gazit with a welcome treasure, fifty thousand rounds of ammunition from the S.S. *Nora.*

The two men talked for a few minutes. Narciss promised Gazit that that the Palmach would relieve his weary men at noon. Then, in the graying dawn, Narciss noticed a man lying dead on the hillside below them.

"Who's that?" he asked.

"One of the Arabs we killed last night," Gazit replied.

Narciss crawled down the slope and rolled the dead man over onto his back. Methodically he began to go through his pockets looking for his papers. He found little: a driver's license, one Palestine pound, some notes on a conversation with a United States consul and, in the breast pocket of the shirt, a miniature leather-bound Koran.

As soon as he had withdrawn his men, Ibrahim Abou Dayieh began looking for Abdul Khader. He was nowhere to be found. Thinking he might have gone back to Jerusalem for reinforcements, he sent men to the city searching for him. He was not there. The rumor spread that he was missing. The news leaped from village to village with that special alacrity linked to bad tidings. From Hebron to Ramallah men set out for Kastel to join the search for their leader. In Jerusalem the souks emptied. Everyone who could get a rifle, it seemed, rushed from the city. The price of ammunition shot up to a shilling a bullet. The National Bus Company canceled its services and devoted its vehicles to hauling volunteers to Kastel. Taxicab drivers, truckers, the owners of private cars offered their services to get men to the battle site.

By midmorning, Mordechai Gazit and his exhausted soldiers were under fire from all sides. Before long almost two thousand Arabs were pouring fire onto Kastel. Gazit and his men hardly knew where to shoot. A mystical fervor seemed to be driving their assailants. Shouting, brandishing their arms, their black-and-white checkered kaffiyehs bobbing up everywhere, they surged irresistibly forward.

The ammunition Narciss had brought was tied up in bundles and tossed from window to window, since it was impossible to step outside. Gazit himself staggered through the building kicking his sleeping men to their feet so that they could fire a few rounds before tumbling back to sleep again. Finally, just after one, the commander of the reinforcements the Palmach had been promising him for hours arrived.

"What shall we do?" he asked.

Before Gazit could answer, a soldier burst in shouting, "The Arabs are here!" This time it was true. They had already captured the mukhtar's house only a few yards away.

"What do you suggest?" the Palmach man asked Gazit. "I suggest we get out of here," Gazit replied, indicating their only line of retreat, the steep hillside falling down toward the road. Gazit ordered his men to get out as best they could. He took the three wounded men with him and began rolling them down the terraced hillside, kicking and pushing them along with his hands and feet. It was, he would recall, a terrible experience, twisting them from level to level like sacks of corn, hearing their heads

263

and limbs thud from bump to bump and bang against the rocks of each of the three-foot-high stone walls along their route down.

At the crest of the hill, the victorious Arabs swept into Kastel, yelling and brandishing their rifles in the air. To their exuberant shouts, someone raised the Arab banner from the roof of the mukhtar's house. Once again, after three days of fighting, Kastel was an Arab village.

Almost at the instant the flag was up, a voice screamed out, *"Allah akhbar!"* It was a cry of grief, not triumph. It came from Nadi Dai'es, the coffee boy who had rushed off to help burn the Commercial Center the day after partition. Nadi's propensity for following passing crowds had led him to Kastel. Struggling to join the others at the summit of the village, he had stumbled on the body of Abdul Khader Husseini lying on his back on a low flight of stairs before a little stone house.

His discovery turned the Arab victory celebration into a wake. The exultation of their triumph was replaced by terrified consternation, glee by hysteria. Men swarmed around the body weeping and shrieking their grief, kissing the dead leader's face. Others mashed their heads with the stock of their rifles to mark their remorse.

Abdul Khader was gently placed on a stretcher, his face washed and his clothes straightened out. Then, passed from hand to hand, he was carried down the hillside of his last conquest while behind him the tear-stained villagers he had led so often to battle moaned over and over again, *"Allah akhbar, Allah akhbar."*

Watching the procession as it wound down the hill, a heartbroken Abou Gharbieh, the schoolteacher who had been with him barely twenty-four hours earlier, thought, "We can never replace him. He was our chief, our only chief, and he has disappeared."

The driver's license and the miniature Koran taken by Uzi Narciss from Abdul Khader's body had reached Haganah intelligence in Jerusalem too late to get a warning to Gazit that a furious Arab assault looking for Abdul Khader's corpse was sure to strike him. Yitzhak Levi, Shaltiel's intelligence officer, put the discovery to another use. The Arabs of the Old City, informed only of the recapture of Kastel, were celebrating their triumph. At five-thirty in the afternoon, on Levi's orders, the Haganah's Arabic-language radio broadcast the first word of Abdul Khader's death. Immediately, the celebrating stopped and a shocked silence fell on the Old City.

Haj Amin Husseini received the news of the death of his ablest lieutenant in the midst of a meeting of his followers in Damascus. He stood up.

"Gentlemen" he announced in his quiet voice, "I give you the jihad martyr Abdul Khader Husseini. Rejoice and thank God." For Emile Ghory, listening to him, these words marked "the end of the Palestine resistance movement. There is something in our blood," he thought, "that ascribes such importance to the man, such hero worship to the leader, that when he dies, everything collapses."

22

THE PEACE OF DEIR YASSIN

A PAIR OF CORPSES in each valise wouldn't have been as heavy. Sweating from his effort, the traveler dragged them along, one after the other. Freddy Fredkens, the false pastry cook who had found the crew of Ocean Trade Airways in a Paris bar, was going back to the wars. It had been five years since the former R.A.F. ace had touched the controls of a plane similar to the one discreetly parked in the hangar of a flying club at Toussus-le-Noble Airfield just outside Paris. It was an Anson bomber, the kind of aircraft Fredkens had flown on dozens of missions over Nazi Germany. With the aid of an old R.A.F. colleague, Fredkens had arranged the purchase of four Ansons for the Haganah's fledgling air forces.

He shoved his heavy valises on board and clambered up to the cockpit. His first stop was Rome. There he got the final instructions he needed for the assignment awaiting him. In his twin-engine Anson devoid of any official identification, Fredkens was going to carry out a bombing raid over the Adriatic Sea in the name of a state which did not exist. Packed into the pair of valises he had carried to his Anson with such difficulty were two one-hundred-pound bombs. They would, hopefully, be the weapons with which Fredkens would sink the S.S. *Lino,* a tramp steamer en route from Fiume to Beirut. Packed into the *Lino*'s holds were six thousand Czech rifles and eight million rounds of cartridges, the harvest of Syrian Captain Abdul-Aziz Kerine's mission to Prague.

Sector by sector, Fredkens prowled the Adriatic searching for the *Lino.* To aid him, he had the exact hour of her sailing, her course, and her speed, furnished by Ehud Avriel's agents in Fiume. Despite all that, he failed to discover the ship. After three days of futile searching, Fredkens and his old Anson were grounded by a furious storm.

The following morning he discovered his missing target—as did almost everyone else in Italy—on the front pages of the Italian press. The storm that had grounded Fredkens had driven the *Lino* into the port of Malfetta, north of Bari. There an Italian customs inspector had discovered her secret cargo, and the press immediately announced to the world the arrival of the mysterious shipload of arms in an Italian port. Italy was at that moment in the midst of a hotly contested national election. Ada Sereina, one of Avriel's Italian colleagues, contacted a friend in the ruling Christian Democratic Party. The *Lino*'s arms, she suggested, were probably destined for the Italian Communist Party to help foment an antigovernment rising. The government immediately seized the ship pending an investigation, arrested the crew and towed the *Lino* to Bari, where it was placed under military guard.

The action, of course, presented the Haganah a superb opportunity to destroy the vessel. The task was assigned to Munya Mardor, one of the Jewish organization's boldest agents. Together with an explosives expert, two frogmen, a radio operator and a driver, Mardor rushed off to Bari. Their transport was a G.M.C. disguised as an American Army truck. Their explosives were packed into its spare fuel tank, onto which they had painted the letters "DDT."

It was quickly apparent there was no way to reach the *Lino* by land. The only way to approach the vessel was by sea, at night. A first attempt failed due to the alert Italian surveillance of the ship. A second attempt was set for midnight April 9.

At eleven o'clock at night, Mardor's G.M.C. slipped discreetly up to an isolated corner of the harbor seawall on the Corso della Vittoria. The two frogmen and the explosives expert unloaded their material, inflated a rubber life raft and paddled out to sea.

The explosives expert clutched his bomb tightly to his chest while the frogmen rowed. It was a motorcycle inner tube packed with TNT. Its three detonators were wrapped in prophylactics, an item that had been almost as difficult to find in Roman Catholic Italy as TNT. Each consisted of a ration of potassium corked by a plug of tightly wadded newspaper. Once the tire had been attached to the hull of the *Lino,* the frogmen would turn the three detonators upside down and gently break a vial of sulphuric acid packed into the head of each one. Mardor had carefully determined the length of the newspaper plug between the acid and the potassium. The time it would take the acid to eat through the paper would cover their escape. With unconcealed glee, Mardor had personally chosen the paper for the plugs. It came from the Rome *Daily American,* a journal not noted for its sympathy to the Zionist cause.

The night was perfectly still. Soon the raft slipped into the military port, and the prow of the *Lino* loomed up in the darkness. Above them, the three men could hear the footfalls of its guards pacing its deck. The frogmen slipped into the water and swam silently to the boat. With great care, they attached the bomb to the *Lino*'s hull, just below the waterline. Then they swam back to their raft and paddled to a little fishing port where Mardor and their truck were waiting. A few seconds later they were on their way to Rome.

Shortly after four o'clock the first drop of sulphuric acid terminated its hungry journey through the pages of the Rome *Daily American*. An enormous explosion shook the port, tearing a gaping hole in the *Lino*'s hull. Slowly, Captain Abdul-Aziz Kerine's six thousand rifles and eight million rounds of ammunition went gurgling to the bottom of Bari harbor.

. . .

The charisma which had made Abdul Khader Husseini such an effective leader in life was going to deprive him in death of his last victory. Determined to honor their dead leader by being present at his funeral, the hundreds of Arabs who had swarmed to Kastel in search of him in the morning now poured back toward Jerusalem. By bus, taxicab, weeping in the open vans of trucks, they streamed away, leaving practically deserted the village for which Abdul Khader had died.

Barely forty men, lead by schoolteacher Abou Gharbieh remained behind. "Our attack was chaotic, but our victory is even worse," he remarked bitterly to the last leader to leave, Anwar Nusseibi, elder brother of the man who had given the partition news on the Palestine Broadcasting System. Nusseibi promised to send him relief and supplies as soon as he could.

For the Haganah, retaking Kastel was essential if Operation Nachshon was to continue. Shortly after midnight two companies of Palmach under a brilliant young officer named David "Dado" Elazar moved up to assault the village. Abou Gharbieh saw them preparing their attack. He knew he had no chance of holding them off. Determined to avoid unnecessary losses, he abandoned the village. Once again the men of the Haganah were masters of Kastel.

. . .

Colonel Fouad Mardam grabbed a glass of ice water to dislodge the morsel of shish kebab suddenly sticking in his throat, then reached over and turned up the volume on his radio. The explosion of unexplained origin, continued Radio Damascus' noon news bulletin, had sunk a shipload of arms in the Italian port of Bari. A few hours later, a telegram confirmed the worst of the fears that had interrupted the Syrian Army Quartermaster General's lunch. The famous rifles he had sent Captain Abdul-Aziz Kerine to Prague to purchase were now resting in the silt in Bari harbor.

In view of the gravity of the situation, Mardam himself was dispatched to Italy to try to salvage the lost cargo and arrange for its shipment east on another ship. A few days later, the Syrian watched the first case of his sunken arms store emerge from the murky waters of the Adriatic. Under his orders a squad of frogmen plunged in and out of the wreckage of the S.S. *Lino,* hauling up to the Bari docks everything they could save from its flooded holds. Mardam quickly realized that his eight million cartridges were a total loss. As his rifles began to pile up on the Bari docks, however, his hopes mounted. Most of them could be saved by treating them with an anticorrosive agent. His foes' escapade was not going to yield the result they had sought. Reassured, Mardam left for Rome in search of a ship to continue his rifles' interrupted voyage.

The catastrophe of the S.S. *Lino* had only served to give fresh impetus to the Arabs' arms purchasers and the incredible array of merchants anxious to fill their orders. Convinced of the gullibility of those newly independent Arab states, the world's arms traffickers descended on the ministries of Beirut and Damascus by the dozens. A Czech offered six thousand rifles and five million cartridges for olive oil. A Spaniard proposed twenty thousand Mausers and twenty million cartridges. From Italy came an offer of four hundred 81-millimeter mortars and 180,000 shells. A Swiss suggested antitank guns. An ingenious Hamburg scrap dealer proposed Hitler's personal yacht and a fleet of secondhand submarines. Sometimes these arms were real, sometimes they existed only in the imagination of the man selling them. In all cases, they served to confuse and bewilder the Arabs they were meant to arm.

One of the most colorful dealers was an Italian named Giuseppe Doria. For twenty years his munitions had fueled conflicts in Ethiopia, Spain, Greece, China. So complete was his line of goods that Doria boasted he alone could furnish an entire army. To deliver them, he owned three ultrarapid three-hundred-ton motor launches "capable of delivering, for a modest surcharge, arms to any place in the world." One restriction, however, accompanied Doria's sales. He insisted on being paid in full, in cash, in dollars, in a Swiss numbered bank account before he would deliver a single bullet.

No one, however, rivaled, for sheer imagination, a French World War

Il ace named Commander Duroc. An instructor in Haile Selassie's Air Force, Duroc promised to sell the Damascus Defense Ministry six Mosquito fighter bombers complete with crews, ready to fly from Tangiers, to any airport in the Middle East. In addition, he told the Syrians, he owned an air transport firm composed of six C-46s with French pilots able to fly fifty tons of arms a week. All he asked for his nonexistent airplanes was an enormous amount of cash.

Nor were the Arabs themselves lacking in imagination in the pursuit of arms. A secret report to Lebanon's Riad Solh from one of his colleagues proposed a particularly ingenious way to equip Lebanon with an air force. Recruit a large number of decorated former pilots, urged the report, then send them into Palestine with orders to kidnap the Jews' planes and fly them to Beirut.

Despite the enormous burden of not being able to operate in the open like the Arabs, David Ben-Gurion's arms buyers had a number of notable achievements to their credit. In hotels near the Rome railroad station, under the hot metal roofs in hangars in the airport of Panama City, a hundred pilots anxiously awaited instructions. Idealists, Zionists, mercenaries, adventurers, Jews and non-Jews, they came from the United States, Europe, South Africa and Asia. Their members included a Dutch millionaire, a Persian veteran of the Indian Air Force, a Red Army deserter, a T.W.A. captain, a newspaperman, a milkman, a fireman, and even a Brooklyn cop. They had two things in common, a desire to fight for the new Jewish state and the thousands of hours of flying time they had amassed during the Second World War.

The planes they would fly were as varied as their pilots' background. On the airstrips of Panama City were a practically new Constellation and ten war-surplus C-46s. Two more Constellations, five Mustangs and three Flying Fortresses waited in airports in California, New Jersey and Florida for a chance to escape the surveillance of the F.B.I. and take off for Europe. Twenty-five Norseman transports bought from an American scrap-metal dealer in Germany were hidden on airfields around Europe. Four Beaufighters slipped out of Britain by a fake movie company on the pretext that they were to be used in a film were tucked away in an airport near Ajaccio on the island of Corsica.

To that burgeoning air force was soon to be added its most substantial acquisition, a purchase David Ben-Gurion deemed indispensable for the first phases of the conflict looming before his followers. Ehud Avriel, the young Austrian whose Czech rifles and machine guns had helped open the road to Jerusalem three weeks earlier, was ordered to pay his Czech friends four hundred thousand dollars for the purchase of ten Messerschmitt 109s, and to take an option on fifteen additional aircraft.

Ben-Gurion's envoys had been equally active purchasing armor and artillery for his army. The most important achievements in that domain had been the handiwork of the man who had sent the Haganah its first Polish rifles in a road roller. To facilitate his work, Yehuda Arazi had employed a two-hundred-thousand-dollar bribe to get himself named special ambassador of Nicaragua to the governments of Europe charged with the task of procuring arms for the Nicaraguan Army. It was not Arazi's first venture into the world of diplomacy. In Italy, he had designed for a printer a set of United Nations diplomatic passports for his agents. So impressive had Arazi's false passports been that when the first real United Nations diplomats had arrived they were arrested by the Italian police for traveling on false documents. The Nicaraguan ambassador's first purchases, five 20-millimeter Hispano Suiza antiaircraft guns and fifteen thousand shells, were already being prepared for shipment to Tel Aviv.

From New York and Los Angeles other ships would soon be on their way carrying in their holds the harvest of a massive collection taken up for the Jews of Palestine from one end of the United States to another. Designed to supplement the surplus material purchased in Belgium by Xiel Federmann, the Santa Claus of the Haganah, the goods amassed by "Materials for Palestine" covered everything except arms and ammunition. Run by the "Sonneborn Institute," the association of devoted Zionists so helpful to Haim Slavine in his quest for an armament industry, Materials for Palestine gathered into its depots contributions from every Zionist state organization in America. Wisconsin sent 350,000 sandbags, Ohio 92,000 flares, New Jersey 25,000 helmets, Chicago one hundred tons of barbed wire and ten tons of khaki paint; San Francisco offered mosquito netting, Minneapolis six hundred mine detectors. From New Orleans came salt tablets and penicillin. Norfolk, Virginia, proposed two corvettes, an ice-cutter and, to guide the naval strategists of the future Jewish state, the complete memoirs of Admiral von Tirpitz.

Impressive as his agents' lists of acquisitions might be, David Ben-Gurion well knew they would only have value once they were landed in Palestine. Despite the approaching end of the mandate, Britain's surveillance of the Palestine coast was as vigilant as ever. Increasingly, the Jewish leader realized that his forces would be confronted by a dangerous time gap, the gap between the end of the mandate and the time enough arms to stem an Arab invasion could be brought into the country. It was during that interval, he told himself, that a war would be won or lost.

• • •

Ahmed Eid gently shook his sleeping wife. Then the middle-aged mason quietly knocked on the doors of several nearby houses. It was four o'clock in the morning, the hour at which his wife and half a dozen of her neighbors left to bake *pitas*, flat loaves of unleavened bread, in the communal kiln attached to the mukhtar's home. It was a thankless ritual performed by that handful of women each dawn and one to which, in a few hours, they would owe their lives this April day.

His ancient Mauser slung over his shoulder, Eid returned to his guard post at the entrance to the village. Although no special danger menaced Eid's community, its elders had followed an old Arab custom and designated a score of its inhabitants to share the duties of night watchmen. This evening, along with two other masons, three stonecutters and a truck driver, Eid had spent the night watching over his neighbors' rest. Only the distant echoes of the firing around Kastel and along the road from Tel Aviv to Jerusalem had disturbed their vigil. Their peaceful community hugging its rocky promontory west of Jerusalem had no need to concern itself with those sounds. So successful had its elders been in holding it out of the tumult around it that Jerusalem's Haganah commander David Shaltiel could note that the community had been "quiet since the beginning of disturbances . . . not mentioned in reports of attacks on Jews, and one of the few places which has not given a foothold to foreign bands." Until this Friday morning, April 9, 1948, the primary function of the old Mausers and Turkish rifles cradled by Eid and his six fellow watchmen had been shooting rabbits or providing a noisy backdrop to village feasts. The last time they had been fired had been twelve days earlier to welcome Alia Darwish to their village of Deir Yassin. Serene and confident, the seven men tranquilly awaited the dawn.

Beneficiaries of the community's peaceful reputation, virtually the entire village population slept at their feet. Those inhabitants who worked outside Deir Yassin had returned to pass the Moslem Sabbath. Others, like Ahmed Khalil, a worker at the Allenby Barracks, or his brother Hassan, a waiter at the King David, had come because their posts had just been terminated by the departing British. The premature end of the school year accounted for the presence in the village of several young men like Mohammed Jaber, a student at Jerusalem's Ibrahimyeh

School. There was even an unexpected guest in the village this night. The young teacher in the village's girls' school, Hayat Halabes, had been caught in Deir Yassin when the No. 38 bus she took each night for her return to Jerusalem had fallen into an ambush.

The sharp report of a rifle shattered their sleep and the predawn calm. Then a voice screamed, *"Ahmed, Yehud alainou!* The Jews are coming!" On the slope below his post the mason could make out the forms of men moving up the wadi. Suddenly, rifle fire seemed to break out on all sides of the village. It was four-thirty. The peace of Deir Yassin was forever ended.

Moving up from three different directions, the commandos of the Irgun and the Stern Gang were in the process of preparing the assault their leaders hoped would win the organizations greater authority in Jerusalem. The Irgun men had approached Deir Yassin by way of the nearby Jewish suburb of Bet Hakerem to the south while the Sternists attacked from the north. To the east, along the only road leading to the village, was an armored car equipped with a loudspeaker. In all, one hundred and thirty-two men were involved. To mark the occasion, their leaders had selected a password particularly appropriate to their effort this night. It was *Achdut,* "Unity," since they had united their armories for the task. The explosives came largely from the Stern Gang, the Sten guns from the Irgun's clandestine arms shop. The rifles and hand grenades had been furnished by the Haganah in the illusory hope that they might have been used to aid their forces at Kastel.

While the guards of Deir Yassin fired into their ranks or raced from door to door giving the alert, the attackers huddled just beyond the first row of houses waiting for the arrival of the loudspeaker and the signal to open the attack. After a heated debate, the leaders of the two groups had finally decided to warn the population of the village to flee their homes. The armored car with its loudspeaker, however, would never broadcast its warning to the villagers of Deir Yassin. It had tumbled into a ditch behind a row of stones cutting the road into the village. The loudspeaker had been tossed onto its side far short of Deir Yassin's first houses, and its words were lost in the night, heard only by its frightened crew. Finally, a machinegun burst tore into the village. It was the signal. From north and south the attackers moved forward. Operation "Unity" was under way.

"Yehud!" Like a tocsin's ring, that call echoed through the streets of the sleeping village. Barefoot, sometimes with only a robe thrown around them, many of Deir Yassin's inhabitants managed to flee to the west.

Among them was the family of Mohammed Zeidan, a well-to-do merchant who rented several houses in Jerusalem to Jewish tenants. Only the schoolteacher in the girls' school remained behind in his house. Hayat Halabes got dressed and ran to get the first-aid kit in her school. She slipped on its Red Crescent armband and rushed toward the firing. Her race was brief. Hit only a few steps from her schoolroom, she fell to the ground dead, among the first victims in the village in which she had been an unexpected guest.

After a first rush, the Irgun and Sternist attack stalled. The terrorists were used to a different kind of war than the one in which they suddenly found themselves. They had had no experience and little training in operations such as this. Almost every male in the village, following Arab custom, had a firearm of some sort, and the citizens of Deir Yassin staged a surprisingly tenacious defense of their homes. Nearly two hours were required before the attackers could breach the first row of houses and reach the center of the village. There the men of the two groups fell into each other's arms.

Their joy, however, was of short duration. Their ammunition supply was almost gone and the Irgun's homemade Sten guns were jamming one after another. Although in reality their casualties were light—the attack would cost the two groups only four killed—in the heat of the battle they seemed high to the untrained terrorists. Two key leaders were wounded. There was even talk of withdrawing. No one seemed to have imagined it might be considerably more difficult to conquer a resisting village than it was to toss a bomb into an unarmed crowd waiting for a bus. Giora, the leader of the Irgun command, rallied his men for another push forward. Then he too was wounded. A kind of collective hysteria overtook the attackers. As the opposition to their assault finally waned, they fell with increasing fury on the inhabitants of Deir Yassin.

Driven from their home along with thirty-three neighbors, the newly-weds of the village's last feast were among their first victims. They were lined up against a wall and shot, their hands clasped as though to seal for eternity their new love. Twelve-year-old Fahimi Zeidan, one of the few survivors of that killing, explained, "The Jews ordered all our family to line up against the wall and they started shooting us. I was hit in the side, but most of us children were saved because we hid behind our parents. The bullets hit my sister Kadri [four] in the head, my sister Sameh [eight] in the cheek, my brother Mohammed [seven] in the chest. But all the others with us against the wall were killed: my father, my mother, my grandfather and grandmother, my uncles and aunts and some of their children."

Haleem Eid, a young woman of thirty belonging to one of Deir Yassin's principal families, declared she saw "a man shoot a bullet into the neck of my sister Salhiyeh who was nine months pregnant. Then he cut her stomach open with a butcher's knife." She said that another woman witnessing the same scene, Aiesch Radwas, was killed when she tried to extricate the unborn infant from the dead mother's womb. In another house, Naaneh Khalil, sixteen, claimed she saw a man take "a kind of sword and slash my neighbor Jamil Hish from head to toe then do the same thing on the steps to my house to my cousin Fathi." Similar scenes took place in house after house. The survivors' accounts indicated that the female members of the two commando groups matched the savagery of their male counterparts. Bit by bit Deir Yassin was submerged in a hell of screams, exploding grenades, the stench of blood, gunpowder and smoke. Its assailants killed, they looted, and finally they raped.

Safiyeh Attiyah, a forty-one-year-old woman, saw one man open his pants and leap on her. "I screamed," she said, "but around me other women were being raped, too. Some of the men were so anxious to get our earrings they ripped our ears to pull them off faster."

Reaching the scene in midmorning, Mordechai Ra'anan, the head of the Irgun in Jerusalem, decided to wipe out the last houses in which the Arabs were still resisting, with a tactic the Irgun had used against British police posts. They dynamited the buildings from which an occasional shot seemed to ring out. The most important of them was the house of the mukhtar. "Within a few minutes," Ra'anan observed, "the house was a pile of ruins and broken bodies." The kiln, however, thanks to its heavy iron door, survived the Irgun's dynamite. Inside, Ahmed Eid's wife and her terrified friends heard a voice reassure them, "Come out! There's no risk." The women refused. Shafikah Sammour, the mukhtar's daughter, recognized the speaker's accented Arabic.

More than fifteen houses were thus destroyed before the Irgun's supply of dynamite ran out. The terrorized survivors fled to those homes still standing. Then the Irgun commandos began to systematically work their way through those remaining buildings with Sten guns and grenades. Before many of them the earlier brutal scenes were played out again. Just before noon Mohammed Jaber, the youth who was in Deir Yassin because his school had closed early, saw from a hiding place under his bed "the Jews break in, drive everybody outside, put them against the wall and shoot them. One of the women was carrying a three-month-old baby."

Shortly after noon, the attackers threatened to dynamite the kiln on the heads of the women inside if they refused to come out. The mukhtar's daughter opened the door and stepped out first. In the ruins of her home, she found the bodies of her mother and two brothers. Slowly an oppressive silence punctuated only by an occasional cry smothered the village, its ruins warmed by the lovely spring sunshine.

Operation "Unity" was finished. The terrorists of the Irgun and the Stern Gang had secured the victory they sought. Deir Yassin was theirs.*

•   •   •

By the thousands, the Arabs of Palestine poured into Jerusalem for the funeral of Abdul Khader Husseini. The dead leader's body, wrapped with flowers and the flag of his Palestine movement, was exposed in a plain pine coffin in the sitting room of his brother's house, where forty-

---

* The Irgun and Stern gang leadership have always denied the excesses attributed to them by the Arabs of Deir Yassin, maintaining that the killing which took place was a result of the Arab opposition to their attack. Their actions were deplored and condemned by the vast majority of Palestine's Jewish community as representing an outrage on Jewish and Zionist ideals. In the interest of avoiding any Arab tendency to magnify the events in retrospect, the material used in this and subsequent passages on Deir Yassin was taken from Jewish sources, the report of the International Red Cross's Jacques de Reynier and three reports on the incident forwarded to the Chief Secretary of the Palestine government, Sir Henry Gurney, by Richard C. Catling, Assistant Inspector General of the Criminal Investigation Division, on April 13, 15 and 16, 1948. Bearing the dossier number 179/110/17/GS, the designation "Secret" and signed by Catling, they contain the interrogation reports of the massacre's survivors by a team of British police officers together with corroborating physical evidence obtained through medical examination of the survivors by a doctor and nurse from Government Hospital in Jerusalem. A copy of the three reports is in the authors' possession. To the report of April 15, the British interrogating officer appended the following remarks: "On 14th April at 10 A.M., I visited Silwan village accompanied by a doctor and a nurse from the Government Hospital in Jerusalem and a member of the Arab Women's Union. We visited many houses in this village in which approximately some two to three hundred people from Deir Yassin village are housed. I interviewed many of the women folk in order to glean some information on any atrocities committed in Deir Yassin but the majority of those women are very shy and reluctant to relate their experiences especially in matters concerning sexual assault and they need great coaxing before they will divulge any information. The recording of statements is hampered also by the hysterical state of the women who often break down many times whilst the statement is being recorded. There is, however, no doubt that many sexual atrocities were committed by the attacking Jews. Many young school girls were raped and later slaughtered. Old women were also molested. One story is current concerning a case in which a young girl was literally torn in two. Many infants were also butchered and killed. I also saw one old woman who gave her age as one hundred and four who had been severely beaten about the head by rifle butts. Women had bracelets torn from their arms and rings from their fingers and parts of some of the women's ears were severed in order to remove earrings."

eight hours earlier he had written his last letter. Since Moslem tradition demanded swift burial, neither his wife nor his children would reach Jerusalem in time for his interment. Abdul Khader's legacy to them would be a request to honor his debts of six thousand Palestine pounds, run up on his own signature buying arms for his followers.

By the time the funeral procession was ready to set out from his brother's house, the alleys and streets outside were dense with men. There were shepherds in rough wool cloaks and sandals, men in suits and fezzes. Above all, there were hundreds of the men who twice in twelve years had answered the dead leader's call to arms. Clutching their rifles to their chests, dressed in a disparate collection of uniforms but united by the grief contorting their faces, they mourned the leader who had been for them a kind of surrogate father.

As Abdul Khader's coffin left his brother's house, the first member of the procession fired his pistol into the air. His shot was the signal for the wildest outburst of gunfire Jerusalem had yet heard. From every corner of the Arab city, Abdul Khader's followers sent a noisy barrage skyward, snapping telephone cables and electric wires and killing two by-standers. "The waste is appalling," thought Anwar Nusseibi. "We are firing off enough ammunition to conquer half of Palestine."

Thus began the most grandiose funeral Jerusalem had witnessed in generations. In accordance with Moslem customs, Abdul Khader's coffin was passed from hand to hand by his followers. In a sea of waving arms, accompanied by a din of piercing laments, it swayed slowly over their heads as dozens fought for the honor of touching it for even a few seconds. Through Damascus Gate, down Solomon Street and the Via Dolorosa, the unhappy procession flowed toward the great esplanade of the Haram esh Sherif. There, in the octagonal monument of the Dome of the Rock, Abdul Khader Husseini was accorded one last honor. In recognition of his extraordinary career, he was awarded the rare privilege of being in-humed in that Islamic shrine from which the Prophet allegedly ascended to heaven.

All morning, on the esplanade outside, the men wept and talked together, grimly conscious that they had laid to rest not only a man, but many of the hopes his leadership had raised in their hearts as well.

Walking home from the funeral, a depressed and melancholy Anwar Nusseibi suddenly came upon Abou Gharbieh, whom he had last seen in Kastel the evening before.

"Ah, Abou Gharbieh," he said, "did someone relieve you at Kastel?"

"Yes," the schoolteacher replied bitterly. "The Jews did."

277

A few miles from the Mosque of Omar, on Jerusalem's western outskirts, other Arab bodies, these anonymous, were now to be buried. For
the scores of men, women and children killed at Deir Yassin, the graveyard would be the rock quarry which had been the source of the village's
wealth, the pit to which so many of them had gone each day of their adult
lives to hew stones for the homes of Jerusalem.

Jacques de Reynier, the Swiss representative of the International Red
Cross, led the first party to reach the site. It did not take him long to discover that Deir Yassin was in the hands of men with whom he had had
no previous contact. Only the intervention of an enormous German-born
member of the Irgun who told Reynier he owed his life to the Red Cross
got the Swiss past the dissidents' sentries.

The spectacle awaiting him made Reynier gasp. "The first thing I saw
were people running everywhere, rushing in and out of houses, carrying
Sten guns, rifles, pistols and long ornate Arab knives," he wrote that night
in his diary. "They seemed half mad. I saw a beautiful girl carrying a
dagger still covered with blood. I heard screams. 'We're still mopping up,'
my German friend explained. All I could think of was the S.S. troops I'd
seen in Athens." Then, to his horror, Reynier noted, he saw "a young
woman stab an elderly man and woman cowering on the doorstep of
their hut."

Still dazed by that sight, Reynier pushed his way into the first house
he reached. "Everything had been ripped apart and torn upside down,"
he wrote. "There were bodies strewn about. They had done their 'cleaning
up' with guns and grenades and finished their work with knives, anyone
could see that." He suddenly saw something moving in the shadows. Bending down, he discovered "a little foot, still warm." It belonged to a ten-
year-old girl, still alive despite her wounds. Reynier picked her up and
ordered his German escort to carry her to an ambulance. Then he furiously
demanded he be allowed to continue his search for wounded. He found
two more, an elderly woman half paralyzed with fear hiding behind a
woodpile, and a dying man. In all, he estimated he had seen two hundred
corpses. One of them belonged, his diary would record, "to a woman who
must have been eight months pregnant, hit in the stomach, with powder
burns on her dress indicating she'd been shot point blank."

Embarrassed by Reynier's presence, the Irgun and Stern leaders finally
ordered him back to Jerusalem with the wounded he had managed to save
from the ruins. There the few survivors of the massacre were being paraded

through the streets by their captors. Harry Levin saw three trucks "driving slowly up and down King George V Avenue, carrying men, women and children, their hands held over their heads." In the front truck he spotted "a young boy, a look of anguished horror written on his face, his arms frozen upright."

High Commissioner Sir Alan Cunningham received his first report of the incident during the daily session of his Security Committee. He had had enough contacts with the Haganah to know that the organization was incapable of such an action. It was, Sir Alan had no doubt, the work of his enemies, the Irgun and the Stern Gang. "At last," he told his troop commander, General Sir Gordon MacMillan, "you've got those bastards. For God's sake, go up there and get them."

Deir Yassin, however, was going to prove one of Cunningham's "greatest disappointments in Palestine." His fellow Scot kept insisting that he did not have the troops available. Another participant in the meeting, Jerusalem Commissioner James Pollock, quickly realized "MacMillan simply did not want to use his troops." It ran counter to his policy of employing his soldiers only in the pursuit of strictly British interests.

Angrily, Cunningham turned to his R.A.F. chief for an air strike. He readily agreed, but pointed out to the High Commissioner a problem which symbolized to Cunningham "our frustrations of that morning and the hell of our last months in Palestine." The R.A.F. had sent all its light bombers to Egypt the day before and its rockets to Habbaniya in Iraq. It would take twenty-four hours to get them back.

Before the Security Committee had ended its deliberations, however, a new factor had arisen which would rule out the strike. The Haganah moved into Deir Yassin to take over the village. The first party to reach the area was led by Eliyahu Arieli, a scholarly veteran of six years' British Army service who commanded the Gadna, the youth organization. The spectacle he found was, in his eyes, "absolutely barbaric."

"All of the killed, with very few exceptions," he remarked, "were old men, women or children." There was never to be any question in Arieli's mind that "the dead we found were all unjust victims and none of them had died with a weapon in their hands." So appalling was the scene that the man who had fought in the rear guard of Britain's retreat from Greece refused to allow his youngsters into the village to witness it. Instead, he set to cleaning it up with his officers.

Yeshurun Schiff, Shaltiel's adjutant, who had involuntarily provided the terrorists with the tools of their carnage, followed with a large party of men. Instead of the help the terrorists had promised him, they had preferred, he noted, "to kill anybody they found alive as though every living thing in the village was the enemy and they could only think 'Kill them all.'"

"You are swine," he said to the Stern commander. His men surrounded the dissidents in the village square, and the two parties eyed each other menacingly. Schiff gave his report to Shaltiel by wireless. The Jerusalem commander told him to disarm the dissidents. "If they don't lay down their arms, open fire!" he ordered.

Schiff was aghast. Things had reached such a tense state that, he knew, the dissidents would not give up their weapons without a fight. Despite his loathing for what they had done, he could not bring himself to fire on the men of the two groups. Jewish history was too full of stories of fratricidal struggle in the face of an enemy to start that now.

"I can't do it," he gasped.

"Don't tell me what you can or can't do, those are your orders," Shaltiel replied.

"David," Schiff begged, "you'll bloody your name for life. The Jewish people will never forgive you."

Finally Shaltiel relented. The dissidents were ordered instead to clean up the village. As Schiff looked on, they carried the bodies of their victims to Deir Yassin's rock quarry and laid them out on the stones. When they had finished, they poured gasoline over them and set them ablaze.

"It was a lovely spring day," Schiff would recall. "The almond trees were in bloom, the flowers were out and everywhere there was the stench of the dead, the thick smell of blood, and the terrible odor of the corpses burning in the quarry."

The dark pillar of smoke rising from the rock quarry of Deir Yassin would become a stain upon the conscience of a new state. By their actions, the Irgun and the Stern Gang had consecrated the little Judean village for years to come as a symbol of the Palestinians' misery. Few Jewish prisoners in the months ahead would not hear the vengeful scream of "Deir Yassin!" and many would reach their own graves in retribution for the dissidents' crime.

The overwhelming majority of the Jews of Palestine reacted to Deir Yassin with shock and abhorrence. The Jewish Agency immediately disassociated itself from the terrorists' act and roundly condemned it. David Ben-Gurion personally cabled his shock at the incident to King Abdullah. The Chief Rabbi of Jerusalem took the extraordinary step of excommunicating the participants in the attack.

It was the Arabs, however, who had the obligation to announce the tragedy to the world. For hours, Hazem Nusseibi and Hussein Khalidi, secretary of Jerusalem's Arab Higher Committee, agonized over how to present the news. "We were afraid the Arab armies for all their talk weren't really going to come," Nusseibi later recalled. "We wanted to shock the population of the Arab countries into bringing pressure on their governments." And so they decided to broadcast the news of Deir Yassin in all its horror. It was, as Nusseibi would one day admit, "a fatal error." The gruesomely detailed news did not change any minds in the council of the Arab governments. But it stirred a growing sense of panic among the Arabs of Palestine. By their unhappy error of judgment, the Arab propagandists too had unwittingly helped set the stage for a problem soon to haunt the Middle East, the drama of thousands of Arab refugees.

• • •

Fawzi el Kaukji was a man of his word. For the second time in ten days he was, as he had promised Yehoshua Palmon he would be, sending his troops against a key Jewish position in the Valley of Jezreel, the kibbutz of Mishmar Ha'emek. Far from erasing the scar of his earlier defeat at Tirat Zvi, however, his first attack on the colony had ended in disaster. And yet the man who dreamed of being a German general had introduced to the battlefields of Palestine that day a new weapon much prized by his mentors, artillery. For hours his guns had pounded the helpless kibbutz. Prepared by their own energies and Palmon's warning, however, the settlers had been ready. It was not a white flag Fawzi had seen rising from the ruins of their smoldering kibbutz when he stopped the bombardment, but a round of Haganah rifle fire. His troops, sent off in pursuit of an easy victory, had retreated in panic. Only the rage of General Sir Gordon Mac-Millan at learning that Kaukji had broken his pledge had saved the day. The British had imposed a truce in the area.

Now Kaukji was ready to begin the second round. So, too, however, was Yehoshua Palmon. He had entered Mishmar Ha'emek along with a party of reinforcements during the cease-fire. With half a dozen men, he had then slipped around Kaukji's flank toward his rear. From a hilltop he surveyed the Arab's preparations with a pair of fieldglasses. Soon he spotted a car shuttling back and forth carrying, he was sure, Kaukji's orders. Its movements led him to the sight he was looking for, Kaukji's artillery, seven 75-millimeter cannons and three 105s.

As he had expected, they were inadequately defended. Convinced he had before him a glittering opportunity to equip the Haganah with some of the artillery it so gravely lacked, Palmon called reinforcements to his side. Then he launched a slashing attack on the Arab guns.

Palmon's attack did not produce the result he had hoped for. With a hasty effort, Kaukji's gunners managed to save his cannon. Their success would soon allow their leader to train them on the most prestigious target in Palestine, the rooftops of Jerusalem. The assault, however, had other, even more important consequences. Panicked by the sound of firing in their rear, Kaukji's men began to flee the battlefield. Within moments, the Liberation Army's attack on Mishmar Ha'emek collapsed. The triumph its leader so desperately sought would have to await another day and another battlefield.

It remained for Kaukji to provide his superiors in Damascus with a satisfactory explanation of his setback. Taking a pencil, Kaukji drafted a cable to Safwat Pasha. The Jews, he reported, "possess 120 tanks, of which the lightest weighs six tons. In addition, they have twelve batteries of 75s, six squadrons of bombers and fighters with all their equipment. They possess a complete infantry division, of which one regiment is composed of non-Jewish Russian Communists."

When he had dispatched his cable, the embittered Kaukji returned to his headquarters in the village of Jabba. There he was to discover the only consolation of his unhappy day. If Kaukji could not be a German general, he could at least be a German husband. It was his birthday, and waiting for him in his quarters, with a birthday cake and a bottle of champagne she had carried across the Allenby Bridge in a suitcase, was his German wife, Anna Elisa.

23

"SHALOM, MY DEAR . . ."

THE TWO MIDDLE-AGED MEN half ran, half stumbled after the departing convoy. It was too late. Slowly gathering speed, it slid off down the street. One of the two shrugged and gave up. He would catch the next convoy in one week's time.

His companion continued to pound along after the disappearing vehicles, shrieking, "Wait, wait!" Dr. Moshe Ben-David had played a vital role in the development of the two institutions on Mount Scopus to which they were headed, Hadassah Hospital and the Hebrew University. He was not going to let the convoy leave without him.

By a miracle, one of Jerusalem's rare taxis passed by as he ran down the street. Ben-David jumped in. Minutes later, red-faced, his heart pounding, he climbed into one of the buses in the convoy and slumped into a seat.

Supplying the hospital and the university to which Dr. Ben-David was bound had been a problem for the Jewish Agency since partition. The only road to the hilltop passed through the Arab stronghold of Sheikh Jarrah. As early as December, Arab ambushes had forced the Jewish Agency to resort to a weekly armed convoy to keep the two institutions on Mount Scopus supplied. For the past month a tacit truce had ruled along the road, and the passage of the convoys had been relatively free of incidents. There seemed no reason to doubt that the convoy of Tuesday, April 13, would have an equally easy trip.

At the foremost Haganah guard post at the end of the Street of the Prophet Samuel, Moshe Hillman, a Jewish officer, held up the convoy while he made a routine check with a British police inspector named Webb.

"Send the convoy up," Webb told the Haganah liaison officer. "The road's clear. We just patrolled it."

Hillman waved the line of vehicles off on the two-and-a-half-mile trip to Mount Scopus. An armored car led the way. Behind it came an ambulance bearing the red star of the Magen David Adom, the Jewish Red Cross, then two buses, another ambulance, four trucks, and a second armored car to protect the rear. Driving one of the trucks was a stubby little man named Benjamin Adin. For five hundred pounds he had purchased in December the dubious right to run a truckload of goods up the hill once a day. Scooting out of back streets at odd times, banging across open fields and dirt tracks, he had succeeded so well he had won the nickname Mishugana, the Crazy Man. Today, for the first time, the Haganah had forced him to make his run in the convoy. He also had a passenger, a man who had begged him for a ride because his wife had just had a baby at Hadassah Hospital.

Packed into the buses and ambulances ahead of his truck was an astonishing assembly of professors, doctors, researchers and scholars, the most precious cargo a Haganah convoy could carry through the dangerous curves of Sheikh Jarrah to Mount Scopus. Distinguished products of the most famous faculties of Europe, they had fled the persecutions of the Continent to come here and found a prestigious array of hospitals, laboratories and research centers. From Berlin, Vienna and Krakow they had come, bringing an intellectual capital of inestimable value to the fledgling Jewish state. Today they were members of the Faculty of Medicine of Hebrew University or the Hadassah Medical Organization, a philanthropic body founded by an American Jewish woman in 1912 to apply in Palestine the byword of Jeremiah, "Cure my people." Sustained by the contributions of American Jewry, Hadassah had built medical institutions all across Palestine. The most important among them, the temple of Jewish medical science, was the ultramodern hospital on Mount Scopus.

The convoy's most prestigious passenger, the director of Hadassah Hospital, the world-renowned ophthalmologist Chaim Yassky, had characteristically taken one of the most exposed seats, beside the driver of the first ambulance. Behind him were his wife, six other doctors, a nurse and a wounded man on a stretcher.

Yassky was personally familiar with every meter of the roadside along their way. He had lived in Jerusalem for twenty years. Peering through the narrow slit in the ambulance's armor-plated window, he recognized, behind its garden walls, the elegant mansion of the Nashasshibis, a distinguished Arab family with whom he had often dined. Farther on was the house where Katy Antonious had received her guests, its precious salons converted now into a guard post by thirty Jocks of the Highland Light Infantry. None of the ambulance's passengers was more eager to arrive than Yassky. Chaim and Fanny Yassky had a deep affection for their hilltop. From the windows of their residence, they never ceased to admire the view of the

Old City spread below, or the perpetually changing tints of the Mountains of Moab to the east.

Esther Passman, a young American widow riding in the second ambulance, did not share Yassky's eagerness to arrive. The directress of social services at the hospital's Cancer Institute, she was in the convoy somewhat against her will. She had wanted to stay in Jerusalem with her fifteen-year-old son, still recovering from a wound he had received assembling explosives for the Gadna. He had insisted she leave, however, and she had rushed to the Street of the Prophet Samuel just in time to catch the convoy.

When the driver of their ambulance announced that they were almost out of Sheikh Jarrah, she and her fellow passengers relaxed and began to babble happily in the darkened vehicle. Even the two wounded Irgunists riding with them, who had been hit at Deir Yassin, cheered up. A nurse opened a thermos of tea and offered everybody a sip.

Their gaiety was premature. Crouched in a ditch alongside the road, his fingers fixed on the plunger of an electric mine, a tailor named Mohammed Neggar watched the convoy's approach, calculating the instant at which to fire his explosives. Forty-eight hours before, in a bar he frequented, Neggar had been given the date and the hour of the convoy's passage by a British officer. Moreover, the Britisher had told Neggar that if his men attacked the convoy, they would not be molested as long as they did not fire on British patrols.

His words were an invitation to attack it. To the Arabs, Mount Scopus also represented a Haganah strongpoint from which their foes sometimes launched assaults on their rear. All the next day in the back room of his tailor shop, while Neggar shuttled in and out to give his customers fittings, his aides had planned the ambush. Counting on British indifference, they had decided to strike from the roadside ditch near a clump of cypress trees beyond the Orient House Hotel. The road began to flatten out there, and the Jews might be expected to relax their vigilance.

The din of the convoy's motors rose, and finally the lead armored car appeared around a bend on the road. Tensely, Neggar watched it crawl toward him. It seemed to the tailor like "an enormous black beetle." He tightened his fingers until he heard the click of the plunger. An explosion shook his ditch, and a cloud of smoke enveloped the armored car. When it cleared, Neggar blinked. He had pushed his plunger too soon. Instead of destroying the vehicle, he had blown an enormous crater in the road. Unable to stop in time, the heavy vehicle had lumbered forward and tumbled into the hole.

Behind the car, the rest of the convoy ground to a halt. So abrupt was the stop in Esther Passman's ambulance that the nurse dropped her thermos of tea. For a moment, the concerned passengers sat in their darkened vehicles, wondering what was happening outside. A signal from Neggar to the score of men with him in his ditch gave them the answer. A rain of gunfire swept into the stalled convoy.

The explosion, the gunfire, attracted the attention of all Jerusalem. By the scores, then by the hundreds, Arab irregulars poured toward the ambush site from the villages nearby and the walls of the Old City. In the suffocating darkness of their metallic prisons, the passengers began to hear a new sound mingling with the din of the gunfire. It was a guttural clamor, a furious call for vengeance, the name of the Arab village the two wounded men in Esther Passman's ambulance had helped assault three days earlier: "Deir Yassin!"

Less than a mile away, in the courtyard of St. Paul's German Hospice, three companies of the Highland Light Infantry, their officers in the regiment's green-and-yellow kilts, stood to attention. While the units' bagpipes played, an inspecting party walked slowly down their ranks. Suddenly a signalman waving a slip of paper rushed up behind them.

"What's the matter?" a short beribboned colonel snapped at him. The signalman handed him a message from the regiment's soldiers in Antonious House. It had been timed off at 09:35 and gave the British command their first notification of the convoy's plight. The colonel spun on his heels and left to investigate the incident.

A veteran of Dunkirk, the landing in Sicily and a commando mission which had ended in Dachau, Jack Churchill, forty-eight, was a florid-faced, colorful Scot who had begun his career with the Highland Light Infantry in Rangoon in 1926. A pleasant eccentric, he had later distinguished himself marching from Naples to London playing the bagpipes. The second in command of the Highland, Churchill knew as well as Chaim Yassky the terrain between Mount Scopus and Jerusalem. The road linking them had been his unit's responsibility for months. He leaped into his Dingo armored car and set out for the ambush site.

There the driver of Esther Passman's ambulance struggled to turn his vehicle around. To the American widow, the assault outside seemed "like an Indian attack on a wagon train." Behind them, the Crazy One, his tires flattened by a hand grenade, wrestled to force his six-ton truck through the same maneuver. Crouched at his feet, his face white with fear, his passenger whimpered that he was never going to see his newborn child.

Inch by inch, Adin swung his truck around, then started rolling back toward Jerusalem. The three other trucks, Esther Passman's ambulance and the last armored car followed.

By the time Colonel Churchill arrived, the lead armored car, the Yasskys' ambulance and the two buses were caught in Neggar's trap. Armed Arabs were arriving from all sides. The Jews in the armored car were holding them off, firing through the slits of their vehicles. Churchill cupped his hands and yelled for a cease-fire. His words were lost in the clatter of gunfire. He quickly understood the gravity of the situation. The Arabs had occupied the houses all along the road, and, at the rate at which they were arriving, the Jews would soon be hopelessly trapped.

At ten-thirty he radioed Jerusalem headquarters requesting half a troop of Life Guard armored cars, an observation officer to arrange for shelling the houses in which the Arabs had taken position, and permission to use his three-inch mortars. He was denied his last two requests, and it would be almost an hour before the Life Guards would receive orders to move. That baffling indifference to the convoy's plight characterized the British headquarters reaction to the tragedy all day long. Whether from a bureaucratic and inept application of procedures, a subliminal desire to punish the Jewish community for Deir Yassin, or the active complicity at some level in the command of the officer who had given Neggar the green light for the operation, the British would be responsible for an unconscionable delay in coming to the convoy's rescue.

Furious at the answer to his requests, Churchill fumed, "They don't realize we're going to have a tragedy here. If they don't hurry, nobody's going to get out alive." Determined to do what he could to save the trapped Jews himself, Churchill rushed back to St. Paul's Hospice for a truck and a half-track to mount a rescue operation of his own.

His determination to do something was all the more remarkable since the Haganah had not yet realized the urgency of the situation. Another convoy on the opposite edge of Jerusalem had the attention of the organization's leadership that day. It was the second to arrive from Tel Aviv since Operation Nachshon had reopened the road to Jerusalem. Informed of the ambush as he watched the convoy's one hundred and seventy-eight vehicles roll down Jaffa Road, David Shaltiel immediately asked the convoy commander for the loan of the armored cars in his escort. The commander refused. He had strict orders to return to Tel Aviv as fast as possible. All Shaltiel had available was three cars of his own, commanded by a young officer named Zvi Sinai.

The operation turned into a nightmare. The first car was hit by heavy fire, took several wounded and bolted past the trapped convoy to deliver its injured to Hadassah Hospital. The car in the rear turned back to Jerusalem after taking several killed and wounded. Sinai's car, driven by a soldier from Tel Aviv who did not know the road, stumbled onto the mine crater that had trapped the convoy's lead armored car. Only one man remained alive in that car, Sinai discovered, and he was wounded. Then his own car stalled. His driver, paralyzed by fear, refused to start it again.

Calmly Sinai put his pistol to the boy's head. "You have two possibilities," he said. "Either you're going to be killed by the Arabs or you'll be killed by me if you don't start this car." As the stunned youth turned the engine over, however, there was an explosion outside. An Arab mine had torn off a front wheel. Another metal hulk was caught in Neggar's trap. To the prisoners of the Haganah convoy were added the fourteen Palmachniks in Sinai's car.

Meanwhile, Colonel Churchill had returned with a G.M.C. and a half-track. To his immense chagrin, he learned that Dr. and Mrs. Yassky were among the trapped passengers. Barely a week earlier, Churchill had dined with the doctor and his wife on their flower-covered Mount Scopus terrace. His Dingo armored car in the lead, Churchill moved out to the trapped vehicles.

"If the Arabs shoot at me, blow their bloody heads off," he told Cassidy, the half-track gunner. Then he leaned out of his car and banged on the door of the last bus with his swagger stick. He told the nurse who came to the grill to open the doors and run for his half-track.

"Can you guarantee us safety?" asked the nurse.

"No, I can't," replied Churchill. "Open the door and run for it."

"But we'll all be killed!" screamed the nurse.

"If you stay there, you'll all damn well be killed," Churchill told her. Again he urged her to run the few feet between their bus and his half-track, promising that his gunner would cover them.

"But we're all right here," pleaded the nurse.

"You won't be all right very long," Churchill shouted.

Then another voice inside the bus yelled, "Why don't your soldiers chase the Arabs away?"

By now Churchill was furious. At the risk of his life he had come out to save these people, and all he was getting was an argument. Someone else added, "We'll wait here until the Haganah rescues us."

At that instant, Churchill heard a shout behind him. Cassidy, the gunner of the half-track, had been hit in the neck. Churchill gave the trapped passengers a last chance to flee. They refused. Staggered, Churchill backed off to take his dying gunner to Antonious House. The only serious British effort to save the imperiled Jews had failed.

From rooftops, from balconies, from windows, from Government House and Mount Scopus, half of Jerusalem would now witness the dying agony of the convoy. The British remained impassive despite the dozens of beseeching calls pouring down on them. At eleven-thirty, two hours after the first word of the incident, the first Life Guard armored cars reached the scene. The lead car fired one round and its gun jammed. It was two more hours before additional cars arrived. Colonel Churchill did not receive permission to use his mortars until noon. Permission to use anything heavier would never be forthcoming. The Haganah was bluntly informed that its men would be fired on if they tried to intervene.

Inside Zvi Sinai's armored car, the Jews' sole defense against the hundreds of Arabs besieging the convoy, the situation was critical. The first man killed had been the first-aid man. Then one of their machine guns had jammed. By now half the men inside the car were dead or wounded. The floor was covered with blood and bodies. The survivors, jumping from side to side to fire their Stens from the car's slits, stepped indiscriminately on them. "If they shouted, you knew they weren't dead," Sinai grimly recalled. At the rear end of the car, the only machine gun working was being fed by a man who had already lost half a hand. The wounded, with no one to care for them, sat propped up against the sides of the car slowly bleeding to death.

By the side of the road, a thirteen-year-old Arab boy named Jamil Bazian watched the men beside him soaking rags in gasoline to hurl at the trapped cars.

At three-fifteen, Dr. Yassky turned to peer from the slit by the driver's seat of the ambulance. A hundred yards behind him he saw the first results of the scene Jamil Bazian had just witnessed. Great sheets of orange flame were sweeping over the two buses crowded with his friends and colleagues. He turned toward his wife. *"Shalom,* my dear," he said. "It's the end."

Then Yassky pitched forward and tumbled to the floor of the ambulance. His wife rushed to his side. The director of Hadassah Hospital was dead. He had been struck by a bullet passing through the ambulance slit at the moment he had turned to address his wife.

Seconds later, the shocked occupants of his ambulance heard a frantic rap on the door of their vehicle. "Open, quick!" a voice screamed. It was a survivor of one of the blazing buses. He plunged half crazily into their midst, groaning, "Save yourselves! You're all going to be roasted." At his words, the ambulance's Yemenite driver opened his door and slipped outside.

One of his passengers, Dr. Yehuda Matot, decided to follow him. Matot shouldn't have been in the convoy in the first place. His turn in Scopus was next week, but he had agreed to substitute this morning for a colleague. Tumbling into the outside ditch, Matot had a strange thought. "At last," he told himself, "I can light a cigarette." The sight of the dead ambulance driver a few yards away brought him back to his senses. Desperately he started crawling toward Antonious House. Jamil Bazian saw him start his frantic race. Everybody fired on him. One shot struck Matot in the back, but he continued to pull himself forward until he reached Katy Antonious' garden wall. "What good luck!" sighed his thirteen-year-old enemy.

Katy Antonious' house was a scene of wild confusion. Its parquet floors were littered with wounded, Arab, Jewish and even British. One officer of the Highland Light Infantry, Captain James Crawford, had gone up to Hadassah Hospital and returned with a doctor to treat the wounded. As the two men rushed into Antonious House, they stumbled on an elderly Arab dying in the garden, moaning for help. The man had been caught in a crossfire as he walked into town with his donkey. Despite the fact that so many of his colleagues awaited his care inside, despite the risks of pausing in the exposed garden, the Jewish doctor knelt beside him to examine his wounds.

Almost six hours after the explosion of Mohammed Neggar's mine, shortly after half past three, the British command finally authorized the men on the spot to intervene vigorously in the ambush. While Churchill and his soldiers of the Highland provided cover fire, Captain Michael Naylor Leyland led his Life Guard armored cars to the besieged vehicles. When he got in close, he radioed back for smoke to cover their movement. To his fury there "was some interminable chitchat about what kind of smoke." Finally he fired off all his own car's smoke himself.

He and his men then took their car covers and, using them to screen a passage between the trapped vehicles and their cars, got the survivors out. There were barely half a dozen left alive.

One of them was Zvi Sinai. A few minutes later, delirious and barely conscious, suffering from a terrible head wound, Sinai lay on a stretcher in Hadassah Hospital. A doctor walked down the line of wounded men selecting those to be treated first. He peered down at Sinai's face. "No," he said, "that's one of them. It's an Arab." He passed on. Sinai was too weak to protest, too dizzy from loss of blood to care. A nurse passing behind the doctor cast a quick glance at him. She started. "My God," she gasped, "it's not an Arab. It's Zvi Sinai!"

By nightfall it was over. A ghastly silence reigned at last on the bend in the road to Mount Scopus where Mohammed Neggar had detonated his mine. A few ribbons of smoke, the putrid stench of burned flesh, and the carbonized remains of the convoy's trapped vehicles remained to greet the falling dusk. Dr. Moshe Ben-David had been faithful to his appointment in Samarra. The bus after which he had so frantically run had been his coffin. At least seventy-five others, most of them men and women who had come to Palestine to heal, not kill, had died with him. So completely had the flames devoured their victims that twenty-four of their bodies would never be identified.

The following morning, Moshe Hillman, the Haganah man who had cleared the convoy's departure, picked through the ruins, removing a skull, an arm, a hat, a stethoscope, a pair of glasses. When he had finished, he turned the wreckage over to a team of British demolition experts.

"The remaining vehicles were blown up to clear the road," laconically noted the daily log of the Highland Light Infantry, "and the road mended, and reopened to traffic."

As they had in December, the curious crowds collected along Cairo's Kasr al Nil underneath the brightly lit windows of Egypt's Ministry of Foreign Affairs. This time the hot breath of the khamsin licked their faces and sent its fine powder sifting into the room above where once again the leaders of the Arab League debated into the night.

They had reached a critical turning point in the Palestine situation. Their early guerrilla successes had been followed by several recent reverses. The Haganah had succeeded in temporarily reopening the road to Jerusalem and had killed Abdul Khader Husseini. Fawzi el Kaukji's Liberation Army had proved a disappointment. The massacre of Deir Yassin was producing the first hints of an Arab flight from Palestine. Six thousand precious rifles and eight million rounds of ammunition, the principal fruit of their arms-purchasing efforts, had been lost in Bari harbor. To even the most ardent advocates of guerrilla warfare it was apparent that only the coordinated intervention of all the Arab armies could now reverse the situation.

For the past six months their foe's strategy had been based on the assumption that the Arab states would attack a Jewish state as soon as

Britain's Palestine mandate expired. That calculation had determined David Ben-Gurion's planning and had sent Golda Meir on her American fund-raising drive and Ehud Avriel into the arsenals of Eastern Europe. Yet the Arab leaders in Egypt's Ministry of Foreign Affairs were no closer to taking that decision than they had been in December.

They did not have to choose war. Before them was a chance to wrest from the West a more favorable Palestine settlement than they could have dared hope for a few months earlier. If their guerrilla campaign had not defeated the Jews, it had led to the Arabs' first significant diplomatic victory in Palestine since Britain's 1939 White Paper: the United States' attempt to substitute a United Nations trusteeship for partition. Now the United Nations Security Council was appealing to both sides in the conflict for a cease-fire. Implicit in the call was the idea that a cease-fire would be followed by a fundamental reexamination of the Palestine issue. The Arab leadership could seize the opportunity offered by those proposals, take the diplomatic initiative and perhaps force the world to a new Palestine formula more favorable to their cause, or they could commit themselves to war and order their armies to do what Haj Amin's guerrillas were clearly incapable of doing, defeating the Jews.

With the exception of Haj Amin Husseini, a recent addition to their circle, the men who were confronted with those grave choices were moderate and intelligent individuals. None of them belonged to the generation of more extremist leaders whose revolutions would soon alter the character of the Arab world. They were tranquil bourgeois, inclined more to conservatism than to adventure. As individuals, they were often culturally closer to the Westerners of the nations that had once ruled them than they were to the masses they governed. Jamil Mardam's passions were growing apricot trees and reciting Arab poetry. Riad Solh's regular bedside reading consisted of Montaigne, Descartes and Rousseau. Azzam Pasha was a gravely polite, courtly gentleman whose accomplishments included a medical degree and the honor of having been the youngest man ever elected to the Egyptian parliament. Nuri as-Said was more at ease in London than he was in the deserts of Iraq.

Yet collectively those individually capable men were leading their people to disaster. Their persistent tendency to underestimate their Jewish foes, to judge their settlement by a condescending, faintly anti-Semitic standard, had led them into an appalling state of overconfidence. "The idea that they might not be able to lick the Jews simply hadn't occurred to them," observed Britain's able minister in Amman, Sir Alec Kirkbride.

Reasonable and moderate in private, particularly with foreigners, they reverted in public to the overwrought flights of rhetoric that were the coin of their political discourse. Always ready to stir public passions to their private ends, they were now trapped by the passions they had stirred. Leaders of a society in which the Word had an exalted role in every act of life from welcoming a stranger to pronouncing a funeral exhortation, they hurled off their verbal thunderbolts without measuring their impact on the emotional, underdeveloped masses they led. Nor did they measure their impact on their foes. None of the men in the Egyptian Foreign Ministry really meant to be taken literally in threatening to "drive the Jews into the sea." But they failed to remember that their foes had just seen six million of their kind driven into Hitler's ovens. While their threats might not be taken at face value in the salons of Cairo, they were read with total serious- ness on the sidewalks of Tel Aviv.

Azzam Pasha continued to advocate, as he had done for months, mil- itary action in Palestine. Yet in the privacy of his own soul he had con- cluded, "We didn't really want war, but we were putting ourselves in a position in which there was going to be no way out but war." He did not dare urge an alternative on his colleagues, but, with the knowledge of only one among them, Azzam had gone to a secret meeting with British Am- bassador Sir Ronald Campbell to beg him to get Britain to extend her Palestine mandate for another year. Thus Britain, he hoped, might spare his fellow Arabs the confrontation he dreaded but did not dare condemn publicly.

While Jamil Mardam's Syrian government had been nourishing that winter the army pledged to drive the Jews into the sea, his wife had been regularly visiting Jerusalem to have a stomach ulcer treated by her Jewish doctor. Transjordan's King Abdullah had already secretly decided to use his army to aggrandize his kingdom, not attack the Jews. The eviction that interested Egypt's Nokrashy Pasha was not that of the Jews from Palestine but that of the British from the Suez Canal Zone. Iraq's Nuri as-Said had been brandishing his army like a sword for months, yet when the day of decision came that army would be most noted for its absence from the battlefield. No man had more persistently urged military action to thwart partition than Lebanon's Solh. Only Transjordan's Abdullah, however, had more amicable relations with the Jewish Agency than he. In seven months' time, in Paris, in one of his regular secret meetings at 7 A.M. in his hotel room with the Jewish Agency's Tuvia Arazi, he would poignantly express the Arab dilemma.

"Tuvia," he would plead, "you must convince the Americans to force us to make peace with you. We want to do it. But it's only possible for us politically if we are forced to do it."

Azzam Pasha revealed that George Allen, first secretary of the United States Embassy in Cairo, had submitted to him a copy of the American trusteeship proposal with a request for the Arab League's opinions before the special session of the General Assembly that was due to convene in four days, on April 16. Haj Amin Husseini quickly suggested that the proposal be submitted for study to a special committee made up of the representatives of Syria, Transjordan and Palestine. A few minutes later, he succeeded in confiding to the same committee the task of replying to the United Nation's truce call.

The committee's report on both items was ready in forty-eight hours. With minor changes, it was adopted and sent off to New York. The Arabs could have saved themselves the time and trouble. Their reply was couched in conditions so hopelessly unrealistic that any possibility of its receiving serious consideration by even their most ardent backers was eliminated. They would consider a truce only if the Haganah were dissolved, the Stern Gang and the Irgun disarmed, all Jewish immigration stopped and all illegal Jewish immigrants in Palestine deported. As for trusteeship, they would accept it only if it were exercised by the Arab states, not the United Nations, and led swiftly to what they had been asking for years, an Arab Palestine state. With their answer, Loy Henderson's scheme was dead, the last life wrung from it by the very men it had been designed to assist.

Having rejected peace, the logical course of action for the Arab leaders was to prepare for war. Things were not to be as simple as that, however. While the men meeting in Cairo had been willing to vote a joint war chest of four million pounds sterling, they had thus far actually paid up barely ten percent of that sum. With the exception of the Arab Legion, none of the Arab armies had made any significant preparation for war in the past four months. A fifteen-page typewritten document accompanied by three maps constituted the Arabs' most substantial preparation for war. It was a plan for the invasion of Palestine.

The plan had been drafted by Major Wasfi Tell, the young officer who had earlier authored the stern warning on the Haganah's capacities to Safwat Pasha. It called for a northern thrust by the Lebanese, Syrian and Liberation armies, spearheaded by an Iraqi armored force to capture the port of Haifa, while a narrow southern thrust by the Egyptian Army up the coastal plain would seize Jaffa. Thus the new state would be deprived of the ports that Tell knew it would need to bring in men and arms after

294

the British left. At the same time, the Arab Legion and the balance of the Iraqi Army would aim to cut the Jewish settlement in half by thrusting across the coastal plain from the Judean hills to the sea north of Tel Aviv. The campaign was to take eleven days.

To implement it, Tell had asked that virtually all of the Arab armies be placed under a supreme commander. If those forces, prepared or not, were made available, Tell's plan had every chance of success. It was the stuff of which Ben-Gurion's nightmares were made.

Its most ardent advocates, Riad Solh and Jamil Mardam, knew that its implementation depended on the cooperation of two enigmatic monarchs who cordially loathed each other. One was Abdullah. The other sovereign was the court of last resort able to overrule the stubborn history professor who refused to commit the largest army the Arabs possessed to their Palestine adventure.

Farouk sat almost nightly in a building a few doors down the Kasr al Nil from the Foreign Ministry. The only official designation stamped onto its carefully polished brass doorplate were four initials, "A.C.R.E." There, with astonishing regularity, the King of Egypt took his place at a green-baize-covered table of the Automobile Club Royal d'Egypte, an ice-cold bottle of orange soda pop at his side, to play baccarat and chemin de fer. Indicative of his nation's popular indifference to the Palestine drama and the country's long tradition of Arab–Jewish harmony was the fact that almost half of his regular partners were Jewish.

The sovereign who could not be disturbed with the news of the partition vote had just turned twenty-eight in April 1948. He had inherited his throne on his father's death twelve years earlier, coming to it a handsome, athletic young man, adored by his people, seemingly destined to an exemplary reign. Three humiliating circumstances turned his life into a tragicomedy. The first was physical. Nature had given him an undersized sexual organ, a cruel jest on the proud young ruler of a land in which sexual potency was traditionally one measure of a man's ability to lead. The second was political. It occurred in January 1942 while Rommel prepared the offensive with which he hoped to seize the Suez Canal. A revolver in his hand, Britain's ambassador to Cairo had ordered Farouk to replace his pro-German Prime Minister with a man more to Britain's liking. From that moment forward the humiliated Farouk harbored a deep and sometimes blinding hatred of the British. The third was an automobile accident in 1944 which upset his glandular balance and helped turn the vain young King into a corpulent figure of ridicule.

By April 1948, Farouk had fallen far from the promise of his youth, but he was no less ambitious for that. He was the heir to the throne of the pharaohs. He longed to avenge the humiliations of his life and his nation by reviving Egypt's ancient grandeur, by installing her at the head of a proud new caliphate stretching from the Euphrates to the Nile. He regarded his fellow Arab leaders with contempt, but above all he scorned the chess-playing Bedouin in Amman. For Farouk, Abdullah was only the Middle Eastern tool of his hated foes, the British.

Those noble designs, however, did not seem to occupy a preponderant place in the young King's preoccupations that spring. Each evening when his card game was finished, he set off on a tour of his favorite shrines, the nightclubs of Cairo. The grail that Farouk sought on those nightly crusades was the pleasure which nature had contrived to deprive him of, sexual satisfaction. His guide was a wizened little monkey nicknamed "the Stork" because in years of following in Farouk's nocturnal footsteps he had learned to sleep standing up.

Antonio Pulli had begun his remarkable career by getting on the wrong boat. Youngest of a family of nine children, he had left his native Naples to seek his fortune along the Amazon, but wound up by mistake along the Nile. His prolific family had relatives in Egypt as well as Brazil, however, and he went to work as an apprentice to an electrician uncle in the royal palace. One day Pulli was summoned to the royal nursery to repair Crown Prince Farouk's electric train. From that simple act was born a lifelong friendship.

By 1948 he had become the King's Minister of Personal Affairs with a salary two and a half times that of the Prime Minister. One special task accounted for his exalted stipend. In the shadowy corners of the Cairo night, Antonio Pulli procured women for the King of Egypt. The most important rendezvous Pulli arranged for his sovereign in that April fortnight of 1948, however, were with a courtesan of a different sort, and they would alter the history of his adopted land. They were with Riad Solh.

Each night, under Pulli's discreet regard, the two men paced along the giant palms and eucalyptus trees of the Koubeh Palace gardens, Solh, the spellbinding talker, exhorting the King to war, Farouk listening patiently.

Solh knew well the arguments that would stir the King's imagination. When the British left, the Arabs would sweep into Palestine, he said, and restore that land to Arab sovereignty. What a tragedy it would be for the Arab world, for Egypt, for Farouk, if the Arabs' largest army was not present at that historic rendezvous, from which Farouk could emerge the undisputed leader of the Arab world. If he remained aloof from the conflict, Solh warned, it would be at the profit of his enemies, Abdullah and the British. Palestine would soon be under an Arab crown, and it was up to Farouk to decide whether it would be the crown of Egypt or the crown of the Hashemites.

Should he wish, Solh reminded the King, he could install his protégé Haj Amin Husseini in Palestine. Then his influence would reach from Khartoum to Jerusalem, and the stage would be set for the emergence of a modern caliphate, this time with its headquarters in Cairo, not Constantinople.

When their midnight conversations were finished, usually around two or three in the morning, Solh regularly dropped in for a chat with his friends on Cairo's largest paper, *Al Ahram.* One night in mid-April, the paper's young proprietor saw him stride into the city room, his tarboosh cocked at a rakish angle on his head, a jubilant smile across his face.

Solh settled in the editor's chair and clapped his hands for coffee. "You cannot print what I am going to tell you," he said. As usual, he reported, he had been walking for hours in the Koubeh Palace gardens with Farouk.

"This time," he smiled, "I convinced him. I can announce to you the best news the Arabs have had since partition. Egypt is going to war."

24

"ATTACK AND ATTACK AND ATTACK."

ABDUL KHADER HUSSEINI'S DEATH forced major changes in the Arabs' guerrilla tactics and organization around Jerusalem. The Mufti named another member of the Husseini family, Khaled, a forty-year-old officer of the Palestine police force, to succeed him. With none of the personal magnetism of his kinsman, Khaled could not impose any real authority over the collection of chieftains making up the Arabs' Jerusalem command. At the moment when Britain's approaching withdrawal made unity and a central authority imperative, the Arabs' organization thus tended to revert to its system of splintered neighborhood bands. Ibrahim Abou Dayieh, the Hebron shepherd, commanded Katamon. Kamal Irekat, who had organized the ambush of the Kfar Etzion convoy, ran the south. Mounir Abou Fadel, a former police inspector, was in charge of the center of the city with a group of former policemen. Bajhat Abou Gharbieh, the schoolteacher who had been left behind in Kastel, took over the north. To their already divided ranks was added still another chieftain, this one a thirty-four-year-old Iraqi bank clerk named Fadel Rashid, who arrived in the city with five hundred volunteers.

Emile Ghory took over the remnants of Abdul Khader's organization in Bab el Wad. Their leader's death and the assaults of Operation Nachshon had been severe blows for the Arab guerrillas stationed along the road. Deir Yassin had compounded their problem by starting a flow of people out of the hilltop villages vital to the guerrillas. There were "few arms, no money and bad morale," Ghory discovered.

He decided to abandon the ambush tactics which required the support of massive numbers of villagers and go back to the strategy Abdul Khader had once rejected, of closing the road with mammoth barricades defended by a limited number of men. Ghory raised ten thousand pounds sterling from the Arab banks in Jerusalem, then set out from village to village raising paid levies.

Capitalizing on the disarray of their foes, the Haganah had already pushed three major convoys up the road since opening it April 5. Before a fourth could be organized, a cable of major consequence reached Tel Aviv from the Jerusalem Haganah. The British were going to evacuate certain fortified areas in the city before the mandate expired, probably in the last days of April, Shaltiel's intelligence officers reported. To capitalize on the move, Shaltiel asked for the Har-el Palmach Brigade operating around Bar el Wad. With it, he said, "it will be possible to strike a decisive blow in the city. . . . The outcome of our battle in Jerusalem depends on the number of reinforcements you send."

His cable placed the Tel Aviv command before a difficult decision. The brigade still had not cleared many of the Arab villages along the route to Jerusalem. Only one village, Kastel, had actually been destroyed, the mukhtar's house near which Abdul Khader Husseini had fallen being left intact by the departing Palmach as a symbol of their victory there. Nonetheless, at almost the same time as Emile Ghory, Tel Aviv decided on a change of tactics. Yitzhak Rabin was ordered to put his men on the next convoy to the city, leaving virtually unprotected the heights they had been trying to clear and abandoning for the time being the effort to push supplies into Jerusalem.

The last convoy, composed of almost three hundred trucks, left Kfar Bilu before dawn April 20. In addition to their loads of flour, sugar, rice and margarine, its trucks contained stocks of the traditional unleavened bread, matzo, so that Jerusalem could celebrate the coming Passover. Riding at its head, exposed to Arab riflemen in an ordinary car, was perhaps the most important commodity the Jewish people possessed that spring, the white-haired figure of David Ben-Gurion. Silent and unsmiling, he rode through the gorge he had walked four decades before as an ardent young Zionist. The roadside gullies in which he had slept so peacefully were now a clutter of burned-out trucks, blackened relics by which Ben-Gurion could reckon the cost of clinging to the city in which he had once sought inspiration and found instead a Tower of Babel.

The convoy stretched over sixteen miles of road. Its first vehicles reached Jerusalem without incident. Then Emile Ghory's men fell on those coming behind them. The Arab leader was awed by their ferocity. He saw one of them, crawling on his stomach, drag a can of gasoline under a stalled truck. He poured the liquid onto the asphalt and set it ablaze. Then, rolling like a dervish, he raced the flames back toward the roadside gully from which he had come.

All day long in Jerusalem, Dov Joseph recorded in his logbook each truckload of supplies as it reached his warehouses. The goal he had set for himself that night in Tel Aviv when David Ben-Gurion had assigned him his responsibility was three thousand tons. With strict rationing, that reserve, he calculated, would last Jersualem two months. Despite his dictatorial powers, however, he had been able to amass only eighteen hundred tons from Tel Aviv's warehouses before returning to Jerusalem. As the afternoon wore on, the column of trucks that managed to extricate themselves from Ghory's ambush dwindled to a trickle. Even the eighteen hundred tons he had managed to commandeer were not going to reach the Canadian's warehouses. The doors were slamming shut again, and he had been able to get barely half what he considered essential into the city. Noting the figures in his book, he suddenly thought, "It is not enough."

It was dark when the last vehicle entered the city. Back in Bab el Wad, Emile Ghory's men were already at work piling up the roadblocks with which to cut the route for good. Once again Jewish Jerusalem was under siege.

• • •

"He doesn't walk into a room, he stomps into it," thought Chaim Haller.

Eyebrows knit in anger, his forehead furrowed, David Ben-Gurion settled into his place before Jerusalem's senior officials. He was in a fierce, angry mood. First he turned to David Shaltiel's recommendations to pull out of Kfar Etzion and the Jewish Quarter of the Old City. Shaltiel's planning officer, Eliyahu Arbel, noticed that Ben-Gurion was "shaking with fury" at their proposal. "No Jewish settlement will be evacuated!" he shouted at Shaltiel, smashing his fist on the table top.

Courageously Shaltiel tried to defend his thesis, but Ben-Gurion interrupted him, growling, "There will be no retreat." An entire strategic doctrine lay behind Ben-Gurion's refusal. If he acceded to Shaltiel's request, how could he force his lonely Negev settlements to stay put in the face of an Egyptian advance?

Then he turned to the matter which lay at the heart of his presence in the besieged city. His arrival coincided with a basic change in his intentions toward its political destiny. The Jews had, he felt, honestly endeavored to be faithful to the internationalization scheme. After all, among his first instructions to Shaltiel had been the order to accept the United Nations' authority in the city if and when the international body established a presence there. The Jewish Agency had repeatedly pleaded with the plan's backers to put their scheme into effect. The last of those pleas, a letter from Chaim Weizmann to Harry Truman, had been hand-carried to the President by Judge Samuel Rosenman on April 20, the day Ben-

Gurion had had to fight through an Arab ambush at Bab el Wad to get to the city.

> Jerusalem should not be a problem of Jewish defence [Weizmann wrote]. It was the United States which took the lead together with France, Belgium and Holland in urging the Jews to give up their claim that Jerusalem should be within the boundaries of a Jewish state, on the grounds of the city's universal character and its association with Christianity and Islam. The Jews, after deep heart searchings, made that sacrifice: it is now for the United Nations to fulfill the task which they have undertaken.

Ben-Gurion, however, had few illusions as to what the response to this latest plea would be. The indifference of internationalization's backers to the city's plight, the Arabs' repeated threats of war, had released the Jewish people, he felt, from their pledge to internationalize the city. With the Arabs of the city in a state of disarray, the Haganah had a glittering opportunity before it.

Ben-Gurion's confrontation with Shaltiel over Kfar Etzion had undermined his confidence in the city's commander, however. To take advantage of the situation, he decided to place Shaltiel's forces and the Har-el Brigade of the Palmach under the temporary command of Yitzhak Sadeh, the founder of the Palmach. The former circus wrestler who had toasted each passing partition vote with a glass of vodka was a man Ben-Gurion could count on to carry out his new orders to Jerusalem's soldiers: "Attack and attack and attack."

The next morning a green-and-black Hebrew poster appeared on the walls of the city. It announced the creation of an exclusively Jewish Jerusalem City Council. It was the logical consequence of the new Jewish position on Jerusalem, and it heralded the birth of one idea and the death of another. Internationalization was finished. Jerusalem would now belong, not to the world, but to whoever had the strength to claim it.

• • •

Yitzhak Sadeh lost no time in planning an offensive in Jerusalem. Instead of waiting for the British to move, as intelligence had promised they would, Sadeh decided to go into action himself. His objective, he told the Har-el Brigade commander, Yitzhak Rabin, was "to seize the vital areas of the city from the Arabs so that on May 14 Jerusalem will fall into our hands."

"If we can get away with this," he promised, "Jerusalem will be all ours forty-eight hours after the British leave."

Sadeh's plan was split into three phases. The first called for the capture of the peak of Nebi Samuel, from which Kaukji had shelled the city. The second, in the north, called for the capture of the Arab quarter of Sheikh Jarrah to establish a link with Mount Scopus, then as soon as possible to move to the Mount of Olives, clearing the whole northern ridge of the city and cutting the Arab Legion's natural access routes to Jerusalem. Simultaneously, in the south, Rabin's forces would try to seize the Arab quarters of Katamon, German Colony, Talpiot and Silwan, thus virtually encircling the city.

It was a classically simple, straightforward plan, and twenty years later another generation of Israeli soldiers would draw their inspiration from it. Sadeh conferred on it the name that Jerusalem had borne four thousand years before, when it was little more than the campsite of a Semitic tribe. Operation Jebussi had only one drawback. Its success depended on one imponderable: to what extent would the British interfere?

In Cairo, Farouk's Prime Minister, Nokrashy Pasha, was summoned to lunch at the Mohammed Ali Club by members of the King's inner circle. Farouk wanted a declaration of war, he was told. Either Nokrashy would ask parliament for it or the King would get a prime minister who would.

Nokrashy's principal failing, in the eyes of one of his key subordinates, was that "he was a man who wanted to have everything." He wanted to stay out of war, but he wanted even more to stay in his prime minister's office. Despite his misgivings, he let himself be convinced of the wisdom of changing his mind. As a first step, he arranged a conference with the commander in chief of the Egyptian Army, a gruff, genial giant of a man named Mohammed Haidar Pasha. Haidar possessed two qualifications for his high office: he had been director of his nation's prisons and he made Farouk laugh.

The Army, he assured Nokrashy, was prepared for war. In any event, he told the Prime Minister, "there will be no war with the Jews." It would be "a parade without any risk whatsoever." The Army, he pledged, "will be in Tel Aviv in two weeks."

Shortly thereafter another visitor called on Nokrashy. Sir Ronald Campbell arrived with his motorcycle escort in a manner befitting His Majesty's ambassador to Egypt. Great Britain, he informed Nokrashy, according to a minute dictated by the Egyptian after their conversation, did not approve or encourage the coming clash of arms in Palestine. For her part, she was resigned to accepting partition as representing the judgment of the world as expressed by the United Nations. If she were asked for counsel by any of her Arab friends, she would advise them not to participate in the war and to accept partition.

However, Sir Ronald continued, should it be Egypt's decision to enter the war, Great Britain would not oppose her efforts nor hinder the movement of her forces. Then he turned to the question of arms. Should Egypt decide to go to war and find herself in need of additional munitions and armaments, His Majesty's government was prepared to allow the Egyptian Army access to her Suez Canal supply depots on two conditions. The first was discretion. The second was that the two nations continue satisfactory progress toward a solution to the problem which most concerned them, the Sudan.

For a man reaching out, as Nokrashy was, for some justification for a shift in his policy, Sir Ronald's words had a most welcome ring. The Prime Minister succumbed. A few days later, his aides shifted their daily instructions to the Cairo press. Palestine was ordered back onto the front pages of Egypt's newspapers. A popular poster began to appear around the city. It showed a dagger dripping blood; on the hilt was the Star of David.

A few voices tried to warn Nokrashy. One of them belonged to an able newsman named Mohammed Hassanein Heikal. Heikal had been to Palestine, and his dispatches warned that the Jews were courageous, organized foes. Called to Nokrashy's office, Heikal was told his articles were harming morale; no one's more, perhaps, than that of the uneasy history teacher reluctantly preparing his nation for war.

Another Egyptian voice on a long-distance telephone call revealed the real state of preparedness of the army that Haidar Pasha had pronounced ready for war. If Haidar's soldiers were going to parade to Tel Aviv, they would first of all have to find out how to get there. The Egyptian Army, George Deeb, the son of Jerusalem's Buick dealer, was told, had no road maps of Palestine. The man who had organized the defense of the Upper Beqaa neighborhood was assigned the task of stealing fifty maps from the Land Settlement Department so that Haidar Pasha's subordinates could start plotting a route for their march to Tel Aviv.

25

A MESSAGE FROM GLUBB PASHA

"It is the Passover sacrifice for the Lord, who passed over the houses of the children of Israel in Egypt when he smote Egypt and spared our houses." With those words began the 3,388th observance of mankind's oldest continually observed religious ceremony, the Jewish Passover. It commemorated in a sense the night on which the history of the Jewish nation began, and on the evening of April 23, 1948, its celebration seemed heavy with the portents of the nation's imminent rebirth.

Passover's high point is the seder, the family banquet in which each ingredient is endowed with special significance. There is matzo, unleavened bread, a reminder of the haste in which the Israelites prepared the flight from Egypt. Placed on a large plate in the center of the seder table are a roasted bone, for the sacrificial lambs slaughtered on the eve of the flight, a roasted egg for the festival offering of Temple days, bitter herbs to recall the bitterness of the Egyptian bondage, a touch of parsley for the green of spring, salt water for the tears of suffering, and a mixture of chopped apples, nuts and cinnamon symbolizing the bricks made by the Israelites for Pharaoh. The ritual meal is eaten to prayers, hymns, the recital of the Haggadah, the story of the Exodus. For almost two millenniums, since Titus' destruction of the Temple, a dispersed people have ended the ceremony with one symbolic vow: "Next year in Jerusalem."

To the one hundred thousand Jews celebrating the Passover in Jerusalem in April 1948, next year was at hand. Yet for that privileged fraction of the Jewish people, the symbol of their scattered race, the western wall of Solomon's Temple, seemed that night as distant and unreachable as it was for the most dispersed of their brethren. For the first time since Saladin, no rabbi, no Jew, had bowed before the stones of the Wailing Wall. Masters of every access to the site, the Arabs of Jerusalem had refused passage to even a symbolic group of rabbis.

The Jews closest to the wall, trapped in the Old City's Jewish Quarter, celebrated their seder in two shifts, one for the Ashkenazim and one for the

Sephardim, so that all the Haganah soldiers on guard duty could join one or the other.

On their isolated hilltops guarding Jerusalem's southern approaches, the settlers of Kfar Etzion marked the Passover with a special fervor. The tables of the *Neve Ovadia*, the house of God's worker, were spread with some of the first fruits plucked from their orchards. The men on guard duty joined the others at the end of the dinner. When they entered the *Neve Ovadia* carrying their rifles, the words of a psalm sprang from the lips of their fellow settlers: "O God, place guards over Thy city day and night."

In New Jerusalem, Dov Joseph decreed a special Passover Week ration. It consisted of two pounds of potatoes, two eggs, half a pound of fish, four pounds of matzo, half a pound of meat and one and a half ounces of dried fruits. That was hardly the making of a feast, but to the city's famished inhabitants it was nonetheless an extravagant treat.

For many a Jerusalem family, a rap on the door marred the household seder. To some, the knock was eerily suggestive of the mystic visit of the Prophet Elijah, the messenger of the Messiah bringing peace to the world, for whom a goblet of wine was set out on every seder table. The author of those knocks, however, was mortal and his message concerned war, not peace. It was a representative of the Haganah calling a father or a son to prepare for Yitzhak Sadeh's coming offensive.

No seder was as memorable, perhaps, as that held in the cooperative restaurant of the Histadrut labor organization around the corner from the still-blackened ruins of Ben Yehuda Street. Gathered in the restaurant were two hundred and eighty truck drivers, the survivors of the men Bronislav Bar-Shemer and his soldiers had kidnapped three weeks earlier from the streets of Tel Aviv. They were trapped in Jerusalem by Emile Ghory's barricades, condemned now to share the suffering of the city whose hunger they had sought to ease.

A grateful Dov Joseph presided. The banquet was sparse. There was, he would recall, "a soup consisting largely of water with a few matzo balls swimming in it," gefüllte fish made "of matzo meal with a few scraps of fish to glue it together," rice and a little meat. An air of gaiety, however, made up for the cuisine. The son of a local truck driver asked the four ritual seder questions of the eldest of the stranded Tel Aviv drivers. There was, Joseph recalled, "a great deal of hilarity and hymn singing."

At the solemn concluding moment of the banquet, someone opened the door so that Elijah could enter the room. His cup was placed in the middle of the table. Then the truck drivers rose. In a lusty, bellowing chorus, they shouted out their two-thousand-year-old pledge, adding to that ancient promise two significant words: "Next year in Jerusalem—the Delivered!"

• • •

The first phase of Operation Jebussi, designed to set the stage for a Jewish takeover of Jerusalem, proved a costly failure. Thirty-five Palmach-niks lost their lives on the night of April 26 in a vain attempt to drive the Arabs from the heights of Nebi Samuel. Operation Jebussi's second phase, executed the same evening, ran into the opposition of the British. Yitzhak Sadeh's occupation of the Arab quarter of Sheikh Jarrah placed his men astride one of the British Army's evacuation routes from Jerusalem. Brigadier C. P. "Splosh" Jones, the city's troop commander, gave them six hours to withdraw or be forced out.

"Whatever makes Jones think anybody wants to stop them from leaving?" Dov Joseph snorted on reading the brigadier's ultimatum. "Don't the British realize both of us, Jew and Arab, have been trying to get them out of here for years?"

Jones was not bluffing. At exactly six o'clock in the evening of April 27, a battalion of the Highland Light Infantry and a troop of tanks supported by a battery of field artillery started to move along the road on which so many Jewish scholars and physicians had died a fortnight earlier. At the sight of their heavy equipment, so conspicuous by its absence during the agony of the Hadassah convoy, Yitzhak Sadeh's men took their lone British bazooka and withdrew to Mount Scopus.

Jones's reaction prompted Sadeh to revise the aims he had set for Operation Jebussi's third phase and limit his attack to the wealthy Arab neighborhood in which Mishael Shacham had destroyed the Hotel Semi-ramis, Katamon. Shacham's explosion had driven a number of Katamon's prosperous businessmen out of the quarter, but their places had been taken by a group of the Mufti's partisans, under Ibrahim Abou Dayieh, and, recently, a contingent of Iraqi volunteers. Entrenched in Katamon's solid stone villas, they were an Arab beachhead jammed into Jewish Jerusalem's southern flank.

Sadeh's first objective consisted of two buildings surmounted by a spindly Cyrillic cross set on the highest ground in Katamon. There, in a grove of pine and cypress trees, the Greek Orthodox Monastery of St. Simeon looked down a gentle incline toward the heart of Jerusalem.

Sadeh's men slipped along the wadi below the monastery, then attacked straight up its steep briar-covered slopes. Abou Dayieh's guerrillas and his Iraqi allies put up a ferocious resistance, but the Palmachniks, fighting their way from room to room with knives, bayonets and hand grenades, finally drove them out of the monastery into a three-story green-shuttered dwelling a hundred yards away.

There Abou Dayieh rallied his men for a counterattack. Using a train of mules to avoid British surveillance, he brought four three-inch mortars up from the Old City to his new strongpoint. Two hundred villagers led by a twenty-one-year-old sheikh arrived to reinforce his exhausted followers.

The situation inside the monastery grew desperate. So devastatingly accurate was the Arabs' sniper fire that one Jew who waved a hand for an instant outside the monastery had a fingertip shot off. On the roof, six Jewish dead, all killed by the same sniper, lay beside a Czech machine gun while a seventh man, already wounded, struggled to work the gun alone. David Elazar, a young company commander, carried off the roof one of his oldest friends, whose leg had been practically torn from his body by a mortar shell. The friend begged Elazar to kill him, murmuring, "I saw my leg." Elazar offered him what comfort he could, a shot of morphine and a reassuring word. When he returned a few minutes later, his friend was dead. He had rolled to a window, seized a shard of broken glass and cut open one of his arteries.

Before long, scores of dead and wounded lay scattered through the monastery, choking in a stench of blood, smoke and cordite. All of the officers were wounded. The radio was out. The first-aid supplies were exhausted and most of the ammunition as well. Only one member of a relief party sent to bring fresh supplies had managed to break through the Arab lines.

Among the cypress trees and the brambles around the monastery, motionless patches of blue and white, the checkered kaffiyehs of the Arab dead, attested to the high price the Arabs were paying for the losses inflicted on their foes. Hit in the spine by a grenade fragment, the stoic Abou Dayieh continued to lead his men from a wooden chair carried from place to place by two of his followers.

Finally Eliyahu Sela "Ranana," the senior Jewish officer, realized that his troops could not hold the monastery. Surrender was impossible; he was certain it would lead to a massacre. He did not have enough able-bodied men left to get his wounded out. Ranana decided to split the remains of his two companies into three groups. The walking wounded

307

and a covering escort of a few men would try to break out of the rear of the building first. Then the rest of the men still standing, with all the wounded they could carry, would follow. He and his five officers would stay behind with the rest of the wounded to cover the withdrawal. Then they would mine the monastery and blow it up on themselves and their wounded comrades. That at least would spare them the agony of dying by an Iraqi knife.

The first group left. Only one of its thirty members reached safety alive. As the second group prepared to leave, a dazed Ibrahim Abou Dayieh, a few hundred yards away, picked up a telephone. At the other end of the line, in Cairo, was Haj Amin Husseini. Brokenhearted, Abou Dayieh begged the Mufti to let him break off his attack. His men were on the verge of collapse. Only six of his original partisans remained unwounded. His ammunition and mortar shells were practically exhausted. Half sobbing, the little shepherd told the Mufti, "We have lost the battle."

As he uttered those words, a Haganah intelligence officer sat upright in the basement of the Jewish Agency. Haj Amin Husseini was not the only one listening. Minutes later a report of that vital interception was on its way to Shaltiel's headquarters from the room in which a score of men and women listened around the clock to the conversations of Jerusalem's key Arab and British leaders.

Just before the second Palmach party was due to leave the monastery, the radio began working again. The beleaguered men were informed of Abou Dayieh's declaration and urged to hold on. Within a short while, the Arabs' fire began to slacken. By nightfall reinforcements reached the monastery. St. Simeon and Operation Jebussi's first success were secured.

With the Monastery of St. Simeon in Jewish hands, the task of taking over Katamon itself was confided to the officer who had relieved the battered Palmach, Yosef Nevo, a twenty-eight-year-old who had been brought to Palestine as an infant by parents he liked to describe as the only Zionists in Chattanooga, Tennessee. In his varied career, Nevo had been an aspiring chemist, a founding member of a kibbutz, the honor graduate of the first officers' course organized by the Haganah, a sergeant major in the Royal Artillery, a student at the London School of Economics, a fledgling diplomat. He was an ebullient, outspoken young man with a shock of stiff black hair and a voice which, in a different destiny, could have called home the hogs for miles around in Tennessee.

Nevo placed his men on two parallel streets running through the center of Katamon and began working his way through the neighborhood.

At one point, a pair of Arab Legion armored cars swung out of the Iraqi Consulate and opened fire. For an instant Nevo was afraid his inexperienced soldiers would panic. He ordered them into a sturdy building and told them to use their two-inch mortars as bazookas. The cars withdrew and his exultant men continued their advance.

Worn out by the heavy losses of the day before, Abou Dayieh's men collapsed. With astonishing swiftness it was over. Nevo had taken Katamon, the Haganah's first significant conquest in Jerusalem.

His advance was so swift that the Arab civilians still in the neighborhood were forced to flee in minutes, carrying away the possessions they could stuff into their pockets or clutch in their hands. As soon as he learned the news, Dov Joseph ordered teams of men into the captured area to seize every scrap of food they could find. The scenes that greeted them in those abandoned homes were extraordinary. They found tables set, meals half eaten, forks full of food resting on the plates, ovens still lit, the food they contained blackened, gas burning under coffeepots, bathtubs overflowing, a hundred small reminders of the precipitous flight of Katamon's Arabs. Those homes yielded up a precious store of food and fuel for the city's hungry Jews. Leon Angel, the city's leading baker, uncovered a five-day supply of flour for his ovens. Dov Joseph's sugar and cooking-oil supplies, severely depleted, were suddenly replenished. One house yielded a barrel of caviar, a delicacy strictly prohibited to orthodox Jews as nonkosher. The epicurean commander of Jerusalem's hungry soldiers, David Shaltiel, could not bear the thought of letting it go to waste. He ordered it put into a marmalade vat and served up as breakfast jam at his Schneller base.

Following in the footsteps of Joseph's men, spurred by the lure of those elegant homes, came a different horde, scavengers in search of loot. Despite Nevo's orders to his men to shoot them in the legs on sight, looters sprang up everywhere like mushrooms after the rain, picking the homes bare of silver, crystal, linen, furniture, rugs, anything that would move. The following morning, one of the Arabs who had fled Katamon had an opportunity to measure the extent of their activities. The Jewish colleague with whom he shared an office telephoned him after checking on the condition of his home for him. "There is nothing left," he announced sorrowfully. "They've even taken the front door off its hinges."

· · ·

"Politics is like chess," Transjordan's King Abdullah liked to remark. "You cannot rush your pawns across enemy territory. You must look for a favorable opening." Stroking his goatee, his pale face impassive, the sovereign scrutinized the Arab leaders arrayed around him with his intense black eyes, pondering whether the moment had come to advance his pawns on the Palestine chessboard. In his immaculate white linen waistcoat and black trousers, his gold-flecked turban knotted on his head in the style peculiar to his Hejazi ancestors, the little King appeared almost out of place in the assembly gathered in his palace, a relic left over from another Arabia, an Arabia of desert tents and camel-borne warriors.

He was not what he seemed, however, and his fellow leaders of the Arab League had congregated in Amman on this May Day to obtain from Abdullah what they had obtained from Farouk, a promise to make war on the Jews. Their presence in his spare throne room placed the Hashemite ruler in an exquisitely delicate position, as complex as any of the chess problems he so enjoyed solving. With a subtlety as Oriental as the aroma of the Indian perfume he ordered regularly from Bombay, Abdullah was maneuvering on many levels. He had his special relationship with the British, and, through the periodic visits of his personal physician, Dr. Mohammed el Saty, to Jerusalem, he had maintained his contacts with the Jewish Agency. He was the only Arab leader who understood the inevitability of partition. Yet, while he might whisper his acceptance of the scheme to Briton or Jew, he did not dare recommend it to his fellow Arabs. Such advocacy, he well knew, might cost him his life or his throne. Nor did he have any intention of revealing to the men around him his plan to annex the Arab part of Palestine to his kingdom. Nonetheless, he was determined to warn his fellow Arab rulers of the perils inherent in the course they contemplated.

Should fighting be necessary, he promised, he would "be among the soldiers fighting at the front." But before plunging into war, he declared, "my advice is: stop shooting at the Jews and demand an explanation from them. Has anyone even tried this, just to find out what possibilities it offers?" he asked. The Haganah, he warned, was "perfectly trained and equipped with modern weapons." Palestine's Arabs were "emigrating by the hundreds and thousands. The price of a room in Irbid is now six dinars.* They are emigrating while the Jews advance. Tomorrow the Jews will arrive by the thousands. They will push along the coast to Gaza and up to Acre. How will the Arabs stop them? Yes, let the Arabs try to

---

* A town in the northern corner of his country. A dinar was the equivalent of a pound sterling.

confront them and thrust them back after the English leave and say to them, 'We don't recognize you,' and then God will do as he wills.

"I swear to you," he said, "if tomorrow groups of Arabs coming from Jaffa, from Haifa or someplace else come forward and miserably demand an understanding with the Jews, the reins of the affair will escape the Arab leaders, the Arab states and the Arab League."

That was not the sort of language the Arab leaders had come to Amman to hear, however. Their minds were already made up that May afternoon. The situation David Ben-Gurion had envisaged, and had begun to prepare for six months before, had come to pass. The Arabs were irrevocably bent on war.*

Indeed, they had become so confident that a conviction was rising that they need only mass their armies on Palestine's borders when the British left and the Jewish will to resist would collapse. Each of them had brought to Amman his nation's senior military men to discuss such an eventuality. The latter had waited in an anteroom while Abdullah presented his futile brief for peace. Now, after thanking the King for his words, Azzam Pasha proposed calling in the soldiers. The time had come, he said, to begin a discussion of the military problems relevant to an invasion of Palestine.

Their conference lasted all afternoon. Fully confident of the outcome of the forthcoming conflict, each leader claimed for his nation's army the preponderant role in the march to Tel Aviv. Huddled over their enormous maps of Palestine, they discussed their lines of advance, the zones of operation in which each army would maneuver, and the forces they planned to commit to the campaign.

Then politicians and generals turned together to the most difficult problem facing their coalition: selecting a joint command and a supreme commander. The rivalries infecting the Arabs' political exchanges were mirrored in their military relations. Abdullah had no intention of letting his Arab Legion, for which he had his own plans, be placed under foreign command. Farouk would not consider subordinating his army to his Bedouin rival. None of the Arab military men present trusted the most capable soldier available, John Glubb.

Hoping to exercise military control over an enterprise he had not

---

* Britain's minister in Amman, Sir Alec Kirkbride, assessing Arab intentions, noted that "they were determined to attack the Jews no matter what anybody said. If you tried to warn them disaster might be ahead, that the Jews were tough, you were a Zionist agent trying to demoralize them. Their whole attitude was: 'The sooner you British get out and leave us to deal with the Jews the better!'"

311

succeeded in restraining politically, Abdullah modestly suggested that he himself be appointed commander in chief. An embarrassed silence greeted his proposal. Aware of how utterly unacceptable such an idea was, Azzam Pasha saved the situation with a graceful phrase. "We will all be guests in Abdullah's country," he said, "and so, of course, he commands us all."

His words were never committed to paper, but they served at least to mollify Abdullah. But graceful phrases do not make efficient commands, and the answer finally adopted by the Arab soldiers left their problem unresolved while offering the illusion of a solution. Each nation, it was decided, would appoint a liaison officer to a joint operations center at the Arab Legion base of Zerqa, outside Amman.

When the conference was over, Lieutenant Colonel Charles Coker, one of the Legion's British officers, drove a high-ranking Iraqi back to the center of Amman.

"How did the meeting go?" he politely asked his passenger.

"Splendid!" was the reply. "We all agreed to fight separately."

• • •

While the leaders of the Arab armies planned their invasion of Palestine in Amman, fifty miles away in the kibbutz of Naharayim on the opposite side of the Jordan River an officer of an Arab army, in civilian clothes, began an extraordinary secret dialogue with a representative of the Haganah. While his sovereign was being shoved reluctantly toward a war, John Glubb had ordered a secret emissary to the Jewish kibbutz to propose a way to keep the Arab Legion out of the coming conflict.

To an astonished Shlomo Shamir, Colonel Desmond Goldie suggested that an arrangement could be made for the peaceful division of Palestine, with the Arab Legion taking over the Arab parts of the country, the Haganah the Jewish parts, and both staying out of Jerusalem.

The Legion, Goldie informed Shamir, was prepared to delay at least two or three days before crossing any partition boundaries, to allow the Haganah time to arrange things on its side of the border and thus hopefully avoid a war. Stressing the fact that he spoke in Glubb's name, Goldie asked what were the Haganah's intentions in Palestine. Did they intend to stay within the borders assigned the Jewish state or did they intend to expand beyond them?

Shamir's reply was deliberately noncommittal. Borders, he said, were the work of politicians, not soldiers, but if it chose to do so the Haganah was capable of conquering all of Palestine. If the Arab Legion did not attack Jerusalem there would be no need for fighting there. He would

312

immediately deliver a full report on Goldie's message to his superiors, he promised.

• • •

The ebullient young officer who had led the Haganah through Katamon confronted conquests of a different sort now. They involved a middle-aged woman welcoming him into her daughter's flat with ill-concealed distaste. For three years Yosef Nevo had been trying, with a singular lack of success, to persuade that woman to become his mother-in-law.

Nevo had first met her in the winter of 1945, when, as a student at a British Army course near London, he had been invited along with several fellow Palestinians to her home for her daughter Naomi's birthday party. One month later, while crossing a street in London, he had proposed to the pretty redheaded Naomi.

To her mother, however, Nevo was a brash, ungainly young man with a haphazard academic background, no discernible financial future, and none of the qualifications she had in mind for an aspirant for her daughter's hand. She coldly refused to sanction the match. Even a trip to Palestine, ostensibly to study the kibbutz movement, had not freed Naomi from her mother's surveillance. Her resumed romance with Nevo had been interrupted shortly after she had settled in Jerusalem by a cable announcing her mother's forthcoming arrival.

To the young couple's growing horror, she had found life in tension-filled Jerusalem entirely to her liking. The danger, the food shortages, the air of excitement, she had informed her daughter, reminded her of the exalting experience of living through the Blitz in London. As the convoys to the coast had dwindled, then stopped entirely, she had remained impervious to her daughter's pleas that she leave. Steadfast, upper lip resolutely stiffened, she had preferred to stay in besieged Jerusalem with her daughter and her daughter's unsuitable suitor.

Now Yosef Nevo was a hero, and he was determined to wed with or without the approval of his future mother-in-law. On the evening after his conquest he informed Naomi, "We're getting married."

Naomi paled. She knew from his determined air that the moment of decision had arrived. All right, she sighed, get a rabbi, and they would marry in secret in a girl friend's apartment.

A British-inspired cease-fire had concluded Yosef Nevo's other, martial conquest in Katamon and brought an end to Operation Jebussi. Yitzhak Sadeh left Jerusalem, turning command of the city back to David Shaltiel.

His departure and Jebussi's limited achievements gave fresh importance to Shaltiel's plans to seize the key buildings in the center of Jerusalem the day the British withdrew. He had assigned that task to a methodical, self-effacing police officer named Arieyeh Schurr. Schurr already had one notable triumph to his credit. A major in the military courts had slipped him a copy of the British Army's Jerusalem evacuation plan. The enormous document gave Schurr the order of departure of all British units in the city, the routes they would use, and their key assembly points. Unfortunately, it left blank a series of vital spaces. Completed by hand at the last minute, they would contain the information Schurr wanted most, the exact hour and minute of the evacuation of each British-held building in the city.

Schurr persuaded a number of the Jewish workers in the city's vital installations to remain on the job until the British walked out, so that they could hold the buildings for a few precious minutes until his troops arrived. Repairmen, typists, operators, often with no military training at all, they were baptized the "Players Brigade," after the firearm with which they would have to defend themselves while they waited for Schurr's soldiers: a box of Players cigarettes stuffed with TNT and a crude detonator. Six hundred of those primitive hand grenades had been smuggled into the General Post Office, the telephone exchange, Barclays Bank, and the court buildings.

One of the men preparing those charges for Schurr was Carmi Charny, the rabbi's son from the Bronx who had had so much difficulty persuading the Haganah to enlist him. After being trained as a machine-gunner, Charny had been assigned to the grenade manufacturers, a group of chemistry students from Hebrew University whose "factory" was a kitchen near Levi Eshkol's home. Their operation, it seemed to the young American, was "half Rube Goldberg, half mad young chemistry geniuses." One of their specialties was a flashlight, its batteries replaced with TNT and capped with a vial of sulphuric acid set in a pod of potash. A twist of the flashlight tip and a pin broke the acid vial, setting off the TNT.

Carmi's job was assembling the finished product on an empty roof on Ben Yehuda Street. Each flashlight's tip had to be screwed down to the precise point at which one more sharp twist would burst the vial. When Carmi had reached what he thought to be the proper point, he would hold the flashlight to his ear. If he heard nothing, he knew he had gauged correctly. If he heard a persistent *psst,* he had twisted too far. It was time to leave the roof as quickly as possible.

Those primitive weapons and the risks their inventors took in making them would only serve as vehicles for a number of Jewish suicides, however, if Schurr did not succeed in filling in the blank spaces on the evacuation plan handed him by his British major, so that he could get to his Players Brigade before the Arabs overran them. Two buildings in particular concerned him: the fortresslike Russian Compound, at the heart of Bevingrad, and the Italian Hospital, whose towers dominated central Jerusalem. The compound was commanded by a British police officer known to be pro-Arab. Schurr decided to handle this officer himself. The task of subverting the major commanding the hospital was assigned to a garrulous architect named Dan Ben-Dor. Ben-Dor had served four years as an officer in the Royal Engineers, and his name was celebrated from Baghdad to Benghazi—everywhere in the Middle East, in fact, where a British soldier had taken a shower in the past five years. By perforating the bottom of a beer can, he had developed a device immortalized as Ben-Dor's Beer Bomb, to replace the Army's irreplaceable and constantly stolen brass shower heads.

Ben-Dor quickly discovered that the major had a proper British affection for the sporting life. Striking up a conversation with him one night while strolling along the barbed wire ringing the hospital, he invited him to tea. Then he arranged to have his brother pop in on them unexpectedly with his pet Great Dane, a handsome animal named Assad V—"Young Lion" in Arabic. The Britisher fairly leaped from his seat at the sight of the magnificent black beast.

"What a superb creature!" he cried.

"Ah, yes," replied Ben-Dor sadly. "What a shame that we shall soon have to put him away." Food, and particularly meat, was so desperately short in Jewish Jerusalem, he explained, that rather than see Assad V suffer slow death by starvation they would be forced to destroy him.

"You'll do nothing of the kind," replied the Britisher. Under Ben-Dor's approving eyes, he took his calling card from his pocket, wrote a few words on it and handed it to the architect. "Take this to my mess sergeant at the hospital," he said. "He'll see the dog is fed regularly."

And so began an evening ritual for Ben-Dor. Promptly at six o'clock each night, tugged along by the hungry Dane, he set out for the hospital kitchen. There the mess sergeant opened a nightly tin of bully beef for the dog. Watching the meat disappear down his dog's throat, Ben-Dor tried to stifle the hunger pains contorting his own empty stomach by chatting with the British soldier.

• • •

United States Secretary of State George C. Marshall led his visitor to the map of Palestine on his office wall. "Here you are surrounded by Arabs," he said, indicating the Negev. "Here you are surrounded by other Arabs," he continued, pointing to Galilee. "You have Arab states all around you, and your backs are to the sea. How do you expect to withstand their assault?

"Believe me," the distinguished soldier said to the Jewish Agency's foreign secretary, Moshe Sharett, "I am talking about things about which I know. You are sitting there in the coastal plains of Palestine while the Arabs hold the mountain ridges. I know you have some arms and your Haganah, but the Arabs have regular armies. They are well trained and they have heavy arms. How can you hope to hold out?"

The evident sincerity of the Secretary, the man's unquestioned military competence, shook the Jewish diplomat. His words reflected an urgent American desire to persuade the Jewish Agency to postpone proclaiming a Jewish state. If the Jews acquiesced, the department was convinced, a truce could then be arranged in Palestine between the Agency and the Arab states which would forestall an invasion.

All Marshall's Middle Eastern envoys were advising him that an Arab assault was inevitable if a Jewish state was proclaimed when the British mandate expired in one week's time. Only American military intervention could then save the Jews of Palestine from extermination, they warned. Their warnings were taken with the utmost seriousness in Washington. At the highest levels in the American government active consideration was being given to the possibility of landing United States troops in Palestine within a fortnight. The previous day, President Truman had sent a top-secret memo to his legal adviser Ernest Gross for a brief on his executive power to order American soldiers into Palestine without waiting for Congressional approval.

Faced with such a dismaying prospect, the State Department had gone to extraordinary lengths to get the Jewish Agency's agreement to its scheme for postponing statehood and organizing a truce. Marshall had even offered the Presidential plane, *The Sacred Cow,* to Sharett to fly him to Jerusalem together with representatives of the United States, France, Belgium * and the Arabs, to try to arrange a truce. Sharett had declined the offer, but had come instead to Washington to meet personally with Marshall and Lovett before returning to Jerusalem.

When Marshall had finished, Lovett turned to Sharett. If the Agency

* The three nations had been named by the Security Council to a Palestine Truce Commission.

refrained from proclaiming a state and the Arabs attacked, then the United States would have some justification for intervening on the grounds that she was aiding a group of individuals, not taking sides in a war between nations. Should, however, the Agency persist in its announced intention of proclaiming a state, he explained, then the Jews of Palestine could not look to the United States for help in the event of an Arab invasion. Having proclaimed their state, they would have to assume by themselves the obligation of defending it.

The Jewish diplomat's reply was deliberately noncommittal, since the decision of whether or not to declare a state would be taken by the Jewish Agency's thirteen-member governing body in Tel Aviv. In his heart, however, Sharett was a worried man. Marshall had convinced him. The next day in New York, he told his Agency colleagues they should consider the secretary's proposal. A surprisingly large number of them agreed.

Just before he boarded his aircraft to return to Tel Aviv, a loudspeaker paged Sharett to take an urgent call. It was Chaim Weizmann telephoning from his sickbed at the Waldorf-Astoria. Weizmann was privy to a secret which would not be revealed until ten years after his death. When Judge Samuel Rosenman had carried his recent letter to the White House, the President had told him, "I have Dr. Weizmann on my conscience." If a Jewish state was declared, Truman had promised, he would do everything in his power to see that the United States recognized it as soon as it was proclaimed. Then he had extracted Rosenman's pledge to repeat his words to only one man, Chaim Weizmann.

His voice grating with illness and passion, the man so many of his colleagues had once accused of indecision now hurled a final injunction at Sharett. "Don't let them weaken," he growled, "don't let them spoil the victory. Proclaim the Jewish State, now or never!"

• • •

In Jerusalem, the crash of artillery fire marred the city's life. Unable to conquer the kibbutzim of Galilee, Fawzi el Kaukji had brought his army south to the hilltops of Judea. From Nebi Samuel, the height that Yitzhak Sadeh's men had failed to conquer, his gunners trained their cannon on the most prestigious target he could offer them, the rooftops of Jewish Jerusalem.

His exploding shells provided an inauspicious counterpoint to a secret and ancient ceremony about to be performed in the city below his guns. Yosef Nevo was ready to marry at last the redheaded girl whose mother had so long refused to agree to their union. Naomi's wedding dress was a frilly white blouse she had bought for the occasion and a white skirt she had managed to sneak past her mother's curious eyes. At the last moment, realizing she had forgotten a veil, she had torn one from a girl friend's hat.

Now, as the ceremony was about to begin, the rabbi whom Nevo had brought to the apartment of one of Naomi's friends reminded the couple of a salient point they had forgotten in their obsession to keep their marriage secret. There could be no wedding without a minyan, the ten-man quorum required for public worship, and there were only four males in the room.

Bride, groom, best man and rabbi rushed down the stairs to look for volunteers. In the streets, deserted because of Kaukji's gunfire, they found only four Palmachniks passing nearby. They were pulled upstairs and assigned the task of holding the poles of the traditional wedding canopy over Naomi and Yosef's heads. To get the remaining men, one of Naomi's girl friends set out on a run for the Jewish Agency. "Quick," she shouted, racing from office to office, "ten men for a minyan!"

Her tactic succeeded; the required males were found. As the ceremony was about to begin there was a knock on the door. Answering it, the owner of the flat found before her an English employee of the Agency, an intimate friend of Naomi's mother. He was clad in a sober suit and dark tie. "My poor child," he whispered, "I understand you want ten men for a minyan." In the inexorable logic of that Jerusalem springtime, he had assumed that the only religious office for which a minyan would be needed was a funeral.

At the conclusion of the ceremony Nevo crushed a glass under his heel, a symbolic gesture of grief for the destruction of the Temple whose ruins lay barely three miles away. He gave Naomi a fervent kiss. Then Nevo returned to duty with the Haganah, and Naomi went back to her mother. The conqueror of Katamon might be married at last, but until he could find a way to smuggle the woman who still did not know she had become his mother-in-law past the Arabs besieging Jerusalem, his share of marital bliss was going to be limited to the fervent kiss he had just given his bride.

President Harry S Truman surveyed the men around his desk as a magistrate might contemplate the litigants before his bench. Indeed, the scene in his office bore its resemblance to a trial. Forty-eight hours after Moshe Sharett's departure for Tel Aviv, Truman had assembled his advisers to debate the most urgent foreign-policy issue before his government: if the Jewish Agency spurned Marshall's advice and proclaimed a Jewish state on May 14, should the United States extend the new state diplomatic recognition?

For Harry Truman, there was no question. He yearned to recognize the new state and honor the pledge he had secretly sent to Chaim Weizmann on the eve of Passover. But he could not undertake so major a decision without the concurrence of his principal advisers. Persuaded that the arguments in favor of recognition were overwhelming, he had summoned them for a "full, complete and exhaustive discussion," convinced that the outcome would be a decision to recognize a new state. On one side of his desk sat Secretary of State George C. Marshall and Undersecretary Robert Lovett. Opposite them were the President's special counsel, Clark Clifford, and his political adviser, David Niles.

Marshall began by putting forward the case against recognition. The professional diplomats in the department he represented were almost unanimous in opposing the move. One of his Middle Eastern ambassadors, George Wadsworth, had cabled his colleagues that he wished "to go on record as saying if the United States recognizes a Jewish state and continues its uncritical support of Zionist policy, then the Russians will be the dominant force in the Middle East within the next twenty years." His cable had brought a wave of supporting messages pouring into Washington from his fellow ambassadors. The Secretary could not easily ignore such an overwhelming manifestation of their opinion. In addition, despite his personal sympathies for the Zionists, he did not believe, as he had told Sharett, that their state could hold out against the Arabs. Withold recognition and all it implied, Marshall counseled Truman, until the new state had demonstrated to the world its viability.

When he had finished, Clifford presented the other side. He urged Truman not only to recognize the state but to strive to be the first nation to recognize it. Such a gesture would be only logically consistent with the United States's policy in Palestine, he argued.

To Clifford's dismay, Marshall responded not by rebutting his arguments, but by attacking the very fact that they were arguing. "Is this a contested proceeding?" he asked the President. Recognition was not, he said, "a matter to be determined on the basis of politics. Unless politics were involved, Mr. Clifford would not even be at this conference. This is a serious matter of foreign-policy determination, and the question of politics and political opinion does not enter into it."

It quickly became apparent that instead of a debate on recognition, Truman's meeting had turned into a debate on the prerogatives of the

Secretary of State. Marshall made it clear that he considered their debating of recognition an invasion of the jurisdiction of his office, an affront to his dignity. To overrule him now, Clifford realized, would be tantamount to calling for his resignation.

Crestfallen, the President began to gather up the papers on his desk. There was no man in his Administration on whom he depended more than Marshall. However deep was his desire to recognize the state, however he longed to make this last gesture to "the old doctor" he so esteemed, he could not do it if the price were going to be a rupture with his Secretary of State.

"Thank you all for your contributions," he said. "I accept your recommendation, General. The United States will not at this time recognize a new Jewish state in Palestine."

26

"WE SHALL COME BACK."

His BLACK ROBE and shoulder-length white wig fixed firmly in place, Sir William Fitzgerald stared down from his Chief Justice's bench at the courtroom before him. On this warm spring morning the last case to be heard by the British court system in Palestine lay before Sir William. The sound of intermittent gunfire outside punctuated the proceedings. No litigation could have symbolized the agony of Palestine better than that final suit at law on Sir William's docket. The litigants were an Arab and a Jew, and the issue at dispute between them was a quarrel over a piece of land.

His decision rendered, Sir William rose and left the courtroom. When it had been cleared, he returned to take down with his own hands the royal coat of arms. Carefully he laid out on his bench the shield bearing two lions and a unicorn, thinking that with his gesture "British justice in Palestine was ending." Then he returned to his chambers, hung his robe and his wig on their hook, cast a last glance at his legal volumes and his ornate gold inkstand, and started out the door. He paused. Instead of shutting it, he left it open, the key hanging from its unturned lock "for whoever would come to claim it."

Thus in a hundred different offices in Jerusalem did the British administration in Palestine begin to go through the last rites of a thirty-year sojourn in the Holy Land. By the end of the first fortnight in May, Britain would have evacuated 227,178 tons of merchandise from Palestine, including items as diverse as fifty-nine tons of maps and twenty-five tons of official archives. And if Britain was leaving, then the appurtenances of British life would leave with her. The unsold cigarettes, whiskey, marmalade and Indian tea from the Naafi stores, the British Army's equivalent of the PX, were crated up for the voyage home.

For Sir Alan Cunningham, those last weeks were a trying ordeal. "We had no instructions from anybody on what to do," he would recall. He had hoped Jerusalem's internationalization at least would be put into effect, but he noted sadly, "No one did anything to carry it out. The Christian world was not sufficiently interested in the problem to provide the cooperation and assistance necessary."

He himself had devoted most of those last days to trying to arrange a truce in the Holy City. But just as, earlier, the Arabs sensing victory had refused to listen to truce calls, so now the Haganah, under Ben-Gurion's resolve to capture the city, was indifferent to his appeals.

There seemed, indeed, to be almost as many peace plans as diplomats in Jerusalem. Jacques de Reynier, the Red Cross representative, concocted a scheme to protect the city by placing it under a Red Cross flag. The counsels of the United States, France and Belgium, representing the Security Council, ceaselessly sought to reconcile the warring parties. The United Nations' Pablo de Azcarate tried to use his influence, but, in addition to local indifference, he was plagued by the naïveté of his superiors in New York. While he was trying to stop people from killing each other, he noted in his diary, his United Nations Palestine Committee was arguing about bus services for Jerusalem. "Does someone have to shout at them," he wrote, "to make them understand that a war is raging in Palestine and if they don't take steps to stop it, the whole of Palestine, including Jerusalem, will become a battlefield?"

None of those efforts, however well-intended, would produce anything enduring. As their futility became apparent, Sir Alan turned increasingly to about the only activity left him, saying goodbye to old friends. Among them were Sami and Ambara Khalidy, the Arab College head and his wife. After a last lunch, they strolled a few moments in his garden, talking, Ambara would remember, "of roses and the Iliad, as though nothing was happening, really."

One afternoon, the mandate's senior civil servants, Arab and Jewish, came to the Residence for a final ceremony. "Gentlemen, there is not much left for you to do," Cunningham said with fine understatement. "Goodbye and good luck." Then he offered each a parting handshake, a gesture which for many of those men terminated decades in the service of His Majesty's government.

Another visitor came to see him that afternoon. Despite the problems separating them, a mutual sense of esteem and respect had characterized the relationship between Sir Alan and Golda Meir. And so, when they had finished their business, Sir Alan allowed himself a personal comment.

"I understand your daughter is in a kibbutz in the Negev," he said. "There will be war, and they stand no chance in those settlements. The Egyptians will move through them no matter how hard they fight. Why not bring her home to Jerusalem?" he suggested.

Golda Meir was touched by his gesture. "Thank you," she replied, "but all the boys and girls in those settlements have mothers. If all of them take their children home, then who will stop the Egyptians?"

"Jerusalem is like one big kibbutz." Thus did one of its residents describe life in the Jewish city on the eve of Britain's departure. It was a sorely tried, desperately hungry kibbutz. The jubilation that had welcomed the Nachshon convoys was gone. The eighteen hundred tons of foodstuffs they had brought to the city, not even half the total that Dov Joseph estimated as indispensable to withstand a siege, were locked under armed guard in his warehouses. From them once a week a miserable portion of his hoard was distributed to the population. The ration issued for the last week of Britain's mandate was an indication of how critical Jewish Jerusalem's plight was. It consisted of three ounces each of dried fish, dried beans, lentils and macaroni, and one and a half ounces of margarine.

The open-air market at Mahane Yehuda was empty. There was simply no fresh food of any kind left. By night, secret emissaries of Dov Joseph visited half a dozen friendly Arab villages in search of a few boxes of vegetables or a lamb or two to slaughter. Jerusalem's twenty-nine bakeries were consolidated into five to save fuel. They were allowed to produce twenty-five thousand loaves of bread a day for the civilian population, a quarter of a loaf for each Jerusalemite. To maintain the strength of the city's workingmen, Joseph's committee set up a community kitchen serving five thousand meals a day, enough to give each worker two reasonably nutritious meals a week. On Ben Yehuda, the cafés known for their thick chocolate cake or sugar-crusted apple strudel could offer their clients only a slice of gray bread smeared with a sweet paste. Inevitably, a black market sprang up. One egg was worth seven olives. A man with a can of peaches to barter away was rich. A handful of British Jews chose evacuation with their departing compatriots; some of them, their neighbors noted bitterly, sold their food reserves at several times their real value. There were a few defeatists. Harry Levin encountered one survivor of Dachau who despaired, "This is our fate wherever we live, even here."

In most Jerusalem homes, however, the prevailing mood was a determination to hang on, a grim conviction that, painful as the city's situation was, the alternatives were worse. A popular watchword was a warning that Haganah officers often gave their recruits. "If you can't face death," it went, "you can run. But remember, if you run, you can't run just a mile. You must run a thousand miles."

Just as serious as the food shortage was the fuel situation. Buses stopped moving at nightfall. Taxis had disappeared. Most private cars had already been taken over by the Haganah. Few people had kerosene left for cooking. The handful of cans still available were black-marketed for as much as twelve pounds a can. People cooked out of doors in gardens or back yards over campfires, and Dov Joseph's committee taught the population how to build box ovens to keep food warm without artificial heat.

For weeks, Alexander Singer, the power-plant manager, had had to watch the brightly lit Arab quarters from his own darkened Jewish city. He had deliberately cut the current coming into Jewish Jerusalem, to force the power plant, while still in British hands, to economize on the fuel supply in its storage tanks. Still, when he had been able to reenter the plant after the capture of Katamon, Singer found only four hundred tons of fuel left. Now, to stretch that precious reserve as far as possible, he closed down all the station's diesel generators except one, and fed the city's vital installations in rotation off that unique generator.

More than anything else, however, one dramatic incident, on the afternoon of May 7, one week before the mandate was due to expire, drove home to every resident of Jerusalem just how precarious the city's situation was. Suddenly, without warning, there was not a single drop of water left in the faucets of Jerusalem. Miles away at Ras el Ein, the Arabs had cut the city's waterline, trying to make good a boast of the Arab Higher Committee "to kill the Jews of Jerusalem from thirst."

Only the foresight of Dov Joseph and his water expert Zvi Leibowitz stood between the city and disaster. Since January, Leibowitz had been building up his emergency reserve in the city's cisterns. His stock now stood at 115,000 cubic meters, enough to last the city 115 days on the spartan ration Leibowitz had proclaimed for his fellow citizens. Leibowitz had determined it by locking himself and his wife in their house and decreasing their own water consumption until he reached what he considered to be the minimum ration allowable, two gallons per person a day in the furnace heat of a Palestine summer. That would allow each Jerusalemite four pints of drinking water daily. Every demand of cooking, toilet flushing, washing and personal hygiene would have to be met with what was left.

From the beginning, Leibowitz had been persuaded that the best way to avoid panic was to bring the water to his consumers instead of sending the consumers to water. He had mobilized a team of civilian volunteers to man his donkey- and horse-towed water tanks. Suddenly they appeared in Jerusalem's Jewish neighborhoods, regularly delivering each householder a three-day ration. They would soon be an institution. For weeks, through the searing heat of summer, between bursts of Arab shellfire, Jerusalem's housewives would line up with their bottles, their teakettles, saucepans and milk cans, to wait for the neighborhood donkey cart and their precious water ration.

Jerusalem being Jerusalem, the city could not endure a siege without some manifestation of Providence. In April, before the Nachshon convoys arrived, a weed called *khubeiza* had provided a miraculous relief to the hungry population. The spinachlike herb sprang up wild in the fields after the spring rains. It was nutritious, filling and full of vitamins. Women scoured the fields of the city looking for it, and before it disappeared it had even made its appearance on the menu of the Hotel Eden as "spinach croquettes." Suddenly, just before the British left, a wholly unseasonable three-day rain struck Jerusalem, bringing a new and totally unexpected crop of *khubeiza* pushing up from the soil. "Ah," said the city's solons, "the Lord is with us. The last time when we left Egypt, he sent us manna. This time he sent us rain for the cisterns and the *khubeiza.*"

There was no *khubeiza* in the cobbled alleyways and obscure courtyards of the Old City. The seventeen hundred residents of the Jewish Quarter and their two hundred defenders lived in a peculiar world of contrasts, of echoing rifle fire blending with the psalmody rising from its synagogues. On its domed rooftops, young soldiers leaped from building to building in pursuit of Arab snipers, while in their musty yeshivas below aged rabbis pursued the wisdom of the Torah. Behind Haganah headquarters, an elderly rabbi, using one leg as a writing table, eating only bread and water in the custom of his exalted calling, spent his days copying sacred texts a few feet from the building where other men drew plans to defend his quarter.

The very concept of defending the quarter, protected until now from the Arabs all around it by British strongpoints, was controversial. Shaltiel considered the place indefensible and had repeatedly urged its evacuation. Many of its elderly residents thought they could arrange a solution to their problems with their Arab neighbors if the Haganah would leave. Sir Alan Cunningham had tried to persuade Jerusalem's Chief Rabbi Isaac Herzog to abandon the area. His refusal echoed the deep emotion those few hundred square yards of soil evoked. Its defenders, he replied, were "trustees guarding the heritage of all past generations of Jews."

Avraham Halperin, the officer arrested after leaving Rabbi Weingarten's house, had never been able to return. His place as commander had been taken by Moshe Russnak, a soft-spoken Czech. Russnak's headquarters were in the Tipat Chalav, the "Drop of Milk," a social service founded to provide milk for underprivileged children. Many of Russnak's men had

325

first entered that building as infants in their mothers' arms. They came from a variety of backgrounds. The most magnetic officer in the command was a handsome, blond twenty-one-year-old Hebrew University student, a native of the Old City, named Emmanuel Meidav. An exuberant, outgoing youth, he was adored equally by the children of the quarter and the pious older residents, who loved the sound of his resonant voice booming out the Sabbath hymns. Emmanuel had an extraordinary faculty for picking apart weapons and explosives. He had, his awed comrades claimed, "golden hands."

None of Russnak's soldiers seemed more out of place than a quietly determined, dark-haired twenty-two-year-old English girl named Esther Cailingold. Born in London into a devoutly orthodox household, she had spent the Blitz serving beside her father in a volunteer fire brigade. Deeply moved by the victims of the death camps after the war, she had come to Palestine to teach in1946. Soon she was serving full time in the Haganah. All during the winter and spring of 1948 she had been obsessed by one desire, to fight at the symbolic center of the dispersed nation she had come to Palestine to help revive. Just after Passover, her request had been granted. Disguised as a nurse, Esther Cailingold had been sent to the quarter she so wanted to defend.

The heart of the quarter was the Street of the Jews. It ran from the Old City walls one hundred yards below Zion Gate to Lubinsky's House, a building spanning its six-foot width at its northern end as a Venetian overpass might span a canal. Underneath the span an iron gate erected after the 1936 riots marked the dividing line between the Arab and Jewish quarters. West of the street, the Jewish Quarter continued up a gentle incline toward the compoundlike outline of the Armenian Quarter. To the south, it was protected by the Old City walls, falling away to the Valley of Kidron. Its western defense depended to a large degree on the Armenians' preventing the Arabs from using their neighborhood to assault it. Its most exposed flanks were the north and the east, and their defense depended on two key positions. The first, in the quarter's northeastern corner, was the Warsaw Building, a collection of three-storied structures built around a courtyard with the contributions of Warsaw's Jewish community. They included a synagogue, and study rooms and living facilities for its scholars, all now evacuated to turn the compound into a Haganah strongpoint.

East of the Warsaw, a narrow alley called the Street of the Stairs ran along a row of low, one-story houses to the other key position, the Nissan

Bek Synagogue, the highest building in the quarter, a huge rectangular edifice surmounted by a cupola donated by the Austrian Emperor Franz Josef in 1870. From the cupola, five windows looked in every direction. Ringing the base of the cupola was a gallery, supported by three arches, that had been the synagogue's women's section. Its circling tier made it an ideal position for its Haganah defenders. An extraordinary array of murals looked down on them from the synagogue walls as they crouched at their posts peering out over the Arab rooftops toward the Mount of Olives. Lurid and unearthly, they portrayed the legend of the destruction of the Temple whose Mount lay under their gaze only a few hundred yards away. To defend that perimeter, Russnak's one hundred and fifty men and women and the fifty-odd members of the Irgun and the Stern Gang had a pitifully small armory. It consisted of three machine guns, a two-inch mortar, forty-two submachine guns, three grenade launchers and an assembly of unmatched and often unreliable rifles and pistols.

The Irgun's years of underground warfare stood them all in good stead, however. To stretch out their meager arms supply, one of its members, a schoolteacher named Leah Vultz, manufactured hand grenades in Players cigarette tins. Her former pupils prowled the quarter for empty tins left by British soldiers. She packed them with explosives, and an elderly upholsterer wrapped the detonators with wooden matches and tied the grenades together. She assigned the most dangerous job to her husband. It was cutting the detonators by hand with a small saw. One slip of the saw and the device could blow off a man's hand. Leah knew that her husband had the steady hands the task required. They were the hands of a musician trained for years to caress the chords of a cello.

The vital supplies required by their besieged quarter had been delivered twice a week on board a British-escorted and -inspected convoy. Shaltiel's men had used every ruse imaginable to slip arms to the Old City's defenders aboard the convoy. They had hidden hand-grenade detonators in loaves of bread, pistols in flour sacks, bullets in kidney beans. Their most important smuggling tools, however, were the ten 200-liter barrels of kerosene allowed in with each convoy for the quarter's stoves. Fitted with a special conical device that would allow an inspector's baton to plunge from top to bottom encountering only liquid, those barrels had brought the quarter's beleaguered defenders Sten guns, ammunition and explosives.

With Britain's withdrawal imminent, the quarter's Haganah men needed to smuggle every bullet they could onto their final British-run convoys. To their dismay, at the beginning of May they were informed that there was no kerosene in the New City to fill their fake barrels. "Fill the barrels with water," they begged. "Sprinkle a little kerosene on top to give them the right smell and send them in."

Gershon Finger, disguised as a civilian, supervised the operation for the quarter from the midst of a knot of curious civilians near Zion Gate. It was a scorching hot day. Nervously he watched the ten barrels delivered to the British checkpoint. An officer opened the second barrel and pushed a thin stick into its spout. He repeated the process with two more barrels selected at random. Then he nodded to a group of waiting Jewish porters. They started to roll the barrels down a three-hundred-yard cordon of British troops to the Street of the Jews.

As they did, Finger froze. One of the barrels had sprung a leak, pouring a wet ribbon at the foot of the British troops as it rolled down to the Jewish Quarter. Instead of leaving the dark stain of kerosene, of course, the water evaporated a few seconds after it hit the hot pavement. Trembling nervously Finger waited for an alert Britisher to notice the evaporating "oil" stain at his feet. Not one did. To his relief the leaking barrel disappeared safely into the quarter. As it did, an elderly white-bearded Kurdistani rabbi standing beside Finger looked up.

"Ah," he whispered, "those Englishmen! How many wars did they fight, how many did they kill, how many of their kind did they lose, all for what? For an empire of oil. And what is the difference between oil and water they cannot tell."

●　●　●

Like a suburban housewife on a Saturday-morning shopping spree, the man who would lead the Arab assaults on the Jewish Quarter prowled the souks of Damascus, his knowing fingers picking over the mounds of fuses, detonators, timers and Bickford cord heaped in the gloomy stalls. After the *Palestine Post,* Ben Yehuda Street and the Jewish Agency, Fawzi el Kutub had decided to make the destruction of the Jewish Quarter his personal crusade. It was a task for which he was preeminently suited. Kutub knew its cluttered alleys and misshapen houses better than most of its defenders. He had spent his childhood playing among them. It was there that he had thrown the first hand grenade of his violent career.

In his pocket were fifteen thousand Syrian pounds, a gift from the Mufti with which to launch his operation. In addition, he had a letter from the Arab leader authorizing him to form a group of twenty-five men called the Tadmir, the explosives unit. Those men would carry the mines primed by the devices Fawzi was buying in Damascus from his headquarters in a

Turkish bath near the Mosque of Omar to the targets Kutub selected in the Jewish Quarter.

By the time Kutub had spent the last of his fifteen thousand pounds, he had accumulated enough material to fill three automobiles. He contemplated his purchases with satisfaction. Then he set off for Jerusalem, burning to begin the endeavor that was the inevitable conclusion of his strange and violent life.

. . .

For centuries, the ground on which the troops paraded had been the domain of other marching feet. Now an army of the shadows was at last emerging into the daylight. Faces taut, arms swinging high in imitation of Palestine's British rulers, the marchers strode down an aisle of their cheering compatriots toward the makeshift reviewing stand set up at the Evelyn de Rothschild School. Proudly defiant of British authority, the Haganah was staging the first full-dress parade in its history right through the heart of Jerusalem.

The marchers wore a staggering variety of uniforms. There were men in work shirts and khaki sweaters, girls in shorts, pants or skirts. Their headgear included olive-drab U.S. Army surplus wool caps, British flat helmets, wide-brimmed Australian bush hats, the dark skullcaps of the orthodox. Equally varied was the collection of arms they carried.

His body stiffened in a rigid salute, the man who had ordered their parade watched from the reviewing stand. For David Shaltiel, the march-past was a measure of spiritual nourishment for his city's hungry Jews, a reassuring gesture to the fainthearted who doubted Jerusalem's ability to hang on when the British left. The meticulous Shaltiel had even marked the occasion by having a tailor sew up the immaculate new uniform in which he watched his troops march past. As they disappeared, he turned to the officers on the reviewing stand beside him. With the formality of a French general in his mess, he proposed a champagne toast to the success of their arms.

The disparate group of soldiers to whom the former Foreign Legion sergeant had raised a glass of champagne represented almost all the forces he would be able to muster in the critical days ahead.

They consisted of three Haganah battalions, a battalion of the Har-el Palmach Brigade, the Irgun and Stern Gang's quasi-independent forces, the Gadna youth formations and the Home Guard. Their arms, by the terrifying standards to which its conflicts had accustomed the world, might seem derisory. Three years after Hiroshima, the conquest of the Holy City was

329

going to hinge on an armory that included fifty-five Sten guns, seventy light machine guns, three Austrian heavy machine guns, six three-inch mortars, three Davidkas, eight thousand homemade grenades and the better part of one million rounds of rifle ammunition delivered under a truckload of vegetables by an Arab from Ramallah.

Unimpressive though they might seem, those forces were nonetheless superior to those available in the city to Shaltiel's dispirited and disorganized foes. The key to operations in the days ahead would lie in the complex character of the commander Ben-Gurion wanted to "attack and attack and attack." For four vital days, history was going to offer him the same opportunity it had offered Godefroy de Bouillon and Saladin—that of being the conqueror of Jerusalem.

Shaltiel, however, was a conservative man, and he was terribly aware that if his fragile force were shattered in an unsuccessful attack, all Jerusalem would lay open to the Arabs. Rather than gamble everything on the kind of bold, all-out assault Ben-Gurion wanted, Shaltiel preferred to move on deliberately classic lines. When the British left, he would launch a three-pronged movement called Operation Pitchfork, designed to create a continuous line from north to south in the major part of the city. In the north, he would capture Sheikh Jarrah and establish a link to the institutions on Mount Scopus. In the south, his men would take Britain's Allenby Barracks and isolate the Arab neighborhoods below Katamon from the rest of the Arab city. The most vital task was the occupation of the public buildings of Bevingrad dominating central Jerusalem.

When those three objectives had been achieved, Shaltiel would feel ready to consider the capture of Old Jerusalem itself. His cautious hopes and careful plans would depend, however, on an element that rarely favors the designs of conservative men, time. It was the amount of time he would have between the moment the British left and the moment the first sand-colored armored cars of the Arab Legion appeared on the ridge lines above Jerusalem.

• • •

The headquarters of David Shaltiel's Arab foes were in a school built upon the piece of ground which had witnessed the beginning of the most famous drama in Jerusalem's history. It was the site of the Antonia, Herod's palace, the point from which Jesus Christ set out on his march to Calvary and from which, in a sense, the Christian religion might date its incredible rise throughout the world. Upon the uneven stone slabs over which the Arab leaders scurried, Rome's soldiery had left the marks of their hopscotch games and had cast the bone dice with which they chose the victims for their Saturnalias.

Adjacent to the Ecce Homo Arch, two hundred and fifty yards inside the Old City walls, the Rawdah School was one of Jerusalem's most famous Arab institutions. Many of the men occupying it had received their first exposure to the tenets of Arab nationalism on its wooden benches and had flocked from its classrooms to participate in their first demonstrations for the cause they now led.

If David Shaltiel's headquarters represented at best the approximation of a military organization, the command post of his rivals looked like a bazaar. Pieces of mortars, machine-gun bullets, Sten-gun clips, lay scattered around the building. Rifles leaned in corners, pistols were tossed on classroom benches under hand-lettered verses from the Koran. Cases of hand grenades and ammunition, often the private hoards of one or two men, were locked into closets and the cellar. From the street outside came the constant honking of horns and shouts of *"Balak, balak!"* to clear a passage for an ancient Dodge taxi or a loaded donkey signaling the arrival of still another local chieftain with his offerings of a few hand grenades or a case of cartridges for the altar of the Rawdah School.

More than arms and ammunition, however, the men in Rawdah School lacked leadership. The one man who might have supplied them that leadership lay buried in the Mosque of Omar a few hundred yards away, beyond a brilliant burst of mimosa under the schoolroom windows. Abdul Khader Husseini's successor, Khaled Husseini, inspired little more than indifference in his followers. Convinced that the men in the Rawdah School were all British agents, Fawzi el Kutub had embarked on his personal crusade against the Old City's Jewish Quarter. Everybody loathed Fadel Rashid, the Iraqi, who was accused of devoting most of his time to expanding his collection of Persian carpets. Ibrahim Abou Dayieh had been crippled by the wound he had received in Katamon. Instead of a single commander, each neighborhood had its leader in Rawdah, each defending his quarter's needs.

As a result, the rivalries sundering the Arab leadership on a higher level found their reflection on a plane as local as the headquarters. Men rushed in and out of its converted classrooms in an air of disarray and tumult, constantly shouting and quarreling, the din of their fervid arguments stilled only by the intermittent calls of the muezzin from the nearby minarets of Al Aqsa.

The leaders of the Arab school had available approximately three thousand men: two thousand supporters of the Mufti, six hundred Iraqi volunteers, and four hundred former policemen led by a former police officer named Mounir Abou Fadel. The state of their morale—and the measure of the opportunity before David Shaltiel—was reflected in a cable from Safwat Pasha to Kaukji on May 9, less than a week before the mandate was due to expire. "The situation of the defenders of Jerusalem has become desperate," it said. "Our forces there have had enormous losses. Much of their armament has been lost. Jerusalem must be protected at any cost even at the price of abandoning ground elsewhere."

No less than their Jewish foes, the Arabs were aware of the importance of seizing the vital areas in the center of the city when the British left. As he had once plotted accident sites on his maps in police headquarters, Mounir Abou Fadel had indicated on a huge map of the city the 138 posts and buildings his men would have to seize when the British left. He had, however, no concerted plans to equal the careful preparations being made on the other side of the city by Arieyeh Schurr and David Shaltiel. As in so many other areas, that responsibility was left to individual initiative.

Incongruous among the kaffiyehs, jodhpurs, old battle jackets and khaki shirts mingling in the Arab headquarters was the black cassock of a Roman Catholic priest. The son of a woodworker who had carved rosary beads from the olive trees of Bethlehem, Father Ibrahim Ayad bore a passionate devotion to the Arab cause that was exceeded only by his devotion to his Church. His talent for intrigue had been perfected in the Terra Sancta, the custodian's office for the Holy Land where for generations the clans of Christianity had conspired for control of their common shrines. Thanks to an Italian colleague there, he now carried in the folds of his cassock a letter from the Italian consul and a key, the instruments that promised the Arabs access to at least one of Jerusalem's vital buildings, the Italian Hospital to which Dan Ben-Dor walked his black Great Dane each night for a tin of bully beef.

Curious fact in a headquarters so resolutely Arab, one of Rawdah's dominant personalities belonged to a woman. Nimra Tannous' husky voice was as familiar to the Haganah operatives eavesdropping on Arab conversations in the basement of the Jewish Agency as it was to her colleagues in the school. For the last six months, to the Haganah operatives' despair, her principal concern as a Jerusalem telephone operator had been breaking in on the calls of the city's garrulous Arab leaders to warn them that an enemy might be listening.

Daughter of a woman who had lost twenty-two children during pregnancy, she had been given at birth, on the advice of an astrologer, the name of a ferocious animal to insure her survival. Inspired by the role her sister telephone operators played in the Jewish community, Nimra "Tigress" Tannous had been determined to make a similar contribution to the Arab cause. Together with an Armenian engineer, she had installed Rawdah's communications system, carrying its components piece by piece from the central post office in her handbag or concealed under her skirt. For a fortnight, a stray kitten cradled in her lap, a small revolver on the table before her, she had been the voice of Jerusalem 25290, the telephone number of the Rawdah headquarters.

As was the case in the Jewish Agency, the most pressing calls to filter through her little switchboard dealt with arms. The largest consignment to reach Rawdah, a personal gift from Farouk, had doubled the Arabs' heavy arms. It consisted of fifteen machine guns, two two-pounder guns, and seven two-inch mortars.

As did many another educated Jerusalemite, Dr. Hassib Boulos, a surgeon at Government Hospital, looked with concern on the disarray in the Rawdah headquarters. Like most of his fellows, however, Boulos listened regularly to the radios of Damascus, Cairo and Beirut. Their speeches, military music and bellicose slogans eased the doubts Jerusalem's defenders inspired in the young doctor. Nightly they promised the Arabs of Palestine that their armies were ready, that soon the hour would arrive to "let the sword speak."

. . .

Fumbling with the radio in his hand, the civil servant who had told himself on Partition Night, "The British will never leave," locked his front door. Sami Hadawi's thoughts that night had been wishful thinking; the British were leaving and so was he. Casting a last glance at his front yard, its garden bursting with unpicked calla lilies, his children's sandbox still littered with toys, he hurried off to join his family in the safety of the Old City.

His was not an isolated gesture in the Arab neighborhoods of Jerusalem during those closing days of the mandate. It was not the specter of famine or thirst that drove people from their homes. Their food and water supplies were adequate. They were frightened by something else, the speed with which the Haganah had moved through most of Katamon, and the knowledge that only a British cease-fire had stemmed the Jews' advance.

The outflow was an acceleration of the movement which, since Christmas, had seen people drifting away to Beirut, Amman, Damascus. Some had been driven out by telephone threats or a bomb. Others had left out

333

of a concern for their own well-being or a desire to ride out the coming storm in calmer ports. With rare exceptions, it had been the well-to-do who had left. They had been followed by the Mufti's political leaders. Only two members of his Arab Higher Committee remained in Jerusalem, a pair of worthy but ailing septuagenarians. The rest of the leaders who had so frequently proclaimed their willingness to drive the Jews into the sea now preferred to leave that task to others and follow the struggle from the safety of some distant Arab capital.

Inside the Old City's walls, a nucleus of able men headed by Anwar Nusseibi struggled to create a municipal administration, but their efforts were stymied by the dimensions of the task, the lateness of the hour, and a lack of skilled help. The inevitable result of that atmosphere of doubt, confusion and growing fear was the new wave of departures. Some people, like Hadawi, found a sanctuary only a few yards from their homes; for others, it would be at the end of a long journey to a neighboring Arab country.

A strange coming and going of trucks and carts preceded their departure. Inevitably, their journeys led them to one of Jerusalem's convents or monasteries. The spartan cells and austere rooms of men and women who had renounced the world and its works began to overflow with crystal, silverware, carpets and porcelain. Emile Kashram, the owner of a women's store on the Mamillah Road, chose the Convent of the Little Sisters of Charity as the repository of his stocks. In an hour, nuns in whose humble life a bar of yellow laundry soap was a luxury found their convent crammed with nylon stockings, silk bras and girdles, a dozen different kinds of French perfume, toilet soap, lipstick, rouge, mascara, all the accouterments of a life totally alien to their existence.

A night of heavy firing frightened Brahim Abou Hawa into rushing to the Allenby Barracks to buy from a British soldier the indispensable supplement to the taxi fare out of Jerusalem, a jerrican of gasoline. Then he loaded his six children into a cab. Before leaving, his wife had carefully packed everything away, draped their easy chairs with dust covers, and stuffed her savings into her bra. As she started out the door, she reached for two of her favorite possessions, a portable sewing machine and a radio. Brahim ordered her to leave them behind. Like most departing Jerusalemites, he had the unshakable conviction that their departure was temporary, that soon they would return to a city occupied by the Arab armies. In eight days, he assured his doubting wife, they would be safely settled in their home once again.

Jamil Tukan, a veteran of twenty years' service in the Land Settlement

334

Department, had his illusions quickly dispelled. From the Old City retreat to which he had retired with a single suitcase, Tukan picked up a telephone and dialed 2026, the number of his abandoned flat. After a few seconds, an unknown voice answered. *"Shalom,"* it said.

Some people, of course, refused to budge. The three sons of Mrs. George Deeb, Jerusalem's Buick dealer, were determined to leave their Upper Beqaa home to carry on their fight elsewhere. She refused to accompany them. As they hurried off she was digging a hole in the garden in which to bury three broken pistols they had left behind. They would not see her again for three years, until, dying of cancer, she was carried from her home on a stretcher.

Her eyes filled with tears, Ambara Khalidy snapped tight the shutters of the little library in which she had translated the Iliad into Arabic and had followed the partition debate with her husband. Sami Khalidy's bookshelves were bare now, his precious texts already hidden for safekeeping in an Old City monastery. After a parting glance around the room, Ambara went to the kitchen and kissed Aziza, her cook.

"We'll be back when school opens," she murmured. Then she went to the door. It was a gray, overcast day. The windows of her husband's college were taped over, and armed guards paced the lawn where his students had strolled. To her left were the new wings he had just completed, their labs and dormitories ready to receive their first students in the fall, concrete incarnations of his ambition to make his Arab College a fitting rival to Hebrew University.

One by one, her husband leading the way, the six members of the family walked to a waiting taxicab. The car started and Ambara turned to look again at her home. "How happy I have been here," she thought. "Here I have known Paradise." Up front, red-faced and totally silent, her husband stared straight ahead, refusing to turn back for a last glimpse of the institution to which he had devoted his life. On one side of Ambara, a daughter clutched a doll in her lap, on the other her youngest son, Tarif, hugged a worn teddy bear. As the last cypress tree rolled past the taxi windows, Ambara could no longer control herself. She burst into tears.

"La tibki, Mama," murmured the children beside her, *"ha nerjaa baden.* Don't cry, Mama, we shall come back."

• • •

Ambara Khalidy's children were wrong. They would never return to the college to which their father had given so many years of labor. They were all unwitting participants in a new Middle Eastern tragedy whose consequences would haunt the conscience of the world for years to come, that of the Palestine refugees. Talented and persevering, the Khalidys would overcome the rigors of their exodus and contribute a new generation of scholars to the educational institutions of another Arab society in Lebanon. For thousands of their less fortunate compatriots, however, the road away from Palestine would lead only to the endless anguish of a refugee camp.

The catalyst behind their exodus was the Haganah's decision to occupy a series of vital areas before the Arab armies could hurl their promised invasion at them May 15. Most but not all of those sites were inside the boundaries assigned the Jewish state by the United Nations and contained substantial Arab populations anxiously awaiting the invaders.

The first major town to fall had been Tiberias, the ancient resort of Roman emperors, on April 18. Hardly had the Haganah secured the town when a victory of far greater consequence took place. After twenty-four hours of intense fighting, the Jewish Army seized control of the port city of Haifa. Safed, the ancient city of the Cabala, was occupied early in May. Dozens of smaller towns and villages in Galilee then came under Jewish control.

In only one instance did the British intervene in force to check the Jewish advance—in the port of Jaffa, next to Tel Aviv. Stung by Arab criticism of Britain's passivity, Foreign Secretary Ernest Bevin gave Sir Gordon MacMillan "a direct, unequivocal order to bloody well put troops in there and get Jaffa back for the Arabs."

His command forced MacMillan to do what he had been reluctant to do since partition, commit British soldiers to an Arab–Jewish action. His troops checked the advance, largely an Irgun operation, but MacMillan soon found that there were virtually no Arabs left in Jaffa to whom his troops could return the city. By early May, sixty-five thousand of the port's seventy thousand residents had fled.

That unhappy situation was being repeated all over Palestine, and its causes were varied. Sometimes it was the result of a calculated Haganah policy. Anxious to clear Upper Galilee of Arabs to check the Arab invasion routes without using his own exhausted troops, the Palmach's Yigal Allon turned to psychological warfare. "I gathered all the Jewish mukhtars who had contacts with the Arabs in different villages," he recorded later in the Palmach history *Sefer ha-Palmach,* and "asked them to whisper in the Arabs' ears that a great Jewish force had arrived in Galilee and that it was going to burn all the villages of the Huleh [the Lake Huleh region].

They should suggest to those Arabs that they flee while there was still time." The tactic, he noted, "attained its goal completely."

On occasion, the Jewish leaders actively sought to persuade their Arab neighbors to remain in their midst. In Haifa, Tuvia Arazi even took the exceptional step of obtaining the Chief Rabbi's permission for Jewish bakers to violate the Passover prohibitions by baking bread for the Arabs in the quarter captured by the Haganah. Yet despite such gestures thousands of Haifa's Arabs streamed into the port, clambered aboard any seaworthy vessel they could find, and fled to Beirut.

Contributing to the exodus everywhere was the exodus that had already taken place, that of the Arabs' middle- and upper-class leaders. Like their brothers in Jerusalem, most of those who left were convinced that their departure was temporary, that they would soon return in the avenging van of the Arab armies.

Above all, fear and uncertainty fueled the Arabs' flight. Panic has no nationality, and fear is not the property of any one people. Just as fear of the coming occupants had seized the French and the Belgians of 1940, so now fear seized the less sophisticated Arabs of Palestine, hurling them onto the roads by thousands. As the French and the Belgians had repeated to each other on the highways of their exodus stories of German soldiers raping nuns and slaughtering children, so the Arabs nourished theirs with the images of the atrocities of Deir Yassin.

And so by thousands they fled, poor, bewildered people, clutching a few belongings in a cardboard box, a sack, a suitcase, carrying their bawling young in their arms. In dilapidated buses whose roofs were crammed with their possessions, in taxis, on foot, on bicycles, on donkeys, they poured out of the country thinking that, unlike their Jewish neighbors, they had somewhere to go, vowing, like Ambara Khalidy's children, "We shall come back." They were wrong.

27

"THROW STONES AND DIE."

CLUSTERS OF POLICE surrounded Egypt's massive Parliament Building despite the supposedly secret nature of the meeting beginning inside. Their presence attested to the success of the press campaign unleashed the month before to stir the population's martial ardor. It had been so successful that Egypt's authorities feared the extremists of the Moslem Brotherhood might at any moment hurl Cairo's aroused masses onto the streets of the capital.

Even King Farouk had made his contribution to the military mood embracing the city. Now he stalked its nightclubs in a garment more appropriate to its new atmosphere than his usual dinner jacket—a field marshal's uniform. So that his entire entourage might share in the temper of the hour, Farouk had even proclaimed uniforms *de rigueur* in his court and had awarded military ranks to his sisters and half a dozen of his favorite courtesans.

Inside the royal parliament, however, the mood was grim and businesslike. His face set in a somber mask, his hands clutching the speech he had spent the morning preparing, Mahmoud Nokrashy Pasha rose from his place below the Speaker's stand and stared at the men arrayed in the circular chamber. It was six o'clock in the evening, Tuesday, May 11, 1948. The moment Nokrashy Pasha had once hoped to avoid was at hand. Calmly he asked the men before him for a declaration of war on the as yet unborn Jewish state in Palestine.

As he droned through his speech, only one dissenting voice rose to protest his call. "Is the Army ready?" asked his predecessor, Ahmed Sidki Pasha.

Amid the chorus of jeers and catcalls that greeted the question, Nokrashy quietly replied, "I will take the responsibility that the Army is ready."*

In two hours it was over. The secret session had voted Nokrashy Pasha a war, a state of siege, and six million additional dollars for his army.

---

* Sidki's pertinent query earned him a scornful nickname—"El Yahud" (The Jew).

Fifteen thousand members of that forty-thousand-man army were already concentrated in an Egyptian Expeditionary Force around the seaside community of El Arish in the Sinai Peninsula. Though it now had road maps of Palestine, the army that Nokrashy believed prepared had yet to receive a single mobile kitchen from which to feed the men he was sending to war. Protesting that only four battalions of the two brigades gathered in El Arish were ready for action, the force's deputy commander, a pipe-smoking Sudanese colonel named Mohammed Naguib, warned his superiors they were courting disaster.

Nonsense, replied Major General Ahmed Ali el Muawi. There would be little fighting and no real opposition.

At the opposite end of the Palestine coastal strip, in the Lebanese port of Sidon, the eight hundred members of another armed force debarked to take their place in the gathering ranks of the Arab armies. Beige woolen burnooses over their shoulders, a Koran in a leather pouch hung around their necks, these Moroccan volunteers represented North Africa's contribution to the coming jihad. Pointing dramatically south toward the city that had beckoned to them in their Magrib, Lebanon's Prime Minister Riad Solh set them on the road to Jerusalem. Then the man who had convinced Farouk to enter the war returned to his capital to perform another action poignantly illustrative of the fratricidal nature of the conflict overtaking the Middle East: he ordered a detachment of his tiny army to protect the citizens of Beirut's ancient and populous Jewish Quarter.

Faithful to its historic tradition, the city of the Ommayad caliphs was the most warlike capital in the Middle East. Daily the vehicles of Syria's armored brigade paraded through Damascus to the noisy accolades of thousands of its citizens. Responding to an impassioned plea by Jamil Mardam, the Syrian parliament in its turn readied a declaration of war and announced that the nation's borders would be closed to civilian traffic two hours before the mandate expired. To flesh out the Syrian Army with an additional five thousand recruits, the parliament appropriated six million Syrian pounds from an account surprisingly well provisioned in a nation so anxious to wage war, that containing the funds paid by young Syrians to avoid the draft.

In the Orient Palace Hotel, Haj Amin Husseini continued to glide mysteriously from salon to salon, his thin figure protected by the folds of his bulletproof vest. The Mufti had hoped for a different resolution to Palestine's problems than the one at hand. He had wanted to see his Jihad Moqhades poised now to drive his Jewish foes into the sea. Instead they were barely able to defend the ground they held, and Palestine's fate lay in other hands, those guiding the Arab armies and above all those of his rival Abdullah.

After two days of furious argument in the Arab League War Council, Abdullah succeeded in thwarting Haj Amin's most cherished scheme, the proclamation of an Arab state in Palestine with as its government his Arab Higher Committee. Instead the War Council announced that the Arab portions of Palestine and the Jewish territory soon expected to be under Arab control would be administered by the Arab League.

A furious Haj Amin cabled his benefactor, King Farouk, his congratulations on Egypt's declaration of war and sent a secret messenger to Egyptian Army headquarters in El Arish. His task was to urge the Egyptians to follow the right road on the maps of Palestine that George Deeb had furnished them. It led to Jerusalem, not Tel Aviv. After twelve years in exile, Haj Amin longed to return to the city of which he was nominally the Mufti. He knew that if his rival Abdullah took Jerusalem his chances of reclaiming the seat of Al Aqsa were as slim as they would be if it fell to his Jewish foes.

The pier's weary old spans crept across a sea shimmering under the unrelenting sun. Its worn shafts had been driven into the Gulf of Aqaba to receive the arms of an earlier Arab conquest, T. E. Lawrence's drive up the Hejazi railway to Damascus. Now the munitions to fuel another campaign were being unloaded on Lawrence's jetty. They represented a vital part of the stores John Glubb had purchased with the subsidy his countrymen had given the Arab Legion in February.

Waiting to receive it was one of the men recruited with that subsidy, an adventuresome young lieutenant named Nigel Brommage. Brommage had corralled twenty-seven trucks, every truck in southern Transjordan, to cart the millions of rounds of rifle ammunition being unloaded from the ship in Aqaba harbor across the desert to the railhead in Ma'an. And in forty-eight hours another, even more vital cargo was due to arrive, thousands of shells for the Arab Legion's artillery.

Those two shiploads of ammunition represented one phase of the Legion's preparations for the coming crisis. The British government had agreed officially to give the Transjordanians enough ammunition to fight a thirty-day war. Unofficially, the Legion had also been able to get a good deal more. For the past six weeks, the British had been nightly dumping their spare ammunition into the Dead Sea. Thanks to Glubb's contacts, much of it instead had been dumped into the waiting trucks of his Legionnaires.

The Legion itself had been expanded to 7,000 men, of whom 4,500, divided into four mechanized regiments, could be counted on for front-line service. The distinctive red-and-white kaffiyeh that the Legionnaires wore was the most coveted piece of clothing a Transjordanian might possess, the badge of honor to which the Beni Sakr and Howeitat tribesmen roaming Abdullah's kingdom assiduously aspired. All volunteers, tightly disciplined, well trained, they were the only Arab force that inspired doubt in the soldiers of the Haganah.

The British arms they employed had proven their value on other deserts in conflict with the Afrika Korps: six-pound antitank guns, 25-pounder field artillery, three-inch mortars and a fleet of fifty Marmon Harrington armored cars. To lead them, Glubb had recruited a nucleus of able British professional officers, men who had fought in Burma, Crete, El Alamein and the Rhineland.

The decision of the Amman conference gave the Legion responsibility for the central section of the front from Jerusalem to Nablus. The Egyptians were responsible for the south up to Bethlehem, and the Syrians and the Iraqis, Glubb noted sardonically, were supposed "to descend like the wolf on the fold in Galilee."

Yet the man who commanded that Legion from a small office with French windows on a hilltop in Amman had no intention of ordering it to Tel Aviv or the sea. The limits that John Glubb had set on his armored cars' advance had been written on the map of Palestine on November 29, 1947. As Colonel Goldie's secret mission to the Haganah had indicated, Glubb's primary concern was executing the agreement between Ernest Bevin and Prime Minister Abou Hoda. He had already quietly given his British officers firm orders to stay inside the areas assigned the Arab state when they moved over the Jordan.

Pondering the tactical problem before him, Glubb knew that from the east of Haifa south to Beersheba a long mountain ridge had offered, from time immemorial, the ideal obstacle to an army trying to reach the heartland of Palestine from the sea. Since Glubb's intention was "just to make a semblance of war," his idea was to move his army along that mountain screen, shifting it from spot to spot to plug any Jewish effort to break through its passes.

The one imponderable in Glubb's planning was Jerusalem. John Glubb had no particular feeling for the city. His Arabs lived in the desert. For

341

both military and political reasons, he was determined to keep the Arab Legion out of the Holy City. His men's superior firepower would be wasted in a house-to-house fight. His Jewish foes with their urban backgrounds were better adapted to city fighting than his Bedouin tribesmen. Glubb reckoned that capturing Jerusalem would require two thousand men, almost half his force. And Britain, to whom Glubb owed his first allegiance, still harbored hopes for its internationalization. Thrusting his Legion into its precincts might place in jeopardy Transjordan's private arrangement with Ernest Bevin, and none of Glubb's orders to his British officers was more categoric than those involving Jerusalem. The vision haunting David Shaltiel's planning might be an illusion. If John Glubb had his way, the sand-colored armored cars of the Arab Legion would never appear on the ridge lines of Jerusalem.

•   •   •

Other voices, however, contested John Glubb's resolve to offer his Legionnaires only "the semblance of a war" in the days ahead. Fed on the same intoxicating diet of propaganda and belligerent boasts as the crowds of Cairo, Baghdad and Damascus, the souks of Amman clamored for war—a real war, not a pretense.

Fueling their emotions were the stories brought to Amman by the Arabs fleeing Palestine, and a constant flow of men looking for arms and ammunition. Among them was a delegation of Jerusalem's leaders. Swallowing their pride, those followers of the Mufti went to Abdullah's palace to beg for weapons. Embarrassed and ill at ease they told the King how depleted their armories were, how serious a blow to the Arab cause the loss of the city would be.

The monarch listened to them with scant pleasure. He did not need to be reminded of Jerusalem's importance. It figured prominently in his own ambitions. But he could not conceal his distaste for the men before him. Turning to the treasurer of the Mufti's Arab Higher Committee, he observed, "You used to collect funds for the Mufti's criminals, and now you dare come here and ask me for money."

Disconcerted, his visitors launched again into a lurid description of the state of their supplies. "Our ammunition is almost gone," they pleaded. "We'll have to defend the city by throwing stones."

"Then throw stones and die," coldly replied the little King.

That same evening a car slipped discreetly up to the side entrance of the residence of Sir Alec Kirkbride. It had come to take the British minister in Amman to a meeting in a private house on the other side of the city. Waiting for him was Azzam Pasha, the secretary general of the Arab League. Azzam appeared to Kirkbride that night "a very worried man, uncertain of the wisdom of going to war." Indeed, what he sought from the British diplomat was reassurance about the course of action on which the Arabs were embarked.

Unaware of the conversation between Nokrashy Pasha and Sir Ronald Campbell, Azzam asked Kirkbride if he would assure him that the British Army would not disturb Egypt's line of communications in the Suez Canal Zone during the coming conflict. The British envoy replied that it would be inconsistent with His Majesty's government's policy as he understood it for Britain to do so. He told Azzam he would ask London for a formal reply, but added that if the Army intended to interfere they clearly wouldn't say so, so that in any event the answer to his query would be No.

Instead of reassuring the Arab leader, his words, Kirkbride noted, seemed only to further perplex and puzzle Azzam. Yet they were an excellent reflection of Britain's policy. The British Foreign Office was not totally displeased by the Arabs' decision to go to war. With the exception of the disappointing showing of the Palestinians, things seemed to be working out about as the Foreign Office had anticipated. The coming conflict, Whitehall estimated, "would be of relatively short duration and would eventually be checked somehow by the United Nations." Indeed, Ernest Bevin had privately warned a Palestinian Arab friend, "Make sure that whatever efforts you undertake, you undertake in two weeks. For two weeks, perhaps, we can help you. After that we can only help you diplomatically."

Bevin and his associates did foresee "some considerable Arab successes in the fighting." In particular, his deputy Sir Harold Beeley would later recall, "We were doubtful about the fate of Jewish Jerusalem. Their situation looked very precarious and we thought they would go under. We were not trying to warn the Arabs off going to war, but we were cautious," Beeley noted. "It would be correct to say that if we did not encourage the Arab states to go to war in Palestine, we did not discourage them, either."

The view of His Majesty's representative in Amman was considerably more candid. Two decades after, Sir Alec Kirkbride would still think, "We were waving the green flag at the Arabs." *

---

* It is interesting to note, in retrospect, how fallacious some of the considerations dominating Britain's Middle East policy in 1948 turned out to be. "Centuries of wise British diplomacy have kept the Russians out of the Middle East," noted a

Seventy-five miles northwest of Amman, another black car drew up to an Arab Legion checkpoint. The Legionnaire on duty peered inside toward the heavyset, black-veiled woman sitting in the back seat. Beside her was a bulky man in a curly black astrakhan hat. The driver leaned toward the soldier and whispered one word: "Zurbati." That was not a password but a name, the name of the driver, an illiterate Iraqi Kurd who had become King Abdullah's most trusted servant. Respectfully, the soldier stiffened to a salute and waved the car forward.

The car was stopped ten times on its three-hour drive to Amman. Each time Zurbati's name whispered in the night sped its passage forward. In the back seat the passengers remained silent. Peering over her veil, the woman's dark eyes followed intently the shadowy outlines of the Arab Legion armor headed in the opposite direction, toward the Jordan River. In Amman, the two went straight to an ornate stone house above the road to the airport, across a wadi from the royal palace. There they were ushered into a lime-green circular salon dominated by a huge black-tiled fireplace. As they sipped a welcoming cup of tea, the frail silhouette of the man they had journey to Amman to see appeared in the doorway. The woman in the black veil rose and uttered a one-word greeting to the King of Transjordan: *"Shalom."*

Golda Meir had come to Amman at the risk of her life for a last confrontation with the Bedouin sovereign, hoping to find a key to the elusive state extolled in the greetings of their languages—*"Shalom"* in Hebrew, *"Salam"* in Arabic. The woman who had arrived in New York with ten dollars in her pocketbook and left with fifty million had been sent to Abdullah by David Ben-Gurion for something more valuable than all the Zionist funds in the world, an agreement that would keep the Arab Legion out of the approaching war.

Given Abdullah's and Glubb's intentions, it would not have seemed difficult. Much had changed, however, in the ten days since Glubb had sent Colonel Goldie to his meeting with the Haganah. The man Golda Meir saw before her that evening was a "sad and nervous king." The strident calls for war rising from the impassioned mobs of his souks had shaken his resolution. His fellow Arab leaders had so enmeshed him in their plans that his freedom of maneuver was now drastically reduced. If

British Army intelligence report in April 1948. "American Demagogy, blind to all but electoral consideration, is letting them in. In vain have the Greeks and Turks warned of the futility of using their countries as barriers to block the front door against Russian aggression while leaving open the pasture gate in Palestine. *Once British troops have left, there will be no one to control or prevent an unlimited immigration of Jewish communists from Russia."* (Authors' italics)

Abdullah still hoped to carry out his schemes, the new circumstances had forced a change in his tactics. He wanted to find a way to talk his fellows out of the war in which they sought to involve him. Through his physician-courier Dr. el Saty he had sent a message to the Jewish leadership. Give him some concession, he asked, so that he might in turn display to the rest of the Arab leadership the advantages of pursuing peace instead of war.

His message had prompted Golda Meir's trip. Dressed in a pair of coveralls, she had flown out of besieged Jerusalem in an open plane. In Haifa a dressmaker had hastily sewn up the black Arab dress that had disguised her on her journey.

Now the representatives of the two branches of the Semitic race, a Bedouin king who traced his descent to the Prophet and whose ancestors had dwelt on the Arabian Peninsula for centuries, and the daughter of a carpenter from Kiev so physically alien, yet so spiritually rooted in this ancient land of her Hebrew forebears, began their last effort to prevent a collision between their peoples.

The King reiterated the concessions his messenger had suggested: postpone proclaiming a Jewish state, keep Palestine united, with the Jews autonomous in their areas, and work out its destiny through a parliament composed equally of Arab and Jewish deputies. He desired peace, he told his visitor, but if his proposals were not accepted he feared war was inevitable.

They were not acceptable, Golda told the monarch. The Jews of Palestine sincerely wanted peace with their Arab neighbors, but not at the price of abandoning the most elemental of their aspirations, a land of their own. However, if they could return to the idea alluded to in their November conversation, the annexation scheme Abdullah still secretly intended to carry out, an understanding between them would be reached. The Jewish Agency was ready to honor the frontiers drawn by the United Nations as long as there was peace. Should war come, she gently warned, then her people would reach out and fight wherever they could as long as their strength lasted, and, she told the King, that strength had increased immeasurably in the past months.

The King said he realized the Jews would "have to repel any attack." But the situation had changed radically since their last meeting. Deir Yassin had inflamed the Arab masses. "I was alone then," he said. "Now I am one of five and I have discovered I cannot make any decision alone."

Golda and the man who had accompanied her, a brilliant Orientalist named Ezra Danin, tactfully reminded the King that Jews were his only real friends.

"I know that," he replied. "I have no illusions. I believe with all my heart that Divine Providence has brought you back here, restoring you, a Semitic people who were exiled in Europe, and have shared in its progress to the Semitic East which needs your knowledge and initiative. But," he said, "conditions are difficult." Be patient, he urged.

The Jewish people, Golda quietly remarked, had been patient for two thousand years. Their hour of statehood was at hand and could not be postponed now. If an understanding between them could not be reached on another basis and His Majesty wanted war, then, she said, "I am afraid there will be war." She was confident they would win, and perhaps they would meet again after the conflict as representatives of two sovereign states.

It was the critical moment of their conversation. Had the King revealed his real intentions to his visitors, they might have moved on to an agreement. He did not, and the proud little sovereign would carry to his grave the explanation of his silence. Perhaps he was convinced that May night that the course on which he was embarked was so perilous that he dared reveal his plans only to the handful of non-Arabs who would be responsible for carrying them out, John Glubb and the British officers of his Arab Legion. "I am sorry," he told his visitors. "I deplore the coming bloodshed and destruction. Let us hope we shall meet again and not sever our relations."

The conversation that might have prevented the first Arab–Jewish conflict was ended. Before leaving on her dangerous journey, Golda Meir had told her escort, Danin, that she would "walk to hell" if there was a chance of saving one Jewish soldier's life by her action. She rose to her feet sadly aware that she had saved no lives this night.

At the doorstep, Danin turned to Abdullah. They had been friends for years. "Your Majesty," he said, "beware when you go to the mosque to worship and let people rush up to kiss your robe. Someday a man will shoot you like that."

"*Habibi,* dear friend," replied the King, "I was born a free man and a Bedouin. I cannot leave the ways of my father to become a prisoner of my guards."

The trio shook hands. The last glimpse Danin and Golda would have of the King was standing on the stairs in his white robe and headgear, "slowly, sadly, waving goodbye."

28

BY JUST ONE VOTE

THE MELANCHOLY NOTES of an accordion rose through the darkness in the settlement of Kfar Etzion. Sometimes nostalgic, sometimes defiant, Zvi Ben-Joseph, a Viennese poet, played one of his own songs to the hushed band of young people gathered around him. "If I fail, friend, take my gun and avenge me," he sang. Softly, moodily, the boys and girls of the Haganah before him took up each chorus, sending Ben-Joseph's words through the shell holes in their *Neve Ovadia* into the night beyond. Few words could have captured better the spirit of the 545 settlers and soldiers waiting in the Etzion bloc that night of May 11 for a final tidal wave to break upon their unfortunate hills.

Much had happened in the six weeks since the settlement's convoy had been lost at Nebi Daniel. On April 12 the colony was assigned the task for which, in a military sense, it had been founded: to harass Arab traffic between Jerusalem and Hebron. Then, on April 30, the settlers received the order that would seal their fate. The men of Jerusalem's southern bastion were told to cut the road to prevent reinforcements from reaching the city from Hebron during the Palmach's attack on Katamon.

His dour face marked by his years in Nazi concentration camps, Kfar Etzion's commander, Moshe Silberschmidt, had urged his men to the dangerous job with one phrase: *"Netsach Yerushalayim"*—for the eternity of Jerusalem. Throwing up barricades, cutting telephone communications, ambushing passing vehicles, they had succeeded in their task, so completely that the Arabs could not ignore the challenge. At dawn on May 4 the inevitable had happened. Only this time, for the first time in Palestine, Jewish soldiers saw in their rifle sights the image of the war David Ben-Gurion had so long prophesied, uniformed regular soldiers moving at them behind a screen of armored vehicles. Determined to wipe out the strategically placed settlement before May 14, the Arab Legion was attacking.[*]

Two squadrons of armored cars began to pour point-blank fire into the

---

[*] The survivors of the assault affirm that in addition to the Legion forces at least one British tank joined in the shelling of their settlement.

347

settlers' advanced posts in an abandoned Russian Orthodox monastery along the Jerusalem–Hebron road. Then, backed up by hundreds of Arab villagers, the Legion's Bedouin infantry moved to the attack. The monastery's defenders had been forced to fall back on their colony, leaving only five hundred yards between their foes and the heart of their settlement.

A hastily scribbled message had saved the colony that day. Anxious to reopen the Hebron road, not to engage in a major battle, Glubb Pasha ordered the officer directing the attack to break off action and return to his base. Deprived of a victory he had believed within his grasp, Major Abdullah Tell had vowed to the villagers around him, "We will be back."

The following morning, beside the common trench dug into their lands beneath the colony's flowering fruit trees, Moshe Silberschmidt had had the sad task of eulogizing twelve more dead settlers of Kfar Etzion. "What are our lives worth?" the young officer asked his sorrowing soldiers. "Nothing compared to our task. Remember: It is the ramparts of Jerusalem we defend here."

The men and women who had vowed not to rest until they had covered Kfar Etzion's barren ridges with blossoming fruit trees now faced the cruel prospect of becoming, according to their commander, "another Masada," the legendary repair of the last Jewish Zealots holding out against the Romans. "At least," one of them wrote in a last letter that night, "we can rejoice at being able to do what the youth of the ghettos of Europe could not do, rise up against our enemy with our arms in our hands."

Yet on the evening of May 11 when Zvi Ben-Joseph's accordion was finally put away in the *Neve Ovadia*, the sound of young laughter rang out again across the settlement. For a few hours, before a spell of guard duty or a brief nap, Kfar Etzion's youthful defenders had managed to forget.

Not for long. Saying goodbye to his girl friend, a nurse he had walked back to the hospital, Yaacov Edelstein had a premonition. He had fought with the partisans against the Wehrmacht in the forests of his native Poland, and he had instinctive feeling for the kind of menace under which Kfar Etzion lived.

"Listen," Edelstein told his girl. "I'm sure they're about to come for us. I'm afraid we shall not see each other again."

He was right. The Legion was coming back. Unknown to its British commander, dozens of its soldiers were at that moment mounting their armored cars and half-tracks. In Hebron and the surrounding villages, the irregulars too boarded their trucks. All of them were heading for Kfar Etzion.

• • •

Their attack began at 4 A.M. Wednesday, May 12. Shaken from his bunk by the first exploding shells, Yaacov Edelstein rushed to his post in his pajamas. Tumbling into his position, he saw the first gray light of dawn on the horizon through the halos of fog clinging to the hills around him.

He had been right. Kfar Etzion's last battle was beginning. True to the vow he had uttered eight days earlier, Major Tell was ready to destroy the colony at all costs. He had used a ruse to justify his attack to the Legion's hesitant commander. He had told his subordinate Captain Hikmet Muhair in Hebron to radio Glubb that one of his convoys was under fire from the colony.

Muhair began the attack with a company of infantry, a squadron of armored cars and hundreds of irregulars. One platoon was to seize a piece of high ground called the Mukhtar's Saddle, then work its way to a grove of umbrella pines and cypress trees south of the buildings of the main kibbutz. His principal force would follow the lines of the May 4 assault. After a heavy shelling by his armored cars, his men would seize the Russian Orthodox monastery from which the Haganah had harassed passing traffic on the Hebron road. Then his armored cars and a band of irregulars would push to a ridge north of the settlement called Lone Tree after the enormous oak on its crest. Once there, Muhair would have split Kfar Etzion off from its three satellite settlements, Massuot, Ravadim and Ein Tsurim.

His attack on the monastery was brief and devastating. Their sandbagged positions shelled apart, their trenches destroyed, their strongpoints shattered by cannon fire, the buildings' defenders were forced to withdraw, leaving their wounded behind. The survivors made their way back toward the main kibbutz, leaping from shell hole to shell hole. Zvi Ben-Joseph, the poet whose songs had animated the *Neve Ovadia* the evening before, was mortally wounded as the retreat began. A comrade grabbed his Sten gun from Ben-Joseph's dying grasp and continued the flight back toward Kfar Etzion. Minutes later another bullet ended Moshe Silberschmidt's determination to live another Masada. The survivor of four years in Nazi Germany's concentration camps fell a few yards from the body of his poet friend.

Once the monastery was in their hands, Muhair's men set out for the first obstacle on their path to Lone Tree. It was a strongpoint set on a knoll between the monastery and Lone Tree, holding eighteen men, a Spandau machine gun and the settlement's only mortar. Within an hour, the commander of the post was dead, the machine gun jammed and the mortar broken. The knoll's defenders in their turn fell back on Kfar Etzion.

Paving the way with another deluge of shells, the Arabs rushed toward Lone Tree, where Kfar Etzion's one old British bazooka waited for them. Its half-dozen shells had no effect on the advancing armored cars. From there the Arabs swept up a short rise littered with white stones to the telephone exchange. When their last ammunition was gone, the operators on duty smashed their switchboard with an ax and fled. Telephone communication between the bloc's four settlements was cut. In a few moments all land contact was, too.

Muhair had completed the first phase of his plan. He had split up Kfar Etzion into four isolated settlements. Now he had only to wipe them out one by one.

● ● ●

In the cluttered Tel Aviv library in which he had pondered most of the major decisions of his life, David Ben-Gurion prepared for what well might be the most important meeting he had ever attended. On this May afternoon, the Council of Thirteen, a body he had created to replace the Jewish Agency Executive and to serve eventually as a provisional government, would decide whether or not to proclaim a Jewish state when Britain's Palestine mandate expired. Secretary Marshall's grave warning and the menacing presence of the Arab armies drawn up on the borders of Palestine had found their audience. A strong current of opinion in the Council favored accepting Marshall's truce proposal and agreeing to postpone the proclamation of a state. So closely aligned were the votes on the issue that Ben-Gurion had taken the extraordinary precaution of sending a Piper Cub to Jerusalem to fly one of the Council members, an orthodox rabbi on whose vote he knew he could count, to the meeting.

For Ben-Gurion there was, of course, no question. He was in complete agreement with the elderly scientist he had so often disputed for the leadership of the Zionist movement: proclaim the Jewish state, now or never. If the Jewish people hesitated it might prove fatal, he felt, to the state for which they had worked so long. Implicit in the United States's proposals was the idea of using a truce period for still another reappraisal of the Palestine question, a reappraisal which might put back into question his people's dreams of statehood.

Despite his esteem for Marshall, Ben-Gurion did not believe that postponing their state would halt the Arabs' invasion. State or no state, truce or no truce, he believed the Arabs would invade, and when they did, the mechanisms of statehood would be indispensable to the Yishuv's survival. With a state, they would be able to buy arms openly as the Arabs did, to run their own maritime commerce to bring them to Palestine. A state would give his people a national identity to buoy their spirits in the difficult times through which they would have to pass.

His opponents in the Council of Thirteen favored a truce as a means of buying time. By rushing ahead now, by triggering an Arab onslaught, the Yishuv, they argued, risked losing everything that the Jewish people had for years striven to attain. Another thought weighed on them as they considered the decision they would have to make Wednesday, May 12. Having just lost six million people in the Nazi holocaust, could they accept the risk of another slaughter? They were also keenly aware that the army on which their settlement depended was beset by internal divisions.

With the advent of a state and the conflict its birth would produce, the Haganah would have to become an army. The army after which Ben-Gurion wanted his soldiers to pattern themselves was Britain's. To Ben-Gurion, it seemed that much of the Haganah leadership, nurtured in the underground, had not grasped "what a state was, what a war was." They had been trained to defend settlements, not to fight a war, and they didn't understand the difference. In war, Ben-Gurion thought, "you take a man from Tel Aviv and put him in front of Beersheba and it's for the state, not Beersheba, that he must be ready to give his life." In trying to prepare the Haganah for its new role Ben-Gurion placed the greater part of his confidence in those officers who had fought with the British Army during the war instead of in those who had remained in Palestine.

That had stirred resentment among the 5,200 men of the Palmach, the elite of the Jewish forces. An intense and special kind of camaraderie bound its members, officers and men alike, together. Disdaining the external trappings of military discipline, they were united by a highly developed sense of interdependence and mutual confidence. That gave them great resiliency and flexibility in battle. It also gave them a sense of superiority over the rest of the Haganah. Palmach officers were not above disputing and, on occasion, ignoring, orders passed to them by Haganah officers whose judgment they questioned. They had no inhibitions about strengthening their armories by raiding the supplies of nearby Haganah units. Their tactics had proven highly successful in the Palestine of the mandate. In the new situation, Ben-Gurion feared, they could lead to disaster. In addition, the Palmach's leadership was drawn largely from the kibbutzim of Ben-Gurion's political rivals of the Mapam party, a more left-wing Socialist body than his own Mapai. One day the Palmach might be the instrument of a left-wing *coup d'état,* he suspected. He had already taken steps to bring it under tighter control.

351

He had begun by eliminating the job of Israel Galili, the man who represented the Palmach in the Haganah high command. The ensuing outcry had forced Ben-Gurion to backtrack and reinstate Galili, but the Jewish leader had made his point: the days of an independent Palmach were numbered.

On paper, the Jewish position was not as desperate as it might have appeared. The Haganah had a trained-manpower pool of sixty thousand people. A third of those citizen soldiers had had wartime experience in the Jewish Brigade or some other military group. Twenty-eight thousand immigrants, many of them of military age, waited in Britain's Cyprus detention camps for the boats that would deliver them to Palestine after the end of the mandate. Others, packed into overcrowded vessels, were already on their way from Europe.*

Yet, on the twelfth of May, the Haganah had only 18,900 men fully mobilized, armed and in position to meet the Arab onslaught. They were divided into nine brigades, three in the north to defend the Galilee and the seacoast north of Haifa, two protecting the southern approaches to Tel Aviv, two in the Negev, one in Jerusalem and one in the bitterly disputed Bab el Wad bottleneck.

In almost every instance the Arabs held the superior terrain. In Tulkarm they were less than ten miles from the sea and the possibility of cutting the Yishuv in half. The Arab communities of Lydda and Ramle were only minutes from the heart of Tel Aviv. The Negev seemed wide open to Egypt's armor. Jerusalem, above all, remained completely cut off. Another effort to reopen the road as Nachshon had done was on the brink of failure.

Those considerations paled beside the Haganah's gravest problem, its shortage of arms. If only twenty thousand of the sixty thousand trained Jews in Palestine were mobilized, it was because there were not enough weapons in the country to equip the rest. To the 10,000 rifles in the Haganah's central reserve, the S.S. *Nora* and the secret flight of Ocean Trade Airways had added 4,500 rifles and 400 machine guns. Haim Slavine's underground factories had managed to produce an additional 7,000 Sten guns. That represented virtually all the Haganah's small arms. Yet the organization was rich in hand weapons compared to its shortage of heavy equipment. Its field artillery was made up almost exclusively of the homemade Davidka and a few bought or stolen three-inch mortars. There

* The Arab armies, despite the fact that the populations from which they were culled vastly outnumbered the 600,000 Jews of Palestine, totaled only 80,000 men. Of them, 23,000 had been committed to the invasion of Palestine.

was not a single warplane in the country. Joseph Avidar's workshops had buckled protective armor-plating onto six hundred assorted vehicles, effective enough in running the gauntlet of Arab ambushes, but worthless against Glubb's armored cars or Egypt's armored force.

Two folders lying on the Jewish leader's desk contained the details of the Haganah's only hopes of victory and the arguments with which Ben-Gurion hoped to persuade his fellows to proclaim their state. They were the summaries of the arms purchased abroad by Ehud Avriel and Yehuda Arazi. Stockpiled in Europe, awaiting the legal sanction of Jewish statehood to begin their journey to Palestine, they could alter the tide of the conflict. Somewhere on the waters of the Mediterranean beyond Ben-Gurion's windows, the first shipload of those arms waited just outside Palestine's territorial water. The holds of the S.S. *Borea* contained the Haganah's first field-artillery pieces, five 65-millimeter mountain guns and 48,000 shells. Ben-Gurion was going to propose to his hesitant fellows a gamble, a gamble on their ability to withstand the Arabs' onslaught until the caravan of ships of which the *Borea* was a harbinger could reach their ports. Clutching the reports on which his arguments and the proclamation of a Jewish state would stand or fall, David Ben-Gurion set off for his historic meeting in the Tel Aviv headquarters of the Jewish National Fund.

*   *   *

"They're closing in. Urgent you send aviation to help us."

In the command post of the kibbutz of Kfar Etzion, the fingers of Eliza Feuchtwanger, the colony's young Polish-born radio operator, skimmed over still another despairing plea for help. Her desperate stream of S.O.S.'s indicated the gravity of the kibbutz's plight. "Situation in regard to men, arms and ammunition grave. Do everything you can tonight. We can no longer attend the dead and wounded," pleaded one. The shellfire of the Legion's armored cars had already ravaged most of the kibbutz's biuldings. Half of the roof of the *Neve Ovadia* was torn off. The dining hall, the kitchen, the hospital, the library and most of the dormitories were in ruins. Only the headquarters itself, installed in a solid stone building that had housed the German Benedictine monks from whom the Jewish National Fund had bought part of Kfar Etzion, had survived intact.

The structure swarmed with breathless messengers, wounded, fighters numb with fear and fatigue grabbing an instant's rest. The constant din of shellfire, the acrid pall of smoke from the kibbutz's burning buildings, the disorderly movement of people shouting for arms, ammunition or help, gave the building an atmosphere of despairing hysteria. The bloc's new commander, a curly-haired sabra named Abbras Tamir, had been seriously wounded May 4. Carried to the command post from the hospital after Moshe Silberschmidt's death, he had to give his orders from a stretcher.

On the other side of the fighting lines, Captain Hikmet Muhair too sent a message. As he had agreed with Tell, he radioed Legion headquarters a lurid account of his situation and called for reinforcements. Two more platoons were sent to bolster his forces.

Toward the end of the afternoon, the Legion's shellfire began again with increased fury, followed by another sortie of Muhair's armored cars. On Rock Hill, the principal outpost before the kibbutz itself, a two-inch mortar being used as a bazooka and two light machine guns hurled a barrage of fire at the oncoming cars.

Despite the shellfire exploding all around them, Rock Hill's defenders held on, training their inadequate weapons on the only vulnerable part of the machines advancing toward them, their tires. Their tactic succeeded. Like a pack of wounded animals, Captain Muhair's cars began to limp back to Lone Tree on their flat tires. The tenacious resistance of the handful of men on Rock Hill had earned their fellows in Kfar Etzion a precious gift, the chance to survive another night.

David Ben-Gurion scrutinized the faces of the nine men gathered around him in the headquarters of the Jewish National Fund. In the absence of three members of the national Council of Thirteen unable to attend their meeting, those leaders of Zionism's supreme body would in a few moments determine whether or not the Jewish people would have a sovereign state of their own. The burden of making that decision had fallen on those individuals around Ben-Gurion for a variety of reasons. Three of them were rabbis representing on the Council the religious consciousness of a people whose attachment to the land of Palestine was originally a profound manifestation of their spiritual heritage. Some, like Golda Meir, Eliezer Kaplan and Moshe Sharett, were veterans of years of service on the body which had preceded the Council, the Jewish Agency Executive. Others were relative newcomers appointed in case the Council became a provisional government.

Ben-Gurion was disturbed by the concern and uncertainty he sensed in the faces of his nine fellow leaders. Sharett's description of his meeting with Secretary of State Marshall had shaken the determination of at least a third of the representatives of Ben-Gurion's own Mapai party. Golda Meir's report of her visit to Abdullah had added its ration of doubt. Now, at the request of the Council, Yigal Yadin presented the Haganah's assessment of their chances in a conflict with the Arab armies.

If the truce proposed by General Marshall would give them time to bring arms into the country, then it was worth accepting it, Yadin indicated. If they did not accept and war broke out immediately, the Haganah would be sorely tried. They knew what the Syrians would do, because intelligence had penetrated Syrian headquarters, but the plans of the Iraqis, the Egyptians and the Arab Legion were unknown. At best, he gave the Haganah a fifty-fifty chance of victory.

Ben-Gurion grimaced at the stunned gasp that followed Yadin's words. The doubting members, he noted, were more frightened than they had been before his speech. He took over the meeting himself.

"I fear for our morale," he told his hesitant colleagues. The Yishuv had been spoiled thus far: the enemy had failed to capture any of its centers. There was no need to regret that, but in the event of heavy casualties, a loss of ground in the future, he feared the Yishuv's morale would be shaken. The trial ahead would certainly lead to those losses, he warned, both in territory and in manpower. They might produce serious repercussions among the public. He paused. Then he opened the files containing the two reports he had studied earlier in his library. He knew something, he revealed, that Marshall had not known when he issued his warning to Sharett. He knew that the Yishuv now possessed arms that could alter the situation.

Slowly, dramatically, he read out the contents of his files, letting the effect of each figure make its impression on the men around him. Avriel, he revealed, had purchased 25,000 rifles, 5,000 machine guns, 58 million rounds of ammunition, 175 howitzers and thirty airplanes. Arazi had succeeded in buying ten tanks, thirty-five antiaircraft guns, twelve 120-millimeter mortars, fifty 65-millimeter cannons, 5,000 rifles, 200 heavy machine guns, 97,000 artillery and mortar shells of assorted calibers, and nine million rounds of small-arms ammunition.

As he had hoped they would, those figures instilled a new air of confidence in the circle of his colleagues. If the arms were stockpiled in Palestine, he continued, they might contemplate the situation more calmly. However, they were not, and the time needed to bring them to Palestine would be decisive in determining not only the outcome of the war but also its duration and the number of casualties they would suffer. The Arab armies would probably march into the country before the arms arrived in any significant quantity. The Jews would have to steel themselves for severe losses and shocks. But, he growled, in view of the prospects of their grow-

355

ing strength, flouting his own experts, "I dare believe in victory. We shall triumph!"

Transfixed by the magnetic personality of their chief, the other leaders fell silent. Ben-Gurion called for a vote. The question was whether to accept Marshall's call for a truce and with it a temporary postponement of statehood. If the vote went against accepting the truce, then it would automatically mean the proclamation of a state. The closeness of the vote, in spite of the power of Ben-Gurion's final oration, was the measure of how near the people in the Jewish National Fund headquarters had come to turning away from statehood. At his call for those in favor of accepting the truce, Ben-Gurion saw four hands go up. The motion had failed by just one vote. On that one vote had hung the rebirth of the Jewish state.

The Council turned to the consequence of its vote, the protocol of proclaiming a state. Someone suggested that the declaration should stipulate that the state's borders would be those contained in the United Nations partition resolution.

Ben-Gurion rejected the idea. The Americans, he said, had not announced the frontiers of their state in the Declaration of Independence. Despite considerable reservations, particularly on the internationalization of Jerusalem, the Jews had accepted the partition resolution. The Arabs had not and by their action they had forfeited their right to the partition plan. The borders of their state would be those that would come out of the war. "We have before us," he said, "a chance to get a state whose borders will be practical ones. The state we are proclaiming is not the state that resulted from the United Nations decision but the *de facto* situation existing today."

Then the group chose a name for the new state. Two names, Zion and Israel, were before them. On Ben-Gurion's urging, the choice finally fell on Israel.

One last decision remained: fixing the exact hour at which they would announce to the world the news for which the Jewish people had been waiting for almost two millenniums. Technically their state would come into existence at midnight Friday, May 14. That would be in the midst of the Sabbath, and the orthodox among them would not be able to travel in an automobile or even affix their signature to a proclamation of statehood at that hour.

One of the participants took from his pocket the chart carried by all Jews wishing to be scrupulously exact in their observance of the rites of their religion. Studying its figures, he announced that in order to conclude before the official hour of the setting of the sun, the ceremony proclaiming the birth of a new Jewish nation in the land of Israel should begin at precisely four o'clock on Friday, May 14, 1948, the fifth day of the month of Iyar in the year 5708 of the Hebrew calendar.

• • •

In the silent night of Kfar Etzion, the anguished eyes of the settlement's defenders studied the star-filled sky. They clung to a last desperate hope, the thought that somehow the Haganah might fill that sky with planes bringing them the instruments of their salvation. Those hopes were illusory. The few light airplanes the Haganah could put into the evening sky had no chance of saving an entire colony. Most of the parachutes of arms and medicine they tried to drop to the settlers fell beyond their lines.

Using the cover of darkness, a team of sappers laid on the approaches to the kibbutz what mines the settlement had left. Abbras Tamir decided to send his thirty-five wounded to one of the other colonies. Volunteers carried those who couldn't walk. Led by Dr. Aaron Windsberg, a former surgeon in the Red Army, the pitiful procession of injured stumbled off over the stones and scrub brush of a goat track, trying to limit the noise of their passage to the groans of the dying. Tamir himself was carried on his stretcher past the Arab lines to Massuot, where he hoped to find enough men to organize a counterattack for the morning.

Toward midnight, a shell set fire to the stable and the barn. There was no water left to put it out. The macabre ballet of those flames reminded some of Kfar Etzion's deeply religious settlers of the burning of the Temple sanctuary. Eliezer Sternberg relived for a few grim instants a more recent tragedy, the end of the Warsaw ghetto.

All night, occasional bursts of tracer bullets poked their orange fingers through the dark sky. "It was a lovely spring night," Yaacov Edelstein would recall. The only sounds in the darkness were the shrill fluttering of cicadas and the occasional guttural mumble of the Arabs massed all around them. Some of Kfar Etzion's exhausted defenders slept. Others prayed. They prayed that the night might never end.

In an army camp near Jericho, the faint ring of a field telephone roused a sleeping Arab soldier. At the voice of his orderly exclaiming, *"Ah, ya Pasha!"* as he picked up the phone, Major Abdullah Tell leaped from his bed and took the receiver from the soldier's hands. There was only one pasha in the Arab Legion and only one pasha in the life of Abdullah Tell. He had been waiting for Glubb's call. In his familiar, faintly hesitant voice, the only Englishman who spoke Arabic with a perfect Bedouin accent ordered the commander of his Sixth Regiment to round up the rest of his men and rush to Kfar Etzion. Captain Muhair, Glubb reported, was "in serious difficulty."

Tell smiled. The ruse had worked. He ordered his men, already in a state of alert, to get ready. Then, picking up his talisman, an ebony swagger stick topped by a hand-worked ornate silver knob, he mounted his command jeep. Burning with an intense desire to personally supervise the Arab Legion's first conquest in Palestine, Tell waved his column of vehicles forward.

No ambition might have seemed beyond the reach of that thirty-year-old officer setting out at the head of his men for the besieged kibbutz of Kfar Etzion. If the face of the young actor disfigured on Ben Yehuda Street might have incarnated the face of a new Jewish nation in Palestine, so Tell could well have offered the visage of its older, Arab civilization. With his perfectly spaced features, his dark moustache, his brown eyes, his white teeth showing through his spacious smile, his head swathed in the perfectly draped folds of his red-and-white kaffiyeh, Tell might have seemed the leading man in some Hollywood drama of the Arabian desert. He had the age, almost, of the emirate he served. His mother had often told him that one of her first gestures after his birth had been to hold him up to the window so that his infant eyes might witness a turning point in his people's history, the retreat of Turkey's soldiers through the streets of his native Irbid. Like so many of his generation, an eighteen-year-old Tell had gone to jail for demonstrating against the power that had replaced Turkish influence in the Middle East, Great Britain. Yet, seven years later, he sought to wear the coveted British battle dress and red-and-white kaffiyeh of the army founded by Lawrence's heirs. In action against Iraq's Golden Square rebels, on duty in Palestine, one single-minded obsession dominated the young Tell: "to resemble as closely as possible a British officer, to be as admired by my men as Glubb was by his Bedouins."

On November 30, 1947, listening to a radio announce the results of the partition vote in a British officers' mess, Tell had had the opportunity to measure the limits to which he might push that resemblance. None of the Englishmen around him appeared moved by the news. Years later, he would still recall his shock at realizing that he alone in the mess was concerned. The Arabs would have to take their destiny into their own hands, he told himself. His determination to seize Kfar Etzion without his British commander's knowledge or blessing was going to be a first manifestation of the young officer's resolution that day to "wipe out the injustice of partition."

29

THE LAST SUPPER

EVERY MORNING for twenty-eight years Fouad Tannous'
working day had begun with the same little ritual: a cup of Turkish coffee,
a glance at the morning paper, and a few jokes on what it contained with
his colleagues in the Jerusalem testing laboratories. On this Thursday
morning, May 13, only two of his fellow employees remained to share for
the last time that rite with Fouad Tannous. There were no jokes that
morning. Sad and solemn, the three men "sat there looking at each other."
There was absolutely nothing for them to do. Yet, totally faithful to the
British training that had been the focal point of his adult existence, Tannous remained on duty until the laboratory's final closing hour. A few
minutes before the end, he went to the office of the director of medical
services at Government Hospital to get his certificate of service. The
director handed it to him with three words: "Here it is." That was all.
No handshake, no thank-you, no goodbye, no "Good luck." For Fouad
Tannous twenty-eight years of service to the British Empire had ended in
that curt phrase.

He went back to his lab to close up. Usually his last gesture was to
lock the large iron cupboard containing almost a year's supply of chemicals
and pharmaceuticals. This time, he slipped the key into the cupboard door
and left it there. "What's the use?" he thought. "The Jews will get it anyway. They'll get the chemicals. They'll get the building. They'll get the
whole country."

A few hundred yards away in the Municipality Building at the foot of
Jaffa Road, an equally brief gesture marked the end of Jerusalem's existence as a united municipality. The city's British controller gave checks for
27,500 pounds sterling, half the balance in the municipality's bank account,
to representatives of the Arab and Jewish communities. Anton Safieh
gasped at the size of his check. It represented more money than the Christian Arab had earned in his adult life. Trembling with the heavy responsibility it thrust upon him, he rushed to deposit it in the safest place he

359

knew, the vault of the Municipality Building. That task accomplished, Safieh turned to a more prosaic chore. With two comrades, he spirited away thirteen municipal vehicles, most of them garbage carts, and placed them just inside the entrance to Jaffa Gate.

The coolest head in the Jerusalem city administration that morning belonged to Safieh's brother, Emile. Inspired by that special respect for sound procedures he had absorbed in his years as a British civil servant, Emile Safieh carried away to safety the archives on which he had worked most of his life. Safieh well knew that no nation, no county, no municipality no matter how small, could hope to exist without such documents. They constituted, in a sense, the finest baptismal offering he could make to Jerusalem's new Arab entity—the complete income-tax records of its Arab inhabitants.

As he did every day, the mandate's official spokesman, Richard Stubbs, met in his office at the Press Information Office this Thursday morning with Jerusalem's press corps. Blandly, he assured the men before him that the British administration in Jerusalem would end May 15, and that a substantial British military presence would remain in the city for at least another week.

His statement was a hoax. Anxious to slip out of the city swiftly so that his rear guard would not get caught in the fighting sure to follow his departure, Brigadier C. P. Jones planned to begin his evacuation at midnight. If all went well there would not be a single British soldier or official left in Jerusalem when the city's journalists reached Stubbs's empty office for their daily briefing the following morning.

Stubbs's words were part of an effort to tranquilize the populace by persuading it that British forces would remain in the city for some days to come. That same morning, the government's Chief Secretary Sir Henry Gurney smilingly informed the United Nations' Pablo de Azcarate, "Absolutely nothing will happen for a few days yet." Thus reassured, the United Nations diplomat set off on an overnight trip to Amman, certain he would be back before the British left.

From the rooftop of the Haganah's Red House headquarters a pair of anxious men followed with binoculars the progress of a dumpy little steamer plodding toward Tel Aviv harbor. It was the S.S. *Borea,* the forerunner of the fleet of ships David Ben-Gurion had promised his colleagues would eventually bring them the arms to secure a Jewish state. So pressing was the need for the five guns and 48,000 shells her hold contained that the

Haganah's leadership had decided to take the risk of running her into port forty-eight hours before the end of the mandate.

Suddenly one of the two men on Red House roof groaned. Joseph Avidar had just spotted in his glasses the outline of a British destroyer steaming toward the *Borea*. On the Red House radio, Avidar followed the ensuing drama. British customs officers boarded the vessel and called for the *Borea*'s manifest of tomato juice, potatoes and the inevitable load of onions. Not satisfied, they ordered the ship to Haifa for inspection.

Avidar radioed the captain to send a crewman to the engine rooms to smash some vital piece of machinery so that they could tell the British the vessel couldn't move. No such gesture was going to stay the firm hand of the British mandatory authority, however. Although the mandate may only have had a few hours left to live, her customs agents were going to see that the regulations by which they had sought to prevent arms from reaching the Jews of Palestine remained in effect until the very last of those hours had elapsed. A second destroyer was called up to take the *Borea* into tow. With despairing glances, the chiefs of the Haganah watched as the little steamer and their five field guns began to move slowly off up the coastline of Palestine toward Haifa.

Eyes reddened with strain, limbs numb with fatigue, another group of Haganah soldiers watched the arms that would soon overwhelm them surge toward their posts. For the one hundred and fifty soldiers and settlers left alive in the principal settlement of Kfar Etzion, the slow approach of the armored cars of Abdullah Tell destroyed any lingering hopes that some miracle might save their colony.

Still, the situation that the commander of the Sixth Arab Legion Regiment had found at Kfar Etzion had been much less favorable than his foes imagined. Captain Muhair had scattered his armored cars over so much ground that he had forfeited their effectiveness; his Legionnaires, mixed in with the undisciplined irregulars, had been infected with their passion for looting; and Muhair had so completely surrounded the central kibbutz that some of his men were firing into each other's positions.

Tell immediately took charge of the operation. He separated his infantry from the irregulars and regrouped his armored cars to concentrate their firepower around the Lone Tree. From that vantage point, they could pulverize the handful of men on Rock Hill who had checked the advance of Muhair's cars the afternoon before.

At 11:30 A.M. he began his assault. The Jews, as he would later recognize, fought "with incredible bravery." In the main kibbutz they rushed the

361

sole machine gun from post to post to support the battered men on Rock Hill. Hammered by round after round, the strongpoint defenders fought until their ammunition was gone. Then they destroyed their weapons and fled. The door to the central settlement of Kfar Etzion was open.

At its main gate, Nahum Ben-Sira saw the lead armored cars start down the road from Lone Tree. In the hands of the young man who had come to Kfar Etzion from the Mauthausen death camp with the survivors of his shattered family was the kibbutz's bazooka, a stovepipelike device with a primitive gunsight. Neither Ben-Sira nor his companion, Abraham Gessner, had ever fired it. His heart pounding, his finger tensed on the trigger, Ben-Sira followed the advancing armored car. When it was fifty yards away, he fired. Nothing happened. While Ben-Sira held his aim, Gessner desperately shook the tube. The rocket refused to budge. Despite their efforts, Kfar Etzion's bazooka remained silent. Ben-Sira crawled to the plunger of the mine hidden behind the roadblock barricading the entrance. As the car smashed into its stones, he squeezed the plunger. But, like his bazooka, the mine refused to work. So many shells had torn up the ground around the entrance that the wire commanding it had been cut.

The car pushed aside the stones of the barricade and rumbled into the kibbutz itself. Two well-aimed Molotov cocktails finally stopped its progress. Gessner and Ben-Sira's string of bad luck had finally ended. Their victory was brief. From behind the thick smoke wrapping the burning car came the rumble of other cars, and in their wake a screaming horde of irregulars rushed toward the gate.

At the command post, Eliza Feuchtwanger radioed Jerusalem: "The Arabs are in the kibbutz. Farewell." Reading her words in his headquarters, David Shaltiel, the man who had urged Kfar Etzion's evacuation, felt tears come to his eyes. Then the young Polish girl added a few words to her message. "The Arabs are everywhere," she said. "There are thousands of them. They are blackening the hills."

Minutes later, her silhouette appeared on the roof of the command post waving a bloody sheet which she attached to the radio's antenna. Since the men in the positions around the kibbutz couldn't see her white flag, messengers dashed out to tell them they were surrendering. Gradually the firing died out, and one by one the colony's exhausted defenders staggered up to the command post. Some of them seemed relieved by the decision. Others, like Zipora Rosenfeld, a beautiful blond Polish survivor of Auschwitz, cried. Yaacov Edelstein smashed his rifle in protest.

Fifty survivors finally reached the little square before the headquarters. Among them was Eliza Feuchtwanger, whose messages would soon become a legend throughout Palestine. Yaacov Edelstein looked for the nurse he had walked to the hospital two days before. As he had feared, they would not meet again. She was dead. Yitzhak Ben-Sira searched for the five brothers and sisters he had brought to Kfar Etzion from Europe's death camps. Only one, Nahum, was still alive. Zipora Rosenfeld leaned against the husband she had refused to leave when the colony's mothers had been evacuated, thinking certainly of her infant son, Yosi, born only a few weeks before on the promised land of her new country.

Scores of irregulars swarmed around them, shrieking, "Deir Yassin!," ordering them to sit down, stand up, sit down again. Edelstein saw one of them step forward. With a click of the shutter of his camera, he registered the saddest spectacle in the long and painful history of Zionism's efforts to settle the hills of Kfar Etzion.

Suddenly a machine gun began to fire. Edelstein saw bodies tumbling all around him. "It's the end," he thought. The sight of a bayonet plunged into a comrade's chest spurred him to action. With a leap, he sprang up from the mound of dying men and women and started a wild flight, shoving his way past the startled Arabs surrounding them. Spurred by his gesture, half a dozen others followed in a wild, instinctive flight. "There was no place to go," Edelstein recalled, "because the whole area swarmed with Arabs."

Nahum Ben-Sira stumbled exhausted into a little vineyard at the edge of the kibbutz, only a few paces from a path along which the Arabs raced up and down in search of loot and survivors. He would huddle there until nightfall, tensed for the shout of *"Yahud!"* which would precede a fatal burst of gunfire.

Edelstein and three others crawled over the stone fence at the end of the settlement and darted into a little glade, called the Song of Songs because it was the favorite sanctuary of the kibbutz's lovers. They burrowed among its boulders and closely spaced trees, hoping somehow that the boughs that had sheltered their lovers' trysts would now save their lives. Suddenly the snapping of a twig told Edelstein they had been discovered. Above him was a wrinkled, toothless old Arab. "Don't be afraid," he told them.

Then a group of irregulars rushed up and threw Edelstein and Yitzhak Ben-Sira, who had hidden with him, against a wall. The old Arab stood in front of them, protecting them with his body. "You have killed enough," he said.

"Silence," one of the irregulars yelled, "or we'll kill you too!"

"No," replied the old man, spreading his arms over the two Jewish prisoners. "They are under my protection." While they argued, a pair of Legionnaires came up. As they led Edelstein and Ben-Sira off to captivity, Edelstein heard shots from the lovers' glade. The irregulars had found the two others who had fled with him.

Eliza Feuchtwanger had thrown herself into a ditch behind the school with half a dozen others. The Arabs rushed to the trench and began to empty their Sten guns at the helpless survivors inside. A piercing shriek from Eliza interrupted their slaughter just long enough to allow one of them to yank her from the trench. A knot of men surrounded her, disputing the privilege of raping her with the Arab who had pulled her from the ditch. Finally two of them dragged her away from the others and pushed her screaming through the smoking ruins of the kibbutz to a clump of wood. There they began to claw at her, tearing at her clothing, unable to agree who would assault her first.

Suddenly two bursts of gunfire interrupted their fight. Eliza saw the two Arabs drop dead at her feet. Stunned, she looked up and found before her an Arab Legion officer, smoke still curling from the mouth of his Sten gun. Lieutenant Nawaf Jaber el Hamoud took a piece of bread from his pocket.

"Eat this," he said. When she had done so, he told her, "Now you are under my protection," and marched her to his armored car.

The only sound in the kibbutz as they left was the shrieks of the looters fighting for each item they tore from the ruins. The shaken Eliza was the only member left alive of the Palmach force assigned to the principal kibbutz. Of the eighty-eight settlers present in the colony when Tell's attack had begun, three had survived, Yaacov Edelstein and Nahum and Yitzhak Ben-Sira.

The grim prophecy of Moshe Silberschmidt had been realized. One hundred and forty-eight people had soaked with their blood the earth they had vowed to cover with fruit trees, deeding to a new generation the legend of a modern Masada, the kibbutz of Kfar Etzion.*

. . .

A haze of dust stirred by the advancing column hung in the air and frosted the trucks with a fine gray powder. In the outskirts of Amman, in the country villages and crossroads, huddled on rooftops, hanging from

* Among the dead were Zipora Rosenfeld and the husband whose side she would not leave. Nineteen years later, after the Six-Day War, a Rosenfeld came back to the bleak hills of Kfar Etzion to carry on the project for which the parents he had never known had given their lives. Yosi Rosenfeld is today an electrician in the resurrected kibbutz of Kfar Etzion.

windows, clustered by black Bedouin goatskin tents, the excited crowds cheered the men on. The Arab Legion was going to battle.

From Mafraq and Zerqa in central Transjordan, the men and vehicles of the army that had just overwhelmed the last defenders of the Etzionbloc's principal settlement moved down the Mountains of Moab to the staging area by the Jordan River from which they would cross into Palestine.

For three uninterrupted miles their cavalcade covered the roads of Transjordan, five hundred vehicles, trucks, jeeps, signal vans, mobile kitchens, armored cars, troop carriers. It was an impressive display, and the throngs went wild at the sight. From behind their black veils, the women warbled the tremulous *"Yo yo yo"* war cry that had sent Moslems into battle since the Prophet's warriors first streamed out of the deserts of Arabia twelve hundred years before. Men clapped and cheered. Children threw flowers and scampered along behind the passing vehicles. In the countryside riders galloped beside the column on horse or camelback wildly firing into the air.

Jubilant and excited, the troops responded in kind, cheering and waving to the crowds. Some of their trucks were hung with pink oleander and green palm sprays. All of them were infected by the excitement of the populace. Looking at their faces, Captain Ali Abou Nuwar, adjutant of the Second Regiment, thought, "All their hopes are on us." To Youssef Jeries, a platoon leader elated at the thought of "rescuing our Palestine brothers," it was as though they were "going to a wedding."

Riding along with his men, John Glubb thought the procession "looked more like a carnival than an army going to war." For a man who knew the Arabs as well as Glubb did, that was a surprisingly inaccurate reading of his men's mood. It was not a "semblance of war" his Bedouin officers and soldiers wanted. They wanted to fight, to march on Tel Aviv, to drive their armored cars down to the shores of the Mediterranean, and their martial mood was going to challenge the English general's plans in the days just ahead.

At the Zerqa camp from which some of Glubb's Legionnaires had just set out, the atmosphere in the Arab armies' joint headquarters was considerably less reassuring. The place, Azzam Pasha noted, "brewed with confusion." The brigadier sent by the Egyptians as their liaison officer appeared to have no idea of what his army's movements would be. The Iraqi hadn't even shown up yet.

To compound their troubles a cable arrived at noon May 13 from General Safwat Pasha in Damascus. "Firmly convinced that the absence of agreement on a precise plan can only lead us to disaster," it announced. "I submit my resignation." Azzam replaced him with another Iraqi, a Kurd who at least bore a propitious name, that of one of Saladin's generals, Nurreidin Mahmoud. In Zerqa's disturbing atmosphere the worried secretary general of the Arab League found only one voice to reassure him. It belonged to the Arab Legion's British liaison officer. "Don't worry," he kept promising Azzam, "we're going to lick them."

For other Britons, packing to leave the following morning, their war was ending at last. Many of them had been fighting practically without pause in one part of the world or another since 1939, and the next day would offer them their first peace in a decade. In Jerusalem, the souks of the Old City swarmed with British soldiers searching for a last souvenir of their service in Palestine. Colonel Jack Churchill, the officer who had tried to save the victims of the Hadassah convoy, had long had his eye on two carpets. The Middle Eastern veteran knew how to barter, but this afternoon he didn't have to. Into the hands of the merchant who had been asking one hundred pounds he thrust four ten-pound notes, saying "take it while you can. Tomorrow the Jews will be here and they'll get them for nothing."

For a handful of British soldiers, the coming departure forced to the surface a decision as old as men and arms: whether to leave behind a girl or desert and accept a new life in exile. Mike Scott did not hesitate. For months, once a week in a darkened Jerusalem movie house, he had slipped his Jewish fiancée documents from his office in Army Intelligence. Ordered home, he had immediately volunteered his services to the Haganah's Vivian Herzog. Was there anything, he inquired, that he might bring along with him when he came? With the understatement of his years of service with the Guards, Herzog had modestly suggested that the Haganah could do with a cannon.

And so, on the afternoon of May 13, accompanied by a crane, a truck and three British soldiers, Major Mike Scott strode into the Army's main weapons park in Haifa. The Jerusalem command, he told the commanding general, had just lost a twenty-five-pound gun in a road accident outside Ramallah and wanted an immediate replacement in case of trouble during the withdrawal.

"Help yourself," said the general, waving to his artillery park. A few minutes later in a garage on Mount Carmel, the army that had been deprived of five precious guns by a zealous British naval officer got its revenge for the seizure of the *Borea*. The Haganah took possession of its first piece of field artillery.

No woman lay behind the decision of other British soldiers to remain in Palestine. The war in which they had been supposed to play the role of impartial policemen had become a cause for them, and its passions and divisions had become theirs. They now deserted to one side or the other. Three soldiers in civilian clothes, carrying their weapons and ammunition, calmly walked into the home of Antoine Sabella, an Arab leader in the area around the railroad station, and offered their services.

In the Jewish Quarter of the Old City, an army private named Albert suddenly seized a Bren gun and bolted away from his mates into the stunned arms of the Haganah. He had brought not only his weapon but also a precious piece of information. The Army would evacuate the quarter in just one hour. Thus, when the bagpiper began to march the British out of the Old City, and the last detachment headed to Mordechai Weingarten's house to offer the elderly rabbi the key to Zion Gate, the Haganah was ready. Kicking aside empty beer cans, whiskey bottles and cigarette boxes, they slipped into the British posts as each was cleared. By nightfall, Operation Shfifon (Serpent) had achieved all its objectives. The Haganah controlled all the abandoned British Army posts that had surrounded the quarter, Zion Gate, and a key cupola called the Cross Position on the edge of the Armenian Quarter, dominating the western flanks. The first skirmish in the struggle for Jerusalem had been an unqualified Jewish success.

Hiding behind a pile of crates in the Schneller School, Yosef Nevo followed with glee the only British departure from Jerusalem which interested him, that of his mother-in-law. It was the result of some of the young officer's most intense strategic thought. In a neat gray suit and daintily flowered hat, she was the only civilian in a convoy of unkempt Palmachniks off to break through the Arab blockade and make a dash for the seacoast. As soon as the convoy disappeared, Nevo and his bride, Naomi, fell into each other's arms. "I am moving in tonight," announced the exultant bridegroom.

Some strange feminine premonition gripped Naomi. "No," she said. "Wait one night. I'll meet you tomorrow morning at ten o'clock at the Café Atara."

A deathly silence wrapped the hills of Kfar Etzion. The fall of the main kibbutz had deprived its three satellites, Massuot, Ein Tsurim and Revadim, of their principal source of strength. Smaller, less well-armed and protected, they now waited helplessly for their turn to come.

It would not, however, be the men of Abdullah Tell who would over-

367

run them. Persuaded that he had successfully stamped out the colony, under orders to get back across the Jordan River before the British mandate expired, Tell had withdrawn his men to Jericho, leaving the satellites to the irregulars.

Before turning to that task, however, the thousands of villagers swarming through the wreckage of Kfar Etzion had an easier job to complete. Toward late afternoon, the settlers of Massuot saw a column of trucks and farm wagons drive into the vanquished settlement. When the column left an hour later, they rushed to study it with binoculars, expecting to see their fellows being carted off to captivity in its vans. Instead, they saw the remnants of the kibbutz itself go rolling past their eyes. Spilling over with goods, the incredible column of pillage stretched on for kilometers. It seemed to one observer that Arabs were carrying away Kfar Etzion "down to the last nails." There were beds, mattresses, cooking utensils, furniture, cows, mules, bales of straw, roofing. Even the Torah of the demolished *Neve Ovadia* was carted off to decorate some neighboring Arab village.

When they had finished, Abdul Halim Shalaf, Haj Amin's principal deputy in the Hebron region, began to assemble his partisans to exterminate Kfar Etzion's three satellites. Determined not to fall into their vengeful hands, Ein Tsurim informed Shaltiel's headquarters that the survivors would try to break through the ring around them during the night and reach Jerusalem by foot.

Convinced that the tactic would lead to still another massacre, Shaltiel begged the settlers to remain where they were. He began instead a race against time to save them through the intervention of the Red Cross and the consuls of Belgium, France and the United States.

• • •

From the Romanesque bell tower of the Church of the Holy Sepulcher, the resonant chimes of the Angelus tolled another sunset. Equally faithful to the watches of Islam, the muezzin's plaintive call reverberated down the alleyways of the Old City, beckoning believers to evening prayer. In their barracks and residences, the British soldiers and civil servants still left in Jerusalem heard those sounds for the last time. Thirty years, five months and four days after General Sir Edmund Allenby's arrival at Jaffa Gate, the British presence in Jerusalem entered its final evening.

Each Englishman would mark it in his own way. At Goldschmidt's boardinghouse at the edge of Zone B in Rehavia, a group of army officers gathered, guests of the man who had once served in their ranks, Vivian

Herzog. To Herzog, their meeting was a small measure of the gratitude he felt toward those men, commanders of some of the key buildings in downtown Jerusalem. Each of them had, in one way or another, aided him in preparing for their takeover by the Haganah in a few hours.

Herzog would always remember their jovial gathering as the "last supper." It was a singularly skimpy last supper. If whiskey was abundant, the plates of Herzog's guests were an accurate reflection of the desperate food situation in the city they were leaving behind. All he was able to offer them was an omelette made of powdered eggs.

In the officers' mess of the Highland Light Infantry in the massive old French Hospice of Notre-Dame, the regiment's officers donned their tartan kilts and mess jackets for a final, formal dinner accompanied by their traditional drink, Athol Brose, a mixture of whiskey, honey, oatmeal and cream. The shouts of a gigantic farewell poker game rising from a street corner in Yemin Moshe marked the final gathering in the Press Club. Its dreary little bar had become the last place in Jerusalem where Arabs, Jews and Britons mingled. That bar had been the scene of not a few monumental drinking bouts in recent weeks. And huddled in its chairs, Gabe Sifroni, dean of the city's Jewish press corps, and his Arabic counterpart, Abou Said Abou Reech, had reached many a discreet agreement to help a newsman's friend or relative threatened by the Mufti's men or the Irgun and the Stern Gang.

Now their last emotional embraces and the cries of the poker game mingled with the noise of a radio blaring in the corner. Between martial airs and exalting Arabic odes, the Palestine Broadcasting System, now Arab-run, was informing its listeners to stand by for an important announcement from the mandatory government at nine o'clock. The British, a few of the cynical newsmen decided, were about to announce they were not leaving after all.

An intimate and elegant last supper in the King David Hotel united a handful of the government's senior officials—the Chief Secretary, the Attorney General, Chief Justice Sir William Fitzgerald. Offered by the hotel's Swiss manager, it was, Fitzgerald would recall, "a sad and silent meal." When it was over the little group strolled to the bay window. There, spread at their feet, its domes and spires glistening in the moonlight, was the most haunting panorama in Palestine, the rooftops of the Old City of Jerusalem. Intuitively, each raised his wineglass in a silent toast to that capital of mankind, their brief reign over which was ending this night.

For Assad V, the magnificent black Great Dane of architect Dan Ben-Dor, it was a last supper, too, and it would reward his master for all his evening walks to the British mess in the Italian Hospital. After the mess sergeant had opened a final can of bully beef for the dog, he took a case of tins from the shelf.

"Here," he said to Ben-Dor, "take this. It's the last time I can feed him. We're leaving tonight."

"Oh, really?" said Ben-Dor, as casually as possible. "What time?"

"Twelve-thirty," replied the cook. Half an hour later, alerted by Ben-Dor, a unit of the Haganah was in position in the streets around the hospital.

In the magnificent state dining room of Government House, the chandeliers blazed over Sir Alan Cunningham's farewell dinner. Clad in dress uniforms and decorations as though they might be staying on in Jerusalem for years to come, his senior staff officers chatted their way through a last meal together, their mood lightened by the sprightly airs of the Highland Light Infantry's regimental band.

Shortly before nine o'clock, a black Rolls Royce escorted by a pair of armored cars drove up to the studios of the Palestine Broadcasting System. Peering from his office windows, Raji Sayhoun, the station manager, understood that the man who was to make the "important announcement" for which he had been preparing the public had arrived.

His ruddy face set in a somber mask, Sir Alan Cunningham stepped from the vehicle in which, a few minutes before, he had left his dinner guests. The Arab station manager escorted him to Studio A, a tiny broadcasting booth equipped with a microphone, a chair and a table. At precisely nine o'clock, Sayhoun cut the recorded Arabic march the radio was playing and announced "an important declaration by his Excellency the High Commissioner." Beside him, the technician flipped the switch on Sir Alan's microphone and with a sharp wave of his finger indicated to the High Commissioner that he was on the air.

At his first words, Sayhoun felt his throat tighten with emotion. The High Commissioner, he realized, was saying farewell to the people of Palestine. His speech was brief and poignant. When he had finished, the men in the studio watched in stunned silence as he stepped from the booth.

Respectfully, Sayhoun asked Sir Alan if he wished him to add a few phrases in Arabic before resuming their regular broadcasts.

"No," quietly replied the High Commissioner, "just play 'God Save the King,' please. It's perhaps the last occasion you'll have to play it."

370

In his little study in Tel Aviv, David Ben-Gurion labored late into the night. Spread on the desk before him was the text which, a few hours hence, would announce to the world that the seat of power left vacant by Sir Alan Cunningham and the nation he represented would be filled by a new authority. It was the draft of the official proclamation of a Jewish state.

30

THE FIFTH DAY OF IYAR

WHISPERING INTENTLY, the two men paced beside the coils of barbed wire lining the street. Already the first gray shafts of dawn picked at Jerusalem's skyline, defining the rooftops rising from the shadows just behind them. One of the two was the British officer commanding those imposing structures of Bevingrad. The other was the ex-policeman to whom David Shaltiel had given the task of seizing them in the footsteps of their departing British occupants.

Arieyeh Schurr hung on each of the Englishman's words as he reviewed once again the final details of the evacuation due to begin in a few minutes. "I have to be going now," the officer concluded. "Good luck."

Before he could turn to leave, Schurr said, "Wait. There is something I want to give you as a measure of our gratitude for what you have done for us. Perhaps you've helped us save the Jews of Jerusalem from a massacre." The Haganah man reached into his pocket and drew out the most appropriate gift he had been able to discover in his beleaguered city, a gold wristwatch. On it was inscribed the Englishman's name, the date and one phrase to remind him in the years he would wear it of the army that had offered it to him: "With gratitude from H."

With a parting handshake, Schurr returned to his headquarters. In it he had assembled a self-contained telephone network. Its twenty-four phones linked to three separate switchboards tied Schurr to the observers he had stationed on rooftops all around central Jerusalem, and to the apartments along the perimeter of Bevingrad in which he had hidden his waiting soldiers. In addition, a group of post-office technicians, carrying portable phones, were ready to follow his men on their advance into Bevingrad so that Schurr would be able to keep abreast of their progress almost room by room. The meticulous Schurr had even found a merchant who had a stock of hundreds of British Army surplus wirecutters. Purchased for two shillings apiece, these tools would allow his men to swiftly hack their way through the dense forest of barbed wire on the Jewish side of Bevingrad.

Now Schurr's weeks of preparation were about to pay off. One of the lights on his switchboard lit up. It was an observer calling. He had just noticed the first British soldiers begin to move out of the General Post Office. Schurr glanced at his watch. His British friend had been true to his word. As he had promised, it was exactly four o'clock.

In Notre-Dame and Bevingrad, in the Allenby and El Alamein Barracks, on the Hill of Evil Counsel and in the nearly deserted lobby of the King David Hotel, the departing British had begun to stir to life as soon as the first shafts of sunlight fell on the city. Soldiers heaved a last duffle bag onto their trucks, civilians packed away their last belongings and souvenirs for their trip home. All over the city, motors coughed to life, vehicles fell into columns and men marched toward their assembly points.

To Brigadier C. P. Jones, the last act of the British Army in Jerusalem would be "a straightforward military movement." To designate the city during the operation, his signals officer had selected a code word barren of even a hint of the history, the religious vocation, the prestigious nature of the community his compatriots were leaving. Jerusalem, on this Friday morning, May 14, 1948, was "Cod."

By seven the first columns were ready to move. The yellow silk regimental colors which had been carried in battle against the Maoris of New Zealand a century before at the head of their procession, the men of the Suffolk Regiment marched down Mount Zion to their embusing point. Kilts packed away in favor of battle dress, bagpipes leading their procession, the men of the Highland Light Infantry in turn marched solemnly out of the Hospice of Notre-Dame. Captain Michael Naylor Leyland, the officer who had rescued the last survivors of the Hadassah convoy, led the vehicles of his First Life Guards Armored Car Squadron through the barbed wire that had separated their British Zone from the inhabitants of Jerusalem. Entering the city, Naylor Leyland noted a little sadly that "there was practically no one out to watch us go."

The last images those Britishers would take away from Jerusalem were mingled with relief at leaving a place in which, as one of them thought, they "had been a football being kicked about between two sides." For some, the last impression they would take away from the Holy City would be religious. For others, like Lieutenant Robert Ross, it would be the memory of the unlikely spot in which the young Scot had been shot at for the first time in his life, the Garden of Gethsemane. For Lance Corporal Gerald O'Neill of Glasgow, it would be the knowledge that he was going to be the last British soldier to leave Jerusalem. For Captain Naylor Leyland it would be the blood of one of his men still coating the inside of the armored car in which the unfortunate soldier had been killed a few days before. For Lieutenant Colonel Alec Brodie, a veteran of dozens of campaigns, it would be something as banal as a desperate search for a piece of rope to bind up a last suitcase.

For Major Dan Bonar it would be the last act of the military career he had opened thirty years earlier, on another May morning in 1918. That day in the little French hamlet of Adinfen he had raised the Union Jack after the battle of the Somme. The intervening years had taken him to Archangel, to Ireland, to Egypt, to Dunkirk, to Normandy, the Ruhr and Palestine, and now he closed them with an act paralleling the gesture with which they had begun: he lowered the Union Jack from its last perch in Jerusalem.

For Captain James Crawford, it was the sight of an elderly sheikh, hand upraised in a perfect military salute, a gesture Crawford saw "as a mark of respect to the comrades I was leaving behind who had given their lives in a fight that was not really theirs."

For General Jones, it was wandering through the empty rooms of Government House on a last inspection, each room as neat and spare as a pin, Sir Alan's office with its bare desk and empty chair looking "as though no one had ever lived or worked here."

For Chief Justice Sir William Fitzgerald it was an image in a bend of the road on the edge of town, an image as old as Palestine, a fellah on an ass plodding down to Bethlehem, his weary head not even raised to watch them go. Studying him from his bus window, Sir William suddenly asked himself, "Did we really change anything in our thirty years here?"

• • •

Theirs were not the only departures taking place that morning. Seizing the microphone over which Sir Alan Cunningham had delivered his parting address a few hours earlier, Raji Sayhoun proclaimed, "A new era for Palestine begins today. Long live a free and independent Palestine!" Then he left the broadcasting station for what would henceforth be its new headquarters in the Arab community of Ramallah.

As he drove out of the city, he cast a last look at its center from the heights of Sheikh Jarrah. The object that caught his eyes was hardly an auspicious omen for the new era he had so proudly announced a few minutes before. Flying over his former office at the Palestine Broadcasting System on Queen Melisande's Way was the blue-and-white Zionist banner.

It marked the first stage of the advance of Arieyeh Schurr's soldiers through the pie-shaped wedge of Bevingrad. The wedge's outer rim was a 350-yard arc that ran along Queen Melisande's Way between Jaffa Road and St. Paul's Road. Its sides, barely a quarter of a mile long, followed the narrowing course of those two roads to the point at which they met opposite the walls of the Old City between New and Jaffa Gates. Most of Schurr's targets were inside that triangle. He had also to seize a strip of buildings, including the General Post Office and the telephone exchange, that ran like a continuous cement barrier down Jaffa Road just across the street from Bevingrad. His last major objective was the Hospice of Notre-Dame, vacated by the Highland Light Infantry. Built in the shape of an E, it lay next to the point of the Bevingrad wedge opposite the Old City wall. From its high wings, gunmen could control both the Old City to the southeast and the heart of New Jerusalem to the west. To carry out his assignment, Schurr had four hundred Haganah men and six hundred Home Guard volunteers.

By eight o'clock, his first units had crossed Queen Melisande's Way and slipped into Bevingrad's northwestern perimeter, the rim of the pie-shaped wedge. At the same time, he sent some of his men with their wirecutters to cut the carpet of barbed-wire coils blocking access to its buildings. Others with ladders began to scale its walls. One unpleasant surprise greeted them: the British had planted a second layer of barbed wire inside Bevingrad itself. Nonetheless, Schurr's men were in possession of the buildings along the northwestern perimeter before the British troops had finished marching out the other side into Suleiman's Way opposite the Old City.

In the General Post Office building, the forty men of Schurr's Players Brigade took over the instant the British withdrew. Its telephone switchboard quickly became an important psychological weapon. His men would telephone the Arabs in the buildings ahead and try to frighten them into fleeing. As each building was taken, a soldier would grab a phone and call Schurr to tell him, "Cross it off your list."

Thus, within the first hour of full-scale operation, Schurr had taken over half of the targets assigned him. Only two areas gave him concern. Along St. Paul's Road bordering the Arab neighborhood of Musrara, the Arabs managed to get a thin foothold inside Bevingrad around the Central Prison. Opposite the walls of the Old City, a band of irregulars broke into Notre-Dame and drove out the handful of Haganah men who had reached it first.

Elsewhere in Jerusalem, David Shaltiel's three-pronged operation designed to secure a continuous north–south front through the city had begun almost as auspiciously. Assigned responsibility for the north, Shaltiel's intelligence officer Yitzhak Levi followed from the rooftop of his headquarters in the Histadrut Building the last British convoys heading for Haifa. As soon as they had disappeared over the ridge line beyond Mount Scopus, he ordered his men, waiting in the streets of Mea Shearim, into action. So swift was their advance that they seized almost without opposition their first objectives, the buildings of the Palestine Police Training School and Sheikh Jarrah from which the British had driven Yitzak Sadeh's Palmachniks seventeen days earlier. By midmorning, Levi had managed to reestablish communications with the besieged university and hospital on Mount Scopus.

In the south, Avram Uzieli had been ordered to take the sprawling grounds of the Allenby Barracks. Its capture would cut the Arab neighborhoods of German Colony, Greek Colony and Upper Beqaa off from the rest of the Arab city, and with it the Haganah would hold a continuous front in the south from the railroad station through the captured barracks and the Jewish neighborhoods of Mekor Hayim and Talpiot to the settlement of Ramat Rachel at the southern entrance to the city. To take the barracks, Uzieli had two platoons, a Davidka, three shells and not enough time. A group of Iraqi volunteers got to the barracks first and stopped his initial attack.

The Iraqis' prompt reaction was an exception. Nearly everywhere else the Arabs had been surprised by the alacrity with which the British had left and Shaltiel's men had attacked. Proudly displaying the pontifical flag and his note of authority from the Italian consul, Father Ibrahim Ayad rode up to claim the Italian Hospital in the name of the Mufti, only to discover that Dan Ben-Dor's men were already there. Mounir Abou Fadel, the former police officer in charge of the Old City's defenders, realized that the British were leaving when he saw their passing convoys as he walked his bulldog, Wolf, along the walls of the Old City.

Trapped behind a tombstone in Mamillah Cemetery after an unsuccessful attempt to reach the buildings already in Schurr's hands, Anwar Khatib caught a glimpse of Sir Alan Cunningham's departing limousine. How desperately he had wanted to see that sight, the Arab thought, and how uncertain he was of the future now that he was witnessing it.

Back in the Rawdah headquarters, Khatib found "no coordination, no one running things, just a lot of people shouting at each other."

Fadel Rashid the Iraqi and Khaled Husseini the nominal commander wouldn't budge from the headquarters. Mounir Abou Fadel's authority in the Old City was being contested by a twenty-five-year-old cobbler's son named Hafez Barakat, called "the General" by his followers. Emile Ghory had planned to lead six hundred men down the slopes seized by Yitzhak Levi's forces. One miscalculation had frustrated his plan. He had figured the British were leaving May 15, and his men were still hours away from Jerusalem. Only in the American Colony, a wealthy neighborhood below Sheikh Jarrah, and Musrara, an Arab quarter outside the Old City walls between Damascus Gate and Notre-Dame, did the Arabs react effectively. There schoolteacher Bajhat Abou Gharbieh, leading a mixture of Syrian Moslem Brothers, Iraqis and Lebanese volunteers, offered Shaltiel's men their only serious opposition.

. . .

If the morning had been an almost unmitigated disaster for the Arabs of Jerusalem, ten miles south of the city thousands of other Arabs were about to secure a victory whose repercussions would deprive the Haganah of the pleasure their successes in Jerusalem should have brought them. The three surviving satellites of Kfar Etzion were about to surrender.

Shortly before dawn a barely audible radio message had informed the settlers that the negotiations to save them from a massacre similar to the one that had befallen their comrades in the central kibbutz had succeeded. They too, however, were going to pay the price for having sought to cultivate the barren hills of Kfar Etzion. In a few hours they would begin an experience familiar to generations of their people. They would be going to captivity in Amman.

From the rooftop on the infirmary of Massuot, Uriel Ofek, a poet enlisted in the Palmach, had watched the Arabs swarm toward the kibbutz for hours. They were so numerous that it seemed to Ofek that all the villages between Jerusalem and Hebron must have been drained of men.

A fragile cease-fire arranged by the Red Cross had been in effect since 4 A.M. Sensing the ease of the victory before them, the hordes clamored for the chance to submerge the three colonies while their tense defenders watched their growing buildup with despair. The Red Cross delegation sent to arrange the surrender was swamped in a sea of shouting people before they could even get near the first kibbutz. When they did, its leaders, aware of the massacre that had taken place at Kfar Etzion, insisted on surrendering to the Arab Legion.

An emissary was sent to a Legion detachment left behind in Hebron in violation of the army's orders to leave Palestine before the mandate expired. It was a breach of orders for which the settlers left in Kfar Etzion would later have cause to be grateful. The detachment and its transport finally arrived at noon and the surrender began. At each settlement, the Haganah officers refused to hand over their arms until their women and wounded were in ambulances and their men safely aboard the Legion's trucks. At Ein Tsurim, a settler went back to the dining hall, already filled with looting irregulars, to take the Sefer Torah from the walls. At Massuot a rabbi began to recite the Sabbath prayers. Tears streaming down their faces, the men around him replied, ". . . the Lord is righteous, my Rock in whom there is no evil." In the radio room, an operator tapped out a last message: "Tonight we shall no longer be here. So ends the chapter of the Etzion bloc."

As the trucks rolled off each hill, the prisoners caught their last glimpse of the buildings on which they had labored so hard. One by one they burst into flames. Then, like a swarm of locusts, the Arab multitudes descended on their orchards and vineyards. As if to eradicate forever the last trace of that foreign intrusion upon their ancient hills, they tore out by the roots the settlers' young trees, beginning to blossom with the fruit of their first harvest.

* * *

Miles away, in Haifa harbor, a pair of greasy hawsers consummated another Haganah setback at the hands of a different enemy. As soon as the port's stevedores had firmly secured the S. S. *Borea* to a quay, a platoon of British troops marched up and formed an arc around the ship. No one, the platoon's commander informed the captain, would be allowed on or off the ship.

* * *

Half from relief, half from sorrow, tears filled David Shaltiel's eyes when the news of Etzion's end reached him. Neither the Jerusalem commander nor his men, however, had time to mourn their loss. On all sides, their progress through Jerusalem continued.

Arieyeh Schurr's men gradually pushed the Arabs from the footholds they had managed to secure in the Bevingrad triangle. Behind them, other teams of Haganah men rushed into the buildings they had captured. To the ill-equipped men of the Jerusalem command, it was like a voyage into some bewildering cave of Ali Baba. Despite the precision of their organization, the British had left behind stores astounding in their variety and occasional abundance. In one building the Haganah found forty thousand pairs of

378

shoes, two pairs for every soldier in the Jewish army. Another office revealed enough flashlights "to light up half of Palestine." Netanel Lorch found a beautiful handworked sword in Police Headquarters. It would soon be used at the inauguration of a Jewish state's first President. The young officer also found to his delight boxes of engraved stationery belonging to the government's Chief Secretary Sir Henry Gurney. Its handsome folds would be the joy of Lorch's correspondents for months. Murray Hellner, ordered to climb the Palestine Broadcasting System's forty-foot tower to take down its antenna, received a bizarre reward for his dangerous mission. In a studio closet he found two British state mourning flags. He immediately appropriated them for bedsheets for his army cot.

Outside Government Hospital, a soldier of the Irgun stumbled on a prize of a different sort, a flock of sheep. They belonged to Dr. Hassib Boulos. The young Arab surgeon was certain they were the key to his staff's survival in the days ahead. Pointing to his Red Cross armband, he asked the Irgunist to help him round up the frightened animals.

"Do those sheep have Red Cross armbands, too?" the Irgunist asked. At Boulos' stunned silence, he said, "Then tough luck. They're mine."

British journalist Eric Downton, moving through the compound with another Irgun veteran, participated in an extraordinary incident. The soldier pushed open a door in Police Headquarters. There before the two men was a chilling sight, the gallows tree, its loop of cord suspended motionless from its crossbar, its silent trap waiting only to be sprung. The Irgunist began to weep. Turning to Downton, he whispered, "This is where you hanged my friends."

None of Jerusalem's Arabs was more surprised by the speed of Schurr's advance than Anton Safieh. Trying to dodge his way through the shooting around Jaffa Gate, Safieh learned that the Municipality Building, "the safest place in Jerusalem," in whose vault he had deposited his £27,500 check, had just fallen to the Jews. Physically sick, he sought out his municipal comrades to inform them that their brand-new municipality was bankrupt.

In the southern section of the city, the Arabs announced an even more startling piece of news. The first of Avram Uzieli's three Davidka rounds failed to explode, but the second did, producing an enormous roar and almost no damage. The stunned Iraqis in the Allenby Barracks shouted over the telephone that the Jews had a weapon like the atomic bomb and begged for help. Informed of the remark by a switchboard operator who had overheard it, Uzieli fired his last round and sent his men rushing toward the barracks. The Iraqis fled, and Uzieli's soldiers in their turn stumbled on a hoard of abandoned British supplies ranging from bully beef to Players cigarettes.

To the north, Yitzhak Levi secured the approaches to the city on the line he had established from Sanhedria, the ancient Jewish burial grounds, through the Police Training School barracks, Sheikh Jarrah and Mount Scopus. In defiance of Ben-Gurion's order that no Jewish settlement was to be abandoned, he authorized the isolated settlers of Neve Yaacov north of the city to fall back into his lines. He had no intention of seeing another Kfar Etzion in his command.

His only setback came in Musrara, where Bajhat Abou Gharbieh's mixed irregulars refused to budge. The Arab schoolteacher had split his seventy men into three groups, the Syrians in a school, the Iraqis in a hotel and the Lebanese along St. Paul's Road opposite the Russian Compound. His Browning machine gun was aimed against the Haganah entrenched in a property destined to become a symbol of a divided Jerusalem, the home of a wealthy businessman named Mandelbaum.

By late afternoon, as the fighting calmed down, Shaltiel was able to radio Tel Aviv that most of his objectives had been secured and "the defense of the enemy was very weak." At about the same time, the accuracy of Shaltiel's message was being confirmed in a cable from Jerusalem's Arab command to Haj Amin Husseini. The situation "was critical," it said. "The Jews have reached almost to the gates of the Old City."

Whistling joyfully, the happiest man in Jerusalem marched up Ben Yehuda Street to the Café Atara. In the two hours he had managed to seize away from his unit, Yosef Nevo would now have two auspicious beginnings to celebrate, the beginning of his married life and the beginning of a new era for Jerusalem. His first glimpse of the waxen face of his bride warned him, however, that he might have overestimated the number of blessings he had to celebrate this day. Her first words confirmed his fears.

"She's back," Naomi gasped. "The convoy didn't get through."

An almost equally unpleasant discovery awaited Pablo de Azcarate on his return to Jerusalem that morning from Amman. The British administration had bid farewell with a lie to Azcarate's United Nations mission which it so disdained. Despite Sir Henry Gurney's assurances, the British were gone. Bitterly Azcarate noted in his diary: "The time for the plunge into the unknown has come."

In New York, the international organization that had sent Azcarate to

Palestine groped toward the only answer it could find for the chaos in the land whose problems it had sought to solve. If the United Nations could not offer Palestine a messiah, it proposed the only alternative of which it seemed capable, a mediator. Their hopeful action, however, would only add one more name to the long list of men martyred for Jerusalem, that of Count Folke Bernadotte.

The long and dolorous road followed by the Hebrew people from the land of Ur of the Chaldees to Pharaoh's Egypt, Babylon and all the corners of the earth led at last to a simple stone building on Rothschild Boulevard in the heart of Tel Aviv. There, on this humid Friday afternoon in May, the leaders of the Zionist movement prepared to accomplish perhaps the most important gesture in the history of their people since an obscure warrior king named David brought the Ark of the Covenant "with shouting and with the sound of the trumpet" from Abou Gosh to a tabernacle in Jerusalem.

The building, a museum, had been the home of Meir Dizengoff, first mayor of Tel Aviv. Appropriately, its galleries contained not the pottery shards, stone relics and religious vessels of a dead Jewish civilization, but the bold modern art of the new one about to be brought forth in its precincts. Outside, a detachment of Haganah military police meticulously checked the credentials of the two hundred selected guests who would be privileged to witness the ceremony scheduled to take place in the building. The backgrounds of those men were as diverse as the race they represented. Some of them had almost died of malaria clearing the Huleh swamps. Others had survived the death camps of Germany. They came from Minsk, Cracow and Cologne; from England, Canada, South Africa, Iraq and Egypt. They were bound together by a common faith, Zionism, a common heritage, Jewish history, and a common curse, persecution. Looking down upon them as they gathered was a portrait of the black-bearded Viennese newspaperman who had founded the movement that had brought them to the Tel Aviv museum's main gallery. Barely fifty-three years had passed since the January day when Theodor Herzl had witnessed the public humiliation of Alfred Dreyfus. They had been years of anguish for his people, and the most apocalyptic of the visions he could have imagined that morning on the Champs de Mars had just overwhelmed them. Yet they had been years of triumph too, and because his followers had willed it the Jewish people were about to have a state of their own.

At precisely four o'clock, David Ben-Gurion rose and sharply rapped a walnut gavel on the table before him. Clad in a dark suit, a white shirt and, in deference to the solemnity of the occasion, a tie, the Jewish leader picked up a scroll of white parchment. Indicative of the haste with which this ceremony had been prepared was the fact the Tel Aviv artist commissioned to prepare the scroll had had time to finish only the decoration. The text Ben-Gurion was about to read had been typed on a separate piece of paper and stapled to the parchment.

"In the Land of Israel the Jewish people came into being," he began. "In this land was shaped their spiritual, religious and national character. Here they lived in sovereign independence. Here they created a culture of national and universal import and gave to the world the eternal Book of Books."

He paused an instant to insure a properly purposeful tone to his delivery. Always the realist, Ben-Gurion was not carried away by the exultation of the moment. In a few hours he would note in his diary: "As on November 29, I mourn among the happy ones." He had lived for two years with the declaration he was reading. He was saying the words, but, as he would one day recall, there "was no joy in my heart. I was thinking of only one thing, the war we were going to have to fight."

"Exiled from the land of Israel," he said, "the Jewish people remained faithful to it in all the countries of their dispersion, never ceasing to pray and hope for their return and the restoration of their national freedom. Impelled by this historic association, Jews strove throughout the centuries to go back to the land of their fathers and regain their statehood." In recent decades, he reminded his audience, "they returned in their masses. They reclaimed the wilderness, revived their language, built cities and villages . . ."

It was, he continued, "the self-evident right of the Jewish people to be a nation, as all other nations, in their own sovereign state." Accordingly, he said, "by virtue of the natural and historic right of the Jewish people and of the Resolution of the General Assembly of the United Nations, we hereby proclaim the establishment of the Jewish state in Palestine, to be called Israel."

One by one, he set out the principles that would guide the new nation: "principles of liberty, justice and peace as conceived by the Prophets of Israel"; full social and political equality for all citizens without distinction of religion, race or sex; freedom of religion, conscience, education, language and culture; safeguarding of the Holy Places of all religions; and the loyal upholding of the principles of the United Nations charter.

Crammed into the only space they had been able to find for their transmitters, a toilet just off the museum's main room, the technicians of the new nation's radio service felt their throats constrict with emotion. Except for the labored breathing of a handful of old men, the main gallery was silent, as though even a foot scraping on the floor might detract from the grandeur of this moment so long awaited by so many. Later, to some of those present the intense silence of their gathering would seem a mystic evocation of their six million dead.

"We appeal to the United Nations to assist the Jewish people in the building of its state and to admit Israel into the family of nations," Ben-Gurion read. "We offer peace and amity to all the neighboring states and peoples . . . Our call goes out to the Jewish people all over the world . . . to stand by us in the great struggle for the fulfillment of the dream of generations, the redemption of Israel.

"With trust in the Almighty," he concluded, "we set our hand to this declaration at this session of the Provisional Council of State . . . in the city of Tel Aviv on the fifth day of Iyar, 5708, the fourteenth day of May, 1948."

When he had finished he said, "Let us all stand to adopt the Scroll of the Establishment of the Jewish State."

Choking with emotion, an elderly rabbi offered thanks to "Him who hath kept and sustained us and brought us unto this time." One by one the leaders in the room put their signatures on the scroll. Then Ben-Gurion announced that the British White Paper of 1939 with its restrictions on Jewish land purchase and immigration was annulled. Otherwise, all mandatory laws would remain in effect for the time being.

It was 4:37 P.M. The entire ceremony had taken barely half an hour. Once more Ben-Gurion picked up his gavel and rapped the table.

"I hereby declare this meeting adjourned," he said. The state of Israel had come into being.

At almost the same time, on the banks of the Nile, another ceremony was taking place. Its focal point, too, was a scroll—the diploma of the Royal Egyptian Army Staff College. Few men's lives would be affected as much by the declaration that had been read in Tel Aviv as that of a distinguished thirty-year-old graduate of that course. The cataclysm it would produce would drive him to the forefront of world politics and lead his fellow Arabs to hail him as their people's greatest leader since Saladin. For the moment a simple joy filled the heart of Captain Gamal Abdel Nasser. He had just received his first major assignment. Within forty-eight

383

hours he was to report for duty as staff officer of the Sixth Battalion on its march to Tel Aviv and the destruction of the state proclaimed by David Ben-Gurion.

. . .

Dusk was beginning to fall. Away to the south, caught between the mountains of Moab and Judea, the motionless waters of the Dead Sea cast back the sun's last light like a silver mirror. Five miles to the east of the assembly area that John Glubb had chosen for his Arab Legion, in the rhododendrons and rushes of the perennially green Wadi Shueib, lay the Allenby Bridge and the Jordan River. On the other side of the river Glubb could see the brown stone rooftops of Jericho and beyond them the imposing four-thousand-foot-high wall of the Palestine mountains.

Just behind Jericho, between the Mount of Temptation and Kerith Brook where the ravens had fed Elijah, a little spur ran up that mountain wall. Glubb studied it intently. It was his secret pride. For four thousand pounds, the villagers beyond Jericho had turned it into a track capable of taking his armored cars and vehicles—and unmarked on his foes' maps. At midnight, the 4,500 men of his Arab Legion now lined up before him in parade formation would begin moving into Palestine over that mountain spur, along which, twenty-five centuries before, Joshua had led the children of Israel in the invasion of the Promised Land.

Glubb looked at that line of troops before him with pride and a broken heart. He had known some of those men since they were infants placed in his arms by their proud fathers. The Arab Legion was Glubb's life, and he despaired at the thought of its being torn apart in a war. Yet he understood the terrible pressures building up in the Arab capitals. Already he had begun to doubt his ability to make only "the semblance of a war" as he wanted. The situation was "so hopeless, so confusing," he felt that night. He hadn't "the vaguest notion what the Syrians and the Egyptians were going to do." Even his precious shipload of artillery shells for his new guns had not yet arrived in Aqaba.

As Glubb meditated, a black sedan with a pennant fluttering from its fender drove up. The man for whom he had assembled his troops had arrived. Dressed in his British Army uniform, King Abdullah marched to a simple wooden platform above the flat, barren plain on which his troops were drawn up. As he did, on the horizon to the south a dark pillar climbed toward the sky, the funnel of an approaching sandstorm. The band began to play Transjordan's lilting national song. The King saluted the men before him, the men who might deliver him at last from the sandy confines of the kingdom which that anthem extolled, the desert cage in which the British had placed him. As much as the simplest of his Bedouin soldiers perhaps, Abdullah was stirred by the emotions of that moment, by the contrived exaltation of military assembly.

Suddenly, almost from nowhere, the sandstorm came shrieking down on the gathering. In seconds visibility was reduced to twenty-five yards. Whipped by the sands, the men in the ranks squinted and strained to hear. Months later Major Abdullah Tell would think the sandstorm "was a protest from God against the conspiracy that was sending us into Palestine not to fight but to add land to Abdullah's kingdom." Tell himself heard only the first three words the King uttered: "My dear sons." The rest was lost in the wind.

The King finally abandoned his efforts to speak. Instead he pulled his pistol from its holster and fired it into the air. As he did, caught, perhaps, by the emotion of the instant, he shouted the magic cry with which so many of history's conquerors had inflamed their soldiers' spirits. Although his men had strict orders to avoid it, Abdullah cried, "On to Jerusalem!"

• • •

Carried by the transmitter tucked into the toilet of the Tel Aviv museum, the words of David Ben-Gurion's speech had been delivered all across the territories of the newly reborn Jewish state. In the Galilee and the Negev, men who were braced to repulse an Arab invasion listened to it, their arms by their sides. On Tel Aviv's Dizengoff Boulevard the crowds were dancing their triumphant horas before the ceremony had ended. In Jerusalem, David Shaltiel and his senior aides followed its scratchy, barely audible tones in the broadcast room of the Jewish Agency. "We knew what a state was," one of them would remember later. "It called for blood and we had already given a full measure at Kfar Etzion."

At the French Consulate, where he had been the Jewish representative in a day-long, unsuccessful effort to install a cease-fire in the city, Vivian Herzog stood up and solemnly informed his colleagues that henceforth he was the representative "of an independent Jewish state." As they congratulated him Herzog noticed an extraordinary sight. On her hands and knees to avoid the occasional bullet passing through the consulate windows, Madame Neuville, ever the gracious hostess, was crawling toward them with a tray of champagne glasses to toast the occasion.

In the Old City, Rabbi Yitzhak Orenstein's son, Avraham, an officer in the Haganah, brought him the news. The pious man immediately recited a *shechiyanu,* a prayer of thanks to God "for having let us live to see this day." The rabbi would not be allowed to live many days in the state he was acclaiming. He would figure in the heavy price the Jewish people would have to pay to secure it. Ten days hence, he would be killed by an Arab artillery shell.

Elsewhere, as a young Haganah officer noted, "there was no time for celebrating. There were wounded and killed." That sober reaction was characteristic of the effect of the announcement in most of the new state's territory. The state would be under attack within hours and there was no time for the wild outbursts of joy that had followed news of the partition vote.

Just beyond the center of Jerusalem, near the area soon to be known as the Mandelbaum Gate, a score of young men gathered in an abandoned house. Members of a religious company of the Gadna youth defending Mandelbaum, they followed the traditional service marking the arrival of the Sabbath eve. Without religious candles to illuminate the room that was their improvised house of worship, they huddled together in the semidarkness. They had only a couple of prayer shawls and two or three prayer books which they passed from hand to hand. Yet for their leader, Jacob Ben-Ur, their impoverished service would always be the most memorable religious ceremony of his life. Their rifles stacked at the door, the sound of gunfire ringing through their half-ruined building, the news of Ben-Gurion's declaration still fresh in their minds, Ben-Ur and his teenage soldiers began to chant the ancient words: "Blessed art Thou, O Lord, who spreadest the shelter of peace over us and over all Thy people, Israel, and over Jerusalem."

For the 359 survivors of the Etzion bloc, the Sabbath eve that marked the rebirth of the land to which they had dedicated their lives would be a painful memory. Covered with insults, spit, and an occasional blow, they were marched through the streets of Hebron, its angry populace screaming for their blood. Only the vigilance of their Arab Legion guards prevented a new massacre from marring this historic Sabbath eve. And for those men and women, many with flesh still scarred by the numbers of Auschwitz, Dachau and Buchenwald, that interminable corridor of hate would lead, not to the freedom they had sought here, but to the barbed wire of still another camp.

Just outside Bethlehem, a bus bore their seriously wounded in the opposite direction, back to Jerusalem. Abbras Tamir, who had commanded the settlement from a stretcher, saw an Arab Legion sergeant leap onto the bus during a momentary pause. Half conscious from the blood he had lost, Tamir watched as the man shouted to them in Arabic, "Your Ben-Gurion has just declared a Jewish state, but we'll finish you in seven days." It was Tamir's first news of the state. He tried to sit up to cry his joy, but, too weak, he fell back exhausted. As he did, he felt tears of pride and pleasure fill his eyes and his mouth twist into a sob.

• • •

An immaculately uniformed British naval officer climbed up to the bridge of the S.S. *Borea* in Haifa harbor and smartly saluted her captain. With a glance at his watch he announced, "It is ten o'clock. In exactly two hours' time His Majesty's government's mandate in Palestine is due to expire. I have been requested to inform you that at that time your guard will be withdrawn and this vessel and all she contains returned to your custody."

While the *Borea*'s stunned captain struggled to assimilate this final gesture of the dying administration, the officer saluted once again. "Good luck," he said and marched off the bridge.

At the end of a promontory pointing into Haifa harbor from under the shadows of Mount Carmel, a solitary figure stood looking out to sea. On a rainy November night in 1917, wrapped in a poncho on a hilltop above Jerusalem, James Pollock had witnessed the opening act of Great Britain's Palestine drama. Tonight Jerusalem's last district commissioner had come to this lonely outcropping to witness the last act of the regime to which he had devoted his adult life.

In the harbor, on board the cruiser *Euralyus,* Sir Alan Cunningham climbed slowly up the passageway leading to the bridge. There the ship's captain motioned him to a large wooden platform in its center. As Cunningham mounted it, the ship's crew cast off the ropes holding her to the shore. Slowly the ship moved into the channel, where an aircraft carrier and half a dozen destroyers of the British Mediterranean Squadron lined her passage out to sea. On their decks, in dress whites, their crews moved to a salute. At a signal, all their searchlights fell on the lonely man on the bridge of the *Euralyus*. Gathering speed, the cruiser slipped along the majestic line of ships. As she drew abreast of the aircraft carrier, a band on the quarterdeck played "God Save the King."

Listening to the strains of his nation's anthem fill the night, hearing the swish of the water sliding under the *Euralyus'* keel, Cunningham thought, "It's the end of the show." Overwhelmed by the poignancy of the moment, he kept his regard fixed on the magnificent bulk of Mount Carmel slowly receding behind him. As the hymn finished, the band, in honor of Cunningham's Scottish blood, began to play him out of the harbor to "The Highland Lament." Hearing its melancholy strains come drifting across the water, the departing High Commissioner felt tears fill his eyes. How fitting, he thought, that he should be going home to the sad notes of that tune.

It had all begun so well and ended so badly. What a world of squandered hopes between Lord Allenby's magnificent gesture, dismounting his horse at Jaffa Gate because he would not ride over the stones on which his Savior had carried His Cross, and his own hurried departure from Jerusalem this morning. How much had gone into this land, how many Britons had died to conquer it, to govern it in the name of an impossibly contradictory set of promises! And now "after all those disappointments, after all those years, after so many efforts, it had all been a failure, we're leaving, and the end is war and misery."

As Sir Alan's cruiser finally reached the three-mile limit, she hove to for the act that would officially mark the end of Great Britain's Palestine mandate. From one end of the ship to the other, an enormous spray of fireworks arched into the Mediterranean sky, sprinkling the dark night with ribbons of orange, red and yellow. When the last spark tumbled hissing into the sea, Sir Alan thought, "That's the end. It's all over."

He glanced at his watch. Then he gasped. It was only eleven o'clock. Britain's star-crossed Palestine mandate had not been able to end without one final error. It had been terminated one hour too soon. The ship's captain had forgotten to take into account the difference between British summer time and Palestine time.

THE INDOMITABLE ARCHITECT OF A JEWISH STATE

Tenacious, inflexible, irascible on occasion, David Ben-Gurion provided the Jewish settlers in Palestine with a priceless asset the Arab foes could not match—sound leadership. It was thanks largely to his foresight in preparing his people for a conflict with five Arab armies that the state of Israel was able to survive the first critical weeks of its existence in May–June 1948.

THE WOMAN WHOSE MISSION SAVED A NATION

Political secretary of the Jewish Agency in 1948, Golda Meir was sent to the United States on an urgent mission—to raise the funds needed to buy arms to defend the still-unborn Jewish state. She arrived in New York with ten dollars in her pocketbook and left a month later with fifty million. "The day when history is written," Ben-Gurion told her, "it will be recorded that it was thanks to a Jewish woman that the Jewish state was born."

ISRAEL'S SECRET EMISSARIES TO THE WORLD'S ARSENALS

EHUD AVRIEL, 31, was ordered to Europe by Ben-Gurion the day after the United Nations' partition vote, to set up a clandestine organization to handle the purchasing and shipment of arms. Thanks to Avriel's ingenuity and tenacity, the Haganah's impoverished armories received enough weapons to hold off the Arab invasion that followed the proclamation of the state of Israel on May 14, 1948.

33

34

FREDDY FREDKENS, 40, a former pilot in the Royal Air Force, helped Avriel to organize an airlift to bring arms to Palestine. Using an abandoned Luftwaffe base near Prague, a French airport in Corsica and a deserted R.A.F. landing strip in Palestine, they flew to the Haganah the equipment needed to force an opening in the Arab blockade of Jerusalem.

390

HAIM SLAVINE, 41. Three years before the birth of Israel, Slavine was sent to the United States by Ben-Gurion to purchase an armament industry for their nonexistent state. From coast to coast, he visited junkyards and factories, buying up machine tools about to be disposed of as war-surplus material. Smuggled past British customs, his machines were hidden in an underground factory beneath the fields of a kibbutz. By May 1948 they were producing hundreds of submachine guns a day.

35

36

YEHUDA ARAZI, 41, began the Zionists' clandestine arms procurement in Poland in 1936 by stuffing with rifles a steam boiler destined for Haifa. In 1948, disguised as an ambassador from Nicaragua, he negotiated the purchase of the Haganah's first artillery pieces—five old French mountain guns nicknamed "Napoleonchiks."

37

38

During the winter and spring of 1948, Arab and Jewish terrorists waged a cruel war in the streets of Jerusalem. Principal technician of the Arab attacks was a 30-year-old Palestinian Arab named Fawzi el Kutub [39], a graduate of an SS commando course in Nazi Germany. On February 1, 1948, he succeeded in destroying the *Palestine Post* building [37] with a booby-trapped police truck. Three weeks later, another of his bombs, transported by a team of British deserters, tore apart Ben Yehuda Street in the heart of Jewish Jerusalem [38], killing 57 people and leaving 88 wounded. Finally, on March 11, Kutub penetrated the most closely guarded Jewish building in Jerusalem, the Jewish Agency [40], using a U.S. Consulate car and its Arab driver to carry his bomb. The resulting explosion killed 13 people and severely damaged the buildings.

A TERRORIST'S HARVEST

39

40

41

42

43

FOOD FOR JERUSALEM'S FAMISHED JEWS—
AT A TERRIBLE PRICE

"We will strangle Jerusalem," vowed the Palestinian Arabs' most effective leader in 1948, Abdul Khader Husseini. For weeks the city's 100,000 Jews endured the ordeals of a siege, their meager water ration distributed by tank truck [44]. A few convoys [41] managed to struggle past the Arab ambushes, while the Haganah strove to claw a relief route, baptized the "Burma Road," across the Judean hills [42]. Most Jewish trucks, like the burning vehicle in [43], fell victim to the Arabs' ambushes. Their rusted ruins [45] still stand along the highway to Jerusalem, silent memorials to the sacrifices the young men and women of the Haganah made to keep the Jews of the City of David alive.

45

A MEASURE IN STONE OF THE FURY
OF THE FIGHT FOR JERUSALEM

Built to harbor French pilgrims to the Holy Land, the 546 cells of the Hospice of Notre-Dame de France [46] constituted a veritable fortress dominating central Jerusalem. During the first critical days following the proclamation of the state of Israel in May 1948, the building changed hands time and time again. The devastation wreaked on its solid stone framework by the hits of over 300 artillery shells bears witness to the intensity of the fighting waged in the heart of Jerusalem [47].

JERUSALEM'S RIVAL COMMANDERS

DAVID SHALTIEL, commander of Jerusalem's Haganah, received his military training as a sergeant in the French Foreign Legion. Arrested by the Gestapo while on a secret Haganah mission to his native Germany before World War II, he kept his sanity during the long weeks of torture and confinement by teaching himself Hebrew. To him David Ben-Gurion had one order: "Attack and attack and attack."

ABDULLAH TELL, 30, Shaltiel's opponent, was the youngest Arab major in Glubb Pasha's Arab Legion. The son of a landowning family in Transjordan, he dreamed of "undoing the injustice of partition." When Old Jerusalem was about to fall to Shaltiel's men, King Abdullah ordered him to "go save Jerusalem."

THE ACCOMPLISHMENT OF A 2,000-YEAR-OLD DREAM: THE REBIRTH OF ISRAEL

At four o'clock in the afternoon of May 14, 1948, in a museum in Tel Aviv, David Ben-Gurion solemnly proclaimed the rebirth of a Jewish state in the ancient homeland of the Jewish people. Over his head was a portrait of Theodor Herzl, the Austrian newspaperman who had founded the Zionist movement barely half a century before [50].

The first hours of Israel's existence scarcely augured well for the new state. Five Arab armies drawn up along its borders vowed to destroy it by arms. Their invasion just after midnight May 14 formally began a conflict that would go on for decades. Outside Jerusalem, the Arab Legion and hundreds of Palestinian irregulars seized the kibbutz of Kfar Etzion, the Haganah's outpost south of the city [51]. Arab Legion commander Major Abdullah Tell (right) and Captain Hikmet Muhair posed with two of the four survivors of the 150 Jewish men and women who had defended the kibbutz's principal settlement [52].

51

52

53

WAR BESIDE THE WAILING WALL

For two weeks, fewer than 200 Jewish men and women, virtually without arms, held off the furious assaults of hundreds of Arabs on the Jewish Quarter of the old walled city of Jerusalem. Only a few yards from their advance posts was the western wall of King Solomon's Temple, Judaism's most revered shrine. Despite numerous efforts, their Haganah colleagues in the New City of Jerusalem were unable to come to their rescue, and on May 28, 1948, the quarter's leadership [55], headed by Rabbi Mordechai Weingarten (with beard), surrendered to Major Tell of the Arab Legion (with binoculars). Tell's Legionnaires protected the 1,300 surviving residents of the quarter, mostly elderly rabbis and their young students [56], as they prepared to leave their ancient quarter. For nineteen years after their departure, there would be no Jews living inside the walls of Old Jerusalem.

54

THE GUNS GROW STILL,
BUT A NEW TRAGEDY BEGINS

A United Nations–imposed cease-fire finally brought an end to the 1948 conflict which would be known in Israel as the War of Independence. Moshe Dayan (with eye patch) and Abdullah Tell (wearing a checkered kaffiyeh, with the back of his head to the camera) set the cease-fire lines which left Jerusalem a divided city [57]. If the war was temporarily over, however, a new tragedy faced many an Arab and Jewish family in Jerusalem—exodus. For scores of Jews like the orthodox Yemenite [58], there would be no return to the Old City's Jewish Quarter where their families had lived for generations. For many an Arab like the man in [59], contemplating from a distant height the home he was constrained to flee in Katamon, there would be no return either. Hundreds of thousands of others like him from all across Palestine were left to molder in the squalor of the Arab refugee camps. Their sons would become the Palestine Fedayeen.

58

59

60

A BROKEN DOOR BETWEEN TWO HOSTILE WORLDS:
THE MANDELBAUM GATE

For nineteen years after the end of the 1948 hostilities, the Mandelbaum Gate, next to the ruins of the home of a wealthy Jewish merchant, was the symbol of the Holy City's division into Arab and Jewish halves. It was the only open door between Israel and the hostile Arab states surrounding her who refused to acknowledge the existence of the new state.

PART FOUR

JERUSALEM: A CITY DIVIDED

May 15, 1948 — July 17, 1948

31

"THESE SHALL STAND."

THE SHRIEK of a locomotive whistle swept down the ill-lit station platform. With a series of metallic clangs the long line of cars lurched forward. All along the platform, the wives, parents, friends and children of the departing troops cheered and clapped. Leaning from the train's windows, the men of Egypt's Sixth Infantry Battalion laughed and waved back. They were heading to the Sinai, to war, but their mood was as gay as that of the crowds seeing them off in Cairo's Abassya Station. Lieutenant Mohammed Rafat, the battalion's twenty-six-year-old intelligence officer, was certain they were "off on a promenade." In a month, he had assured his fellows, they would be back to a reception even gayer than the one marking their departure.

Everywhere in the Egyptian capital other rituals of war were being performed. At midnight, after playing the march from *Aida,* Egypt's national anthem, Cairo Radio announced the imposition of martial law, and the sheikh of Al Azhar proclaimed, "The hour of the Holy War has struck." All Arab fighters, he said, must look upon the struggle for Palestine as a religious duty. Prime Minister Nokrashy Pasha announced that the nation was invading Palestine "to save it from Zionism and bring peace back to its borders." A few minutes later the Egyptian Foreign Ministry officially informed the United Nations Security Council that with the termination of the British mandate "Egyptian armed forces have started to enter Palestine." At Almaza Airport, crews were already loading the bays of Egypt's half-dozen bombers for the first air raids of the war.

A discordant reminder of the conflict marred even the candlelit roof garden of the Semiramis Hotel overlooking the waters of the Nile. A group of uniformed men in capes clustered around a table in one corner of the music-filled terrace. Proudly attired in his field marshal's uniform, a pretty girl by his side, King Farouk studied with his operations staff the first moves of his army's triumphant march to Tel Aviv on the map spread before him.

After its round of bellicose proclamations was finished, Cairo Radio

407

turned its microphone over to a vibrant, husky female voice. No speech, no martial air, no heroic poem could move the masses of the Arab world as that voice did. It belonged to a plump middle-aged balladeer named Om Khalsum. In every corner of the Arab world, radios switched on in that early morning of May 15 to hear her sing. Appropriately, the long and plaintive ballad she had chosen to perform extolled a site as universal in its appeal to her audience as her legendary voice: Jerusalem.

In his home in Beirut, the Prime Minister of Lebanon woke his sleeping daughters so that they could hear the tremulous accents spilling from the radio. When Om Khalsum had finished her evocation of the Prophet's ascent to heaven from the Dome of the Rock, Riad Solh's eldest daughter, Alia, saw tears in her father's eyes. "My God, my God," he murmured, "let the Rock remain in our hands always."

Across the mountains, in Damascus, the Syrian government closed its frontiers, proclaimed martial law and gave its radio over to the nonstop broadcast of military marches. In Baghdad, Nuri as-Said, the man whose aides had vowed that his army would take Haifa in two weeks, had thus far dispatched only two thousand troops to Palestine. Sir Alec Kirkbride scathingly denounced their commander "as an incompetent idiot incapable of commanding a squad of infantry." Nuri, however, vowed that between two and three million tribesmen were ready to march on Palestine. Even the Arab League's Azzam Pasha, who privately abhorred the turn events had taken, was swept up by the emotion of the hour. "This will be a war of extermination and a momentous massacre," he predicted in a phrase that would haunt him for years, "which will be spoken of like the Mongolian massacres and the Crusades." Haj Amin Husseini's spokesman Ahmed Shukairy announced the Arabs' goals as "the elimination of the Jewish State." The foreign press was not immune to the spell cast by the Arab orators. Reuters from Cairo referred to an Egyptian Army of 200,000 men. The New York Times correspondent in Damascus described a Syrian brigade "speeding toward the Galilee after a lightning feint toward the Mediterranean."

At exactly five minutes after midnight, the advance party of the Arab Legion left the staging area in which a few hours before a sandstorm had drowned out the final exhortation of King Abdullah. Riding at the head of the main column in an open jeep was the adjutant of the Fourth Regiment, Captain Mahmoud Rousan. There was almost no moon, and the column moved without headlights. The only sound Rousan could hear was the low rumble of the engines. Ahead of him, he could just make out the ruby glow of the taillight of the last vehicle in the advance party. At the Jordan River, the military policemen controlling the movement silently waved him across Allenby Bridge. "It was," the young captain would later think, "the most exalting moment of my life." He was certain that "within fifteen days" they would be coming back across that bridge "a triumphant army having undone the wrong of partition."

. . .

As he had on Partition Night, David Ben-Gurion went to sleep early on May 14 to conserve his energies for the trials ahead. Once again he was awakened by a messenger bringing him news from the New World. Shortly after one o'clock, a telephone call informed him that the United States had officially recognized the new state. He understood at once that the gesture would be "a great moral encouragement to our people."

That announcement greeted by Ben-Gurion with so much pleasure was the culmination of five days of intensive activity in Washington to alter the decision taken in President Truman's office May 9. Largely through the efforts of Clark Clifford, Secretary of State Marshall had been persuaded to reconsider his stand and recommend to the President that the United States recognize the new state. Delighted, Truman had ordered Clifford to set the machinery of recognition in motion. At the same time that the independence ceremony was beginning in the Tel Aviv museum, Clifford had called the Jewish Agency's Washington representative, Eliahu Elath. "You'd better write a letter asking us for recognition," he told him.

Almost two thousand years had elapsed since the last diplomat in some dim corner of history had written an official letter on behalf of a Jewish state, Elath thought as he started to draft his request. It presented only one problem: Elath did not know the name of the state for which he was requesting recognition. Solving the problem by calling it simply "the Jewish state," he had dispatched his letter to the White House. Hardly was it out of his office door when the radio announced the name of the new nation. Elath sent a second messenger racing after the first one. His letter was intercepted at the White House gate and the word "Israel" added to it in ink. At 6:12 P.M. twelve minutes after Britain's mandate expired, President Truman had announced American recognition of the reborn Jewish state.

That would not be the only news to interrupt Ben-Gurion's sleep that night. Over the furious pleas of Paula Ben-Gurion, Yaacov Yanai, the

Haganah's communications chief, pushed into his bedroom three hours later to ask the Jewish leader to make a radio broadcast to America. The sleepy Ben-Gurion stumbled out of bed and pulled a coat over his pajamas while Paula got him his shoes and stockings.

He had barely begun his broadcast from a secret Haganah transmitter when the planes being loaded in Cairo a few hours before arrived over Tel Aviv. The crash of their falling explosives shook his studio and echoed into his microphone. The sound they had just heard, Ben-Gurion dramatically told his audience, was the explosion of the first bombs dropped in the new state's war for independence.

As soon as he had finished, he drove off to inspect the damage. Riding through areas hit by the raid, he scanned the faces of his countrymen peering from their windows as he had once scanned the faces of Londoners during the Blitz. Were they afraid? he asked himself.

Worry and concern he saw on those faces, but no tears, no panic. Returning home, Ben-Gurion entered two words in his diary. They summed up the relieved Prime Minister's impressions of his countrymen's reactions to their first exposure to modern warfare. *"Eleh yamduh.* These shall stand," he wrote.

• • •

In the march of the Arab armies into Palestine, one was moving in the opposite direction to all the others. It was leaving Palestine. There was no role in the coming offensive for the general who had sworn to capture Tel Aviv or die at the head of his troops. The only laurels Fawzi el Kaukji would take back from the campaign that was to have made of him a general in the Prussian mold were the splintered ruins of a few homes in Jerusalem. In accordance with the orders he had received from Damascus, he prepared to lead his army back across the Jordan, where an honorless dissolution awaited it. Just before dawn, his withdrawing columns crossed an advancing group of Arab Legion vehicles in the sleepy streets of the town of Ramallah. Kaukji was sure they were moving up to replace him in the positions from which he had just retired.

Held now by only two hundred irregulars under Haroun Ben-Jazzi, those hilltop positions controlled the most important crossroads in Palestine. Below them, in the wheatfields and vineyards of the Valley of Ayalon, the principal roads from the north, south and west joined to form the highway that ran up to Jerusalem through the gorge of Bab el Wad. Since Biblical times, the destiny of Jerusalem had been decided on the ridge lines of Latrun.

It was there on the evening of his terrible battle that Joshua had bade the sun stand still to give him time to complete his victory over the Canaanites. From there the Philistines had terrorized the Hebrews of Saul's time. Here Judas Maccabaeus, Judas the Hammer, had begun his war to liberate his people. Herod had defeated the Jews on these hills, and Vespasian had installed his legions along its crests. Richard the Lionhearted had built on one of its peaks "a vigilant citadel along the route of the Caliphs," only to have it razed by Saladin on his own march to Jerusalem. Nine centuries later, in 1917, Prussians and Turks had tried to stem on its ridges the advance of General Allenby. Only the fact that they were held by the British and not the Arabs had kept them from becoming the focal point of Operation Nachshon a month earlier.

Now, as the sun of Joshua began to rise over the Valley of Ayalon on the first morning in the life of a new Jewish state, Fawzi el Kaukji's withdrawal had presented to the soldiers of Israel a glittering opportunity to seize the heights that were the key to the road to Jerusalem.

• • •

Squatting on his prayer carpet in the predawn grayness, King Abdullah fondled his pet, a one-eyed cat, and ruminated with his newspaperman guest.

"All right" he said, "the Arab countries are going to war and we must naturally be at their sides, but we are making a mistake for which we will pay dearly later. One day we will live to regret that we did not give the Jews a state to satisfy their demands. We have been following the wrong course and we still are."

The King paused a moment. Then, smiling faintly at the guest in his Amman palace, he added, "If you quote me on that, I will deny it publicly and call you a liar."

• • •

The principal concern of Jerusalem's Haganah on the first day of the new state's existence was the determined resistance still being put up by Bajhat Abou Gharbieh in the quarter of Musrara outside the Old City's northwestern wall. At seven o'clock in the morning a Haganah attack wrested from the Arabs the Hospice of Notre-Dame, overlooking one side of Musrara, and soon loudspeakers warned its inhabitants, "Return to the Old City or you'll be killed."

Despite the warning and an order from his chieftains at the Rawdah School to withdraw, Abou Gharbieh refused to abandon the neighborhood

411

in which he had been born. For the next two hours, he and his men waged a furious combat with the Haganah, its epicenter a curious location, the basketball court of a Swedish school.

Elsewhere, in the Arab neighborhoods of Greek Colony, German Colony and Upper Beqaa, cut off by Avram Uzieli's capture of the Allenby Barracks, the day was characterized by the outburst of an ancient malady that had followed conquering armies in the Holy City since time immemorial —looting. For Naim Halaby, as for most of the Arabs left in those middle-class neighborhoods, the memory of that May 15 would always be associated with a sight he watched from his window, "an orgy of looting." Their first visitors were simply hungry Jews literally begging for something to eat. But then, as word spread, others swarmed in behind them.

Halaby saw one group bring a horse and a cart up to his next-door neighbor's abandoned home and systematically strip it bare. Down the street other looters carried away tires, furniture, kerosene and heaps of clothing from another house. Halaby's worst shock, however, came when he saw a green Willys drive by his window. It was his. He had left it in a friend's garage with its distributor cap removed, thinking that no one would be able to move it.

The father of Hassib Boulos, the surgeon at Government Hospital, looked on helplessly as a wave of looters picked his home clean, even stripping the clothes from his closet. "If I had known," he later lamented, "at least I would have put on a good suit that morning." Daoud Dajani heard a noise outside his house. Stepping out, he saw a man trying to get into his home through a little door under its eaves. He yelled and the frightened looter tumbled at his feet. It was a Yemenite truck driver from the Dead Sea Potash Works who had been a customer of Dajani's grocery store for years. Late in the afternoon, Emile Hourani overheard two elderly women who were looting his neighbor's house bitterly complain, "The rich people took all the good things and left nothing for us."

Unprepared for what was happening, preoccupied with the city's military situation, the Haganah made only cursory efforts to curb the looting. The terrorist organizations complicated their problem. One Arab automobile dealer brought the Haganah a slip of paper in Hebrew given him by the men who had "requisitioned" 180 new tires from his cellar. "It's the Irgun," the Haganah people told him. "There's nothing we can do."

The blare of sirens rising above the gunfire denoted another aspect of the agony overtaking Jerusalem. On both sides of the city her inhabitants, Arab and Jewish alike, were paying with blood for their attachment to

Jerusalem. The emergency clinics and operating theaters established in the New City by the Magen David Adom were already overflowing. Deprived of their facilities on Mount Scopus, the Jewish medical establishment had converted their neighborhood clinics into military hospitals. They had even rented the classrooms of the St. Joseph Convent School to supplement their limited hospital space.

Bandages, plasma, antibiotics and two thousand flasks of blood had been divided among the clinics. Water was desperately short. What had been used to scrub wounds was meticulously saved to wash the floors. Since laundries couldn't work, sheets were taken from the dead to welcome the wounded. As there was almost no electric power, operations were performed by flashlight. Antitetanus serum and morphine were almost non-existent.

To the nurses in the St. Joseph clinic, the agony of one young Haganah soldier represented much of the suffering besetting their city. His wounded brother was in the bed beside him. His father had been killed in the withdrawal from Neve Yaacov a few hours before. And he, he was going to lose both his legs with, as his only anesthesic, one shot of morphine and the blocks of ice in which his heartbroken mother had wrapped his mangled limbs.

The Jews of Jerusalem had one priceless resource, however: the skill of their doctors who had survived the Hadassah ambush. They were men like Dr. Edward Joseph, a brilliant abdominal surgeon in the clinic of the Street of the Prophet. Twice, in 1929 and 1936, the gray-haired graduate of the University of Edinburgh Medical School had cared for his fellows wounded defending their city. Almost speechless with fatigue, he labored hour after hour on the battered bodies of the Haganah wounded.

A few hundred yards away, an Arab doctor struggled to imitate the movements that had made Dr. Joseph world famous. Dr. Ibrahim Tleel had never operated on the abdomen. He had no assistants, and his only nurse was busy somewhere else. As in so many other domains, the confusion and disorder in his improvised hospital were part of the price the Arabs were paying for their failure to organize their society. Only after repeated warnings from the British and the Red Cross had they established an emergency clinic in the Austrian Hospice on the Via Dolorosa by the Fourth Station of the Cross. It lacked almost everything: fuel, electricity, water, bandages, blood, penicillin, anesthetics, plaster, even food. Volunteers were going from door to door in the Old City begging for a jar of kerosene, a box of sugar, a sheet or a mattress. Its equipment, brought in haste by the young Dr. Tleel three days earlier, consisted of an antiquated

413

sterilizer, one old operating table, some plasma, penicillin and morphine. Cut off from Government Hospital and the other institutions on which they had relied in the New City, the Arabs could offer their wounded little more than a stopping-off place on the way to the grave.

Even the men on whom they had counted were absent. Dr. Hassib Boulos, who could have performed the operation haunting Dr. Tleel, was trapped in Government Hospital. Despairing, the young Palestinian took the only course open to him. He ran up the stairs to his bedroom and grabbed one of the six enormous volumes on his bookshelf. Tleel had bought them in London for six guineas. Frantically he plunged into the pages of Love and Bailly's *Emergency Surgery* in search of the knowledge that would save the man dying on his operating table.*

Assiya Halaby, the woman who had gone to the King David to say goodbye to her British colleagues, was among the volunteers who came to Tleel's aid. Her first wounded was a Syrian. Someone had stuffed an old rag into the gaping hole in his head. Assiya called for scissors to cut it away and clean the wound. There were none. She ran out into the souks, dashing from stall to stall until she finally found a pair. Tied around her neck with a black ribbon, they became for the woman who had left her home with a copy of *The Arab Awakening* a kind of weapon, the symbol of her participation in the struggle enveloping the city.

* * *

All day John Glubb had fretted over the failure of his second ammunition ship, the one bearing thousands of rounds for his artillery, to arrive in Aqaba. Late in the afternoon, a telephone call from the commanding general of Britain's Middle Eastern forces in Port Said provided him the explanation for its absence.

"I say, old boy, your allies seem to be pinching your ammunition," the general said. The Egyptians, he reported, had ordered the departing ship back to the dock and were unloading its cargo. The shells its hold contained were going to wind up in the cannon of King Farouk and not in the guns of the Bedouin rival he so despised.

No event in Jerusalem during that first full day of the Jewish state's existence would have as much bearing on the city's struggle as a discovery

---

* His patient, suffering from a perforated colon, was saved. In the trying days ahead, confronted by cases which went far beyond his experience and lay well outside his specialty, the twenty-nine-year-old Tleel would have many an occasion to be grateful for his purchase. Using the texts, he also succeeded in saving several men with lung wounds and one with a head injury.

in the hills abandoned the evening before by Fawzi el Kaukji. A unit of the Palmach's Givati Brigade, surprised by the lack of response to a couple of probing mortar shots, began to push cautiously up the slope. To their stupefaction, the men found no opposition. In a few minutes they were inside the heavily fortified British police station commanding the road for which they had made such sacrifices six weeks before during Operation Nachshon.

From the police station, they crossed through the grove of olive and cypress trees wrapping the Trappist Monastery of Latrun in a protective belt of greenery and scaled the summit behind the abbey's buildings. There they came under a furious attack, not from their Arab foes, but from hundreds of bees in the monks' hives.

Faces puffed from their assault, the Palmach conquerors of Latrun prudently withdrew to the police station to ponder their exploit. They immediately radioed Tel Aviv that the road for which they had been fighting so desperately was unexpectedly open and the key heights of Latrun were empty of the enemy. Kaukji's assumption as he passed through Ramallah had been wrong.

Latrun did not, for the moment, figure in the strategy of the commander of the Arab Legion. By an extraordinary coincidence it was not going to figure in the strategy of the Haganah either. Instead of the interminable column of trucks they had hoped to see rushing up to Jerusalem on the road that now lay open, the frustrated men on the heights of Latrun and Bab el Wad would see only one truck pass below them. It would become known in Israeli legend as the Orphan Convoy.

Even more inexplicable to some was the decision to abandon the Latrun ridge a few hours later. To the Chief of Operations of the Israeli Army, however, the new state resembled that afternoon "a nude girl with only a handkerchief to cover herself." As the girl would have to decide what to hide, so Yigal Yadin had to decide what to defend. The young archaeologist was convinced on Saturday, May 15, that the gravest danger Israel faced was not the situation in Jerusalem, but that created by the Egyptian Army columns pouring into the country from the south.

Rejecting Yitzhak Rabin's plea to hold Latrun in force by adding a battalion of the Givati Brigade to Rabin's battered Fifth Battalion, he ordered the Givati troops south to meet the forces of King Farouk. Thus for a few hours, abandoned in turn by the Arabs and the Haganah, the vital heights of Latrun would be virtually empty. They would not be for long.

• • •

Thousands of miles from the shores of the new state of Israel, in a suite in the Waldorf-Astoria Hotel in New York, a small group of friends stood around the sickbed of Chaim Weizmann. The long struggle of Zionism's most distinguished spokesman had culminated with an honor no man deserved more than he. Raising a glass of champagne to the ailing scientist, his secretary, Joseph Linton, proposed, "for the first time in two thousand years," a toast to "the President of a Jewish state."

32

"THE MOST BEAUTIFUL MONTH OF THE YEAR"

IN THE BEDROOM overlooking the Austrian Hospice, in which he had taken refuge, an out-of-work Arab civil servant patiently twisted the dials of his battery-powered radio. Since May 14, Aladin Namari had been the self-appointed Minister of Information of Arab Jerusalem. The two days in which he had discharged his function had been marked by one Arab setback after another in the city. Its citizens had an important consolation, however, and its source was the crackling voices pouring out of Namari's radio as he moved the dial from one Arab broadcasting service to another.

As soon as he had switched off the radio, Namari began to compose the bulletin he would mimeograph for his fellow Jerusalemites. This Sunday, May 16, it would inform them that, according to Palestine Radio in Ramallah, "the Arab armies continued to advance on all battlefields, winning victory after victory."

Baghdad had announced, "Iraqi forces have captured the Rutenberg power plant which supplies most of Palestine with electric power."

Cairo claimed that "the Egyptian Army arrived in Gaza via Khan Yunis and advanced beyond in its successful march."

Beirut proudly declared that the Lebanese Army "continued its advance triumphantly, destroying the fortifications of the Jewish settlements on its way."

To that litany of Arab triumphs Namari appended only one local note, an urgent appeal for donations to relieve the shortages in the Austrian Hospice below his windows.

It was the only accurate item in Namari's bulletin that morning. The Rutenberg power plant "captured" by the Iraqis was inside Transjordan, while Khan Yunis and Gaza were purely Arab communities. Reading Namari's bulletin and later hearing of other Egyptian "victories" in Beersheba, Hebron and Bethlehem, George Deeb would angrily ask a friend, "Can't they read the maps I sent them? All their conquests are Arab!"

417

If the Arabs' victories to date were largely in their own minds, the situation facing the Jewish state was still extremely grave, and the diary of David Ben-Gurion that Sunday corroborated the tone, at least, of Namari's bulletin. In the north, he noted, "we have one hundred and fifty casualties in a battalion of five hundred." In Upper Galilee the situation was "dire." Morale in many units was low. Egyptian attacks were reported in Nir Am, Nirin and Kfar Darim, and the settlements, he recorded, were "sure they will not be able to hold out." There was "news of Egyptian columns along the shore," Ben-Gurion concluded, and "the south is open."

One of the men moving up with those advancing columns was Lieutenant Mohammed Rafat, the twenty-six-year-old intelligence officer of the Sixth Battalion who had so cheerfully waved goodbye to his family in the Cairo station. He was a confused young man. He had been ordered to prepare a dawn attack on a Jewish kibbutz that wasn't even marked on his map.

With no reconnaissance, led by a colonel who had never commanded a unit in the field, Rafat and his men set out in search of their missing Jewish settlement. After walking nine miles through the desert, they stumbled on it just after dawn. That example of the helpless Jewish colonies that were supposed to line their route to Tel Aviv was surrounded by barbed wire and sandbagged strongpoints. A devastating wave of fire swept out from its trenches, causing the Egyptians heavy losses. Nailed to the desert floor under a battering sun, they suffered for hours until darkness allowed them to stagger back across the desert to their base. There one final shock awaited them. There was no water in the camp. Exhausted, racked with thirst, the embittered young Rafat realized that his "promenade" to Tel Aviv was over.

•　•　•

The struggle for Jerusalem had brought pandemonium into the lives of a special category of its citizens, those men and women dedicated to a religious vocation. Priests, monks and nuns whose cellars already overflowed with goods given them for safekeeping now found their convents and monasteries clogged with refugees. On this Pentecost Sunday, communities which had chosen to detach themselves from the temporal world were forced by the crisis enveloping the city to come to grips with its most ferocious aspects.

None of them had their life as completely disrupted as a group of twenty-nine cloistered French nuns who had the immense misfortune to live in what was probably the most exposed building in Jerusalem. The architect of their convent had made it a kind of modern assault tower, its front end extending beyond the Old City's walls next to New Gate and its rear actually inside the Old City itself.

Its community of Soeurs Réparatrices lived a life so isolated from the world that the only male many of them had seen for half a century was their priest. Their only ventures into the streets of Jerusalem were walking to their convent on the day of their arrival and leaving it at their death for the graveyard beyond Gethsemane. Their Holy City was the chapel in which they prostrated themselves in perpetual adoration before a host representing the Savior who had been crucified a few hundred yards from their altar. Overnight, the peaceful haven of their convent had become an appealing target to both sides. Those sheltered nuns, who barely remembered what a man was, now saw men streaming through their convent by the dozens, Arabs from one side, Jews from the other. In the first forty-eight hours of fighting, the building and its rooftop vantage points were seized first by the Arabs, then by the Haganah, then by the Arabs again. At each intrusion, the *mère supérieure* and her assistant the *mère econome* valiantly tried to scold the invaders out of their convent with a perfectly futile declaration of their neutrality.

Finally, on this Pentecost Sunday, with the Haganah preparing to wrest the building back from the Arabs, the mother superior decided to suspend her followers' vows. The war was going to return the Soeurs Réparatrices to the world for five minutes, just the time needed to rush through the streets of Jerusalem to the Roman Catholic Patriarchate. Once there, they were installed in the Archbishop's reception hall. Each of the nuns was assigned a huge red velvet chair which she turned to the wall to form a temporary cell in which to practice the meditations of her order. That evening in the Patriarchate's chapel, they resumed their rigid routine. Arms extended in a cross, they recited the rosary. Then, in unfeigned joyfulness, they sang an old French hymn: "It is May. It is the month of Mary. It is the most beautiful month of the year."

* * *

Fawzi el Kutub was ready to launch his personal crusade against the Jewish Quarter of the Old City. Behind the Arabs' explosives expert was the bomb he had prepared for his assault at his headquarters in a Turkish bath: twenty-five homemade mines. Each consisted of thirty-five pounds of dynamite stuffed into metal cans and armed with one of the detonators he had purchased in the souks of Damascus. Kutub was going to blow his way into the quarter building by building.

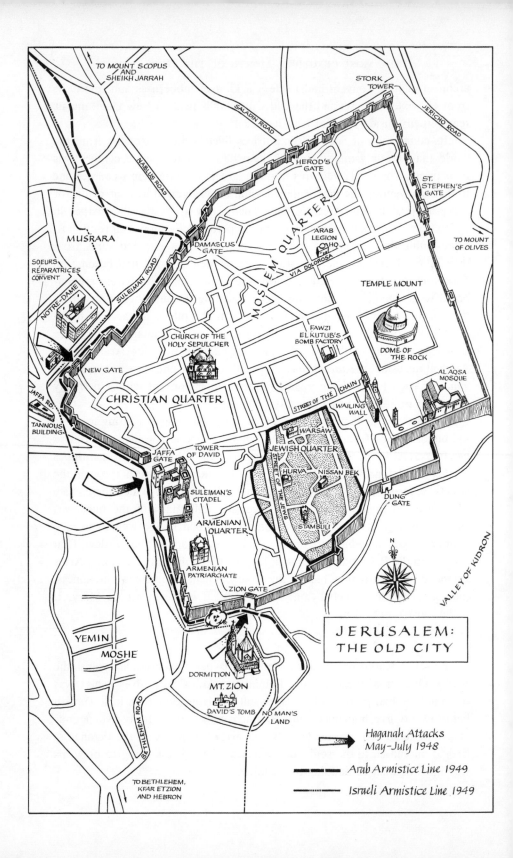

TO MOUNT SCOPUS
AND
SHEIKH JARRAH

STORK
TOWER

SALADIN ROAD

JERICHO ROAD

NABLUS ROAD

HEROD'S
GATE

ST.
STEPHEN'S
GATE

MUSRARA

M
O
S
L
E
M

Q
U
A
R
T
E
R

ARAB
LEGION
HQ

TO MOUNT
OF OLIVES

SOEURS
RÉPARATRICES
CONVENT

DAMASCUS
GATE

VIA DOLOROSA

SULEIMAN ROAD

NOTRE-DAME

TEMPLE MOUNT

CHURCH OF THE
HOLY SEPULCHER

FAWZI
EL KUTUB'S
BOMB FACTORY

DOME OF
THE ROCK

NEW GATE

AL AQSA
MOSQUE

JAFFA RD.

CHRISTIAN QUARTER

STREET OF THE CHAIN

WAILING
WALL

TANNOUS
BUILDING

WARSAW

JAFFA
GATE

TOWER
OF DAVID

JEWISH QUARTER

STREET OF THE JEWS

HURVA   NISSAN BEK

SULEIMAN'S
CITADEL

STAMBULI

DUNG
GATE

ARMENIAN
QUARTER

N

VALLEY OF KIDRON

ARMENIAN
PATRIARCHATE

ZION GATE

JERUSALEM:
THE OLD CITY

YEMIN
MOSHE

BETHLEHEM ROAD

DORMITION

MT. ZION

DAVID'S TOMB   NO MAN'S
LAND

Haganah Attacks
May–July 1948

Arab Armistice Line 1949

Israeli Armistice Line 1949

TO BETHLEHEM,
KFAR ETZION
AND HEBRON

His first target was the Haganah position in the Warsaw Buildings, barely a hundred yards from the spot where he had been born. To set an example for the twenty-five volunteers he had recruited for his Tadmir unit, Kutub lit a cigarette, stuck it into his mouth and raced forward with the first mine. As he did, the metal scraps of an exploding booby trap peppered his face. Kutub lit the mine with his cigarette, heaved it at its target and sprinted to cover. His face smeared with blood, seized by an almost hysterical frenzy, he grabbed a second bomb and thrust it at Kadour Mansour, "El Tunsi," his whiskey-drinking truck driver. Pulling out his pistol, he pointed it at the trembling Tunisian's temple and ordered him to run. The bomb balanced on his head like a safari porter's load, El Tunsi staggered off.

Three times Kutub forced the Tunisian to repeat the gesture. After the third, the man told him, "Shoot me. I don't give a damn. I'm not going back."

Kutub turned to another member of his unit, a fourteen-year-old boy named Sabah Ghani, and ordered him to go. Inspired by a parade of volunteers marching through Damascus, Ghani had run away from his Syrian home to join his father and brother, already fighting in Palestine. Knees trembling, he started out. As he did, an elderly man leaped forward, grabbed the bomb from his arms and, screaming, "*Allah akhbar!*," rushed off in his place. Two Haganah men in a concealed tunnel cut the old man down with a Sten-gun burst. Then they drove the rest of Kutub's men back to cover.

It was only a momentary respite. On all sides, the Arab irregulars hammered the beleaguered quarter. The most serious attacks were along its western flank, where the Jewish and Armenian Quarters ran side by side. The Arabs had occupied the cross-shaped belfry of the Church of St.-Jacques, which the Old City Haganah had been ordered to abandon by Shaltiel's headquarters after a series of vociferous Armenian protests. As a result the vital Haganah post at Zion Gate had come under a crossfire and had to be given up, too. Using the Cross Position for support, the Arabs then drove down the little slope on which Rabbi Weingarten lived toward the heart of the Jewish Quarter, the Street of the Jews. As they advanced, they tried to lure the Israelis into the open with offers of tomatoes and bread. The fighting was desperate, from room to room and street corner to corner; despite the Haganah's determined resistance, the Arabs progressed steadily.

As composed as if she were still walking the streets of her native London, Esther Cailingold moved through the fighting, bringing ammunition, food and a cheering word to each post. Discovering in one a tray of sandwiches covered with dust, she quietly admonished its occupants. In England, during the Blitz, she told them, they had had to learn to make sure precious food wouldn't spoil. Fifteen minutes later she brought them a new set of sandwiches, all carefully wrapped.

On one of her trips a ricocheting bullet struck her hip. Insisting that the Arabs' attack was too intense to allow anyone to leave a post, she limped off to the hospital unaided.

None of the losses the Haganah would suffer that day would have a more depressing effect on morale than that which occurred shortly after noon in an abandoned building in the line of the Arabs' advance. To try to check their assault, Emmanuel Meidav, the boy with the "golden hands," had returned to booby-trap the building with one of the Irgun's homemade bombs. Emmanuel had had no experience with the device and something went wrong. A frightful explosion shook the building.

An hour later, his fiancée, Rika Menache, finally found him in the hospital. Dr. Abraham Laufer, the Old City's surgeon, sorrowfully took her to a table on which Emmanuel lay on a stretcher, his face swathed in bandages.

"Will he live?" Rika whispered. Laufer nodded. She sank to his side and began to caress his broken body. The energetic, vital young man who had been her fiancé could hardly breathe. One of his "golden hands" had been amputated; the other was a useless claw. Worse, the handsome face under the bandages would never see again. The explosion had torn out both of Emmanuel's eyes.

Outside, the Arabs continued to push their way toward the quarter's principal artery, the Street of the Jews. In one day's fighting, they had brought almost a quarter of the neighborhood's surface under their control. The frightened residents who had lived in the areas they had captured crowded into the Stambuli Synagogue. Relations between them and the Haganah had deteriorated since the English had left. On Saturday, May 15, some of them had even refused to dig fortifications for the quarter, shouting *"Shabbos!* Sabbath!" at the Haganah.

Now panic overtook many of them. Crowded together, reciting psalms while frightened mothers scurried after missing children, they began to chant in unison, "Surrender. Wave a white flag. Save our souls." To the Haganah men guarding them they insisted, "We lived in peace with the Arabs. If we surrender we can live in peace with them now."

Their insistent pleas for surrender, the gains made by the Arabs in one day's fighting, exacted a toll on the morale of the quarter's Haganah leadership. Their messages to the New City grew increasingly urgent. "The situation is desperate," said one. "They are breaking in from all sides." "Send help immediately," read another later in the day, "otherwise we will not be able to hold out."

In that atmosphere of growing despair, Rabbis Weingarten, Mintzberg and Hazan marched into Haganah headquarters to ask their shaken commander for his agreement to the opening of surrender negotiations. Further resistance was futile, pleaded Weingarten; they should surrender to avoid a massacre of innocent civilians. Appalled by the idea of assuming responsibility for such a slaughter, disheartened by what he felt was a lack of understanding and guidance in Shaltiel's headquarters, Russnak finally agreed.

"All right," he told the rabbis in a half-whisper, "go ahead."

Half an hour later, Alberto Gori, an Italian priest at Terra Sancta, the custodian's office for the Holy Land, received a telephone call from Weingarten asking him to find out the Arabs' surrender terms. The request fell on the dispirited leaders in the Arab headquarters like a breeze on a pile of dying embers. The situation in the rest of Jerusalem was grim. Their untrained irregulars had been expending ammunition at an appalling rate. None of their pleas to the Arab Legion for help had shaken Glubb's determination to keep his soldiers out of the city. Outside of their attacks on the Jewish Quarter, their sole offensive gesture this Pentecost Sunday had been performed by the few gunners Fawzi el Kaukji had left behind in Palestine. To bolster the Arabs' sagging morale, they had resumed their indiscriminate shelling of Jewish Jerusalem from their position on Nebi Samuel.

Elated at the thought of their first victory in the city since the British departure, the Arab leaders informed Gori that the quarter's inhabitants could be returned to New Jerusalem under Red Cross supervision and combatants taken prisoner. When Gori telephoned the Arabs' terms, Weingarten was crestfallen. Like everyone else in his quarter, Weingarten was haunted by the specter of the slaughter committed by the Arab villagers at Kfar Etzion. It was the soldiers of John Glubb, not the partisans of the Mufti, to whom he wanted to surrender. "But where is the Arab Legion?" the puzzled rabbi asked.

The absence of the Arab Legion delighted another Jewish leader in Jerusalem that Sunday. To David Shaltiel, each hour in which its sand-colored armored cars failed to appear on the ridge line above Sheikh Jarrah was a precious gift taking him one step closer to the conquest of the city.

Operation Pitchfork, his three-pronged assault keyed to the departure of the British, was largely complete. He was ready to thrust his men against the Old City itself. As their target he had picked what seemed to be the most impregnable part of its walls, Jaffa Gate, dominated by the three imposing towers of Suleiman's Citadel. Shaltiel, however, had a secret tactic to storm the Citadel. It had been suggested to him by a lady archaeologist, the wife of an officer on his staff. Thanks to her studies, she knew that at the base of the Citadel, outside the wall, was an almost forgotten iron grill. Behind it a secret passageway six feet high and three feet wide led to the interior of the Citadel's courtyard.

Shaltiel's plan was simple. He would send his "armored force"—two British armored cars and a scout car commanded by Yosef Nevo—toward the Jaffa Gate. While they riveted their fire on the gate's defenders, a team of sappers would blow the grill. Then his infantry would dash for the passageway and take the Arabs in the Citadel from behind.

Shaltiel's calculations were determined by the despairing, almost hysterical messages that had been pouring into his headquarters all day long from the Old City. One had even warned that the Jewish Quarter could not hold out more than a quarter of an hour. Still unaware of the rabbis' surrender negotiations, persuaded that he was involved in a race with time, Shaltiel had given up the more logical but time-consuming scheme of trying to surround the entire Old City. Once his men had secured the Citadel, they would have a relatively easy job moving through the Armenian areas to relieve the Jewish Quarter. To keep the Arabs from grouping at Jaffa Gate, Shaltiel planned two diversionary assaults, one on the left at New Gate by the Irgun and the Stern Gang, the other on the right on Mount Zion by the Palmach.

From the outset, Shaltiel ran into difficulties. The Irgun, the Stern Gang and the Palmach all suspected that he had assigned them to diversionary attacks to keep the glory of seizing the Old City for his own forces. The Palmach's Yitzhak Rabin and Yosef Tabenkin didn't believe his plan would work. To Rabin, attacking Jaffa Gate was like "banging your head against a stone wall." He and Tabenkin urged instead that they put all their forces into an assault from the Mandelbaum house to the northeastern corner of the Old City, which would give them control of the principal access routes to Jerusalem.

"I don't want your advice on how to conduct this war," Shaltiel told them. "All I asked was, Are you ready to make a diversion or not?"

Even the members of his own staff did not share Shaltiel's confidence in his scheme. Yitzhak Levi warned him that one Arab machine gun on

David's Tower of the Citadel would stop the attack. The first officer he asked to command the operation, Zelman Mart, refused, saying the plan wouldn't work.

None of their criticisms, however, shook Shaltiel's resolve. So confident was he of the operation's outcome that he had already prepared two elements essential to celebrating its success. One was a flag of the new Jewish state which Shaltiel intended to have raised on the top of David's Tower. The other was a baby lamb secreted in the back of Shaltiel's Jewish Agency quarters. A far more exalted destiny than that originally intended for it by its Arab shepherd awaited the animal. Shaltiel was going to sacrifice it at the base of David's Tower as soon as he had returned the ramparts of Jerusalem to Jewish hands.

33

"GO SAVE JERUSALEM."

IT WAS A TRANQUIL, moonless night. Somewhere in the silence, in a building perched on one of Amman's seven hills, a man rose from the mattress spread on the floor on which he slept, and unfolded his prayer rug. It was 4 A.M., Monday, May 17. As he always did, King Abdullah of Transjordan began a new day by resuming his solitary dialogue with the God of whom one of his distant ancestors had been the messenger.

His dialogue was interrupted by his aide de camp, Hazza el Majali, bursting into the bedroom. He had just received a telephone call from Jerusalem. Weeping, Ahmed Hilmi Pasha, one of the two members of Haj Amin Husseini's Arab Higher Committee still in the city, had begged for the Legion "to come to our assistance and save Jerusalem and its people from a certain fall."

It was the second call Majali had received that night from Hilmi begging for help, the climax of a series of pleas that had been pouring in for the past twenty-four hours. "The Jewish flag will fly over the tomb of your father if you do not send troops," one distraught Jerusalemite had warned the King.

Those words had not left the little sovereign unmoved. Though he had resigned himself to the partition of Palestine, the internationalization of Jerusalem was a project which pained him no less than it did Ben-Gurion. Only the constant pressure of Great Britain, the nation whose support and subsidy were vital to his throne, had kept him from sending his Bedouin soldiers to El Kuds, the Holy City. Jerusalem's fall would be a bitter blow to him personally and would have a disastrous effect on his prestige. What good, after all, was the best army in the Arab world if its soldiers were not to defend the third city of Islam?

Abdullah's palace was not the only place where Jerusalem's fate was being debated that night. In the army camp of Zerqa, just outside Amman, the worried leaders of the Arab League had been summoned from their sleep by the cry for help from the Holy City. An Egyptian volunteer fight-

426

ing in Jerusalem had come to Azzam Pasha to tell him it would fall if the Arab Legion did not intervene. The city was desperately short of ammunition, and the loss of most of the New City had been devastating to morale. One concerted Jewish attack, he warned, and "all Jerusalem will be theirs."

In pajamas, occasionally shouting at each other in the heat of their exchanges, the League leaders debated his message in the sitting room of Azzam's cottage. Finally, exasperated, Azzam turned to Iraq's Crown Prince Abdul Illah. "If you don't go immediately and convince your uncle to send troops to Jerusalem," he threatened, "and if Jerusalem falls for want of them, I will tell the world the Hashemites are Arab traitors even if I hang for it." His outburst spurred them to action. They all decided to dress and rush to Abdullah's palace.

Meanwhile, in a simple stone house in Djebel Amman, a sleepy Tewfic Abou Hoda stumbled from his bedroom and gaped at the figure before him. Transjordan's Prime Minister had come to expect unusual gestures from the eccentric monarch he served, but nothing had prepared him for the sight of Abdullah standing in his living room in the middle of the night. The shock did not, however, disturb his presence of mind. Any interference in Jerusalem, he told Abdullah, would in his view constitute a breach of the agreement he had concluded with Bevin and the British.

His reply disturbed the King. Those were not the words he had come to his Prime Minister's home in the middle of the night to hear. As anxious as Abdullah was to send his soldiers to Jerusalem, he was not yet prepared to do it if it meant defying his only allies.

Meditating morosely on his problem, he returned to his palace, to stumble upon the angry delegation of his fellow Arab leaders. Once again the outspoken Azzam repeated the threat he had made at Zerqa to Abdul Illah. This time he added that if the Arab Legion saved Jerusalem, "I will not oppose declaring you king of Jerusalem and I will put the crown on your head with my own hands even though my own sovereign will oppose it."

The King leaped from his chair and embraced him.

"You will not be disappointed," he promised.

. . .

Netanel Lorch eyed the five Four Square cigarettes before him with suspicion. The young officer who had told himself on Partition Night that "dancing is for the innocents" knew that three was the daily ration. There would be a price to pay for the two extra cigarettes, he thought. Before

427

he had had time to enjoy the first one, he found out what it was. He was summoned to a conference at the Schneller base to be briefed on his role in David Shaltiel's attack on Jaffa Gate.

It was, Lorch would recall, a "very solemn, very formal" briefing. Neat and cool in a freshly pressed uniform, Shaltiel looked on while Ephraim Levi, the young officer he had chosen to lead the assault, explained the operation on a map of Old Jerusalem. Levi himself had at first thought that "the whole thing was crazy"—trying to "break into the Old City through this little window leading to some stairs which no one was really certain were there or not." Pondering it, Levi had become convinced that despite the heavy casualties he was certain they would take, they would somehow get in.

The Irgun and the Stern Gang would strike at New Gate, the Palmach at Mount Zion, he explained, while the main Haganah force would wait in the Tannous Building opposite Jaffa Gate. As soon as the sappers had blown the grill with a bangalore torpedo, they would make for the tunnel under the protective fire of Nevo's "armored force." The first group would seize the northwest tower of the Citadel, controlling Jaffa Gate. The second, Lorch's, would take the southeast tower, then the police headquarters just beyond it.

When Levi had finished, David Amiran, the man whose archaeologist wife had furnished the idea for the attack, gave them a lecture on the Citadel's architecture, stirring in Lorch an unexpectedly passionate interest in archaeology. Then Shaltiel presented them a flag of their new state. "Tomorrow morning," he promised his young officers, "this flag of Zion will fly from the Tower of David."

• • •

John Glubb scrutinized the slip of red paper reserved in the Arab Legion for urgent communications. "His Majesty the King orders an advance towards Jerusalem from Ramallah," it said. "He intends by this action to threaten the Jews in order that they may accept a truce in Jerusalem." Half an hour later, at noon, a still more explicit cable reached Glubb, stressing that the King was "extremely anxious" to "ease the pressure on the Arabs and incline the Jews to accept a truce for Jerusalem. . . . His Majesty," the cable concluded, "is awaiting swift action. Report quickly that the operation has commenced."

Those two cables were as far as Abdullah dared go in manifesting to his English troop commander his growing desire to get his soldiers into Jerusalem. For forty-eight hours, Glubb had been opposing both the

King and the government on Jerusalem for reasons that were "partly political, partly military." He did not believe the situation in the city was as desperate as its leaders claimed. To Glubb, with his ingrained dislike of city Arabs, they were incompetent, semihysterical men more adept at overestimating their foes' strength than at using theirs.

Elsewhere, his hopes of waging only a semblance of a war had been notably successful. His Legion had been inside Palestine for over forty-eight hours without a single engagement of any consequence. Some of his regiments had not even fired a round of ammunition.

But they were paying a price for their inactivity, and it was growing with each passing hour. In Amman, the city crowds, spurred by the non-stop, triumphant bulletins emanating from their neighbors' radio stations, were beginning to scream for victories of their own. The Arab officers and soldiers to whom Abdullah had cried, "On to Jerusalem!" added their protests to the crowds'. The proud Bedouins who had ridden down to the Jordan through a cheering crowd now found their campsites surrounded by jeering women calling them cowards. There had been a significant number of desertions to the ranks of the irregulars. At least one unit was close to mutiny, and everywhere relations between British and Arab officers were strained. When Colonel T. L. Ashton invoked the example of India in an argument with his subordinates, his adjutant Captain Ali Abou Nuwar replied with a curt phrase that summed up the sentiments beginning to rise in many of his fellows: "India was not your country. And this is ours."

Despite those pressures, Glubb remained steadfast in his determination to stay out of Jerusalem. He clung to the hope that the Consular Commission might still arrange for a cease-fire in the city and save the internationalization scheme from collapse. More than ever he was haunted by the idea of using his precious troops in an urban conflict. But he could not ignore the King's cables. He would send Jerusalem's population a reminder of the force that lay just beyond the Judean hills ringing their city—one of the 25-pounder guns purchased with the subsidy he had received in London. Perhaps, as Abdullah hoped, a few shells from that field piece would sober the city's Haganah command and spare him the need of sending his army to Jerusalem.

* * *

Netanel Lorch was furious. The good Jewish mothers of Jerusalem, his own at their head, had, at an enormous sacrifice of their own skimpy rations, prepared hundreds of sandwiches for their hungry compatriots in the Jewish Quarter of the Old City. In addition to the ammunition, water and first-aid kits already weighing down the men of his platoon, Lorch was ordered to give each man a sack of sandwiches to carry.

The first preparations for the attack that was going to deliver those sandwiches were hardly auspicious. Moving up to their positions, Lorch's men came under a withering enfilade fire from an Arab machine gun. "Headquarters said the Arabs have no automatic weapons and they're never wrong," one of his men yelled from the back of the bus in which they were being transported. "That's not a machine gun—it's ten Arabs firing in order." With that, his men leaped from their buses into the burned-out ruins of the Commercial Center. Then they began to blow their way from shop to shop up to the Tannous Building, their assigned jump-off point. There an Arab sniper killed one of Lorch's men. Afraid of the effect his death might have on the inexperienced platoon's morale, Lorch propped the dead man up in a corner of the room and, pretending that he was only wounded, began a running conversation with his corpse.

Looking at the city spread below the crest of Nebi Samuel, Mohammed May'tah felt an extraordinary emotion seize him. The only time the artillery officer of the Arab Legion had seen Jerusalem, he had been on his white horse Sabha riding through its cheering crowds in a parade to celebrate Britain's victory at El Alamein. Now, on Glubb's orders, he was going to open the Arab Legion's war on the city with the 25-pounder behind him.

Shouting "Fire!," he told himself, "I am the first."

As his shells screamed into Jerusalem, another Arab officer of the Legion appeared at the Arab radio station in Ramallah. He handed Raji Sayhoun a communiqué. "The artillery of the Arab Legion has just begun to shell the Jewish positions in Jerusalem," it read. "Our shelling will not cease until the four-color flag of Palestine floats over the entire city."

Eight artillery shells on Jewish Jerusalem were not, despite Glubb's and Abdullah's hopes, going to influence the thinking of the Haganah. Shaltiel's command had far more pressing problems to deal with that day. Early in the morning, Rabbi Weingarten had informed Terra Sancta that the Jewish Quarter would surrender to the Arab Legion only, and the furious irregulars had reopened their attacks with new energy. Meanwhile, through the Belgian consul, the Jewish Agency got its first indication that the quarter Shaltiel was planning to save was already negotiating its end.

For the quarter, the day was, as one leader would observe, an "unrelieved disaster." Only their shortage of ammunition and their failure to press their attacks instead of looting and burning each building as they captured it prevented the Arabs from penetrating into the very heart of the quarter. Its exhausted defenders fought bitterly for each room they yielded up. The unfulfilled promises of help which arrived almost hourly from Shaltiel's headquarters did little to raise their morale. One, the evening before, had even promised relief in an hour and a half. Late in the afternoon the quarter's defenders angrily informed the New City, "Help will soon be useless. The need is now. The hour and a half has already continued thirty-six hours. What watch are you going by?"

. . .

Bobby Reisman, the American paratrooper from Buffalo who had come to Palestine almost by mistake, talked quietly beside an armored bus with his close friend Moshe Salamon. In a few minutes one of them would have to get into that bus to lead the most dangerous phase of an attack that neither of them believed in, blowing out the secret gate at the base of Suleiman's Citadel.

"Suppose we do get in?" Salamon said to Reisman. "What do we do then? We won't last ten minutes."

Reisman shrugged. "Maybe they've got another operation," he said. "Maybe we're just a diversion."

Salamon drew a shilling from his pocket. "Heads I take them in, tails you get the job," he said.

He flipped the coin. It was heads. Salamon ordered onto the bus the men who would help him blast the grill. As Salamon climbed on board himself, Reisman called "Good luck" to his disappearing figure.

In the Synagogue of Yemin Moshe, the four platoons of the Palmach who were going to be the diversion waited for the order to assemble for their assault on Mount Zion. Uzi Narciss, the man who had captured Kastel, was in charge. His four under-strength platoons were all that was left of the Har-el Brigade's Fourth Battalion after six weeks of constant combat.

Just before moving his men out, Narciss got a call from Shaltiel. The Haganah commander asked him if he had a flag.

"In fact, no," answered Narciss. "Why the hell would I have a flag?"

"To put on Mount Zion if you capture it," Shaltiel replied.

"Well," grumbled Narciss, "I just didn't think about it."

431

Ephraim Levi had his flag tied around his waist, planning to raise it before dawn on the medieval tower which loomed before him in the darkness. With Yosef Nevo, he contemplated from a blown-out window of the Tannous Building the outlines of the walls of the city against which he was about to launch the first attack of a Jewish army in almost two thousand years. There was no moon, and in the almost perfect blackness they could see nothing moving. They would have the advantage of surprise. Nevo's two British armored cars, his command car and Moshe Salamon's bus were hidden in the streets below. Levi glanced at his watch. It was a few minutes before midnight. He tapped his friend on the shoulder, and Nevo moved downstairs to his cars.

A cry as old as Jerusalem rang through the Holy City's twisting alleys: "To the walls!"

Kamal Irekat answered its call half dressed, with two barefoot aides running along behind him. As he reached the Jaffa Gate someone yelled, "The Jews are coming! The gate is open!"

Irekat ran up to the entry, the widest in the Old City. Only a few sandbags lined its mouth—not enough to stop a truck. Then he glanced to one side and spotted, along the Citadel wall, the thirteen garbage carts Anton Safieh had rescued from the crumbling municipality May 13. They were a providential gift. Irekat and his followers began to push them into the gate to form an improvised barricade.

On the walls above, there was pandemonium. Men ran up to the wall from every direction, half dressed, pulling their kaffiyehs on as they came, squatting down to fire from any crenellated gunport that was undefended. As their ancestors had spilled boiling oil on the Crusaders of Godfrey de Bouillon, they rolled up wads of paper, set them on fire and dropped them over the wall to illuminate the moonless night. Their principal firearm was a grenade made by Fawzi el Kutub out of a clump of dynamite sticks which could be flung a great distance by whirling them from the end of a cord. Already a relay of women and children were rushing them to the wall as fast as Kutub could manufacture them in his Turkish bath.

Crouched in his window in the Tannous Building, Ephraim Levi watched the outlines of Nevo's car move toward the gate. By the time it got within the circle of light made by the flaming wads of paper hurled from the wall, the Arabs' fire was murderous. Nevo tried to hold his cars out of grenade range, but, not aware of the device the Arabs were using to throw Kutub's bombs, he found them exploding all around him. Ahead of him, his armored cars opened fire on the walls with the twenty-one shells they held between them. Nevo saw a bazooka round zip past his car. Suddenly he realized his Bren wasn't firing. Turning around, he saw his gunner slide onto the floor of the car. The wireless operator crawled to him. With a puzzled regard, he looked back at Nevo. "I think he is dead," he said. He had barely uttered those words when he himself gasped and started to cough. He too had been badly hit.

Nevo's driver chose that instant to slam shut the slit through which he saw outside. Terrified, he refused to open it. Up ahead the young officer saw his lead armored car stop well short of its assigned position, almost on the spot to which Salamon's bus was supposed to move. The car was blocking the column's advance. It had to be moved forward. Salamon and his sappers would have no chance of getting to their iron grill alive in the fire pouring down on them if their bus was forced to pull up short of their jump-off point.

To his anger, Nevo discovered that a bullet had put his wireless out of action. Looking back, he saw Salamon's bus grind to a halt. The whole column was stalled now and heading to disaster if it didn't get moving again. Cursing, he forced his driver, who still refused to open his slit, to move blindly up on the lead car.

Crouched behind a gunport on the wall above, Peter Saleh saw Nevo's car start its move. The wall was a confused hurly-burly of shouting, shooting men. The wounded lay propped up on the floor moaning softly or begging for help. The old stone runway was covered with blood and spent cartridges. Men were stationed every six or seven feet pumping fire into the Israelis below. Ammunition was desperately short. A ramp had been set up so a jeep could climb part way to the wall with crates of ammunition rushed up from Rawdah headquarters.

An old man with his abaya clutched in his hand like a housewife carrying an apron full of apples moved from man to man distributing bullets. Some of Saleh's companions had old Italian rifles that lit up like a flare each time they were fired, providing the enemy a perfect indication of their position. Down the line, a Molotov cocktail splattered on the pavement. As its flames rolled toward Salamon's stalled bus, the Arabs on the walls cheered.

The Rawdah School headquarters was on the verge of collapse. Yelling, shouting men rushed in and out screaming for arms and help. Its leaders shrieked angrily at each other, and a growing state of panic gradually paralyzed their effectiveness. At her switchboard, convinced that the Jews would soon be inside the walls, Nimra Tannous personally called the royal palace in Amman. To her astonishment, she was able to get the King.

"Your Majesty," she cried, "the Jews are at the gates! In a few minutes Jerusalem will be theirs!"

The Jews were, indeed, at the gates, but their assault was in trouble. Yosef Nevo had managed to get his command car abreast of the stalled armored car. Opening his door, he saw that the car's turret was shut and three of its tires shot out. There was no sign of life inside. He screamed over the din of fire; there was still no answer. He leaned out and beat on the car's panels. Still no reaction. The only course open was to try to save the car by pushing it out of the line of fire with his own vehicle.

Salamon, meanwhile, radioed Levi he was taking heavy casualties in his bus. The Arabs' fire was slicing through its thinly armored roof. Then, as they talked, Levi heard his old friend gasp, "I am hit." Seconds later, Salamon's radio operator told Levi that his friend was dying.

On the walls the situation was desperate, too. Dozens of dead or wounded littered the Citadel and Jaffa Gate. One of the dead was the irregular manning the gunport next to Peter Saleh's. Watching a pool of blood form at the base of his skull, Saleh thought how strange it was—he did not know the man or even where he came from. They had barely exchanged two words in all the time they had stood next to each other on the firing line.

A sense of despair had spread like a disease along the walls. "This time," Saleh thought, "they'll break in." Behind him, Irekat raced from gunport to gunport, begging his men to save their ammunition, with little effect. His untrained followers fired off their rounds as fast as they could get them, as if, it seemed to Saleh, "by firing hard we could keep their shots away from us."

Below Saleh, Yosef Nevo saw men spilling out of Salamon's bus and fleeing back to Tannous. The attack, he told himself, was collapsing. By this time, Levi too had decided their assault was failing. He had two urgent tasks on hand, getting the wounded men out of Salamon's bus and bringing Nevo's "armored force" to cover.

In the stalled attack, only one operation was going according to plan. Uzi Narciss' Palmachniks had rapidly swarmed up the hilltop whose name had symbolized their lost homeland to twenty generations of Jews. Huddled on Mount Zion behind the graves of the Armenian Cemetery, yards from the tomb of Jerusalem's founder, King David, they and the Arabs threw grenades at each other, the metallic bombs bouncing around the tombstones in the midst of the wounded.

"Jerusalem is falling. Where is the Son of the Prophet?" screamed a frightened group of men bursting into the Jericho police station where Abdullah Tell was sleeping. The officer who had conquered Kfar Etzion leaped from his bed. One of his visitors was weeping. All of them were shaking. Jerusalem, they told Tell, was in a horrible state, its irregulars exhausted, its ammunition gone, its population close to panic. Tell told his orderly to make them coffee and urged them to rush to Amman. Picking up his phone, he warned the palace they were on the way.

In Jerusalem, Fadel Rashid, despairing of help from King Abdullah, sent a desperate radio message to Fawzi el Kaukji. "The situation is perilous," it said. "The enemy has launched a generalized attack on all sectors of the city. We are bombarded from all sides. We must have help or it is our end. Our End, I assure you once again, it will be the end." The general who had been ordered to withdraw his forces from Palestine replied immediately: "I am warning Syria and Transjordan of your message. Resist, I'm coming at your call, O Divine Mosque."

Meanwhile a chilling new sound filled the darkness around Jaffa Gate. One of the armored cars had missed a turn moving back to the Commercial Center and had crashed against the city walls. There a Molotov cocktail had killed its crew, and a short circuit had activated its horn. Now, like some mournful foghorn, its wail shook the night, grating with equal effect on both Arab and Jewish nerves.

Netanel Lorch and three of his men groped through the wreckage of Moshe Salamon's bus toward the wounded officer. The man who was in the car on the toss of a coin guided them through the blackness, smoke and confusion with his soft whispers. When they had taken the dying man back to the Tannous Building, Lorch set out after Nevo's wounded radio operator.

He found the wounded man by groping through the darkness, refusing to use his flashlight so as not to draw Arab fire. Lorch felt the man's body with his fingers until he located his head wound. He bandaged him as best he could, then reached down and felt for his pulse. There was none. He had just bandaged a dead man. For just a second, he cast his flashlight's beam on his face. As he did, he gasped. It was his cousin.

• • •

It was just after two o'clock in the morning when the telephone rang in Abdullah Tell's headquarters. The young officer's orderly shook as he handed Tell the receiver. "It is our master," he said.

This time King Abdullah was convinced. The deep emotions conjured up by Jerusalem had overcome at last the reasons of state entailed in his agreement with the British. Persuaded that the city was going to fall and that the flag of the new state of Israel might indeed soon fly over the mosque in which his father was buried, Abdullah now wanted his men to take Jerusalem, not just threaten it. Deliberately ignoring his army's chain of command, he chose to give his order not to its English commander, who might raise again his wise objections, but to a man whose emotions he knew would lead him to act within the hour, a fellow Arab like himself.

"*Ya habibi,* my dear," he told Tell, "I saw the Palestinian leaders you sent me. We cannot wait any longer. Go save Jerusalem."

In Jerusalem, the temporary lull in the firing had not reassured the Arabs. At his gunport on the wall above Jaffa Gate, Peter Saleh waited for the rush that would carry his foes inside the city. Hundreds of frightened civilians gathered at St. Stephen's Gate waiting to flee if the wall was breached. From Mount Scopus, Haganah observers caught an occasional glimpse of others who had already begun their flight plodding toward the Mount of Olives.

On the other side of the city, Shaltiel's headquarters and Ephraim Levi debated whether or not to renew the attack. Although none of Salamon's sappers had gotten close to the gate at the base of the Citadel, his assault platoons were largely unscathed. Shaltiel urged him to try one more time. Levi resisted. The Arab irregulars' inability to conserve their dwindling ammunition supplies was about, perhaps, to deprive their foes of the Old City of Jerusalem for two decades. Since their fire had not slackened in pace with their disappearing supplies, Levi had no way of knowing how desperate the Arabs' situation was. To attack again, he argued, would lead to unacceptable casualties. Shaltiel finally agreed.

It would be twenty years before an Israeli flag would fly from the Tower of David.

A few minutes later, at Rawdah School, a call from Amman informed Mounir Abou Fadel that the Legion was on the way. A noisy celebration immediately revived the dispirited Arab headquarters. Abou Fadel sent an order to the men on the walls: "Hold on at all costs. Help is coming. Our brother Arabs are on the way."

Opposite Jaffa Gate, Netanel Lorch and his men were ordered to barricade the windows of the Tannous Building with sandbags. Lorch could not find any dirt inside the building, and it was too dangerous to dig outside. He ordered his men to stuff their bags with an unlikely filling in a city as hungry as Jerusalem, the sandwiches made at such sacrifice by the mothers of the city. In a few days, Lorch reasoned, they ought to be hard enough to stop a rifle bullet.

34

"A LAMENT FOR A GENERATION"

MAJOR ABDULLAH TELL stared down the Mount of Olives to the darkened community at his feet, its skyline illuminated by the occasional flash of an exploding grenade. "The most important city in the world," Tell thought, and it had just been entrusted to his care. An avid student of history, Tell knew that it was on this hilltop that the Caliph Omar, son of a black slave, become the successor of Mohammed, had accepted the city's surrender and brought it its first Islamic rule. How much blood had the centuries mixed with its soil? he wondered, aware he would soon add still more to it.

One of Tell's infantry companies, ordered to the Mount of Olives at sunset, had followed from the hilltop the sound and glare of the battle for Jaffa Gate. Tell had no intention of throwing his battalion piecemeal into Jerusalem, but the urgency of Abdullah's call and the pleas of the irregulars rushing to the Mount of Olives from the city led him to order Captain Mahmoud Moussa to send fifty men into Jerusalem immediately. He reasoned that their presence would bolster its defenders' sagging morale until the rest of his men arrived.

Tell and Moussa watched the shadowy figures move slowly down the Mount of Olives toward the Garden of Gethsemane and St. Stephen's Gate. Forty minutes later, at 3:40 A.M. on Tuesday, May 18, a lime-green signal flare cut a parabola across Jerusalem's black skyline. Although John Glubb still did not know it, the men of the army he had wanted to keep out of Jerusalem were now on the ramparts of the Old City.

At about the same time, a laconic four-word message was being relayed to David Shaltiel's headquarters. "We have Mount Zion," it read. If Shaltiel's assault on Jaffa Gate had failed, Uzi Narciss' diversion, at least, had succeeded. The ideal springboard into the Old City was in Jewish hands. Barely fifteen feet separated Narciss' Palmachniks and the walls of the Old City itself.

Listening to the despairing pleas for help from his besieged comrades only yards away, Narciss resolved to break into the Jewish Quarter as

438

soon as possible. His men's fatigue and an Arab mortar round on a truck bringing him a Davidka ruled out his hopes of a daytime attack. He was certain, however, he could break in under cover of darkness. He promised Shaltiel that he would smash through Zion Gate and establish a corridor along the rear of the Armenian Quarter to the Street of the Jews. Once he had, the Jerusalem commander would have only to provide the forces to hold the gate and the corridor. By midmorning, Narciss announced to his men that everything was ready. Shaltiel's headquarters would provide a force to exploit their success. This time it was sure. That night they would relieve the siege of the Jewish Quarter.

At about the same time on the other side of the Old City walls, Captain Moussa made a startling discovery. The towerlike structure of Zion Gate through which Narciss' men would rush into the city was deserted. Its irregular defenders had fled after the fall of Mount Zion. Moussa rushed to reoccupy it, together with the buildings adjacent to the gate itself. The door into the Old City, left briefly ajar by the fleeing irregulars, had been slammed shut.

Yosef Atiyeh, a bespectacled schoolteacher, was about to go home for lunch when he was ordered to the courtyard of the Schneller School.

It was going to be almost a year before Yosef Atiyeh would get home for lunch. With the half-trained men around him, he was, as one of Shaltiel's subordinates declared, going "to save the Old City." Some of the men gathered at Schneller barely knew how to handle a rifle, but they represented the only force Shaltiel was able to find in his strained command to exploit Uzi Narciss' attack on Zion Gate. The man he had selected to lead them, Mordechai Gazit, was appalled by his first sight of these men, dressed in ordinary street clothes, without any organization or structure. He appointed the most martial-looking among them as his sergeant major. The choice turned out to be a poor one. The man would desert in a few hours.

Shaltiel issued each man a new Czech rifle, eighty rounds of ammunition and four hand grenades. It was, Atiyeh noticed, the first ammunition some of his comrades had seen. As uniforms, they were issued British left-behinds captured in Bevingrad and U.S. Navy gunnery helmets. Designed to be worn with earphones under them, they wobbled like soup tureens on the men's heads.

From the beginning there was confusion about their task. Gazit thought their job was to reinforce Mount Zion. Narciss expected them to man Zion Gate and push into the Armenian Quarter. Most of the men thought they would be porters bringing supplies to the Jewish Quarter and would return home at dawn.

While this unlikely troop assembled, two men puzzled over a maze of metal spread on the floor of one of the classrooms of the Schneller School. They represented the parts of two Czech machine guns flown to Jerusalem by Piper Cub to give covering fire to the attack. Bobby Reisman had recruited Carmi Charny, the soft-spoken rabbi's son from the Bronx, to man one of them, but neither man had any idea of how to assemble the guns. Swallowing their pride, the two Americans finally sent for the foremost expert on machine guns in Jerusalem, a former ordnance sergeant of the Red Army.

• • •

Once the ochre wings of Ramallah's Grand Hotel had welcomed to its luxuriant gardens the gourmets of Jerusalem. It was not its Moroccan couscous or chicken Musaghan that had drawn to its terraces a uniformed group of men this Tuesday evening, May 18. The Grand Hotel was the headquarters of John Glubb's senior deputy, Brigadier Norman Lash.

Confronted by the King's *fait accompli* in ordering Abdullah Tell to Jerusalem, Glubb had meditated all day on the dilemma before him. Clearly, he could not rescind the King's command and order Major Tell to leave Jerusalem. Committed to the city, he now had to make certain that the force stationed there was large enough to rule out the possibility of defeat. "I have decided to intervene in force in Jerusalem," he cabled Lash. The die, as he was later to write, was cast.

Pouring himself a whiskey and soda, Lash told the officers around him that a task force composed of a score of armored cars and three infantry companies would move south from the Ramallah area to join Tell's men in the city. Lash wrote out the task force's assignment on a sheet of paper. Behind a dawn artillery barrage, it would drive the Haganah from Jerusalem's northern buttress, the Arab quarter of Sheikh Jarrah, and proceed to Damascus Gate to link up with Tell's forces.

A few minutes later, Colonel Bill Newman, the Australian commander of the Legion's Third Regiment, and Major Bob Slade, his Scottish deputy appointed to lead the task force, assembled their Arab officers under an apricot tree outside the village of Kalandia. Spreading his maps in the white glare of a storm lantern, Newman stabbed his finger at Jerusalem. "That's where we're going," he said. An explosion of joy and shrieks of delight drowned his words. Newman looked up astonished. Beside him

Lieutenant Fendi Omeish, an artillery officer, noticed tears in the Australian's eyes.

"Why?" the lieutenant said. "It's wonderful."

"No," replied Newman in a half-whisper. "They're sending my Bedouins into a fight they're not trained for."

As Newman finished his briefing, the news of the regiment's mission raced through the bivouac. By their tents, trucks and armored cars, his Bedouin soldiers began to sing, to dance the *dabke,* to pray. The villagers who a few hours before had jeered at their inactivity rushed up with fruit, flowers and sweets for these men whom Allah had chosen to defend the Holy City.

In less than twenty-four hours, there would be over one thousand of those soldiers in the city with their armored cars and artillery. The assault that a score of exhausted Palmachniks were preparing to launch on Zion Gate was going to be David Shaltiel's last chance to seize Jerusalem. By nightfall tomorrow the Haganah's hopes of capturing its ancient ramparts would have disappeared. Then the situation would be reversed and it would be Shaltiel who, with a dwindling ammunition supply and a half-starved city behind him, would have to cling to the stones of Jerusalem until help could reach him.

A tightly rolled map of Palestine pinned like a swagger stick under his arm, John Glubb gravely walked into the residence of Sir Alec Kirkbride, Britain's resident minister in Amman. The two men were close friends. Defying the snide remarks of detractors who were certain he came to receive orders from His Majesty's government, Glubb frequently called on the diplomat, whose wisdom and experience he appreciated.

Tonight Glubb needed all the consolation he could get. His hopes of offering his soldiers only the semblance of a war were collapsing. Carefully he unrolled his meticulously drafted British Army map on Kirkbride's dining-room table. Traced upon it was a sweeping curve joining Bethlehem, Ramallah and Nablus, its arc passing well outside Jerusalem. It indicated the limited objectives he had assigned to his forces on their entry into Palestine, and it was well inside the area assigned to an Arab state by the partition plan. As he had secretly informed the Haganah a fortnight earlier, he had hoped to wait out a diplomatic agreement between the warring parties in those positions. Now the crisis in Jerusalem had confronted him with a new situation. He had committed his men to the city; he would have to fight for it. As Abdul Khader Husseini's guerrilla campaign had shown, the key to Jerusalem lay in the gorges of Bab el Wad. Morosely, Glubb asked Kirkbride what he thought of the situation.

Kirkbride leaned over Glubb's map. "Well," he said after a brief reflection, "you've had to go into Jerusalem, and it seems to me what happens in Jerusalem is going to be decided in Latrun. You'll have to go down there."

Glubb hesitated a moment. Placing his Legion in strength on the historic hills would pose a challenge that the Jewish army could not ignore. It would have to drive him off those heights or lose Jerusalem.

"You're right," he said quietly, "but you realize that if I move into Latrun, that means we're going to have a real war on our hands."

A strangely peaceful carillon rolled down the darkened hills that were the center of Glubb's and Kirkbride's preoccupations. As they did every night, the church bells of the Trappist Monastery of the Seven Agonies of Latrun summoned the community's forty monks to herald the birth of a new day with the mournful mutter of their Latin matins.

Those monks and their predecessors had built with their own hands the imposing array of buildings whose arched windows looked down upon the strategic crossroads of Latrun. Just three miles from their monastery, after cutting across the fringe of their six-hundred-acre domain, the road to Jerusalem entered the treacherous gorge of Bab el Wad. Kaukji's troops had dug into the crest line above their buildings, and it was through their wheatfields and vineyards that the soldiers of the Givati Brigade had moved to their brief conquest of the abandoned British police station at the limit of their estate.

From October 31, 1890, when seventeen French Monks had reached that hilltop over the Valley of Ayalon to found their monastery on its historic slopes, the sleep of Latrun's Trappist community had been regularly marred by that nightly summons to prayer. It marked the ritual beginning point in a life dedicated to silence, prayer and labor on the land. With half a century of effort, Latrun's monks had turned their fields into an agricultural enterprise as flourishing as any of Palestine's kibbutzim. Their twenty Dutch cows and the bees whose angry attack had startled the men of the Palmach had helped return their valley to its Biblical promise as a land of milk and honey.

The monastery owed its real renown to yet another product of its domain, a product sought after by the connoisseurs of the Middle East. Swollen by the sun that had stood still for Joshua, the grapes of Latrun's vineyards were transformed into Pommard, Chablis or cognac by a Belgian theologian whose two passions were the dogma of the Incarnation and the mysteries of enology. The caves of Father Martin Godart stretched for dozens of yards below Latrun's vital crossroads. In that troubled May of 1948 when the Valley of Ayalon was about to revert to its ancient calling as a battleground, Father Godart's cellars harbored a treasure that could have reconciled all the claimants to Latrun's crossroads in a common alcoholic euphoria: 78,200 liters of Pommard and Chablis, 26,000 liters of cognac and 12,000 liters of vermouth, curaçao and crème de menthe.

His back bent under forty pounds of plasma and ammunition, Yosef Atiyeh stumbled through the darkness toward the crest of Mount Zion. Breathing heavily from the unaccustomed exertion, the eighty middle-aged men and young recruits who, with Atiyeh, were supposed to save the Old City struggled along behind him. Uzi Narciss exploded with fury when they reached the top. Was this sorrowful troop the company of men Shaltiel had promised him? he asked Gazit.

Seething with anger, he called Shaltiel. To the Jerusalem commander's pleas that he too was short of men, Narciss replied, "Don't bring me your bloody troubles, I've got enough of my own. You damn well organize your men yourself."

"What the hell," he told Gazit, "take your men inside as reinforcements." Gazit protested that his men weren't prepared, that they had been promised they wouldn't be away from their families for more than twenty-four hours. Narciss shrugged. It was too late for that now. Take over Mount Zion, he ordered Gazit, so that he could assemble his exhausted Palmachniks for the assault.

There were forty of them, all that remained of four hundred who had set out for Jerusalem in Operation Nachshon six weeks before. David "Dado" Elazar, the young officer who had led the assault on the monastery in Katamon, had to call for volunteers for the first time in his career. He picked twenty-two, twenty men and two girls. Like everyone else in the Palmach, they had been living for days on Novadrin pep pills and had reached a state of such total exhaustion that a pill now had no more effect than an aspirin.

At twenty minutes past two a Davidka and three two-inch mortars opened fire on Zion Gate. One of the Davidka shells fell short and its explosion deprived the attacking force of two of its members. As the barrage lifted, two sappers ran forward and placed 165 pounds of explosive at the base of the gate. They exploded in a whistling blast of stone and shattered masonry.

Dado sprang up. "Follow me!" he shouted to the men hunched along the wall of the Armenian Cemetery behind him. As he raced forward, he suddenly made a disconcerting discovery. No one was following him. He looked back and through the darkness saw his men still slumped against the wall. He ran to the first one. A strange sound was rising from the line of soldiers. It was snoring. They were all sound asleep. He went down the line kicking them awake one by one. Then, with twenty grumpy, half-sleeping soldiers, he charged Zion Gate for a second time.

From a window in the Armenian Convent, Lieutenant Nawaf Jaber el Hamoud saw half a dozen of his men scramble toward him from the tower of Zion Gate. "The tower, the tower!" he cried. "Don't abandon the tower. Go back."

It was too late. Dado Elazar's men had already seized it. Twenty exhausted men and two women had done something no Jewish soldier had done since the days of Judas Maccabaeus—they had breached the walls of Jerusalem. Zion Gate was back in Jewish hands, its portals opened not by the rusting key proffered by a British officer but by an explosive manufactured in the cellars of Jewish Jerusalem. In small groups, Elazar's men leapfrogged down the line of Armenian shops to the Street of the Jews. Just after three they radioed Narciss, "We're in."

Lieutenant el Hamoud debated whether to launch a counterattack. Captain Moussa, after suffering three flesh wounds, had withdrawn to the Mount of Olives, leaving him in charge. Troubled, Hamoud decided to remain in his positions until Moussa returned. The passage into the besieged Jewish Quarter was secured.

The quarter's elated inhabitants swarmed over the Palmach men. Hundreds of depressed and homeless people packed into the Rabbi Jochanan ben Zakai Synagogue began to weep and embrace them. The company's garrulous political officer, Benny Marshak, thought he had "never gotten so many kisses." Some of the quarter's defenders, assured that they were about to be relieved, began to pack their suitcases.

Outside, on Mount Zion, Gazit was ordered to "get your people and get in quickly." Carrying their loads of plasma and ammunition, their bulky U. S. Navy helmets giving them a grotesque look, Gazit's protesting men were driven in as fast as he could round them up. At Zion Gate, some of them refused to go in, claiming that they were their parents' only sons and thus exempt from combat. The Palmachnik at the gate forced them ahead with a wave of his Sten gun.

Shmuel Bazak was greeted on arriving by Esther Cailingold, who offered him a glass of warm milk. Yosef Atiyeh, sent to relieve the guard at the

Porat Yosef Synagogue where his father had been the head of a yeshiva, found himself deluged by his father's former pupils.

The excitement of the Palmach's breakthrough brought everyone rushing out of the hospital. Only the nurse beside him heard the muffled cry escaping from the bandage-shrouded figure of Emmanuel Meidav. She shook awake his fiancée, sleeping at the feet of the handsome young officer who had been so admired in the quarter. Since Emmanuel had been wounded, Rika Menache had not left his side, feeding him liquids with a spoon, sponging the sweat from his fevered body.

In the doorway another nurse appeared with a bearded Palmachnik. "Look," she said, pointing to him, "they broke in. We're saved!"

At that moment an anguished scream from Rika filled the room. "Don't, don't," she pleaded. The two nurses looked at her. The Palmach had arrived too late for the boy with the golden hands. Rika was already sobbing on the chest of her dead fiancé.

When Mordechai Gazit, now the senior officer in the Old City, arrived at headquarters, Moshe Russnak informed him, "I'm going to sleep." He had been without sleep for five days, he said. His deputy, Mordechai Pincus, promptly imitated him. Gazit was unable to arouse the exhausted men. Then he got the worst news of his trying day. The Palmach was withdrawing back to Mount Zion.

The decision was an agonizing one for Narciss to take, but Elazar's exhausted men were incapable of going on without rest. Leaving them at Zion Gate would only lead, Narciss feared, "to a lot of blame and a lot of dead." Shaltiel had failed to send him the men who could hold the gate. He felt he had no choice.

Jerusalem was going to pay for the rivalry and lack of communication between the Palmach and the Haganah.

Staggering with fatigue, the bone-weary Palmachniks came out at dawn. The Jewish Quarter was once more in a state of siege. It would be two decades before a Jewish soldier would breach those walls again— "a lament for a generation," in the words of the man who breached them that night, Dado Elazar.*

---

* Narciss saw Shaltiel's failure as a breach of promise and would always suspect that Shaltiel had not been prepared because he had not really believed the Palmach could break in. To Shaltiel, Narciss' decision to withdraw was placing the priorities of the Palmach above those of the city.

35

"YOSEF HAS SAVED JERUSALEM!"

THE RUMBLE of artillery ripped apart the fragile silence shrouding the Judean hills. Once again the cannon of the Arab Legion pounded Jerusalem, this time opening the way for the Legion's entry in force into the city. In the darkness, a file of armored cars, motors turning, waited for the barrage to lift. Behind them in trucks and half-tracks, the infantry of Lieutenant Abdullah Salam nervously watched for the order to move forward. Salam, a dark-skinned Bedouin from Iraq, had requested the honor of leading the attack. It was the most memorable moment of the young officer's life. He was about to enter the Holy City of Jerusalem for the first time.

With the methods taught them by their British Army instructors, the Legion's gunners walked their fire forward, shifting it to the orthodox quarter of Mea Shearim. The deep barks of three-inch mortars joined the barrage. The streets of Mea Shearim suddenly filled with frightened, half-dressed people thrown from their beds by the shelling, desperately scurrying about in search of a shelter or rushing toward the center of town. Everywhere a terrible rumor swept the crowd: "The Legion is coming!" Nor were the civilians alone in their fright. Some of the members of the Irgun defending the Police Training School at the entrance to Sheikh Jarrah began to flee, too.

At four-thirty, at about the time the last of Uzi Narciss' Palmachniks were withdrawing from Zion Gate, the fire stopped and Major Bob Slade ordered his men into Jerusalem. On the rooftops of the Palestine Broadcasting System building from which his Beza machine gun had been giving the Palmach cover fire all night, Carmi Charny saw them come. The sight made his blood run cold. Majestically they rolled toward the heart of Jerusalem, "as imperturbably as if they were in a parade."

On the rooftop of Mea Shearim's Tipat Chalav, in which he had installed his advance headquarters, Yitzhak Levi, the man who had driven the Arabs from Sheikh Jarrah five days earlier, also watched the line of advancing armor. A far more dismaying sight held the attention of Shal-

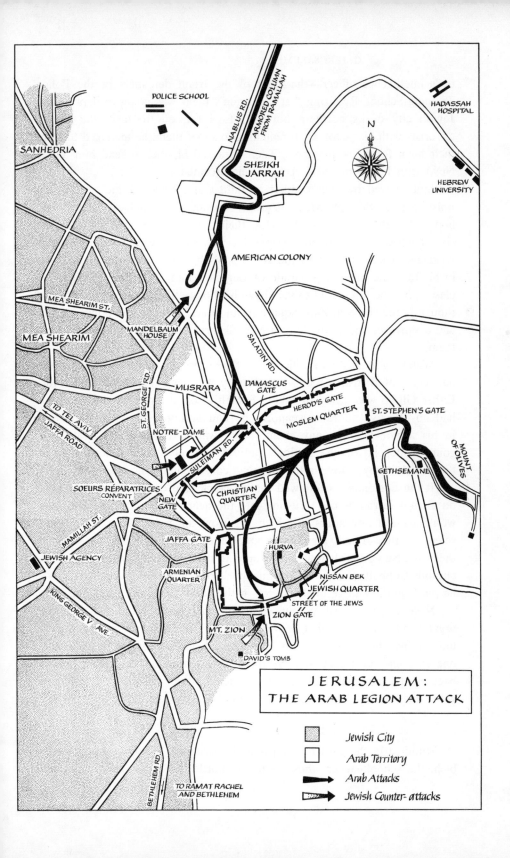

POLICE SCHOOL

SANHEDRIA

NABLUS RD.

ARMORED COLUMN FROM RAMALLAH

SHEIKH JARRAH

N

HADASSAH HOSPITAL

HEBREW UNIVERSITY

AMERICAN COLONY

MEA SHEARIM ST.

MEA SHEARIM

MANDELBAUM HOUSE

ST. GEORGE RD.

SALADIN RD.

MUSRARA

DAMASCUS GATE

HEROD'S GATE

MOSLEM QUARTER

ST. STEPHEN'S GATE

TO TEL AVIV

JAFFA ROAD

NOTRE-DAME

SULEIMAN RD.

MOUNT OF OLIVES

SOEURS RÉPARATRICES CONVENT

GETHSEMANE

CHRISTIAN QUARTER

NEW GATE

JAFFA GATE

HURVA

MAMILLAH ST.

JEWISH AGENCY

ARMENIAN QUARTER

NISSAN BEK

JEWISH QUARTER

STREET OF THE JEWS

KING GEORGE V AVE.

ZION GATE

MT. ZION

DAVID'S TOMB

JERUSALEM:
THE ARAB LEGION ATTACK

BETHLEHEM RD.

TO RAMAT RACHEL AND BETHLEHEM

Jewish City

Arab Territory

Arab Attacks

Jewish Counter-attacks

tiel's intelligence officer—the flight of the Irgun defenders of the Police Training School. Realizing that the Irgun's flight was going to deprive the Jewish city of its northern bulwark, Levi ran out to meet the fleeing terrorists with his pistol. By threatening to shoot them, he managed to stem their flight for a few moments. Then he asked Shaltiel to send him Yosef Nevo with his "armored force" as reinforcements.

Still scarred by their combat at Jaffa Gate, Nevo's vehicles staged a noisy parade through Mea Shearim. Jerusalem's unluckiest bridegroom hoped that the sight of his vehicles, their turrets hastily painted with the six-branched star of the new Army of Israel, would reassure its distraught residents. Then he went to the rooftop of the Tipat Chalav, to discover in his turn the oncoming parade of Legion armor. Watching through his glasses, he, too felt a cold shiver shake his body. "If they keep coming," he thought, "they'll be in Zion Square in an hour." Beyond the police station and a skirmish line below him in Mea Shearim, there was nothing to stop them.

Watching them, Nevo noticed that they were violating one of the cardinal tenets of British tactics—the infantry was lagging behind the armor. Either Glubb was afraid of taking casualties or, aware that the Haganah had no effective antitank weapons, he had accepted the risk of moving in his armor first. In any event, Nevo was sure Jerusalem's fate was going to depend on the Legion's faithful adherence to another adage of the British Army: Move in the morning, consolidate in the afternoon.

If the Legionnaires followed that principle and consolidated their hold on Sheikh Jarrah before thrusting into the heart of the city, the Haganah would have a few hours in which to throw up a defense to save Jerusalem. If they didn't, then Nevo knew they would not be able to stop them. All New Jerusalem would be open to them. Nevo telephoned his conclusions to Shaltiel. The city commander's response was straightforward— he put Nevo in charge of the sector, with orders to stop the Legion.

Nevo hung up and announced to the men in the confused and disorganized headquarters that he was in charge. He named the most military-looking man in the room as his adjutant and ordered him to throw everyone who had no urgent business there out of headquarters. Then he ran back to his command car to survey for himself the slender resources with which he was supposed to check Glubb's armored cars.

• • •

Huddled in the garden of an American seminary, Bajhat Abou Gharbieh, the schoolteacher whose disparate horde of Syrians and Iraqis had been the only Arab force to effectively resist the Haganah in Jerusalem, wondered if the shells dropping around him were Arab or Jewish. Looking back toward Sheikh Jarrah, he too discovered the imposing column of armored cars grinding toward the city. He snorted his satisfaction. Then, as he lowered his weary eyes, his gaze fell on a rose. The ferocious little warrior leaned over, plucked it, stuffed it into the muzzle of his submachine gun, and lay down to sleep. Jerusalem's fate, he thought with relief, was now in better armed hands than his.

On the hilltop above Sheikh Jarrah, Lieutenant Abdullah Salam threw himself on the ground at his first glimpse of Jerusalem's skyline. The devout Bedouin kissed the earth three times in fervent thanks to his One and Merciful God. The same mystic sense of mission ran through the Arab soldiers behind him. Inspired by those beckoning rooftops of the Holy City, the column plunged forward.

Major Slade's men encountered little opposition from the Police Training School, and soon, he would recall, "we were having ourselves a fine little attack." At the first turning in Sheikh Jarrah, Slade came upon an imposing barricade of stones, logs and barbed wire. He jumped out of his car to help his men dismantle the roadblock. As he did, a crashing explosion tore the ground at his feet. One of his units' mortar rounds had fallen short. His back and buttocks lacerated by shrapnel, Slade fell to the ground unconscious. Behind him, his body pointing toward Jerusalem, another officer lay dead. Lieutenant Abdullah Salam would not reach the city that had fed the dreams of his boyhood in the deserts of Iraq.

From a rooftop in Mea Shearim, Yosef Nevo watched in astonishment as the advancing chain of cars ground to a halt, then began to pull back toward the ridge above Sheikh Jarrah. Begun with such élan, the Legion's attack was faltering at the sudden disappearance of two key officers. Nevo, of course, could not know the reasons behind the action, nor did he bother to wonder. Only one thing mattered. The Legion was offering him the gift he needed most: time.

• • •

Pinchas the Strong peeped cautiously from his trench at the southern end of the Street of the Jews, the Jewish Quarter's main street. Ahead was the tower of Zion Gate. To his astonishment, Pinchas caught a glimpse of a red-and-white kaffiyeh fluttering between the crags of the tower. Like most of the quarter's defenders, he didn't know that the Palmach had pulled back to Mount Zion. "Hey, men," he whispered, "are the Arabs up there?"

449

The reply was the slap of a sniper's bullet smacking into the wall above his head. Captain Mahmoud Moussa, his wounds treated, had returned to the city at sunup with the rest of his company. He had immediately ordered Zion Gate retaken and had launched a probe of the quarter's defenses to measure the reinforcements that had slipped in during the night. Pinchas the Strong and his fellows were quickly driven from their trench back into the quarter's lifeline, the Street of the Jews.

They leaped over the sandbag barricades set up in the middle of the street while, behind them, hastily called-up reinforcements jumped into doorways and shop windows and onto rooftops. Little boys scurried after them carrying boxes of Leah Vultz's homemade grenades. From a nearby roof, other children called corrections to a grenade launcher set up in a courtyard below, their nervous, high-pitched cries cutting through the roar of the firing like the shriek of seagulls over the pounding of a heavy surf.

Mordechai Gazit joined the reserves heading for the Street of the Jews. With one of his new command's most able fighters, a curly-haired Kurdish Jew nicknamed Yitzhak the Bren Gunner, he led a successful counterattack.

Then Gazit climbed up the tile roof of a Talmud Torah * to watch the Legion's retreat. As he did, one of his girl soldiers called out, "Don't go there!"

It was too late. A sniper's shot hit the quarter's new commander full in the chest. Staggering under the blow, Gazit saw blood spurting from his chest like water from a hose. As he began to lose consciousness, an anguished thought slipped through the young diplomat's mind: Was he simply fainting or was he living the very last moments in his life?

As he had been taught in his machine-gunner's course, Carmi Charny's first action after his night's firing was to break down and clean his new Beza machine gun. Its parts were scattered around a bedroom opposite Fink's Restaurant when Charny received an urgent message: Get the gun to Sheikh Jarrah, the Legion was attacking.

Imitating the movements of the machine-gun expert who had helped him the night before, Charny tried to reassemble his gun. It was hopeless. Every ten minutes a frantic knock on the door reminded him to hurry. Unwilling to expose the gun's state, Charny answered each frantic appeal with the promise that the Beza was almost ready. Finally Charny was

---

* A religious school devoted to Biblical studies.

forced to open the bedroom door and admit that the Beza was in pieces. Once again the American was obliged to send out an embarrassed call for help to the city's Red Army arms expert.

Yosef Nevo had urgent need for Charny's gun. Since he obviously did not have the forces to hold a line all along Mea Shearim, he had decided on a gamble and the machine gun figured prominently in it. Betting that the Legion would continue to advance its armor first and its infantry second, Nevo decided to prepare for an armored assault. The Legion had two logical axes of attack. One was across an open field from the Police Training School to the neighborhood of Sanhedria, at the northern end of Mea Shearim. It was the shortest route and the one that would lead most directly to the heart of Jewish Jerusalem. The other was through Sheikh Jarrah, up to the vital intersection commanded by the Mandelbaum house, leading into Mea Shearim. Over that route the advancing Legion would have only one exposed flank, and it was there that Nevo guessed they would attack. He decided to divide his forces between Sanhedria and Mandelbaum, with his best weapons at the second position. His center he would leave virtually unprotected.

At Mandelbaum, his force consisted of Jacob Ben-Ur and the teenage soldiers of the Gadna who had greeted the Sabbath of May 14 in their improvised synagogue. Nevo ordered them to smash holes in the second-story windows of the house so that they could hurl Molotov cocktails on the cars. Under cover of darkness, he would conceal the most effective part of his miserable "armored force," two armored cars, a pair of bazookas and a Davidka, in hidden positions dominating the intersection. He also instructed the Gadna to mine a pair of houses on St. George Road below their positions. By blowing them up after a few cars had passed, Nevo hoped to split the lead vehicles off from the rest of an attack force. At Sanhedria, Nevo posted a pair of machine guns. If the Legion chose to attack them, he told his gunners, they would just have to hold out until he could get help to them. As for Charny and his Beza, he would be Nevo's central reserve, to be brought out once the Legion had committed itself.

By midnight, most of Nevo's preparations were completed. He briefed his men by candlelight in the cellar of his Tipat Chalav headquarters. Nevo had two concerns: that the Legion would throw its infantry against his almost undefended center or launch a two-pronged attack against Sanhedria and Mandelbaum. In either case, the result was easy to predict. They would break through.

He did not reveal his fears to his subordinates. Listening to him, Carmi Charny marveled at how calm and assured he seemed to be. There was,

Charny knew, "an air of dread and fear" hanging over them all that night. Nevo's tranquil air, he reasoned, must be "the calm of despair."

Well before first light, the Legion's mortars began to methodically work over Mea Shearim once again. The quarter's residents who had returned to their homes after Nevo's intervention the day before showed signs of renewed panic. Some began to flee the neighborhood without even waiting for the dawn. Trying to catch a few hours' sleep in the cellar of his headquarters, Nevo was awakened by the first explosions. Lying in the darkness, he realized that the providential pause the Legion had offered him was over. They would be on him with the sunrise.

In the hills above Mea Shearim, Major John Buchanan, Slade's replacement, assembled his men for a new push into the city. In the lead armored car, Lieutenant Mohammed Negib fidgeted nervously. An artillery observer, Negib was urgently needed in the center of the city to help correct the army's mortar fire. Negib's driver, Mohammed Abdallah, shared his impatience. A Bedouin from northern Transjordan, Abdallah had never been to Jerusalem. The route he was to take into the city, however, had been clearly set out for him. After the hairpin turn at the base of Sheikh Jarrah, he would go straight down Nablus Road to Damascus Gate.

Nevo watched the cars move slowly, ponderously, down the hill into Sheikh Jarrah "as though they had all the time in the world." "The bastards are trying to frighten us," he thought. "They think they're unbeatable." Fright, in any event, was the effect they had on the thirty men Nevo had held with him at Tipat Chalav as a reserve. Some of them shook so badly that they couldn't stand up. All refused to leave the safety of the headquarters cellar.

Nevo pulled out his pistol and pointed it at the first man. "Get out of here before I count three or I shoot," he warned. As he began to count, the trembling man started out the door.

When all the men were outside, Nevo ordered them to attention and gave them a loud oration. Then, in the cellar, Carmi Charny heard their shaking voices begin to sing "Hatikvah." As their song gained in strength, Nevo marched them off singing to their positions.

When he came back, he announced to Charny, "O.K., it's your turn now."

Charny felt his mouth go dry and his knees shake as he stood up. Carrying his heavy machine gun on his back, the aspiring poet followed Nevo. Behind him, two friends hauled belts of cartridges for the gun. Nevo took them to a rock-strewn field at the edge of Mea Shearim. Three hundred yards ahead was a road and, looming behind it, the Police Training School. "Crawl out into that field as far as you can go and pick a rock to give you some cover," Nevo ordered. "When you open fire, give them long bursts. Make them think you've got all the ammunition in the world."

Charny tried not to think. He was terribly frightened, and each forward movement seemed to demand an immense ration of willpower. At the barbed-wire fence marking the entry into the field, he paused to catch his breath. "Keep moving," Nevo shouted. He crawled on. As he neared the rock outcropping on which he had decided to place his weapon, he passed a line of riflemen lying in the fields. One was a friend. They nodded *shalom*. Hands trembling and his breath coming in quick, nervous gulps, Charny set up his gun. When he had finished, he turned to look at his friend. He was lying on his back, his mouth hanging open, his head torn asunder as though it had been parted by a meat ax.

At that horrible image, a strange change came over the terrified Charny. Looking at his dead friend, he thought, "That's it. That's the worst that can happen." Suddenly he became totally calm and detached, as cool and rational as if he were preparing to write a dissertation on the Law.

Two Legion armored cars pulled out of the advancing line and began to swing down a dirt track some fifty yards from Charny's gun. They were so close that he could see the trademarks on their tires. As Nevo had ordered, he opened fire in long bursts as though his Beza were a Sten gun. "Wholly, fanatically, concentrated," he watched his rounds hitting the car and its tires.

Not far away, on the second floor of the Mandelbaum house, one of the Gadna teenagers cried, "There they are!"

The young men who six days earlier had been praying that peace might descend on Jerusalem clutched their bottles of Molotov cocktails and pressed their backs to the wall of the house. Jacob Ben-Ur started to count as one by one the Legion armored cars slid into view on the road through Sheikh Jarrah. In a chorus of growing awe, the boys around him began to repeat each number after him. As the count mounted past ten, someone asked, "How many shells do they have for the bazooka downstairs?"

"Three," someone replied.

"No," came another, more satisfying answer. "Seven." Ben-Ur's count continued until he had reached the terrifying total of seventeen Legion armored cars.

Mishka Rabinovitch, a twenty-eight-year-old Russian-born veteran of the British Army, crouched with the bazooka behind a pile of stones, looking down St. George Road. Rabinovitch had his seven shells, but the Haganah was deprived that morning of one of its prime assets, the accuracy of its best gunner. A few days earlier, the premature explosion of a Davidka shell had torn off part of Rabinovitch's right hand. To answer Nevo's call, he had fled the hospital.

If he couldn't shoot his bazooka, he could at least aim it. Peering through its lens, he sighted on a sign fifty yards down St. George Road reading "Jerusalem—one kilometer." Turning to the young Pole beside him, he whispered, "When 'Jerusalem—one kilometer' disappears behind the first car, fire."

Nevo, from his headquarters' roof, watched the "slow, maddeningly confident march forward" of the cars. The line advanced to the intersection of St. George Road and Nablus Road. There was a moment of hesitation. Then Nevo felt his throat go taut. The column was moving up St. George Road, straight into his trap.

Eliyahu, the young Pole next to Rabinovitch, watched the lead car creep slowly toward his bazooka. That car should not in fact have been in the gunsight of his weapon. It was there because in his haste to get into the Holy City, the Bedouin driving the lead car, Mohammad Abdallah, had taken the wrong turn. The imposing line of cars moving into town that morning was not supposed to conquer Jewish Jerusalem. Buchanan's orders to his men were to reach Damascus Gate and establish a continuous Arab line from Sheikh Jarrah to the Old City walls.

Rabinovitch held his breath as the youth slowly squeezed his trigger. The rocket leaped forward. Hit head on, the lead car was tossed to the side of the road. At that instant, Nevo noted with satisfaction, "all hell broke loose." The youth's shot unleashed the action which Nevo had been expecting but which the Legion had not planned for. Half a dozen cars moved to attack in aid of the crippled vehicle.

Inside, Lieutenant Negib, the artillery forward observer on his way to Damascus Gate, was dead. Mohammed Abdallah too had paid a terrible price for turning right instead of heading straight down Nablus Road. He pulled himself from his car and huddled for an instant behind his turret. From a nearby hotel window, British journalist Eric Downton watched his mates calling to him to jump to the ground and run. Then Abdallah, a grotesque dwarf with both legs reduced to bloody stumps by the bazooka shell, slid down the car to die in the street.

In the British Daimler armored car he had helped to steal a few weeks earlier, Reuven Tamir watched the other Legion cars moving up behind the smoking vehicle. He closed his eyes and fired his cannon. When he opened them, he saw only a hole in the house down the street. He fired again with no more luck. With the third shot, he shouted in triumph. Flames were gushing from the turret of a second armored car.

An intense battle swirled around the Mandelbaum house. Anxious to help their comrades, the Legion infantry rushed forward. When their red-and-white kaffiyehs moved into view, the teenagers of the Gadna hurled their remaining Molotov cocktails. From one window, Jacob Ben-Ur fired their sole machine gun. From another, his fiancée, Sarah Milstein, the daughter of a devoutly orthodox family, caught the figure of an advancing Legionnaire in her gunsight. She had never fired a weapon at a living thing. She was a nurse by training. "I can't kill him," she thought. She fired at the pavement at his feet. The Legionnaire turned and fled. Sarah lowered her rifle with a sigh of relief.

Surprised by the ferocity of the resistance to an attack they had not planned to make, the Legionnaires drew back to regroup and resume their original line of advance. At the sight of their cars withdrawing, a series of triumphant shouts echoed from the Mandelbaum house.

Nevo too watched with satisfaction. John Glubb's army had paid dearly for stumbling into his trap. Two cars were knocked out near Nevo's positions at Mandelbaum; a third, crippled by Carmi Charny's fire, lay farther down the road.

The news of the victory spread through Jerusalem in minutes. Its psychological importance was enormous. A group of Gadna teenagers had turned back the enemy the city feared most—the armored cars of the Arab Legion. The relief, the reassurance their action brought the city would be of incalculable importance in the days ahead. Its impact could be measured in the manner in which Naomi Nevo heard the news. A friend rushed up to her, weeping for joy, and threw her arms around Naomi's neck. "Naomi, Naomi," she cried, "Yosef has saved Jerusalem!"

36

"TAKE LATRUN."

Studiously ignoring the crash of the Arab Legion artillery fire in the streets outside, Dov Joseph continued his sermon to the men around him in one of the Jewish Agency's conference rooms.

"Idleness is the source of depression," he warned. "People should be encouraged to lead normal lives insofar as possible." He wanted civilians to continue going to their offices, shopping and otherwise living as they usually did. Despite the fact that Jerusalem was now under daily shellfire and they had nothing to sell anyway, Joseph decreed that food shops would remain open every day from eight to four. To keep people informed, they should publish a daily news bulletin. It would be called *The Voice of the Defender*.

No one gave a more convincing display of determined normalcy than the Canadian lawyer become Jewish Jerusalem's civilian chief. His cufflinks were fastened, his shoes were brushed, his tie was precisely knotted; only his soiled shirt betrayed the strain under which they all lived. In a Jerusalem short of water, it had not been laundered for a fortnight. Tenacious, taciturn, as sparing of his words as he was unsparing of his energies, Joseph was a dedicated, demanding leader who set an example he expected all around him to follow. He was, as one of his subordinates would observe, a man who "truly put Jerusalem above his highest joys."

Nothing escaped him. If a truck driver wanted five gallons of gasoline, Joseph wanted to know why. If a bakery was ten loaves short in its day's production, Joseph demanded an explanation. His day began with a phone call from Avraham Picker, his food expert, at 4 A.M. At seven o'clock, Joseph was in his office. His staff consisted of a personal assistant and two secretaries. Keeping up with him, one of them recalled, was "terribly hard." He never showed a sign of weakness, and he tolerated none in his subordinates.

Once, one of his exhausted secretaries began to doze as he dictated. "Mr. Joseph," she begged, "if you don't give me a little rest, I'll faint."

"If you do," he replied, "I'll throw water on you and we'll go on."

Half an hour after the daily food distribution was completed, Joseph entered the day's outlay himself on the chart in the orange folder he kept locked in his desk. There was no identifying label on its cover. No one else had access to the grim knowledge it contained, and Joseph had arranged his organization so that very few people knew the real state of the city's food supply. Like his employees, Joseph lived on the daily ration furnished by the Agency canteen, a sandwich of marmalade and halvah, and a cup of weak tea. The working day which began at four in the morning ended close to midnight with Joseph working alone in his office by the light of a single, battery-powered bulb.

Whenever he had a free moment, Joseph would walk through the city, repeating over and over again a phrase that had become his personal psalm: *"Yihiyeh tov.* It will be all right." Above all, in his dedicated pursuit of normalcy he urged his fellows to sit down three times a day in front of an unwashed plate and go through at least the motions of eating a meal.

The little that Joseph was able to put on those plates was an indication of how abnormal in fact the situation in Jerusalem was. The ration of the citizens of Jewish Jerusalem by May 20 amounted to nine hundred calories a day, just over half the daily ration of the Japanese civilian population in the last year of World War II, only two hundred calories more than the daily ration at the concentration camp of Bergen Belsen, about the equivalent of the ration given the inmates of Japan's prisoner-of-war camps.

The Arab shelling and the search for food were the city's preoccupations. By day the streets were deserted and, as Joseph observed, "a great stillness pervaded the city." Without electric current, its nights were dark and gloomy. To minimize both the effects of the Arab shelling and evaporation, the water ration was distributed in the middle of the night; nevertheless, six volunteer water carriers would be killed by shellfire during the siege. There was even a black market in water, at $2.65 a quart.

The Café Vienna was the city's trading exchange. Cigarettes were its currency, and by May 20 one cigarette was worth a loaf of bread, two cans of sardines or one can of herring. There were strange windfalls. One factory happened to have a supply of glucose. It was mixed with water to make a kind of energy-giving candy for the children.

Each Jerusalemite would have his special memory of these tragic days. For Ziporah Borowsky it was her return from a trip to downtown Jerusalem to pick up the one egg each that was allotted to her and her fellow students in a Bet Hakerem boardinghouse. Chosen by a lottery so that only one person would be exposed to Arab shellfire, she fell with her precious bundle on the boardinghouse steps. She promptly scraped up the broken eggs and converted them into a muddy omelette.

For Zev Benjamin, an enduring image would be the sight of Jerusalem's dogs. "They were so thin," he would recall, "they couldn't understand what was happening. They would run from garbage can to garbage can, only to find them as dry as they had been when they had come off the assembly line."

* * *

Carmi Charny and the machine-gun crew with which he had halted two Legion armored cars studied the thick walls of the building in which they had been ordered to set up their gun. Here at least, Charny thought, they'd be safe from the Legion's shellfire.

Exhausted after forty-eight hours of almost nonstop combat, the New Yorker stretched out on the floor to catch a few moments' sleep. As he began to doze, a strange and delicious odor tickled his nostrils. It was the smell of a delicacy so rare he had almost forgotten its existence—chocolate. Charny leaped up and with his comrades plunged into the next room. To their astonishment, they discovered they were in an abandoned chocolate factory. Frantically they began to search the building for some scrap of that precious substance left behind by the factory's owners. It was a fruitless search. All they found were a few bars so rancid that even the rats in the building wouldn't touch them.

A few hundred yards away, three other Haganah men crawled through the darkness in pursuit of a different treasure. Elbows and knees bleeding, their clothes torn, Yosef Nevo, Jacob Ben-Ur and Mishka Rabinovitch crept up on three dark shapes scattered down St. George Road. With their turrets full of ammunition, their cannons, their radios, the three abandoned Legion armored cars represented a potential windfall. If they could somehow be put back into service they would double Nevo's armored force, and he was determined to drag them back into his lines.

From a window of the Mandelbaum house, Sarah Milstein covered the trio with her fiancée's Bren gun. Convinced that an Arab sniper was tracking them, the nervous Rabinovitch thought he could hear the bones in his head cracking. He crawled to a pile of rubble for cover, then started, terrified. Pointing starkly into the night sky from the pile, like a tree ravaged by a forest fire, was a bone. He had hidden behind the remains of a Legionnaire caught by one of the Gadna's Molotov cocktails.

For fear that the cast on his wounded arm was shimmering in the starlight, Rabinovitch smeared it with mud before continuing his advance. He and Nevo fixed a rope to the car's front axle. With Jacob Ben-Ur manning its Bren gun, the Haganah's stolen British police armored car slipped down the road to pick up the tow. Rabinovitch climbed into the Legion car and slipped its gear into neutral. Slowly the lead car began to tug it up the road toward the Mandelbaum house.

A few minutes later, the operation was repeated with the second car. As it started to move, another dark object began to roll along the road in the opposite direction. It was the third car. While Nevo and his companions had been pursuing their salvage operation, Lieutenant Zaal Errhavel of the Arab Legion had been doing exactly the same thing a few dozen yards away, at the other end of the street.

.   .   .

Two thousand miles from Jerusalem, other men too were concerned with arms, the arms David Ben-Gurion had promised would turn the tide of the combat in which their new state was engaged. The site of their activities was the little Czech town of Žatec, until recently a part of the Nazi-occupied Sudetenland. Its outskirts harbored Ehud Avriel's latest achievement. To make sure that the men, planes and equipment of an air service supposed to bring salvation from the sky to Israel reached their destination in time, Avriel had persuaded his Czech friends to lend him a complete air base. While the United States and the Soviet Union were sliding into the quagmire of the Cold War, under Avriel's direction a largely American-staffed airfield was coming into being behind the Iron Curtain.

Thursday, May 20, marked, in a sense, the beginning of operations in Žatec's hastily converted Luftwaffe base. For three days Ben-Gurion had been pressing Avriel to start shipping his Messerschmitt fighter planes to Israel. The skies of the new Jewish state were still the exclusive domain of the Egyptian Air Force. Nightly its planes were bombing Tel Aviv, their attacks virtually unchallenged. Forty-one people had been killed only forty-eight hours earlier when a bomb had fallen in the city's bus depot.

Summoned to Žatec from Paris, where they had been resting after their last trip to Palestine, the crew and owners of Ocean Trade Airways' one plane watched Avriel's men with awe. They were trying to maneuver into the door of their DC-4 the most unusual cargo they had been called on to carry in their turbulent career, the stripped-down fuselage of a Messerschmitt 109. Six weeks after having flown the Haganah its first load of Czech arms, the Ocean Trade Airways crewmen were scheduled to deliver the Israeli Air Force's first fighter plane.

They were, that is, if a way could be found to force it into their DC-4. No matter how Avriel's men maneuvered the fighter's fuselage, it always managed to stick in the door.

Petrified by the thought that his precious Messerschmitts might remain grounded on his little airstrip two thousand miles from the country in which their appearance was so anxiously awaited, Avriel followed the work with anguished eyes. Maneuvering their cranes with the precision of a watchmaker's drill, his men slipped, pushed, pulled on the bulky fuselage until, without anyone quite knowing how, it slid into the hold of the DC-4. Israelis, Czechs and Americans let out a triumphant cry. Then, so that the plane could go into action as soon as it arrived, the DC-4 was stuffed with bombs and machine-gun rounds. The Israeli Air Force's first fighter pilots, Mordechai Hod and Ezer Weizman, climbed on board. Along with them went a pair of Czech mechanics to reassemble the plane.

Eight hours later as it approached the Israeli coastline, the DC-4 got an astonishing welcome. A salvo of tracer shells fired by the Hispano-Suiza antiaircraft guns of "Don José" Arazi suddenly bracketed it. Egypt's mastery of the skies over Tel Aviv was so complete that no Jewish antiaircraft gunner could imagine that the plane approaching was anything but Arab.

Twisting through the shellbursts, the pilot set course for the former R.A.F. field of Akir, not far from the airfield where he had landed during the night of March 31. No one on board was more anxious to see this historic flight end than the DC-4's pilot. Indifferent for the moment to the importance of his mission to the survival of Israel, the former Milwaukee accountant had only one thing on his mind—an acutely painful souvenir of his Paris visit given to him by a pretty young lady. To one of the joyous Israelis rushing up to congratulate him, he mumbled, "Quick, get me a doctor and some penicillin!"

The dockers of the port of Haifa looked with rising incredulity at the pile of pack racks they had pulled from the cargo hold of the S.S. *Isgo* and wondered what contribution they could possibly make to the country's war effort. Purchased almost as an afterthought on Christmas Day in Antwerp by Xiel Federmann, they had arrived along with a more substantial product of his activities, two dozen half-tracks.

The half-tracks of the S.S. *Isgo,* three other boatloads of auxiliary equipment and Ocean Trade Airways' Messerschmitt represented the only elements of the Haganah's overseas stockpile to reach Israeli ports in the first week of Israel's existence. The problem of getting their arms from one end of the Mediterranean to the other was even more difficult than the Haganah's planners had imagined. Wary of the conflict raging in the Middle East, shippers, insurers and captains were proving extremely reluctant to handle cargoes bound for the new state. In some countries, particularly the United States, strictly enforced embargoes on arms deliveries to the belligerents had forced the Haganah into complicated and time-consuming transshipments. The result, despite a daily stream of angry cables from Ben-Gurion's office, had been an agonizing series of delays.

Yet as each day passed, the need for those arms grew more desperate. Despite the Haganah's tenacious resistance, the Arabs' superior firepower and armor were inexorably turning the balance against the Jewish army. Forty-eight hours after the war had begun, Ben-Gurion had asked his young Chief of Operations if the Haganah could hold out for two more weeks without further arms. Yigal Yadin had bluntly replied that it was not certain.

The most serious situation was in the south, where two Egyptian columns pushed steadily northward. They were composed of over ten thousand men, supported by fifteen fighter planes, a regiment of Sherman and British Matilda tanks, and 25-pounder field guns. Only five of the twenty-seven Jewish settlements in their area of operations contained more than thirty defenders. The army defending them consisted of just two Haganah brigades. The first, the Negev Brigade, contained eight hundred men with two 20-millimeter guns and two Davidkas with ten shells. The second, on the seacoast, had 2,700 men, but not a single antitank weapon except mines and Molotov cocktails.

After encountering furious opposition at the first two settlements he had attacked, the commander of the column heading for Tel Aviv had decided to bypass the kibbutzim along his way if their locations did not menace the coastal road. By the time the Haganah's first Messerschmitt reached Israel, his column was assaulting the one kibbutz it could not bypass, Yad Mordechai, one of the oldest settlements in the Negev. Named for the leader of the Warsaw ghetto uprising in 1943, the settlement stood right alongside the coastal road. Once the Egyptians had overwhelmed it, they would be able to advance all the way north to Ashkelon, only thirty miles from Tel Aviv.

The second Egyptian column, composed mainly of Moslem Brotherhood volunteers under Colonel Ahmed Abdul-Aziz, had been advancing through purely Arab territory. Ironically, his forces were following almost the same route taken by the Children of Israel in their flight from Pharaoh's Egypt to the Promised Land. The natural lack of opposition had not prevented Abdul-Aziz from announcing a "victory" with each Arab town

461

he entered. Now his men had passed through Hebron. With Kfar Etzion in Arab hands, not a single Jewish soldier stood between Abdul-Aziz' forces and the settlement of Ramat Rachel, barely two miles from the heart of New Jerusalem.

That the Jewish situation was not yet desperate was due to the relative inactivity of the other Arab forces. The Arab Legion's thrust into Sheikh Jarrah May 19 had been the only real action of the Legion so far. The Iraqi Army that was supposed to have reached Haifa in a fortnight had confined itself to sporadic artillery and air attacks on its foes.

However, in the north, the Syrian Army, led by thirty armored vehicles, including French Renault tanks, had captured three Jewish settlements and was in the process of assaulting two more, Degania A and B. This attack led to one of the most anguished moments in David Ben-Gurion's life. The leader of Degania B, one of his oldest friends, came to him to beg for just one field gun to turn back the Syrians' armor. Almost sick with sorrow, Ben-Gurion told him, "We have no guns. If I had one, I'd give it to you. Maybe tomorrow we'll have one. But today there are none. You'll have to go back and tell your people to fight with what they've got."

Ben-Gurion knew his words meant that men would die in a hopeless fight. Watching his friend's figure disappear, he felt, for the first time in his adult life, tears on his cheeks.

It would be almost two decades before he would shed tears again—on the day when he would announce to his people his retirement from public life.

.   .   .

The exploit of Yosef Nevo and his Gadna youngsters had stopped the first rush of the Arab Legion, but other grave problems were accumulating for David Shaltiel. The most important was in the south, where Abdul-Aziz' armor had reached Bethlehem. Foreshadowing the storm about to break in that sector, the Egyptians' artillery began to shell the kibbutz of Ramat Rachel on the afternoon of Friday, May 21.

The second critical area was the Jewish Quarter of the Old City. Arrayed against it was Major Abdullah Tell's battalion and fifty guerrillas led by ten Yugoslav, English and German volunteers whose commander was a former S.S. lieutenant named Robert Brandenburg. In addition, Tell could call on Fawzi el Kutub's explosives units and dozens of Haj Amin's irregulars.

The Arab Legion commander had taken over the Rawdah School headquarters on his arrival, quietly but firmly inviting its disorganized occupants to get out. On the wall of his office Tell had installed a huge map of the Old City. Around the Jewish Quarter was a chain of red pins, indicating the positions held by his men. Instead of the haphazard attacks of the irregulars, Tell decided to squeeze the quarter methodically from all sides. And as each Jewish strongpoint was captured, he ordered it destroyed. That way his foes would not be able to reclaim it, and the territory held by his enemies would be steadily reduced. Tell's chain of red pins would creep forward with deliberate slowness. He had chosen this tactic for one reason: it would save the lives of many of his men.

Moshe Russnak understood his tactic immediately. Slowly and inexorably, he saw, he was being driven deeper and deeper into the territory left to him. The days since the Palmach had left Zion Gate had brought him other bitter discoveries too. The reinforcements he had been sent were reluctant combatants. Some had disappeared into the cellars of the synagogues with the civilian population. Others complained that they were not supposed to be there at all, causing Russnak to lament that instead of eighty fighters he had received eighty new mouths to feed and listen to.

The third target of the Arab Legion was the most massive building in Jerusalem, the three-story Hospice of Notre-Dame de France. With its 546 cells, named for French saints and the philanthropic Frenchmen who had provided the funds to build it, Notre-Dame was a honeycomb of rooms and windows, a kind of pilgrims' Hilton in the heart of Jerusalem. Above all, its great granite wings were a superb manifestation of the material and political considerations underlying much of nineteenth-century Christian Europe's spiritual attachment to the Holy City.

The building had been launched with a collection taken on a homeward-bound steamer after one of the "Pilgrimages of Penitence" undertaken by French Catholics following the Franco-Prussian War. "It is not simply a question of building a *pied-à-terre* for pilgrims," noted the first fund-raising appeal, "but of opposing to those of our rivals our own national monument, vast in its proportions, grandiose in its architecture, a colossal witness to our solicitude for Jerusalem and for the secular rights we possess there." In every parish in France, Catholics were urged to "donate a franc, sacrifice a gold Napoleon" so that France in Jerusalem "would no longer be a nomad camped under a tent . . . but ensconced in her own palace, equal to her rivals; represented not only by spiritual but by material interests." Its crowning glory was a twenty-foot, six-ton statue of the Virgin offering her infant son to the Jerusalem skyline and, by no accident, towering over the three onion domes of the nearby Russian church. On Notre-Dame's inauguration in 1888, so that no one would misunderstand its significance,

463

the French consul had proclaimed the building "a great monument to Catholic France, here where Russia has crushed us under her millions and her buildings." It was indeed a prodigious monument to the glories of France, and each stone of Notre-Dame was going to pay for its grandeur.

The building had been retaken by the Haganah on the night of May 19 after a bitter struggle. Since then, its defenders, as at Mandelbaum, had been a unit of Gadna teenagers. They were supplemented by middle-aged Home Guardsmen, doctors, lawyers, businessmen, many of whom had to be taught how to shoot by their seventeen-year-old comrades.

To John Glubb, Notre-Dame was the pivot on which Jerusalem turned. He was persuaded that his men could not move into the New City so long as it was in Jewish hands. Indeed, the armored cars which had stumbled by error into Yosef Nevo's trap at Mandelbaum should have led an assault on the building. If his Bedouin soldiers could capture Notre-Dame without heavy casualties, Glubb would feel confident enough to unleash them in a house-to-house drive to seize the New City. If they could not, he would have to find other tactics to subdue Jerusalem.

Almost across the street from Notre-Dame, another French institution was already living its ordeal. Learning that their convent was unoccupied, five of the cloistered Soeurs Réparatrices who had fled their dwelling on Pentecost Sunday had returned in the hope that their presence might somehow keep the building out of the fighting. It was a vain hope. Snipers on both sides observed their figures in what they had all assumed was an abandoned building. Each, persuaded that the other had occupied the convent, opened fire on it.

Caught in the crossfire, the terrified nuns huddled for safety in the vaulted chapel in which they had so often prostrated themselves before the Blessed Sacrament. Their leader, Sister Emérence, had what seemed to her a particularly felicitous idea: she hung the convent's yellow-and-white papal flag from a window.

That served only to further confuse the Arabs and the Haganah. Ignorant of the flag's meaning, both assumed it was hostile and intensified their fire. An incendiary bullet from one of their exchanges set a wing of the convent ablaze. Desperately the nuns gestured from the convent window until Dr. René Bauer, director of the French Hospital across the street, saw them and opened his door. Gathering up their skirts, they rushed under fire to the hospital.

Their anguish was not quite ended, however. The next day, Sister Emérence noticed that the Haganah had strung a net of cables from Dr.

Bauer's office to the convent. Over the French physician's protest, the army had occupied the hospital. What, asked Sister Emérence, were the cables for? Bauer shrugged. The Haganah was probably putting in a telephone in their convent, he said. Not quite. Short of mines, without antitank weapons, the Haganah had to use any tactic it could to close Jerusalem's main streets to the Arabs' armor. Before Sister Emérence's horrified eyes, the convent in which she and her colleagues had planned to spend the rest of their lives exploded. From it a cascade of masonry, stones and timber spilled out into Suleiman Street, a firm and blessed barrier to the free movement of John Glubb's armored cars.

. . .

David Ben-Gurion pondered with distress the pile of cables littering his glass-topped desk. All day long, the front which claimed priority in his preoccupations had been sending him a series of urgent warnings. Between its growing shortage of food and ammunition, the menace of the Legion from the north and that of the Egyptians from the south, the situation in Jerusalem was so alarming that a disaster was inevitable if some way was not found to get help to the city.

Ben-Gurion was determined to find a way. "At last we had a state," he would later write, "but we were about to lose our capital." He was irked by what he felt was the Haganah's underestimation of the danger to Jerusalem. "They don't see the importance of Jerusalem," Ben-Gurion thought. "They are used to defending villages."

"I knew," he would later recall, "that if ever the people of the country saw Jerusalem fall, they would lose their faith. They would lose their faith in us and in our hopes of winning." He had never before directly intervened in a tactical problem of the Haganah. Tonight he was going to. Despite the lateness of the hour, he summoned to his office Yigal Yadin and his senior officers.

Three weeks earlier, on his way to the besieged city, Ben-Gurion had studied for himself the exact nature of the tactical problem confronting Jerusalem. Like John Glubb and Sir Alec Kirkbride, David Ben-Gurion was persuaded that the key to Jerusalem was Latrun. The sudden appearance on its heights of the soldiers of the Arab army he feared most added immeasurably to the city's perils. Unaware that the men of the Palmach had held those heights for a few brief hours, he now told his Chief of Operations, "I want you to occupy Latrun and open the road to Jerusalem."

Yadin stiffened. For the young archaeologist who had over-all direction of the Haganah, other fronts that night had priority over Jerusalem. The

Egyptian advance would menace Tel Aviv if Yad Mordechai fell. All of Galilee seemed threatened by the Syrians. Jerusalem, he was persuaded, could hold on. "If we follow his idea," Yadin thought, "we'll save our capital and lose our state." Once they had checked the onrushing Egyptians and Syrians, then they could turn their attention to the capital. In any event, he told Ben-Gurion, "you simply cannot take Latrun by a frontal attack. We have to take a longer period and hit them by the flanks."

Ben-Gurion insisted. Yadin's timetable was not his, and their clash was violent and acrimonious. "Jerusalem can't hold out," the Jewish leader said. "By the time we capture Latrun under your plan there won't be any Jerusalem left to save!"

At those words, Ben-Gurion saw his young subordinate's face pale. With a sweep of his arm, Yadin crashed his fist down on the desk, shattering its glass cover. The young man wiped a few flecks of blood from his fist and stared at his leader.

"Listen," he said, his voice low with fury and barely controlled passion. "I was born in Jerusalem. My wife is in Jerusalem. My father and mother are in Jerusalem. Everybody I love is there. Everything that binds you to Jerusalem binds me even more. I should agree with you to send everything we have to Jerusalem. But tonight I don't because I'm convinced they can hold on with what we've given them and we need our forces for situations far more dangerous than the one in Jerusalem."

Shaken by Yadin's unexpected outburst, Ben-Gurion drew his head down into his shoulders like a wrestler, the certain sign of his unshaken determination. Pushing aside the shards of glass on his desk, he sat back in his chair and quietly studied Yadin. Then he gave him a straightforward, unequivocal order: "Take Latrun."

37

TICKET TO A PROMISED LAND

THE TASK of carrying out Ben-Gurion's order was given to the phlegmatic Haganah veteran who had earlier received the secret messenger of Glubb Pasha at the kibbutz of Naharayim. Shlomo Shamir, to whom Colonel Desmond Goldie had hinted of Glubb's hopes for a peaceful division of Palestine, was now to lead the first military formation raised by the new state of Israel against the entrenched forces of Glubb's Legion.

The thirty-three-year-old Russian-born Shamir had been a shopkeeper, a printer, an artist, an electrician and a globetrotter before undertaking full-time service with the Haganah. What had led Ben-Gurion to appoint him commander of the Seventh Brigade was not his Haganah background, however, but his service in the British Army.

Before attacking the Legion, the newly appointed commander of the Seventh Brigade first had to assemble his brigade. Half of it was to be made up of companies assigned to him from existing units; the rest would have to be recruited from training depots and reserve headquarters, or simply, as Shamir observed, "on the sidewalks of Tel Aviv."

With a few hundred pounds issued by the Haganah's paymaster to set up his headquarters, Shamir requisitioned three rooms in the Hotel Bristol, in the center of Tel Aviv. Using the telephone, prowling the sidewalk cafés of Dizengoff Street, sending scouts north and south, he managed to recruit a skeleton force of officers for his brigade. Since the best men were already taken, he had to dig through his memory for the names of friends he had met and admired during the war. The first was that of Vivian Herzog, the elegant former Guards officer who had been the Haganah Intelligence Service's liaison with the British in Jerusalem. Rushed to Tel Aviv by Piper Cub, Herzog became Shamir's chief of operations. The atmosphere he discovered in the three rooms of the Bristol Hotel bore little resemblance to the British headquarters he had known. "It had an air of happy chaos," he remembered, "with men without rank hitting each other on the shoulder, trying to get done in two days what the British would have taken nine months to do."

To lead two of his battalions, Shamir managed to get his hands on a pair of fellow Russians. The first was Haim Laskov, twenty-nine, a former captain in the Jewish Brigade and an assiduous student of Clausewitz. He had discovered his taste for the military as a boy collecting buttons that had fallen from the uniforms of Napoleon's soldiers by the banks of the Berezina. The battalion he was assigned to lead was a former Palmach unit whose noncommissioned officers, preferring to stick with their Palmach brothers fighting in the south, had disappeared. His armor was a heteroclite assembly of twenty vehicles hastily plated up in Joseph Avidar's workshops, and a dozen of the half-tracks which had just arrived on the first boat sent by Xiel Federmann, the Santa Claus of the Haganah.

His vehicles lacked light machine guns, munitions, radios and tool kits. His drivers didn't know how to drive with their lights out or their armored slits down. Some of them, Laskov noted, "didn't even know how much air to put in their front tires." Pompously designated as the 79th Motorized Battalion, his command was, in Laskov's own words, a parody of an armored force.

Even more difficult was the task assigned Shamir's second battalion commander, twenty-nine-year-old Zvi Hurewitz, a veteran of Orde Wingate's specially created night assault units. His 72nd Infantry Battalion existed only in the hopeful imagination of its planners. He would have a hundred recruits in various stages of training as the nucleus of the battalion. To get them, Hurewitz rushed to Tal Hashomer, a hospital outside Tel Aviv used as a training center. He reported to Shamir that the scene there was like "an Oriental bazaar. Brigades were fighting over men as though they were scraps of bread, and if you didn't get in and fight yourself, you got the crumbs."

With his first hundred men under his wing, Hurewitz asked Shamir where the rest were to come from. Shamir threw his arms to the sky. "Who knows?" he said. "Tomorrow we'll find an answer."

In Jerusalem, the Arab Legion's assault on the Jewish Quarter of the Old City continued unabated. Abdullah Tell had placed his armored cars and six-pound antitank guns on the Mount of Olives to support his attacks. They were hurling two hundred shells a day into the quarter.

The first major Haganah stronghold to fall was the Nissan Bek Synagogue, the splendid building whose dome had been donated by the Emperor Franz Josef. It was essential to Russnak's defense plan, and the Haganah fought tenaciously to hold on to it. From all over the quarter, reserves came to help. The girls gave an extraordinary demonstration of courage to the men. Esther Cailingold dashed from post to post carrying ammunition and tending the wounded. Sixteen-year-old Judith Jaharan, trained as a nurse, was forced into the role of an infantryman to defend the street in which she had been born.

Unable to spot all of the positions from which they were directing fire at his men, one Arab officer turned for help to a man who owed his intimate knowledge of the quarter's buildings to his little-loved calling as a rent collector. Dressed in a business suit and a red tarboosh as though he were off on his rounds, the rent collector was picking out buildings when a sniper, presumably firing from one of his tenants' windows, killed him.

Fawzi el Kutub finally ordered eight of his men to rush across an open space and place a charge at the base of the synagogue. All of them were killed or wounded. No one would volunteer for a second try. Hoping to force his men's hands by his example, Kutub sprinted across the space himself. When he got to the base of the synagogue, he saw that no one had followed him. Like a spider, he pressed himself up against its wall until finally the Tunisian to whom he had promised a wife rushed out to him carrying a fifty-five-pound charge.

The explosion barely chipped the wall.

Three more unsuccessful attempts were required before Kutub managed to blow a hole in the synagogue wall and a party of Legionnaires rushed through the smoke into Nissan Bek's interior.

Sure that the Haganah would counterattack and that the irregulars swarming into the synagogue would quickly turn to looting, Kutub decided to destroy it with a 220-pound charge. His strongest follower, a one-eyed former porter in the railroad station nicknamed the Whale, staggered up with the explosive. A terrible roar shook the quarter and blew out the heart of the building. As the smoke cleared and the frightful devastation caused by the bomb became apparent, Kutub heard a cry of consternation rising from the Jewish posts around him.

It was quickly replaced by a triumphant yell. A small group of Haganah led by Judith Jaharan counterattacked and took the smoking ruins of Nissan Bek from the Arabs. As Kutub had suspected, the irregulars had spent their time looting the synagogue. The Haganah found the bodies of Arab irregulars killed in their counterattack with altar cloths around their waists, pages of the Torah stuffed into their shirts, pieces of chandeliers and lamps in their pockets.

More than courage such as that displayed by the defenders of Nissan Bek was going to be needed if the quarter was to survive. Two more efforts to break through Zion Gate had failed and a sense of defeat was beginning to grip many defenders. That night, after Nissan Bek had fallen again, two of the quarter's senior rabbis sent a despairing, almost hysterical message to their colleagues in the New City: "The community is at the end of a slaughter. In the name of the residents, a desperate cry for help . . . Shake the higher institutions and the whole world to save us."

An equally grave warning cry rang through the Jewish suburb of Beth Hakerem that same night. Like coast watchers warning seafront residents of an incoming tidal wave, the neighborhood's Home Guardsmen raced from door to door shouting the news that Ramat Rachel had fallen. The Egyptians were, quite literally, at their doorsteps. After his long chain of Arab conquests, Colonel Abdul-Aziz had finally added a Jewish one to his laurels: with almost twenty-four hours of continuous shelling to pave the way, his men had swept through the ruins of the settlement at nightfall. Now his armor was reported heading for Beth Hakerem.

Boys ran from house to house calling for anybody with "two arms and two legs" to come out and build barricades. Women came in bathrobes and pin curlers, men in pajamas or a pair of pants hastily pulled on, children in undershirts and sandals. By early morning, under the full moon, the entire neighborhood was at work. Sixty- and seventy-year-old men with hernias and bad hearts heaved stones onto the fortifications. Twelve-year-olds struggled to push heavy wheelbarrows up to the barricades while younger children raced along behind them with the heaviest stones they could carry. Women scoured the fields, filling their shopping baskets with rocks. If Beth Hakerem was going to become the second Jewish community of Jerusalem to face an Arab army, its residents were determined to give the rest of the city an example. Abdul-Aziz' men would have to pay a price for every Jewish home they seized.

Slowly, like an old man out of breath, the rusty hulk rescued from a cluster of ships waiting for the scrap-metal dealer, plodded across the majestic bay, a black cloud from its funnel huddling over it like an umbrella. Built long before the war to carry eight hundred first-class passengers, the decks, passageways and holds of the S.S. *Kalanit* crawled today with two thousand men contemplating in awe and silence the spectacle before them: the port of Haifa and beyond it the green slopes of Mount Carmel. For those men the port culminated a dream of years and a voyage begun somewhere in Central Europe seven, eight, nine years earlier in the wake of Hitler's drive east. Some of them had managed to flee to the forests, where, like hunted animals, they had fought alongside the partisans

470

until the hour of liberation. Others, swept into the death camps of Nazi Germany, had awaited their liberation at the portals of the gas chambers in which six million of their kind had perished before their eyes.

The Allied victory they had so desperately awaited had delivered them from one barbed-wire camp to another, and it was in the displaced-persons centers that the Haganah had found most of them. Zionist and non-Zionist, orthodox and atheist, Communist and capitalist, they were animated by the desire to join their fellow Jews outside a Europe in which they no longer had confidence, and in which they had been so consistently betrayed to their Nazi oppressors.

The Haganah had offered them that opportunity, demanding only one thing in return for their passage to Israel—that they fight. Organized by the networks of the underground army's illegal immigration service, they were secretly directed to assembly areas where some of them received a rudimentary military training, then shipped to their ports of embarkation. The most important was Sète, near Marseilles; from its wharves some of the men aboard the *Kalanit* this morning had set out for Haifa seven months earlier on another equally overcrowded vessel. The prow of the *Exodus,* however, had never anchored in the waters below Mount Carmel, and its unhappy human cargo had been returned to Europe to be dispersed again in a new set of camps.

On the high seas, the immigrants of the *Kalanit* had shouted cries of triumph at the news that the country toward which their old steamer was bearing them had conquered the right to receive them openly, legally. No fanfare, no speeches, no pretty girls with bouquets of flowers were on hand to welcome them on the docks of Haifa. The only sight that greeted them, as they stared down from their decks, was the line of yellow roofs of the column of old buses waiting for them.

Matti Megid, the young officer of the Haganah who had accompanied the immigrants from Germany and Rumania, noticed a black Oldsmobile slide up to the quay and heard someone calling his name. Two hours later, in a pinkish building by the Tel Aviv seafront, Megid was hurried into an office filled with people and noise. At one end of the room, behind a table, Megid saw the disorderly white tufts of hair of a familiar head poring over a list of names, the passenger list of the *Kalanit*. Without looking up, the white-haired man began to question Megid.

"How many are they?" Ben-Gurion asked.

Ben-Gurion wanted to know everything: who they were, where they came from, how old they were, what kind of military training they had. Then the old leader suddenly lifted his massive head and looked at Megid.

471

"Do you know why they're here?" he asked. As Megid nodded, Ben-Gurion added, "Because we need them."

"But not right away?" questioned the young officer, concerned for the first time by the turn the conversation was taking.

The Jewish leader gazed at Megid, somewhat surprised by his remark. "That's not your concern," he replied.

Suddenly realizing that the immigrants he had brought to Israel were going to have to buy their right to enter their new country by risking their lives in a conflict for which they were not yet prepared, Megid begged Ben-Gurion not to throw his men into combat too quickly. His comment clearly disturbed Ben-Gurion.

"You can't judge," Ben-Gurion said. "You don't know how serious the situation is."

Then, sadly, he added, "We need them all."

As Shlomo Shamir had predicted, the new day had brought an answer to Zvi Hurewitz' manpower problems. Taken directly from the docks of Haifa to Tel Hashomer, four hundred and fifty immigrants of the *Kalanit* were to constitute the rank and file of Hurewitz' 72nd Battalion. The Russian-born officer studied them as they scrambled down from their yellow buses and lined up before him. They were all young. Those who had spent time in the British detention camps in Cyprus were tanned. The others were gray and pale. They clutched in their arms everything they owned, stuffed into a little cloth sack or a frail valise.

There were blue-eyed Poles, Hungarians, Rumanians, Czechs, dour Bulgars, Yugoslavs, Russians with hair as blond as sun-bleached straw. They were uniformly thin, and a certain furtiveness in their regard betrayed the painful pasts which had preceded their arrival in Haifa.

Hurewitz lined his four hundred and fifty recruits up in the hospital courtyard and decided to mark their arrival in this new camp with an attention that had rarely honored their unhappy lives at their other, earlier destinations. He bade them welcome. But as Hurewitz began to talk, he realized from their uncomprehending stares that his battalion was a Tower of Babel in which apparently only one language, Hebrew, was not spoken.

He sent for the Polish sergeant who was his clerk and had him translate his words into Yiddish and Polish. "Welcome to the ranks of the Army of Israel," Hurewitz began again. "We have been impatiently awaiting your arrival. Time is short and Jerusalem is in danger. We are going to her rescue." As he uttered his last words, Hurewitz felt a tremor of emotion seize him. The pale faces of the remnants of a condemned people suddenly came alive and from the mouths before him rose a spontaneous, triumphant shout.

He split the men into four companies and issued rifles to them. Although a third of his men had had some military training, none of them had ever used the weapon with which they were equipped, the British Lee Enfield. The companies were split into platoons and squads, keeping men who spoke the same language in the same unit as far as possible. Each man was issued a rudimentary uniform. Since nobody knew anyone else and there was no way of telling noncoms from officers or soldiers, Hurewitz ordered his sergeants and corporals to sew a red ribbon on the shoulder of their shirts.

The most difficult problem of all was that of language. The platoon and squad leaders were all sabras who spoke only Hebrew. How, Hurewitz asked himself, could they be expected to lead into battle men who couldn't understand their orders? He assembled them to study the problem. Finally he said, "Look, we haven't got much time. We'll have to get along with the kind of thing we'd do with children. Teach them just a few simple words, the words they'll have to know to fight." Soon, Hurewitz noted, a strange murmur began to rise from the esplanade of Tel Hashomer, the sound of hundreds of voices slowly articulating a succession of syllables. In the language of the Judges and the Prophets, the recruits of his 72nd Battalion were trying to learn the words with which they hoped to save Jerusalem.

Hauled up to the Old City walls with great effort, two of John Glubb's six-pound guns peeped through the gunports designed four centuries before by the architects of Suleiman the Magnificent for wars of bows and arrows. Farther along the ramparts, near Damascus Gate, were a pair of Vickers machine guns. On the ground below waited a battery of eight two-inch mortars. In front of Herod's Gate, protected by a natural depression, was the most important piece of all, a 25-pounder field gun. It was noon, Sunday, May 23, and without exception every muzzle of that array of artillery was fixed on one target. Notre-Dame de France, built by the "Pilgrims of Penitence," was about to do penance for the grandiose ambitions of its founders.

Lieutenant Fendi Omeish took a last look through the 25-pounder's gunsight. It was pointed straight at the center of Notre-Dame's façade, right at the statue of the Virgin. He adjusted its aim to the left. "Try not to hit Mariam," he told his Moslem gunners, who had, too, a certain veneration for the Virgin. Then he ordered the shelling to begin.

473

Soon Notre-Dame's mammoth shape was enveloped in a cloud of dust. To John Glubb's trained eyes, however, his guns seemed to have the effect of "a peashooter" on Notre-Dame's solid masonry. "The Holy Catholic Church," he observed glumly, "seemed to have built for eternity."

For the men inside the building, the shelling had a different aspect. To Netanel Lorch it was like "a continuous earthquake." Stonework, masonry, timber, plaster rained down on its defenders. Dust and smoke choked the teenagers of the Gadna and their middle-aged fellow fighters. The roar stunned many of them. For two hours it went on, half a dozen shells a minute, until Notre-Dame's proud eastern façade was pockmarked and shattered.

As the roar of the Legion's artillery finally died away, another, more terrifying sound rose up to Notre-Dame's defenders, the rumble of motors. Four armored cars of Lieutenant Zaal Errhavel were advancing up Suleiman Street from Damascus Gate toward the building. On the third floor, Mishka Rabinovitch watched them with the homemade periscope he had devised out of two pipes and a broken mirror. The solid walls of Notre-Dame had protected Rabinovitch and the building's lone Piat antitank gun during all the shelling. Rabinovitch, his arm still in a cast, aimed the weapon for the Gadna teenager beside him, as he had at Mandelbaum.

The tension was enormous. Lying on the floor, they could hear the steady drone of the advancing cars' engines and the snap of rifle fire all around them. Everyone in the building waited for the Piat's first shot, knowing that once the gun's position had been revealed, it might not get a second chance. Looking at the two of them lying on the floor, Zelman Mart, one of Shaltiel's deputies, thought, "The kid's never going to be calm enough to hold on and wait until he's sure of his shot."

The four cars came closer. Coached by Rabinovitch, the Gadna teenager patiently held on under Mart's admiring gaze until they were only a hundred yards away. Coolly, he squeezed off his first round. The lead car spun to the side. His assistant gunner dropped a second shell into the Piat. He fired again and a second car ground to a stop.

"My God," thought Mart, "if he can do that, anybody in this command can."

In the cars, Errhavel's gunners found that at that range they could not elevate their guns to an angle wide enough to shell Notre-Dame's top floor. Errhavel ordered his two damaged vehicles to withdraw and pulled the other two cars back out of the Piat's range.

Meanwhile, the infantry, led by Lieutenant Ghazi el Harbi, a burnished veteran of hundreds of tribal skirmishes in his native Saudi Arabia, opened its assault. His men got to the hospice's garden wall, broke in and rushed to the base of the building itself. From the dozens of cell-like rooms above, bearing names like Notre-Dame de Lourdes, Sainte Françoise Romaine, Sainte Eulalie, came an uncharitable rain of hand grenades.

Despite the intense fire, a party of Harbi's men managed to get a foothold on the ground floor. Watching from the Old City walls, the United Press's Samir Souki could see them trying to push forward in one room while through another's windows he could see Jewish soldiers rushing forward to check their advance. The fighting was savage, with grenades and bayonets; yet the Gadna youngsters, many of them only sixteen and in action for the first time, succeeded in holding the Legionnaires to half a dozen rooms.

Inside Notre-Dame, Mishka Rabinovitch was beckoned to a window by a seventeen-year-old French boy named Jacques. The little Frenchman, a veteran of the Maquis, had already acquired an extraordinary reputation. He was, one of his commanders noted, "continually engaged either in fighting or in looting." He was covered with pink brick dust from the shattered hospice and looked to Rabinovitch more like a clown than a fighter.

There was nothing comic about the sight to which Jacques was pointing, however. It was a Legion armored car maneuvering below the window. Silently, Rabinovitch pointed his good arm to a Molotov cocktail and gestured to Jacques to throw it.

Lieutenant Fendi Omeish had just leaped from the car to help a wounded man at New Gate when he turned and saw the bottle arching gracefully through the air to smash onto the pavement in front of the car. Since it was on a slight incline, the burning liquid rolled down under its bumper and fired its engine. From the window above, the dark-moustached Rabinovitch and Jacques, "looking like a pink Picasso," peered down with pride on the boy's handiwork. Its turret crammed with munitions, the car began to explode in sheets of blue flame and the stench of burning rubber. "Everything I have," moaned Omeish, "my blankets, my toothbrush, my soap, my wife's picture, and there it goes."

There, too, went the car's driver, Ali. Disgusted by the turn the war had taken, he scrambled from his turret, dashed through New Gate and, presenting himself as a civilian, kept right on going until he reached his Arabian home.

South of the city, Shaltiel's reserves had retaken Ramat Rachel, catching Abdul-Aziz' men in the act of looting the kibbutz. Then, concerned by the Legion's assault on Notre-Dame, Shaltiel had felt he could not have his last two reserve platoons so far from the city's center, and he had replaced them by Home Guardsmen. Once again the Arabs had attacked and captured the settlement.

And once again Shaltiel's reserves repeated their attack. Incredibly, they found the Egyptian Moslem Brothers busy looting what they had not been able to carry away the first time. Once again they routed them. By dawn, the Israeli flag was back on the blackened chimney of the kibbutz's ruined dining hall.

In that same dawn of May 21, the Legion's attack, stalled the night before, began again at Notre-Dame. Once again the Jews held their ground. Gradually, the Arabs' casualties began to mount at a worrying rate.

John Glubb, disturbed by his army's long delay in capturing Notre-Dame, observed the attack from the Old City with increasing apprehension. Just after noon, his Third Regiment's Australian commander, Bill Newman, brought him a distressing piece of news. Half of the two hundred men who had launched the attack the day before were dead or wounded. It was a jarring revelation. "Our business is fighting in the open country, not slogging from room to room," Glubb told himself. He ordered the attack stopped and Harbi's men withdrawn to Musrara.

The Saudi Arabian was heartbroken. When he had pulled his men back, he sought out Glubb in the Old City and begged him to allow him to attack one more time. The Pasha was adamant; their failure before the walls of Notre-Dame was a crucial turning point in Jerusalem. Once and for all, he was sure the Legion did not have the men or the training to fight its way from house to house and room to room through New Jerusalem.

John Glubb knew, however, that a house-to-house fight was not the only way to take Jewish Jerusalem. There was another way: blockading it. The key to that was the vital crossroads he had studied with Sir Alec Kirkbride a few nights before. There, on the plains below Latrun, the Bedouins of his Legion would at last meet their enemies in the open country that was their natural fighting environment.

476

38

"EXECUTE YOUR TASK AT ALL COSTS."

SLOWLY, METHODICALLY, Lieutenant Colonel Habes Majali, commander of the Fourth Regiment of Glubb's Arab Legion, panned his field glasses over the vast panorama at his feet. From his observation post, some of the most famous generals of history had scanned the approaches to these heights of Latrun. Ibn-Jebel, one of the Caliph Omar's lieutenants, had even built his tomb in the field of wild lavender surrounding Majali. The young colonel had climbed onto a pile of stones left from a fortified château built on these heights by Richard the Lionhearted, then razed by Saladin, to scan the countryside in his latest attempt to discern the intentions of his enemy.

The commander of the Fourth Regiment had little doubt as to what those intentions were. To get help to the 100,000 besieged Jews of Jerusalem, the Haganah, he was sure, would have to storm his positions and break open a passage to the city. By midday of May 24, Majali sensed that their attack was imminent.

His soldiers had been preparing for it for days. The hillside so precipitously abandoned by Fawzi el Kaukji was now well seeded with machine-gun nests. The trenches in which the Turks had fought off Allenby's attacks on Latrun had been cleaned out, deepened and reoccupied. Mines and rolls of barbed wire covered the slopes before them. Antitank guns controlled the principal approaches to the crest. Three Vickers machine guns had been posted on the roof of the old British police station west of Latrun's Trappist monastery controlling the plain rolling down toward Tel Aviv. In the village of Yalu, the Ayalon of Biblical times, Majali had hidden his three-inch mortars.

Nightly his adjutant, Captain Mahmoud Rousan, had been sending deep penetration patrols out into the plain to uncover the Haganah's positions and intentions. Rousan had even stationed a detachment of men in the police station of Artouf, a village three miles south of Latrun on the road to Beersheba. On this evening of May 24, he intended to send a major patrol across the valley to Artouf to destroy the one bridge on the

477

road leading to the village and thus eliminate any possibility of its being used as an access road to Jerusalem.

To supplement his own manpower, Majali had reorganized Haroun Ben-Jazzi's irregulars and the local villagers into auxiliary units. It was a task for which Majali, son of the paramount sheikh of Transjordan's most important Bedouin tribe, was particularly suited. In the formalist tongue of the desert, the first Arab to be honored with the command of an Arab Legion regiment had given each group of irregulars the name of an animal whose ferocity was legendary. Thus, Majali's Lions, Tigers, Wolves and Falcons, equipped with new rifles, had been attached to his regular companies.

The core of Majali's force was hidden under camouflage nets in an olive grove near the hamlet of Beit Nuba. From that piece of high ground, his six 25-pounder field guns commanded all of the roads converging like the tributaries of a river on the single ribbon of asphalt leading up to Jerusalem. Like Majali, their young commander was the son of one of Transjordan's most famous Bedouin tribes. Mahmoud May'tah, the brother of the officer who had opened fire on Jerusalem, had initiated his illiterate Bedouin gunners into the mysteries of geometry and ballistics with an old French seventy-five captured in the struggle with Vichy France in Syria. So expert had they become that two smoke shells fired on their arrival in Latrun had sufficed to range their guns on the targets selected for them by May'tah. He had had no difficulty in picking the targets. The subject of May'tah's last prewar maneuver had been the conquest of Latrun.

Standing on his observation post, Colonel Majali contemplated Latrun's amber stands of ripening wheat, then to the northwest the square minaret of Ramle and, farther on, at the edge of the horizon, the rooftops of Tel Aviv and Jaffa outlined against the sea. As his glasses moved carefully back across the green Plain of Sharon toward the Valley of Sorec, homeland of Delilah, one of his aides brought Majali a radio message. It was from brigade headquarters and it informed Majali that three companies of the Second Regiment with artillery support were en route to Latrun to reinforce his positions. A satisfied Majali resumed his scrutiny of the vista before him. This time his binoculars stopped on a grove of pine and cypress trees five miles distant. Through their branches Majali could pick out a series of red-tiled roofs. Lowering his glasses, he consulted his map. As he suspected, they belonged to a Jewish settlement, the kibbutz of Hulda, the last Haganah stronghold on the road to Jerusalem.

Calmly, Dov Joseph looked at the group of ultra-orthodox rabbis gathered before him in the Jerusalem home of Chief Rabbi Isaac Herzog and waited for one of them to break the silence.

Finally the exasperated Chief Rabbi said to the assembly, "You wanted to speak to Dr. Joseph. Here he is. Speak."

Embarrassed, the group's leader, an elderly man, began by giving Joseph a lecture on Jewish moral precepts and the value attached by the Jewish faith to preventing the loss of a human soul. Mea Shearim had been badly hit by the Legion's shelling, he said; many women and children had been killed. While clearly the Haganah could not be expected to abandon the struggle with the Arabs, perhaps they, in the quarter, could go to the Arabs and make some arrangement whereby it might be excluded from the fighting.

Joseph sensed immediately what was coming, a plea for a partial surrender. He knew he could not tolerate such a gesture. The result might be a wave of panic that would infect the whole city. Awkwardly the man before him stumbled toward his conclusions. At least, under his plan, their women and children would be spared further suffering and many innocent souls saved. What did Joseph think of his proposition?

The Canadian fixed him with a steady gaze.

"You do what you believe to be right," he answered, "and I shall do what I believe to be right."

There was a long silence. And what, Joseph's interlocutor inquired, did Joseph think was right?

"I think that if anyone attempts to raise the white flag, he will be shot," he said.

The forces whose intentions Colonel Habes Majali had attempted to discern were in the process of assembling this Monday, May 24, in the kibbutz of Hulda. Zero hour for the Jewish attack on Latrun had been fixed for midnight, and, as they had so often before, the officers of the Haganah had turned to the Bible for a name for their operation. It was "Bin Nun," for Joshua, the son of Nun, for whom the setting sun had stood still on the Valley of Ayalon so that he could complete his victory over the enemies of Israel. To conquer the same valley, the officers of a modern Israeli Army might well have prayed for the rising sun to stand still, for the success of their operation would depend above all on carrying it out under the cover of darkness.

Undertaken in an atmosphere of anarchy and argument, the preparations for the attack hardly seemed to augur well for its outcome. Originally set for midnight May 23, zero hour had had to be pushed back twenty-four hours because the Seventh Brigade's manpower had not been assembled at Hulda nor its armament delivered. The strike force of the brigade, an infantry battalion detached from the Palmach's Alexandroni Brigade, hadn't even arrived at Hulda at six o'clock on the evening of the twenty-third. Those farmers from the Plain of Sharon were the only members of the brigade with real military experience, and Shamir had assigned them the key role in the attack, the capture of the police station west of the Monastery of Latrun.

Haim Laskov's homemade armored cars and half-tracks had not been ready to participate in the attack, either. They still had not received their machine guns, ammunition or radios. As for the immigrants of Zvi Hurewitz' 72nd Infantry Battalion, delivered to Hulda by buses requisitioned from Tel Aviv's No. 5 bus line, they had had neither packs, helmets nor canteens. The battalion's officers still did not know their men nor the men their arms. And, as at Tel Hashomer, the immigrants continued to mutter the few words they had been able to learn in Hebrew, the words on which their survival might soon depend. Faced with such an impossible situation, Shamir had been obliged to advise Yadin that he was postponing his attack for twenty-four hours.

When his missing Palmach battalion finally arrived at Hulda at noon the following day, Shamir and his staff welcomed them with relief. Their pleasure, however, turned to stupefaction as they saw the men getting off their buses. Ten days after its creation, the new state of Israel possessed an army still fundamentally organized for clandestine combat, a series of baronies in which commanders often interpreted superiors' orders according to their own estimate of the situation. Before allowing its battalion to leave for Hulda, Alexandroni's Palmach commanders had systematically stripped their men of all their arms and equipment. Twelve hours before they were due to attack the Legion, they had showed up without a single rifle, "a battalion of beggars," as Vivian Herzog bitterly observed.

No one was more horrified by the lamentable state of the Seventh Brigade's preparations than Yigal Yadin, who had argued so hard with Ben-Gurion against the attack. Flying up to inspect the brigade, Yadin saw that its battalions were in fact companies lumped together without reserves, support or communications. Its artillery was made up of a pair of old French Army mountain guns nicknamed "Napoleonchiks," the 25-pounder stolen for the Haganah on May 13 by the Australian Mike Scott, four three-inch mortars without sights and a Davidka no one knew how to use. Yadin also saw to his horror that there was no effective medical service: the brigade had no doctors, no ambulances, not even enough stretchers.

In the few days since May 14, the prodigious efforts of the Haganah's overseas arms-buying missions and the support of American and world Jewry had not yet begun to make themselves felt in Israel. Beset on every side by the Arab invasion Ben-Gurion had so long predicted, the new state was confronted by so many simultaneous tasks that the spirited improvisation and ingenuity which had been the Yishuv's greatest assets had been overwhelmed.

Sensing a tragedy, Yadin decided to make one more effort to change the mind of the only man who could now stop what he saw as a suicidal attack. The answer to his radio message was an unequivocal "No." Yadin was still not ready to go ahead. At two o'clock his Auster took off from Hulda's improvised landing strip for Tel Aviv, carrying both Yadin and Shamir. The Haganah's Chief of Operations hoped that Shamir might be able to convince Ben-Gurion of the folly of the attack, or at least secure a delay of a few days in which to prepare his troops. Before they went into the old man's office Yadin told Shamir, "It all depends on what you tell him. He's in a kind of trance about this thing and I can't argue with him any more. He just won't listen to me. He's sure Jerusalem will fall if we don't attack, and nothing I say seems to shake him."

Before Shamir could even finish describing his brigade's problems, Ben-Gurion was on his feet and launching into an impassioned description of Jerusalem's plight. Not a day, not an hour could be lost in opening up the road to the city, he said. His eloquence swept Shamir along with him. When he had finished, the Russian said simply, "Your will is my command. I will follow any order you give."

As they left, Yadin exploded. "Who the hell asked you to tell him you'll follow orders?" he said. "Of course you will. You were supposed to tell him what you think, dammit!"

It was too late for second thoughts now. The two men flew back to Hulda. On their arrival, they learned that at least the machine guns for Laskov's half-tracks had arrived, but it would take hours to scrape off the protective grease with which they were still covered. More hours of labor would be needed to load the loose ammunition into cartridge belts. Those and many other tasks like them had so burdened the officers of the Seventh Brigade for the past forty-eight hours that they had had neither the time nor the manpower to probe the foe's defenses with patrols.

481

Deeply concerned, Yadin remained in Hulda all afternoon, watching Shamir's preparations. Before leaving, he sent one last plea to Ben-Gurion, begging for a twenty-four-hour postponement in the operation. Then, brokenhearted, convinced that the brigade was doomed, Yadin flew back to Tel Aviv.

At seven o'clock, Shamir assembled his officers in the kibbutz's main building, converted into a temporary operations center. A 1:200,000 map of Latrun was hung on the wall. Before his dozen aides, Shamir ceremoniously began his final briefing according to the procedures employed by commanding officers in His Majesty's Army. Written in pencil, the document he held in his hand was the first operational order of the Army of Israel. It answered the four classic questions of a battle plan: the state of the enemy's forces, the state of their own forces, their objectives and the means they would employ to achieve them.

The objective was clear: to occupy a three-mile stretch of the Jerusalem road from Latrun to Bab el Wad, to secure it, then to push through to the capital the enormous convoy waiting on the highway between Kfar Bilu and Rehovot.

The information which Shamir then transmitted to his officers on the state of the enemy's forces was brief. The Jewish intelligence service, which had acquitted itself so brilliantly while operating underground against the British, had yet to adapt itself to the exigencies of military intelligence. "The enemy holds in unknown numbers the Latrun high ground," said Shamir's intelligence report, "and he has *perhaps* * some artillery." The area around Bab el Wad, estimated the report, "is probably held by irregular forces." That was all.

Shamir then began to analyze the assault plan. As he did, a runner interrupted their conference with a message from Tel Aviv. Reading the few words hastily scribbled on the piece of paper the messenger handed him, Shamir shuddered. It was an urgent communication from Yadin timed at 7:30 P.M.: "Enemy wheeled force of 120 vehicles including large number of armor and gun carriers left Ramallah apparently for Latrun. They are now at map coordinates 154-141." The arrival of Colonel Majali's reinforcements had been spotted by the Haganah.

Shamir walked over to his map and swiftly plotted the convoy's location. He estimated that it would reach Latrun in one hour. They would have to attack before those new troops were in position. "Gentlemen,"

* Authors' italics.

482

he said, "we must advance zero hour by two hours." Instead of midnight it would be 10 P.M.

Shamir then resumed his briefing. Their jump-off point was on the Hulda–Latrun road, not quite two and a half miles below the Latrun crossroads. From there his two battalions would advance in different directions. The battalion borrowed from the Alexandroni Palmach Brigade would advance straight ahead, seizing the village of Latrun, the police station and the hamlet of Amwas to prevent reinforcements from reaching Latrun over the Latrun–Ramallah road. Once it had obtained its objectives, the battalion would dig in and give protection to the Jerusalem-bound convoy.

Shamir was about to turn to the mission of Zvi Hurewitz' immigrant battalion when a runner arrived with a second message from Yadin. "The position in Jerusalem is critical. You have to break through tonight," it read. For the third time in three days, the soldiers of Colonel Abdul-Aziz had seized the kibbutz of Ramat Rachel at the city's southern entry. Once again an Arab flag flew over its ruined buildings. More menacing still for the city's situation was the fact that the Arab Legion had joined the attack this time.

Shamir ordered petrol lamps brought into the room and once again, in the uneven light, returned to his briefing. Zvi Hurewitz' battalion would make a long sweep east from the jump-off point until it was opposite the point where the Jerusalem road entered Bal el Wad. It would cross the road and move up the slopes of Bab el Wad to the crest dominating the gorge, seizing the villages of Deir Ayub, Beit Nuba and Yalu. Then they too would secure their positions and give cover to the Jerusalem convoy.

Captain Laskov's armored force would give limited support to their attack; only three of his armored cars and two of his half-tracks were ready to take to the road. Shamir concluded by announcing that the immigrants' battalion and Laskov's cars would follow the convoy up the gorge to Jerusalem. The meticulous commander had even set out the composition of the column. Behind Laskov's three armored cars would come buses carrying the third, still incomplete battalion Shamir was holding in reserve, his own headquarters and the immigrants. Laskov's two half-tracks would act as the rear guard. Shamir predicted that dawn would just be coming up when the drivers of Laskov's lead cars saw the rooftops of Jerusalem before them, if the attack went off according to his hopeful previsions.

As Shamir finished, a sergeant of the Alexandroni battalion arrived to announce the first of the imponderables that always complicate any military plan. In their withdrawal from the Latrun police station ten days earlier, the men of the Givati Brigade had sown the Hulda road with mines. They would have to be dug out before Shamir's Tel Aviv city buses could move his men to their jump-off point. Without a mechanical mine detector, the job would take several hours and cause a worrisome delay. There was no choice. Shamir set zero hour back to midnight, the time he had originally chosen for the attack, hoping that some major obstacle might arise to cancel it altogether.

Instead, at twelve-thirty the commander of the Seventh Brigade got his third message from Yadin. The Haganah's Chief of Operations had received a reply to his last plea to postpone the attack. He had immediately transmitted its substance to Shamir. "You will execute your task at all costs," it read.

39

THE WHEATFIELDS OF LATRUN

No SOUND beyond the metallic concert of the cicadas and the occasional baying of a dog broke the silence. Not a ripple of air moved the stands of maturing wheat or picked at the cypress trees. It was a breathless, suffocating night, but its quiet was deceptive. Shortly after the Trappist monks of Latrun began to chant their predawn vigil, the soldiers of Shlomo Shamir's brigade set out in quest of the road to Jerusalem.

They were already three precious hours late, and the four hundred men Shamir had finally been able to put into the field were far less than the number Ben-Gurion had counted on to seize the most vital crossroads in Palestine. The commander of Shamir's best Palmach battalion had collapsed two hours before the attack. Shamir had replaced him with Haim Laskov, who didn't know any of the men in his command.

Under a full moon, Laskov and his three companies set off across the plain on the attack's most important assignment, seizing the Latrun high ground, the fortresslike former British police station and the ridge above the Trappist monastery. As soon as they had left, Zvi Hurewitz and his immigrants began their eastward trek up the valley toward the narrow road running along the base of the Judean hills from Artouf to Bab el Wad. When they hit it, a few hundred yards above Bab el Wad, they would turn north, cross over the entry to the notorious gorge and begin their attack on the heights and villages above it.

At the upper end of the little road toward which the Jewish soldiers were moving, Lieutenant Qassem Ayad of the Arab Legion's Fourth Infantry Regiment cursed the stupidity of his engineers. They had forgotten a pair of unused detonators under the road's only bridge, which Lieutenant Ayad and his reinforced patrol of fifty men had been assigned to destroy. Before blowing it, Ayad had sent them back for the missing detonators, a tactic which would delay his return to Latrun by almost an hour.

The men who had spent barely seventy-two hours on the soil of a land they had dreamed of for years were going to suffer for Lieutenant Ayad's missing detonators. Heading back down the road toward Bab el Wad, the Arab lieutenant suddenly caught sight of a series of suspicious shadows in the plain to his left. Peering through the darkness, he made out the silhouettes of a long column of men moving toward Bab el Wad. He rushed to his radio. "The Jews are attacking," he informed headquarters. Ayad's accidental discovery of Zvi Hurewitz' immigrants had deprived the Israelis of the most important element in their attack, surprise. It was four o'clock in the morning of Tuesday, May 25.

The first battle of Latrun had just begun.

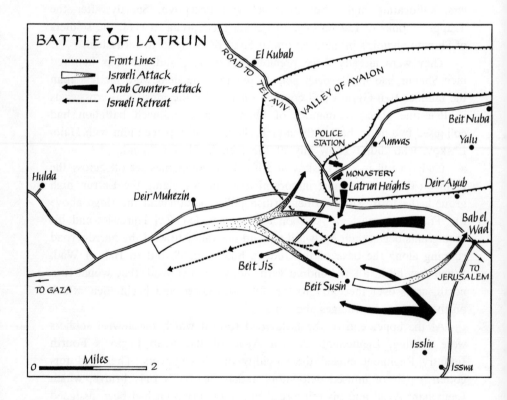

In his observation post on the hilltop from which Colonel Majali had studied the valley the afternoon before, Lieutenant Mahmoud May'tah could not believe the sight before him in the first gray haze of dawn. Moving through the wheatfields of Latrun, almost under the muzzles of his field guns, were dozens of Jewish soldiers.

From May'tah's guns, from the regiment's mortars, from rifles and machine guns all over the hillside, a devastating fire swept down on the hapless Jews trapped by the first light of a sun that would not stand still. Stunned by the Arab outburst, their forward progress stopped. None of the principal objectives had been reached or even approached. In the center of Laskov's sector, the men of his lead company had not even reached the Latrun–Bab el Wad road. They threw themselves for cover into the tomatoes and stringbeans of the Trappists' vegetable garden, waiting for the shelling to stop. To their left, the second company was caught outside the hamlet of Latrun below the police post. Up the road, near Bab el Wad, Lieutenant Ayad's men, bolstered by a number of villagers, fell on the unprotected flank of Hurewitz' immigrants.

In his Hulda command post, Shamir heard his men's pathetic appeals for artillery support to silence the Arab batteries hammering their ranks. A few minutes later in his classroom in the monastery at Latrun, Father Martin Godart, the abbey's viticultural expert, was interrupted in his lecture on the dogma of the Incarnation by a series of violent explosions. The two old French mountain guns, the 25-pounder of Mike Scott, the three-inch mortars without sights and a handful of light mortars were doing their best to silence the guns of Habes Majali.

Desperately short of ammunition, the Jews' counterfire was brief. Their infantry was soon alone before the machine guns and cannons of the Legion.

A pale sun climbing into a leaden sky overhead heralded the arrival of still another enemy, the cruelest the Jewish soldiers would face that morning. It was the hot, burning wind of the khamsin rolling up from the depths of the Arabian Desert to wrap Palestine in a mantle of fire. The wind brought along with it wave after wave of tiny black mosquitoes called *barkaches*. They infested the men's nostrils, their mouths, their eyelids, every exposed inch of their skin, driving some of them half mad with their sharp little bites.

Studying the battlefield from Hulda, Shlomo Shamir realized that his first battle as an Israeli officer was lost before it had really begun. His forces were much too weak to take Latrun in a daytime frontal attack. The only thing left was to minimize his men's losses and suffering by organizing a rapid retreat. Before giving the order, Shamir waited for the results of a desperate effort of Laskov's lead company to outflank Latrun village and reach the Latrun–Ramallah road. But the vicious fire from the Vickers machine guns on the roof of the police station and a Legion counterattack thwarted his attempt. Without waiting for an order from Laskov, the commander of the company told his men to withdraw. With their radio communications cut, most of the units along the front started to do the same thing.

The plain came alive with crawling, running men as the Haganah began an agonizing retreat. To cover the withdrawal, Laskov ordered the men who had taken cover in the monks' vegetable garden to move across the plain to a rocky crest called Hill 314 just opposite the Latrun heights. From there he hoped they could protect the immigrants' retreat. As soon as the company started to move, the Arabs opened fire. All around the men, the wheatfields which had once been fired by the flaming tails of Samson's jackals were set ablaze by Arab tracers and phosphorus shells.

Trapped by flying shrapnel, bullets, the withering heat, the dense smoke of the burning fields, tortured by thirst and clouds of *barkaches,* men collapsed of sheer exhaustion. Some were not able to get up. The others crawled and dragged themselves, pulling their wounded with them, trying to jump from one rock to another for cover. The survivors who finally struggled to the crest of Hill 314 saw that they were on a desert of rocks. With no entrenching tools, they had to dig the emplacements for their guns with their fingers. Their fire kept the Legion from circling around the hilltop to fall on their retreating comrades, until their machine guns jammed. Ezra Ayalon saw their commander take his Sten gun and leap behind a tree to continue his fire. While his men pulled back, he remained there, covering their withdrawal. For half an hour, it seemed, Ayalon could hear the burst of the Sten gun. Then there was silence.

From their observation posts near the Tomb of Ibn-Jebel, Lieutenant Colonel Habes Majali and Captain Mahmoud Rousan followed the attack. "My God," thought Rousan, "the Haganah must really want Latrun to throw themselves in front of our guns like this." Rousan was particularly awed by the Israelis' determination to take their dead and wounded off the battlefield with them. Six times he saw a group of men on Hill 314 trying to get down its forward slopes to pick up their dead comrades. "Each effort," the Arab officer noted, "cost them a couple more dead." Their retreat seemed without pattern, the flight "of a flock without a shepherd."

Majali ordered his mortars to concentrate their fire on the hill while his field guns worked over the passages just behind it. There Zvi Hurewitz was trying to lead his immigrants back to Hulda. For many of those men the road away from the ghettoes and death camps of Europe was ending on the sun-scorched plain of Latrun. The Promised Land had offered them nothing but a brief and fatal exposure to its unrelenting sun, its savage swarms of mosquitoes and the tortures of thirst. Like packs of wolves, the Arab villagers followed their retreating footsteps, using their knives on the wounded or those who fell from exhaustion.

In the terror of the Arab shelling, many of the immigrants had forgotten the few words of Hebrew hastily learned on their descent from the *Kalanit*. Matti Megid, who had begged Ben-Gurion to give his men more time for training, tried to gather some of them and lead them to safety. They were like frightened animals. "They didn't even know how to crawl under fire. Some of them didn't know how to fire the rifles that had been thrown at them a few hours before. Their section leaders had to run from man to man under fire to show them how to take their safeties off." Many who did know how to fire their rifles could not sight them. Hurewitz picked up one exhausted survivor of his battalion mumbling in Yiddish, "I saw him, I saw him, but I couldn't hit him."

Megid saw the familiar face of a seventeen-year-old boy he remembered from the *Kalanit*. He was lying in a ditch, dying. "Oh," he whispered to Megid, "we must have disappointed you." Farther on, he came on a boy who had mimeographed a news sheet for him in a D.P. camp in Germany. Weeping, the youth was clawing through the weeds looking for the thick glasses without which he was helpless.

The survivors of Laskov's first company and the debris of Hurewitz' battalion finally found themselves huddled together on the slopes of Hill 314. At eleven o'clock, their ammunition virtually gone, they were authorized to withdraw and move south to the Arab village of Beit Jiz, now occupied, according to Laskov, by friendly forces. There they would at last find water—none of them had been issued canteens—and buses to get them back to Hulda.

From all sides the survivors struggled toward Beit Jiz. To provide cover, Laskov took his armored cars and half-tracks bouncing across the open plain toward the village. Buffeted by the khamsin, literally dying of thirst, the Jewish soldiers fainted one after another in the parched plains; even the indomitable Laskov, dizzy with heat and exhaustion, felt his own strength beginning to ebb. The sight of one of Hurewitz' company commanders driving his immigrants toward safety at gunpoint revived him.

489

Men ran, fell, got up, stumbled over the dead and dying, turned to fire a round or two, collapsed. A deadening sense of lassitude spread through their ranks. The wounded begged the living to kill them.

Others didn't get up. Asher Levi came on two immigrants collapsed side by side, a haunted expression in their eyes. "Leave us alone. We want to stay here," one of them mumbled. Levi resorted to the only tactic he thought might save them. He began to club them with his rifle butt until they staggered to their feet to escape his beating.

At the promised haven of Beit Jiz, there was neither water nor transport nor Haganah men to greet the pitiful flock staggering back from Latrun. There was only another rank of Arab guns. The village had been occupied by the Arab irregulars, and their fire caused the last Jewish casualties of the retreat.

It was two o'clock in the afternoon when the first survivors finally stumbled back to the buses they had left twelve hours before. All day Laskov and his half-tracks, dodging Arab shellfire, combed the blackened fields for the last survivors.

In his headquarters, Captain Mahmoud Rousan thumbed through the dozens of identity cards recovered from his foes' bodies by Lieutenant Ayad's patrol. "They belong to Jews from every part of the world," the wondering Rousan noted, "who had come here to fight for this land of milk and honey."

No one would ever know how many of those immigrants had purchased with their lives the right to enter their new country. In the confusion that had preceded the attack, there had been no time to compile accurate rosters for their companies. Officially, the Haganah would admit to seventy-five dead. Unofficially, its historians acknowledged years later that their losses had far exceeded that. The Legion claimed that eight hundred of the attackers had been killed, clearly an exaggerated figure, but they did capture 220 rifles. Their own losses were insignificant.

Whatever the true figures, the immigrants of Shlomo Shamir's Seventh Brigade, assailed by a determined foe, by the khamsin and the *barkaches,* had suffered the bloodiest defeat an Israeli unit would receive in three wars with the Arabs.

40

". . . REMEMBER ME ONLY IN HAPPINESS."

THE CENTER of Amman was dense with the crowds. Clapping their hands in rhythm to their slogans, they danced from street to street chanting their army's victory. Their jubilant chorus gave the men in the hotel conference room opposite the Roman arena of ancient Philadelphia a pleasant pause. The triumph of Latrun was not the only Arab victory the members of the Arab League's Political Committee had to celebrate. The same day that Colonel Majali's men had turned back the Israelis at Latrun, the kibbutz of Yad Mordechai, after five days of heroic resistance, had fallen to the Egyptian Army. Only in the north, where the Israelis had driven the Syrians from Galilee, had the Arab armies suffered an important reverse.

The sense of coming triumph did not dispose the Arab leaders to look with favor upon the paper presented to them by the League's secretary, Azzam Pasha: an appeal from the United Nations Security Council for a cease-fire within thirty-six hours.

Since May 14 the United States had been seeking to get a cease-fire call through the Security Council. The American efforts had been persistently thwarted by Great Britain. Persuaded that the Arabs might be on the threshold of substantial gains, the British showed no disposition to hasten the end of the fighting. As one of Britain's senior diplomats told an American colleague, the situation "should be allowed to seek its own level for a while."

Finally, on May 22, the United States and the Soviet Union had pushed a cease-fire appeal through the Security Council after British opposition had thwarted their plea for an "order" to stop fighting with severe sanctions if it wasn't followed.

In Tel Aviv, David Ben-Gurion polled his military on the advisability of accepting it. Their arms situation had improved slightly. Five more Messerschmitts had been flown into Israel, and the first major shipment of arms to arrive by sea had reached Haifa harbor. Nonetheless, Ben-Gurion's advisers were unanimous: a cease-fire was much to be desired.

Quite a different sentiment animated the Arab leaders meeting in Amman. Convinced that Jerusalem was about to fall to their forces, they categorically rejected the cease-fire appeal. Instead, the Arab leaders issued to the United Nations an ultimatum of their own: they gave the world body forty-eight hours to devise a new Palestine solution which would not include a Jewish state.

. . .

In the Jewish Quarter of Jerusalem's Old City, the rabbis who four days earlier had begged their superiors to "shake the world and save our souls" urged the quarter's Haganah commander to surrender. "We have been saying psalms all the time, yet the battle continues," one of them sadly told Moshe Russnak. Clearly, it was God's will that they surrender.

Russnak's situation was indeed desperate. Abdullah Tell's relentless pressure had deprived his men of position after position. The quarter's limited space had now been reduced to half its original dimensions. Their water was almost gone. The electricity supply had failed. The sewers no longer worked and it was impossible to collect garbage. In the May heat, the quarter's alleys were heavy with the stench of decomposing human excrement. An even worse smell, the putrefying odor of dead flesh, clung to every stone around the hospital. Unable to bury their dead, the quarter's doctors had ordered them wrapped in old sheets and stacked in a court-yard behind the hospital. Among them were Rabbi Yitzhak Orenstein and his wife. While their son and their fifteen-year-old daughter, Sarah, were fighting on the quarter's perimeter, the rabbi who had greeted Israel's birth May 14 with a *shechiyanu* had been killed with his wife by a shell falling on their home. Young Avraham Orenstein had been able to leave his post just long enough to say the Kaddish, the prayer for the dead, over his father's body.

In the hospital, even the last bottles of blood plasma had been lost when the power failed. There was no anesthetic left, and operations were performed without it by flashlight. The old vaulted rooms of Misgav Ladakh were crowded with over one hundred and fifty wounded, fighters and civilians alike. On one of those beds, her back torn open by a mortar fragment, was the English girl who had wanted so much to be a part of the Old City's defense, Esther Cailingold.

Uprooted from their homes because the Arabs had either captured them or made life in them unbearable with shellfire, most of the quarter's seventeen hundred residents huddled together in three synagogues just

492

inside the Haganah's lines. They cooked on the floor, slept on dirt-encrusted, vermin-filled old mattresses, weeping, praying or gazing off into space.

Yet despite his grim situation, Russnak would not yield to the rabbis' pleas for surrender. Time and time again since May 18 he had been promised help, and time and time again it had failed to arrive. So categoric had been the promises made to him this morning, however, that Russnak was persuaded to hold on. Tonight, he told the rabbis, help had to arrive.

Instead of reinforcements, it was a surprise sent by the Arabs that the next twenty-four hours would bring Russnak.

Dissatisfied with the results being obtained by his artillery on the Mount of Olives, Abdullah Tell had decided to bring his guns to the heart of Jerusalem, where the penetrating effect of their shells would be devastating. Past the Stations of the Cross of the Via Dolorosa, using sandbags to smooth over stairways, Tell succeeded in moving two of his armored cars where only mules and goats had gone before, through the crooked alleyways of the Old City.

Their appearance bewildered the Haganah's weary soldiers. "We didn't know what hit us, it was all new to us," Yehuda Choresh recalled. There was not a single antitank weapon in the quarter's depleted armory. Choresh and his comrades fled to the rooftops. There they threw their handful of Molotov cocktails at the cars, hoping that the narrow, rubble-filled passageways below would stop them.

Thirty-three days after Passover, the Jewish feast of Lag B'Omer commemorates the miraculous halt of a plague sweeping Judea during the Roman wars and the last struggle of the Jewish people to wrest their independence from Rome. As that normally festive day dawned in the Jewish Quarter Thursday, May 27, it was clear both to its deeply religious inhabitants and to its exhausted defenders that only a similar miracle could save them.

Taking a post-by-post survey of his perimeter, Moshe Russnak discovered that of the two hundred fighters with whom the struggle had begun and the eighty reinforcements who had come in with Gazit, thirty-five men remained unwounded. Together they had an average of ten bullets per man. There was no ammunition left for the Bren guns. Leah Vultz's factory had converted the last Players cigarette tin and tomato can in the quarter into her homemade grenades. Only one remained in her reserve and it would not leave its hiding place. Leah was determined to kill herself with it when the end came.

Russnak's pitiful perimeter included the hospital, his headquarters and

493

the three ancient synagogues, into whose cellars the demoralized residents were packed. Only one other major synagogue remained in Jewish hands, the Hurva, the principal temple of the Ashkenazim, considered the most beautiful in all Jerusalem and, indeed, all Palestine. As the dome of St. Peter's dominated the skyline of Rome, its graceful eighteenth-century parabola towered over the roofs of Old Jerusalem. Anxious to avoid the opprobrium of destroying it, Abdullah Tell had written Otto Lehner of the Red Cross forty-eight hours before to warn that unless the Haganah abandoned its positions in the synagogue and its adjoining courtyard, he would be forced to attack it.

Russnak could not agree to his request. The Hurva was the key to the last stretch of ground he controlled. Once it fell, the Arabs would be fifteen yards from the seventeen hundred civilians he was defending. He would fight for it as long as he could.

Even in the despair and filth of the crumbling quarter, the normal events of life went on. A woman gave birth to a baby girl and named her "Reinforcements," for that thought was uppermost in everybody's mind. The doctors at the hospital could spare her a bed just long enough to let her deliver her child. Then, carrying the new infant under her arm, she returned to the Rabbi Jochanan ben Zakai Synagogue and started cooking for her family.

As he did every morning, Jacob Tangy, an orderly in the hospital, tagged with identity cards the shrouds wrapping the night's dead. Then, in the clean shirt he had saved for the occasion, Tangy ran to the cellar of the Gates of Heaven Yeshiva for a ceremony symbolizing life's continuance and, above all, in Tangy's mind, Jewish life in their shattered quarter. It was his wedding.

His bride had arrived from her front-line post a few minutes before, just in time to change from her khaki uniform to a dress. By the light of a candle quivering from the shock of exploding shells, the two young people exchanged their vows, praying according to their Jewish marriage service that soon "there may be heard in the cities of Judah, in the streets of Jerusalem, the sound of joy and gladness."

• • •

Abdullah Tell's company commanders were unanimous in their reports at their daily conference that morning: With one concerted push, the quarter would fall.

There was no doubt in Tell's mind where the attack should be made. Confident that he had discharged his moral obligations in his unanswered letter to the Red Cross, he told his men, "Get the Hurva Synagogue by noon."

"If we do," replied Captain Moussa, "promise us you will have tea in it this afternoon."

"*Insh' Allah!* God willing!" said Tell.

The destruction of the ancient synagogue would be the final achievement of Fawzi el Kutub's savage career.

To blow his way through the walls surrounding it, he strapped to a ladder a 200-liter barrel filled with explosives. Four men, among them Nadi Dai'es, the coffee boy who had discovered Abdul Khader's body at Kastel, grabbed the ends of the ladder as though it were a stretcher. Pistol in hand, Fawzi led them across a fifty-yard strip of open ground to the base of the synagogue's courtyard wall. As they ran for cover, Fawzi waited an instant to make sure the fuse he lit with a cigarette was burning. Then he ran for shelter.

The explosion blew a gaping hole in the synagogue wall. For forty-five minutes, a dozen Haganah soldiers kept the Legion from bursting through it, hurling every hand grenade they possessed into the breach. Finally their fire stopped and the Legionnaires burst in. They found a rare booty, a pile of rifles. For the first time, the quarter had had more arms than men. There simply had not been enough fighters to carry them away.

The Legionnaires entered the synagogue itself and tried to scramble to the top of its dome to plant an Arab flag. Three of them were shot by Haganah snipers, but the fourth succeeded. Clearly visible in the New City, their flag over the skyline of the Old City signaled the Legion's triumph.

With the capture of the Hurva, twenty-five percent of the territory remaining to the Haganah had fallen to the Arabs. Only one thing saved the quarter from annihilation. The captured area was full of shops, and a looting party was soon in full sway.

Profiting from the respite the looting gave him, Russnak decided to make a desperate effort to reestablish a defense by taking back a small building on the flank of the synagogue. Called the Defense Club, its windows offered the Haganah a vantage point from which they might at least slow the Legion's advance.

Russnak decided to get his best surviving fighter, Yitzhak the Bren

Gunner, to lead the attack. He sent a dark-haired girl lieutenant with his order. "I can't," said Yitzhak, who had fought in almost all the quarter's battles. "All this means nothing now. In the end we'll surrender."

"Yitzhak, it must be done," pleaded the girl. "The Arabs are only fifteen yards away. If you don't, they'll sweep everything away in an hour. There are women and children."

Furious, resigned, the young Kurdish Jew got to his feet, called five men and left. Two minutes later he was dead. The quarter's last offensive was over.

A few minutes later, a gigantic explosion shook Jerusalem. A thick cloud of red-gray dust billowed up from the heart of the Old City, darkening the horizon before the Jewish Quarter and sprinkling its alleys with a brick dust. As the smoke finally cleared, a thousand anguished Jewish voices began to chant in the basements of the three remaining synagogues Judaism's holiest prayer, the Shema Yisrael. It had been Fawzi el Kutub and not Abdullah Tell who had come to tea at the Hurva Synagogue. Using the last explosives left in his Turkish bath, Kutub had wreaked his final revenge on the neighbors against whom he had waged his lifetime's crusade. The skyline of Jerusalem had lost one of its great monuments. He had reduced what was left of the city's most precious synagogue to ruins.

As if the destruction of their synagogue was the final act of their destiny, a strange reaction swept over the quarter's residents, now huddled in their dark cellars. They broke out the last few treasures they had been hiding. In every corner of the fetid, sweaty basements of the three synagogues still standing, people broke into their reserves of wine, sweets, chocolates, cigarettes, lentil soup, noodles. In a few moments the cellars were alive with the merriment of a gigantic feast of the damned.

From his headquarters Russnak sent a clear warning to the New City: if help did not arrive that night it would be all over. But the only help to come over the wall that night was sent in the casing of a Davidka shell with its explosives removed. In it two Palmachniks put the one thing that might aid the beleaguered comrades they could not reach, bullets. On top they slipped a note reading: "Strength and courage. We are with you." Then they fired their Davidka.

The shell fell inside the Arabs' lines.

• • •

A few minutes past nine o'clock Friday, May 28, the telephone rang in Major Abdullah Tell's headquarters at Rawdah School. It was Captain

Moussa. "Two rabbis," he said, "are coming out of the quarter with a white flag."

Walking into Moussa's headquarters in the Armenian School of the Holy Translators, Tell found himself face to face with the first Jews he had ever met: the seventy-year-old Rabbi Reuven Hazan and the eighty-three-year-old Rabbi Zeev Mintzberg. As Jerusalem's Arab mayor had surrendered the city to the British with an old bedsheet thirty-one years earlier, the two had come to prepare their quarter's surrender to the Arab Legion.

Their arrival climaxed a two-hour struggle inside the quarter. The Haganah had thwarted with gunfire the rabbis' first effort to cross the battle line, wounding Hazan. Undaunted, they insisted that Russnak would have to kill them to stop them from going to the Arabs. "It makes no difference who kills us," Hazan declared. "The situation is hopeless."

The hard-pressed Russnak summoned a meeting of his staff. The situation was indeed hopeless. The Legion was six yards away from the synagogue in which the residents huddled; the hospital was out of virtually every form of medicine. His men had ammunition for no more than another half hour. After that, seventeen hundred people would be at the mercy of the Arabs. Russnak decided to try to stall for time by talking. He authorized the two rabbis to ask for a cease-fire for the removal of the dead and wounded.

Politely but firmly, Tell ordered Rabbi Hazan back to the quarter to bring Rabbi Weingarten and a representative of the Haganah. On his side, Russnak delayed as long as he dared, then ordered an Arabic-speaking officer, Shaul Tawil, back to Tell.

Tell had meanwhile invited the Red Cross's Otto Lehner and the United Nations' Pablo de Azcarate to witness the proceedings. Azcarate was deeply moved. He found Tell "without a single word or gesture which could have humiliated or offended the defeated leader in any way," Tawil "calm, strong, showing not the slightest sign of submission or resentment." Tell was not prepared to enter discussions, however. His terms were simple. All able-bodied men would be taken prisoner. Women, children and the aged would be sent to the New City. The wounded, depending on the extent of their injuries, would be held prisoner or returned. Although he knew there were many women in the ranks of the Haganah, he would take no women prisoners. Tell dictated his terms to Nassib Boulos, a bilingual Arab correspondent of *Time* magazine; then he gave the Haganah until four o'clock to accept his offer.

While they had been talking, a phenomenon had occurred which was to shatter any hope Russnak still had of prolonging negotiations on until nightfall. The residents huddling in the cellars of Rabbi Jochanan ben Zakai Synagogue had learned of the surrender delegation. Shrieking shouts of joy and thanksgiving, they rushed past their Haganah guards into the street. Within minutes, Arabs and Jews who had been killing each other hours before were embracing in the street, old friends greeted each other with tears of relief, the Legionnaires moved out of their posts and began to mingle with the men of the Haganah, Jewish shopkeepers opened their stores. Bitterly, Russnak noted that some of them who had given his men a glass of water begrudgingly were offering cakes and coffee to the Arabs. Seeing the two peoples so completely intermingled, Russnak realized that surrender was already an accomplished fact. It only remained to perform the act that would consecrate it.

Sadly Russnak smoked his last cigarette in his candle-lit office, then assembled his officers. All except the representative of the Irgun agreed to surrender. Armed by their votes, Russnak put on an Australian battle blouse and a beret, strapped an old Parabellum to his waist, and set off to surrender to his Arab foes the oldest patch of Jewish soil in the world.

Their shoes brushed, their uniforms straightened, the thirty-odd Haganah men who had survived unscathed lined up in three ranks on one side of the courtyard designated by Tell for the surrender ceremony. Opposite them, the residents had begun to assemble children, sacks of clothes, scraps of furniture with which to remember their homes.

Surveying the pitiful lines of his foes, Tell told Russnak, "If I had known you were so few we would have come after you with sticks, not guns." Then, seeing the worry on the faces of the residents, Tell realized they all feared they would be the victims of another massacre. He began to move down their ranks, quietly seeking with a gesture or a word to reassure them. In the hospital, one of his officers read in the eyes of the wounded "the terrified conviction that we would massacre them all." The United Press's Samir Souki, picking his way through that same roomful of misery, nauseated by the terrible stench of death, heard a voice calling his name. Looking down, he recognized a taxicab driver he knew, trembling with fear of a coming massacre. Souki stooped down and offered him a cigarette and the assurance that all would be well.

Their fears would indeed prove unfounded. Tell's only victims would be Arab, not Jewish—looters who had thrown themselves with too much haste on the booty.

498

The shortest, saddest exile in modern Jewish history began just before sunset. Two by two, some thirteen hundred residents of the Jewish Quarter started over the five hundred yards separating them from Zion Gate and the New City. Their departure marked the end of almost two thousand years of continuous Jewish residence—interrupted only by a sixty-year period in the sixteenth century—inside the Old Walls of Jerusalem. Abandoned behind them was the ruined wall over which they and so many generations before them had been sorrowing sentinels. As the villagers of Hebron had uprooted the orchards of Kfar Etzion to eradicate the last traces of Jewish settlement from their hills, so the last vestiges of Jewish residence inside Jerusalem's walls would be effaced from their ancient quarter. As the refugees passed through Zion Gate, sparks from the first of their fired buildings sputtered into the sky.

Tell's Legionnaires offered them the protection of their bodies along the narrow passageways and staircases so familiar to them, holding back the excited Arab crowds. They helped the aged, carried bundles or children for overburdened women. They drove back the excited mob with their rifle butts, arrested those who tried to pelt the Jews with stones, and, on one occasion, fired over the crowd's head to hold them back.

Some of those people abandoning their homes had never been outside the Old City. One 100-year-old man had left it ninety years earlier to look at the first houses built outside its walls; he had never left since. Saddest sight of all were the bearded old men, leaving a lifetime of study behind them. Some, fortunate enough to pass their own homes on their way into exile, stopped to reverently kiss the mezuza, the blessed inscription on the lintel of their front door.

At the gate, an elderly rabbi suddenly burst from the lines and thrust a three-foot-high package into the hands of Antoine Albina, a Christian Arab. "It is something holy from the synagogue," he said. "I give it to you. It is a trust." It was a seven-hundred-year-old Torah twenty-three yards long, written on gazelle parchment. Albina would keep it for eleven years, until he was able to hand it over to the first rabbi to visit Arab Jerusalem in a decade.*

On the other side of the city, a desperate rush was under way to prepare to receive the refugees. Having decided to lodge them in the homes abandoned by the Arabs in Katamon, Dov Joseph sent his assistant

---

* The rabbi, Dr. Elmer Berger, a distinguished scholar, noted for his anti-Zionist convictions, in turn presented it to a New York synagogue.

Chaim Haller to scour the neighborhood for sheets and blankets. In one Catholic home, Haller found an enormous hoard of candles. Realizing how much it would mean to those orthodox refugees to have a Sabbath candle to light their new homes, Haller took them all, vowing not to reveal their unsanctified origins to their recipients.

Until well into the evening, the sad procession continued through Zion Gate, the flames of their burning quarter illuminating their faces. Masha Weingarten thought, "It is the end of my life." Her father insisted on leaving with the prisoners, carrying off with him into captivity in Amman the key to Zion Gate given him by a British officer only a fortnight earlier.

Avraham Orenstein and his sister went to the home in which their parents had been killed. "It was full of books, full of childhood memories" for Avraham. He wanted to take something, some souvenir of his dead parents, but he couldn't think of anything. Sarah picked up "some silly object." Then they parted, she heading to the New City, he to prison camp with 293 others.

From a street corner near Zion Gate, the man who had led so many destructive forays against their quarter watched the last Jewish refugees leave. All his life Fawzi el Kutub had been used to seeing Jews in the streets of his native Old Jerusalem. Suddenly he understood that he was seeing them there for the last time. Their pathetic parade was the final triumph of the strange and vicious career he had begun twelve years earlier, only a few yards from the doorway in which he now stood, hurling a homemade hand grenade at a Jewish bus.

Among the last people through the gate was Leah Vultz. The Legion had not given her cause to use her final grenade.

Looking at the flames of the quarter she had fought so hard to defend, she thought of "the Jews of Spain leaving their burning ghettoes." Bitterly she cried to the first man on the other side, "Jews! You remained here, and we had to surrender."

As night fell, only the quarter's 153 wounded remained in the Old City, crowded in their wretched hospital, waiting for the inspection by a team of doctors to determine which of them would be returned to the New City and which would go to prison camp. Soon the fires raging in the looted quarter began to creep up on their sanctuary. Persuaded that the hour of their massacre had come, the wounded saw a company of Legionnaires march into the building. They had come, however, to carry their injured enemies to the safety of the nearby Armenian Patriarchate.

At his headquarters, Abdullah Tell received the final accolade of his triumphant day. It was a telephone call from Amman. Warm and paternal, the King personally congratulated the young officer he had sent to the city ten days before.

Beyond the Old City walls, Chaim Haller went from room to room trying to comfort the refugees in their strange New City surroundings. They were "totally shattered." But, to his astonishment, he discovered it was not the closeness of their brush with death, nor the loss of the only homes most of them had ever had, that had so totally demoralized them. The cause of their deep grief was the fact that it was Friday evening and in riding from Zion Gate to Katamon most of them had desecrated the Sabbath for the first time in their lives.

Haller offered them the only comfort he could. Into the hands of those devastated men and women he pressed the candles blessed by the priests of another faith rooted in the soil of Jerusalem. Tears in his eyes, he watched their faces as they lit them, overjoyed to have honored at least one Sabbath commandment after having violated so many others.

Racked by a high fever, in terrible agony, Esther Cailingold lay dying this Sabbath eve on the floor of the second story of the Armenian monastery with the rest of the wounded. There was no morphine left to ease her pain, and the wounded man beside her saw one of the orderlies bend over and offer the only sedative he had, a cigarette. She lifted her hand and started to take it. Then her hand fell back.

"No," she whispered. *"Shabbat."*

They were her last words. A few minutes later she lapsed into a final coma. Under her pillow was a letter she had written to her parents five days earlier anticipating the possibility of her death in the fighting enveloping the quarter. It was the only legacy the English girl would leave.

> DEAR MUMMY AND DADDY,
>
> I am writing to beg you that whatever may have happened to me, you will make the effort to take it in the spirit I want. We had a difficult fight. I have tasted hell but it has been worthwhile because I am convinced the end will see a Jewish state and all our longings. I have lived my life fully, and very sweet it has been to be here in our land . . . I hope one day soon you will all come and enjoy the fruits of that for which we are fighting. Be happy and remember me only in happiness.
>
> Shalom.
> ESTHER

The red-bearded giant lying on the floor beside her wept as her labored breathing slowly faded away. Outside the monastery, the flames of the burning quarter for which she had died reddened the night sky and sent streams of sparks dancing skyward like a whirl of snowflakes caught in a beam of light. Stretched out in the darkness, Shar Yeshuv Cohen thought of a Biblical line he had often chanted as a boy. He began to sing it now, over and over again, softly at first, then stronger, until finally it rolled from his pallet with all the power of his deep bass voice. The other wounded lying around him in the darkness took it up, too. Gradually building in strength, it became a proud, defiant roar, reverberating through the vaulted chamber of the monastery.

"Out of blood and fire Judea will fall," they sang, "and out of blood and fire it will be reborn."

41

"GOOD NIGHT AND GOODBYE FROM JERUSALEM"

CAPTAIN EMILE JUMEAN studied the twenty-five selected targets on the 1:25,000-scale British Army map on the floor of an unfinished schoolhouse three miles north of Jerusalem. From his schoolhouse the Arab Legion officer commanded the force which now represented the most immediate military threat to Jewish Jerusalem, twelve 25-pounder field guns. The meticulous Arab officer had designated each of their targets with a code name. Notre-Dame was "Whiskey," after the favored liquor of its former Scots residents. The Jewish Agency was "Flower." The Schneller School was "Diamond."

Major Abdullah Tell had hoped to follow the conquest of the Old City with a push into New Jerusalem. Mindful of the losses he had incurred at Notre-Dame, Glubb categorically rejected his suggestion. Angrily, Tell decided to rely on Jumean's guns to obtain the result he wanted to secure himself. By pounding the city daily he hoped to disrupt its existence, to make civilian life unbearable, and finally to force its surrender.

Jumean spread his guns on three key hilltops controlled by a trio of observers: one on a rooftop in Sheikh Jarrah, one on a minaret in Nebi Samuel and one in a house on the Mount of Olives. In addition to his own guns, he also controlled a pair of Iraqi six-inch howitzers on Nebi Samuel. With an allotment of ten shells a gun a day, he could hurl almost 150 rounds into Jerusalem's confined New City every twenty-four hours, enough to make life hell for its inhabitants.

It was a weapon against which the Jews were helpless. Jumean's cannons were far beyond the reach of the Haganah. The city was to be saved, ironically, by an old British ordinance promulgated in 1920 by Sir Ronald Storrs. It required all new homes in Jerusalem to be built of stone to preserve its special character. But no ordinance could save the lives of its Jewish residents. As day after day Jumean's shells whistled into its streets, Jerusalem's casualty toll mounted until, at the end, it would represent, on a proportional basis, five times the toll suffered by London in the worst year of the Blitz.

The only reply the Haganah could offer was in an abandoned brewery in Givat Shaul. Eliahu Sochaczever, who had carried off the Menorah Club's Turkish cannon, had installed a small explosive plant in its precincts. His treasure was a store of chlorate KCL 63 that had been used as a weed killer. By a complex electrolysis system, he had managed to break down its elements, which, mixed with organic materials, gave him a homemade Cheddite to pack the city's mines, grenades and Davidka shells.* As Sochaczever labored early one morning a religious Jew, a blanket around his shoulders like a prayer shawl, stumbled into his laboratory. Seeing Sochaczever's Davidka shells, he kissed and blessed each one.

David Shaltiel was forced to hoard those precious shells with the parsimony of a miser. As each day dragged by with the road to the sea closed, his ammunition reserve dwindled. No one in his command was allowed to fire a three-inch mortar or a Davidka without his personal approval. Occasionally, when one of his units asked for cover fire, Shaltiel waited until an Arab shell had fallen near its positions, then informed his men it had been one of their own rounds. His machine guns and Brens could not be used on automatic fire without clearance from headquarters. At Notre-Dame the defenders were forbidden to fire at targets more than a hundred yards away. One night, ammunition reserves at Notre-Dame were down to five rounds per man.

Throughout the command there was an absolute ban on discussing the situation by radio or telephone, in case the Arabs were intercepting their communications. The few cases of rifle ammunition reaching the city by Piper Cub were jealously seized by Shaltiel's arms expert, a portly Yemenite cheesemaker named Yaffe. He hid their reserves in a series of hiding places known only to him and to the Jerusalem commander. Their final "iron ration" was locked in the basement of the Jewish Agency, to be used only in the last resort. How close they were to breaking into it was revealed to Yitzhak Levi on May 29, the day after the Old City's surrender. That morning, their ammunition report showed there were eight three-inch mortar shells and a reported average of forty rounds of ammunition per rifle left to the city.

That crucial situation was overshadowed in the public eye by the other

---

* In 1949, Sochaczever took some of his product to the French town of Cheddes for whose factory it was named. The astonished Frenchmen found that his product was even purer than theirs.

shortages which affected everybody in the city—those of food and water. The gesture of General Jones's departing British communications officer in assigning to the city the code name "Cod" had been singularly appropriate. Jerusalem reeked of one of the rare commodities in Dov Joseph's warehouses, dried fish. The critical lack of food touched everybody. At Notre-Dame, Netanel Lorch almost came to blows with a fellow officer in arguing whether a looted sausage should be left at a position or whether it should leave with its departing occupants. Shaltiel had to tell his men, who ocasionally fainted from hunger at their posts, that their rations were minimal because "Jerusalem has been besieged for two months and our reserves are critically low. . . . You must remember," he said, "Jerusalem's elderly, her women and children, are hungry, too."

There were all kinds of improvisations. With the *khubeiza* gone, some people tried to make a kind of spinach by boiling grape leaves. A common dish was crushed matzo sprinkled with oil, spread on more matzo and called "monkey fat." Ruth Erlik grew radishes on her windowsill, watering them with the last of her water ration after it had been passed through its four traditional stages. Mrs. Joseph Rivlin, a distinguished hostess, offered her occasional callers a cup of water passed through her ancient samovar, hoping that somehow the memory of the gallons of tea it had boiled over the years would leave an imprint upon it. Because the shelling made food distribution difficult, the meager bread ration was often stale. Mothers with babies had to soften it with water so that their children could eat it. The city was filled with sick infants for whom the hospitals, overflowing with wounded, had no room.

Dov Joseph asked Ben-Gurion if there was any possibility of airlifting supplies. Ben-Gurion replied they might be able to fly in three tons a week. Joseph exploded. "Jerusalem's minimum needs to keep the population alive for a week are 140 tons of flour, three tons of powdered eggs, ten tons of powdered milk, ten tons of smoked or salted fish and ten tons of yellow cheese," he cabled Ben-Gurion. "The three tons which you suggeest will solve nothing whatsoever."

Anguished, Ben-Gurion replied in a cable addressed to the city: "Help will come . . . The moral effort as well as the physical effort of the Army will save and liberate our capital. Courage and strength."

The other shortages plaguing the city were equally vexatious. Without fuel for trucks, there was no garbage collection. Waste rotted in the May heat all over the city, and, with the Arab shelling, burning it was a hazardous procedure. The tinkling bell of the waterman announcing the arrival of the water ration became unforgettable music to every Jerusalemite. The hospitals faced one shortage after another. Clinics designed to handle fifty or sixty patients had four or five times that number as the Arab shelling began to take a frightening toll. Dizzy with hunger, Professor Edward Joseph and his assistants performed an average of twenty-one abdominal operations a day, working twenty-four hours nonstop, then sleeping eight.

Cigarettes had disappeared. Even Shaltiel, a chain smoker, had none. One night his adjutant, Yeshurun Schiff, found a treasure, three butts, in the street. He ran to Shaltiel's room at Greta Ascher's boardinghouse. Like schoolboys, the two officers cut them apart and rolled their tobacco into one precious smoke.

In the midst of all the problems besetting Jerusalem, there were still determined islands of normalcy. Kol Jerusalem, the radio station, broadcast regular news bulletins in Hebrew, Arabic, English and French.

The most famous members of its staff were the thirty musicians in its orchestra. Although there was no current for their broadcasts, they insisted on continuing their Tuesday concerts, playing in the streets outside their studio for anyone brave enough to defy the Arabs' shelling. If it became too intense, they simply moved inside and continued to play by candlelight.

Their radio station provided a constant and memorable reassurance to Jerusalemites of their capacity to withstand the siege. Many, like Aaron Elner, would never forget sitting night after night, in darkened bedrooms or cellars, the sound of Arab shells bursting in the streets outside, listening to the calm voice of the announcer repeat once again the reassuring phrase "Good night and goodbye from Jerusalem."

• • •

Jerusalem's Arab population too was beset by problems, though none of them were as serious as those facing the Jewish parts of the city. The gravest was that caused by the refugees from the Arab neighborhoods seized by the Haganah on May 14 and 15. Almost thirty thousand people were crammed into the Old City and Sheikh Jarrah, and if the Haganah's shellfire was only sporadic, it still had devastating results in such a small, densely populated area.

The hospital in the Austrian Hospice remained desperately short of almost everything. Most graveyards were under Jewish fire, and the dead were buried in gardens and back lots. Father Eugene Hoade, an Irishman, buried in the Garden of Gethsemane two of his countrymen who had deserted from the British Army to fight with the Arabs. The priestly veteran of El Alamein also took time from his ecclesiastical chores to teach a group of Arab Legionnaires how to use a bazooka.

With the power station in Jewish hands, the Old City was without electricity except that furnished by a generator at Terra Sancta, the custodian's office for the Holy Places. The city was temporarily without water too, as it had lived on the same source cut below Bab el Wad. The Arabs, however, were able to reactivate an abandoned source at Ein Fara nine miles from the city.

George Deeb handled the food problem by purchasing five thousand tons of foodstuffs from Steele Brothers in Beirut. By selling it at a ten percent premium, the municipality was able to overcome its most embarrassing shortage, caused by Anton Safieh's lost check—its total lack of funds.

• • •

Sadly, his regard full of reproach, Tewfic Abou Hoda passed the slip of paper on his desk to John Glubb. It was a communication from the War Office. His Majesty's government, it noted, having taken cognizance of the fighting in Palestine, would be most embarrassed if any British subjects were taken prisoner. All British officers seconded to the Arab Legion were therefore to be immediately withdrawn across the Jordan River.

"Is this the kind of allies the British are?" Abou Hoda sorrowfully asked.

The order represented an almost complete reversal of Britain's position. "After waving the green flag for weeks we suddenly started sawing the branch off on them," Sir Alec Kirkbride would bitterly recall. In one swoop, London was depriving Glubb of more than two-thirds of the officers who had made his Legion such an effective fighting force. His brief session with Abou Hoda would be remembered by Glubb as "one of the most painful and humiliating" interviews of his life.

The dispatch in Abou Hoda's hand was to be followed in a few hours by a second, even more important announcement. Britain was imposing an embargo on arms deliveries to the Middle East. Even the continuation of Britain's subsidy to the Arab Legion would be brought under review, the Foreign Office announced, if Transjordan was found to be defying the United Nations.

London's change of mind was the direct result of Britain's relations with the United States. Washington had gone so far as to hint at cutting off all economic aid to England's war-shattered economy if Britain did not fall in line on the Middle East. Two decades later, British diplomats would still recall with bitterness the intensity of those pressures exerted by America to force a change in Britain's policy.

To Glubb, the change was "absolutely catastrophic." That evening he summoned one of the men affected by it, Colonel Hugh Blackenden, to his office and ordered him to leave immediately for London to persuade the War Office to lift the arms embargo and to set up a recruiting office to find replacements for their lost officers.

"We have been left here to implement a British government plan," Glubb explained to Blackenden. "We must try to salvage what we can from this debacle by setting the foundations of a viable Arab state here under Abdullah which will have reasons to maintain its association with England." If the Legion was deprived of munitions and officers, Glubb pointed out, they would have to either run the risk of a defeat or start yielding ground.

Thirty-six hours later, at 6 Upper Fillimore Gardens, London, Colonel Blackenden opened his recruiting office. One of the first men in the door was Geoffrey Lockett, an angular, red-faced man with "a monumental hangover and a breath to curdle milk." He had been Orde Wingate's aide de camp, however, and Geoffrey Lockett was authorized to wear enough gallantry decorations to make a man a hunchback. Like most of the men Blackenden would recruit, he drank a little too much or owed too much money, but his military qualifications were above question. Three hours later he was on a plane heading east.

Whatever his allies' infidelities, King Abdullah remained the courteous Bedouin monarch. The day the British officers were withdrawn, he made it a point to call on the two Britons wounded in his service. After ceremoniously shaking Major John Buchanan's hand, he graciously handed the Englishman an enormous bouquet of flowers. As the King left, Buchanan fondly noted the paper in which the sovereign had wrapped his bouquet. It was an old Arabic newspaper.

42

"WE'LL OPEN A NEW ROAD."

THE BALD and wrinkled man bursting into the nursery of the kibbutz in which Shlomo Shamir had installed the headquarters of his Seventh Brigade was not an Israeli. He was a graduate of West Point, a veteran of the Normandy landing, the holder of numerous British and American decorations. David Marcus' presence in the Hulda nursery was the result of one of the most secret of David Ben-Gurion's preparations to arm his people for the conflict breaking over them. Aware that modern warfare required experienced men as well as advanced weapons, he had ordered his representatives in the United States to recruit a number of high-ranking officers as a nucleus for the Haganah's general staff.

Among the distinguished officers prepared to offer their services to the new state had been Brigadier General Walter Bedell Smith, Eisenhower's chief of staff in Europe during World War II. A formal veto of the plan by the Defense Department, however, had prevented their departure. Only Colonel Marcus, determined to aid his Jewish brothers, had defied the ban, walking away from a prestigious post in the Pentagon.

Aware of the terrible urgency of Jerusalem's situation, the Jewish leader had given Marcus the same orders he had earlier given Yadin: take Latrun and open the road to Jerusalem. In the pocket of Marcus' fatigues this May morning was an order naming him commander in chief of the Jerusalem front, responsible for all the men from the city to Latrun. The same order made Marcus the first general of a Jewish army since the Maccabean revolt, assigning him the newly created rank of *aluf.*

He had come to Hulda to prepare a new attack with Shamir. The two men decided to use basically the same tactics that had been employed in the first, unsuccessful assault—with one important modification: this time, they intended to run the attack according to a rigid timetable.

They began by occupying the two Arab villages on their line of attack, Beit Jiz and Beit Susin. They forced their officers to study the terrain scrupulously and through a series of patrols obtained the intelligence on the Arabs' defenses that had been so seriously lacking the first time.

To improve their forces, they substituted a battalion of the Givati Palmach Brigade for the battered Alexandroni battalion. Led by Jacob Prulov, a Palmach veteran, the battalion was assigned the decisive role in the attack. It would seize the heights of Bab el Wad, occupy the Arab villages of Deir Ayub, Yalu and Beit Nuba, then circle around behind the Legion's positions at Latrun to the Ramallah road. To bolster Prulov's force, Shamir assigned him the survivors of Hurewitz' immigrant battalion.

Latrun itself would be hit by the first armored attack ever made by the Army of Israel: thirteen half-tracks purchased by Xiel Federmann in Antwerp Christmas Day and the twenty-two locally made armored cars.

In three days of frantic effort, Haim Laskov had succeeded in organizing his unit into three assault groups. They would draw the Legion's forces to their front with a concerted attack and facilitate Prulov's strike at Bab el Wad. The one on the left would seize the Arab village of Latrun, the one on the right the junction of the Tel Aviv, Jerusalem and Ramallah roads. To the strongest group in the center would go the most difficult assignment: seizing the former British police station on the Latrun hillside.

With stones, sand and huge packing crates, Laskov meticulously reconstituted the entire Latrun hillside in a field near the kibbutz. Everything was there: the ruins of the Crusader château on its crest, the Trappist monastery, the blockhouselike police post. By an extraordinary coincidence, Laskov himself was familiar with its interior. A year before, as an employee of the Palestine Electric Company working on a high-tension line, he had been invited by its British occupants to visit the installation.

The post's principal entry was a massive armored door. Above it a fortified tower protected the station's flanks. To blow in the door, Laskov counted on a charge of 250 kilograms of TNT. The tower he would neutralize with a far more terrifying weapon, one he himself had employed in action against the Wehrmacht outside Rome—flamethrowers.

Made to his design in the Haganah's Tel Aviv workshops, Laskov's flamethrowers were mounted on his half-tracks. They could shoot a jet of napalm twenty-five yards and would be fired a yard ahead of the vehicle by an incendiary bullet. It was a complex weapon, and its use involved disadvantages as well as advantages. Because he had overlooked one of them, a disaster was going to overtake Laskov's half-tracks in the midst of his attack.

Unlike its predecessor, Operation Bin Nun II began with precision. At exactly 11 P.M. Sunday, May 30, the mortars and "Napoleonchiks" of

Shlomo Shamir began to rake the Latrun promontory while, off to the right, Jacob Prulov's men moved toward Bab el Wad.

Almost thrown from his bed by the first explosions rocking his abbey, Father Martin Godart pulled on his robes and sandals and rushed from his cell. It was not fear for his own well-being or for the sacred objects in the abbey chapel that prompted his precipitous flight. Rushing along corridors already strewn with broken glass, he headed for the room which harbored his most valuable treasure, those winemaking instruments thanks to which he had given the abbey a special renown on the best-spread tables of the Middle East. He carted off his retorts and alembics to the deepest corner of his wine cellar.

The monastery's cloister, freshly decorated by the monks with flowers and olive branches so that, as one of them wrote, "Jesus will not see His Palestine is at war," was covered with broken glass and tiles from shells landing nearby. A suffocating odor of cement dust and smoke choked the members of the community who had tried to take refuge there. Finally, a candle in one hand, straw mattress in the other, the monks filed down into Father Godart's cellars to find safety among his barrels of Pommard and Chablis.

From his observation post on the crest behind the monastery, Colonel Habes Majali and his staff studied the shells streaking through the night. As the barrage died, the clank of treads rose from the valley below. The Jews were attacking.

Majali turned to the frail man with a Vandyke beard and rough-spun robe standing beside him. "Pray Allah that he grant us another victory," he ordered his regiment's imam.

Haim Laskov too listened to the reassuring sounds of his half-tracks' treads as the vehicles pushed through the night toward Latrun. He looked at his watch. It was midnight.

In the third half-track, a pair of earphones clamped on her head, a nineteen-year-old Polish girl peered at the somber ridge line rising before her. Hadassah Limpel had walked across half the world for the privilege of riding in a half-track this night toward the crest barring the road to Jerusalem. Nine years earlier, the armored vehicles of Nazi Germany had terminated Hadassah's childhood and cast her onto the roads of Poland and Russia. From Siberia, along with a miserable flock of fifteen hundred Polish children no one wanted, she was herded across the Soviet Union to Iran, then to Karachi. From there a journey on a dilapidated old steamer took her to Bombay, Aden, Port Said and finally the docks of the Promised

511

Land. There was no familiar figure on those quais among the hundreds of adults who had come in hopes of finding a missing child or relative lost in the chaos of war. Sent to a kibbutz, Hadassah became determined to resemble as closely as possible the vigorous young sabras who now surrounded her. In pursuit of that goal, she had enrolled in the Palmach's youth movement.

During all the harsh springtime of 1948, armed with a Sten gun and a pair of grenades, she had served with the Furmanim, escorting Jerusalem-bound convoys past the ambushes of Abdul Khader Husseini. Caught in Tel Aviv when the road was finally cut, she had volunteered for an operator's course to learn how to work the radios purchased by Xiel Federmann. It was, in her mind, a final symbol of her acceptance in the army of her new country.

Nervous and tense, Captain Izzat Hassan tried to follow the sound of the advancing treads across the Latrun plain. Commander of Majali's support company, he was in charge of the antitank guns and mortars that were supposed to stop their attack. Their eyes fixed to their gunsights, his gunners peered into the darkness, looking helplessly for some moving form. Hassan's hopes now lay on a little ridge below the police station on which he had zeroed in his guns. If he could spot the Haganah's vehicles crossing that ridge, he was confident he could destroy them all.

On the tower of the police station, behind his Vickers machine gun, Sergeant Yossef Sa'ab, a Druze, also stared through the night at the ridge. All around him, crouched behind sandbags, grenades in their hands, other Legionnaires watched for the vehicles those advancing treads propelled toward them. Below them behind the ring of sandbags guarding the entrance to the building, Mahmoud Ali Rousan, a cousin of the regiment's adjutant, held a bazooka tube tightly against his cheek.

All of those men were in for a brutal shock. Protected by a series of smoke grenades and the moonless night, Laskov's vehicles passed over the ridge without receiving a single hit. From his command car, code-named "Yona," Laskov heard the quiet, poised voice of Hadassah Limpel announce, "We're crossing their wire."

At that instant, Laskov's attention was diverted by a green flare popping into the sky to his right. A smile spread over his face. It was Prulov announcing he had taken his first objective, the village of Deir Ayub, overlooking Bab el Wad. Laskov was reassured. In a few minutes, Prulov would be in position to begin circling behind the Arab positions his armor was attacking. A few minutes later, coming from the same direction as Prulov's flare, Laskov heard a series of violent explosions. "They've run into resistance," Laskov thought.

At Latrun itself, his attack was moving ahead exactly as he had hoped. "The lead half-track is fifty yards from the gate," Hadassah announced.

While the Legionnaires on the roof of the police station pummeled them with hand grenades, the sappers in the lead half-track ran to the door and placed their charge. It was a useless gesture. The door was unlocked. A few hundred yards away, Captain Hassan followed the fighting with anguished eyes. In the darkness he could barely distinguish forms. He was afraid of placing his fire too close to the police post and killing his own men.

"Flamethrowers ready," the voice of Hadassah Limpel from Yona, the command car, announced. Suddenly a fantastic stream of flame lit up the night, clearly illuminating the façade of the police post. Watching the sight, Captain Rousan thought, "The Jews are using acetylene torches to cut the door from its hinges." Their real tool, the sappers' charge, went off with a roar. An assault team leaped from the second half-track and rushed for the door.

A savage hand-to-hand battle with grenades, Sten guns and knives soon left the ground floor of the building littered with dying men.

It was outside, however, that the Haganah's assault was encountering its gravest problem. The terrifying bursts of flame on which Laskov counted to drive the post's defenders from its roof had set fire to its façade. The flames lit up the building and the area around it like a stage. The frustrated Captain Hassan was startled to see illuminated before him five perfect targets, Laskov's half-tracks. In the brilliant light, Captain Rousan even caught a glimpse of "a blond woman with a radio helmet on her head."

In her quiet voice, Hadassah Limpel continued to describe the attack for Laskov. The force commander had just left the car to see what was happening in the building. He had covered only a few feet when a burst of fire from the roof killed him. His deputy, a young immigrant who had fought in the Red Army, tried to take over, but in the inferno no one could understand him. He spoke only Russian. Then, from only yards away, Captain Hassan's antitank guns opened fire.

One after another the half-tracks were reduced to flaming wrecks. Laskov heard a stifled gurgling in his earphones, then nothing. "Yona, Yona," he called. There was no answer from his shattered command car. All of its occupants were dead. Hadassah Limpel's long journey had ended in front of the police station at Latrun.

A pair of haggard men stumbling into his command post brought Laskov the news of still another disaster that had struck his men. The engineers had demined the road before the buses carrying his infantry, but they had put the mines into a roadside ditch without disarming them. Leaping into the ditch, the first soldier out of the bus had set off a terrible explosion that had killed twenty of his fellows and sent the rest rushing to the rear.

A few minutes later Laskov got a radio message that ended the Seventh Brigade's second unsuccessful effort to seize Latrun. "Your pal has disappeared," Shamir informed him. Laskov understood that Prulov and the men he was counting on to sweep around the Legion's rear had somehow vanished into the night. Just after firing off his first flare, Prulov had stumbled on a Legion machine-gun nest, which had killed three of his men. Considering those losses too much for an operation in which his battalion had been detached from its regular Palmach command, Prulov had broken off action on his own initiative.

In front of the police station, the flamethrowers that had turned a potential victory into a disaster were out. None of the assault team that had stormed into the ground floor of the police station would come back alive. In the welcome darkness, the survivors of the vehicles struggled to organize a retreat under a hail of fire from the Legionnaires on the roof, making their way as best they could back down the Latrun slopes.

Once again the Haganah had failed to break the Arab Legion's hold on Latrun. Five days had elapsed between the first attack and the second, five days in which Jerusalem's rations, like the sands in an hourglass, had continued to flow out of Dov Joseph's warehouses. Yet the Israeli Army was no closer to relieving the city now than it had been the night Ben-Gurion had ordered Yigal Yadin, "Take Latrun." It was out of the question for Shamir to hurl his shattered brigade at the Legion still a third time. Their two defeats had made one thing clear: Jerusalem was not going to be saved at Latrun.

• • •

The jeep scraped, whined, backfired, bucked, skidded, and spun its wheels in dumb mechanical protest. Two of the men inside leaped out to lighten its load and guide it from rock to rock. Clutching the steering wheel, a young Palmach officer named Amos Chorev guided the jeep which carried David Marcus and Vivian Herzog like a kayak in a riptide. At the bottom of the ravine they began to force their way up the other side, the aroma of burning rubber and oil curdling the freshness of the moonlit night. They finished their grueling climb by pushing the jeep themselves up the last few yards.

Exhausted, they could see in the moonlight two and a half miles away the verdant promontory against which they had unsuccessfully thrown their forces the night before. Below the little clearing around the Monastery of Latrun, they could make out in the moonlight the road to Jerusalem skirting the foot of the Trappist estates up to Bab el Wad. The punishing passage along which they had just pushed their jeep paralleled that road. After running through the abandoned Arab hamlet of Beit Susin, it started through the wadis and steep mountain slopes leading up to the Judean heights. A passage for shepherds since Biblical times, it ran through the wild mustard, thyme and cyclamen without any discernible pattern.

Gasping for breath, Amos Chorev looked at the dark mounds of the mountains still before them. "If only we could find a way through there," he sighed, "we'd have another way of getting to Jerusalem."

"You think it could be done?" Herzog wondered.

Marcus snorted. "Why not?" he said. "We got across the Red Sea, didn't we?"

A few hours later the sound of another motor suddenly woke the three men, who had stopped to sleep a couple of hours before pushing ahead with their explorations. They picked up their Sten guns and crept to the cover of a little clump of wild olive trees. There, on the reverse slope of their crest, they saw a silhouette guiding another vehicle up the hill toward their position. Chorev crawled cautiously forward to study the oncoming forms. Suddenly, with a whoop of joy, he leaped up and rushed down the hill. He had recognized the driver of the jeep and his comrade. They were fellow Palmachniks from the Har-el Brigade and they were coming from Jerusalem.

Their accidental meeting was a revelation to all five men standing on the desolate Judean ridge. Each vehicle had covered half the distance separating Jewish Jerusalem from its salvation.

If the routes they had followed could somehow be made passable for men and vehicles, Jerusalem might be saved.

Listening to the three filthy, unshaven men, David Ben-Gurion understood immediately. David Marcus, Amos Chorev and Vivian Herzog had come directly to the Jewish leader's office on their return to Tel Aviv,

515

to give him a firsthand account of their trip in the hills beyond Bab el Wad. They had found the answer to the problem that had haunted them all since December—the isolation of Jerusalem.

But with his terrible realism, Ben-Gurion knew well that a track over which they could somehow take a jeep was not going to save a city of one hundred thousand hungry people; they needed a road, a real road to Jerusalem. Turning to the man who had served in the army which in the course of just one war had laid more miles of road around the globe than all the armies since Alexander, Ben-Gurion said, "You've got to build a road, a real road."

Then, alert to the moral value that even a single jeep arriving from Tel Aviv might have on his isolated Jerusalem command, Ben-Gurion ordered Amos Chorev to repeat their journey that night. This time, Chorev was to go all the way to Jerusalem!

For Yitzhak Levi the report being read out that first morning in June by David Shaltiel's ammunition officer would always be "the blackest piece of listening" to which he had ever been subjected. It was, almost bullet by bullet, an enumeration of the munitions left in their reserves. Making a swift calculation, Levi figured that that reserve might get them through twenty-four hours of intense fighting. Nor was that the end of the day's bad news. A few minutes later, in Dov Joseph's office, he was told that the city's reserves contained enough flour to continue their spartan bread ration for just seven more days. "Clearly," Levi told himself, "we have to be resupplied and resupplied quickly or we're going to collapse."

While Levi pondered those grim statistics, the first jeep to reach Jerusalem over the shepherds' path lurched up to the Palmach base at Kiryat Anavim. Amos Chorev had made it all the way from the sea. He had proved that it was possible to take a vehicle to the city over the goat track he and his friends had found almost by accident twenty-four hours earlier.

Learning that Chorev's Palmach comrades were going to try to duplicate his feat in the opposite direction, Levi urged Shaltiel to let him join their party. He wanted to warn Ben-Gurion personally of the catastrophic state of their supplies and to see if there were any way of supplying themselves across the forbidding hills by wheel or foot. The few cases of munitions being delivered by Piper Cub or parachuted from a DC-3 were not going to save them. "If we are not resupplied we are doomed," Levi reminded Shaltiel.

At ten o'clock, Levi and a dozen Palmachniks set out. The little intelligence officer rode off into the night in the one jeep in Jerusalem that seemed capable of the grueling run down the Judean hills. The vehicle was camouflaged a light sandy beige; its previous owner had died in a desperate attempt to seal shut the very exit Levi was trying to open. It was Abdul Khader Husseini's jeep, captured in the fighting May 14.

By five o'clock in the morning, after seven tortuous hours, Levi was in Rehovot, twelve miles from Tel Aviv. The exhausted officer stopped in a café in Rehovot for a cup of coffee.

"Where did you come from?" its proprietor asked.

"Jerusalem," said Levi.

"Jerusalem!" screamed the café owner. At his words everyone in the café swarmed over the dazed Levi, kissing him, hugging him, cheering him as though he had "conquered Mount Everest." As the crowd parted, the famished Levi saw the owner bearing down on him with an extraordinary welcoming gift, a huge plate of strawberries and cream.

Levi went straight from his strawberries to David Ben-Gurion's office.

"Will we be able to hold Jerusalem or will it fall?" Ben-Gurion asked.

Levi's reply was equally blunt. There was terrible hunger in the city, he said. People were not yet starving to death, but the situation was going to get worse and it might come to that. "The fate of Jerusalem does not depend on food this morning," he said. "It depends on ammunition. If there is a serious Arab attack we will simply run out of ammunition." Looking at the man on whose shoulders so many burdens weighed, Levi said gravely, "We will be overwhelmed."

Ben-Gurion called Joseph Avidar, the Ukrainian miller's son who ran the Haganah's supply branch, to join them. If one jeep could get across the mountain, twenty could. The loads they delivered might be a pittance compared to Jerusalem's needs, but they could at least bring Shaltiel the reassurance that everything humanly possible was being done to relieve him. Ben-Gurion ordered Avidar to requisition all the jeeps he could find in Tel Aviv, load them with arms and ammunition and give them to Levi for a return run through the mountains that night.

Avidar's military policemen rushed out to the principal crossroads of Tel Aviv to intercept these precious vehicles. As if by magic, Tel Aviv's jeeps disappeared from its streets. An entire day's search turned up exactly one jeep, in lamentable condition. Furious at his compatriots' lack of collective spirit, Ben-Gurion told Avidar, "Take mine at least."

"Tell Shaltiel," he ordered Levi, "to hold on. We'll organize things here. We'll open a new road to save Jerusalem."

An hour later, the officer whose men had barely a pocketful of bullets to hold off the Arabs ringing their city discovered the warehouses of the Haganah in Hulda. "My God," he thought, staring at what seemed to him a mountain of supplies, "what a difference it would make to have all that in Jerusalem."

Like a child in a candy store, Levi didn't know what to take. Finally he loaded thirty Czech machine guns and 100 three-inch mortar shells into his jeeps and headed back.

An unexpected drone cut across the silence of Amman's night sky, the drone of airplane engines. High-pitched and feeble, they might have been the sound of mail planes winging down to Cairo. They belonged, however, to two Messerschmitt 109s about to carry out the first bombing raid of the Israeli Air Force.

Half a dozen Messerschmitts had now arrived in Israel. One of the unstable planes had crashed on takeoff, and another had been shot down. But a third had served notice that Arab control of the skies over Tel Aviv was henceforth going to be challenged: it shot down two Egyptian DC-3s. Now, on Ben-Gurion's orders, the two warplanes of the Israeli Air Force were going to give Amman a taste of what Tel Aviv had suffered since May 14.

In the city below, the lights of Abdullah's Ragdan Palace blazed as though a formal ball were under way. The sovereign was giving a banquet to his fellow Arab leaders. He had stubbornly refused to consider a blackout, saying, "Never will it be said that I, a Hashemite, have dimmed my lights before a Zionist menace." Now, for the edification of his guests, the little sovereign provided his own reply to Ben-Gurion's air raid. Grabbing a bodyguard's gun, he ran out into the night and began gleefully firing up into the sky.

In the headquarters of the Haganah, a Russian, Joseph Avidar, and an American, David Marcus, presided over a tense meeting. Under their supervision, the people who had walked through the Red Sea and crossed the deserts of the Exodus were about to embark on an extraordinary engineering adventure. As David Ben-Gurion had promised Shaltiel's intelligence officer, they were going to try to achieve with sweat, ingenuity and mechanical skill what they had failed to accomplish with arms—opening a road to Jerusalem.

Given the limited material means at their disposal, it was a gigantic undertaking. It meant carving out of those tortured goat tracks zigzagging through the wadis and precipitous hills of Judea a road that bypassed the Jerusalem highway and lay beyond the control of the Arab Legion.

It could not be a trail open only to a daringly driven jeep; a dozen jeeps a night were not going to save the one hundred thousand Jews of Jerusalem. It had to be a road that could take fully loaded trucks; it had to be built quickly; and it had to be built under the constant menace of Arab shellfire from Latrun.

For once, the Haganah did not turn to the Bible in search of a name for one of its undertakings. Inspired by the 750-mile highway that Chinese coolies had constructed from the jungles of Burma across the mountains to China, they decided to call the road with which they hoped to save Jerusalem the Burma Road.

43

"THE ARAB PEOPLE WILL NEVER FORGIVE US."

AS REMORSELESS as an oncoming tide, the plague of hunger crept over Jewish Jerusalem. At Notre-Dame, the famished Gadna youths kept their field glasses trained on the adjacent Arab quarter of Musrara, looking for a stray chicken scurrying through the yard of an abandoned home. Musrara was a kind of no man's land, and at night the hungry youths would risk their lives going after the chickens they had picked out.

Those forays could be dangerous. One night Netanel Lorch learned that one of his men had been killed by a Legion mortar shell as he crept back from Musrara with a sack of rice and a Persian carpet on his back.

They could also lead to bizarre happenings. One group of Notre-Dame's Gadna youths broke into the store of an Armenian shopkeeper in Musrara, gulping down enormous bottles of what those desperately thirsty youngsters assumed to be pink lemonade. A few hours later Shaltiel's headquarters got a despairing call. "The Legion is using poison gas," the youngster said. "We need help desperately." Shalom Dror rushed to the building. Indeed, the kids were all sick, retching on the floor or lying in a stupor. Picking up a bottle of the lemonade they had been drinking, Dror sipped it and found the Legion's poison gas. They were all drunk. The bottle contained pink champagne. Products of rigidly orthodox households, none of the youngsters had known what it was.

Few Jerusalemites outside of the Haganah dared venture into Arab-held territory no matter how painful their hunger. The Arab homes in the areas occupied by the Haganah's rush forward May 14 and 15 had long since been picked clean of food. Joseph ordered engineers, pretending to be looking for shell damage, to make a house-to-house survey of the Jewish city in quest of unusual food hoards seized by looters.

A small community of forty-one people, at least, was spared the cruel hunger gripping Jerusalem's one hundred thousand Jews. Not surprisingly, they were all French. Trapped in their consulate, they had a secret food supply behind the Arab lines—a farm run by the Assumptionist Fathers of St.-Pierre in Gallicante on the slopes below Mount Zion. Built over the grotto in which Saint Peter had allegedly wept his remorse at having denied Jesus three times before the cock's crow, the church and its farm contained seven cows, one hundred pigs and six hundred chickens. Nightly its director, Brother François, slipped along the Valley of Silwan up to Sir Alan Cunningham's old residence, now occupied by the Red Cross, with a sackful of food for the consulate. One evening Brother François decided to bring his besieged compatriots a special treat, three suckling pigs. At Job's Well, one of his pigs squirmed out of his sack. Under the insults and threats of the disgusted Legionnaires watching him, the monk chased around after the fleeing animal.

This night, no one from the French Consulate was on hand to greet Brother François at Government House. Undaunted, he continued across the fields toward a Jewish kibbutz to see if he could contact the consulate from there. The gesture almost cost the good monk his life. He had forgotten that he had dressed as an Arab for the first half of his trip. When his frightened cries in French had finally calmed the kibbutz's defenders, they tore open his sack, then recoiled in disgust. Its contents were as loathsome to their hungry orthodox stomachs as they had been to the Legionnaires' at Job's Well. A few hours later, roasted in Madame Sabine Neuville's ovens, Brother François's unpopular piglets made a triumphant appearance on the consulate table.

There was practically nothing left to put on the other tables of Jewish Jerusalem, however. On Friday, June 4, Dov Joseph transmitted to David Ben-Gurion the grimmest alarm he had been forced to send Tel Aviv. By reducing the population's already spartan bread ration from 200 to 150 grams, he would have enough flour to supply his citizens bread for five more days. "We can't rely on miracles," he warned. "I ask you to order the transportation of bread any way possible. Minimum seventeen tons per day. Try to send it by jeep or by camel."

Despite Dov Joseph's words, Jerusalem was going to have to rely on a miracle to survive, and the instrument with which David Marcus would have to perform it was before him—a solitary bulldozer belonging to the Solel Boneh construction firm. The Haganah was not the American Army, and that machine was the sole representative of the parade of road levelers, scrapers and hydraulic shovels he had hoped to see converge on the Arab village of Beit Jiz, the beginning point of Marcus' Burma Road.

The American colonel waved toward the looming crags of the Judean hills. "There," he told the driver, "it's through there we've got to go."

Beit Jiz became a construction camp overnight. Ahead, the bulldozer tore away yard by yard at the first hill along its route. Slowly, steadily it shoved aside the topsoil, rolled stones out of the way, terraced the slope, uprooted tree trunks. Lacking machines, Marcus and Shlomo Shamir used men. Sweating and choking in the red dust raised by the bulldozer, an army of laborers and stonecutters followed behind the bulldozer, filling in holes, leveling the ground, widening with axes and saws the path hacked out by the bulldozer's blade.

They worked around the clock, one shift sleeping in Beit Jiz while the second worked. By day a cloud of dust marked their advance into the hills. By night it was the clang and snort of the bulldozer echoing from crest to crest up toward the ridge of Latrun.

Sure that the noise and the dust would alert Colonel Majali to their activities and lead him to shell the area or attack it, Marcus set up outposts and laid ambushes all around the work site. Each night, as soon as darkness and a total blackout covered their activities, the jeeps came up, fifteen or twenty of them, weighed down with three-inch mortar shells, rifle ammunition and Beza machine guns. While the workers slapped their metal sides as a man might whack a pony's flank, they rolled through the darkness over the stretch of road workers had built toward the forbidding hillside still untamed by their shovels.

Marcus received a second bulldozer to speed the work. But the terrain was so rough, the inclines they had to pass were so steep, that each hundred yards forward required three hundred yards of winding road. Marcus despaired. The miracle was going to take too much time. Before he could tear out of the resistant hills of Judea a road over which a loaded truck could pass, Jerusalem was going to be shelled or starved into submission.

· · ·

The daily quota of shells hurled into Jerusalem by Emile Jumean's guns had now been supplemented by a second menace. The fieldpieces of Colonel Abdul-Aziz' Egyptian army in the south were battering the city with airbursts which flung showers of shrapnel through its streets. In lives, in morale, in property damage, the shelling was taking a frightful toll. The Arabs were apparently aware of the bread and water distribution schedules. Every time one started, a new flood of wounded submerged the desperately overcrowded hospitals. Wounded were packed into every available corner. In the growing heat, flies became a major problem. After attempting to drive them off for a while, hospital inhabitants, both patients and staff, grew apathetic. Wounded and doctors alike lived on a cup of tea, a slice of bread and a spoonful of jam three times a day.

The intensity of the shelling had forced an end to the normality Dov Joseph had sought to maintain. Most shops were closed now and Jerusalem's streets almost as deserted in the daytime as they were at night. People slept in cellars or in the hallways of their homes, and Jerusalem's citizens became adept at identifying the sound of incoming shells and judging their point of impact.

Dana Adams Schmidt of *The New York Times* found the incessant shelling more terrifying than anything he had been exposed to during four years of reporting the European war. Shells seemed to select their victims at random. One, Schmidt noted, crashed through a barbershop window, killing the barber and the client in his chair but leaving unscathed another client waiting in the corner. One of his acquaintances spent an entire day scouring the city for a cup of condensed milk for her pregnant sister. On her way home with her treasure, she was knocked down by the concussion of an exploding shell. She was badly hurt, but her cup of milk remained unspilled.

Certain categories of citizens became local heroes. Among them were Zvi Leibowitz' water carriers and Alexander Singer's repair crews for the high-tension lines feeding the hospitals and the bakeries. Fourteen- and fifteen-year-old Gadna youths carried messages under shellfire from one Haganah post to another. One of them, Tova Goldberg, a dark-haired, big-framed girl, always ran to her destination thinking that if she did the shells had less chance of finding her. She could not run fast enough. One morning an Arab shell caught up with her. When the stunned girl recovered her senses, she saw her hand, severed from her wrist, lying on the ground before her, its fingers still folded around her message. She picked it up and staggered to the Haganah post to which it was addressed. "Here is your message," the sixteen-year-old girl said, passing her severed hand to a soldier. "Now please get me a doctor."

Jerusalem's Jewish population would not easily forget that the centers of Western Christianity, which had clamored for their city's internationalization, now ignored their agony. The Vatican, the Church of England, the councils of Orthodoxy, the governments of those nations that had supported internationalization did not see fit to launch a storm of protest over what was happening to them in New Jerusalem. To the city's besieged residents, it seemed that the outside world was more interested in saving Jerusalem's Christian stones than in saving its Jewish inhabitants.

As the city's casualties grew, a walk through Jerusalem's streets became a painful as well as a dangerous experience. Its walls and telephone poles were covered with death notices and with pictures of the young men and women who had died defending the new state. One of them one day early in June bore the photo of a young girl killed in the fighting in the south. The following morning her father was at his desk promptly at seven o'clock, as he was every day. Even the loss of his daughter could not be allowed to interrupt Dov Joseph's terrible task.

On Saturday, June 5, he was forced to make still another cut in the city's ration. It was the last he would be able to make: when it was gone, there would be nothing left. Henceforth his fellow Jerusalemites would get 150 grams a day—four thin slices—of a soggy, crumbling mass called bread, and, for a week, eight ounces of dried beans, peas and groats.

• • •

On the other side of the city, Major Abdullah Tell waited patiently. Inspecting his men's positions each day, his swagger stick in his hand, his pearl-handled Smith and Wesson revolver strapped to his waist, the young officer was sure that he was slowly squeezing the Jewish city into submission. The intelligence he was able to glean from the city's diplomats, the two desperate attacks of the Haganah at Latrun, revealed how grim his foes' situation was. And on June 5 he received his first indication that events were heading toward a conclusion. The Belgian consul discreetly sounded him out on his surrender terms.

Only one faint worry disturbed him. It was a report brought him by a peasant from a village near Bab el Wad. "The Jews," he said, "are building a secret way to Jerusalem."

Colonel Habes Majali had already observed the bulldozers' advancing column of dust and heard their motors' echoes at night. For several days, villagers near Latrun had been informing him that large numbers of Jewish civilians were assembling in Beit Jiz and Beit Susin. When Tell relayed the peasants' words to him, they confirmed his growing suspicions. Majali had only to order his 25-pounders to open an intense fire in the area and he could have devastated Marcus' project and killed dozens of workers. But he could not undertake a major action without the agreement of his brigade commander and a major addition to his ammunition supply. He sent his adjutant, Captain Rousan, to the English colonel, T. L. Ashton, commanding the brigade, for permission to bombard the area. Rousan explained to the Englishman their conviction that the Jews were building a road to Jerusalem that could bypass the Latrun salient.

Ashton shrugged his shoulders with indifference. "The terrain is too tough," he said. "It's too mountainous. They'll never get a road through there."

Before sending Rousan back to his regiment's headquarters, Ashton gave the young officer a handwritten order for Colonel Majali. "Under no condition," it said, "are you to waste your 25-pounder ammunition in the sector Beit Jiz–Beit Susin."

• • •

By Monday, June 7, Dov Joseph was desperate. As the first week of June slipped by, he had watched in a growing fear and apprehension the steadily shrinking figures in each column of the orange folder locked in his desk. One by one, the last of the commodities each of these columns represented had disappeared and he had drawn a double line under the column indicating it was finished.

They were, Joseph thought, "coming to a perilous end." There was three days of food left in his warehouses. The prospects were so horrible he didn't dare contemplate them. "I was mentally bracing myself for that terrible moment when I'd have the women of Jerusalem on my doorsteps crying out for food for their children and I would have nothing to offer them but empty warehouses," he would one day recall. "Whatever would I say to them?"

On the outskirts of Jerusalem it was already coming to that. Leon Angel, one of the city's bakers, found on his doorstep, begging for a piece of bread for her children, a woman who had walked through the Arab shelling. Reuven Tamir, taking a few tins of canned meat to his fellow soldiers, saw families crying in the street from the pains of hunger.

Aware of how desperate the city's situation had become, the Haganah was preparing still another assault at Latrun. Jerusalem, Joseph feared, could not even wait for that. He was not an emotional man, but on this June morning he poured out all his concern and anger in a cable to Ben-Gurion:

Do we have to be satisfied with only hopes and possibilities? I've been warning for weeks that there is a need to send food supplies and nothing has arrived. I suggested a few ways and you didn't respond. You managed to send other things, why not food? Why not draft those hundreds who

525

are sitting in cafés in Tel Aviv for Jerusalem's sake? I ask you what will happen if, God forbid, the operation doesn't succeed. If we do not receive flour by Friday, there will be starvation in the city.

• • •

So brief was the delay proposed in that cable that there was no question of waiting for the Burma Road. Ben-Gurion summoned his closest collaborators to find a way of nourishing the famished city. There was only one. Three miles of steep ravines and sharp inclines separated the farthest point to which Marcus had been able to push his bulldozers and the point to which vehicles coming down from Jerusalem could penetrate into the hills. Since it was totally impossible to push a truck through those three miles, the survival of Jerusalem's one hundred thousand Jews would have to be entrusted to another form of transport, the most ancient in the world: two marching feet.

Ben-Gurion's experts calculated that if they could round up six hundred men and marched them through the darkness each night over those three miles of terrain with a forty-five-pound sack on their backs, they might get enough food across the hills to save the city.

An hour later, Pinhas Bracker, a forty-year-old meter reader for the Palestine Electric Company, like scores of others, got a call ordering him to report immediately to the headquarters of Histadrut, the labor organization. Bracker assured his wife he'd be home for dinner. He was used to such summonses; he had been a member of the Home Guard since 1940.

A line of buses waited for Bracker and the scores of men called up with him. As soon as they arrived, they were loaded into the buses for what they were informed would be "a very short but very special mission." They were a rich variety of types: bank clerks in dark suits, civil servants in shirtsleeves, workers, shopkeepers. Even Mordechai Zeira, Israel's best-known folk singer, was among them.

Most of them shared two characteristics. They were city dwellers and had rarely walked more than half a mile at a time. They were middle-aged or older; the legs and backs which would have to nourish Jerusalem were all close to retirement age.

The buses took them to Kfar Bilu, the old British Army camp from which the Nachshon convoys had set out. The camp was already brimming with activity when they arrived. Called in haste from the nearby kibbutzim, women were frantically stuffing flour, rice, sugar, dried vegetables and chocolate into the sacks the men would carry.

526

Their leader, Joseph Avidar, gathered them for a briefing on the job ahead. As he spoke, he began to see signs of fear and doubt creeping into the faces of some. The Russian miller's son who had lost a hand making grenades for the Haganah stalked up closer. In a voice hoarse with emotion he told the men before him that the entire ration distributed to their brothers in Jerusalem that morning had consisted of four slices of bread. Pointing dramatically to the pile of sacks awaiting them, he proclaimed, "Each one of you is going to carry on your back the food to keep a hundred Jews alive another day."

Avidar had one more surprise. The three hundred pack racks Xiel Federmann had bought for twenty cents almost as an afterthought on Christmas Day in Antwerp had found at last a utilization. Avidar ordered the hastily mobilized men to lash their sacks to a rack and get back into their buses. They were off to the hills of Judea.

. . .

There was still another way by which Jerusalem might be saved, and Ben-Gurion was determined to seize it if he could. It was a cease-fire. After the Arabs had summarily rejected the United Nations' first cease-fire call, Britain had placed before the Security Council another, calling for a four-week truce. Two of its terms, providing for an embargo on the shipment of arms and of men of military age into the area during the truce, displeased Tel Aviv. It was, indeed, to be able to do just that that the Israelis wanted a cease-fire.

The Arabs, despite Britain's change of mind, continued to resist the appeal, and the problem of getting both sides' agreement was thrust into the lap of the United Nations mediator, Count Folke Bernadotte. The Swedish diplomat had made a hurried trip to Cairo, Beirut, Amman and Tel Aviv seeking agreement. On this Monday morning, June 7, Bernadotte had submitted to the Arab League and Tel Aviv a new truce plan. It made one concession to the Israeli position. Men of military age would be allowed into the area provided they had not been formed into military units before the truce.

Ben-Gurion felt he had no choice but to accept. There was no doubt in his mind that "we were at the end of our rope." Supplies "were running out everywhere." They had suffered two defeats at Latrun, lost the Old City and suffered what would have been a serious defeat against the Iraqis in Jenin if their enemies had pursued it. The Egyptians were twenty-five miles from Tel Aviv. Only in the north, where they had captured Acre, driven to the Lebanese border and chased the Syrians out of Galilee, had they been successful. Everywhere their units needed time to regroup, reorganize and reequip. And above everything else loomed the problem of Jerusalem. Despite the heroic efforts of Marcus' road builders and his porters, Ben-Gurion had a growing fear that "the Arabs were going to get Jerusalem." Hoping his foes would do the same, he cabled his acceptance of the plan to Bernadotte.

• • •

As they had a few days earlier, the Arab League's leaders gathered in Amman to debate the mediator's proposal. This time they were bitterly divided.

On the surface, there seemed little reason for the Arabs to accept a cease-fire. If their gains were considerably less than their enflamed propaganda had indicated, they still had the Israelis on the defensive almost everywhere. The reality, however, was not as promising.

The Egyptian Army had captured great stretches of territory, but it had conquered relatively few settlements. A whole string of Israeli colonies lay menacingly to the army's rear. The ferocious resistance of each settlement's underarmed defenders gave evidence of the high price the Egyptians would have to pay to conquer them. A determined Israeli counterattack had finally checked their advance south of Tel Aviv. The campaign had exposed the army's inefficiency and the corruption of its suppliers. Medicine, food, water, gasoline, munitions, all were lacking. Rifles jammed and grenades exploded prematurely in men's hands. The higher-ranking officers preferred the shelter of their tents to sharing the heat of the desert with their men. Morale was low. The army's younger officers felt bitterly that they had been thrown into a war for which they were unprepared and unequipped, while in Cairo the country's rulers continued to live a life of undiminished ease and luxury.

The Iraqis had been a total disappointment to their fellow Arabs. The Lebanese, after a few gestures on May 14, had been inactive, and the Syrians, as Major Wasfi Tell had predicted, were soundly defeated. Although the Arab Legion had some notable successes to its credit, it had failed in the streets of Jerusalem. The Iraqis, Egyptians and Transjordanians all were dependent on Britain for supplies, and with an embargo looming they were running short of arms, supplies and spare parts. Now the nation which had made no effort to stop the conflict on May 14, Great Britain, was actively counseling her Middle Eastern friends to accept the cease-fire.

Events had not worked out quite as Ernest Bevin's Foreign Office had predicted. The Israelis had been tenacious, the Arabs less aggressive than expected. A beleaguered Israel turning to Britain to extricate her, at the price of handing the Arabs the Negev or some other part of her territory, was no longer likely.

Ironically, in Amman it was the leaders of the nations that had made the smallest contribution to the war, Syria and Lebanon, who were most anxious to pursue it. Haj Amin Husseini's Arab Higher Committee also opposed a cease-fire bitterly, fearing that it would deprive the Arab drive of its momentum and shatter the delicate alliance that had driven them to fight. So, too, did Azzam Pasha. He now felt that the war had to be pursued because he was sure a pause would favor their foes. Given the state of world opinion, he felt that the Arabs would be unable to resupply themselves during a cease-fire, while the Israelis would.

Glubb was "rather pleased" by the prospects of a cease-fire. His Legion was intact and he noted that "we had accomplished rather more than I had hoped we might accomplish when I went into the war with such misgivings."

The decisive position was that adopted by the history professor who had been talked into asking for a declaration of war. Farouk's limited patience had been strained by his army's failure to win a swift triumph, and Nokrashy was now free to express his second thoughts on their original decision.

"We went into this war when we never should have," he told his colleagues. It was time to accept the United Nations cease-fire and "use the four weeks to improve the state of our armies. Then perhaps we can hope to win the war."

"You are talking nonsense," Azzam Pasha exploded. "Your army is twenty-five miles from Tel Aviv. You haven't been defeated and you want to catch your breath. What do you think the Jews will do with a cease-fire? Do you think they will do nothing? They will use it, too, and you will find them twice as strong as you are afterward."

Nokrashy was adamant. "Azzam," he said, "my decision is based on the advice of my Chief of Staff. I'm not going to take your advice over my soldiers'."

"You're getting your advice from the most ignorant man in Egypt when it comes to warfare," Azzam snorted in reply. The League's secretary general feared that Nokrashy's stand was simply a pretext to abandon the war altogether. He knew, too, that the Egyptian masses, fed a daily barrage of misleading communiqués, were going to be enraged if a cease-fire deprived them of their expected triumph. Just as bellicose propaganda was in part responsible for getting the Arab leaders into the war, it now threatened to keep them in it. It was Azzam's ace in the hole.

When it became apparent that the truce was going to carry the day and that only the Syrians were prepared to go on fighting, Azzam grabbed a piece of paper from his desk. Angrily he wrote out his resignation and threw it on the table. He was going to publicly denounce the men who had forced a cease-fire on the League, he said, as he stalked from the meeting.

White-faced, Nokrashy leaped up and rushed after him. He caught up with Azzam in the corridor. Tugging his sleeves, he said, "Azzam, do you know what you are doing? You are killing me. If I go back to Cairo with your resignation and a cease-fire, I will be assassinated."

Azzam was shattered by his words. He knew how much truth there was in what Nokrashy had just said. Despite their bitter political differences, they were friends and they had lived through many tribulations together.

"All right," he said, "I'll accept. But the Arab people will never forgive us for what we are about to do." Then, wordlessly, Azzam walked back into the meeting room and tore up his resignation.

. . .

A nervous silence prevailed in the buses. Like many of the men around him, Pinhas Bracker, the meter reader of the Palestine Electric Company who had promised his wife he would be back for dinner, wondered what anguish his prolonged absence was going to cause his family. From Kfar Bilu their bus had gone through Hulda, then up toward Latrun. Two miles below the crossroads which the Seventh Brigade had twice tried to wrest from the Arab Legion, the bus had turned east up a dirt track to Beit Jiz.

It was midnight as the first buses started into the Judean foothills. A chill wind rolled down from the plateau, sending shivers through these men dressed in shirtsleeves for the humid sidewalks of Tel Aviv. Ahead, green, pink and yellow streaks of light danced across the dark skies, signal flares announcing, perhaps, their arrival to some hidden Arab gunner. At the first whistle of a few random shots fired by Mahmoud May'tah's mortars, the men threw themselves onto the floor of the bus.

The convoy struggled through cyclamen and lavender up to the village of Beit Susin, easternmost terminus that night of the Burma Road. There the men got down and slung their sacks on their backs.

Bronislav Bar-Shemer, the officer who had kidnapped the trucks of Tel Aviv for Operation Nachshon, arranged them in single file. Each man was instructed to take hold of the shirttail of the man before him so that they would not get lost in the darkness. Then, Bar-Shemer at their head, they started forward into the night.

Watching them disappear, Vivian Herzog was struck by a strange detail, "the total silence of those men who belonged to the world's most talkative people." To David Marcus, their disappearing silhouettes evoked the image of "the caravans of antiquity on King Solomon's highways."

The column passed through the zone where Marcus' two bulldozers and his army of laborers fought, as they had for nights, to push the road forward. Some of them were already laying the first segments of a pipeline which would soon deliver water over the hill to tank trucks run down from Jerusalem. The pipeline that would eventually ease Jerusalem's collective thirst had originally been destined to replace the pipes of London blown out by the Blitz.

After a slight decline, the track straightened out to assault the steep incline leading up to the first crest. It was there that the porters' martyrdom began. Without any light, the men stumbled on hidden stones, slipped to the ground, grabbing a clump of wild carrots or a bush to keep themselves from rolling down the hillside. Felled by a heart attack, one man tumbled back down the ravine, bouncing helplessly from rock to rock. The men behind him stepped over his body to attack in their turn the slope that had killed him.

Some, too exhausted to go on, sank to the ground by the side of the path. The strongest struggled to the top, laid down their loads, then came back down to help them. To forget the pain of his ascent, Pinhas Bracker forced himself to remember a happy picnic he had had in these hills as a young family man. Others remembered Avidar's words, that they carried on their aching backs the ingredients of one hundred thousand Jews' survival. Still others thought only how to move one foot forward after the other. Mixed with the scraping and stumbling noise of their feet was a bizarre sound, the panting of their middle-aged lungs. At points the slope became so steep that the men literally had to pull themselves forward by tugging on stone ledges or grasping the roots of the rare shrubs along their route. The one that offered the best support was a kind of wild strawberry plant with deep roots, called because of its red flower "Blood of the Maccabees."

Some men crawled forward on their hands and knees. On the reverse slopes, those who couldn't hold on slid down the hillside on their stomachs, moving like crabs from rock to rock so that the precious load on their backs would not be lost.

531

Without a word, without a cry, the column continued along its way. At its head, Bar-Shemer prayed that the guns of Latrun would remain silent and not turn their expedition into a disaster with a few mortar shells. Finally, after three hours, he saw ahead in the predawn grayness the silhouettes of a team of porters brought out from Jerusalem to load their sacks onto waiting trucks and jeeps. Dov Joseph's desperate appeal had been heard. The efforts of Bar-Shemer's three hundred men from Tel Aviv would give thirty thousand Jews in Jerusalem food for another day.

At dawn, Arieh Belkind, the manager of Dov Joseph's warehouses, arrived at his principal depot at the Evelyn de Rothschild School. All he had that morning of Tuesday, June 8, was a few crates of matzo. On his way to work, his thoughts had been on their "impending tragedy." Walking in the door, he suddenly discovered a pile of sacks sitting on the warehouse floor. Belkind bent down, opened one, and ran his fingers through its contents. It was flour. Overcome, he began to cry.

44

A TOAST TO THE LIVING

"THIS IS Mahmoud Rousan. The Jews have captured the police station. Open fire on it with all available artillery."

Hearing that name on the Arab Legion's radio net at Latrun, a man sat bolt upright in the midst of the heavy assault straining the Legion's positions. Grabbing his microphone, Captain Mahmoud Rousan, the real one, said, "This is Mahmoud Rousan. The Jews are trying to fool us. I forbid anyone to fire on the police station. Our men are still inside."

The discovery of their ruse would deprive the Haganah of a success they were close to winning on the night of June 9. For the third time, the Jewish Army was trying to wrest the heights of Latrun from the Arab Legion and reopen the Jerusalem road before a cease-fire could freeze their enemy in his commanding positions. To carry it out, a fresh brigade, one of the best in the Palmach, had been brought down from Galilee to replace the shattered battalion of the Seventh Brigade. Their task was to try to take the Arab positions from behind while a smaller, diversionary attack fixed Arab attention once again on the police station. Paradoxically, the latter effort, due to an error on its commander's part, came closer to bringing the Haganah success at Latrun than either of the two previous efforts.

Turning up the wrong valley, the diversionary force stumbled on the Legion's headquarters. They seized the artillery control center and were within a few yards of overrunning Colonel Habes Majali's command post when their attack faltered for lack of reinforcements. Just before dawn, a hastily assembled group of Arab cooks, clerks and signalmen, rallied by the cries of "*Allah akhbar!*" from the regiment's imam, took the crests back. For nineteen years they would remain in the hands of the Legion.

When news of the Haganah's third defeat at Latrun reached Jerusalem, a pall descended on the city. To Leon Angel, one of the two bakers still working, it seemed on that Thursday, June 10, as though "death was stalking the city. Everything was silent. Shutters were closed." The hunger-weakened population, he surmised, "was probably staying inside, trying not to move to save energy."

To finish baking his bread that morning, Angel had used his last reserves. He had swept the flour on the floor to fill out his ration. All the heroism of the middle-aged men struggling up the hills from Beit Susin was not going to save Jerusalem. The flour they had been able to deliver had been a tonic to the city's morale, but it could not fill Jerusalem's stomachs and its warehouses. Those warehouses contained that morning flour for about thirty thousand loaves of bread, a third of a loaf per person, enough perhaps to allow the city to survive another forty-eight hours. Their situation was so grim that Joseph and Shaltiel had to consider the awful question of whom to stop feeding first, the civilians or the soldiers. At the Schneller base, the ration that Thursday morning consisted of six olives, a slice of bread and a cup of tea.

Most families' hidden reserves were gone. Even the black market had dried up. Famine was truly at Jerusalem's doorstep. Certain elements in the city's Oriental population were close to panic, and a food riot might have a catastrophic result, by showing the Arabs how desperate the situation was. It might even lead them to dismiss the cease-fire Dov Joseph counted on to save the city. Dan Ben-Dor suggested that Joseph cut the ration of Jerusalem's European Jews still further to give a bit more to the Orientals. The Westerners, he argued, would better understand the need to hang on.

"What?" yelled Joseph. "Give them the price of their weakness? Never!"

Even if they could get more flour, they would have nothing to bake it with. That morning Alexander Singer had extracted the last barrels of fuel from his tanks by cutting the sludge at their bottoms with kerosene. The resulting mixture would give him a few spasms of current—enough to keep Jerusalem's bakeries and hospitals powered for perhaps thirty-six more hours. Only the water reserves of Zvi Leibowitz were capable of going on a bit longer.

For the twenty-sixth consecutive day, Arab shellfire racked the city. In the past forty-eight hours, Emile Jumean's guns had dropped 670 rounds in its streets. David Shaltiel, his ammunition supply still critically low, could answer the deluge with only a few desultory rounds. Jumean, however, was gracious enough to make up for his failure to reply. Hoping to provoke a worldwide storm of protest against the Jews, he sent two of his own shells at the Church of the Holy Sepulcher and the Dome of the Rock, sure that the Haganah would be blamed for the outrage.

In the midst of the chaos produced by the shellfire and their hunger, the city's population clung to one hope, the thirty-day cease-fire ordered by the U. N.'s mediator, Count Folke Bernadotte. It was scheduled to begin the following morning, Friday, June 11, at ten. The news drew no celebrations. Twice before, the mediator had set cease-fire dates, and twice the Arabs had ignored them.

Dov Joseph refused to contemplate what would happen if they spurned it again. As poised and calm as he had been all during the struggle, he spent the evening in the most hopeful exercise he could find, reviewing the supplies he wanted rushed into the city when a cease-fire took effect. It was, he reflected, the only worthwhile thing left to do. If a cease-fire did not go into effect, it was going to be all over anyway.

• • •

Twenty miles from Dov Joseph's office, in the darkness above Bab el Wad, a pair of American newspapermen clung desperately to a swaying jeep. Painfully they made their way along the vague track which David Marcus' bulldozers had hacked out of that terrible terrain. With their passage, the Burma Road was pronounced officially open for traffic.

The news bore little relation to the real state of the road. The Israelis had chosen to reveal to the world their secret route for a very specific reason. They had now established that the Burma Road had linked Jewish Jerusalem to the plains before the cease-fire took effect. They could henceforth maintain that it would not fall under the jurisdiction of the United Nations truce supervisors.

A few miles ahead of the jeep, near the church of the Christian Arab village of Abu Gosh, the sound of gunfire shattered the night. A Jewish sentry at the command post of the Haganah forces operating between Bab el Wad and Jerusalem rushed toward the white-robed figure he had just shot. David Marcus would not live to see the "inauguration" of the road on which he had labored so hard. The first Jewish general since Judas Maccabaeus was dead, mistaken for an Arab because he had wandered out to urinate in the fields by his tent wrapped in a bedsheet.

• • •

It was shortly after eight o'clock in the morning of Friday, June 11, when another newspaperman, this one Arab, walked into the office of Major Abdullah Tell. Before Abou Said Abou Reech could put a question to the Arab officer, the telephone rang.

"Yes, Your Majesty," he heard Tell say. Then the expression of the

535

handsome Arab officer's face changed to shocked disbelief. "Your Majesty," Tell gasped, "how can I stop these men? They feel victory is within reach."

Aware of the delicate problems Tell would face in enforcing a Jerusalem cease-fire, not only on his own men but on the Mufti's partisans as well, the King had made the exceptional gesture of calling him personally. Abou Reech heard the sovereign's voice rasping through the phone.

"You are a soldier and I give you an order," the King told Tell. "You must order a cease-fire at ten o'clock." Then, to underscore the serious-ness of his words, he said he intended to come to Jerusalem for noon prayers at the mosque.

Heartbroken, Tell hung up. Dabbing at his eyes with the edge of his kaf-fiyeh, he rushed wordlessly past Abou Reech into the street.

For the next two hours Jerusalem was racked by almost constant gun-fire, as though both sides, realizing that a cease-fire was imminent, now sought to empty their armories before it began. At ten o'clock it burst into a last spasm. Then the fire began to slacken like the rain of a fading thunder-storm. Behind the battlements of the Old City a word fled from one Legion-naire's lips to another: *hudna,* truce. At Mandelbaum, at Notre-Dame, on Mount Zion, David Shaltiel's exhausted men lowered their weapons at the sound of sirens blown throughout the Jewish city. By 10:04, a strange, almost oppressive silence shrouded Jerusalem.

In the Arab Old City quarters, the first reaction to the cease-fire was shocked disbelief, then grief and fury. Little groups of people began to gather protesting, demonstrating against the politicians who had deprived them of their victory. A few of the Mufti's snipers opened fire in an effort to sabotage the truce. Tell's Legionnaires silenced them, but they had their own profound misgivings. They expressed them by beginning a Bedouin funeral dance in the streets.

To watch the reaction on the other side, their commander climbed up to the tower on which David Shaltiel had hoped to plant an Israeli flag. Bitterly Abdullah Tell looked for the first person he could see moving in that city now freed from the menace of his shellfire. It was a woman, her head bent, running fast with a basket in her hand, off to get food for her family. Watching her go, Tell suddenly saw his victory disappearing with her fleeing figure. Never again would he be as close to conquering all Jerusalem as he had been that morning.

Dazed, numbed almost, by the silence, the inhabitants of New Jerusalem crawled from their cellars and shelters, not quite believing after so many false alarms that the firing had really stopped. There was no jubilation, no celebrating. They were too weak with hunger for that. The streets were littered with broken glass, masonry, stacks of refuse. Jerusalem's stone dwellings had survived well, but a shattered roof or gaping black hole at each street corner bore evidence to the severity of the struggle the city had undergone.

Dov Joseph barely paused in his routine to savor the truce. He dispatched a message to Ben-Gurion with an urgent reminder to get a food convoy in immediately, holding its contents to absolute essentials. Reflecting an instant, he told himself, "It has been a people's struggle and we survived because our people struggled."

A few doors away in his own Jewish Agency office, David Shaltiel assembled his staff officers. From the bottom drawer of his desk he took out a bottle of French champagne one of his men had found on their advance May 14, and poured a glass for each man. Solemnly he proposed a toast to the men whose lives had been saved by the cease-fire. Then he warned that it was of a limited, four-week duration. Each day of that respite would have to be used to prepare for a new outbreak of hostilities. The next round, he promised, was going to be theirs.

As he had said he would King Abdullah had arrived in Jerusalem for noon prayers in the Mosque of Omar. Afterward, in one of the classrooms of the Rawdah School, the city's leaders offered a Bedouin banquet in his honor. As was the custom, a whole roast sheep on a pile of steaming rice was set before the sovereign. A special lore enveloped Abdullah's banquets: when he found a partner too talkative, he plucked the tongue from the sheep's head and passed it to him; to guests whom he considered dull or whose ideas displeased him, he proposed the brains. Today, however, he had only honors to propose, and the first man to receive them was Abdullah Tell. He announced Tell's promotion from major to colonel.

As King Abdullah got up to leave, each man filed past him to kiss his hand. Normally he offered it palm down. When he was angry he extended his fist. To the young officer he had ordered to "go save Jerusalem," he offered the highest of accolades. He gave him his hand palm up.

For another young officer who had saved Jerusalem, June 11 was also a day of triumph. Riding in the back seat of a Palmach jeep on the very first convoy to leave the besieged city was a prim and proper middle-aged Englishwoman in a flowered hat. It had taken all of Yosef Nevo's connec-

537

tions and prestige to get her there. It was his mother-in-law, and this evening he would be able to celebrate at last an event which he had looked forward to for five weeks, his wedding night.

Several miles down the road, above the intersection for which so many men had fought and died, the Trappist monks of Latrun chanted the Mass of Saint Barnaby with a particular fervor. Then, reinstalled in their damaged refectory, they decided that in honor of the truce they would climax their usually austere meal with a little cordial from the cellars of Father Godart.

To David Ben-Gurion in his study in Tel Aviv, the thirty-day respite the cease-fire had won his beleaguered nation was a "golden dream." As on Partition Night, as on May 14, he had no time for celebration. Before him was a report from Ehud Avriel announcing a third shipload of arms ready to leave Yugoslavia. They had bought 100-millimeter mortars in France. The Czechs had agreed to train pilots, paratroopers and armored experts for them. Planes had arrived that could fly nonstop from Prague to Tel Aviv.

His state had survived and he knew the tide was turning, a new phase in his country's history beginning.

His foes had made that day "a mistake, a fateful mistake."

45

THE THIRTY-DAY PAUSE

THE SPOT DESIGNATED for the first encounter between the two men whose forces had struggled for the control of Jerusalem for almost a month was singularly appropriate. It was in the middle of a street named for another soldier who centuries before had shared their dream of conquering Jerusalem, Godefroy de Bouillon.

David Shaltiel, the sophisticated Jew from Hamburg, and Abdullah Tell, his handsome young Arab rival from Transjordan, paused for a silent instant to appraise each other. Then they saluted and shook hands. The task before them at that first meeting was to fix a cease-fire line in one part of their disputed Holy City, the Arab quarter of Musrara. The evening before, a last Haganah attack had pushed its irregular defenders back two hundred yards. Shaltiel insisted that the demarcation line must include their gains.

"If these are your positions, where are your fortifications?" a skeptical Tell asked.

"Our bloody shirts are our fortifications," Shaltiel quietly replied.

Impressed, Tell told his rival, "Very well, I will accept your word as an officer and a gentleman."

In Jewish Jerusalem, life staggered slowly back to normal. Stores opened, the broken glass and the rubble were cleaned from the streets. The *Palestine Post* reappeared and a fragmentary bus service was instituted. Above all, the cease-fire checked the famine menacing its population. As the first convoys came up from the coast, Jerusalem began to eat again. For Ruth Erlik, Professor Joseph's operating-room nurse, a knock on her door marked the end of her hunger. It was a friend from Tel Aviv, and "if Elijah the Prophet had stood there," the young woman thought, he would not have impressed her more favorably—for the friend handed her a package of chocolate and canned food. A similar surprise awaited David Shaltiel one night. Returning to his room at Greta Asher's boardinghouse, he found the wife he had left in Tel Aviv months before. Yehudit Shaltiel had brought her husband a Camembert cheese, unhappily converted into a pool of yellow sludge by her long, hot trip up the Burma Road.

Dov Joseph's first concern was establishing a working relationship with the United Nations mediator, Count Folke Bernadotte. The Swede's interpretation of how the cease-fire should be implemented made their relations difficult. He insisted that Jerusalem's food supply at the end of the cease-fire should be the same as it had been at the beginning and that food coming into the city over the Burma Road should be included in the totals when the final tally was made. It was a convention Joseph had no intention of accepting. The nightmare of the last few days was not going to be repeated if he could help it. He was going to pull every ounce of food he could into Jerusalem during the next four weeks. The Burma Road did not come under United Nations jurisdiction, he maintained, and in any event, he told the Swede, "You are not going to tell us how much we can eat after weeks of starvation."

David Shaltiel immediately ordered his planners to start drawing up plans and laying in the supplies they would need to go on the offensive when the four-week truce ended. This time he intended to be in a position to seize all Jerusalem for his new state.

David Ben-Gurion's first gesture was to summon all the senior commanders of the Haganah to Tel Aviv for a full-scale conference. Exhausted, pushed to the edge of physical and mental endurance by the test they had just undergone, they nonetheless had cause for satisfaction that morning of June 12. They had survived, and that in itself was an achievement.

The price had been heavy. Their casualties had been higher than anyone had expected, and at the end they had been stretched to the breaking point. Moshe Carmel, the commander in the north, summed up the sentiments of all of them, remarking that the truce "came to us as dew from heaven."

Deficiencies of every sort had surfaced which would have to be corrected before the next round. Arms and ammunition had been in short supply almost everywhere, while cases of goods piled up unused on the docks of Haifa. The almost universal lack of antitank weapons had been a disaster. Men had fought without shoes, in pajamas, with hats which failed to protect them from the desert sun.

Patiently, David Ben-Gurion listened to the long list of complaints. Then he took over, his voice a familiar, confident growl. They had thirty days ahead of them and they would use every one. Thirty days, he believed, were enough to train a Jewish soldier. Despite the restrictions of the cease-fire, they would use them to bring in their arms and their manpower reserves from Cyprus and Europe. Their real problem, he said, was not hats that failed to prevent sunstroke, or poor shoes. It was their lack of discipline. How many positions had they lost, how many opportunities had they missed because of that shortcoming, he wondered. "If we had one army instead of a number of armies," he said, "if we had operated according to one strategic plan, we would have more to show for our efforts."

That would not be allowed to happen again. The next time, he warned, they "must have a plan for victory, otherwise we will be defeated."

"If the battle is renewed," he proclaimed, "and it must be assumed it will, we shall be entering the decisive phase."

• • •

In Amman, John Glubb was serenely confident that the war would not be resumed. He had good reason to think as he did. At about the time the Haganah chiefs were assembling in Tel Aviv, Prime Minister Tewfic Abou Hoda categorically informed Glubb, "There won't be any more fighting." He and Nokrashy, Abou Hoda said, were determined not to let the war break out again. There was going to be "no more fighting and no more money for soldiers."

It was a point of view with which Glubb was wholly in accord. The fighting had proved to him that there was no future for the Arabs in throwing their populations into conflict with the Jewish state. The principal factor in the situation, in Glubb's view, "was that you had a modern European population opposed to a much more numerous local population which was without technical knowledge and modern skills, and which was uncontrollably excitable and emotional." The behavior of the Arabs facing Israel, it seemed to Glubb, "had been similar to that of the Jews during the Maccabean and Roman revolts." The Arabs were "forever splitting up into little groups. No one would take orders from anyone else and then when something went wrong, somebody had to be a traitor because that was the only possible explanation of why things had gone wrong."

"It makes it terribly difficult to operate a war against an external enemy," he would later note with bitterness, "when you are under the constant menace of hysterical riots by your own people." Until the Arabs had produced more mature societies, economies and populations, they would be no match for their new Jewish neighbors, Glubb felt, and they had best keep out of war with them.

• • •

541

Despite Glubb's observation, the most significant accomplishment of the Israelis during the four-week cease-fire was achieved thanks to sweat, not sophistication, and artisan skill rather than technology. With almost frantic energy, work went forward on the Burma Road. Additional bulldozers and laborers were recruited. A pair of powerful tractors were installed on two grades to tow trucks to the top. By June 19, less than three weeks after work had begun, the Burma Road was ready for its real, working inauguration. On that day, 140 trucks, each carrying a three-ton load, reached Jerusalem traveling over a highway carved from terrain a British brigadier had scornfully dismissed with the words "They'll never get a road through there."

Since U. N. truce supervisors were carefully checking the food convoys passing through Latrun to make sure they carried no arms, the first trucks up the Burma Road were assigned to David Shaltiel's forces. To the man who had once had to order his men not to fire on targets more than one hundred yards distant, they brought an impressive variety of weapons. Forty tons of dynamite, hundreds of rifles, Sten guns, Czech machine guns, cases of hand grenades and ammunition came pouring into the Haganah's armories. Behind them came two-, three- and six-inch mortars. Next time, Jerusalem's Haganah was going to answer the cannon of the Arab Legion not with the sporadic and inaccurate fire of the Davidka, but with a murderous counterfire from its own guns. Watching the first of those fieldpieces arrive, an awed David Shaltiel kept repeating over and over again to his adjutant Yeshurun Schiff, "Oh, my God! Oh, my God!"

As traffic increased, other convoys began pouring in with food for Dov Joseph's warehouses. In the first full week of operation, the Burma Road delivered Joseph a staggering 2,200 tons of food, enough to last the city almost four months on the minimum supply of 140 tons he had needed during the desperate closing days of May. The final symbol of the city's triumph over the threat to "strangle Jerusalem" uttered by Abdul Khader Husseini six months earlier was a chain of trucks June 22 bringing Jerusalem a forgotten luxury—oranges.

Alongside those passing convoys, 150 men labored to complete a sixteen-mile pipeline that would ensure Jerusalem the other element essential to its survival: water. Divided into four teams under Moshe Rochel, a Polish-born engineer who had built pipelines for the Iraq Petroleum Company, they worked fourteen hours a day, laying their pipes above ground, contour-welding, and pacing off distances by foot, without tape measures. In nineteen days they had finished. Rochel went to Jerusalem and, beaming with pleasure, watched the first drops of water pour from the city's faucets. The event was so extraordinary that he was asked to mark the accomplishment with a press conference. He refused. "There's nothing to say," he said. "It's done."

• • •

The supplies rolling up the Burma Road to Jerusalem were a mere token of things to come. At last the arms David Ben-Gurion had promised his colleagues May 12 were beginning to pour into the country in considerable number—and, evidently, in open violation of the terms of the cease-fire. On June 15, one of Yehuda Arazi's ships delivered ten 75-millimeter cannon, ten Hotchkiss tanks, the first real armor to reach Israel, nineteen 65-millimeter cannon, four antiaircraft guns and 45,000 shells. A second ship delivered 110 tons of TNT, ten tons of cordite and 200,000 detonators.

From Mexico, the S.S. *Kefalos* brought thirty-six 75-millimeter cannon, five hundred machine guns, seventeen thousand shells, seven million rounds of ammunition and, as an extra dividend, 1,400 tons of sugar used to hide its real cargo in case the British tried to seize the ship at Gibraltar. Materials for Palestine sent from the United States included two boatloads of war-surplus jeeps, trucks and half-tracks, bombsights, chemicals for the production of explosives, a radar set and the machine tools require to manufacture bazookas. The indefatigable Yehuda Arazi also bought thirty surplus Sherman tanks in Italy. To his consternation, he discovered that there was no crane in the ports of Israel capable of swinging their weight ashore. Not a man to be put off by details, Arazi went out and bought a fifty-ton crane.

In Prague, Ehud Avriel continued his purchasing activities. During June alone, he bought eight million rounds of ammunition, twenty-two light tanks and four hundred machine guns. The air force which had started out with a handful of pleasure planes now possessed fifteen C-46s, three B-17 Flying Fortresses, three Constellations, five P-51 Mustang fighters, four Boston A-20 bombers, two DC-4s, ten DC-3s, twenty Messerschmitts, seven Ansons and four Beaufighters. To fly them, volunteers and mercenaries, Zionists and non-Zionists, Jews and non-Jews, were pouring into Avriel's Žatec airbase. Begun by a letter to Ben-Gurion from his next-door neighbor, the Haganah Air Service had become in less than six months the most powerful air force in the Middle East. In Israel, the miniature arms industry bought surreptitiously in the United States by Haim Slavine was in full production, turning out, among other things, nine hundred mortar shells and six thousand bullets a day. Equally important, the men to man

543

those weapons were being mobilized in Israel and arriving every day from Europe and Cyprus.

As Ben-Gurion had foreseen, the tide was turning, and it was turning fast.

Cut off from their principal source of arms in Britain, deprived of the support of a sympathetic world opinion, the Arabs were unable to make anything more than a few marginal acquisitions of arms during the four-week cease-fire. Glubb flew to Suez and literally begged his old friend who was commanding the British forces in the Middle East for an illegal supply of arms. "His feelings were all with me," Glubb later acknowledged, "but his orders were blunt and unequivocal: not one cartridge."

Glubb did arrange to "steal" a substantial number of small-arms stores from the R.A.F. in Amman. But to face an enemy now receiving artillery shells by the thousands, Glubb was not able to procure a single shell for his 25-pounder guns.

The midnight requisitions of the Egyptian Army in the Suez Canal Zone were also discontinued. An Egyptian officer in the Negev noted that during that period "we were getting chocolate, biscuits and tea from Cairo, but no bullets."

As the Israelis had been earlier, the Arabs were now forced into a kind of cottage industry for the production of arms. Colonel Desmond Young, a one-eyed Burma veteran serving with the Arab Legion, set up a clandestine production center in the Science Laboratories of the American University in Beirut with a rabidly anti-Semitic German as his chief chemist. The ingenious Young also had a group of Palestinian tinsmiths in Zerqa make antipersonnel mines out of bicycle pumps stuffed with scrap metal.

But there was one aspect of their arms program in which the Arabs could take satisfaction. It was going on in Bari harbor. With great patience, Colonel Fouad Mardam supervised the cleaning of the rifles salvaged from the hulk of the S.S. *Lino*. Freshly greased and recrated, they were being kept under guard in a Bari warehouse while Mardam tried to charter a ship to take them to Alexandria. Despite all his efforts, Mardam was unable to find a charter in Bari. Thanks to the proprietor of his hotel, however, he finally got the name of a shipping agent in Rome who might help him.

Two days later, as discreetly as possible, making sure he was not being followed, Mardam walked into the offices of the Menara Shipping Agency on the Via del Corso in Rome. For one million lire, he secured a charter on a 250-ton corvette, the S.S. *Argiro*. Relieved that his mission was accomplished and his ill-fated Czech arms en route at last to their final destination, Mardam cabled Damascus the good news.

The news was not quite as good as all that. Mardam's Czech arms were indeed on their way to their final destination, but it would turn out to be Tel Aviv, not Alexandria. The Menara Shipping Agency, whose name had been so kindly furnished Colonel Mardam by the owner of his hotel, had neglected to inform the Syrian of one salient detail. The S.S. *Argiro*'s owners were the Israeli Navy.

*   *   *

David Ben-Gurion and his fellow leaders could face the future with growing confidence. Each passing day of the truce period saw their forces increasing and their prospects of victories in a new period of hostilities improving. But their optimism was going to prove slightly premature. More painful than the invasion of five Arab armies, an ancient curse befell the Jewish state—civil strife, the menace which had plagued its ancient predecessor and had finally led to its downfall. The terrorists of the Irgun who had sought to assert their authority in Jerusalem in the slaughter of Deir Yassin were now going to imperil the domestic stability of their new nation. The arrival off Israel of a freighter of the Irgun, the *Altalena,* detonated the conflict. In its holds were five thousand rifles, five half-tracks, three hundred Bren guns and nine hundred men. Landing the men and arms it carried would be an open challenge to the authority of Ben-Gurion's government. The order establishing the Army of Israel prohibited the maintenance of separate armed organizations, and the Irgun and the Stern Gang had been invited to place their men in the ranks of the Haganah. The Irgun, whose leader, Menahem Begin, had denounced the truce as "a shameful surrender," nonetheless continued to operate as an independent, private army.

Ben-Gurion considered the ship's arrival a challenge he could not ignore. He gave orders that the arms it carried be landed and placed in government warehouses. Begin refused. He wanted them in Irgun warehouses under Irgun guards and he wanted twenty percent of them shipped to his men in Jerusalem, which was outside the sphere of his agreement with Haganah. Despite the warning that his actions would have grave consequences, he ordered the ship unloaded June 20 at Kfar Vitkin. Six hundred men of the Alexandroni Brigade surrounded the unloading party, and firing broke out. The *Altalena* hastily set sail.

Dodging the Israeli Navy ships sent out to intercept her, she headed south to Tel Aviv, where her captain tried to run her aground on the beach. He got to within a hundred yards when the vessel grounded itself on the ruins of a prewar immigrant ship sunk by the British. Its presence there on the waterfront of Israel's first city brought on the crisis. The Irgun's chief of operations began to mobilize his men to "take over the government." Ben-Gurion summoned his Cabinet.

The Irgun move, he warned, "endangers the very existence of the state." He told Yigal Allon, the chief of the Palmach, "Tel Aviv is in danger of falling to rebel forces. Your new assignment may be the toughest one you've had so far. This time you may have to kill Jews."

Allon did. In one bloody day's fighting, eighty-three people were killed and wounded. For a few hours the control of Tel Aviv was for all practical purposes in the Irgun's hands. Allon was outnumbered in the city, but the situation was saved for him by a quick artillery hit which set the *Altalena* ablaze and deprived the Irgun of its prize and the reason for this factional strife. Slowly Allon brought the city back under control. In one blow, Ben-Gurion had ended the gravest threat to the new nation's domestic stability. The gun that had sunk the *Altalena,* he later proclaimed, merited "a place in Israel's War Museum."

• • •

Dressed in an immaculate white robe, a cherubic smile on his face, King Abdullah climbed aboard a dark-gray Vickers Viking. He was off for Riyadh, the capital of Saudi Arabia, to make his peace with the warrior King who had driven his family from the sacred cities of Mecca and Medina. Packed inside the plane were the gifts which would consecrate his historic gesture, a golden dagger, a porcelain tea set and an embossed silver tray flown to him from London by a Jewish silversmith.

If the divisions of the Arab world were at the moment less evident than those in Israel, they were nevertheless real, and Abdullah's trip was a manifestation of them. The King was convinced of the folly of going back to war with the Israelis and he had good personal reasons for his sentiment. Count Bernadotte was in the process of formulating a peace proposal which fulfilled all his own ambitions. It would give him Jerusalem, the Negev, a free port in Haifa and a free airport at Lydda, while giving western Galilee to the Israelis. To win Ibn-Saud's support for the plan, Abdullah was prepared to make an extraordinary gesture—he was going to renounce his family's claims to the ancient homeland from which Ibn-Saud's warriors had evicted them.

While Abdullah visited with his old foe, the prime ministers of the Arab

546

League in Cairo were rejecting Count Bernadotte's plan. It took the Arab leaders just one session on June 27 to unanimously decide "in deep sorrow" that the Arab League could "not accept these proposals as a convenient basis for negotiations." Bernadotte's plan, they maintained in a three-page memorandum, was just a reworking of partition with its unacceptable provision for a Jewish state.

With their summary rejection of Bernadotte's proposals, the Arabs were once again foreclosing their options. They had again been trapped by their own propaganda. In Jerusalem, the Arab crowds were repeating a new slogan, "Wait until the ninth of July," the date the cease-fire was to expire. Once again the civilians of Palestine were sapping the Legionnaires' morale by calling them cowards for having stopped fighting. In Bethlehem, one of Glubb's officers watched the Moslem Brothers chanting for a resumption of the Holy War.

Nowhere was the menace of the crowds more keenly felt than in Cairo. The predictions of Azzam Pasha in Amman on the eve of the cease-fire were being fulfilled. Wary of the Moslem Brotherhood's extremists, Egypt's Prime Minister Nokrashy Pasha reversed himself once again. Egypt, he declared, was prepared to resume hostilities.

This time, the country that had made no effort to prevent the Arabs from embarking on war May 14 strongly counseled them against resuming the conflict. Britain made it clear that the Arabs would not be able to get arms in England for a second round.

Before Transjordan's Tewfic Abou Hoda left for Cairo, Glubb had warned him, "We have no ammunition. For God's sake, no matter what happens, don't agree to resume fighting." Afraid of being diplomatically isolated, Abou Hoda joined the others in voting to resume fighting July 9 if the mediator did not submit a more satisfactory peace plan in the meantime.

On his return to Amman, Abou Hoda was greeted by a furious Glubb. "Good heavens," Glubb said, "why did you agree to resume fighting? Whatever are we going to use for ammunition?"

"Well," said the Prime Minister after a moment's reflection, "don't shoot unless the Jews shoot first."

• • •

With his arms supply secured and the Irgun crushed, Ben-Gurion devoted his time to ensuring that Israel had one army, not a number of armies, and one basic strategic plan. On June 29, the Israel Defense Force officially came into being, an army with ranks, pay scale, and messes like any other. The recalcitrant Palmach was brought under stricter supervision in the new organization. The strategic plan concentrated above all on Jerusalem.

Despite the U. N., 7,500 tons of food and 2,800 tons of fuel, enough to last almost a year, had been stocked in the city's warehouses during the cease-fire period. This time no one was going to menace Jewish Jerusalem with starvation. But the long-term solution for the city depended on more than its ability to withstand a siege. "King David chose one of the most difficult places in the country for his capital," Ben-Gurion told his Cabinet. He deplored the fact that Zionism's pioneers had not resolved the problem by linking Jerusalem to the sea with a chain of settlements. In the next round of fighting, the objective would be to capture all the city, and to establish a broad territorial link to the plains, seizing enough of the country-side around the city to give it breathing space.

"We must mend in this war," he said, "what we neglected in peace-time."

. . .

The Arab's swift rejection of Bernadotte's proposals spared the Israelis the onus of being the first to turn down a U. N. plan which, this time, was as unacceptable to them as it was to the Arabs. On July 6, Moshe Sharett gave Bernadotte Israel's formal rejection of his scheme.

The following day, in a last effort to preserve peace, Bernadotte called on both sides to accept a prolongation of the truce. The Israelis had no reason to accept. Both sides had violated the truce whenever possible, but the Israelis' efforts had been far more successful than the Arabs' had. The Iraqis and the Egyptians had each managed to add about ten thousand men to their forces; otherwise there had been no substantial changes on the Arab side. But Israel was now ready to put sixty thousand men into the field. For the first time, the Jews would both outnumber *and* outgun the Arabs.

Reviewing the situation, Ben-Gurion "knew it was finished. I knew we had won. They couldn't conquer us. It was only a question of how far we could go." Yet he knew that his state's reputation and the ideals to which it subscribed obliged him to take a decision against which all his fibers rebelled. He accepted Bernadotte's proposal. Israel would not resume firing.

"I was afraid of one thing that day," he would remember two decades later, "that the Arabs would accept the truce, too."

. . .

Ben-Gurion need not have worried. As so often before, his Arab foes obliged him. In a last unsuccessful effort to head off a resumption of hostilities, King Abdullah invited Lebanon's Riad Solh, Syria's Jamil Mardam, Egypt's Nokrashy Pasha and the Arab League's secretary general to his palace in Amman. Much as he wanted to avoid war, Abdullah felt, as he had in May, that he could not stand alone. He had to persuade the others to join him.

Patiently Abdullah reminded them that they had all accepted the cease-fire because their ammunition was running low. During the past four weeks all their information indicated that their enemies had received enormous quantities of arms. The Arab Legion, for its part, had gotten virtually nothing. Perhaps, suggested Abdullah, his fellow Arab leaders might be able to indicate what new provisions they had received to justify going back to war with a vastly strengthened enemy they had not been able to defeat even when they enjoyed a clear margin of superiority.

Riad Solh exploded. They had to go back to war. Their people wanted it. Arab pride, honor and dignity demanded it. If they lacked grenades and ammunition, then, he declared, "we shall pick the oranges from the trees and hurl them at the Jews to fight and save our honor."

A silence followed his impassioned words. Abdullah sighed.

"Thank you, Riad Bey," he said, "for your sentiments and such a delicate expression of our national spirit. I must, however, remind you of something you seem to have forgotten. We are now in the month of July. There will be no oranges on the trees of Palestine before September."

46

THE FLAWED TRUMPET

THE JAGGED SHARDS of metal were still warm. Twisting
one of them between his fingers, Major Abdullah Tell studied it with the
appraising eye of a pawnbroker scrutinizing a piece of jewelry. It took Tell
only a few seconds to realize that these scraps marked the end of one era
in Jerusalem and the beginning of another. "The Arabs' hopes of capturing
New Jerusalem," he would later note, had disappeared with their arrival.
They came from the shattered casing of a six-inch mortar shell. Less than
an hour after the expiration of the cease-fire, they confirmed Tell's fears
that his was no longer the only artillery in Jerusalem. Now it would be
his enemy's turn to take the offensive and try to drive him from the
ramparts of Suleiman the Magnificent.

Bent on giving Jerusalem's Arab population a taste of the shelling that
the New City had endured for four weeks under the Arab Legion's cannon,
David Shaltiel's men poured round after round of artillery into the Old
City. Now it was the Austrian Hospice which was submerged in a wave
of victims. Aladin Namari, the city's self-appointed Minister of Information,
saw one woman, her stomach torn apart by a direct hit on her car,
hysterically shrieking for her six children. Near her stretcher was a hamper
full of human fragments, all that remained of her family.

All night the firing continued. By dawn, Jerusalem's stunned and shell-
shocked Arab population had understood what Abdullah Tell had realized
in the first minutes after the cease-fire had expired. The ninth of July for
which they had clamored with such impatience was going to prove the
beginning of a time of trial, not triumph.

The mortars of Jerusalem were an indication of what was happening
all over the country. Everywhere the Israeli forces were going over to
the offensive. In the south they captured several villages from the stunned
Egyptians. In the north, four Israeli columns struck at the Syrians holding
their colony of Mishmar Hayarden below Lake Huleh, while others routed

the refurbished Liberation Army of Fawzi el Kaukji and took the ancient city of Nazareth.

By far the most important gains were made in the area north of Latrun, around the Arab cities of Lydda and Ramle. Within three days the two cities and the surrounding countryside were in Jewish hands. Vital to the Israelis' quick success were the spectacular tactics of a commando unit led by a one-eyed officer whose face was destined to become a symbol of his country's military prowess—Moshe Dayan.

In the wake of the sudden Israeli triumph, tens of thousands of Arab refugees began swarming up the hills toward Ramallah. This time their flight was not a result of fear, but of a calculated Israeli policy to drive them out. The earlier Arab departures had made it all too clear that the land seized by the Israelis was more valuable without the embarrassing presence of its Arab inhabitants. Loudspeaker vans roamed the streets telling the Arabs to leave. Arab leaders were summoned to Israeli Army headquarters and bluntly advised to get out. Buses were promised to transport their people to Arab lines. In Lydda, after many Arabs, persuaded that the Legion was counterattacking, turned on the Israelis to whom they had just surrendered, large parts of the population were physically evicted from their homes and ordered onto the road to Ramallah.

Under a boiling sun, clutching what few possessions they had had time to gather, an occasional Israeli bullet whistling overhead to keep them moving, the miserable column of human beings stumbled over the rock- and thorn-strewn hillside toward Ramallah. An unknown number of the aged and the young died during their trek.

When the news of their flight and the fall of Lydda and Ramle reached the Arab world, riots broke out everywhere. In Amman, thousands of angry young men screaming "Treason!" marched on the King's palace. Defying his shocked aides, the King walked straight into the face of the advancing mob, marched up to one of its chanting ringleaders and slapped his face sharply.

In the stunned silence that followed, the King glared up at him. "You want to fight the Jews?" he asked. "Go enlist in the Arab Legion." With a wave, he pointed out a recruiting office. "If you don't," he said, "go home and shut up." With that, the King ordered the mob out of his palace grounds and strode back to his office.

• • •

The plane's wings bore the little-known insignia of the air force of Panama. Its navigator was picking out landmarks with a map taken from a Baedeker bought in a secondhand bookstore in Prague. The B-17 Flying Fortress's machine guns were Czech-made Skodas, and seven out of its ten Israeli, English, American and South African crewmen were fainting because the welder's oxygen provided for them on their departure at Ehud Avriel's Žatec air base was inadequate for high altitudes.

Bought as U.S. war surplus, the plane was one of three B-17s smuggled out of the United States despite F.B.I. surveillance. With its two companion planes it was en route to Tel Aviv. On the way, the Israeli Air Force had decided to bomb Cairo to show the Egyptians that its nation's new offensive spirit was not confined to its ground forces.

The big bomber's pilot, Ray Kurz, a former Brooklyn policeman, knew these Mediterranean skies well. He had been flying them for the past two years as a flight engineer for Trans World Airlines. At exactly 9:40 P.M. he set his radio to the familiar frequency of Cairo's Almaza Airport.

"Cairo Control," he announced, "this is TWA Flight 924. May I have the runway lights, please?"

At his words, an obliging pool of light illuminated the B-17's target. "Roger, TWA 924," answered Cairo Control. "Please land on Runway Four."

Kurz's South African bombardier, Johnny Adir, fixed the airport in the crosshairs of his German bombsight. Setting his course straight down the tarmac on which he had so often landed, Kurz held the B-17 steady while Adir blanketed the unsuspecting airport with high explosives. Banking off toward Suez on a ten-degree compass heading, Kurz could not resist calling back a parting message.

"Cairo Control," he asked, "do you still want me to land on Runway Four?"

• • •

An unusual animation stirred the little Lebanese mountain resort of Aley on the evening of July 14. Around the dining-room table of a large villa, Lebanon's Prime Minister Riad Solh had welcomed the cause of so much activity in Aley—his fellow leaders of the Arab League. Their meeting was an urgent response to a kind of ultimatum issued to the warring parties in the Middle East by the United Nations Security Council, calling for an immediate and indefinite end to the fighting.

This time, the Arab leaders had every reason to accept it. As Abdullah had predicted barely a week earlier, the balance of power had been rudely upset during the four-week cease-fire. Now their forces were being thrown back everywhere by the Israelis. To Azzam Pasha's secretary, Whalid el

Dali, the meeting seemed as if "it was a funeral and they had all come to bury some dear relative."

In a sense they had; for their reply that night finally interred the Arab Armies' hopes of conquering Palestine. Even the usually bellicose Syrians agreed, although for a special reason. The nation's President, Shukri al Kuwatli, had revealed to his colleagues that Syria would soon be in a position to lead a new jihad. She now possessed a locally made atomic bomb. It had been manufactured, he confided to them, by an Armenian blacksmith in Damascus.

Just before midnight, Whalid el Dali rushed through the darkened corridors of Beirut's General Post Office, kept open past its closing time on orders from Riad Solh. Azzam Pasha's secretary shook the sleeping telegraph operator in the cable office and handed a short cable addressed to Trygve Lie, Secretary General of the United Nations.

It announced the Arab League's willingness to accept an immediate and indefinite end to the fighting in Palestine.

• • •

The swiftness of the Arab reply deprived the officer who was planning to conquer all Jerusalem of one of the assets he counted on most, time. Instead of the month he had estimated he would have, David Shaltiel learned on the morning of July 15 that he would have less than forty-eight hours. The United Nations mediator had fixed the cease-fire in Jerusalem for 5 A.M. Saturday, July 17, forty-eight hours before it would take effect in the rest of the country.

Shaltiel immediately summoned his staff. It was clear to them all that this cease-fire would end the war and that what they did not get now might be lost for years, perhaps generations, to come. The Jerusalem commander reminded them of the historic importance that the conquest of the Old City would have for the state of Israel and for the Jewish people.

"What glory will fall upon us," he said, "if it is we who conquer Jerusalem for our generation and all the subsequent generations of Jewry."

The plan they had prepared for taking Old Jerusalem called for two wide, encircling movements, followed by an artillery barrage to provoke a panicked flight of its residents. To Shaltiel, the scheme posed a major drawback: it would take three or four days to carry it out—two more days than he had.

The alternative was a direct attack on the walls. It was more risky and it would certainly cost more lives. To Shaltiel's adjutant, Yeshurun Schiff, the frontal attack was like poker: you won or lost everything in one high hand. He knew that for Shaltiel, with his ingrained sense of the dramatic, it had an almost irresistible appeal. Although almost every officer in the room opposed the plan, Shaltiel announced, "We shall attack directly at the Old City. Start preparing the plans immediately."

Like any good poker player, David Shaltiel had an ace in the hole. Called the "Conus," because it bore a resemblance to a cone, it was a hollow charge designed to have a devastating penetrating effect. The idea for it had come from one of the world's most distinguished physicists, Joel Racah. The elderly scientist had come upon it in an Italian textbook. A prototype of the device had been built to Racah's specifications in a Beth Hakerem laundry. It weighed 335 pounds and rested upon a metallic tripod. To be effective, it had to be exploded precisely six inches from its target, but Racah assured Shaltiel that it would tear a gaping hole in the walls of the Old City.

Since the assault was scheduled to take place almost 2,500 years after the Babylonians of Nebuchadnezzar had breached Jerusalem's walls, it was baptized Operation Keddem—Antiquity. As Joshua's trumpets had blown down the walls of Jericho in another battle of antiquity, so the invention of a twentieth-century physicist would blow down the walls of Jerusalem for Keddem and return its alleys to Jewish rule for the first time in two thousand years.

While his commanders completed the detailed arrangements for the attack, Shaltiel and his headquarters staff prepared for an historic burden: giving Jerusalem's Old City its first Jewish government in twenty centuries. Totally confident of the success of their operation, they labored with meticulous care to prepare every facet of their occupation. Provisional currency was hastily printed. Shaltiel named a whole military government to administer the city. A set of posters in Hebrew, Arabic and English had been prepared, and a team of Gadna youths was already selected to paste them on the walls of the city.

For the role of military governor, Shaltiel had chosen a soft-spoken chemistry professor named David Amiran. Amiran had assembled his staff and had set out in step-by-step detail the actions he would take as Jerusalem's military governor. He would begin by proclaiming a curfew. Then, conscious of a grave warning from David Ben-Gurion to see that no harm came to the city's shrines, he would surround them with military police. He had drafted a ten-point "order to the population," already printed in three languages. It called for the handing over of all arms, the surrender of regulars and irregulars, and a return to normal life as quickly as possible. Each member of his staff had been provided with a handsome blue-and-white Military Government armband. Amiran had even designated on a huge map of the Old City the location of his headquarters. He had chosen the Austrian Post Office just inside Jaffa Gate.

Aware of the awesome burdens that would soon be his, Amiran decided to go to sleep at sunset so that he could be up at dawn "ready to act swiftly and decisively" in his new role.

David Shaltiel too had prepared physically and psychologically for the burdens his historic victory would impose on him. As on the night of his assault on Jaffa Gate, a lamb stood ready for the ritualistic sacrifice at the Temple Mount. The Jerusalem commander had also carefully drafted the speech announcing the Old City's fall to the world from the Tower of David. At sundown, he assembled his staff to listen to him rehearse it.

"I have the supreme honor to announce," it began, "that the forces of the city of Jerusalem have liberated all of the city and we hand it over to the people of Israel with pride."

• • •

The man who was determined to thwart the promise of Shaltiel's speech nervously paced up and down in his headquarters at the Rawdah School. For Abdullah Tell as for David Shaltiel it would be a night of decision. He knew his foes must soon launch the assault he had been expecting for days. Just after 10 P.M. a first mortar shell fell into the Old City. Within minutes it was followed by a score of others. Soon Tell was under the heaviest artillery barrage he had ever known, the certain prelude to the attack he had been awaiting.

The depth of Tell's emotional attachment to the city was no less profound than Shaltiel's. In his desk he too had an order of the day drafted for this moment. Tell ordered it radioed to all his positions. "Let every True Believer resolve to stand or die," it said. "We shall defend the Holy City to the last man and the last bullet. Tonight there will be no retreat."

For the next three hours, five hundred shells rained into the Arab city, as much in an hour as the New City had received in a day during the Arab Legion's daily shelling of Jewish Jerusalem. For the medical staff of the Austrian Hospice "it was a night out of hell." The mobile patients were taken to its cellars, and the litters of those who couldn't be moved were dragged into the hallways. One of the first shells destroyed the hospital's ambulance; another set the trees in its courtyard ablaze so that stretcher-bearers couldn't move outside. "Women were screaming in terror all over the place," Dr. Hassib Boulos would recall. "The living, dead and dying were mixed pell-mell throughout the city with no way to get them help."

In New Jerusalem, in an office opposite Zion Cinema, Zvi Sinai, named by Shaltiel to command the attack, ran through his last-minute preparations. His objectives were "Moscow," "Paris" and "Berlin," the code names assigned to the three spots at which his task force would breach Jerusalem's walls. Using conventional explosives to open their way, one hundred and fifty men of the Irgun would rush from Notre-Dame into New Gate—"Paris." The Stern Gang would attack "Moscow"—Jaffa Gate. The bulk of his men, five hundred soldiers of a newly formed battalion, would rush from Mount Zion through the hole that the Conus would blast in Jerusalem's wall just past the Zion Gate at "Berlin."

Commanding one of the assault companies was Mishka Rabinovitch, the bazooka expert, his wounded arm now healed. As he briefed his men on their role in the attack, one of them, a deeply religious soldier, asked, "What happens if we get to the Wall and the Temple Mount?" The Temple Mount, of course, now contained two of Islam's great mosques.

Rabinovitch thought a moment. "We'll take off our shoes and go on fighting barefoot," he answered.

Riding toward Barclays Bank, their assembly point, a group of Stern Gang's soldiers had other plans for the Temple Mount. In defiance of Ben-Gurion's charge to see that no damage came to the Holy Places, they planned to destroy the Dome of the Rock and El Aqsa Mosque, and thus pave the way for the reconstruction of the third Temple.

As Sinai's troops moved into their position, an agonizing problem arose for the young officer. In the haste to manufacture the Conus, no one had thought to provide a means to move it forward. Finally a pair of iron bars were slipped under its tripod base and, with men at each end, the explosive was carried off like a litter.

The climb up Mount Zion was a torture. The trench through which men usually reached the summit was just one foot too small to take the Conus, and its porters had no choice but to carry it in the open, fully exposed to the Arab Legion's shells.

Mishka Rabinovitch was ordered to help speed its arrival. He split a platoon into three groups of eight men. One staggered forward with the Conus for twenty yards, then ran ahead fifty yards to give covering fire while another rushed up to repeat the process. Hands bleeding, their legs and backs aching, grunting under their dangerous load, Rabinovitch's men slowly heaved the Conus up the hillside.

It was well after two o'clock when the assault began with the Irgun's attack at New Gate. A few minutes later, a triumphant message announced to Zvi Sinai his first success. "Paris" was in the hands of the Irgun. By telephone he ordered his battalion on Mount Zion to attack as soon as the Conus had battered a hole in the wall. Then, despite the Arab shellfire, he stepped to the balcony of his headquarters to watch for the explosion. Hidden in his advance command post, a ditch near Yemin Moshe, David Shaltiel too kept his eyes fixed on the site chosen for the explosion on which all his hopes depended.

From the walls of the Old City, Captain Mahmoud Moussa suddenly saw an extraordinary apparition surging toward him out of the darkness. It was a group of men trying to lug what looked to him like a vegetable vendor's cart through the Armenian Cemetery. All around him his men began to hurl grenades.

One of them set fire to a clump of thistles in the cemetery. To the men advancing "through almost the light of day," it was "total hell." The Arabs on the walls were throwing grenades and shooting, the fire was burning and at any moment their 350 pounds of explosives might blow up.

At the place selected for it, a slight bulge in the wall where they were protected from enfilade fire, they discovered that the Conus' base was too short. Under fire they raised it with stones so that the charge stood at the proper height and distance from the wall. Then they connected three fuses and bolted for cover.

"Conus primed," Rabinovitch shouted as he slid to safety behind the cemetery wall. "Get ready."

An incredible blaze of light lit up the sky and a roar shook the city. Seeing the explosion's flash, Zvi Sinai on his balcony in New Jerusalem threw up his hands in glee. "The wall has been breached," he told himself. "They're moving in."

From his trench, David Shaltiel, overwhelmed, had seen the fantastic flash and, his radio operator puffing after him, started up Mount Zion. On its summit, waiting to attack, Avram Uzieli thought it was "just like Jericho. The walls are coming down before our trumpets." The battalion commander, Avraham Zorea, heard one of his forward posts shriek in delight, "It worked!"

"Get in," Zorea ordered his forward company. "I'll bring the rest of the battalion in behind you."

As Zorea rushed through the Armenian Cemetery, he suddenly saw a bewildered man running toward him through the smoke gushing up from the explosion site. It was the commander of his assault company. "My God, my God," gasped the dazed man, "I don't understand. All that noise and there's no hole. All it did was leave a black smudge on the wall!"

For the officers of Israel's new Army there was to be no miracle in that July dawn. This time their trumpet had failed. The miraculous device on which all their hopes had rested had turned out to be a noisy firecracker.

When a messenger ran to give him the bad news, David Shaltiel, it seemed to his adjutant, aged ten years. It was almost five o'clock, and the cease-fire would soon be on them. So confident had they all been in their Conus that there was no alternative plan of attack. Almost broken by the admission, Shaltiel declared, "We have no choice. Now we must follow the cease-fire."

The Jerusalem commander immediately went to Zvi Sinai's headquarters. Sinai begged Shaltiel to let him take the battalion off Mount Zion and put it through the opening the Irgun had forced at New Gate. To do so, of course, would have meant violating the cease-fire. Shaltiel put his hand on his young officer's shoulders. Their orders were clear. They would have to obey them.

Overwhelmed by "a terrible sense of failure," Sinai picked up his phone and told his units they would cease fire as scheduled.

In the Jewish Agency, someone woke the man who should by then have been the military governor of Old Jerusalem. David Amiran walked into the office that was to have been his and looked at the currency, the posters, the decrees, the armbands of the first Jewish occupation of Old Jerusalem in two thousand years. Sadly he selected two examples of each for the archives of the Israeli Army. Then, with a bitter laugh, he marked the rest for destruction.

Outside, the sky was already gray and the guns began to cease firing. Peace crept uncertainly back into the skyline of Jerusalem. Hearing the sound of firing fade away, David Shaltiel whispered to Yeshurun Schiff, "Thank God, at least nobody will die today. But we did not take the Old City."

Behind its walls, Abdullah Tell sadly contemplated his wounded in the Austrian Hospice. His happiness that he had held Jerusalem's walls was mingled with the compassionate thought that "so many Jews had lost their lives for nothing."

The last firing came from the Irgun's foothold inside New Gate. Surrounded, without hope of reinforcement, they finally drew back to the New City on Shaltiel's orders, leaving Old Jerusalem's ramparts to the Arab Legion. From Sheikh Jarrah in the north to Ramat Rachel in the south, their action left Jerusalem split in half. The ancient prophecy of Isaiah was fulfilled: Jerusalem had "drunk at the hand of the Lord the cup of His fury." The line drawn down her heart would divide the Holy City for years to come.

EPILOGUE

THOUGH THE PEACE descending upon Jerusalem that July morning would prove fragile, its divisions would endure. Two more outbursts of fighting in the Negev and one in Galilee were undertaken before the United States's Dr. Ralph Bunche on the island of Rhodes negotiated armistice agreements between Israel and Egypt, Lebanon, Jordan and Syria early in 1949. Those agreements put a formal end to the hostilities. They did not end the war, and the Arab states resolutely continued to proclaim their intention of one day terminating the existence of a state they would neither accept nor recognize.

What the Israelis would call their War of Independence thus came officially to an end. The young nation's survival had been bought at a terrible cost. Approximately six thousand people, military and civilian, had lost their lives in the fighting. Those losses would have represented, on a proportional basis, two million Americans, more men than the United States lost in two World Wars. The end of the fighting left Israel occupying 500 square miles of land and 112 villages assigned to the Arabs by the partition plan; the Arabs held 129 square miles of territory and fourteen sites allotted the Jewish state.

None of the legacies left by the war would be as long-festering or as bitterly disputed as the one symbolized by the Arab families who had fled their homes in Jerusalem in the first weeks of the partition, that of the Arab refugees. Even their number could never be agreed upon. The Arabs claimed that up to a million people had left. More conservative estimates set the figures at between 500,000 and 700,000. According to a note in his diary, Ben-Gurion was informed on June 5, 1948, that 335,000 Arabs had fled. That, of course, was before the flight from Lydda and Ramle. In any event, on that June night David Ben-Gurion set the tone of his government's policy on the issue for years to come. He ordered his aides to "see to the settling of the abandoned villages." Later in the year, on the urging of Tuvia Arazi, the man who had sought to persuade the Arabs to stay in Haifa, Ben-Gurion agreed to the return of 100,000 compassionate cases at the signature of a final peace treaty. Persuaded that a more substantial return would alter the fundamental nature of their state and pose

561

an unacceptable security risk, successive Israeli governments refused to go beyond his offer.

The Arab states displayed no haste to succor their suffering brothers. The Lebanese, afraid that the predominantly Moslem refugees would upset their nation's delicate balance between Christian and Moslem, persistently refused them. The Egyptians kept them crowded into the Gaza Strip. Syria and Iraq, whose resources made them the countries best equipped to receive the refugees, turned their backs on them. Only Jordan, poorest of the Arab states, made a genuine effort to welcome them into its ranks.

An element of political propaganda for the Arabs, a grating embarrassment for Israel, the refugees were left to fester in squalid refugee camps, the wards of international charity administered by the United Nations. But if the world forgot them, they did not forget. A generation was born and raised in the misery of those camps, nourished by dreams of vengeance and a return to a lost land they had never known. In the aftermath of the 1967 Six-Day War, that generation emerged on the Middle East scene as the Palestine *fedayeen*.

The conflict born the day the representatives of thirty-three nations, assembled in an old ice-skating rink outside New York, decided to partition Palestine would claim other victims. The first to fall was the man who had hoped to restore peace to the Holy Land, United Nations mediator Count Folke Bernadotte. He was assassinated by the Stern Gang on September 16, 1948, as he drove to a meeting with Dov Joseph.

Mahmoud Nokrashy Pasha, the hesitant history professor who wanted to keep Egypt out of the war but had not dared to place his convictions above his ambitions, fell as he had predicted he would, to an assassin's bullet, fired by a member of the Moslem Brotherhood as he left his office in Cairo on December 28, 1948.

Lebanon's Riad Solh, who had urged King Abdullah to fight with oranges, was killed in his turn in the summer of 1951.

On an evening of that same summer, Thursday, July 19, 1951, King Abdullah attended a reception in Jerusalem. The monarch had long since realized his dream: he had been proclaimed king of "Arab Palestine" on December 1, 1948, and thirteen days later his parliament had confirmed the union of Transjordan and the remnants of Arab Palestine into the Hashemite Kingdom of Jordan. That night, contemplating the city he had so yearned to add to his kingdom, Abdullah was a sad and melancholy man. Pointing to his grandson Hussein, he told his Prime Minister, "If anything ever happens to me it is he who must carry on the house of the Hashemites."

The Prime Minister protested that there was no reason to talk of his succession.

"No" said the little King, "I feel my time is near."

It was.

At noon on the following day, as Ezra Danin had predicted the night he and Golda Meir had secretly visited the King, Abdullah was shot dead by an assassin on entering the Mosque of Omar for his Friday prayers.

The last of the 1948 Arab leaders to meet a violent death was Iraq's Nuri as-Said. Deafer than ever to advice he did not wish to take, the man the Arabs considered Britain's spokesman in the Middle East was overthrown by a *coup d'état* in July 1958. Captured while trying to flee his capital disguised as a woman, he was murdered and his body dragged through the streets of Baghdad behind a jeep.

One man outlived all the others. An occasional rust-colored hair still peeping from his white beard, still remarkably slender, Haj Amin Husseini lives quietly in the hills above Beirut, surrounded by his bodyguards and the latest manifestation of his lifelong preoccupation with his physical security, an atomic shelter. The leadership of the movement he launched in the souks of Jerusalem has long passed to other, younger hands, but amidst his diaries and his chickens he remains implacable in his hatred of Briton and Jew, persuaded that it may yet be Allah's will to return him to his domains in Jerusalem.

As David Ben-Gurion guided his people's struggle for independence, so he presided over the extraordinary transformation of their tiny state into a viable economic entity. Prime minister with an interruption of only two years from 1948 to 1963, he watched his nation's population more than double, his immigrants reclaim hundreds of acres of land from the Negev he had fought so hard to join to the country, and his businessmen give to Israel a vigorous industrial base. Now retired, he lives in quiet simplicity in the kibbutz of Sde Bokher in the Negev. There, in a sparely furnished room, its walls lined with books, he remains withdrawn from the world, but constantly aware of it, preparing his memoirs and reading the papers and letters he receives from all over the world. Like any other member of the kibbutz, he performs his daily chores. One fixed activity is the daily pole of the old man's life, his visit to the grave of his wife, Paula.

The child of a carpenter in the Russia of the czars returned to her homeland in 1949 to become Israel's first ambassador to the Russia of the

Soviets. For years in Jerusalem and the United Nations, Golda Meir was the architect of Israel's diplomacy. Summoned from retirement and ill-health to become prime minister in 1969 on the death of Levi Eshkol, she runs her high office with the simplicity that has always marked her life. Not a few of the most important decisions in the Middle East are now decided over a cup of coffee in the kitchen where Golda Meir counted the votes of the partition debate in 1948.

In Jerusalem itself, the Mandelbaum house, where Jacob Ben-Ur and his Gadna youngsters stopped the armored cars of the Legion, became an international symbol of the divisions separating the world's most cherished city. A strange crossing point, the Mandelbaum Gate was the one spot where the Arab and Israeli worlds opened onto each other. For years the stern guardian of the Arab side of that crossing was Assiya Halaby, the woman who had fled her home on May 14 with a copy of *The Arab Awakening* under her arm.

Battlements and barbed wire became a permanent part of Jerusalem; the great scars of no man's land marred its center with ruins and uncharted minefields. For almost twenty years, the rusting wreck of the armored car lost on the night of the Jaffa Gate attack lay against the walls of the city, the bones of its crew whitening in the sun.

To those battlements came the the pious elders of orthodox Jewry every Sabbath eve to stare across the rooftops toward the hidden stones of their lost Wall. Others, on the anniversary of the death of a wife or a child, climbed to a height in Mea Shearim to look longingly toward the cemetery they could no longer visit on the Mount of Olives. Among them was Rabbi Mordechai Weingarten, the man to whom a British officer had handed the key to Zion Gate. From the fall of the Old City until his death, the elderly rabbi lived his life in accordance with the rigid principles of Jewish mourning, his personal sign of grief for the loss of the quarter over which he had presided for so many years.

On the other side of the city, the Arabs too came to the walls to stare at the homes they had lost, occupied now by a tide of new immigrants. The Moslems among them looked in their turn at the cemetery they too could no longer reach in the heart of a thriving Israeli city.

In 1949, the government of Israel began to move its offices to Jerusalem, proclaiming the New City its capital in defiance of the United Nations and the United States, both of which still clung to the hope of internationalizing it.

Behind Old Jerusalem's ramparts, the Wailing Wall was deserted, its only guardians the black-robed women slipping past it, an occasional tourist or the Arab children playing in the narrow alley running past its ancient stones. The ruins of the Jewish Quarter, picked clean of every object of value, lay exposed to the sun like the upturned stones of a desecrated cemetery, convincing evidence, the Arabs would sometimes say, of how permanent had been its residents' eviction from their quarter.

It was not to be as permanent as they had hoped. In June 1967, after twice warning King Hussein to stop the shelling of New Jerusalem, Israel went to war with Jordan. The paratroopers of Uzi Narciss, the man who had ordered his Palmach back from Zion Gate in May 1948, captured the Old City after forty-eight hours of fighting. In the wake of their victory, a parade of Israelis flocked to the walls. Sweating paratroopers, ecstatic old rabbis, government ministers, and bearded teenagers joined in that emotional hour when an ancient people at last regained the most vital landmark of their existence. Among the first to contemplate its stones were the two men who had hoped to cling to them in 1948, Dov Joseph and David Shaltiel.

All across the city, the first days following the end of the June war witnessed an extraordinary intermingling of peoples, of Arabs and Jews renewing old friendships, rediscovering sights, sounds, smells and landscapes. In that brief euphoric hour, the battlements and gunports were dismantled, the barbed wire was rolled up, no man's land rehabilitated. Once again Jerusalem was a united city, its two halves rejoined in their common whole, the ugly scars of war removed. The blessing of its newfound unity would be disturbed, however, and the euphoria that had burst out in the aftermath of the war would be of limited duration.

The government of Israel, anxious to place its new occupation of its ancient capital beyond question, formally annexed the conquered portions of the city. New immigrants were encouraged to move to Jerusalem and plans were developed to link it more closely to the Jewish state by surrounding it with new settlements. Jerusalem, the Israeli government made it clear, could not be considered negotiable in a peace settlement with Arab states, although special measures for the protection of its shrines would be contemplated.

For their part, the Arabs, angered by what they sensed was an effort to diminish their numbers and role in the city, withdrew into a muted hostility toward Jerusalem's new regime. The rise of the *fedayeen* elsewhere inevitably had its effect in Jerusalem, and the awful wreckage of terrorist bombs once again scarred the city in the marketplace of Mahane Yehuda, the dining room of Hebrew University, a supermarket crowded with Sabbath shoppers . . .

And so, while the barbed wire and the battlements were gone, the line dividing the city's heart remained. As the image of ancient Jerusalem had decorated the walls of Jewish homes in the Diaspora, a portrait of the Dome of the Rock now graces Arab homes from Beirut to Baghdad— and unless Arab and Jew can display more tolerance and understanding of each other than they have done in the past, the ancient prayer "If I forget thee, O Jerusalem" may well become a war cry for future generations of another Semitic people.

Written for the great Hebrew King who made the city his capital, the words of the ancient psalm of David remain as true today as when they were first sung:

> Pray for the peace for Jerusalem . . .
> Peace be within thy walls, and prosperity within
> Thy palaces.

WHERE ARE THEY NOW?

ARABS

ABOU GHARBIEH, Bajhat: The defender of the Musrara quarter is active in the Palestine guerrilla movement in Amman.

ABOUSSOUAN, Dr. Samy: The survivor of the explosion of the Hotel Semiramis is now a dentist in Beirut.

ANTONIOUS, Katy: She returned to the city in which she had been such a noted hostess and continued her activities on the Arab side of Jerusalem until the Six-Day War in June 1967. Since then she has lived in Beirut.

AZZAM Pasha, Abdurrahman: Retired as secretary general of the Arab League in 1956.

DEEB, George: The man who furnished the Egyptian Army its road maps of Palestine is today a businessman in Amman.

GENNO, Abou Khalil: The man who helped destroy the *Palestine Post* is a wealthy businessman in Jerusalem today. In the aftermath of the Six-Day War, he tried for a time to promote Arab–Israeli harmony.

GHORY, Emile: Now a member of the Jordanian parliament, Ghory maintains close ties with the Mufti and has served as an intermediary between the government and the *fedayeen*.

HALABY, Assiya: The woman who bid the last British goodbye remains in Jerusalem. She has been jailed twice in the past two years for her protests against the city's annexation to Israel.

IREKAT, Kamal: The organizer of the ambush of the Nebi Daniel convoy is today the Speaker of the Jordanian parliament.

JUMEAN, Emile: Jumean continues to serve in the Arab Legion. Most recently he has been the aide of King Hussein's brother, Prince Mohammed.

KAUKJI, Fawzi el: The commander of the Liberation Army lives in seclusion outside Beirut.

KHALIDY, Mrs. Ambara: The Khalidy family settled in Beirut. Sami Khalidy never fully recovered from the shock of leaving Jerusalem and died shortly thereafter. Among Ambara Khalidy's sons are a distinguished historian and a prize-winning chemist.

KUTUB, Fawzi el: Kutub pursues his career as an explosives expert in Damascus, where his services are at the disposal of the Palestine *fedayeen*.

MAJAJ, Hameh: Never remarried, the man who lost his wife to Uri Cohen's bomb at Jaffa Gate lives quietly with his two children in Amman.

MAJALI, Habes: The commander of the Arab Legion at Latrun remains active in military affairs. He was called in by King Hussein to serve as minister of defense when the Jordanian Army moved against the *fedayeen*.

MARDAM, Colonel Fouad: Mardam was condemned to death by a Syrian tribunal after the war for his role in the loss of the Arab League's arms at Bari Harbor. His Israeli enemies, to establish the fact that he was innocent of wrongdoing in the affair, revealed their role in the capture of the *Argiro* and Mardam's life was subsequently spared.

PULLI, Antonio: Spared by the 1952 Nasser *coup d'état* which overthrew Egypt's King Farouk, the indefatigable organizer of Farouk's night life now runs a pastry shop in a Cairo suburb.

ROUSAN, Mahmoud: A member of parliament from Irbid, Rousan, Majali's adjutant at Latrun, was dismissed from the Jordanian Army on the charge of having been involved in pro-Nasser activities. He fled to Syria in 1971 after King Hussein crushed the *fedayeen*.

TANNOUS, Nimra: The "Tigress" of the switchboard at the Arabs' Rawdah School headquarters now is employed by the Jordanian government in its Refugee Department.

TELL, Abdullah: The Arab Legion's Jerusalem commander went into voluntary exile in Cairo in 1950 after his popularity among the Palestinians led to his dismissal from his Jerusalem command. Sentenced to death in absentia for a role he always denied playing in the assassination of King Abdullah, he remained in Cairo until 1967, when King Hussein pardoned him.

TELL, Wasfi: The officer whose warnings were ignored so frequently in 1948 was assassinated in Cairo in December 1971.

BRITISH

BEELEY, Sir Harold: Bevin's senior aide in 1948 retired in 1969 after a long and distinguished diplomatic career, including ambassadorships in Moscow and Cairo.

CHURCHILL, Colonel Jack: Retired from the British Army, the man who attempted to rescue the Hadassah convoy lives quietly outside London.

CUNNINGHAM, General Sir Alan: The last High Commissioner in Palestine lives in retirement outside London.

GLUBB, General Sir John Bagot (Glubb Pasha): Glubb was summarily dismissed by King Hussein in 1956 at the instigation of a group of the Legion's Arab officers led by Ali Abou Nuwar, the young man who had told his British superior, "India is not your country." Returning to England, he was knighted and has led an active life writing and lecturing about a subject few men know better than he, the Arab world.

JONES, Brigadier C. P.: Jerusalem's last British commander is now the Governor of London's Chelsea Pensioners Hospital.

KIRKBRIDE, Sir Alec: Sir Alec continues to call on his long years of service in Amman in his role as a director of the British Bank of the Middle-East.

MACMILLAN, General Sir Gordon H. A.: Retired from active service, the last commander of the British forces in Palestine lives in Scotland, where he heads the MacMillan clan.

ISRAELIS

ALLON, Yigal: The commander of the Palmach in 1948 went on to a political career and is now deputy prime minister. With Moshe Dayan, he is considered one of Golda Meir's heirs apparent.

AVIDAR, Joseph: The man who ran the Haganah's supply efforts in 1948 now is a director of the nation's trade-union organization, Histadrut.

AVRIEL, Ehud: Avriel served for years as Israel's ambassador to Rome. The man who was responsible for the purchase of so many arms is now a member of the International Zionist Action Committee.

CHARNY, Carmi: The man who helped stop the Legion's armor at Sheikh Jarrah still lives in Jerusalem and has become one of Israel's outstanding Hebrew poets.

CHOREV, Amos: Chorev, who helped discover the "Burma Road," remains in active service as a general in the Israeli Army.

COHEN, Uri: Now a senior pilot with El Al Israel Airlines, the man who was an Irgun terrorist in 1948 recently helped thwart an Arab terrorist attempt to throw a grenade into an airport bus in Frankfurt, Germany.

ELAZAR, David "Dado": The officer who had to kick his men awake during the attack on Zion Gate is now Chief of Staff of the Israel defense forces. During the Six-Day War he commanded the forces on the northern front.

FEDERMANN, Xiel: The Santa Claus of the Haganah presides today over the largest chain of luxury hostels in Israel.

GAZIT, Mordechai: Gazit returned to the civil service after spending months recuperating from the wound he received in the Old City. He is now involved in the settlement of new immigrants in Israel.

HERZOG, Chaim (Vivian): The former Guards officer pursues a varied career today as businessman, diplomat and commentator on military affairs.

HOD, Mordechai: One of the first two pilots to arrive with Avriel's Messerschmitts, Hod commanded the Israeli Air Force during the Six-Day War.

JOSEPH, Dov: Jerusalem's Civil Affairs Chief's experience stood him in good stead. During Israel's lean years after the 1948 war, Joseph applied it on a national scale and his name became a household word in Israel. He now lives in semiretirement in Jerusalem, where he maintains his law practice.

LASKOV, Haim: The commander of Israel's first armored columns today is the chairman of the Citrus Marketing Board.

LEVI, Yitzhak: Shaltiel's intelligence officer now manages his own publishing firm in Jerusalem.

LORCH, Netanel: The young man who thought "dancing is for the innocents" is today in charge of the Israel Foreign Office's United Nations Relations Department. He is also the author of the Israel Army's official history of the 1948 war, *The Edge of the Sword*.

NARCISS, Uzi: Retired from the Israel Army after the Six-Day War, the man who withdrew his Palmachniks from Zion Gate is now in charge of Israel's new-immigrants program.

NEVO, Yosef: Long and happily married, Nevo remained in the Army until after the Six-Day War. Now mayor of Herzlia, he is a military-affairs commentator.

RABIN, Yitzhak: The commander of the Har-el Brigade climaxed a long and distinguished career by leading his nation's army to victory in the Six-Day War. Rabin is now Israel's ambassador to the United States.

RUSSNAK, Moshe: The Old City's commander lives quietly in Jerusalem, where he is an employee of the Hadassah organization.

SHALTIEL, David: Jerusalem's Haganah commander died in 1969 after a long diplomatic career in Europe and South America.

SHAMIR, Shlomo: The commander of the Seventh Brigade has recently retired after a long and distinguished military career.

SINAI, Zvi: The commander of Operation Keddem remained in the Army and is now at GHQ Tel Aviv, involved in military history.

SLAVINE, Haim: Ben-Gurion's arms-manufacturing expert who scoured the United States for surplus machine tools is today supervising a more peaceful activity, the assembly of prefabricated houses.

WEIZMAN, Ezer: One of the first two pilots to reach Israel with Ehud Avriel's ME-110s, he later became Minister of Transportation. Today he is a member of the Gahal Party and serves in the Knesset.

YADIN, Yigal: Yadin's current preoccupations are not the state he helped defend as chief of operations in 1948 but its ancient predecessor. He followed in his father's footsteps and is today one of the world's leading archaeologists.

THE OTHERS

REYNIER, Jacques de: Retired today from the Red Cross, Reynier is living in Geneva.

ACKNOWLEDGMENTS

Rarely have authors been as indebted to as wide an array of people and sources as we have been in preparing *O Jerusalem!* The research for the book took us two years of intensive efforts in the Middle East, the United States and Europe, and it would be quite impossible to enumerate all those people who so kindly gave us of their time and help. In addition, for political reasons, many of them would prefer to remain anonymous. If space compels us to be brief, we beg the indulgence of the many we have not been able to mention, with the assurance of our gratitude and esteem.

In Israel, Lieutenant Colonel Eli Bar-Lev of the Defense Ministry Information Department and his assistants were particularly helpful in arranging appointments for us. Colonel Gershon Rivlin, editor of the Israeli military publishing house *Maarachot,* gave us much valuable guidance to documents and written records. Teddy Kollek, Jerusalem's mayor, put the resources of his municipality at our disposal.

Mr. David Ben-Gurion kindly granted us two four-hour interviews, painstakingly reviewing for us his memories of 1948, according us the rare privilege of opening his diaries and reading us extracts from his entries of the time. Despite her busy Prime Minister's schedule, Mrs. Golda Meir gave us a lengthy interview, even pushing back an appointment with a departing diplomat to extend our conversation.

Mrs. David Shaltiel kindly put at our disposal her husband's voluminous files, logbooks and military documents, which were invaluable to us in recreating the situation in Jerusalem in 1948. Ehud Avriel took great amounts of time to painstakingly reconstruct with us his arms-purchasing activities, opening up his cornucopia of memorabilia, invoices, bank deposit slips, his "Ethiopian" purchase orders, all of which gave us the impression of being in Prague in the springtime of 1948. Joseph Avidar exhumed his long-buried Haganah archives to review with us almost machine gun by machine gun in their meticulously kept pages the gradual evolution of the underground army's stores.

Invaluable were our long walks through Jerusalem with Jacob Tsur as he patiently explained street by street and neighborhood by neighborhood the city's quirks and complexities. At Hulda, in the countryside around Latrun, Vivian Herzog graciously reconstructed the terrible battles of Latrun.

In Amman, Peter Saleh, chief of the Jordan Information Department, and Ibrahim Izzidine, press officer at the royal palace, were particularly kind and helpful to us. His Majesty King Hussein graciously offered us access to the files of the Arab Legion. Abdullah Tell was a source of enormous help, patiently sitting with us for hours in his home in Amman, reviewing day by day his activities during the fighting in Jerusalem. As Vivian Herzog had, Mahmoud Rousan reconstructed for us with his diaries and his maps the battles of Latrun as he had witnessed them from his Arab Legion positions.

Emile Ghory and Bajhat Abou Gharbieh were particularly helpful, devoting to us long hours in which they reviewed the role of the Palestine irregulars in 1948 and particularly that played by their dead leader, Abdul Khader Husseini.

Two of Lebanon's leaders, Dr. Charles Malik and Camille Chamoun, were good enough to review for us in detail the United Nations debate in which they participated, and to unearth the reports and cables they compiled at the time. In Cairo, we owed a special debt to the assistance of Mohammed Hassenein Heikal and to Mrs. Abdul Khader Husseini, who showed us her husband's last letters, as well as to Antonio Pulli Bey for his insights into King Farouk's court.

Sir John Glubb took time from his own busy writing schedule to review with us the vital role he played in the events of 1948. Sir Alec Kirkbride, Sir Alan Cunningham, Sir Gordon MacMillan and Sir Harold Beeley were all most kind in offering their time and counsel.

In the United States, among the many people who assisted us, we would like to particularly thank Mr. Clark Clifford for giving us permission to review his personal papers, and the helpful and professional staff of the Truman Library in Independence, Missouri. Jacques de Reynier of the International Red Cross kindly gave us his private diary and helped with his recollection of Deir Yassin.

Our most particular thanks go to those collaborators who worked with us on the book and without whose aid it would have been impossible to accomplish our task. First and foremost among them was Miss Dominique Conchon, our inestimable companion and collaborator along the hard three-and-a-half-year route which led to this *O Jerusalem!* With care, intelligence, and a constant faith in our task, she oversaw the organization of our files of notes, recordings and documents, supervising translations, assembling in well-ordered dossiers over eight thousand pages of original research. During the long and lonely months required to write the book, she was a cheerful friend and valued critic overseeing the typing of our manuscripts.

We owe an equally substantial debt to our researchers, Lily Rivlin, an able and determined interviewer whose work made a great contribution to our task in Israel; Mr. Suleiman Moussa, a distinguished historian in his own right; and our Palestinian friend Diana, who interviewed many of her compatriots for us. René Clair of the French Academy kindly read the French version of the manuscript and gave us the benefit of his good counsel. Madame Colette Modiano, author of another soon-to-be-published work on the Middle East, was a constant source of support.

Hélène Fillion, Catherine Guyon, Jeanne Conchon and Jacqueline de la Cruz were yeomanlike in the long hours of work they devoted to typing our manuscripts and translating from English to French. To Ginette and René Dabrowski and Paulette and Alexandre Isart, who looked after our well-being during many arduous months, our special thanks.

Finally, without the encouragement and support of our friends at *Reader's*

Digest, headed by Fulton Oursler, Jr., it would not have been possible to accomplish our task. To them, and to our friends and editors Peter Schwed, Mike Korda and Dan Green in New York and Robert Laffont and Pierre Peuchemaur in Paris, and our agents Irving Lazar and Nicholas Thompson goes our deep gratitude.

La Biche Niche,
Les Bignoles,
Ramatuelle, France

CHAPTER NOTES

PROLOGUE

Interviews: Rabbi Shar Yeshuv Cohen; Masha and Rivka Weingarten, daughters of Rabbi Mordechai Weingarten; Lieutenant Colonel G. W. Harper, commanding officer of the Suffolk Regiment; Assiya Halaby; Sir William Fitzgerald; Sir Alan Cunningham; Sir Gordon MacMillan; Brigadier C. P. Jones; Richard Chichester, aide to Sir Alan Cunningham; Dana Adams Schmidt, *The New York Times;* Eric Downton, the London *Daily Telegraph.*

Written sources: *Ma'ariv;* the *New York Herald Tribune; The New York Times.*

CHAPTER 1:
DECISION AT FLUSHING MEADOW

Material on the United Nations partition debate and its background came from, on the Arab side, interviews with Dr. Charles Malik, Camille Chamoun, Farid Zeinedine, Jamal Husseini, and Azzam Pasha of the Arab League; on the Jewish side, interviews with Dov Joseph, Michael Comay, Moshe Tov, Rose Halprin, Walter Eytan, Morris Rivlin, and Arthur Lurie, who served with the Jewish Agency at Lake Success and in New York, and Joseph Linton and Eliahu Elath, the Agency representatives in London and Washington. An interview with Sir Harold Beeley provided information on the British position. Interviews with Loy Henderson, Robert Lovett, Raymond Hare, Judge Samuel Rosenman and Carlos Romulo contributed to the material on the U. S.'s role.

Written sources: Alan R. Taylor, *Prelude to Israel; The Forrestal Diaries;* Jon Kimche, *Seven Fallen Pillars;* Dov Joseph, *The Faithful City;* Sumner Welles, *We Need Not Fail;* Anny Latour, *The Resurrection of Israel;* Sami Hadawi, *Bitter Harvest;* Zeef Sharaf, *Three Days;* Harry S Truman's *Memoirs;* Maurice Samuel, *Light on Israel;* Fred J. Khouri, *The Arab–Israeli Dilemma;* the private papers of Riad Solh and Jamil Mardam; cables and correspondence of Camille Chamoun and Dr. Charles Malik between New York and Beirut; Report of the United Nations Special Committee on Palestine; the Central Zionist Archives, Jerusalem, bibliographical material on Rabbi Abba Hillel Silver; the Truman Library, Presidential correspondence and cables, 1947; *The New York Times,* the *New York Herald Tribune, The Times,* London.

Most of the material for the passage on the Arab and Zionist backdrop to 1947 is from written sources. Also included, however, is material from interviews with David Ben-Gurion, Azzam Pasha, Sir John Glubb, Anthony Nutting, Sir Alec Kirkbride and Sir John Martin. The written sources are Jon Kimche, *Seven Fallen Pillars;* John Marlowe, *The Seat of Pilate;* Sami Hadawi, *Bitter Harvest;* Fred J. Khouri, *The Arab–Israeli Dilemma;* Dov Joseph, *The Faithful City;* Geoffrey Furlonge, *Palestine Is My Country: The Story of Musa Alami;* Christopher Sykes, *Crossroads to Israel;* Maurice Samuel, *Light on*

Israel; Jean-Pierre Alem, *Juifs et arabes: 3000 ans d'histoire;* Report of the United Nations Special Committee on Palestine, and a survey of Palestine prepared for the committee by the mandatory government, June 1947; Leonard Stein, *The Balfour Declaration;* Michael Adams, "The Twice Promised Land," Manchester *Guardian,* Nov. 9, 1947; Anny Latour, *The Resurrection of Israel;* Marius Modiano, *Les Juifs, le judaïsme;* Christopher Sykes, *Orde Wingate;* Cecil Roth, *History of the Jews.*

CHAPTER 2:
"AT LAST WE ARE A FREE PEOPLE."

Interviews for the events in Jerusalem on Partition Night came from Ambara Khalidy, Samy Aboussouan, Nassereddin Nashasshibi, General Abdul-Aziz Kerine, Dr. Rajhib Khalidy, Gibrail Katoul, Nassib Boulos, Katy Antonious, Sami Hadawi, Hazem Nusseibi, Hameh Majaj, Haidar Husseini, Meir Rabino-vitch, Gershon Avner, Netanel Lorch, Uri Cohen, Mona and Issac Givton, David Ben-Gurion, Golda Meir, Reuven Ben-Yehoshua, Zev Benjamin, Ruth Kirsch, Heinz Gruenspan, Yaacov Salamon, Reuven Tamir, Uri Saphir, Ezra Spicehandler, Uri Avner, David Rothschild. Interviews with Emile Ghory and Israel Amir provided material for each side's first preparations.

The description of events in Cairo came from Said Mortagi, then an attaché at Farouk's palace, and from a senior member of Nokrashy Pasha's staff who must remain anonymous.

Published sources: *The New York Times;* the *New York Herald Tribune; L'Orient,* Beirut; *Haaretz,* Tel Aviv; the *Jerusalem Post;* Anny Latour, *The Resurrection of Israel;* Walter Lever, *Jerusalem Is Called Liberty;* Dov Joseph, *The Faithful City;* Benoist Mechin, *Le Roi Saud; Eretz Israel,* Vol. 8, Sukenik Memorial Volume.

CHAPTER 3:
"PAPA HAS RETURNED."

Material for the passage on the Mufti of Jerusalem came from interviews with the Mufti himself, his kinsmen Haidar, Daoud and Jamal Husseini, Rassam Khalidy (who was imprisoned with him), Rashid Berbir (his host at his last lunch in Berlin), Emile Ghory and numerous Palestine Arab sources among his friends and foes. Sir Alec Kirkbride provided British background, and Tuvia Arazi and Moshe Pearlman information from the Jewish side. Written sources include Dov Joseph, *The Faithful City;* Christopher Sykes, *Crossroads to Israel;* Walter Lever, *Jerusalem Is Called Liberty;* Jon and David Kimche, *Both Sides of the Hill;* Joseph B. Schechtman, *The Mufti and the Fuehrer;* Netanel Lorch, *The Edge of the Sword;* Lukasz Hirszowicz, *The Third Reich and the Arab East;* Minutes of Session No. 63, Criminal Case No. 40/61, District Court of Jerusalem: *The Attorney General of the Government of Israel v. Adolf, the son of Adolf Karl Eichmann.* In addition, portions of the Mufti's diary are available in Arabic in Beirut.

Material on the Commercial Center riots was provided on the Arab side in interviews with Haj Amin Husseini, Emile Ghory, Kamal Irekat, Jamil Tukan, Nassib Boulos, Khazem Khalidy, Nadi Dai'es, Kay Albina, Zihad Khatib, Dr. Samy Aboussouan and others; Zvi Sinai, Yosef Nevo and Israel Amir contributed on the Haganah side. An interview with Jerusalem District Commissioner James Pollack was also used. Written sources are the *Palestine Post; Haaretz,* Tel Aviv; *L'Orient,* Beirut; *The New York Times;* the *New York Herald Tribune; The Times,* London.

CHAPTER 4:
TWO PASSENGERS TO PRAGUE

Material for the passages related to Arab and Jewish arms gathering comes from interviews with David Ben-Gurion, Ehud Avriel, Eliahu Sacharov, Joseph Avidar, Shaul Avigour, Haim Slavine, Rudolf G. Sonneborn, Azzam Pasha, General Abdul-Aziz Kerine, Fouad Mardam, Colonel Sami Shoucair, and Ahmed Sherabati. The passage about the road to Jerusalem includes interview material from Yigal Yadin and Mishael Shacham.

Written Sources: Edgar O'Ballance, *The Arab–Israeli War, 1948;* reports of Eliahu Sacharov to David Ben-Gurion on the arms-purchasing mission, 1947–48; personal archives of Ehud Avriel, Shaul Avigour and Joseph Avidar; Munya Mardor, *Strictly Illegal;* the private papers of Jamil Mardam; the *Jerusalem Post; Haaretz,* Tel Aviv; *L'Orient,* Beirut; *The New York Times;* the *New York Herald Tribune.*

CHAPTER 5:
TWO PEOPLES, TWO ARMIES

Material for the passage on the Haganah includes interviews with Israel Amir, Netanel Lorch, Eliyahu Arbel, Shalom Dror, Colonel Gershon Rivlin, Zvi Sinai, Bobby Reisman, Carmi Charny and Jacob Tsur. Material for the Arab passage includes interviews with George, Raymond and Gaby Deeb, Hazem Nusseibi, Abou Khalil Genno, Kamal Irekat, Emile Ghory, Bajhat Abou Gharbieh, Kassem el Rimawi, Haidar, Daoud and Haj Amin Husseini, and Peter Saleh, all of whom participated in one way or another in Jerusalem's Arab defense structure, and Izzat Tannous and Youssef Sayegh, who were involved in the Arab Higher Committee's financial activities.

Written sources: Dov Joseph, *The Faithful City;* Netanel Lorch, *The Edge of the Sword; Sefer ha-Palmach* (Book of the Palmach); Jon and David Kimche, *Both Sides of the Hill;* Fred J. Khouri, *The Arab–Israeli Dilemma;* Edgar O'Ballance, *The Arab–Israeli War, 1948;* Jon Kimche, *Seven Fallen Pillars;* Aref el Aref, *El Nakla* (The Tragedy).

CHAPTER 6:
"WE WILL STRANGLE JERUSALEM."

In the passage on the Arab League, and in subsequent passages on the organization, the private papers of Riad Solh and Jamil Mardam and a set of the minutes of the League's sessions were used extensively—the minutes for the meetings themselves, the papers for an Arab evaluation of them. Of the principal participants, only Azzam Pasha and King Feisal are still alive. Azzam and his private secretary Wahid el Dali were extensively interviewed.

Material for the Haganah meeting comes largely from interviews with David Ben-Gurion and a number of other men who participated in it.

In this chapter and subsequent chapters much of the material dealing with King Abdullah comes from interviews with a number of men close to him: his physician and confidant Dr. el Saty, his private secretary Nassereddin Nashasshibi, Azzam Pasha, Sir John Glubb and Sir Alec Kirkbride; the family of his late Foreign Minister, Fawzi el Mulki; Arab historians Khazem and Walid Khalidy and Aref el Aref; and a number of newsmen who interviewed him frequently during the period, including Nassib Boulos of *Time* and Samir Souki of the United Press. A translation of his memoirs is also available in English.

The passage on Sir Alan Cunningham comes largely from interviews with the last High Commissioner, with Sir Harold Beeley and with Sir Gordon MacMillan, and from the latter's final report to the War Office.

Material on Abdul Khader Husseini here and elsewhere comes largely from interviews with his principal lieutenants, notably Kamal Irekat, Emile Ghory, Kassem el Rimawi, Mounir Abou Fadel and Bajhat Abou Gharbieh. Aref el Aref's *El Nakla* (The Tragedy), an Arabic history of the 1948 war, contains much background material on him. His widow, Madame Wajiha Husseini, made available his letters and writings in her home in Cairo.

CHAPTER 7:
"ARE WE NOT NEIGHBORS . . . ?"

Descriptive material on life in Jerusalem in December 1947 includes interviews with Jacob Tsur, Dov Joseph, Max Hesse, Heinz Kraus, Youssef Sayegh, Hilda Shiber, Hazem Nusseibi and Naim Halaby, and unused material from the original *Time* magazine files of Don Burke and Nassib Boulos.

Written material includes Dov Joseph, *The Faithful City;* Daniel Spicehandler, *Let My Right Hand Wither;* Walter Lever, *Jerusalem Is Called Liberty; The New York Times;* the *New York Herald Tribune;* the *Palestine Post, The Times,* London. The passages on transportation, early Haganah strategy in Jerusalem and the first skirmishes are based on interviews with Ruth Givton, Zvi Sinai, Zelman Mart, Israel Amir, Abbras Tamir, Yosef Nevo, Mordechai Gazit and Shalom Dror of the Haganah, and with David Ben-Gurion, Emile Ghory and Kamal Irekat.

The Old City passage contains material from interviews with Isser Natanson, Mordechai Pincus, Baruch Agi, Daoud Alami, Avraham Banai, Nadi Dai'es, Gershon Finger, Yisrael Lehrman, Moshe Russnak, Rivka and Masha Weingarten, Yehuda Choresh, Rabbi Shar Yeshuv Cohen, Dr. Avraham Orenstein, Zohar Vilbush, Ellie Lichenstein and James Pollock. Written sources include Adina Maarechot, *Megillat Heir Haatika* (Notes on the Scroll of the Old City); Aharon Liron, *Yerushalayim Haatika Bematzor Be-Bakran* (Old Jerusalem in Siege and Battle); *The Jewish Quarter in the Old City of Jerusalem,* published by the Israel Exploration Society, Jerusalem (1968); the communications logbook of the Jerusalem Haganah headquarters; Dov Joseph, *The Faithful City;* Edgar O'Ballance, *The Arab–Israeli War, 1948.*

The story of the old Syrian is based on an interview with Gaby Deeb. The Irgun passage includes material from interviews with Uri Cohen, Yehoshua Zetler and Yeshua Ophir. Written sources includes *The New York Times* and Menahem Begin's *The Revolt.*

The passage relative to intelligence gathering in the city is based on interviews with Shalhevet Freir, Yitzhak Navon, Herman Mayer, Benyamin Gibli, Yitzhak Levi, Chaim (Vivian) Herzog and Emile Ghory.

CHAPTER 8:
THE SANTA CLAUS OF THE HAGANAH

The Christmas passage is based on interviews with Mishka Rabinovitch, Gershon Avner, Samy and Cyril Aboussouan, James Pollock and Berthe Malouf. Written sources include *The New York Times,* the *New York Herald Tribune,* the *Palestine Post* and the files of *Time* magazine's Jerusalem correspondent, Don Burke. The Antwerp passage is based on an interview with Xiel Federmann.

CHAPTER 9:
JOURNEY TO ABSURDITY

The passages relating to the destruction of the Hotel Semiramis and the bombing at Jaffa Gate are based on interviews with the participants and the survivors of the actions. Yitzhak Navon of Haganah intelligence identified the source on which the decision to destroy the hotel was based. Emile Ghory confirmed his presence there with Abdul Khader Husseini's jeep the day before the decision was made. There were in fact no Arab irregulars in the hotel at the time of its destruction. Mishael Shacham, Israel Amir and Avram Gil described the action from the Haganah viewpoint. Wida Kardous and Samy Aboussouan described it from the viewpoint of the hotel's occupants.

Uri Cohen and Hameh Majaj were the principal sources of information on the Jaffa Gate bombing. The incident on the road New Year's Eve is based on an interview with Golda Meir.

CHAPTER 10:
"BAB EL WAD ON THE ROAD TO THE CITY"

The descriptions of Jerusalem life and its preparations for a siege is based on numerous interviews, among them those with Dov Joseph, Zvi Leibowitz, Alexander Singer, Arieh Belkind, Avraham Picker, Ruth and Chaim Haller, Max Hesse, David Rothschild, Ambara Khalidy, Abbras Tamir and Yosef Nevo. Written sources included Dov Joseph's *The Faithful City,* the private papers of Riad Solh and the diary of Jacques de Reynier. Among these whose interviews contributed to the passage on Bab el Wad were Haroun Ben-Jazzi, Emile Ghory, Major Michael Naylor Leyland of the Life Guards, Yehuda Lash and Reuven Tamir.

The working documents of the U. N. Working Committee on Jerusalem are available at the U. N. Copies of the British documents referred to on page 150 are on file with Haganah intelligence in Tel Aviv. The report of the Jewish Agency's request for 500 marines and Chief Secretary Gurney's quote are contained in declassified cables from the U. S. consul general in Jerusalem to Washington.

CHAPTER 11:
GOLDA MEIR'S TWENTY-FIVE "STEPHANS"

The account of the Haganah's and the Àrabs' arms-procurement activities are based largely on interviews with Eliahu Sochaczever, Avner Treinin, Jonathan Adler, Eliahu Sacharov, Emile Ghory, Raymond Deeb and Joseph Avidar and on the latter's voluminous personal archives. A detailed account of the Haganah's Jerusalem arms activities is also to be found in Pinhas Vaze's *Ha-Mesima: Rechesh.*

The passage on the formation of the Liberation Army in Damascus was based primarily on interviews with men who served there, notably Safwat Pasha, Wasfi Tell, Mike Elissa, Khazem Khalidy, Fawzi el Kaujki, Azzam Pasha and Haidar Husseini. Excellent newspaper accounts on the army's activities were compiled at the time by Dana Adams Schmidt of *The New York Times,* by Samir Souki of the United Press and, in Arabic, by Ali Nasseridine.

The description of Golda Meir's trip to the United States is based primarily on an interview with the Israeli Prime Minister. A more detailed account may be found in Marie Syrkin's *Golda Meir.*

CHAPTER 12:
"SALVATION COMES FROM THE SKY."

The details contained in the passage on the Haganah's arms-purchase activities in Europe are based largely on interviews with Ehud Avriel and Shaul Avigour and on study of their voluminous personal files. For the section on the development of the Haganah Air Service, interviews with Aaron Remez, Ezer Weizman, Mordechai Hod, Jerry Renov, Al Schwimmer and Amy Cooper were indispensable. A detailed and excellent account of the Haganah's arms-procurement activities in the U. S. may be found in Leonard Slater's *The Pledge.*

CHAPTER 13:
"WE SHALL BECOME AS HARD AS STONE."

The account of the destruction of the *Palestine Post* was compiled from interviews with those in the building or involved in the attack, including Fawzi el Kutub, Salah el Haj Mir, Abou Said Abou Reech, Emile Ghory, Abou Khalil Genno, George and Gaby Deeb, Ted Lurie and Shimshon Lipshitz. Excellent contemporary accounts of the explosion are to be found in the *Post* itself, *The New York Times* and the *New York Herald Tribune.* An interesting footnote to the explosion took place at a dinner party in Ramallah shortly after the Six-Day War. Among those attending were Ted Lurie, the paper's editor, and Abou Khalil Genno, who had fired the explosives that destroyed it.

The description of the Mufti's life in Cairo was compiled from interviews with Haj Amin himself and several of his collaborators, notably Emile Ghory and Haidar Husseini. Most of the material on Abdul Khader's Cairo visit was furnished by his wife.

The passage on David Shaltiel's arrival in Jerusalem was compiled largely from his voluminous personal papers, which contained copies of all his command's communications and to which we were given access by his widow, Dr. Yehudit Shaltiel, and his literary executors Avriel Katz and Arye Levavi,

Israel's ambassador to Bern. In addition, material from interviews with Mrs. Shaltiel and his close collaborators, notably Yeshurun Schiff, are included.

CHAPTER 14:
A FLASH OF WHITE LIGHT

The background to the U. S. State Department's reversal on the partition of Palestine is covered in detail in a number of works, including President Truman's *Memoirs, The Forrestal Diaries,* Christopher Sykes's *Crossroads to Israel,* and *The Impossible Takes Longer,* by Chaim Weizmann's widow, Vera Weizmann. In addition, a great deal of material on the incident is contained in the papers of Harry S Truman and Clark Clifford on file at the Truman Library in Independence, Missouri. Mr. Jacobson's role is covered at great length in a letter dated April 1, 1952, from Jacobson to Josef Cohn of the Weizmann Archives. A copy of the letter is on file at the Truman Library. Interviews with Clark Clifford, Loy Henderson, Sir Harold Beeley, Judge Samuel Rosenman and Raymond Hare also were used.

The description of the explosion on Ben Yehuda Street is based largely on interviews with the victims and the perpetrators. On the Jewish side, they included Dov Joseph, David Rivlin, Heinz Gruenspan, Uri Saphir, Uri Avner and Yaacov Orlovsky. On the Arab side, they included Bajhat Abou Gharbieh, Fawzi el Kutub, Kamal Irekat and Emile Ghory. Certain aspects of the role of the English deserters Brown and Madison were furnished by Don Burke, formerly of *Time,* to whom they gave their story, and by a former officer of British Intelligence in Palestine who requested anonymity. Good newspaper accounts of the incident are contained in *Haaretz* and the *Palestine Post.* Aref el Aref's *El Nakla* (The Tragedy) has an account of the explosion seen from the Arab side.

CHAPTER 15:
AN UNLIKELY LAWRENCE

Material on the personality and role of John Glubb in 1948 was accumulated in extensive interviews with the Pasha himself and over thirty of the officers, English and Arab, who served under him in the Arab Legion. An account of his interview with Ernest Bevin, expanded upon in conversation with the authors, is to be found in Glubb's memoir of the period, *A Soldier with the Arabs.* Supplementary information was also obtained in interviews with Sir Harold Beeley and Tewfic Abou Hoda's private secretary Hamad Bey Farhan.

The account of Pablo de Azcarate's treatment on his arrival in Jerusalem is based on an interview with him and his own description of the incident in his book *Mission in Palestine.* In a letter to the authors July 17, 1969, Sir Alan Cunningham referred to the treatment accorded Azcarate in the following terms: "I wish to make it perfectly clear why we acted as we did with the Spanish diplomat sent to Jerusalem by the U. N. I was personally prepared to give him any help and information he wanted but what I must make clear is that the British Government had made it perfectly clear to me and to others that we would not be responsible for implementing the U. N. plan."

The description of Fawzi el Kaujki's entry into Palestine is taken from interviews with Kaujki, Sir Gordon MacMillan and Yehoshua Palmon and from the diary of Jacques de Reynier of the Red Cross, who visited Amman just after Kaujki passed through Transjordan and was given a description of his passage by diplomats who witnessed it.

Copies of David Shaltiel's initial observations on the Jerusalem situation and his recommendations to Tel Aviv are on file in his personal archives, and the quotations used on pages 202 and 203 are from those archives. The account of his meeting with Yoshua Zetler was furnished by the latter. Jacob Tsur provided a description of his meeting with Jerusalem's rabbis. The passage on the seizure of the Schneller Compound is based on an interview with Nahum Stavy.

CHAPTER 16:
THE HABERDASHER FROM KANSAS CITY

The account of the Jewish Agency explosion is based on interviews with Chaim (Vivian) and Aura Herzog, Fawzi el Kutub, Yitzhak Navon, Bajhat Abou Gharbieh, Gershon Avner, Yitzhak Levi, Emile Ghory and Robert Bowie and on an exhaustive investigation into the incident made by the U. S. Consulate in Jerusalem.

The passage on the U. S. reversal on partition contains excerpts from the Jacobson letter referred to in the notes on chapter 14, the papers of Clark Clifford on file at the Truman Library—including his report on how Austin's speech was made—and interviews with Clifford, Loy Henderson and Judge Samuel Rosenman. For Chaim Weizmann's account of his conversation with President Truman, see Vera Weizmann's *The Impossible Takes Longer.*

CHAPTER 17:
THE CONVOY WILL NOT ARRIVE

The quotes from Haj Amin Husseini's letter to the governments of Egypt, Syria and Lebanon are taken from the Lebanese copy of the letter contained in the personal archives of Riad Solh. The report of the Lebanese consul in Jerusalem is contained in the same archives. Madame Neuville's personal scrapbook and diary provided most of the details of her farewell dinner. Interviews with Fawzi el Kutub, Emile Ghory and Bajhat Abou Gharbieh provided material for the description of the Montefiore explosion. Dov Joseph, Haroun Ben-Jazzi and Moshe Rashkes furnished information about the convoy ambush. Both Rashkes and Ben-Jazzi later recorded their versions of the ambush, Rashkes in an unpublished English manuscript and Ben-Jazzi in a private memoir in Arabic for his tribe.

CHAPTER 18:
A HOUSE IN THE MIDDLE OF HELL

A detailed history of the settlement of Kfar Etzion, containing extensive quotes from settlers' diaries and the kibbutz's archives, may be found in *Siege in the Hills of Hebron,* edited by Dov Knohl. The account of the convoy's dispatch and subsequent ambush was compiled from over a score of interviews with actors in the drama. They included Yitzhak Ben-Sira, Yigal Yadin, Mishael Shacham, Eliyahu Arbel, Yitzhak Levi, Uzi Narciss, Amos Chorev, Benjamin Golani, Chaim (Vivian) Herzog, Yehuda Lash, Uriel Ofek, Shmuel Matot, James Pollock, Colonel George W. Harper, Lieutenant Nigel Brommage, Kamal Irekat, Anwar Nusseibi, Abou Said Abou Reech and Yousef Abdou. Also used were the communications dispatched between Jerusalem Haganah headquarters and Tel Aviv contained in David Shaltiel's archives and certain descriptive material from the diary of Jacques de Reynier.

David Ben-Gurion's meeting with the chiefs of the Haganah was reconstituted in an interview with Mr. Ben-Gurion, who called on the entries in his diary of the time for information.

CHAPTER 19:

"HANG ON TO JERUSALEM WITH YOUR TEETH."

For the figures from Dov Joseph's famous chart summarizing Jerusalem's food reserves, we are indebted to his assistant for food supplies, Arieh Belkind, who allowed us to make a copy of his personal copy of the chart, given to him as a souvenir by Dov Joseph. Interview material from our conversations with Dr. Joseph was used extensively in the opening and closing passages of the chapter. For the account of Ocean Trade Airways' flight to Beit Darras we are indebted to interviews with Freddy Fredkens, Ehud Avriel, Aaron Remez, Amy Cooper and Shimon Avidan. The description of the meeting at which Operation Nachshon was decided contains material from interviews with Joseph Avidar, Yigal Yadin and David Ben-Gurion. Parts of Mr. Ben-Gurion's speech quoted in the passage are from his diary or from Netanel Lorch, *The Edge of the Sword*, the Israeli Defense Force's authorized history of the 1948 war.

Yitzhak Rabin provided much material on objectives and tactics of the operation, as did an extensive analysis he prepared of it for a lecture at the Israeli Defense Force's War College, later published in the I.D.F.'s monthly bulletin. The account of Abdul Khader Husseini's trip to Damascus is based on interviews with Safwat Pasha, Wasfi Tell and three men who accompanied Husseini—Emile Ghory, Kassem el Rimawi and Mounir Abou Fadel.

CHAPTER 20:

SIX WORDS ON A BUMPER

The description of the opening phases of Operation Nachshon and the arrival of the first convoys is based on interviews with Dov Joseph, Uzi Narciss, Emile Ghory, Kamal Irekat, Yitzhak Rabin, Yosef Tabenkin, Chaim Haller, Harry Jaffe, Bronislav Bar-Shemer, Shimon Avidan, Iska Shadmi, Amos Chorev, Mordechai Gazit and Haim Laskov. Excellent material on the operations is also to be found in Netanel Lorch, *The Edge of the Sword*. *Haaretz* and the *Palestine Post* contain contemporary accounts of the convoy's arrival.

CHAPTER 21:

"ONE OF THE ARABS WE KILLED LAST NIGHT"

The account of Abdul Khader Husseini's death is based on interviews with survivors of the fighters for Kastel: Kamal and Rashid Irekat, Bajhat Abou

Gharbieh, Mordechai Gazit, Uzi Narciss, Nadi Dai'es, Yigal Arnon and Kassem el Rimawi. Abdul Khader's last letter quoted at the beginning of the chapter was furnished by his wife.

CHAPTER 22:
THE PEACE OF DEIR YASSIN

The story of the sinking of the S.S. *Lino* is based on interviews with Freddy Fredkens, Munya Mardor and Fouad Mardam. A detailed account of the incident is also to be found in Mardor's memoir *Strictly Illegal*. The details of the arms offers, real and spurious, including some of the original documents, made to the Arabs are contained in the personal archives of Riad Solh and Jamil Mardam. Tuvia Arazi kindly gave us access to his late brother's papers and memoirs for the details of his arms-purchasing activities recounted in this chapter.

As explained in the footnote on page 276, the survivors' stories of the massacre of Deir Yassin are quoted from the official British investigation of the incident made shortly after it took place. Although the authors interviewed, with some difficulty, a number of survivors of the massacre in Jerusalem in 1969, only the account of Ahmed Eid was used. This was because of the fear that perhaps over the years the survivors' accounts of what happened might have been altered to conform with some of the propaganda excesses associated with it. In any event, their accounts related in 1969 amply confirmed the details in the British report. Also used in the passage on Deir Yassin were interviews with two Haganah officers, Yeshurun Schiff and Eliyahu Arieli. Although neither man saw evidence of rape, both confirmed the wantonness, savagery and amplitude of the slaughter. The diary of the Red Cross's Jacques de Reynier, written on the evening of his trip to Deir Yassin, provides further corroboration of the slaughter.

Shaltiel's report to Tel Aviv on the attack, contained in his archives, makes these observations: "There was no military advantage in their plan and it did not fall into the general defense of the Yishuv. . . . No forces of Haganah participated in this action . . . the exhibition of women and children of Deir Yassin in the streets of the city was a degrading spectacle." After the war, appearing before a board of fellow officers compiling a history of the 1948 conflict, Shaltiel made the following statement: "I can't say I didn't know about it [Deir Yassin]. One day before, Yeshurun Schiff told me about it. I met with the commander of Lechi [the Stern Gang] and informed him of my opposition; I emphasized that the village was friendly to us; they insisted; I said, if so, you must hold the village. I suggested they help us with Kastel, they refused. During the battle I was forced to order a unit of Palmach to assist them with cover fire in order to extricate them."

The Irgun, of course, has always denied that the slaughter took place, claiming that whatever killing occured in Deir Yassin was a result of legitimate military action.

An account of Deir Yassin from the Irgun's standpoint is contained in Menahem Begin's *The Revolt*. A more detailed reconstruction of the affair was published by Uri Millstein in *Haaretz* August 30, 1968. In addition to those individuals already mentioned, Sir Alan Cunningham, Sir Gordon Mac-Millan, Brigadier C. P. Jones, James Pollock, Zelman Mart of the Haganah,

Yeshua Zetler of the Stern Gang, and Menachem Adler, Mordechai Ranana and Amnon Lapidot of the Irgun were also interviewed.

Fawzi el Kaujki's cabled explanation of his defeat at Mishmar Ha'emek was found in the papers of Jamil Mardam.

CHAPTER 23:
"*SHALOM*, MY DEAR . . ."

Vital in compiling the story of the ambush of the Hadassah convoy were the report, issued May 5, 1948, of the committee of inquiry formed by the Jewish Agency to investigate the attack, Colonel Churchill's report to his superior, and the diary entries of the Highland Light Infantry for the day, a copy of which was furnished the authors by Colonel Churchill. Among the survivors interviewed were Mrs. Esther Passman, Mrs. Fanny Yassky, Sonia Astrachan, Dr. Yehuda Matot, Malka Zakagi, Benjamin Adin and Dr. David Ullman; among the attackers, Mohammed Neggar, Daoud Alami, Bajhat Abou Gharbieh, Yahia Zouwi, Mohammed Da'ud and Jamil Bazian; among the British, Colonel Churchill, Michael Naylor Leyland, Captain James Crawford, James Pollock, Sir Alan Cunningham and Sir Gordon MacMillan; among the Haganah, Zvi Sinai, Yitzhak Levi, Moshe Hillman, and Zelman Mart.

The account of the Arab League's Cairo meeting is taken largely from interviews with Azzam Pasha and his secretary Wahid el Dali, and from the minutes of the meeting itself. The description of Farouk and Riad Solh's meetings was provided by Antonio Pulli and is referred to at length in a letter from Solh to his Foreign Ministry in Solh's papers. The description of his visit to *Al Ahram* was provided by the paper's owner at the time, Bishara Takla.

CHAPTER 24:
"ATTACK AND ATTACK AND ATTACK."

The passage relating the shift in Arab and Haganah tactics and the arrival of the last Operation Nachshon convoys is based on interviews with Yigal Yadin, Yitzhak Rabin, Dov Joseph, Josef Tabenkin, Uzi Narciss and Emile Ghory, and on cabled exchanges between Jerusalem and Tel Aviv, one of which is quoted, contained in David Shaltiel's papers. The account of David Ben-Gurion's meeting with the Jerusalem Haganah is based on an interview with Mr. Ben-Gurion, his diary entry of the time and an interview with Eliyahu Arbei. A copy of the Weizmann-Truman letter referred to on page 301 was given to the authors by Judge Rosenman.

The chapter's concluding passage on Egypt's war preparations is based on interviews with Said Mortagi, King Farouk's senior military aide, with Mohammed Hassanein Heikal, now editor of *Al Ahram*, with George Deeb and with a highly placed member of the Prime Minister's entourage.

CHAPTER 25:
A MESSAGE FROM GLUBB PASHA

The precise details of the Passover rations and of other weekly rations cited later in the book were taken from the files of Arieh Belkind. The account of the fight for the Monastery of St. Simeon at Katamon was compiled from interviews with Peter Saleh, Abou Farouk, Gaby Deeb, Brigadier C. P. Jones, Yitzhak Rabin, David Elazar, Uzi Narciss, Benny Marshak, Uri Ben-Ari, Yosef Tabenkin, Eliyahu Sela, Yitzhak Navon and Yitzhak Levi.

The description of the Arab League meeting in Amman includes interview material from Azzam Pasha, Dr. Mohammed el Saty and Colonel Charles Coker. The quotes attributed to King Abdullah were found in the personal archives of Riad Solh. Colonel Desmond Goldie and his Haganah interlocutor Shlomo Shamir furnished the account of their meeting in Naharayim. Interviews with Ariyeh Schurr, Carmi Charny and Dan Ben-Dor form the basis of the passage describing preparations for the takeover of central Jerusalem. President Truman's message to his legal adviser concerning the dispatch of U. S. troops to Palestine is on file with his papers in the Truman Library. We are indebted to Eliahu Elath for his description of the meeting between Moshe Sharett and Secretary Marshall at which he was present.

CHAPTER 26:
"WE SHALL COME BACK."

The opening passage on preparations for Britain's departure from Jerusalem includes interview material from Sir Alan Cunningham, Sir William Fitzgerald, Golda Meir, Pablo de Azcarate and Ambara Khalidy. The description of life in Jewish Jerusalem is based on interviews with numerous Jerusalemites plus Dov Joseph and his key aides: Zvi Leibowitz for water, Alexander Singer for electric power, and Dan Ben-Dor, Arieh Belkind and Avraham Picker for food. Among those whose interviews were used in preparing the Old City passage were Moshe Russnak, Avraham Orenstein, Leah Vultz, Gershon Finger and Fawzi el Kutub. For the material on Esther Cailingold in this and future chapters we are indebted to her mother, Mrs. Moshe Cailingold, and her brother and sister, Asher Cailingold and Shulamit Kogan.

The outline of Shaltiel's Operation Pitchfork and the details of his arms and troops strengths were found in documents in his archives. The description of the Arabs' Rawdah School headquarters is based on numerous interviews, including those with Emile Ghory, Bajhat Abou Gharbieh, Mounir Abou Fadel, Anwar Khatib, Ibrahim Abou Dayieh and Nimra Tannous. The stories of the various Arab departures from Jerusalem were recounted by the people who lived them. The cause of the Arabs' flight has been much disputed in the years since 1948. For some time the Israeli government maintained that they were ordered to leave by Arab radio broadcasts to make way for the Arab armies. A careful study of the BBC's recorded archives of all broadcasts of the time by two independent sets of researchers indicates no trace of any such broadcasts. To the contrary, there is documentary evidence that the Mufti's Arab Higher Committee sought (see page 215) to check the outflow and force the earlier refugees to return to Palestine. Unfortunately the Mufti's appointees were most often the first to flee. In Haifa and Acre his commanders disappeared as soon as the fighting began, to Damascus ostensibly in search of arms. There is no doubt the massacre of Deir Yassin played an important role in the creation of a climate of fear and uncertainty among the Arabs. It was also apparent from our interviews with dozens of Arabs that the great majority of those who fled were persuaded they would be returning in a very short time in the van of the conquering Arab armies.

CHAPTER 27:
"THROW STONES AND DIE."

The brief description of Egypt's war preparations and the parliament's declaration of war is based on interviews with Antonio Pulli, with Said Mortagi, Farouk's military aide, and with Ali Amin, a member of parliament present when war was declared. Riad Solh's daughter, Alia, who accompanied her father, described his greeting to the Moroccan volunteers. An account of Syria's preparations and Jamil Mardam's declaration of war is contained in his personal papers. The passage on the Arab Legion's preparations and John Glubb's strategy is based on two lengthy interviews with General Glubb and interviews with his English officers Nigel Brommage, R. K. Melville, Desmond Goldie, Hugh Blackenden, Charles Coker and John Downes. Azzam Pasha and Sir Alec Kirkbride provided largely identical accounts of their Amman conversation.

The account of Golda Meir's visit to King Abdullah is based on interviews with Mrs. Meir and Ezra Danin. Ahmed Zurbati showed us the room in his home where the meeting took place, but declined to comment on it. Dr. el Saty provided some insight into the King's intentions, based on the messages he had carried for him to the Jewish Agency in Jerusalem.

CHAPTER 28:
BY JUST ONE VOTE

The description of the fall of Kfar Etzion contained in this and the following chapter is based largely on interviews with the survivors of the colony, Abbras Tamir, Yaacov Edelstein and Yitzhak and Nahum Ben-Sira, and the Arab officers of the Legion directing the attack: Abdullah Tell, Mahmoud Moussa, Qasem el Nasr, Hikmet Muhair, Nawaf Jaber el Hamoud, and Noaf el Karim Mussalam. Both Tell and Hamoud wrote unpublished memoirs which describe the assault in detail. Copies of the messages referred to are all contained in David Shaltiel's archives. An excellent description of the fall of the colony is also to be found in *Siege in the Hills of Hebron,* edited by Dov Knohl.

The account of the meeting at the Jewish National Fund and David Ben-Gurion's preparations for it is based on the authors' interview with Mr. Ben-Gurion and his own lengthy description of it as recorded in his diary. The figures for arms given in the passage were taken either from Mr. Ben-Gurion's diary or from the actual invoices furnished the authors by Ehud Avriel.

CHAPTER 29:
THE LAST SUPPER

The material in this chapter is based almost exclusively on interviews with the individuals named therein whose experiences on the eve of Britain's departure from Palestine are recounted.

CHAPTER 30:
THE FIFTH DAY OF IYAR

The description of the first day's fighting in Jerusalem and the Haganah's capture of Bevingrad is based on interviews with, on the Jewish side, Arieyeh

Schurr, Yitzhak Levi, Avram Uzieli, Mordechai Faitelson, Shmuel Matot, Netanel Lorch and Murray Hellner; on the Arab side, with Bajhat Abou Gharbieh, Father Ibrahim Ayad, Mounir Abou Fadel, Anwar Khatib, Nassib Boulos, Raji Sayhoun and Emile Ghory. Eric Downton of the *Daily Telegraph* provided the story of the gallows tree.

The description of the proclamation of the Jewish state is based on interviews with David Ben-Gurion and Mordechai Avida, who broadcast it for Kol Israel, contemporary newspaper accounts, notably *Haaretz,* and Ben-Gurion's diary entry for the day. Avraham Orenstein, Chaim (Vivian) Herzog, Avraham Banai and Jacob Ben-Ur were interviewed for the passage relating to the reaction to the proclamation.

The account of the Arab Legion's last formation and King Abdullah's address is based on interviews with John Glubb, Abdullah Tell, Desmond Goldie and Hugh Blackenden.

Sir Alan Cunningham's departure from Jerusalem was reconstructed during an interview with the last High Commissioner.

CHAPTER 31:
"THESE SHALL STAND."

The quotes and declarations issued by the Arab radio at the beginning of the 1948 war are on file in the archives of the BBC. Azzam Pasha's declaration was made in an interview with the BBC May 15. The scene on the Semiramis roof was witnessed by Captains Michael Naylor Leyland and Derek Cooper of the Life Guards. Mohammed Rafat furnished the account of the departure of the Sixth Battalion; Captain Mahmoud Rousan, that of the passage of the Arab Legion's advance party into Palestine.

Clark Clifford and Eliahu Elath contributed the account of U. S. recognition of the new state. The description of David Ben-Gurion's receiving the news, his speech and his tour of the bombed areas comes from an interview with Mr. Ben-Gurion and his diary entry for the day. The passage on Latrun is based on interviews with Yigal Yadin, Yitzhak Rabin, John Glubb, Haroun Ben-Jazzi and Fawzi el Kaujki as well as the official study of the battle by the Israeli Defense Force's Historical Section.

The extent of Jewish looting of the captured Arab areas in Jerusalem and the apparent unwillingness or inability of the city's leadership to stop it was the subject of much criticism in 1948. The incidents described here are based on the accounts of eyewitnesses. Jon Kimche, a distinguished Zionist author, called the looting a "shame." The United States consul general, in a dispatch to the State Department May 18, noted: "Looting in the captured Arab areas has now been so widespread and has been regarded with such indifference by the authorities that it is difficult not to think that it is being officially tolerated."

Joseph Linton, Chaim Weizmann's secretary, described his champagne toast to Israel's first President.

CHAPTER 32:
"THE MOST BEAUTIFUL MONTH OF THE YEAR"

The quotes from the news bulletin of Aladin Namari were taken from a copy of his original bulletins, a set of which was furnished the authors. The quotes on the following page are from Ben-Gurion's diary. Mohammed Rafat furnished the description of his first action. The account of the flight of the Soeurs Réparatrices is based on the detailed entries made at the time in the convent's diary, which were made available to the authors.

All cables cited in the passage on the Old City are contained in the Shaltiel archives. In addition, interview material from Mordechai Pincus, Moshe Russnak and Father Ibrahim Ayad was included in the passage.

An outline of the plan for the Jaffa Gate attack is contained in David Shaltiel's archives. It was severely criticized at the time by the Palmach's Yitzhak Rabin, Uzi Narciss and Yosef Tabenkin as being unrealistic. Sometime later, defending his plan before a board of fellow officers compiling a history of the war, Shaltiel said he rejected the Palmach's alternative plan because "I had an almost common border with the Old City which I didn't have near the Rockefeller Museum [where the Palmach proposed to attack]. I saw my first and primary target saving the Jews of the Old City . . . I didn't think the Jewish Quarter would hold out. I expected the appearance of a Legion force from the east in a matter of hours."

CHAPTER 33:
"GO SAVE JERUSALEM."

The account of the interventions of Jerusalem's Arab leaders in Amman, the King's predawn visit to his Prime Minister's home and his subsequent decision to order Abdullah Tell to the city is contained in the memoirs of Hazza el Majali, then his private secretary, published in Amman in May 1960 in Arabic. Abdullah Tell, in an interview, contributed his version of the day's events. Copies of the King's cables were published in Glubb's book *A Soldier with the Arabs.* He himself expanded on his efforts to resist sending the Legion into Jerusalem in interviews at his home in England.

A series of cables sent by Jerusalem Haganah headquarters to Tel Aviv, copies of which are in the Shaltiel archives, provide a graphic account of the progress and ultimate failure of the Jaffa Gate attack. A Palmach version of the attack, written by Uzi Narciss, is contained in the Palmach history *Sefer ha-Palmach.* Among those interviewed in preparing this account of the assault were, on the Jewish side, Netanel Lorch, Bobby Reisman, Aryeh Fishman, Ephraim Levi, Yitzhak Levi, Uzi Narciss, Eliyahu Sela, Uri Ben-Ari, David Elazar, Yosef Nevo, Avraham Bar-Yefet, Yigal Arnon and David Amiran; on the Arab side, Nimra Tannous, Abou Eid, Anwar Nusseibi, Mounir Abou Fadel, Peter Saleh, Kamal Irekat, Nadi Dai'es, Hafez Barakat, Daoud Husseini and Daoud Alami.

CHAPTER 34:
"A LAMENT FOR A GENERATION"

Interviews with Abdullah Tell and Mahmoud Moussa, coupled with Tell's memoirs, provided material for the account of the Legion's entry into Jerusalem. Major Bob Slade, who described the Arab Legion assembly at Ramallah, still possesses Brigadier Lash's handwritten order for his movement to Jerusalem. The meeting between Glubb and Kirkbride was described by the two men in separate interviews.

589

The account of the Palmach's breach of Zion Gate is based on interviews with, on the Jewish side, Yosef Atiyeh, Mordechai Gazit, Avraham Bar-Yefet, Benny Marshak, Eliyahu Sela, Shmuel Bazak, David Elazar, Mordechai Pincus and Moshe Russnak; on the Arab side, with Nawaf Jaber el Hamoud, Mahmoud Moussa and Abdul Karim Mussalam.

For the details on the history of the Trappist Monastery of Latrun and the monks' life in 1948, we are indebted to R. P. Marcel Destailleur, abbot of Latrun, for access to the monastery's enormously detailed 1948 diary.

CHAPTER 35:
"YOSEF HAS SAVED JERUSALEM!"

The account of the fighting near the Mandelbaum house is based almost entirely on interviews with those who participated in it. From the Haganah they include Yosef Nevo, Mishka Rabinovitch, Jacob and Sarah Ben-Ur, Carmi Charny, Bobby Reisman, Kalman Rosenblatt, Yitzhak Levi and Reuven Tamir. From the Arab Legion they include Majors Bob Slade and John Buchanan, Lieutenant Zaal Errhavel, Lieutenant Abdul Razzak Sherif and Sergeant Eit Matar.

CHAPTER 36:
"TAKE LATRUN."

A carefully kept protocol of each of the almost daily meetings of Dov Joseph's Jerusalem Commission is on file in the Israel Prime Minister's Archives in Jerusalem. They are the source of Joseph's quotes on page 456 and numerous specific details such as the price of black-market water and the daily calorie ration on page 457.

The account of the Haganah's and the Legion's joint efforts to rescue the three armored cars is based on interviews with Yosef Nevo, Jacob and Sarah Ben-Ur, Mishka Rabinovitch and Lieutenant Zaal Errhavel.

The description of the Žatec air base and the flight of the Israeli Air Force's first Messerschmitt is based on interviews with Ehud Avriel, Mordechai Hod and Ezer Weizmann. The background to the struggle for Notre-Dame includes interviews with John Glubb and Netanel Lorch, and material from the archives of the hospice, the diary of Dr. René Bauer and that of the Soeurs Réparatrices. The account of the meeting between Yigal Yadin and David Ben-Gurion is based on Mr. Ben-Gurion's diary and interviews with the two men.

CHAPTER 37:
TICKET TO A PROMISED LAND

For the preliminaries on the battle of Latrun, see the notes for the following chapter. The account of the fighting for Notre-Dame de France was assembled from interviews with participants in the engagement: for the Haganah, Zelman Mart, Netanel Lorch and Mishka Rabinovitch; for the Arab Legion, Fendi Omeish, Zaal Errhavel, Eit Matar, Fawzi el Kutub and Sir John Glubb.

CHAPTER 38:
"EXECUTE YOUR TASK AT ALL COSTS."

and

CHAPTER 39:
THE WHEATFIELDS OF LATRUN

The three battles of Latrun, the first of which is described in these two chapters, constituted perhaps the most important and certainly the most controversial series of engagements of the first Arab–Israeli war. As a result, a great deal of literature is available to the researcher interested in the subject. The most important probably is a lengthy study of the battles compiled on the basis of interviews with Israel's senior commanders conducted by the Historical Section of the Israel Defense Forces. After the capture of the Latrun salient in the Six-Day War a series of studies on the 1948 Latrun struggle appeared in the Israeli press. The most important of them were: "Attack at all Costs," by Haim Laskov, *Haaretz,* April 30, 1968; "What Happened at Latrun?," by Uri Oren, *Ma'ariv,* June 7, 1968; "Thundering Silence," by the same author, in *Yediot Achronot,* June 14, 1968; and "Latrun: The History of a Battle," a seven-part series that ran in *Ma'arachot* in 1968. In addition there is available for Latrun an excellent and detailed account of the battles seen from the Arabic side based on the diary written at the time by Mahmoud Rousan, the adjutant of the Sixth Regiment. Called *Harbe Bab el Wad* (The Battles of Latrun), it was published in Amman in 1959.

Since most of the men the authors interviewed to compile this account of the fighting at Latrun participated in more than one of the battles, we are, to avoid repetition, listing them all here. They were, for the Haganah, Yaacov Freed, Matti Megid, Benny Marshak, Moshe Klein, Pnina Schneman, Haim Laskov, Shlomo Shamir, Zvi Hurewitz, Chaim (Vivian) Herzog, Zvi German, David Ben-Gurion, Yigal Yadin, Shimon Avidan, Iska Shadmi, Moshe Kellman, Carmi Charny, Uri Zantbank, Hadassah Sussman and David Levinson; for the Arab Legion, Captain Mahmoud Rousan, Colonel Habes Majali, Lieutenant Mahmoud May'tah, Lieutenant Qassem Ayad, Captain Abdullah Salem, Captain Izzat Hassan, Dr. Yacoub Abu Gosh, Lieutenant Abdullah Shwei'ir, Lieutenant Mohammed Na'em, Sergeant Youssef Jeries, Lieutenant Nasr Ahmed and Lieutenant Nigel Brommage.

CHAPTER 40:
". . . . REMEMBER ME ONLY IN HAPPINESS."

Two important accounts of the Jewish Quarter's struggle and fall have been published in Israel and constitute basic reference works on the subject: *Megillat Heir Haatika* (Notes on the Scroll of the Old City) by Adina Maarechot, and *Yerushalayim Haatika Bematzor Be-Bakron* (Old Jerusalem in Siege and Battle) by Aharon Liron. All cables between the New and Old Cities quoted here were located in David Shaltiel's archives. We are indebted to Mrs. Moshe Cailingold for the text of her daughter's last letter. Among interviews used in preparing this account of the Jewish Quarter's fall were, on the Jewish side, Mordechai Pincus, Yehuda Choresh, Avraham Orenstein, Rivka and Masha Weingarten, Uri Ben-Ari, Moshe Russnak, Rabbi Shar Yeshuv Cohen, Chaim Haller, Yosef Atiyeh, and Yechiel and Leah Vultz; and, on the Arab side, Nadi Dai'es, Abdullah Tell, Samir Souki, Nassib Boulos, Mahmoud Moussa, Fawzi el Kutub and Antoine Albina.

CHAPTER 41:
"GOOD NIGHT AND GOODBYE FROM JERUSALEM."

The cable exchanges between Dov Joseph and David Ben-Gurion quoted in this chapter and in chapters 43 and 44 are on file in the Israel Prime Minister's Archives, Military Governor File No. 42. Shaltiel's message to his troops on the food situation is contained in an order of the day for June 2, 1948. The passage on the Arab shelling of the city is based on interviews with Abdullah Tell and Emile Jumean and the daily summaries of shelling by the enemy in Shaltiel's archives. Material for the description of Jerusalem life under siege was taken from interviews with Dov Joseph, Dr. Edward Joseph, Eliyahu Sochaczever, Mr. and Mrs. David Erlik, Mrs. Joseph Rivlin, Aaron Elner, Eliyahu Carmel and Amos Elon. Interviews with Sir John Glubb, Hugh Blackenden, Sir Alec Kirkbride and Sir Harold Beeley contributed to the description of Britain's change of policy.

CHAPTER 42:
"WE'LL OPEN A NEW ROAD."

For the second battle of Latrun, see the notes to chapters 38 and 39. The discovery of what was to become known as the Burma Road was described to the authors by the two survivors of the trio who made it, Amos Chorev and Chaim (Vivian) Herzog. Chorev kindly agreed to retrace with us his footsteps over the road twenty years after its discovery. Interviews with Yitzhak Levi and David Ben-Gurion were used in the closing passages of the chapter.

CHAPTER 43:
"THE ARAB PEOPLE WILL NEVER FORGIVE US."

As in the previous chapters, cables between Dov Joseph and David Ben-Gurion quoted herein are on file in the Israel Prime Minister's Archives, Military Governor File No. 42. Statistics on food supplies remaining in the city or on its rations are contained either in the same file or in the files kept at the time by Arieh Belkind, one of Dov Joseph's food aides. In addition, in the passages in this chapter describing Jerusalem's desperate situation, material was used from interviews with Dov Joseph, Avraham Picker, Arieh Belkind, Reuven Tamir, Leon Angel, Netanel Lorch and Shalom Dror. The odyssey of Brother François Haas and his pigs is recounted in the diary of Notre-Dame de France.

The account of the Arab League's debates in Amman is based on interviews with Azzam Pasha and his secretary Wahid el Dali and the minutes of the meeting itself.

The description of the decision to send men on foot across the hills to Jerusalem and the struggle of the Tel Aviv porters to get food to the city is based on interviews with Bronislav Bar-Shemer, Joseph Avidar, David Ben-Gurion, Pinhas Bracker, Chaim (Vivian) Herzog and Amos Chorev. The account of the Arab Legion's reaction to the Jews' road building comes from Mahmoud Rousan's diary and Abdullah Tell's unpublished memoirs as well as from interviews with Rousan, Tell, Habes Majali and Ali Abou Nuwar.

CHAPTER 44:
A TOAST TO THE LIVING

For the third battle of Latrun, see the notes to chapters 38 and 39. The description of Jewish Jerusalem's plight on the eve of the cease-fire is based on Arieh Belkind's and Dov Joseph's files. The statistics on the amount of flour left in the city were taken from Belkind's copy of the chart listing the food reserves. In addition, material from interviews with Joseph, Belkind, Alexander Singer, Avraham Picker, Dan Ben-Dor and Zvi Leibowitz was used. According to the records of Joseph's committee, 2,000 Jewish Jerusalemites—two percent of the city's Jewish population—were killed or wounded by shellfire during the siege.

The story of the Arab Legion's shell on the Church of the Holy Sepulcher was furnished the authors by the man who fired it, Emile Jumean.

The account of Marcus' death comes from the inquiry into its causes conducted by the Haganah. There was a suspicion at the time, rejected by the inquiry, that he might have been killed deliberately by the Palmach, which resented his and Ben-Gurion's efforts to bring its forces under tighter discipline and convert the Haganah into a regular army. The account of King Abdullah's visit to Jerusalem and the cease-fire seen from the Arab side was prepared on the basis of interviews with Abou Said Abou Reech, Emile Ghory and Abdullah Tell. David Ben-Gurion's appraisal of the Arabs' acceptance of the cease-fire as a "mistake" appeared in an interview with Uri Oren in *Yediot Achronot* June 24, 1948.

CHAPTER 45:
THE THIRTY-DAY PAUSE

The statistics on the quantity of arms and ammunition which reached Jerusalem via the Burma Road during the thirty-day cease-fire were taken from the Shaltiel archives. The quantities and nature of the foodstuffs sent to the city were taken from David Ben-Gurion's diaries, where the Israeli Prime Minister recorded them meticulously each day. The statistics on the amount of arms reaching Israel during the cease-fire and the purchases made in Czechoslovakia were taken from Mr. Ben-Gurion's diaries and from the files of Ehud Avriel. The quotes attributed to Mr. Ben-Gurion in his meetings with the Haganah's commanders and his Cabinet were taken from parts of his speeches as entered in his diary at the time. His mixed emotions at accepting Bernadotte's plea for a prolongation of the cease-fire were described to the authors in an interview.

The accounts of the Arab League's rejection of the cease-fire were taken from the minutes of the League's meetings. The description of the Arabs' difficulties in replenishing their arms stores and of Britain's position includes materials from interviews with Sir John Glubb, Sir Harold Beeley and Desmond Young.

CHAPTER 46:
THE FLAWED TRUMPET

The bombing of Cairo is recounted in detail in *Strictly Illegal,* by Munya Mardor. Yehuda Brieger, a crew member of the B-17, was interviewed by the authors. The description of the Arab League's Aley meetings is based on the minutes of the meeting and interviews with Azzam Pasha and Wahid el Dali.

The account of the final assault on the Old City walls by the Haganah is based on interviews with Zvi Sinai, David Amiran, Yeshurun Schiff, Mishka Rabinovitch, Avram Uzieli, Menachem Adler, Avram Zorea, Shmuel Matot, Abdullah Tell and Mahmoud Moussa. Copies of the proclamation of martial law, Shaltiel's speech to announce the Old City's capture and other documents prepared for its occupation are contained in the Jerusalem commander's files.

BIBLIOGRAPHY

BOOKS

Abd Allah Ibn-Husain (King Abdullah), *My Memoirs Completed (Al-Takmilah)*. Washington, D. C.: American Council of Learned Societies, 1954.

Adin (Edelman), Benjamin, *Adventure at the Wheel*. Jerusalem: Alfa Jerusalem Press, 1965.

Agar, Herbert, *The Saving Remnant*. New York: Viking, 1960.

Alem, Jean-Pierre, *Juifs et arabes: 3000 ans d'histoire*. Paris: Grasset, 1968.

Allon, Yigal, *Battles of the Palmach*. Tel Aviv: Hakibbutz Hameuchad, 1965 (Hebrew).

Amrami, Yaakov, *Tolnot Milchenet Hakomeneut* (History of the War of Independence). Tel Aviv: Shelach, 1951 (Hebrew).

Antonius, George, *The Arab Awakening*. Philadelphia: Lippincott, 1939.

Aref, Aref el, *El Nakla* (The Tragedy), 7 vols. Beirut, 1958.

Attlee, Clement (Earl Attlee), *As It Happened* (autobiography). London: Heinemann, 1954.

Avnery, Uri, *Bisdot Pleshet* (Fields of Palestine). Tel Aviv: Twersky, 1950.

Azcarate y Flores, Pablo de, *Mission in Palestine*. Washington, D. C.: Middle East Institute, 1966.

Baer, Israel, *Carvot Latrun* (Battles of Latrun). Tel Aviv: Maarachot, 1953.

Barodi, Fakhri, "The Catastrophe of Palestine." Damascus: Ibn Zaidon, 1950 (Arabic).

Bar-Zohar, Michael, *The Armed Prophet*. London: A. Barker, 1967.

Begin, Menahem (Menachem Beigin), *The Revolt: Story of the Irgun*. Tel Aviv: Hadar, 1964.

Bemis, Samuel Flagg, *The American Secretaries of State and Their Diplomacy*. New York: Pageant, 1958.

Ben-Gurion, David, *Ben-Gourion parle*. Paris: Stock, 1971.

———, *Israel: Years of Challenge*. New York: Holt, 1963.

Ben-Jacob, Jeremiah, *The Rise of Israel*. New York: Grosby House, 1949.

Ben-Shaul, Moshe (ed.), *Generals of Israel*. Tel Aviv: Hadar, 1968.

Bentwich, Norman, *Israel*. London: Benn, 1952.

Berkman, Ted, *Cast a Giant Shadow*. Garden City, N. Y.: Doubleday, 1962.

Berlin, Isaiah, *Chaim Weizmann*. New York: Farrar, Straus and Cudahy, 1958.

Bernadotte, Folke, *The Curtain Falls*. New York: Knopf, 1945.

———, *To Jerusalem*. London: Hodder, 1951.

Betchy, Mohammed al, *Our Martyrs in Palestine*. Cairo: 1949 (Arabic).

Bilby, Kenneth W., *New Star in the Near East*. Garden City, N. Y.: Doubleday, 1950.

Birdwood, Christopher B., *Nuri as-Said: A Study in Arab Leadership*. London: Cassell, 1959.

Bullock, Alan, *The Life and Times of Ernest Bevin*. London: Heinemann, 1960.

Burrows, Millar, *Palestine Is Our Business*. Philadelphia: The Westminster Press, 1949.

Carlson, John Roy (Arthur Derounian), *Cairo to Damascus*. New York: Knopf, 1951.

Catarivas, David, *Israël*. Paris: Seuil, 1967.

Cattan, Henry, *Palestine, the Arabs and Israel: The Search for Justice*. London: Longmans, 1969.

Cohen, Geula, *Woman of Violence: Memoirs of a young Terrorist, 1943–1948*. New York: Holt, Rinehart and Winston, 1966.

Crossman, R. H. S., *A Nation Reborn*. London: Hamish Hamilton, 1960.

————, *Palestine Mission*. New York and London: Harper & Brothers, 1947.

Crum, Bartley, *Behind the Silken Curtain*. New York: Simon and Schuster, 1947.

Daniels, Jonathan, *Man of Independence: A Biography of Harry S Truman*. Philadelphia: Lippincott, 1950.

Dayan, Shmuel, *Pioneers in Israel*. New York and Cleveland: World Publishing, 1961.

Derogy, Jacques, *La Secrète et Véritable Histoire de l'Exodus*. Paris: Fayard, 1969.

————, and Edouard Saab, *Les Deux Exodes*. Paris: Denoël, 1968.

Dimont, Max, *Jews, God, and History*. New York: Simon and Schuster, 1962. Published in Paris by Laffont as *Les Juifs, Dieu et l'histoire*.

Eddy, William Alfred, *F.D.R. Meets Ibn Saud*. New York: American Friends of the Middle East, 1954.

Edelman, Maurice, *David: The Story of Ben-Gurion*. New York: Putnam, 1965.

Elath, Eliahu, *Israel and Her Neighbors*. Cleveland and New York: World, 1957.

————, *Israel and Elath*. London: Weidenfeld, 1966.

Elissar, Eliahu ben, *La Diplomatie du IIIe Reich et les juifs, 1933–1939*. Paris: Julliard, 1969.

Elston, Roy, *No Alternatives*. London: Hutchinson, 1960.

Eretz Israel (Collection) Vol. 8, Sukenik Memorial Volume.

Eytan, Walter, *The First Ten Years*. New York: Simon and Schuster, 1958.

Farag, Sayed, *Our Army in Palestine*. Cairo: Fawakol, 1949 (Arabic).

Feis, Herbert, *The Birth of Israel: The Tousled Diplomatic Bed*. New York: H. Feis, 1969.

Flaubert, Gustave, *Voyage en Orient*, in *Oeuvres complètes*. Paris: Seuil, 1964.

Forrestal, James V., *The Forrestal Diaries*, ed. Walter Millis in collaboration with E. D. Duffield. New York: Viking, 1951.

Francos, Ania, *Les Palestiniens*. Paris: Julliard, 1968.

Frank, Gerold, *The Deed*. New York: Simon and Schuster, 1963.

Furlonge, Geoffrey, *Palestine Is My Country: The Story of Musa Alami*. London: John Murray, 1969.

Gabbay, Rony E., *A Political Study of the Arab–Jewish Conflict*. Geneva: Librarie Droz, 1959.

Garcia Granados, Jorge, *The Birth of Israel*. New York: Knopf, 1948.

Gervasi, Frank H., *To Whom Palestine?* New York: Appleton-Century, 1946.

Glubb, Sir John Bagot (Glubb Pasha), *Britain and the Arabs*. London: Hodder, 1959.

———, *A Soldier with the Arabs*. New York: Harper & Brothers, 1957.

———, *Story of the Arab Legion*. London: Hodder, 1948.

Graves, Philip P. (ed.), *Memoirs of King Abdullah of Transjordan*. London: Cape, 1950.

Gugenheim, E., *Le Judaïsme dans la vie quotidienne*. Paris: Albin Michel, 1961.

Hadawi, Sami, *The Arab–Israeli Conflict: Cause and Effect*. Beirut-Lebanon, 1967.

———, *Bitter Harvest: Palestine Between 1914 and 1967*. New York: New World Press, 1967.

Haezrahi, Yehuda, *The Living Rampart*. London: Zionist Youth Council, 1948.

Halpern, Ben, *The Idea of the Jewish State*. Cambridge, Mass.: Harvard, 1961.

Hariri, Saleh al, *The Saudi Army in Palestine*. Cairo: Dar el Ketab, 1950 (Arabic).

Hashemi, Taha, *Diary of the War*. Beirut (Arabic).

Hecht, Ben, *A Child of the Century*. New York: Simon and Schuster, 1954.

———, *Perfidy*. New York: Messner, 1961.

Hirszowicz, Lukasz, *The Third Reich and the Arab East*. London: Routledge & Kegan Paul, 1966.

Horowitz, David, *State in the Making*. New York: Knopf, 1953.

Hurewitz, J. C., *The Struggle for Palestine*. New York: Norton, 1950.

Hyamson, H. M., *Palestine under the Mandate*. London: Methuen, 1950.

Hyrkanos-Ginzburg, Devora, *Jerusalem War Diary*. Jerusalem: Wizo Zionist Education Department, 1950.

Jacobovitz, Mordechai, *Heroes Tell Their Stories: Chapters on the War of Independence*. Tel Aviv: Niv (Hebrew).

Jarvis, Claude, *Three Deserts*. London: John Murray, 1936.

Join-Lambert, Michel, *Ancient Cities and Temples: Jerusalem*. London: Elek Books, 1958.

Joseph, Bernard (Dov), *The Faithful City*. New York: Simon and Schuster, 1960.

Josephus, *The Jewish War*. Baltimore: Penguin, 1959.

Kagan, Benjamin, *The Secret Battle for Israel*. New York and Cleveland: World, 1966.

Katz, Samuel, *Days of Fire*. Garden City, N. Y.: Doubleday, 1968.

Keller, Werner, *The Bible as History: Archaeology Confirms the Book of Books*. London: Hodder & Stoughton, 1956.

Khatib, Mohammed Nemr al, *The Result of the Catastrophe*. Damascus: Matba Umomeya, 1951 (Arabic).

Khouri, Fred J., *The Arab–Israeli Dilemma*. Ithaca, N. Y.: Syracuse University Press, 1968.

Kimche, Jon, *Seven Fallen Pillars*. New York: Praeger, 1953.

———, *The Secret Roads*. London: Secker, 1954.

——— and David Kimche, *Both Sides of the Hill*. London: Secker, 1960.

———, *A Clash of Destinies*. New York: Praeger, 1960.

Kirk, George, *A Short History of the Middle East*. London: Methuen, 1961.

———, *Survey of International Affairs, 1939–46: The Middle East in the War*. London and New York: Oxford, 1952.

———, *Survey of International Affairs: The Middle East, 1945–50*. London .and New York: Oxford, 1954.

Kirkbride, Sir Alec, *A Crackle of Thorns*. London: John Murray, 1956.

Knohl, Dov (ed.), *Siege in the Hills of Hebron*. New York: Yoseloff, 1958.

Koestler, Arthur, *Promise and Fulfilment*. New York: Macmillan, 1949.

Kollek, Teddy, and Moshe Pearlman, *Jerusalem, Sacred City of Mankind: A History of Forty Centuries*. Jerusalem, Tel Aviv, Haifa: Steimatzky's Agency Ltd., 1968.

Kotker, Norman, *The Earthly Jerusalem*. New York: Scribner's, 1969.

Latour, Anny, *The Resurrection of Israel*. Cleveland and New York: World, 1968.

Lau-Lavie, Naphtalie, *Moshe Dayan*. London: Vallentine Mitchell, 1968.

Lawrence, Thomas Edward, *Seven Pillars of Wisdom*. Garden City, N. Y.: Doubleday, 1935.

Learsi, Rufus, *Israel: A History of the Jewish People*. New York and Cleveland: World, 1949.

Lever, Walter, *Jerusalem Is Called Liberty*. Jerusalem: Massadah Publication Co., 1951.

Levin, Harry, *I Saw the Battle of Jerusalem*. New York: Schocken Books, 1950.

L'Huillier, Fernand, *Fondements historiques des problèmes du Moyen-orient*. Paris: Sirey, 1958.

Lias, Godfrey, *Glubb's Legion*. London: Evans, 1956.

Lie, Trygve, *In the Cause of Peace*. New York: Macmillan, 1954.

Lilienthal, Alfred M., *What Price Israel?* Chicago: Regnery, 1953.

Liron, Aharon, *Yerushalayim Haatika Bematzor Be-Bakron* (Old Jerusalem in Siege and Battle). Tel Aviv: Maarachot, 1957 (Hebrew).

Litvinoff, Barnet, *The Story of David Ben-Gurion*. New York: Oceana Publications, 1959.

Longrigg, Stephen Hemsley, *Oil in the Middle East, Its Discovery and Development*. London: Oxford, 1954.

Lorch, Netanel, *The Edge of the Sword*. New York: Putnam, 1961.

Loti, Pierre, *Jerusalem*. Paris: Plon, 1957.

Lowdermilk, Walter C., *Palestine, Land of Promise*. New York and London: Harper & Brothers, 1944.

———, *The Untried Approach to the Palestine Problem*. New York: American Christian Palestine Committee Publications, 1948.

Lukan, Kadri, *After the Catastrophe*. Beirut: Dar el Elm, 1950 (Arabic).

Maarechot, Adina, *Megillat Heir Haatika* (Notes on the Scroll of the Old City). Jerusalem, 1949.

Mardor, Munya (Meir), *Haganah*. New York: New American Library, 1966.
————, *Strictly Illegal*. London: Robert Hale Ltd., 1964.
Marin, Max, *Le Retour d'Israël*. Paris: Desclée de Brouwer & Cie., 1935.
Marlowe, John, *Rebellion in Palestine*. London: Cresset Press, 1946.
————, *The Seat of Pilate*. London: Cresset Press, 1959.
McDonald, James G., *My Mission in Israel*. New York: Simon and Schuster, 1951.
Mechin, Benoiste, *Le Roi Saud*. Paris: Édition Albin Michel, 1960.
Meinertzhagen, Richard, *Middle East Diary*. London: Cresset Press, 1959.
Modiano, Marius, *Les Juifs, le judaïsme*. Paris: Édition de Seuil, 1955.
Nadel, Baruch, *Bernadotte*. Tel Aviv, 1968 (Hebrew).
Naguib, Mohammed, *Egypt's Destiny*. London: Gollancz, 1955.
Nasser, Gamal Abdel, *Egypt's Liberation: The Philosophy of the Revolution*. Washington, D. C.: Public Affairs Press, 1955.
Neher-Bernheim, Renée, *La Déclaration Balfour, 1917: Un Foyer national juif en Palestine*. Paris: Julliard, 1959.
O'Ballance, Edgar, *The Arab–Israeli War, 1948*. London: Faber, 1956.
Parkes, J. W., *A History of Palestine from 135 A.D. to Modern Times*. London: Gollancz, 1949.
Pearlman, Maurice, *The Army of Israel*. New York: Philosophical Library, 1950.
Peretz, Don, *Israel and the Palestine Arabs*. Washington, D. C.: Middle East Institute, 1958.
Polk, William R., David M. Stamler, and Edmund Asfour, *Backdrop to Tragedy*. Boston: Beacon Press, 1957.
Rabinowicz, Oskar K. *Vladimir Jabotinsky's Conception of a Nation*. New York: Beechhurst Press, 1946.
Reynier, Jacques de, *À Jérusalem un drapeau flottait sur la ligne de feu*. Geneva: Histoire et Société d'Aujourd'hui, 1950.
Reynolds, Quentin, *Leave it to the People*. New York: Random House, 1949.
Robinson, Donald, *Under Fire—Israel's 20-Year Fight for Survival*. New York: Norton, 1968.
Roosevelt, Kermit, *Arabs, Oil, and History*. New York: Harper & Brothers, 1949.
Roth, Cecil, *History of the Jews*. New York: Schocken, 1961.
Rousan, Mahmoud al, *Harbe Bab el Wad* (Battles of Bab el Wad). Amman (Arabic).
————, *Palestine and the Internationalization of Jerusalem*. Baghdad: The Ministry of Culture and Guidance, 1965.
Sachar, Howard M., *Aliyah: The Peoples of Israel*. New York and Cleveland: World, 1961.
————, *From the Ends of the Earth: The Peoples of Israel*. New York and Cleveland: World, 1964.
————, *The Emergence of the Middle East: 1914–1924*. New York: Knopf, 1969.
Sacher, Harry, *Israel: The Establishment of a State*. London: Weidenfeld, 1952.

Sadat, Anwar el, *Revolt on the Nile*. London: Wingate, 1957.

St. John, Robert, *Ben-Gurion: The Biography of an Extraordinary Man*. Garden City, N. Y.: Doubleday, 1959.

————, *The Boss: The Story of Gamal Abdel Nasser*. New York: McGraw-Hill, 1960.

————, *Shalom Means Peace*. Garden City, N. Y.: Doubleday, 1949.

Samuel, Maurice, *Light on Israel*. New York: Alfred A. Knopf, 1968.

Sayegh, Fayez A., *The Arab–Israeli Conflict*. New York: Arab Information Center, 1964.

Schechtman, Joseph B., *The Mufti and the Fuehrer*. New York: Yoseloff, 1965.

Sefer ha-Palmach (Book of the Palmach), 2 vols., ed. Zrubavel Glass. Tel Aviv: Hakibbutz Hameuchad, 1953.

Shahan, Avigdor, *Kanfer Hanizachon* (The Wings of Victory). Tel Aviv: Am Hasafer, 1966.

Sharef, Zeev, *Three Days*. London: W. H. Allen, 1962.

Sharett, Moshe, *Beshar Haoumot* (The Gates of the Nations). Tel Aviv: Am Oved, 1958.

Sherwood, Robert E., *Roosevelt and Hopkins*. New York: Harper & Brothers, 1948.

Shwadran, Benjamin, *The Middle East, Oil, and the Great Powers*. New York: Council for Middle Eastern Affairs, 1959.

Slater, Leonard, *The Pledge*. New York: Simon and Schuster, 1970.

Smith, Wilfred Cantwell, *Islam in Modern History*. Princeton: Princeton University Press, 1957.

Soustelle, Jacques, *La Longue Marche d'Israël*. Paris: Fayard, 1968.

Spicehandler, Daniel, *Let My Right Hand Wither*. New York: Beechhurst Press, 1950.

Stark, Freya, *Dust in the Lion's Paw*. London: John Murray, 1961.

Stein, Leonard, *The Balfour Declaration*. London: Vallentine Mitchell, 1961.

Steinberg, Alfred, *The Man from Missouri*. New York: Putnam, 1962.

Steinberg, Milton, *Basic Judaism*. New York: Harcourt, Brace, 1947.

Stone, Isidor, *This Is Israel*. New York: Boni, 1948.

Storrs, Sir Ronald, *Lawrence of Arabia: Zionism and Palestine*. Middlesex and New York: Penguin Books, 1943.

Sykes, Christopher, *Crossroads to Israel*. New York and Cleveland: World, 1965.

————, *Orde Wingate*. London: Collins, 1959.

Syrkin, Marie, *Blessed Is the Match*. Philadelphia: Jewish Publication Society of America, 1947.

————, *Golda Meir: Woman with a Cause*. New York: Putnam, 1961.

Talmai, Menahem, *Shayarot Baesh*. (Convoys under Fire). Tel Aviv: Amihai, 1957.

Taylor, Alan R., *Prelude to Israel; An Analysis of Zionist Diplomacy, 1897–1947*. New York: Philosophical Library, 1959.

Tell, Abdullah, *El Nakla Falastin* (The Tragedy of Palestine). Cairo: Dar al Kalam, 1959 (Arabic).

Tharaud, Jérôme and Jean, *Un Royaume de Dieu*. Paris: Plon, 1920.

Trevor, Daphne, *Under the White Paper*. Jerusalem: The Jerusalem Press, 1948.

Truman, Harry S, *Memoirs*, Vol. II: *Years of Trial and Hope*. Garden City, N. Y.: Doubleday, 1956.

Tsur, Jacob, *Prière du matin: L'Aube de l'état d'Israël*. Paris: Plon, 1967.

Vaze, Pinhas, *Ha-Mesima: Rechesh* (Objective: To Acquire Arms). Tel Aviv: Maarachot, 1966.

Vester, Bertha, *Our Jerusalem*, Garden City, N. Y.: Doubleday, 1950.

Vilnoy, Zev, *Hamaaracha Leshichrur Israel* (The Battle to Liberate Israel). Jerusalem: Tor-Israel, 1953.

Weisgal, Meyer W., and Joel Carmichael (eds.), *Chaim Weizmann: A Biography by Several Hands*. New York: Atheneum, 1963.

Weizmann, Chaim, *Trial and Error*. New York: Harper & Brothers, 1949.

Weizmann, Vera, *The Impossible Takes Longer*. New York: Harper & Row, 1967.

Welles, Sumner, *We Need Not Fail*. Boston: Houghton Mifflin. 1948.

Wynn, Wilton, *Nasser of Egypt: The Search for Dignity*. Cambridge, Mass.: Arlington Books, 1959.

Zeine, Z. N., *The Struggle for Arab Independence*. Beirut, 1960.

Zurayk, Constantine R., *The Meaning of the Disaster*. Beirut, 1956.

PAMPHLETS AND ARTICLES

Cattan, Henry, *À qui donc appartient la Palestine?* Beirut: Institute for Palestine Studies, 1967.

————, *The Dimensions of the Palestine Problem, 1967*. Beirut: Institute for Palestine Studies, 1967.

Le Comité International de la Croix-rouge en Palestine. Geneva: Comité International de la Croix-rouge, July 1948.

Khalidy, Walid, *Jerusalem—The Arab Case*. Amman: Hashemite Kingdom of Jordan, 1967.

Maarechot, Adina, *Megillat Heir Haatika* (Notes on the Scroll of the Old City). Jerusalem, 1949.

Maksoud, Clovis, "Israel: The Arab Case," in *New Statesman*, London, August 11, 1967.

Meir, Golda, *Israel's Record at the United Nations*. Beirut: Arab Women Information Centre, 1967.

PERIODICALS and NEWSPAPERS

HEBREW

Haaretz.
Ma'arachot.

Ma'ariv.
Yediot Achronot.

ENGLISH

Daily Telegraph, London.
New York Herald Tribune.
The New York Times.
Palestine Post.
The Times, London.

FRENCH

Le Jour, Beirut.
Le Monde, Paris.
L'Orient, Beirut.

PRIVATE AND UNPUBLISHED DIARIES, DOCUMENTS AND CORRESPONDENCE MADE AVAILABLE TO THE AUTHORS BY THEIR OWNERS

Aboussouan, Dr. Samy: Private diary.

Arazi, Tuvia: Private papers and correspondence relative to the arms-purchasing activities of his brother Yehuda.

Avriel, Ehud: Invoices and contracts of the 1948 Haganah arms purchase, Prague.

Ayad, R. P. Ibrahim: Private correspondence and diary.

Bauer, Dr. René: Private journal of the French Hospital in Jerusalem.

Boulos, Nassib, and Don Burke, correspondents for *Time* magazine in Jerusalem, 1948: Copies of their original cable dispatches.

Christ Church, Jerusalem: Diary, 1948.

Churchill, Colonel Jack: British military documents, logs and message slips relevant to the Hadassah Hospital ambush, April 13, 1948.

Cooper, Major Derek: Daily After-Action Reports, the Life Guards, January 1, 1948–May 14, 1948.

Davis, Professor Eli: Correspondence with Red Cross, U. N. and British authorities relative to the status of Hadassah Hospital, Mount Scopus.

Government of Israel, Prime Minister's Archives: Minutes of Jerusalem Municipality committee meetings, 1948; cable traffic between Jerusalem civilian headquarters and Tel Aviv, 1948; reports of the Jewish Agency, New York, on dealings with the United Nations Special Subcommittee in Jerusalem; Jerusalem Municipality files and correspondence, 1948.

Herzog, Chaim (Vivian): Private documents.

Highland Light Infantry: Regimental Journal, Palestine, 1948.

Hoade, R. P. Eugene: Diary.

Husseini, Haidar: Communication logbooks (5) of Haj Amin Husseini's headquarters, October 1947–August 1948.

Husseini, Madame Wajiha Abdel Khader: Correspondence with her husband, Abdel Khader Husseini.

Kaujki, Fawzi el: Private correspondence, captured Haganah documents and communication logs between his headquarters and Damascus, Jerusalem and Cairo.

Lebanese U. N. Delegates: Camille Chamoun, Foreign Minister, 1948–49 cables and correspondence with Beirut: Dr. Charles Malik, Foreign Minister, 1948 cable traffic between Beirut and New York during the partition debates.

MacMillan, Sir Gordon, commanding general, British Army in Palestine: Official Report to the War Office on the Activities of the British Army in Palestine, November 29, 1947–June 30, 1948.

Mardam, Jamil, Prime Minister of Syria, 1948: Private papers, correspondence, 1948 appointments and private Syrian government files.

Neuville, Madame René: Private papers and diary.

Notre-Dame de France, Jerusalem: Daily journal, 1948.

Nusseibi, Anwar: Private memoirs.

Report of the Jewish Agency's Committee of Inquiry into the Hadassah Hospital Ambush.

Reynier, Jacques de, Red Cross delegate to Palestine, 1948: Private diary.

Rosenman, Judge Samuel: Private correspondence between Chaim Weizmann and President Harry S Truman, 1948.

Sacharov, Eliahu: Periodic reports of the arms-purchasing mission headquarters, Geneva, to Haganah General Headquarters, Tel Aviv.

Shaltiel, David, Haganah commander in Jerusalem: Private papers and correspondence; communication log of Jerusalem's Haganah command; military correspondence between Jerusalem and Tel Aviv, 1948.

Shamir, Shlomo, Haganah commander in Latrun: Private correspondence, cable communications between his command and General Headquarters, Tel Aviv, 1948.

Soeurs de Sion, Jerusalem: Convent diary.

Soeurs Réparatrices, Jerusalem: Convent diary.

Solh, Riad, Prime Minister of Lebanon, 1948: Private papers, correspondence and cables originating from and delivered to the Prime Minister's office, 1948; furnished by his daughter.

Trappist Monastery of the Seven Agonies of Latrun: Daily journal, 1948.

Truman Library, Independence, Missouri: Clark Clifford, personal papers and correspondence; Jonathan Daniel, oral history of the Truman Administration; Eddie Jacobson, personal papers and correspondence; Harry S Truman, personal papers and correspondence.

United States Department of State: Unclassified and declassified cable traffic between Washington and the U. S. consul general in Jerusalem, the U. S. mission to the United Nations, and the U. S. missions to Cairo, Baghdad and Amman, 1947–48.

BIBLIOGRAPHY

SUBMITTED TO THE AUTHORS
BY INDIVIDUALS WHO PREFER THAT
THEIR IDENTITY NOT BE DISCLOSED

Haganah Intelligence: Transcripts of taped Arab and British telephone conversations, Jerusalem, December 1947–July 1948; various British Army and
mandatory orders, reports, intelligence estimates and other official documents.
Verbatim reports of the meetings of the Arab League Political Committee,
October 15, 1947–July 18, 1948.

INDEX

631

PHOTOGRAPH CREDITS

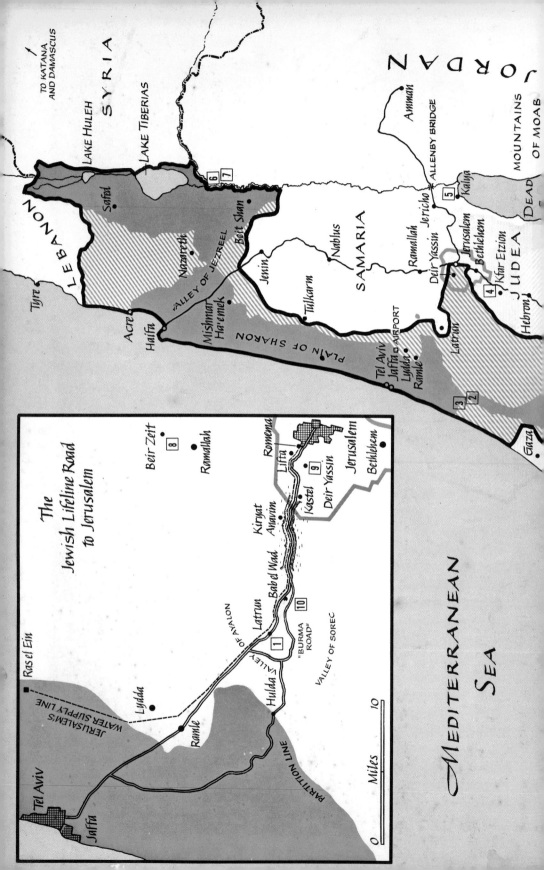

MOUNTAINS
OF MOAB

DEAD SEA

JORDAN

Amman

ALLENBY BRIDGE

Kalya

5

Jericho

Hebron

Kfar Etzion

4

Bethlehem

Jerusalem

Deir Yassin

Ramallah

SYRIA

TO KATANA
AND DAMASCUS

LAKE HULEH

LAKE TIBERIAS

Safal

6 7

Beit Shan

Nazareth

VALLEY OF JEZREEL

Nablus

SAMARIA

Jenin

Tulkarm

Mishmar
Ha-emek

PLAIN OF SHARON

LEBANON

Tyre

Acre

Haifa

Tel Aviv
Jaffa AIRPORT
Lydda
Ramle

Latrun

3 2

Gaza

The
Jewish Lifeline Road
to Jerusalem

Beir Zeit

8

Ramallah

Romema

Lifta

Kiryat
Anavim

Latrun

Bab el Wad

VALLEY OF AYALON

Ras el Ein

Lydda

Ramle

Kastel

Deir Yassin

9

Jerusalem

Bethlehem

"BURMA
ROAD"

10

VALLEY OF SOREC

Hulda

1

VALLEY

JERUSALEM'S
WATER SUPPLY LINE

PARTITION LINE

Tel Aviv

Jaffa

0

Miles

10

MEDITERRANEAN
SEA